IP Networking

Wendell Odom, CCIE No. 1624

Cisco Press

800 East 96th Street

Indianapolis, IN 46240

IP Networking

Wendell Odom, CCIE No. 1624

ISBN-13: 978-1-58714-300-7
ISBN-10: 1-58714-300-3

Library of Congress Cataloging-in-Publication data is on file.

Printed in the United States of America

Fourth Printing: February 2014

Warning and Disclaimer

This book is designed to provide information about IP Networking. Every effort has been made to make this book as complete and as accurate as possible, but no warranty or fitness is implied.

The information is provided on an "as is" basis. The authors, Cisco Press, and Cisco Systems, Inc. shall have neither liability nor responsibility to any person or entity with respect to any loss or damages arising from the information contained in this book or from the use of the discs or programs that may accompany it.

The opinions expressed in this book belong to the author and are not necessarily those of Cisco Systems, Inc.

Trademark Acknowledgments

All terms mentioned in this book that are known to be trademarks or service marks have been appropriately capitalized. Cisco Press or Cisco Systems, Inc., cannot attest to the accuracy of this information. Use of a term in this book should not be regarded as affecting the validity of any trademark or service mark.

Publisher: Paul Boger

Associate Publisher: Dave Dusthimer

Executive Editor: Brett Bartow

Managing Editor: Sandra Schroeder

Development Editor: Andrew Cupp

Senior Project Editor: Tonya Simpson

Copy Editor: John Edwards

Editorial Assistant: Vanessa Evans

Book Designer: Gary Adair

Composition: Mark Shirar

Indexer: Larry Sweazy

Proofreader: Water Crest Publishing

Technical Editors: Elan Beer, Teri Cook, Brian D'Andrea, and Stephen Kalman

Americas Headquarters	Asia Pacific Headquarters	Europe Headquarters
Cisco Systems, Inc.	Cisco Systems (USA) Pte. Ltd.	Cisco Systems International BV
San Jose, CA	Singapore	Amsterdam, The Netherlands

Cisco has more than 200 offices worldwide. Addresses, phone numbers, and fax numbers are listed on the Cisco Website at **www.cisco.com/go/offices.**

Contents at a Glance

Table of Contents

About the Author

Wendell Odom, CCIE 1624, is the author of popular certification books, videos, software, and blogs, all related to computer networking. He is most known as the best-selling author of Cisco certification books from Cisco Press, including books on CCENT, CCNA, CCNP, and CCIE. He helped design key features of the Pearson Network Simulator, used with the IP Networking Lab Manual (a companion to this text), and the Subnet Prep iPhone apps, also from Pearson. Wendell has worked in the networking world for 30 years as a network engineer, consultant, instructor, and course developer, spending part of those years at IBM and Cisco Systems. He is also a 1985 graduate of Georgia Tech. http://www.certskills.com.

About the Technical Reviewers

Elan Beer, CCIE No. 1837, CCSI No. 94008, is a senior consultant and Certified Cisco Instructor. His internetworking expertise is recognized internationally through his global consulting and training engagements. As one of the industry's top internetworking consultants and Cisco instructors, Elan has used his expertise for the past 15 years to design, implement, and deploy multiprotocol networks for a wide international clientele. As a senior instructor and course developer, Elan has designed and presented public and implementation-specific technical courses spanning many of today's top technologies. Elan specializes in MPLS, BGP, QoS, and other internetworking technologies.

Teri Cook (CCSI, CCDP, CCNP, CCDA, CCNA, MCT, and MCSE 2000/2003: Security) has more than ten years of experience in the IT industry. She has worked with different types of organizations within the private business and DoD sectors, providing senior-level network and security technical skills in the design and implementation of complex computing environments. Since obtaining her certifications, Teri has been committed to bringing quality IT training to IT professionals as an instructor. She is an outstanding instructor who utilizes real-world experience to present complex networking technologies. As an IT instructor, Teri has been teaching Cisco classes for more than five years.

Brian D'Andrea (CCNA, CCDA, MCSE, A+, and Net+) has 11 years of IT experience in both medical and financial environments, where planning and supporting critical networking technologies were his primary responsibilities. For the last five years, he has dedicated himself to technical training. Brian spends most of his time with The Training Camp, an IT boot camp provider. Using his real-world experience and his ability to break difficult concepts into a language that students can understand, Brian has successfully trained hundreds of students for both work and certification endeavors.

Stephen Kalman is a data security trainer and the author or tech editor of more than 20 books, courses, and CBT titles. His most recent book is *Web Security Field Guide*, published by Cisco Press. In addition to those responsibilities, he runs a consulting company, Esquire Micro Consultants, which specializes in network security assessments and forensics. Mr. Kalman holds SSCP, CISSP, ISSMP, CEH, CHFI, CCNA, CCSA (Checkpoint), A+, Network+, and Security+ certifications and is a member of the New York State Bar.

Dedication

To Dr. Oliver C. Ibe, one of my college professors who helped me find my way in the world of computer networking.

Acknowledgments

Many people see the name on the front cover and assume that a book was created mainly through the effort of that one person. In reality, it takes many people to create a book like this one. Many people have contributed to this book, both directly and through the creation of the Cisco Press ICND1 and ICND2 Official Exam Certification Guides, from which much of the content of this book was taken.

Thanks to Wen Liu of ITT for the opportunity and for the insights into the world of college textbooks and courses.

Thanks to Brett Bartow, executive editor at Pearson, for getting me into the college textbook business and for guiding me through the business side of publishing. Now on to the next step!

Thanks to Ann Zevnik, quality control manager at Pearson, who helped unravel the world of custom publishing for Brett and me.

Drew Cupp, development editor extraordinaire, got to guide this project through the early stages. Juggling totally new chapters, chapters picked up intact, chapters with material from multiple other books, all in various formats—the list goes on . . . Couldn't have done it without you. Thanks Drew!

Thanks to Elan Beer for his technical edits of the chapters published as new material in this book (mainly the chapters on IP addressing and subnetting). It's always nice to get to work with the best—thanks for the detailed and useful comments.

My good friend and coworker Rich Bennett drew many of the figures created for this book, particularly the figures in seven chapters on IP addressing and subnetting. I'm sure that Robin Williams would consider you a great student of visual design—nice job!

Thanks to Sandra Schroeder and her production team, particularly to Tonya Simpson (senior project editor) and John Edwards (copy editor). Juggling tons of details for any book project is always a challenge, but this one had several unique challenges related to the high percentage of material picked up from other books, plus the transition to new internal systems and processes. Those conditions actually made the project editing and copy edit jobs more difficult for this book in some ways. Thanks for staying on top of it!

Thanks to my wife, Kris, and daughter, Hannah, who light up my day when I come upstairs after a long day in front of the keyboard. And to Jesus Christ, who gives the book-writing work purpose and meaning.

Reader Services

Visit our website and register this book at http://www.pearsonitcertification.com/title/9781587143007 for convenient access to any updates, downloads, or errata that might be available for the book.

Introduction

This book serves as a textbook for a college networking course. The book aims to strike a balance between theoretical knowledge and practical skills useful in the marketplace. It examines a variety of topics related to TCP/IP, first introducing the core concepts and theory. The book also focuses on how to install and configure IP routers and switches, specifically routers and switches from Cisco Systems. Following a ten-unit format, the text takes the student from a broad and basic knowledge of IP addressing and routing to a solid skill level with how hosts, switches, and routers collectively deliver IP packets in modern corporate networks.

As for topics, this text centers on TCP/IP networking, specifically the IP packet-forwarding process, and how to make Cisco routers perform IP routing. The book begins with two units that review and expand the students' knowledge of prerequisite topics, including all layers of the TCP/IP model, with emphasis on LANs, WANs, IP, and TCP. Units 3 through 8 take the students to a much deeper and practical knowledge of IP addressing and routing, two topics that truly need to be understood together. These same lessons examine how to implement various IP features in Cisco routers, building skills that matter in the real world. Finally, the last two units focus on LAN and WAN technologies, respectively, and their roles in how routers and hosts use LANs and WANs to forward IP packets.

Organization of the Text

This text organizes the material into ten units. In many classes, the instructor will teach one unit per week. The text reduces the materials in Units 5 and 6 to account for midterm exams, both for review and for taking the midterm exam. The text assumes that a final class period would be devoted to a final exam following Unit 10.

Each unit contains between two and four chapters. Some units contain topics that obviously relate directly to each other. In some units, the mix of topics is wider, in most cases to balance the amount of theoretical discussion versus practical hands-on experience.

The organization of topics in Units 1 through 7 follows three parallel themes:

- IP Addressing and Subnetting

- IP Routing and Routing Protocols

- Cisco Router Configuration

These first seven units all contain chapters on at least one of these three topics. The reasons are simple. IP routing relies on the concepts behind IP networks and subnets; IP addressing and subnetting rules were designed to make the IP routing process work efficiently. You cannot fully understand subnetting without thinking about routing and vice versa. But learning the theory of both IP subnetting and IP routing does not prepare a student to engineer a modern corporate network, so the text interleaves Cisco router hands-on configuration topics. As a result, the students learn the theory and build practical skills at the same time.

Finally, although this text does not include lab exercises, the book design expects that students do lab exercises related to the relevant topics. In particular, these exercises typically include practice doing the math related to IP subnetting, and using either simulated or real Cisco routers and switches.

In addition to the core of each chapter, which explains a particular set of related topics, the chapters include the following features as appropriate:

- **Key Topic Lists:** Inside the core of each chapter, the margins note the most important topics with Key Topic icons. The list of key topics at the end of each chapter summarizes these topics and provides a handy reference for later study and review.

- **Key Terms:** A list of the most important terms in the chapter.

- **Command References:** For chapters that review commands useful on Cisco routers and switches, these chapters list tables of commands and their purposes.

- **Review Questions:** Multiple-choice questions that review the main concepts and also require critical thinking and application of the topics in the chapter.

Beyond these per-chapter features, the book includes the following features:

- **Appendix A, "Numeric Reference Tables":** This appendix lists useful numbers related to this text, including a binary-decimal conversion table and lists of valid IP subnet masks.

- **Appendix B, "IP Access Control Lists":** This appendix is a chapter taken from another book (*ICND2 Official Exam Certification Guide*, Odom, 2007) in case some instructors decide to add discussions of access control lists to their version of the course.

- **Glossary:** A list of all the key terms from the chapters, plus other networking terms, with definitions.

The author also supplies a support page for this book, mainly for convenience: http://www.certskills.com/IPNetworking. This page includes links to URLs mentioned in this book and links to other useful resources related to book content. This site also includes many links for any students planning to pursue their CCENT or CCNA certifications from Cisco.

This chapter covers the following subjects:

■ **The TCP/IP Networking Model:** This section explains the terminology and concepts behind the world's most popular networking model, TCP/IP, including several example protocols: HTTP, TCP, IP, and Ethernet.

■ **The OSI Networking Model:** This section explains the terminology behind the OSI networking model in comparison to TCP/IP.

CHAPTER 1

The TCP/IP and OSI Networking Models

You can think of a networking model as you think of a set of architectural plans for building a house. Sure, you can build a house without the architectural plans, but it will work better if you follow the plans. And because you probably have a lot of different people working on building your house, such as framers, electricians, bricklayers, painters, and so on, it helps if they can all reference the same plan. Similarly, you could build your own network, write your own software, build your own networking cards, and create a network without using any existing networking model. However, it is much easier to simply buy and use products that already conform to some well-known networking model. And because the networking product vendors use the same networking model, their products should work well together.

This book includes detailed coverage of one networking model: Transmission Control Protocol/Internet Protocol, or TCP/IP. TCP/IP is the most pervasively used networking model in the history of networking. You can find support for TCP/IP on practically every computer operating system in existence today, from mobile phones to mainframe computers. Every network built using Cisco products today supports TCP/IP. And unsurprisingly, the one networking protocol that every network engineer needs to know is TCP/IP.

One other networking model matters to a small extent in today's networks: the Open Systems Interconnection (OSI) reference model. Historically, OSI was the first large effort to create a vendor-neutral networking model. Because of that timing, many of the terms used in networking today come from the OSI model, so this chapter's section on OSI discusses OSI and the related terminology.

TCP/IP Networking Model

A *networking model*, sometimes also called either a *networking architecture* or *networking blueprint*, refers to a comprehensive set of documents. Individually, each document describes one small function required for a network; collectively, these documents define everything that should happen for a computer network to work. Some documents will define a protocol, which is a set of logical rules that devices must follow to communicate. Other documents will define some physical requirements for networking. For example, a document could define the voltage and current levels used on a particular cable when transmitting data.

You can think of a networking model as you think of an architectural blueprint for building a house. Sure, you can build a house without the blueprint. However, the blueprint can ensure that the house has the right foundation and structure so that it will not fall down, and has the correct hidden spaces to accommodate the plumbing, electrical, gas, and so on. Also, the many different people that build the house using the blueprint—such as framers, electricians, bricklayers, painters, and so on—know that if they follow the blueprint, their part of the work should not cause problems for the other workers.

Similarly, you could build your own network—write your own software, build your own networking cards, and so on—to create a network. However, it is much easier to simply buy and use products that already conform to some well-known networking model or blueprint. And because the networking product vendors build their products with some networking model in mind, their products should work well together.

The History Leading to TCP/IP

Today, the world of computer networking uses one networking model: TCP/IP. However, the world has not always been so simple. Once upon a time, there were no networking protocols, including TCP/IP. Vendors created the first networking protocols; these protocols supported only that vendor's computers. For example, IBM published its Systems Network Architecture (SNA) networking model in 1974. Other vendors also created their own proprietary networking models. As a result, if your company bought computers from three vendors, network engineers often had to create three different networks based on the networking models created by each company, and then somehow connect those networks, making the combined networks much more complex. The left side of Figure 1-1 shows the general idea of what a company's enterprise network might have looked like back in the 1980s, before TCP/IP became common in enterprise internetworks.

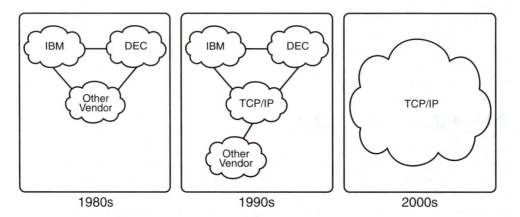

Figure 1-1   *Historical Progression: Proprietary Models to the Open TCP/IP Model*

Although vendor-defined proprietary networking models often worked well, having an open, vendor-neutral networking model would aid competition as well as reduce complexity. The International Organization for Standardization (ISO) took on the task to create such a model, starting as early as the late 1970s, beginning work on what would become known as the Open Systems Interconnection (OSI) networking model. ISO had a noble goal for the OSI model: to standardize data networking protocols to allow communication between all computers across the entire planet. ISO worked toward this ambitious and noble goal, with participants from most of the technologically developed nations on Earth participating in the process.

A second, less formal effort to create an open, vendor-neutral, public networking model sprouted forth from a U.S. Defense Department contract. Researchers at various universities volunteered to help further develop the protocols surrounding the original department's work. These efforts resulted in a competing open networking model called TCP/IP.

During the 1990s, companies began adding OSI, TCP/IP, or both to their enterprise networks. However, by the end of the 1990s, TCP/IP had become the common choice, and OSI fell away. The center part of Figure 1-1 shows the general idea behind enterprise networks in that decade—still with networks built upon multiple networking models, but including TCP/IP.

Here in the twenty-first century, TCP/IP now dominates. Proprietary networking models still exist, but they have mostly been discarded in favor of using TCP/IP. The OSI model, whose development suffered in part because of a slower formal standardization process as compared with TCP/IP, never succeeded in the marketplace. And TCP/IP, the networking model originally created almost entirely by a bunch of volunteers, has become the most prolific network model ever, as shown on the right side of Figure 1-1.

In this chapter, you will read about some of the basics of TCP/IP. Although you will learn some interesting facts about TCP/IP, the true goal of this chapter is to help you understand what a networking model or networking architecture really is and how it works.

Also in this chapter, you will learn about some of the jargon used with OSI. Will any of you ever work on a computer that is using the full OSI protocols instead of TCP/IP? Probably not. However, you will often use terms relating to OSI.

Overview of the TCP/IP Networking Model

The TCP/IP model defines a large collection of protocols that allow computers to communicate, and references other protocols and standards as well. To define a protocol, TCP/IP uses documents called Requests for Comments (RFC). (You can find these RFCs using any online search engine.) The TCP/IP model also avoids repeating work already done by some other standards body or vendor consortium by simply referring to standards or protocols created by those groups. For example, the Institute of Electrical and Electronic Engineers (IEEE) defines Ethernet LANs; the TCP/IP model does not define Ethernet in RFCs, but refers to IEEE Ethernet as an option.

An easy comparison can be made between telephones and computers that use TCP/IP. You go to the store and buy a phone from one of a dozen different vendors. When you get home and plug in the phone to the same cable in which your old phone was connected, the new phone works. The phone vendors know the standards for phones in their country and build their phones to match those standards.

Similarly, when you buy a new computer today, it implements the TCP/IP model to the point that you can usually take the computer out of the box, plug in all the right cables, and turn it on, and it connects to the network. You can use a web browser to connect to your favorite website. How? Well, the operating system (OS) on the computer implements parts of the TCP/IP model. The Ethernet card, or wireless LAN card, built into the computer implements some LAN standards referenced by the TCP/IP model. In short, the vendors that created the hardware and software implemented TCP/IP.

To help people understand a networking model, each model breaks the functions into a small number of categories called *layers*. Each layer includes protocols and standards that relate to that category of functions. TCP/IP actually has two alternative models, as shown in Figure 1-2.

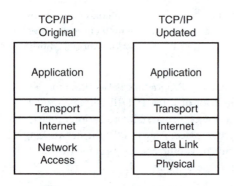

Figure 1-2   *Two TCP/IP Networking Models*

The model on the left, the original TCP/IP model, breaks TCP/IP into four layers. The top layers focus more on the applications that need to send and receive data, whereas the lower layers focus more on the need to somehow transmit the bits from one device to another. The model on the right is a newer version of the model, formed by expanding the network access layer on the left into two separate layers: data link and physical. Note that the model on the right is used more often today.

Many of you reading this book will have already heard of several TCP/IP protocols, like the examples listed in Table 1-1. Most of the protocols and standards in this table will be explained in more detail as you work through this book. Following the table, this section takes a closer look at the layers of the TCP/IP model.

Table 1-1   *TCP/IP Architectural Model and Example Protocols*

TCP/IP Architecture Layer	Example Protocols
Application	HTTP, POP3, SMTP
Transport	TCP, UDP
Internet	IP
Network Access	Ethernet, Point-to-Point Protocol (PPP), T/1

The TCP/IP Application Layer

TCP/IP application layer protocols provide services to the application software running on a computer. The application layer does not define the application itself, but rather it defines services that applications need—such as the capability to transfer a file in the case of HTTP. In short, the application layer provides an interface between software running on a computer and the network itself.

Arguably, the most popular TCP/IP application today is the web browser. Many major software vendors either have already changed or are changing their application software to support access from a web browser. And thankfully, using a web browser is easy—you start a web browser on your computer and select a website by typing in the name of the website, and the web page appears.

HTTP Overview

What really happens to allow that web page to appear on your web browser?

Imagine that Bob opens his browser. His browser has been configured to automatically ask for web server Larry's default web page, or *home page*. The general logic looks like that shown in Figure 1-3.

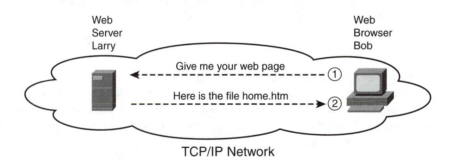

Figure 1-3 *Basic Application Logic to Get a Web Page*

So what really happened? Bob's initial request actually asks Larry to send his home page back to Bob. Larry's web server software has been configured to know that the default web page is contained in a file called home.htm. Bob receives the file from Larry and displays the contents of the file in the web browser window.

HTTP Protocol Mechanisms

Taking a closer look, this example shows how applications on each endpoint computer—specifically, the web browser application and web server application—use a TCP/IP application layer protocol. To make the request for a web page and return the contents of the web page, the applications use the Hypertext Transfer Protocol (HTTP).

HTTP did not exist until Tim Berners-Lee created the first web browser and web server in the early 1990s. Berners-Lee gave HTTP functions to ask for the contents of web pages, specifically by giving the web browser the ability to request files from the server, and giving the server a way to return the content of those files. The overall logic matches the earlier Figure 1-3; Figure 1-4 shows the same idea, with details specific to HTTP.

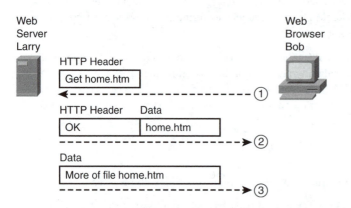

Figure 1-4 *HTTP Get Request, HTTP Reply, and One Data-Only Message*

Note: The full version of most web addresses—also called universal resource locators (URL)—begin with the letters *http*, meaning that HTTP will be used to transfer the web pages.

To get the web page from Larry, at Step 1, Bob sends a message with an HTTP header. Generally, protocols use headers as a place to put information used by that protocol. This HTTP header includes the request to "get" a file. The request typically contains the name of the file (home.htm in this case), or if no filename is mentioned, the web server assumes that Bob wants the default web page.

Step 2 in the figure shows the response from web server Larry. The message begins with an HTTP header, with a return code (200) that means something as simple as "OK" returned in the header. HTTP defines other return codes as well so that the server can tell the browser whether the request worked. (As another example, if you have ever looked for a web page that was not found, you received an HTTP 404 "not found" error, which means that you received an HTTP return code of 404.) The second message also includes the first part of the requested file.

Step 3 in the figure shows another message from web server Larry to web browser Bob, but this time without an HTTP header. HTTP transfers the data by sending multiple messages, each with a part of the file. Rather than wasting space by sending repeated HTTP headers that list the same information, these additional messages simply omit the header.

The TCP/IP Transport Layer

Although many TCP/IP application layer protocols exist, the TCP/IP transport layer includes a smaller number of protocols. The two most commonly used transport layer protocols are the *Transmission Control Protocol (TCP)* and the *User Datagram Protocol (UDP)*.

Transport layer protocols provide services to the application layer protocols that reside one layer higher in the TCP/IP model. How does a transport layer protocol provide a service to a higher-layer protocol? The following sections introduce that general concept by focusing on a single service provided by TCP: error recovery. Later chapters in this book examine the transport layer in more detail and discuss more functions of the transport layer.

TCP Error Recovery Basics

To appreciate what the transport layer protocols do, you must think about the layer above the transport layer: the application layer. Why? Well, each layer provides a service to the layer above it, like the error recovery service provided to applications by TCP.

For example, in Figure 1-3, Bob and Larry used HTTP to transfer the home page from web server Larry to Bob's web browser. But what would have happened if Bob's HTTP get request had been lost in transit through the TCP/IP network? Or, what would have happened if Larry's response, which included the contents of the home page, had been lost? Well, as you might expect, in either case, the page would not have shown up in Bob's browser.

TCP/IP needs a mechanism to guarantee delivery of data across a network. Because many application layer protocols probably want a way to guarantee delivery of data across a network, the creators of TCP included an error recovery feature. To recover from errors, TCP uses the concept of *acknowledgments*. Figure 1-5 outlines the basic idea behind how TCP notices lost data and asks the sender to try again.

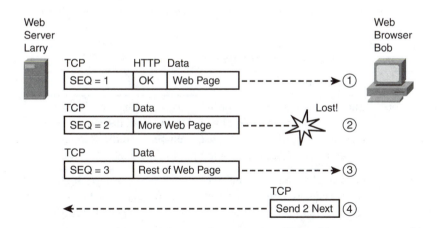

Figure 1-5   *TCP Error Recovery Services as Provided to HTTP*

Note: The data shown in the rectangles in Figure 1-5, which includes the transport layer header and its encapsulated data, is called a *segment*.

Figure 1-5 shows web server Larry sending a web page to web browser Bob, using three separate messages. Note that the TCP header shows a sequence number (SEQ) with each message. In this example, the network has some problem, so the network fails to deliver the segment with sequence number 2. When Bob receives messages with sequence numbers 1 and 3, but does not receive a message with sequence number 2, Bob realizes that message 2 was lost. That realization by Bob's TCP logic causes Bob to send a TCP segment back to Larry, asking Larry to send message 2 again.

Same Layer and Adjacent Layer Interactions

The example in Figure 1-4 also demonstrates a function called *adjacent-layer interaction*, which refers to the concepts of how adjacent layers in a networking model, on the same computer, work together. In this example, the higher-layer protocol (HTTP) needs to do something it cannot do (error recovery). The higher layer asks for the next lower-layer protocol (TCP) to perform the service; the lower layer provides a service to the layer above it.

Figure 1-4 also shows an example of a similar function called *same-layer interaction*. When a particular layer on one computer wants to communicate with the same layer on another computer, the two computers use headers to hold the information that they want to communicate. For example, in Figure 1-4, Larry set the sequence numbers to 1, 2, and 3 so that Bob could notice when some of the data did not arrive. Larry's TCP process created that TCP header with the sequence number; Bob's TCP process received and reacted to the TCP segments. This process through which two computers set and interpret the information in the header used by that layer is called *same-layer interaction*, and it occurs between different computers.

Table 1-2 summarizes the key points about how adjacent layers work together on a single computer and how one layer on one computer works with the same networking layer on another computer.

Table 1-2 *Summary: Same-Layer and Adjacent-Layer Interactions*

Concept	Description
Same-layer interaction on different computers	The two computers use a protocol to communicate with the same layer on another computer. The protocol defined by each layer uses a header that is transmitted between the computers, to communicate what each computer wants to do.
Adjacent-layer interaction on the same computer	On a single computer, one layer provides a service to a higher layer. The software or hardware that implements the higher layer requests that the next lower layer performs the needed function.

The TCP/IP Internet Layer

The application layer includes many protocols, whereas the transport layer includes fewer—most notably, TCP and UDP. The TCP/IP Internet layer includes a small number of protocols, but only one major protocol: the *Internet Protocol (IP)*. In fact, the name TCP/IP is simply the names of the two most common protocols (TCP and IP) separated by a slash (/).

IP provides several features—most importantly, addressing and routing. The following sections begin by comparing IP's addressing and routing with another commonly known system that uses addressing and routing: the postal service. Following that, these sections introduce IP addressing and routing. (More details follow in Chapter 5, "Fundamentals of IP Addressing and Routing.")

Internet Protocol (IP) and the Postal Service

Imagine that you just wrote two letters: one to a friend on the other side of the country and one to a friend on the other side of town. You've addressed the envelopes and put on the stamps, so both are ready to give to the postal service. Is there much difference in how you treat each letter? Not really. Typically, you would just put them in the same mailbox and expect the postal service to deliver both letters.

The postal service, however, must think about each letter separately and then make a decision of where to send each letter so that it is delivered. For the letter sent across town, the people in the local post office probably just need to put the letter on another truck.

For the letter that needs to go across the country, the postal service sends the letter to another post office, then another, and so on, until the letter gets delivered across the country. At each post office, the postal service must process the letter and choose where to send it next.

To make it all work, the postal service has regular routes for small trucks, large trucks, planes, boats, and so on, to move letters between postal service sites. They must be able to receive and forward the letters, and they must make good decisions about where to send each letter next, as depicted in Figure 1-6.

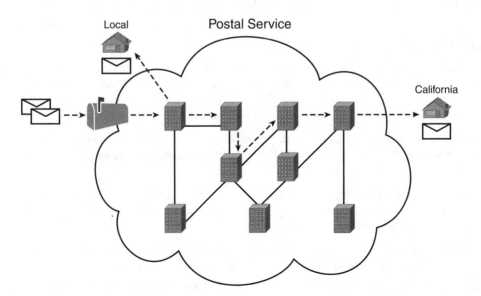

Figure 1-6 *Postal Service Forwarding (Routing) Letters*

Still thinking about the postal service, consider the difference between the person sending the letter and the work that the postal service does. The person sending the letters expects that the postal service will deliver the letter most of the time. However, the person sending the letter does not need to know the details of exactly what path the letters take. In contrast, the postal service does not create the letter, but it accepts the letter from the customer. Then the postal service must know the details about addresses—postal codes that group addresses into larger groups—and it must have the ability to deliver the letters.

The TCP/IP application and transport layers act like the person sending letters through the postal service. These upper layers work the same way regardless of whether the endpoint host computers are on the same LAN or are separated by the entire Internet. To send a message, these upper layers ask the layer below them—the Internet layer—to deliver the message.

The lower layers of the TCP/IP model, the Internet layer and the network access layer, provide the service of delivering those messages to the correct destinations. To do so, these lower layers must understand the underlying physical network because they define the protocols used to deliver the data from one host to another.

So, what does this all matter to networking? Well, the Internet layer of the TCP/IP networking model, primarily defined by the *Internet Protocol (IP)*, works much like the postal service. IP defines addresses so that each host computer can have a different IP address, just as the postal service defines addressing that allows unique addresses for each house, apartment, and business. Similarly, IP defines the process of routing so that devices called routers can do work like the post office, to forward packets of data so that they are delivered to the correct destinations. And just as the postal service created the necessary infrastructure to be able to deliver letters—post offices, sorting machines, trucks, planes, and personnel—the Internet layer defines the details of how a network infrastructure should be created so that the network can deliver data to all computers in the network.

Internet Protocol (IP) Addressing Basics

IP defines addresses for several important reasons. First, each device that uses TCP/IP— each TCP/IP host—needs a unique address so that it can be identified in the network. IP also defines how to group addresses together, just like the postal system groups addresses based on postal codes (like zip codes in the United States).

To understand the basics, examine Figure 1-7, which shows the familiar web server Larry and web browser Bob. But now, instead of ignoring the network between these two computers, part of the network infrastructure is included.

First, note that the figure shows some sample IP addresses. Each IP address has four numbers, separated by periods. In this case, Larry uses IP address 1.1.1.1, and Bob uses 2.2.2.2. This style of number is called a *dotted decimal number (DDN)*.

The figure also shows three groups of addresses. In this particular example, all IP addresses that begin with 1 must be on the upper left, as shown in shorthand in the figure as 1._._._. All addresses that begin with 2 must be on the right, as shown in shorthand as 2._._._. Finally, all IP addresses that begin with 3 must be on the bottom part of the figure.

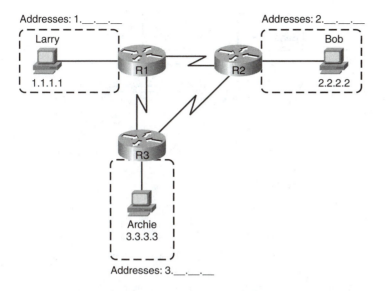

Addresses: 1.__.__.__

Larry
1.1.1.1

Addresses: 2.__.__.__

Bob
2.2.2.2

R1

R2

R3

Archie
3.3.3.3

Addresses: 3.__.__.__

Figure 1-7 *Simple TCP/IP Network: Three Routers, with IP Addresses Grouped*

Additionally, the figure also introduces icons that represent IP routers. *Routers* are networking devices that connect the parts of the TCP/IP network together, for the purpose of routing (forwarding) IP packets to the correct destination. Routers do the equivalent of the work done by each post office site: They receive IP packets on various physical interfaces, make decisions based on the IP address included with the packet, and then physically forward the packet out some other network interface.

IP Routing Basics

The TCP/IP Internet layer, using the IP protocol, provides a service of forwarding IP packets from one device to another. Any device with an IP address can connect to the TCP/IP network and send packets. This section shows a basic IP routing example for perspective.

Note: The term *IP host* refers to any device, regardless of size or power, that has an IP address and connects to any TCP/IP network.

Figure 1-8 repeats the familiar case in which web server Larry wants to send part of a web page to Bob, but now with details related to IP. On the lower left, note that server Larry has the familiar application data, HTTP header, and TCP header ready to send. Additionally, the message now also contains an IP header. The IP header includes a source IP address of Larry's IP (1.1.1.1) and a destination IP address of Bob's IP address (2.2.2.2).

Note: The data shown in the bottom rectangle in Figure 1-8, which includes the Internet layer header and its encapsulated data, is called a *packet*.

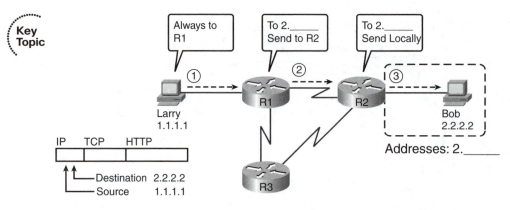

Figure 1-8   *Basic Routing Example*

Step 1, on the left of the figure, begins with Larry being ready to send an IP packet. Larry's IP process chooses to send the packet to some router—a nearby router on the same LAN—and with the expectation that the router will know how to forward the packet. (This logic is much like you or me sending all our letters by putting them into any nearby post office box.) Larry need not know anything more about the topology or the other routers.

At Step 2, Router R1 receives the IP packet and R1's IP process makes a decision. R1 looks at the destination address (2.2.2.2), compares that address to its known IP routes, and chooses to forward the packet to Router R2. This process of forwarding the IP packet is called *IP routing*, or simply *routing*.

At Step 3, Router R2 repeats the same kind of logic used by Router R1. R2's IP process will compare the packet's destination IP address (2.2.2.2) to R2's known IP routes and make a choice to forward the packet to the right, on to Bob.

The TCP/IP Network Access Layer

The TCP/IP model's network access layer defines the protocols and hardware required to deliver data across some physical network. The term *network access* refers to the fact that this layer defines how to access or use the physical media over which data can be transmitted.

Just like every layer in any networking model, the TCP/IP network access layer provides services to the layer above it in the model. When a host or router's IP process chooses to send an IP packet to another router or host, that host or router then uses network access layer details to send that packet to the next host/router.

Because each layer provides a service to the layer above it, take a moment to think about the IP logic related to the earlier Figure 1-8. In that example, host Larry's IP logic chooses to send the IP packet to a nearby router (R1), with no mention of the underlying Ethernet. The Ethernet network access layer protocols must then be used to deliver that packet from host Larry over to Router R1. Figure 1-9 shows four steps of what occurs at the network access layer to allow Larry to send the IP packet to R1.

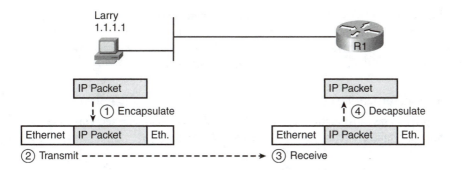

Figure 1-9 *Larry Using Ethernet to Forward an IP Packet to Router R1*

Figure 1-9 depicts the Ethernet as a series of lines. Networking diagrams often use this convention when drawing Ethernet LANs, in cases where the actual LAN cabling and LAN devices are not important to some discussion, as is the case here. The LAN would have cables and devices, like LAN switches, not shown in this figure.

The figure shows four steps. The first two occur on Larry, and the last two occur on Router R1, as follows:

Step 1.   Larry encapsulates the IP packet between an Ethernet header and Ethernet trailer, creating an Ethernet *frame*.

Step 2.   Larry physically transmits the bits of this Ethernet frame, using electricity flowing over the Ethernet cabling.

Step 3.   Router R1 physically receives the electrical signal over a cable and re-creates the same bits by interpreting the meaning of the electrical signals.

Step 4.   Router R1 deencapsulates the IP packet from the Ethernet frame by removing and discarding the Ethernet header and trailer.

By the end of this process, the network access processes on Larry and R1 have worked together to deliver the packet from Larry to Router R1.

Note: Protocols define both headers and trailers for the same general reason, but headers exist at the beginning of the message and trailers exist at the end.

The network access layer includes a large number of protocols and standards. For example, the network access layer includes all the variations of Ethernet protocols, along with several other LAN standards that were more popular in decades past. The network access layer includes WAN standards for different physical media, which differ significantly compared to LAN standards because of the longer distances involved in transmitting the data. This layer also includes the popular WAN standards that add headers and trailers as shown generally in Figure 1-7—protocols such as the Point-to-Point Protocol (PPP) and Frame Relay. Chapter 2, "LAN Fundamentals," and Chapter 3, "WAN Fundamentals," further develop these topics for LANs and WANs, respectively.

In short, the TCP/IP network access layer includes standards related to physical transmission of the data, as well as the standards used to perform other functions less related to physical transmission. The five-layer TCP/IP model simply splits out the network access layer into two layers (data link and physical) to match this logic.

TCP/IP Model and Terminology

Before completing this introduction to the TCP/IP model, the following sections examine a few remaining details of the model and some related terminology.

Comparing the Two TCP/IP Models

The functions defined in the network access layer can be broken into two major categories: functions related directly to the physical transmission of data, and those only indirectly related to the physical transmission of data. For example, in the four steps shown around Figure 1-9, Steps 2 and 3 were specific to sending the data, but Steps 1 and 4—encapsulation and deencapsulation—were only indirectly related. This division will become clearer as you read about additional details of each protocol and standard.

The two alternative TCP/IP models exist. Comparing the two, the upper layers are identical. The lower layers differ in that the single network access layer in one model is split into two layers to match the division of physical transmission details from the other functions. Figure 1-10 shows the two models again, with emphasis on these distinctions.

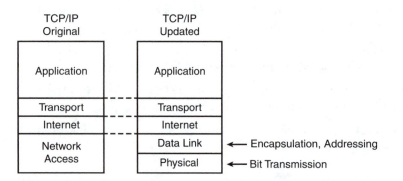

Figure 1-10   *Network Access Versus Data Link and Physical Layers*

Data Encapsulation Terminology

As you can see from the explanations of how HTTP, TCP, IP, and Ethernet do their jobs, each layer adds its own header (and sometimes trailer) to the data supplied by the higher layer. The term *encapsulation* refers to the process of putting headers (and sometimes trailers) around some data.

Many of the examples in this chapter show the encapsulation process. For example, web server Larry encapsulated the contents of the home page inside an HTTP header in Figure 1-4. The TCP layer encapsulated the HTTP headers and data inside a TCP header in Figure 1-5. IP encapsulated the TCP headers and the data inside an IP header in Figure 1-7. Finally, the Ethernet network access layer encapsulated the IP packets inside both a header and a trailer in Figure 1-9.

The process by which a TCP/IP host sends data can be viewed as a five-step process. The first four steps relate to the encapsulation performed by the four TCP/IP layers, and the last step is the actual physical transmission of the data by the host. In fact, if you use the five-layer TCP/IP model, one step corresponds to the role of each layer. The steps are summarized in the following list:

Step 1.   **Create and encapsulate the application data with any required application layer headers.** For example, the HTTP OK message can be returned in an HTTP header, followed by part of the contents of a web page.

Step 2.   **Encapsulate the data supplied by the application layer inside a transport layer header.** For end-user applications, a TCP or UDP header is typically used.

Step 3.   **Encapsulate the data supplied by the transport layer inside an Internet layer (IP) header.** IP defines the IP addresses that uniquely identify each computer.

Step 4.   **Encapsulate the data supplied by the Internet layer inside a data link layer header and trailer.** This is the only layer that uses both a header and a trailer.

Step 5.   **Transmit the bits.** The physical layer encodes a signal onto the medium to transmit the frame.

The numbers in Figure 1-11 correspond to the five steps in the list, graphically showing the same concepts. Note that because the application layer often does not need to add a header, the figure does not show a specific application layer header.

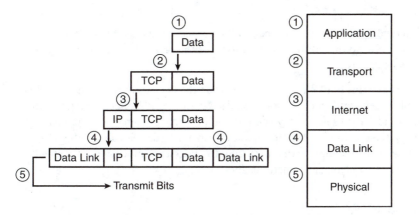

Figure 1-11   *Five Steps of Data Encapsulation—TCP/IP*

Names of TCP/IP Messages

Finally, take particular care to remember the terms *segment*, *packet*, and *frame* and the meaning of each. Each term refers to the headers and possibly trailers defined by a particular layer and the data encapsulated following that header. Each term, however, refers to a different layer—segment for the transport layer, packet for the Internet layer, and frame for the network access layer. Figure 1-12 shows each layer along with the associated term.

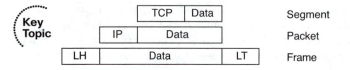

	TCP	Data	Segment
IP	Data		Packet
LH	Data	LT	Frame

Key Topic

Figure 1-12 *Perspectives on Encapsulation and "Data"*

The letters LH and LT stand for link header and link trailer, respectively, and refer to the data link layer header and trailer.

Note that Figure 1-12 also shows the encapsulated data as simply "data." When focusing on the work done by a particular layer, the encapsulated data typically is unimportant. For example, an IP packet might indeed have a TCP header after the IP header, an HTTP header after the TCP header, and data for a web page after the HTTP header. But when discussing IP, you probably just care about the IP header, so everything after the IP header is just called "data." So, when drawing IP packets, everything after the IP header is typically shown simply as "data."

OSI Networking Model

At one point in the history of the OSI model, many people thought it would win the battle of the networking models discussed earlier in this chapter. If that had occurred, instead of running TCP/IP on every computer in the world, those computers would be running with OSI.

However, OSI did not win that battle. In fact, OSI no longer exists as a networking model that could be used instead of TCP/IP, although some of the original protocols referenced by the OSI model still exist.

So, why is OSI even in this book? Terminology. During those years in which many people thought the OSI model would become commonplace in the world of networking (mostly in the late 1980s and early 1990s), many vendors and protocol documents started using terminology from the OSI model. That terminology remains today. So, although you will never need to work with a computer that uses OSI, to understand modern networking terminology, you need to understand something about OSI.

Comparing OSI and TCP/IP

The OSI model has many similarities to the TCP/IP model from a basic conceptual perspective. It has layers (seven total), and each layer defines a set of typical networking functions. As with TCP/IP, the OSI layers each refer to multiple protocols and standards that implement the functions specified by each layer. In other cases, just as for TCP/IP, the OSI committees did not create new protocols or standards, but instead referenced other protocols that were already defined. For example, the IEEE defines Ethernet standards, so the OSI committees did not waste time specifying a new type of Ethernet; they simply referred to the IEEE Ethernet standards.

Today the OSI model can be used as a standard of comparison to other networking models. Figure 1-13 compares the seven-layer OSI model with both the four-layer and five-layer TCP/IP models.

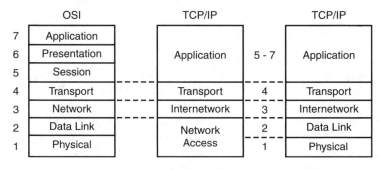

Figure 1-13 *OSI Model Compared to the Two TCP/IP Models*

Next, these sections will examine two ways in which we still use OSI terminology today: to describe other protocols and to describe the encapsulation process. Along the way, the text will briefly examine each layer of the OSI model.

Describing Protocols by Referencing the OSI Layers

Even today, networking documents often describe TCP/IP protocols and standards by referencing OSI layers, both by layer number and layer name. For example, a common description of a LAN switch is a "Layer 2 switch"—with "Layer 2" referring to OSI Layer 2. Because OSI did have a very well-defined set of functions associated with each of its seven layers, if you know those functions, you can understand what people mean when they refer to a product or function by its OSI layer.

For another example, TCP/IP's Internet layer, as implemented mainly by IP, equates most directly to the OSI *network* layer. So, most people say that IP is a *network layer protocol* or a *Layer 3 protocol*, using OSI terminology and numbers for the layer. Of course, if you numbered the TCP/IP model, starting at the bottom, IP would be either Layer 2 or 3, depending on what version of the TCP/IP model you care to use. However, even though IP is a TCP/IP protocol, everyone uses the OSI model layer names and numbers when describing IP, or any other protocol for that matter.

Although Figure 1-13 seems to imply that the OSI network layer and the TCP/IP Internet layer are at least similar, the figure does not point out why they are similar. To appreciate why the TCP/IP layers correspond to a particular OSI layer, you need to have a better understanding of the OSI layers. For example, the OSI network layer defines logical addressing and routing, as does the TCP/IP Internet layer. While the details differ significantly, the TCP/IP Internet layer matches the overall goals and intent of the OSI network layer.

As another example, you might recall that the TCP/IP transport layer defines many functions, including error recovery. The OSI transport layer also defines these same functions as well, although with different details and different specific protocols. As a result, the networking industry refers to TCP as a Layer 4 protocol or a transport layer protocol, again based on the OSI layer number and name.

OSI Layers and Their Functions

Network engineers need a basic understanding of the functions defined by each OSI layer, as well as remembering the names of the layers. It is also important that, for each device or protocol referenced throughout the book, you understand which layers of the OSI model most closely match the functions defined by that device or protocol.

Today, because most people happen to be much more familiar with TCP/IP functions that with OSI functions, one of the best ways to learn about the function of different OSI layers is to think about the functions in the TCP/IP model and correlate those with the OSI model. If you use the five-layer TCP/IP model, the bottom four layers of OSI and TCP/IP map closely together. The only difference in these bottom four layers is the name of OSI Layer 3 (network) compared to TCP/IP (Internet). The upper three layers of the OSI reference model (application, presentation, and session—Layers 7, 6, and 5) define functions that all map to the TCP/IP application layer. Table 1-3 defines the functions of the seven layers.

Table 1-3 *OSI Reference Model Layer Definitions*

Layer	Functional Description
7	Layer 7 provides an interface between the communications software and any applications that need to communicate outside the computer on which the application resides. It also defines processes for user authentication.
6	This layer's main purpose is to define and negotiate data formats, such as ASCII text, EBCDIC text, binary, BCD, and JPEG. Encryption is also defined by OSI as a presentation layer service.
5	The session layer defines how to start, control, and end conversations (called *sessions*). This includes the control and management of multiple bidirectional messages so that the application can be notified if only some of a series of messages are completed. This allows the presentation layer to have a seamless view of an incoming stream of data.
4	Layer 4 protocols provide a large number of services, as described in Chapter 5. Although OSI Layers 5 through 7 focus on issues related to the application, Layer 4 focuses on issues related to data delivery to another computer—for example, error recovery and flow control.
3	The network layer defines three main features: logical addressing, routing (forwarding), and path determination. Routing defines how devices (typically routers) forward packets to their final destination. Logical addressing defines how each device can have an address that can be used by the routing process. Path determination refers to the work done by routing protocols to learn all possible routes and choose the best route.
2	The data link layer defines the rules that determine when a device can send data over a particular medium. Data-link protocols also define the format of a header and trailer that allows devices attached to the medium to send and receive data successfully.
1	This layer typically refers to standards from other organizations. These standards deal with the physical characteristics of the transmission medium, including connectors, pins, use of pins, electrical currents, encoding, light modulation, and the rules for how to activate and deactivate the use of the physical medium.

Table 1-4 lists some example devices and the comparable OSI layers at which most of each device's logic operates. Note that many network devices must actually understand the protocols at multiple OSI layers, so the layer listed in the table actually refers to the highest layer that the device normally thinks about when performing its core work. For example, routers need to think about Layer 3 concepts, but they must also support features at both Layers 1 and 2.

Table 1-4   *OSI Reference Model—Example Devices and Protocols*

Layer Name	Protocols and Specifications	Devices
Application, presentation, session (Layers 5–7)	Telnet, HTTP, FTP, SMTP, POP3, VoIP, SNMP	Firewalls, intrusion detection systems, hosts
Transport (Layer 4)	TCP, UDP	Hosts, firewalls
Network (Layer 3)	IP	Routers
Data link (Layer 2)	Ethernet (IEEE 802.3), HDLC, Frame Relay, PPP	LAN switches, wireless access points, cable modems, DSL modems
Physical (Layer 1)	RJ-45, EIA/TIA-232, V.35, Ethernet (IEEE 802.3)	LAN hubs, LAN repeaters, cables

Besides remembering the basics of the features of each OSI layer (as shown in Table 1-3), and some example protocols and devices at each layer (as shown in Table 1-4), you should also memorize the names of the layers. You can simply memorize them, but some people like to use a mnemonic phrase to make memorization easier. In the following three phrases, the first letter of each word is the same as the first letter of an OSI layer name, in the order specified in parentheses:

■   All People Seem To Need Data Processing (Layers 7 to 1)

■   Please Do Not Take Sausage Pizzas Away (Layers 1 to 7)

■   Phew! Dead Ninja Turtles Smell Particularly Awful (Layers 1 to 7)

OSI Layering Concepts and Benefits

While networking models use layers to help humans categorize and understand the many functions in a network, networking models use layers for many reasons. For example, consider another postal service analogy. A person writing a letter does not have to think about how the postal service will deliver a letter across the country. The postal worker in the middle of the country does not have to worry about the contents of the letter. Likewise, networking models that divide functions into different layers enable one software package or hardware device to implement functions from one layer, and assume that other software/hardware will perform the functions defined by the other layers.

The following list summarizes the benefits of layered protocol specifications:

Key Topic

■ **Less complex:** Compared to not using a layered model, network models break the concepts into smaller parts.

■ **Standard interfaces:** The standard interface definitions between each layer allow multiple vendors to create products that compete to be used for a given function, along with all the benefits of open competition.

■ **Easier to learn:** Humans can more easily discuss and learn about the many details of a protocol specification.

■ **Easier to develop:** Reduced complexity allows easier program changes and faster product development.

■ **Multivendor interoperability:** Creating products to meet the same networking standards means that computers and networking gear from multiple vendors can work in the same network.

■ **Modular engineering:** One vendor can write software that implements higher layers—for example, a web browser—and another vendor can write software that implements the lower layers—for example, Microsoft's built-in TCP/IP software in its operating systems.

OSI Encapsulation Terminology

Like TCP/IP, each OSI layer asks for services from the next lower layer. To provide the services, each layer makes use of a header and possibly a trailer. The lower layer encapsulates the higher layer's data behind a header, and that header includes information use. The final topic of this chapter explains some of the terminology and concepts related to OSI encapsulation.

The TCP/IP model uses terms such as *segment*, *packet*, and *frame* to refer to various layers and their respective encapsulated data (see Figure 1-11). OSI uses a more generic term: *protocol data unit*, or *PDU*.

A PDU represents the bits that include the headers and trailers for that layer, as well as the encapsulated data. For example, an IP packet, as shown in Figure 1-10, using OSI terminology, is a PDU. In fact, an IP packet is a *Layer 3 PDU* (abbreviated L3PDU) because IP is a Layer 3 protocol. So, rather than use the terms *segment*, *packet*, or *frame*, OSI simply refers to the "Layer x PDU," or LxPDU, with "x" referring to the number of the layer being discussed.

Figure 1-14 represents the typical encapsulation process, with the top of the figure showing the application data and application layer header, and the bottom of the figure showing the L2PDU that is transmitted onto the physical link.

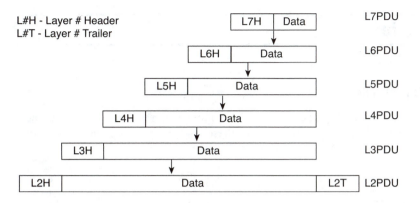

Figure 1-14   *OSI Encapsulation and Protocol Data Units*

Chapter Review

Review Key Topics

Review the most important topics from the chapter, noted with the Key Topic icon in the margin of the page. Table 1-5 lists a reference of these key topics and the page number on which each is found.

Table 1-5 *Key Topics for Chapter 1*

	Description	Page Number
Table 1-2	Provides definitions of same-layer and adjacent-layer interaction	10
Figure 1-8	Shows the general concept of IP routing	14
Figure 1-9	Depicts the data-link services provided to IP for the purpose of delivering IP packets from host to host	15
Figure 1-12	Shows the meaning of the terms *segment*, *packet*, and *frame*	18
Figure 1-13	Compares the OSI and TCP/IP network models	19
List	Lists the benefits of using a layered networking model	22

Define Key Terms

Define the following key terms from this chapter, and check your answers in the glossary:

Adjacent-layer interaction, decapsulation, encapsulation, frame, networking model, packet, protocol data unit (PDU), same-layer interaction, segment

Answer Review Questions

Answer the following review questions:

1. Which of the following protocols are examples of TCP/IP transport layer protocols?

   a. Ethernet

   b. HTTP

   c. IP

   d. UDP

   e. SMTP

   f. TCP

2. Which of the following protocols are examples of TCP/IP network access layer protocols?

   a. Ethernet

   b. HTTP

   c. IP

   d. UDP

   e. SMTP

   f. TCP

   g. PPP

3. The process of HTTP asking TCP to send some data and make sure that it is received correctly is an example of what?

   a. Same-layer interaction

   b. Adjacent-layer interaction

   c. The OSI model

   d. All the other answers are correct.

4. The process of TCP on one computer marking a TCP segment as segment 1, and the receiving computer then acknowledging the receipt of TCP segment 1, is an example of what?

   a. Data encapsulation

   b. Same-layer interaction

   c. Adjacent-layer interaction

   d. The OSI model

   e. None of these answers are correct.

5. The process of a web server adding a TCP header to the contents of a web page, followed by adding an IP header and then adding a data link header and trailer, is an example of what?

    a. Data encapsulation

    b. Same-layer interaction

    c. The OSI model

    d. All of these answers are correct.

6. Which of the following terms is used specifically to identify the entity that is created when encapsulating data inside data link layer headers and trailers?

    a. Data

    b. Chunk

    c. Segment

    d. Frame

    e. Packet

    f. None of these—there is no encapsulation by the data link layer.

7. Which OSI layer defines the functions of logical network-wide addressing and routing?

    a. Layer 1

    b. Layer 2

    c. Layer 3

    d. Layer 4

    e. Layer 5

    f. Layer 6

    g. Layer 7

8. Which OSI layer defines the standards for cabling and connectors?

    a. Layer 1

    b. Layer 2

    c. Layer 3

    d. Layer 4

    e. Layer 5

    f. Layer 6

    g. Layer 7

9. Which OSI layer defines the standards for data formats and encryption?

   a. Layer 1

   b. Layer 2

   c. Layer 3

   d. Layer 4

   e. Layer 5

   f. Layer 6

   g. Layer 7

10. Which of the following terms are not valid terms for the names of the seven OSI layers?

   a. Application

   b. Data link

   c. Transmission

   d. Presentation

   e. Internet

   f. Session

This chapter covers the following subjects:

- **An Overview of Modern Ethernet LANs:**
Provides some perspectives for those who have used
Ethernet at the office or school but have not exam-
ined the details.

- **A Brief History of Ethernet:** Examines several old
options for Ethernet cabling and devices as a point
of comparison for today's cabling, devices, and terminology.

- **Ethernet UTP Cabling:** Explains the options for cabling and cable pinouts.

- **Improving Performance by Using Switches Instead of Hubs:** A more detailed examination of the
performance improvements made by using switches
instead of older Ethernet hubs.

- **Ethernet Data-Link Protocols:** Explains the meaning and purpose of the fields in the Ethernet header
and trailer.

CHAPTER 2

LAN Fundamentals

A typical Enterprise network consists of several sites. The end-user devices connect to a LAN, which allows the local computers to communicate with each other. Additionally, each site has a router that connects to both the LAN and a wide-area network (WAN), with the WAN providing connectivity between the various sites. With routers and a WAN, the computers at different sites can also communicate.

This chapter describes the basics of how to create LANs today, with Chapter 3, "WAN Fundamentals," describing the basics of creating WANs. Ethernet is the undisputed king of LAN standards today. Historically speaking, several competing LAN standards existed, including Token Ring, Fiber Distributed Data Interface (FDDI), and Asynchronous Transfer Mode (ATM). Eventually, Ethernet won out over all the competing LAN standards, so that today when you think of LANs, no one even questions what type—it's Ethernet.

An Overview of Modern Ethernet LANs

The term *Ethernet* refers to a family of standards that together define the physical and data link layers of the world's most popular type of LAN. The different standards vary as to the speed supported, with speeds of 10 megabits per second (Mbps), 100 Mbps, and 1000 Mbps (1 gigabit per second, or Gbps) being common today. The standards also differ as far as the types of cabling and the allowed length of the cabling. For example, the most commonly used Ethernet standards allow the use of inexpensive *unshielded twisted-pair* (UTP) cabling, whereas other standards call for more expensive fiber-optic cabling. Fiber-optic cabling might be worth the cost in some cases, because the cabling is more secure and allows for much longer distances between devices. To support the widely varying needs for building a LAN—needs for different speeds, different cabling types (trading off distance requirements versus cost), and other factors—many variations of Ethernet standards have been created.

The Institute of Electrical and Electronics Engineers (IEEE) has defined many Ethernet standards since it took over the LAN standardization process in the early 1980s. Most of the standards define a different variation of Ethernet at the physical layer, with differences in speed and types of cabling. Additionally, for the data link layer, the IEEE separates the functions into two sublayers:

- The 802.3 Media Access Control (MAC) sublayer

- The 802.2 Logical Link Control (LLC) sublayer

In fact, MAC addresses get their name from the IEEE name for this lower portion of the data link layer Ethernet standards.

Each new physical layer standard from the IEEE requires many differences at the physical layer. However, each of these physical layer standards uses the exact same 802.3 header, and each uses the upper LLC sublayer as well. Table 2-1 lists the most commonly used IEEE Ethernet physical layer standards.

Table 2-1   *Today's Most Common Types of Ethernet*

Common Name	Speed	Alternative Name	Name of IEEE Standard	Cable Type, Maximum Length
Ethernet	10 Mbps	10BASE-T	IEEE 802.3	Copper, 100 m
Fast Ethernet	100 Mbps	100BASE-TX	IEEE 802.3u	Copper, 100 m
Gigabit Ethernet	1000 Mbps	1000BASE-LX, 1000BASE-SX	IEEE 802.3z	Fiber, 550 m (SX) 5 km (LX)
Gigabit Ethernet	1000 Mbps	1000BASE-T	IEEE 802.3ab	100 m

The table is convenient for study, but the terms in the table bear a little explanation. First, beware that the term *Ethernet* is often used to mean "all types of Ethernet," but in some cases, it is used to mean "10BASE-T Ethernet." (Because the term Ethernet sometimes can be ambiguous, this book refers to 10-Mbps Ethernet as 10BASE-T when the specific type of Ethernet matters to the discussion.) Second, note that the alternative name for each type of Ethernet lists the speed in Mbps—namely, 10 Mbps, 100 Mbps, and 1000 Mbps. The *T* and *TX* in the alternative names refer to the fact that each of these standards defines the use of UTP cabling, with the *T* referring to the T in *twisted pair*.

To build and create a modern LAN using any of the UTP-based types of Ethernet LANs listed in Table 2-1, you need the following components:

■ Computers that have an Ethernet network interface card (NIC) installed

■ Either an Ethernet hub or Ethernet switch

■ UTP cables to connect each PC to the hub or switch

Figure 2-1 shows a typical LAN. The NICs cannot be seen, because they reside in the PCs. However, the lines represent the UTP cabling, and the icon in the center of the figure represents a LAN switch.

Note: Figure 2-1 applies to all the common types of Ethernet. The same basic design and topology are used regardless of speed or cabling type.

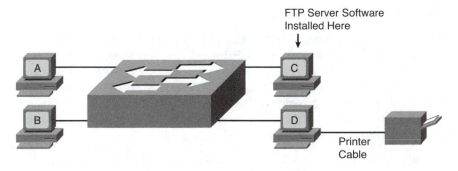

Figure 2-1 *Typical Small Modern LAN*

Most people can build a LAN like the one shown in Figure 2-1 with practically no real knowledge of how LANs work. Most PCs contain an Ethernet NIC that was installed at the factory. Switches do not need to be configured for them to forward traffic between the computers. All you have to do is connect the switch to a power cable and plug in the UTP cables from each PC to the switch. Then the PCs should be able to send Ethernet frames to each other.

You can use such a small LAN for many purposes, even without a WAN connection. Consider the following functions for which a LAN is the perfect, small-scale solution:

- **File sharing:** Each computer can be configured to share all or parts of its file system so that the other computers can read, or possibly read and write, the files on another computer. This function typically is simply part of the PC operating system.

- **Printer sharing:** Computers can share their printers as well. For example, PCs A, B, and C in Figure 2-1 could print documents on PC D's printer. This function is also typically part of the PC's operating system.

- **File transfers:** A computer could install a file transfer server, thereby allowing other computers to send and receive files to and from that computer. For example, PC C could install File Transfer Protocol (FTP) server software, allowing the other PCs to use FTP client software to connect to PC C and transfer files.

- **Gaming:** The PCs could install gaming software that allows multiple players to play in the same game. The gaming software would then communicate using the Ethernet.

The goal of the first half of this chapter is to help you understand much of the theory and practical knowledge behind simple LAN designs such as the one illustrated in Figure 2-1. To fully understand modern LANs, it is helpful to understand a bit about the history of Ethernet, which is covered in the next section. Following that, this chapter examines the physical aspects (Layer 1) of a simple Ethernet LAN, focusing on UTP cabling. Then this chapter compares the older (and slower) Ethernet hub with the newer (and faster) Ethernet switch. Finally, the LAN coverage in this chapter ends with the data-link (Layer 2) functions on Ethernet.

A Brief History of Ethernet

Like many early networking protocols, Ethernet began life inside a corporation that was looking to solve a specific problem. Xerox needed an effective way to allow a new invention, called the personal computer, to be connected in its offices. From that, Ethernet was born. (Go to http://inventors.about.com/library/weekly/aa111598.htm for an interesting story on the history of Ethernet.) Eventually, Xerox teamed with Intel and Digital Equipment Corp. (DEC) to further develop Ethernet, so the original Ethernet became known as *DIX Ethernet*, referring to DEC, Intel, and Xerox.

These companies willingly transitioned the job of Ethernet standards development to the IEEE in the early 1980s. The IEEE formed two committees that worked directly on Ethernet—the IEEE 802.3 committee and the IEEE 802.2 committee. The 802.3 committee worked on physical layer standards as well as a subpart of the data link layer called *Media Access Control (MAC)*. The IEEE assigned the other functions of the data link layer to the 802.2 committee, calling this part of the data link layer the *Logical Link Control (LLC)* sublayer. (The 802.2 standard applied to Ethernet as well as to other IEEE standard LANs such as Token Ring.)

The Original Ethernet Standards: 10BASE2 and 10BASE5

Ethernet is best understood by first considering the two early Ethernet specifications, 10BASE5 and 10BASE2. These two Ethernet specifications defined the details of the physical and data link layers of early Ethernet networks. (10BASE2 and 10BASE5 differ in their cabling details, but for the discussion in this chapter, you can consider them as behaving identically.) With these two specifications, the network engineer installs a series of coaxial cables connecting each device on the Ethernet network. There is no hub, switch, or wiring panel. The Ethernet consists solely of the collective Ethernet NICs in the computers and the coaxial cabling. The series of cables creates an electrical circuit, called a bus, which is shared among all devices on the Ethernet. When a computer wants to send some bits to another computer on the bus, it sends an electrical signal, and the electricity propagates to all devices on the Ethernet.

Figure 2-2 shows the basic logic of an old Ethernet 10BASE2 network, which uses a single electrical bus, created with coaxial cable and Ethernet cards.

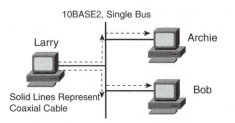

Figure 2-2   *Small Ethernet 10BASE2 Network*

The solid lines in the figure represent the physical network cabling. The dashed lines with arrows represent the path that Larry's transmitted frame takes. Larry sends an electrical signal across his Ethernet NIC onto the cable, and both Bob and Archie receive the signal. The cabling creates a physical electrical bus, meaning that the transmitted signal is received by all stations on the LAN. Just like a school bus stops at every student's house along a route, the electrical signal on a 10BASE2 or 10BASE5 network is propagated to each station on the LAN.

These "rules" are based on your culture: CSMA/CD. Because the network uses a single bus, if two or more electrical signals were sent at the same time, they would overlap and collide, making both signals unintelligible. So, unsurprisingly, Ethernet also defined a specification for how to ensure that only one device sends traffic on the Ethernet at one time. Otherwise, the Ethernet would have been unusable. This algorithm, known as the *carrier sense multiple access with collision detection (CSMA/CD)* algorithm, defines how the bus is accessed.

In human terms, CSMA/CD is similar to what happens in a meeting room with many attendees. It's hard to understand what two people are saying at the same time, so generally, one person talks and the rest listen. Imagine that Bob and Larry both want to reply to the current speaker's comments. As soon as the speaker takes a breath, Bob and Larry both try to speak. If Larry hears Bob's voice before Larry makes a noise, Larry might stop and let Bob speak. Or, maybe they both start at almost the same time, so they talk over each other and no one can hear what is said. Then there's the proverbial "Pardon me; go ahead with what you were saying," and eventually Larry or Bob talks. Or perhaps another person jumps in and talks while Larry and Bob are both backing off. These "rules" are based on your culture; CSMA/CD is based on Ethernet protocol specifications and achieves the same type of goal.

Basically, the CSMA/CD algorithm can be summarized as follows:

Key Topic

- A device that wants to send a frame waits until the LAN is silent—in other words, no frames are currently being sent—before attempting to send an electrical signal.

- If a collision still occurs, the devices that caused the collision wait a random amount of time and then try again.

In 10BASE5 and 10BASE2 Ethernet LANs, a collision occurs because the transmitted electrical signal travels along the entire length of the bus. When two stations send at the same time, their electrical signals overlap, causing a collision. So, all devices on a 10BASE5 or 10BASE2 Ethernet need to use CSMA/CD to avoid collisions and to recover when inadvertent collisions occur.

Repeaters

Like any type of LAN, 10BASE5 and 10BASE2 had limitations on the total length of a cable. With 10BASE5, the limit was 500 m; with 10BASE2, it was 185 m. Interestingly, the 5 and 2 in the names 10BASE5 and 10BASE2 represent the maximum cable length—with the 2 referring to 200 meters, which is pretty close to the actual maximum of 185 meters. (Both of these types of Ethernet ran at 10 Mbps.)

In some cases, the maximum cable length was not enough, so a device called a *repeater* was developed. One of the problems that limited the length of a cable was that the signal sent by one device could attenuate too much if the cable was longer than 500 m or 185 m. *Attenuation* means that when electrical signals pass over a wire, the signal strength gets weaker the farther along the cable it travels. It's the same concept behind why you can hear someone talking right next to you, but if that person speaks at the same volume and you are on the other side of a crowded room, you might not hear her because the sound waves have attenuated.

Repeaters connect to multiple cable segments, receive the electrical signal on one cable, interpret the bits as 1s and 0s, and generate a brand-new, clean, strong signal out the other cable. A repeater does not simply amplify the signal, because amplifying the signal might also amplify any noise picked up along the way.

Note: Because the repeater does not interpret what the bits mean, but it does examine and generate electrical signals, a repeater is considered to operate at Layer 1.

You should not expect to need to implement 10BASE5 or 10BASE2 Ethernet LANs today. However, for learning purposes, keep in mind several key points from this section as you move on to concepts that relate to today's LANs:

- The original Ethernet LANs created an electrical bus to which all devices connected.

- Because collisions could occur on this bus, Ethernet defined the CSMA/CD algorithm, which defined a way to both avoid collisions and take action when collisions occurred.

- Repeaters extended the length of LANs by cleaning up the electrical signal and repeating it—a Layer 1 function—but without interpreting the meaning of the electrical signal.

Building 10BASE-T Networks with Hubs

The IEEE later defined new Ethernet standards besides 10BASE5 and 10BASE2. Chronologically, the 10BASE-T standard came next (1990), followed by 100BASE-TX (1995), and then 1000BASE-T (1999). To support these new standards, networking devices called hubs and switches were also created. This section defines the basics of how these three popular types of Ethernet work, including the basic operation of hubs and switches.

10BASE-T solved several problems with the early 10BASE5 and 10BASE2 Ethernet specifications. 10BASE-T allowed the use of UTP telephone cabling that was already installed. Even if new cabling needed to be installed, the inexpensive and easy-to-install UTP cabling replaced the old expensive and difficult-to-install coaxial cabling.

Another major improvement introduced with 10BASE-T, and that remains a key design point today, is the concept of cabling each device to a centralized connection point. Originally, 10BASE-T called for the use of Ethernet *hubs*, as shown in Figure 2-3.

When building a LAN today, you could choose to use either a hub or a switch as the centralized Ethernet device to which all the computers connect. Even though modern Ethernet LANs typically use switches instead of hubs, understanding the operation of hubs helps you understand some of the terminology used with switches, as well as some of their benefits.

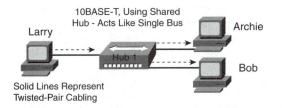

Figure 2-3   *Small Ethernet 10BASE-T Network Using a Hub*

Hubs are essentially repeaters with multiple physical ports. That means that the hub simply regenerates the electrical signal that comes in one port and sends the same signal out every other port. By doing so, any LAN that uses a hub, as in Figure 2-3, creates an electrical bus, just like 10BASE2 and 10BASE5. Therefore, collisions can still occur, so CSMA/CD access rules continue to be used.

10BASE-T networks using hubs solved some big problems with 10BASE5 and 10BASE2. First, the LAN had much higher availability, because a single cable problem could, and probably did, take down 10BASE5 and 10BASE2 LANs. With 10BASE-T, a cable connects each device to the hub, so a single cable problem affects only one device. As mentioned earlier, the use of UTP cabling, in a star topology (all cables running to a centralized connection device), lowered the cost of purchasing and installing the cabling.

Today, you might occasionally use LAN hubs, but you will more likely use switches instead of hubs. Switches perform much better than hubs, support more functions than hubs, and typically are priced almost as low as hubs. However, for learning purposes, keep in mind several key points from this section about the history of Ethernet as you move on to concepts that relate to today's LANs:

■   The original Ethernet LANs created an electrical bus to which all devices connected.

■   10BASE2 and 10BASE5 repeaters extended the length of LANs by cleaning up the electrical signal and repeating it—a Layer 1 function—but without interpreting the meaning of the electrical signal.

■   Hubs are repeaters that provide a centralized connection point for UTP cabling—but they still create a single electrical bus, shared by the various devices, just like 10BASE5 and 10BASE2.

■   Because collisions could occur in any of these cases, Ethernet defines the CSMA/CD algorithm, which tells devices how to both avoid collisions and take action when collisions do occur.

The next section explains the details of the UTP cabling used by today's most commonly used types of Ethernet.

Ethernet UTP Cabling

The three most common Ethernet standards used today—10BASE-T (Ethernet), 100BASE-TX (Fast Ethernet, or FE), and 1000BASE-T (Gigabit Ethernet, or GE)—use UTP cabling. Some key differences exist, particularly with the number of wire pairs needed in each case, and in the type (category) of cabling. This section examines some of the details of UTP cabling, pointing out differences among these three standards along the way. In particular, this section describes the cables and the connectors on the ends of the cables, how they use the wires in the cables to send data, and the pinouts required for proper operation.

UTP Cables and RJ-45 Connectors

The UTP cabling used by popular Ethernet standards include either two or four pairs of wires. Because the wires inside the cable are thin and brittle, the cable itself has an outer jacket of flexible plastic to support the wires. Each individual copper wire also has a thin plastic coating to help prevent the wire from breaking. The plastic coating on each wire has a different color, making it easy to look at both ends of the cable and identify the ends of an individual wire.

The cable ends typically have some form of connector attached (typically RJ-45 connectors), with the ends of the wires inserted into the connectors. The RJ-45 connector has eight specific physical locations into which the eight wires in the cable can be inserted, called *pin positions*, or simply *pins*. When the connectors are added to the end of the cable, the ends of the wires must be correctly inserted into the correct pin positions.

Note: If you have an Ethernet UTP cable nearby, it would be useful to closely examine the RJ-45 connectors and wires as you read through this section.

As soon as the cable has RJ-45 connectors on each end, the RJ-45 connector needs to be inserted into an RJ-45 receptacle, often called an *RJ-45 port*. Figure 2-4 shows photos of the cables, connectors, and ports.

Note: The RJ-45 connector is slightly wider, but otherwise similar, to the RJ-11 connectors commonly used for telephone cables in homes in North America.

The figure shows three separate views of an RJ-45 connector on the left. The head-on view in the upper-left part of the figure shows the ends of the eight wires in their pin positions inside the UTP cable. The upper-right part of the figure shows an Ethernet NIC that is not yet installed in a computer. The RJ-45 port on the NIC would be exposed on the side of the computer, making it easily accessible as soon as the NIC has been installed into a computer. The lower-right part of the figure shows the side of a Cisco 2960 switch, with multiple RJ-45 ports, allowing multiple devices to easily connect to the Ethernet network.

Although RJ-45 connectors and ports are popular, engineers might want to purchase Cisco LAN switches that have a few physical ports that can be changed without having to purchase a whole new switch. Many Cisco switches have a few interfaces that use either Gigabit Interface Converters (GBIC) or Small-Form Pluggables (SFP). Both are small removable devices that fit into a port or slot in the switch. Because Cisco manufactures a wide range of GBICs and SFPs, for every Ethernet standard, the switch can use a variety of cable connectors and types of cabling and support different cable lengths—all by just switching to a different kind of GBIC or SFP. Figure 2-5 shows a 1000BASE-T GBIC, ready to be inserted into a LAN switch.

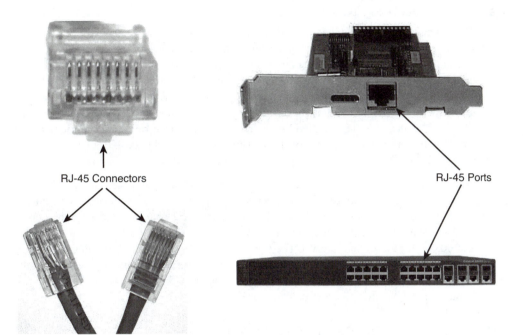

Figure 2-4   *RJ-45 Connectors and Ports*

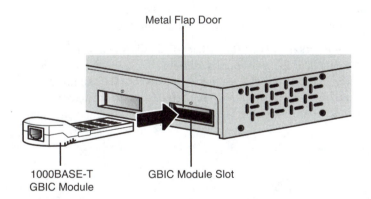

Figure 2-5   *1000BASE-T GBIC with an RJ-45 Connector*

If a network engineer needs to use an existing switch in a new role in a campus network, the engineer could simply buy a new 1000BASE-LX GBIC to replace the old 1000BASE-T GBIC and reduce the extra cost of buying a whole new switch. For example, when using a switch so that it connects only to other switches in the same building, the switch could use 1000BASE-T GBICs and copper cabling. Later, if the company moved to another location, the switch could be repurposed by using a different GBIC that supported fiber-optic cabling, and different connectors, using 1000BASE-LX to support a longer cabling distance.

Transmitting Data Using Twisted Pairs

UTP cabling consists of matched pairs of wires that are indeed twisted together—hence the name *twisted pair*. The devices on each end of the cable can create an electrical circuit using a pair of wires by sending current on the two wires, in opposite directions. When current passes over any wire, that current induces a magnetic field outside the wire; the magnetic field can in turn cause electrical noise on other wires in the cable. By twisting together the wires in the same pair, with the current running in opposite directions on each wire, the magnetic field created by one wire mostly cancels out the magnetic field created by the other wire. Because of this feature, most networking cables that use copper wires and electricity use twisted pairs of wires to send data.

To send data over the electrical circuit created over a wire pair, the devices use an *encoding scheme* that defines how the electrical signal should vary, over time, to mean either a binary 0 or 1. For example, 10BASE-T uses an encoding scheme that encodes a binary 0 as a transition from higher voltage to lower voltage during the middle of a 1/10,000,000th-of-a-second interval. The electrical details of encoding are unimportant for the purposes of this book. But it is important to realize that networking devices create an electrical circuit using each wire pair, and vary the signal as defined by the encoding scheme, to send bits over the wire pair.

UTP Cabling Pinouts for 10BASE-T and 100BASE-TX

The wires in the UTP cable must be connected to the correct pin positions in the RJ-45 connectors in order for communication to work correctly. As mentioned earlier, the RJ-45 connector has eight *pin positions*, or simply *pins*, into which the copper wires inside the cable protrude. The wiring *pinouts*—the choice of which color wire goes into which pin position—must conform to the Ethernet standards described in this section.

Interestingly, the IEEE does not actually define the official standards for cable manufacturing, as well as part of the details of the conventions used for the cabling pinouts. The Telecommunications Industry Association (TIA) defines standards for UTP cabling, color coding for wires, and standard pinouts on the cables. (See http://www.tiaonline.org.) Figure 2-6 shows two pinout standards from the TIA, with the color coding and pair numbers listed.

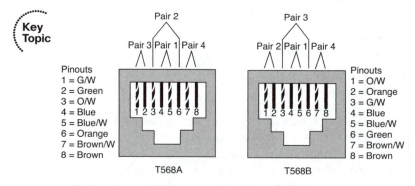

Figure 2-6   *TIA Standard Ethernet Cabling Pinouts*

To understand the acronyms listed in the figure, note that the eight wires in a UTP cable have either a solid color (green, orange, blue, or brown) or a striped color scheme using white and one of the other four colors. Also, a single-wire pair uses the same base color. For example, the blue wire and the blue/white striped wire are paired and twisted. In Figure 2-6, the notations with a / refer to the striped wires. For example, "G/W" refers to the green-and-white striped wire.

Note: A UTP cable needs two pairs of wires for 10BASE-T and 100BASE-TX and four pairs of wires for 1000BASE-T. This section focuses on the pinouts for two-pair wiring, with four-pair wiring covered next.

To build a working Ethernet LAN, you must choose or build cables that use the correct wiring pinout on each end of the cable. 10BASE-T and 100BASE-TX Ethernet define that one pair should be used to send data in one direction, with the other pair used to send data in the other direction. In particular, Ethernet NICs should send data using the pair connected to pins 1 and 2—in other words, pair 3 according to the T568A pinout standard shown in Figure 2-6. Similarly, Ethernet NICs should expect to receive data using the pair at pins 3 and 6—pair 2 according to the T568A standard. Knowing what the Ethernet NICs do, hubs and switches do the opposite—they receive on the pair at pins 1,2 (pair 3 per T568A), and they send on the pair at pins 3,6 (pair 2 per T568A).

Figure 2-7 shows this concept, with PC Larry connected to a hub. Note that the figure shows the two twisted pairs inside the cable, and the NIC outside the PC, to emphasize that the cable connects to the NIC and hub and that only two pairs are being used.

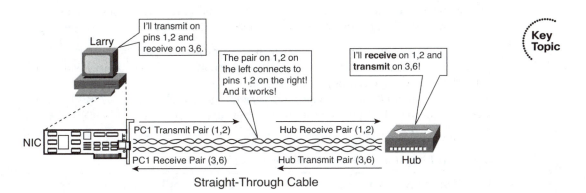

Figure 2-7   *Ethernet Straight-Through Cable Concept*

The network shown in Figure 2-7 uses a *straight-through* cable. An Ethernet straight-through cable connects the wire at pin 1 on one end of the cable to pin 1 at the other end of the cable; the wire at pin 2 needs to connect to pin 2 on the other end of the cable; pin 3 on one end connects to pin 3 on the other; and so on. (To create a straight-through cable, both ends of the cable use the same TIA pinout standard on each end of the cable.)

A straight-through cable is used when the devices on the ends of the cable use opposite pins when they transmit data. However, when connecting two devices that both use the same pins to transmit, the pinouts of the cable must be set up to swap the wire pair. A cable that swaps the wire pairs inside the cable is called a *crossover cable*. For example, many LANs inside an Enterprise network use multiple switches, with a UTP cable connecting the switches. Because both switches send on the pair at pins 3,6, and receive on the pair at pins 1,2, the cable must swap or cross the pairs. Figure 2-8 shows several conceptual views of a crossover cable.

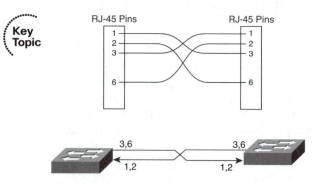

Figure 2-8   *Crossover Ethernet Cable*

The top part of the figure shows the pins to which each wire is connected. Pin 1 on the left end connects to pin 3 on the right end, pin 2 on the left to pin 6 on the right, pin 3 on the left to pin 1 on the right, and pin 6 on the left to pin 2 on the right. The bottom of the figure shows that the wires at pins 3,6 on each end—the pins each switch uses to transmit—connect to pins 1,2 on the other end, thereby allowing the devices to receive on pins 1,2.

You should be well prepared to choose which type of cable (straight-through or crossover) is needed in each part of the network. In short, devices on opposite ends of a cable that use the same pair of pins to transmit need a crossover cable. Devices that use an opposite pair of pins to transmit need a straight-through cable. Table 2-2 lists the devices mentioned in this book and the pin pairs they use, assuming that they use 10BASE-T and 100BASE-TX.

Table 2-2   *10BASE-T and 100BASE-TX Pin Pairs Used*

Devices That Transmit on 1,2 and Receive on 3,6	Devices That Transmit on 3,6 and Receive on 1,2
PC NICs	Hubs
Routers	Switches
Wireless Access Point (Ethernet interface)	—
Networked printers (printers that connect directly to the LAN)	—

For example, Figure 2-9 shows a campus LAN in a single building. In this case, several straight-through cables are used to connect PCs to switches. Additionally, the cables connecting the switches—referred to as *trunks*—require crossover cables.

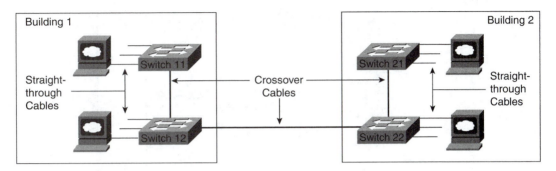

Figure 2-9 *Typical Uses for Straight-Through and Crossover Ethernet Cables*

1000BASE-T Cabling

As noted earlier, 1000BASE-T differs from 10BASE-T and 100BASE-TX as far as the cabling and pinouts. First, 1000BASE-T requires four wire pairs. Also, Gigabit Ethernet transmits and receives on each of the four wire pairs simultaneously.

However, Gigabit Ethernet does have a concept of straight-through and crossover cables, with a minor difference in the crossover cables. The pinouts for a straight-through cable are the same—pin 1 to pin 1, pin 2 to pin 2, and so on. The crossover cable crosses the same two-wire pair as the crossover cable for the other types of Ethernet—the pair at pins 1,2 and 3,6—as well as crossing the two other pairs (the pair at pins 4,5 with the pair at pins 7,8).

Note: If you have some experience with installing LANs, you might be thinking that you have used the wrong cable before (straight-through or crossover), but the cable worked. Cisco switches have a feature called auto-mdix that notices when the wrong cabling pinouts are used. This feature readjusts the switch's logic and makes the cable work. Be ready to identify whether the correct cable is shown in figures.

Next, this chapter takes a closer look at LAN hubs and the need for LAN switches.

Improving Performance by Using Switches Instead of Hubs

This section examines some of the performance problems created when using hubs, followed by explanations of how LAN switches solve the two largest performance problems encountered with hubs. To better appreciate the problem, consider Figure 2-10, which shows what happens when a single device sends data through a hub.

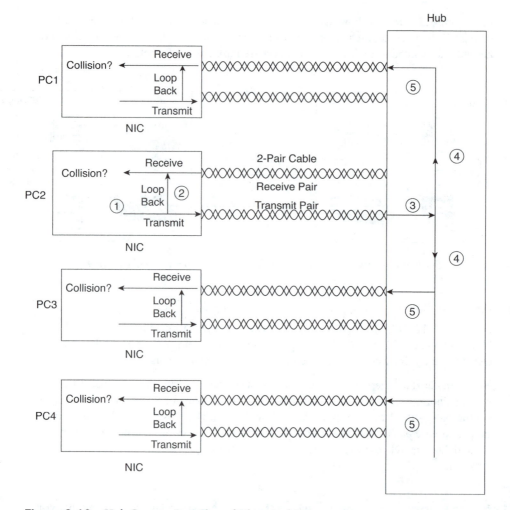

Figure 2-10   *Hub Creates One Shared Electrical Bus*

Note: The figure and the logic describing it apply to any hub, whether 10BASE-T, 100BASE-TX, or even 1000BASE-T.

The figure outlines how a hub creates an electrical bus. The steps illustrated in Figure 2-10 are as follows:

Step 1.   The network interface card (NIC) sends a frame.

Step 2.   The NIC loops the sent frame onto its receive pair internally on the card.

Step 3.   The hub receives the electrical signal, interpreting the signal as bits so that it can clean up and repeat the signal.

Step 4.   The hub's internal wiring repeats the signal out all other ports, but not back to the port from which the signal was received.

Step 5. The hub repeats the signal to each receive pair on all other devices.

In particular, note that a hub always repeats the electrical signal out all ports, except the port from which the electrical signal was received. Also, Figure 2-10 does not show a collision. However, if PC1 and PC2 sent an electrical signal at the same time, at Step 4 the electrical signals would overlap, the frames would collide, and both frames would be either completely unintelligible or full of errors.

CSMA/CD logic helps prevent collisions and also defines how to act when a collision does occur. The CSMA/CD algorithm works like this:

Key Topic

Step 1. A device with a frame to send listens until the Ethernet is not busy.

Step 2. When the Ethernet is not busy, the sender(s) begin(s) sending the frame.

Step 3. The sender(s) listen(s) to make sure that no collision occurred.

Step 4. If a collision occurs, the devices that had been sending a frame each send a jamming signal to ensure that all stations recognize the collision.

Step 5. After the jamming is complete, each sender randomizes a timer and waits that long before trying to resend the collided frame.

Step 6. When each random timer expires, the process starts over with Step 1.

CSMA/CD does not prevent collisions, but it does ensure that the Ethernet works well even though collisions can and do occur. However, the CSMA/CD algorithm does create some performance issues. First, CSMA/CD causes devices to wait until the Ethernet is silent before sending data. This process helps avoid collisions, but it also means that only one device can send at any one instant in time. As a result, all the devices connected to the same hub share the bandwidth available through the hub. The logic of waiting to send until the LAN is silent is called *half duplex*. This refers to the fact that a device either sends or receives at any point in time, but never both at the same time.

The other main feature of CSMA/CD defines what to do when collisions do occur. When a collision occurs, CSMA/CD logic causes the devices that sent the colliding data frames to wait a random amount of time, and then try again. This again helps the LAN to function, but again it impacts performance. During the collision, no useful data makes it across the LAN. Also, the offending devices have to wait longer before trying to use the LAN. Additionally, as the load on an Ethernet increases, the statistical chance for collisions increases as well. In fact, during the years before LAN switches became more affordable and solved some of these performance problems, the rule of thumb was that an Ethernet's performance began to degrade when the load began to exceed 30 percent utilization, mainly as a result of increasing collisions.

Increasing Available Bandwidth Using Switches

The term *collision domain* defines the set of devices whose frames could collide. All devices on a 10BASE2, 10BASE5, or any network using a hub risk collisions between the frames that they send, so all devices on one of these types of Ethernet networks are in the same collision domain. For example, all four devices connected to the hub in Figure 2-10 are in the same collision domain. To avoid collisions, and to recover when they occur, devices in the same collision domain use CSMA/CD.

LAN switches significantly reduce, or even eliminate, the number of collisions on a LAN. Unlike hubs, switches do not create a single shared bus, forwarding received electrical signals out all other ports. Instead, switches do the following:

- Switches interpret the bits in the received frame so that they can typically send the frame out the one required port, rather than all other ports.

- If a switch needs to forward multiple frames out the same port, the switch buffers the frames in memory, sending one at a time, thereby avoiding collisions.

For example, Figure 2-11 illustrates how a switch can forward two frames at the same time while avoiding a collision. In Figure 2-11, both PC1 and PC3 send at the same time. In this case, PC1 sends a data frame with a destination address of PC2, and PC3 sends a data frame with a destination address of PC4. (More on Ethernet addressing is coming up later in this chapter.) The switch looks at the destination Ethernet address and sends the frame from PC1 to PC2 at the same instant as the frame is sent by PC3 to PC4. Had a hub been used, a collision would have occurred; however, because the switch did not send the frames out all other ports, the switch prevented a collision.

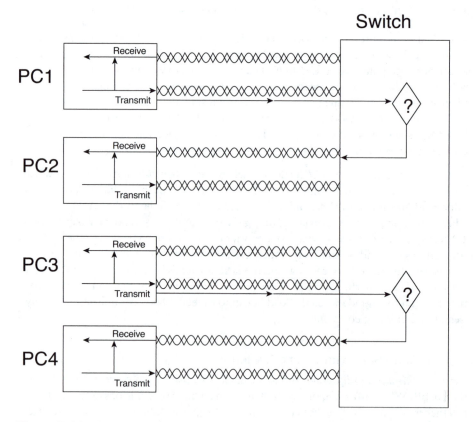

Figure 2-11   *Basic Switch Operation*

> **Note:** The switch's logic requires that the switch look at the Ethernet header, which is considered a Layer 2 feature. As a result, switches are considered to operate as a Layer 2 device, whereas hubs are Layer 1 devices.

Buffering also helps prevent collisions. Imagine that PC1 and PC3 both send a frame to PC4 at the same time. The switch, knowing that forwarding both frames to PC4 at the same time would cause a collision, buffers one frame (in other words, temporarily holds it in memory) until the first frame has been completely sent to PC4.

These seemingly simple switch features provide significant performance improvements as compared with using hubs. In particular:

■ If only one device is cabled to each port of a switch, no collisions can occur.

■ Devices connected to one switch port do not share their bandwidth with devices connected to another switch port. Each has its own separate bandwidth, meaning that a switch with 100-Mbps ports has 100 Mbps of bandwidth *per port*.

The second point refers to the concepts behind the terms *shared Ethernet* and *switched Ethernet*. As mentioned earlier in this chapter, shared Ethernet means that the LAN bandwidth is shared among the devices on the LAN because they must take turns using the LAN because of the CSMA/CD algorithm. The term switched Ethernet refers to the fact that with switches, bandwidth does not have to be shared, allowing for far greater performance. For example, a hub with 24 100-Mbps Ethernet devices connected to it allows for a theoretical maximum of 100 Mbps of bandwidth. However, a switch with 24 100-Mbps Ethernet devices connected to it supports 100 Mbps for each port, or 2400 Mbps (2.4 Gbps) theoretical maximum bandwidth.

Doubling Performance by Using Full-Duplex Ethernet

Any Ethernet network using hubs requires CSMA/CD logic to work properly. However, CSMA/CD imposes half-duplex logic on each device, meaning that only one device can send at a time. Because switches can buffer frames in memory, switches can completely eliminate collisions on switch ports that connect to a single device. As a result, LAN switches with only one device cabled to each port of the switch allow the use of *full-duplex* operation. Full duplex means that an Ethernet card can send and receive concurrently.

To appreciate why collisions cannot occur, consider Figure 2-12, which shows the full-duplex circuitry used with a single PC's connection to a LAN switch.

Figure 2-12 *Full-Duplex Operation Using a Switch*

With only the switch and one device connected to each other, collisions cannot occur. When you implement full duplex, you disable CSMA/CD logic on the devices on both ends of the cable. By doing so, neither device even thinks about CSMA/CD, and they can go ahead and send data whenever they want. As a result, the performance of the Ethernet on that cable has been doubled by allowed simultaneous transmission in both directions.

Ethernet Layer 1 Summary

So far in this chapter, you have read about the basics of how to build the Layer 1 portions of Ethernet using both hubs and switches. This section explained how to use UTP cables, with RJ-45 connectors, to connect devices to either a hub or a switch. It also explained the general theory of how devices can send data by encoding different electrical signals over an electrical circuit, with the circuit being created using a pair of wires inside the UTP cable. More importantly, this section explained which wire pairs are used to transmit and receive data. Finally, the basic operations of switches were explained, including the potential elimination of collisions, which results in significantly better performance than hubs.

Next, this chapter examines the data link layer protocols defined by Ethernet.

Ethernet Data-Link Protocols

One of the most significant strengths of the Ethernet family of protocols is that these protocols use the same small set of data-link standards. For instance, Ethernet addressing works the same on all the variations of Ethernet, even back to 10BASE5, up through 10-Gbps Ethernet—including Ethernet standards that use other types of cabling besides UTP. Also, the CSMA/CD algorithm is technically a part of the data link layer, again applying to most types of Ethernet, unless it has been disabled.

This section covers most of the details of the Ethernet data-link protocols—in particular, Ethernet addressing, framing, error detection, and identifying the type of data inside the Ethernet frame.

Ethernet Addressing

Ethernet LAN addressing identifies either individual devices or groups of devices on a LAN. Each address is 6 bytes long, is usually written in hexadecimal, and, in Cisco devices, typically is written with periods separating each set of four hex digits. For example, 0000.0C12.3456 is a valid Ethernet address.

Unicast Ethernet addresses identify a single LAN card. (The term *unicast* was chosen mainly for contrast with the terms *broadcast*, *multicast*, and *group addresses*.) Computers use unicast addresses to identify the sender and receiver of an Ethernet frame. For instance, imagine that Fred and Barney are on the same Ethernet, and Fred sends Barney a frame. Fred puts his own Ethernet MAC address in the Ethernet header as the source address and uses Barney's Ethernet MAC address as the destination. When Barney receives the frame, he notices that the destination address is his own address, so he processes the frame. If Barney receives a frame with some other device's unicast address in the destination address field, he simply does not process the frame.

The IEEE defines the format and assignment of LAN addresses. The IEEE requires globally unique unicast MAC addresses on all LAN interface cards. (IEEE calls them MAC addresses because the MAC protocols such as IEEE 802.3 define the addressing details.) To ensure a unique MAC address, the Ethernet card manufacturers encode the MAC address onto the card, usually in a ROM chip. The first half of the address identifies the manufacturer of the card. This code, which is assigned to each manufacturer by the IEEE, is called the *organizationally unique identifier (OUI)*. Each manufacturer assigns a MAC address with its own OUI as the first half of the address, with the second half of the address being assigned a number that this manufacturer has never used on another card. Figure 2-13 shows the structure.

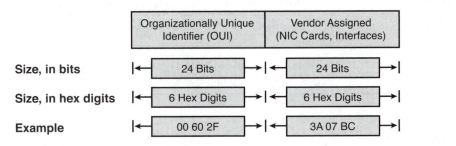

Figure 2-13   *Structure of Unicast Ethernet Addresses*

Many terms can be used to describe unicast LAN addresses. Each LAN card comes with a *burned-in address (BIA)* that is burned into the ROM chip on the card. BIAs sometimes are called *universally administered addresses (UAA)* because the IEEE universally (well, at least worldwide) administers address assignment. Regardless of whether the BIA is used or another address is configured, many people refer to unicast addresses as either LAN addresses, Ethernet addresses, hardware addresses, physical addresses, or MAC addresses.

Group addresses identify more than one LAN interface card. The IEEE defines two general categories of group addresses for Ethernet:

■ **Broadcast addresses:** The most often used of the IEEE group MAC addresses, the broadcast address has a value of FFFF.FFFF.FFFF (hexadecimal notation). The broadcast address implies that all devices on the LAN should process the frame.

■ **Multicast addresses:** Multicast addresses are used to allow a subset of devices on a LAN to communicate. When IP multicasts over an Ethernet, the multicast MAC addresses used by IP follow this format: 0100.5e*xx.xxxx*, where any value can be used in the last half of the address.

Table 2-3 summarizes most of the details about MAC addresses.

Table 2-3   *LAN MAC Address Terminology and Features*

LAN Addressing Term or Feature	Description
MAC	Media Access Control. 802.3 (Ethernet) defines the MAC sublayer of IEEE Ethernet.
Ethernet address, NIC address, LAN address	Other names often used instead of MAC address. These terms describe the 6-byte address of the LAN interface card.
Burned-in address	The 6-byte address assigned by the vendor making the card.
Unicast address	A term for a MAC that represents a single LAN interface.
Broadcast address	An address that means "all devices that reside on this LAN right now."
Multicast address	On Ethernet, a multicast address implies some subset of all devices currently on the Ethernet LAN.

Ethernet Framing

Framing defines how a string of binary numbers is interpreted. In other words, framing defines the meaning behind the bits that are transmitted across a network. The physical layer helps you get a string of bits from one device to another. When the receiving device gets the bits, how should they be interpreted? The term *framing* refers to the definition of the fields assumed to be in the data that is received. In other words, framing defines the meaning of the bits transmitted and received over a network.

For instance, you just read an example of Fred sending data to Barney over an Ethernet. Fred put Barney's Ethernet address in the Ethernet header so that Barney would know that the Ethernet frame was meant for him. The IEEE 802.3 standard defines the location of the destination address field inside the string of bits sent across the Ethernet.

The framing used for Ethernet has changed a couple of times over the years. Xerox defined one version of the framing, which the IEEE then changed when it took over Ethernet standards in the early 1980s. The IEEE finalized a compromise standard for framing in 1997 that includes some of the features of the original Xerox Ethernet framing, along with the framing defined by the IEEE. The end result is the bottom frame format shown in Figure 2-14.

Most of the fields in the Ethernet frame are important enough to be covered at some point in this chapter. For reference, Table 2-4 lists the fields in the header and trailer, and a brief description.

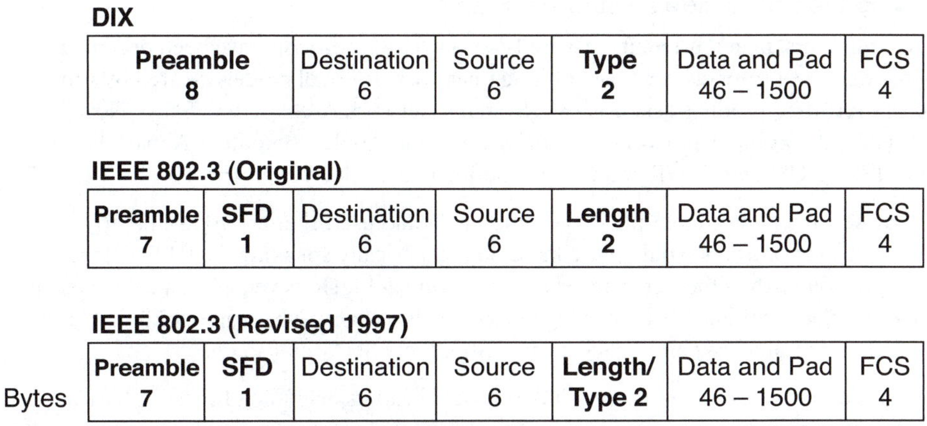

DIX

Preamble 8	Destination 6	Source 6	**Type** **2**	Data and Pad 46 – 1500	FCS 4

IEEE 802.3 (Original)

Preamble 7	SFD 1	Destination 6	Source 6	**Length** **2**	Data and Pad 46 – 1500	FCS 4

IEEE 802.3 (Revised 1997)

Bytes

Preamble 7	SFD 1	Destination 6	Source 6	**Length/** **Type 2**	Data and Pad 46 – 1500	FCS 4

Figure 2-14   *LAN Header Formats*

Table 2-4   *IEEE 802.3 Ethernet Header and Trailer Fields*

Field	Field Length in Bytes	Description
Preamble	7	Synchronization
Start Frame Delimiter (SFD)	1	Signifies that the next byte begins the Destination MAC field
Destination MAC address	6	Identifies the intended recipient of this frame
Source MAC address	6	Identifies the sender of this frame
Length	2	Defines the length of the data field of the frame (either length or type is present, but not both)
Type	2	Defines the type of protocol listed inside the frame (either length or type is present, but not both)
Data and Pad*	46–1500	Holds data from a higher layer, typically an L3 PDU (generic), and often an IP packet
Frame Check Sequence (FCS)	4	Provides a method for the receiving NIC to determine if the frame experienced transmission errors

* The IEEE 802.3 specification limits the data portion of the 802.3 frame to a maximum of 1500 bytes. The Data field was designed to hold Layer 3 packets; the term maximum transmission unit (MTU) defines the maximum Layer 3 packet that can be sent over a medium. Because the Layer 3 packet rests inside the data portion of an Ethernet frame, 1500 bytes is the largest IP MTU allowed over an Ethernet.

Identifying the Data Inside an Ethernet Frame

Over the years, many different network layer (Layer 3) protocols have been designed. Most of these protocols were part of larger network protocol models created by vendors to support their products, such as IBM Systems Network Architecture (SNA), Novell Net-Ware, Digital Equipment Corporation's DECnet, and Apple Computer's AppleTalk. Additionally, the OSI and TCP/IP models also defined network layer protocols.

All these Layer 3 protocols, plus several others, could use Ethernet. To use Ethernet, the network layer protocol would place its packet (generically speaking, its L3 PDU) into the data portion of the Ethernet frame shown in Figure 2-14. However, when a device receives such an Ethernet frame, that receiving device needs to know what type of L3 PDU is in the Ethernet frame. Is it an IP packet? an OSI packet? SNA? and so on.

To answer that question, most data-link protocol headers, including Ethernet, have a field with a code that defines the type of protocol header that follows. Generically speaking, these fields in data-link headers are called *Type fields*. For example, to imply that an IP packet is inside an Ethernet frame, the Type field (as shown in Figure 2-14) would have a value of hexadecimal 0800 (decimal 2048). Other types of L3 PDUs would be implied by using a different value in the Type field.

Interestingly, because of the changes to Ethernet framing over the years, another popular option exists for the protocol Type field, particularly when sending IP packets. If the 802.3 Type/Length field (in Figure 2-14) has a value less than hex 0600 (decimal 1536), the Type/Length field is used as a Length field for that frame, identifying the length of the data field of the Ethernet frame. In that case, another field is needed to identify the type of L3 PDU inside the frame.

To create a Type field for frames that use the Type/Length field as a Length field, either one or two additional headers are added after the Ethernet 802.3 header but before the Layer 3 header. For example, when sending IP packets, the Ethernet frame has two additional headers:

■ An IEEE 802.2 Logical Link Control (LLC) header

■ An IEEE Subnetwork Access Protocol (SNAP) header

Figure 2-15 shows an Ethernet frame with these additional headers. Note that the SNAP header Type field has the same purpose, with the same reserved values, as the Ethernet Type/Length field.

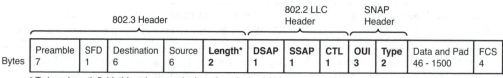

Figure 2-15   *802.2 SNAP Headers*

Error Detection

The final Ethernet data link layer function explained here is error detection. Error detection is the process of discovering if a frame's bits changed as a result of being sent over the network. The bits might change for many small reasons, but generally such errors occur as a result of some kind of electrical interference. Like every data-link protocol discussed in this book, Ethernet defines both a header and trailer, with the trailer containing a field used for the purpose of error detection.

The Ethernet Frame Check Sequence (FCS) field in the Ethernet trailer—the only field in the Ethernet trailer—allows a device receiving an Ethernet frame to detect whether the bits have changed during transmission. To detect an error, the sending device calculates a complex mathematical function, with the frame contents as input, putting the result into the frame's 4-byte FCS field. The receiving device does the same math on the frame; if its calculation matches the FCS field in the frame, no errors occurred. If the result doesn't match the FCS field, an error occurred, and the frame is discarded.

Note that error detection does not also mean error recovery. Ethernet defines that the errored frame should be discarded, but Ethernet takes no action to cause the frame to be retransmitted. Other protocols, notably TCP (as covered in Chapter 6, "Fundamentals of TCP/IP Transport, Applications, and Security"), can notice the lost data and cause error recovery to occur.

Chapter Review

Review Key Topics

Review the most important topics from this chapter, noted with the key topics icon. Table 2-5 lists these key topics and where each is discussed.

Table 2-5   *Key Topics for Chapter 2*

Key Topic Element	Description	Page Number
Table 2-1	The four most popular types of Ethernet LANs and some details about each	30
List	Summary of CSMA/CD logic	33
Figure 2-6	TIA standard Ethernet Cabling Pinouts	38
Figure 2-7	Straight-through cable concept	39
Figure 2-8	Crossover cable concept	40
Table 2-2	List of devices that transmit on wire pair 1,2 and pair 3,6	40
List	Detailed CSMA/CD logic	43
Figure 2-13	Structure of a unicast Ethernet address	47
Table 2-3	Key Ethernet addressing terms	48

Define Key Terms

Define the following key terms from this chapter and check your answers in the glossary:

1000BASE-T, 100BASE-TX, 10BASE-T, crossover cable, CSMA/CD, full duplex, half duplex, hub, pinout, protocol type, shared Ethernet, straight-through cable, switch, switched Ethernet, twisted pair

Answer Review Questions

Answer the following review questions:

1. Which one of the following answers is most accurate about the cabling of a typical modern Ethernet LAN?

    a. Connect each device in series using coaxial cabling

    b. Connect each device in series using UTP cabling

    c. Connect each device to a centralized LAN hub using UTP cabling

    d. Connect each device to a centralized LAN switch using UTP cabling

2. Which of the following is true about the cabling of a 10BASE2 Ethernet LAN?

    a. Connect each device in series using coaxial cabling

    b. Connect each device in series using UTP cabling

    c. Connect each device to a centralized LAN hub using UTP cabling

    d. Connect each device to a centralized LAN switch using UTP cabling

3. Which of the following is true about Ethernet crossover cables?

    a. Pins 1 and 2 are reversed on the other end of the cable.

    b. Pins 1 and 2 on one end of the cable connect to pins 3 and 6 on the other end of the cable.

    c. Pins 1 and 2 on one end of the cable connect to pins 3 and 4 on the other end of the cable.

    d. The cable can be up to 1000 meters long to cross over between buildings.

    e. None of the other answers is correct.

4. Each answer lists two types of devices used in a 100BASE-TX network. If these devices were connected with UTP Ethernet cables, which pairs of devices would require a straight-through cable?

    a. PC and router

    b. PC and switch

    c. Hub and switch

    d. Router and hub

    e. Wireless access point (Ethernet port) and switch

5. Which of the following is true about the CSMA/CD algorithm?

    a.   The algorithm never allows collisions to occur.

    b.   Collisions can happen, but the algorithm defines how the computers should notice a collision and how to recover.

    c.   The algorithm works with only two devices on the same Ethernet.

    d.   None of the other answers is correct.

6. Which of the following is a collision domain?

    a.   All devices connected to an Ethernet hub

    b.   All devices connected to an Ethernet switch

    c.   Two PCs, with one cabled to a router Ethernet port with a crossover cable and the other PC cabled to another router Ethernet port with a crossover cable

    d.   None of the other answers is correct.

7. Which of the following describe a shortcoming of using hubs that is improved by instead using switches?

    a.   Hubs create a single electrical bus to which all devices connect, causing the devices to share the bandwidth.

    b.   Hubs limit the maximum cable length of individual cables (relative to switches).

    c.   Hubs allow collisions to occur when two attached devices send data at the same time.

    d.   Hubs restrict the number of physical ports to at most eight.

8. Which of the following terms describe Ethernet addresses that can be used to communicate with more than one device at a time?

    a.   Burned-in address

    b.   Unicast address

    c.   Broadcast address

    d.   Multicast address

9. Which of the following is one of the functions of OSI Layer 2 protocols?

    a.   Framing

    b.   Delivery of bits from one device to another

    c.   Error recovery

    d.   Defining the size and shape of Ethernet cards

10. Which of the following are true about the format of Ethernet addresses?

   a. Each manufacturer puts a unique code into the first 2 bytes of the address.

   b. Each manufacturer puts a unique code into the first 3 bytes of the address.

   c. Each manufacturer puts a unique code into the first half of the address.

   d. The part of the address that holds this manufacturer's code is called the MAC.

   e. The part of the address that holds this manufacturer's code is called the OUI.

   f. The part of the address that holds this manufacturer's code has no specific name.

11. Which of the following is true about the Ethernet FCS field?

   a. It is used for error recovery.

   b. It is 2 bytes long.

   c. It resides in the Ethernet trailer, not the Ethernet header.

   d. It is used for encryption.

   e. None of the other answers is correct.

This chapter covers the following subjects:

- **OSI Layer 1 for Point-to-Point WANs:** This section explains the physical cabling and devices used to create the customer portions of a leased circuit.

- **OSI Layer 2 for Point-to-Point WANs:** This section introduces the data link layer protocols used on point-to-point leased lines, namely HDLC and PPP.

- **Frame Relay and Packet-Switching Services:** This section explains the concept of a WAN packet-switching service, with particular attention given to Frame Relay.

CHAPTER 3

WAN Fundamentals

As you read in the previous chapter, the OSI physical and data link layers work together to deliver data across a wide variety of types of physical networks. LAN standards and protocols define how to network between devices that are relatively close together, hence the term *local-area* in the acronym LAN. WAN standards and protocols define how to network between devices that are relatively far apart—in some cases, even thousands of miles apart—hence the term *wide-area* in the acronym WAN.

LANs and WANs both implement the same OSI Layer 1 and Layer 2 functions, but with different mechanisms and details. This chapter points out the similarities between the two, and provides details about the differences.

The WAN topics in this chapter describe mainly how enterprise networks use WANs to connect remote sites. Unit 10 of this book covers a broader range of WAN topics, including point-to-point serial links and Frame Relay.

OSI Layer 1 for Point-to-Point WANs

The OSI physical layer, or Layer 1, defines the details of how to move data from one device to another. In fact, many people think of OSI Layer 1 as "sending bits." Higher layers encapsulate the data, as described in Chapter 1, "The TCP/IP and OSI Networking Models." No matter what the other OSI layers do, eventually the sender of the data needs to actually transmit the bits to another device. The OSI physical layer defines the standards and protocols used to create the physical network and to send the bits across that network.

A point-to-point WAN link acts like an Ethernet trunk between two Ethernet switches in many ways. For perspective, look at Figure 3-1, which shows a LAN with two buildings and two switches in each building. As a brief review, remember that several types of Ethernet use one twisted pair of wires to transmit and another twisted pair to receive, in order to reduce electromagnetic interference. You typically use straight-through Ethernet cables between end-user devices and the switches. For the trunk links between the switches, you use crossover cables because each switch transmits on the same pair of pins on the connector, so the crossover cable connects one device's transmit pair to the other device's receive pair. The lower part of Figure 3-1 reminds you of the basic idea behind a crossover cable.

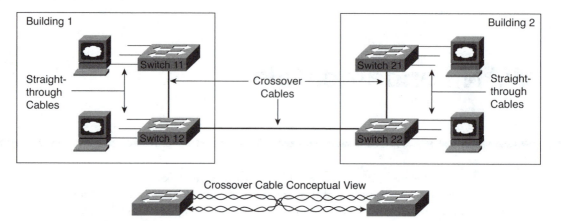

Figure 3-1 *Example LAN, Two Buildings*

Now imagine that the buildings are 1000 miles apart instead of right next to each other. You are immediately faced with two problems:

■ Ethernet does not support any type of cabling that allows an individual trunk to run for 1000 miles.

■ Even if Ethernet supported a 1000-mile trunk, you do not have the rights-of-way needed to bury a cable over the 1000 miles of real estate between buildings.

The big distinction between LANs and WANs relates to how far apart the devices can be and still be capable of sending and receiving data. LANs tend to reside in a single building or possibly among buildings in a campus using optical cabling approved for Ethernet. WAN connections typically run longer distances than Ethernet—across town or between cities. Often, only one or a few companies even have the rights to run cables under the ground between the sites. So, the people who created WAN standards needed to use different physical specifications than Ethernet to send data 1000 miles or more (WAN).

Note: Besides LANs and WANs, the term metropolitan-area network (MAN) is sometimes used for networks that extend between buildings and through rights-of-way. The term MAN typically implies a network that does not reach as far as a WAN, generally in a single metropolitan area. The distinctions between LANs, MANs, and WANs are blurry—there is no set distance that means a link is a LAN, MAN, or WAN link.

To create such long links, or circuits, the actual physical cabling is owned, installed, and managed by a company that has the right of way to run cables under streets. Because a company that needs to send data over the WAN circuit does not actually own the cable or line, it is called a *leased line*. Companies that can provide leased WAN lines typically started life as the local telephone company, or telco. In many countries, the telco is still a government-regulated or government-controlled monopoly; these companies are sometimes called public telephone and telegraph (PTT) companies. Today, many people use the generic term *service provider* to refer to a company that provides any form of WAN connectivity, including Internet services.

Point-to-point WAN links provide basic connectivity between two points. To get a point-to-point WAN link, you would work with a service provider to install a circuit. What the phone company or service provider gives you is similar to what you would have if you made a phone call between two sites, but you never hung up. The two devices on either end of the WAN circuit could send and receive bits between each other any time they want, without needing to dial a phone number. Because the connection is always available, a point-to-point WAN connection is sometimes called a *leased circuit* or *leased line* because you have the exclusive right to use that circuit, as long as you keep paying for it.

Now back to the comparison of the LAN between two nearby buildings versus the WAN between two buildings that are 1000 miles apart. The physical details are different, but the same general functions need to be accomplished, as shown in Figure 3-2.

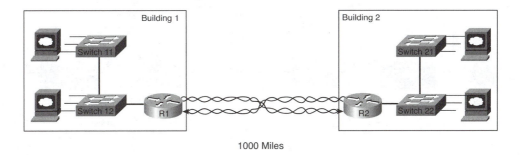

1000 Miles

Figure 3-2 *Conceptual View of Point-to-Point Leased Line*

Keep in mind that Figure 3-2 provides a conceptual view of a point-to-point WAN link. In concept, the telco installs a physical cable, with a transmit and a receive twisted pair, between the buildings. The cable has been connected to each router, and each router, in turn, has been connected to the LAN switches. As a result of this new physical WAN link and the logic used by the routers connected to it, data now can be transferred between the two sites. In the next section, you will learn more about the physical details of the WAN link.

Note: Ethernet switches have many different types of interfaces, but all the interfaces are some form of Ethernet. Routers provide the capability to connect many different types of OSI Layer 1 and Layer 2 technologies. So, when you see a LAN connected to some other site using a WAN connection, you will see a router connected to each, as in Figure 3-2.

WAN Connections from the Customer Viewpoint

In Figure 3-2, you saw that a WAN leased line acts as if the telco gave you two twisted pairs of wires between the two sites on each end of the line. Well, it is not that simple. Of course, a lot more underlying technology must be used to create the circuit, and telcos

use a lot of terminology that is different from LAN terminology. The telco seldom actually runs a 1000-mile cable for you between the two sites.

So, what does the telco do to create a point-to-point leased line? First, the telco antici-
pates that the buildings used by businesses will all need some type of WAN connection.
To be ready for an order for WAN service, the telco has built a large network already and
even runs extra cables from the local central office (CO) to your building. (A CO is just a
building where the telco locates the devices used to create its own network.) Regardless of
what the telco does inside its own network, what you receive is the equivalent of a four-
wire leased circuit between two buildings.

Figure 3-3 introduces some of the key concepts and terms relating to WAN circuits.

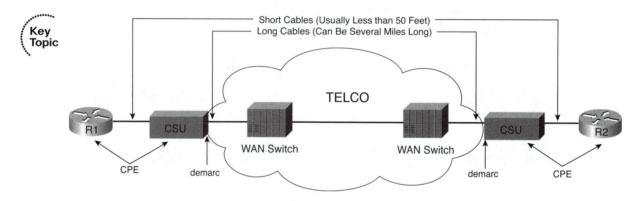

Figure 3-3   *Point-to-Point Leased Line: Components and Terminology*

Typically, routers connect to a device called an external channel service unit/data service
unit (CSU/DSU). The router connects to the CSU/DSU with a relatively short cable, typically less than 50 feet long, because the CSU/DSUs typically get placed in a rack near the
router. The much longer four-wire cable from the telco plugs into the CSU/DSU. That cable leaves the building, running through the hidden (typically buried) cables that you
sometimes see phone company workers fixing by the side of the road. The other end of
that cable ends up in the CO, with the cable connecting to a CO device generically called
a WAN switch.

The same general physical connectivity exists on each side of the point-to-point WAN
link. In between the two COs, the service provider can build its network with several competing different types of technology. However, the perspective in Figure 3-2 remains
true—the two routers can send and receive data simultaneously across the point-to-point
WAN link.

From a legal perspective, two different companies own the various components of the
equipment and lines in Figure 3-3. For instance, the router cable and typically the
CSU/DSU are owned by the telco's customer, and the wiring to the CO and the gear inside
the CO are owned by the telco. So, the telco uses the term *demarc*, which is short for demarcation point, to refer to the point at which the telco's responsibility is on one side and

the customer's responsibility is on the other. The demarc is not a separate device or cable, but rather a concept of where the responsibilities of the telco and customer end.

In the United States, the demarc is typically where the telco physically terminates the set of two twisted pairs inside the customer building. Typically, the customer asks the telco to terminate the cable in a particular room, and most, if not all, the lines from the telco into that building terminate in the same room.

The term *customer premises equipment (CPE)* refers to devices that are at the customer site, from the telco's perspective. For instance, both the CSU/DSU and the router are CPE devices in this case.

The demarc does not always reside where it is shown in Figure 3-3. In some cases, the telco actually could own the CSU/DSU, and the demarc would be on the router side of the CSU/DSU. In some cases today, the telco even owns and manages the router at the customer site, again moving the point that would be considered the demarc. Regardless of where the demarc sits from a legal perspective, the term CPE still refers to the equipment at the telco customer's location.

WAN Cabling Standards

Cisco offers a large variety of different WAN interface cards for its routers, including synchronous and asynchronous serial interfaces. For any of the point-to-point serial links or Frame Relay links in this chapter, the router uses an interface that supports synchronous communication.

Synchronous serial interfaces in Cisco routers use a variety of proprietary physical connector types, such as the 60-pin D-shell connector shown at the top of the cable drawings in Figure 3-4. The cable connecting the router to the CSU/DSU uses a connector that fits the router serial interface on the router side, and a standardized WAN connector type that matches the CSU/DSU interface on the CSU/DSU end of the cable. Figure 3-4 shows a typical connection, with some of the serial cabling options listed.

The engineer who deploys a network chooses the cable based on the connectors on the router and the CSU/DSU. Beyond that choice, engineers do not really need to think about how the cabling and pins work—they just work! Many of the pins are used for control functions, and a few are used for the transmission of data. Some pins are used for clocking, as described in the next section.

Note: The Telecommunications Industry Association (TIA) is accredited by the American National Standards Institute (ANSI) to represent the United States in work with international standards bodies. The TIA defines some of the WAN cabling standards, in addition to LAN cabling standards. For more information on these standards bodies, and to purchase copies of the standards, refer to the websites http://www.tiaonline.org and http://www.ansi.org.

The cable between the CSU/DSU and the telco CO typically uses an RJ-48 connector to connect to the CSU/DSU; the RJ-48 connector has the same size and shape as the RJ-45 connector used for Ethernet cables.

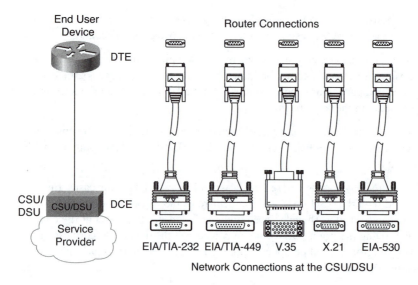

Figure 3-4 *Serial Cabling Options*

Many Cisco routers support serial interfaces that have an integrated internal CSU/DSU. With an internal CSU/DSU, the router does not need a cable connecting it to an external CSU/DSU because the CSU/DSU is internal to the router. In these cases, the serial cables shown in Figure 3-4 are not needed, and the physical line from the telco is connected to a port on the router, typically an RJ-48 port in the router serial interface card.

Clock Rates, Synchronization, DCE, and DTE

An enterprise network engineer who wants to install a new point-to-point leased line between two routers has several tasks to perform. First, the network engineer contacts a service provider and orders the circuit. As part of that process, the network engineer specifies how fast the circuit should run, in kilobits per second (kbps). While the telco installs the circuit, the engineer purchases two CSU/DSUs, installs one at each site, and configures each CSU/DSU. The network engineer also purchases and installs routers, and connects serial cables from each router to the respective CSU/DSU using the cables shown in Figure 3-4. Eventually, the telco installs the new line into the customer premises, and the line can be connected to the CSU/DSUs, as shown in Figure 3-3.

Every WAN circuit ordered from a service provider runs at one of many possible predefined speeds. This speed is often referred to as the clock rate, bandwidth, or link speed. The enterprise network engineer (the customer) must specify the speed when ordering a circuit, and the telco installs a circuit that runs at that speed. Additionally, the enterprise network engineer must configure the CSU/DSU on each end of the link to match the defined speed.

To make the link work, the various devices need to synchronize their clocks so that they run at exactly the same speed—a process called synchronization. *Synchronous circuits* impose time ordering at the link's sending and receiving ends. Essentially, all devices agree to try to run at the exact same speed, but it is expensive to build devices that truly can operate at exactly the same speed. So, the devices operate at close to the same speed and listen to the speed of the other device on the other side of the link. One side makes small adjustments in its rate to match the other side.

Synchronization occurs between the two CSU/DSUs on a leased line by having one CSU/DSU (the slave) adjust its clock to match the clock rate of the other CSU/DSU (the master). The process works almost like the scenes in spy novels in which the spies synchronize their watches; in this case, the networking devices synchronize their clocks several times per second.

In practice, the clocking concept includes a hierarchy of different clock sources. The telco provides clocking information to the CSU/DSUs based on the transitions in the electrical signal on the circuit. The two CSU/DSUs then adjust their speeds to match the clocking signals from the telco. The CSU/DSUs each supply clocking signals to the routers so that the routers simply react, sending and receiving data at the correct rate. So, from the routers' perspectives, the CSU/DSU is considered to be *clocking* the link.

A couple of other key WAN terms relate to the process of clocking. The device that provides clocking, typically the CSU/DSU, is considered to be the data communications equipment (DCE). The device receiving clocking, typically the router, is referred to as data terminal equipment (DTE).

Building a WAN Link in a Lab

On a practical note, when purchasing serial cables from Cisco, you can pick either a DTE or a DCE cable. You pick the type of cable based on whether the router is acting like DTE or DCE. In most cases with a real WAN link, the router acts as DTE, so the router must use a DTE cable to connect to the CSU/DSU.

You can build a serial link in a lab without using any CSU/DSUs, but to do so, one router must supply clocking. When building a lab, you do not need to buy CSU/DSUs or order a WAN circuit. You can buy two routers, a DTE serial cable for one router, and a DCE serial cable for the other, and connect the two cables together. The router with the DCE cable in it can be configured to provide clocking, meaning that you do not need a CSU/DSU. So, you can build a WAN in your home lab, saving hundreds of dollars by not buying CSU/DSUs. The DTE and DCE cables can be connected to each other (the DCE cable has a female connector and the DTE cable has a male connector) and to the two routers. With one additional configuration command on one of the routers (the **clock rate** command), you have a point-to-point serial link. This type of connection between two routers sometimes is called a back-to-back serial connection.

Figure 3-5 shows the cabling for a back-to-back serial connection and also shows that the combined DCE/DTE cables reverse the transmit and receive pins, much like a crossover Ethernet cable allows two directly connected devices to communicate.

As you see in Figure 3-5, the DTE cable, the same cable that you typically use to connect to a CSU/DSU, does not swap the Tx and Rx pins. The DCE cable swaps transmit and receive, so the wiring with one router's Tx pin connected to the other router's Rx, and vice versa, remains intact. The router with the DCE cable installed needs to supply clocking, so the **clock rate** command will be added to that router to define the speed.

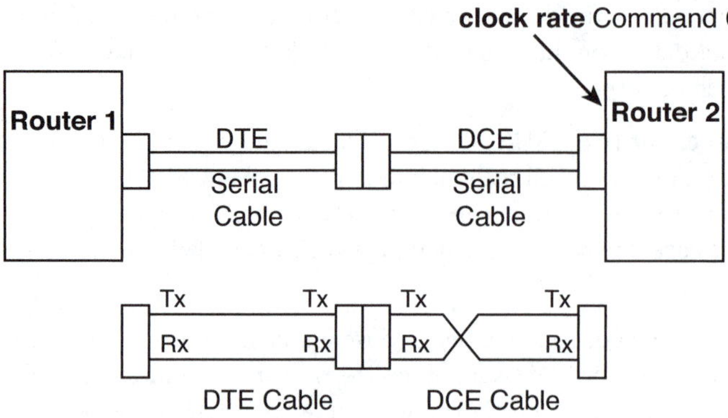

clock rate Command Goes Here

Figure 3-5   *Serial Cabling Uses a DTE Cable and a DCE Cable*

Link Speeds Offered by Telcos

No matter what you call them—telcos, PTTs, or service providers—these companies do not simply let you pick the exact speed of a WAN link. Instead, standards define how fast a point-to-point link can run.

For a long time, the telcos of the world made more money selling voice services than selling data services. As technology progressed during the mid-twentieth century, the telcos of the world developed a standard for sending voice using digital transmissions. Digital signaling inside their networks allowed for the growth of more profitable data services, such as leased lines. It also allowed better efficiencies, making the build-out of the expanding voice networks much less expensive.

The original mechanism used for converting analog voice to a digital signal is called pulse code modulation (PCM). PCM defines that an incoming analog voice signal should be sampled 8000 times per second, and each sample should be represented by an 8-bit code. So, 64,000 bits were needed to represent 1 second of voice. When the telcos of the world built their first digital networks, they chose a baseline transmission speed of 64 kbps because that was the necessary bandwidth for a single voice call. The term digital signal level 0 (DS0) refers to the standard for a single 64-kbps line.

Today, most telcos offer leased lines in multiples of 64 kbps. In the United States, the digital signal level 1 (DS1) standard defines a single line that supports 24 DS0s, plus an 8-kbps overhead channel, for a speed of 1.544 Mbps. (A DS1 is also called a T1 line.) Another option is a digital signal level 3 (DS3) service, also called a T3 line, which holds 28 DS1s. Other parts of the world use different standards, with Europe and Japan using standards that hold 32 DS0s, called an E1 line, with an E3 line holding 16 E1s.

Note: The combination of multiple slower-speed lines and channels into one faster-speed line or channel—for instance, combining 24 DS0s into a single T1 line—is generally called time-division multiplexing (TDM).

Table 3-1 lists some of the standards for WAN speeds. Included in the table are the type of line, plus the type of signaling (for example, DS1). The signaling specifications define the electrical signals that encode a binary 1 or 0 on the line. You should be aware of the general idea, and remember the key terms for T1 and E1 lines in particular.

Table 3-1   *WAN Speed Summary*

Key Topic

Name(s) of Line	Bit Rate
DS0	64 kbps
DS1 (T1)	1.544 Mbps (24 DS0s, plus 8 kbps overhead)
DS3 (T3)	44.736 Mbps (28 DS1s, plus management overhead)
E1	2.048 Mbps (32 DS0s)
E3	34.368 Mbps (16 E1s, plus management overhead)
J1 (Y1)	2.048 Mbps (32 DS0s; Japanese standard)

The leased circuits described so far in this chapter form the basis for the WAN services used by many enterprises today. Next, this chapter explains the data link layer protocols used when a leased circuit connects two routers.

OSI Layer 2 for Point-to-Point WANs

WAN protocols used on point-to-point serial links provide the basic function of data delivery across that one link. The two most popular data link layer protocols used on point-to-point links are High-Level Data Link Control (HDLC) and Point-to-Point Protocol (PPP).

HDLC

Because point-to-point links are relatively simple, HDLC has only a small amount of work to do. In particular, HDLC needs to determine if the data passed the link without any errors; HDLC discards the frame if errors occurred. Additionally, HDLC needs to identify the type of packet inside the HDLC frame so the receiving device knows the packet type.

To achieve the main goal of delivering data across the link and to check for errors and identify the packet type, HDLC defines framing. The HDLC header includes an Address field and a Protocol Type field, with the trailer containing a frame check sequence (FCS) field. Figure 3-6 outlines the standard HDLC frame and the HDLC frame that is Cisco proprietary.

HDLC defines a 1-byte Address field, although on point-to-point links, it is not really needed. Having an Address field in HDLC is sort of like when I have lunch with my friend Gary, and only Gary. I do not need to start every sentence with "Hey Gary"—he knows I am talking to him. On point-to-point WAN links, the router on one end of the link knows that there is only one possible recipient of the data—the router on the other end of the link—so the address does not really matter today.

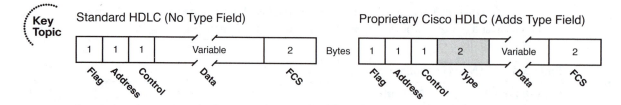

Figure 3-6 *HDLC Framing*

Note: The Address field was useful in years past, when the telco would sell multidrop circuits. These circuits had more than two devices on the circuit, so an Address field was
needed.

HDLC performs error detection just like Ethernet—it uses an FCS field in the HDLC
trailer. And just like Ethernet, if a received frame has errors in it, the device receiving the
frame discards the frame, with no error recovery performed by HDLC.

HDLC also performs the function of identifying the encapsulated data, just like Ethernet.
When a router receives an HDLC frame, it wants to know what type of packet is held inside the frame. The Cisco implementation of HDLC includes a *Protocol Type* field that
identifies the type of packet inside the frame. Cisco uses the same values in its 2-byte
HDLC Protocol Type field as it does in the Ethernet Protocol Type field.

The original HDLC standards did not include a Protocol Type field, so Cisco added one to
support the first serial links on Cisco routers, back in the early days of Cisco in the latter
1980s. By adding something to the HDLC header, Cisco made its version of HDLC proprietary. So, the Cisco implementation of HDLC will not work when connecting a Cisco
router to another vendor's router.

HDLC is very simple. There simply is not a lot of work for the point-to-point data link
layer protocols to perform.

Point-to-Point Protocol

The International Telecommunications Union (ITU), previously known as the Consultative
Committee for International Telecommunications Technologies (CCITT), first defined
HDLC. Later, the Internet Engineering Task Force (IETF) saw the need for another data
link layer protocol for use between routers over a point-to-point link. In RFC 1661 (1994),
the IETF created the Point-to-Point Protocol (PPP).

Comparing the basics, PPP behaves much like HDLC. The framing looks identical to the Cisco proprietary HDLC framing. There is an Address field, but the addressing does not matter. PPP does discard errored frames that do not pass the FCS check. Additionally, PPP uses a 2-byte Protocol Type field. However, because the Protocol Type field is part of the standard for PPP, any vendor that conforms to the PPP standard can communicate with other vendor products. So, when connecting a Cisco router to another vendor's router over a point-to-point serial link, PPP is the data link layer protocol of choice.

PPP was defined much later than the original HDLC specifications. As a result, the creators of PPP included many additional features that had not been seen in WAN data link layer protocols up to that time, so PPP has become the most popular and feature-rich of WAN data link layer protocols.

Point-to-Point WAN Summary

Point-to-point WAN leased lines and their associated data link layer protocols use another set of terms and concepts beyond those covered for LANs, as outlined in Table 3-2.

Table 3-2 *WAN Terminology*

Term	Definition
Synchronous	The imposition of time ordering on a bit stream. Practically, a device tries to use the same speed as another device on the other end of a serial link. However, by examining transitions between voltage states on the link, the device can notice slight variations in the speed on each end and can adjust its speed accordingly.
Clock source	The device to which the other devices on the link adjust their speed when using synchronous links.
CSU/DSU	Channel service unit/data service unit. Used on digital links as an interface to the telephone company in the United States. Routers typically use a short cable from a serial interface to a CSU/DSU, which is attached to the line from the telco with a similar configuration at the other router on the other end of the link.
Telco	Telephone company.
Four-wire circuit	A line from the telco with four wires, composed of two twisted-pair wires. Each pair is used to send in one direction, so a four-wire circuit allows full-duplex communication.
T1	A line from the telco that allows transmission of data at 1.544 Mbps.
E1	Similar to a T1 but used in Europe. It uses a rate of 2.048 Mbps and 32 64-kbps channels.

Also, just for survival when talking about WANs, keep in mind that all the following terms can be used to refer to a point-to-point leased line as covered so far in this chapter:

leased line, leased circuit, link, serial link, serial line, point-to-point link, circuit

Frame Relay and Packet-Switching Services

Service providers offer a class of WAN services, different from leased lines, that can be categorized as *packet-switching services*. In a packet-switching service, physical WAN connectivity exists, similar to a leased line. However, a company can connect a large number of routers to the packet-switching service, using a single serial link from each router into the packet-switching service. Once connected, each router can send packets to all the other routers—much like all the devices connected to an Ethernet hub or switch can send data directly to each other.

Two types of packet-switching service are very popular today, Frame Relay and Asynchronous Transfer Mode (ATM), with Frame Relay being much more common. This section introduces the main concepts behind packet-switching services, and explains the basics of Frame Relay.

The Scaling Benefits of Packet Switching

Point-to-point WANs can be used to connect a pair of routers at multiple remote sites. However, an alternative WAN service, Frame Relay, has many advantages over point-to-point links, particularly when you connect many sites via a WAN. To introduce you to Frame Relay, this section focuses on a few of the key benefits compared to leased lines, one of which you can easily see when considering the illustration in Figure 3-7.

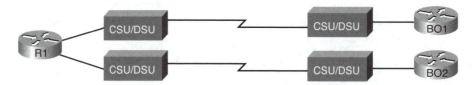

Figure 3-7   *Two Leased Lines to Two Branch Offices*

In Figure 3-7, a main site is connected to two branch offices, labeled BO1 and BO2. The main site router, R1, requires two serial interfaces and two separate CSU/DSUs. But what happens when the company grows to 10 sites? Or 100 sites? Or 500 sites? For each point-to-point line, R1 needs a separate physical serial interface and a separate CSU/DSU. As you can imagine, growth to hundreds of sites will take many routers, with many interfaces each, and lots of rack space for the routers and CSU/DSUs.

Now imagine that the phone company salesperson says the following to you when you have two leased lines, or circuits, installed (as shown in Figure 3-7):

> You know, we can install Frame Relay instead. You will need only one serial interface on R1 and one CSU/DSU. To scale to 100 sites, you might need two or three more serial interfaces on R1 for more bandwidth, but that is it. And by the way, because your leased lines run at 128 kbps today, we will guarantee that you can send and receive that much data to and from each site. We will upgrade the line at R1 to T1 speed (1.544 Mbps). When you have more traffic than 128 kbps to a site, go ahead and send

it! If we have capacity, we will forward it, with no extra charge. And by the way, did I tell you that it is cheaper than leased lines anyway?

You consider the facts for a moment: Frame Relay is cheaper, it is at least as fast as (probably faster than) what you have now, and it allows you to save money when you grow. So, you quickly sign the contract with the Frame Relay provider, before the salesperson can change his mind, and migrate to Frame Relay. Does this story seem a bit ridiculous? Sure. The cost and scaling benefits of Frame Relay, as compared to leased lines, however, are very significant. As a result, many networks moved from using leased lines to Frame Relay, particularly in the 1990s, with a significantly large installed base of Frame Relay networks today. In the next few pages, you will see how Frame Relay works and realize how Frame Relay can provide functions claimed by the fictitious salesperson.

Frame Relay Basics

Frame Relay networks provide more features and benefits than simple point-to-point WAN links, but to do that, Frame Relay protocols are more detailed. Frame Relay networks are multiaccess networks, which means that more than two devices can attach to the network, similar to LANs. To support more than two devices, the protocols must be a little more detailed. Figure 3-8 introduces some basic connectivity concepts for Frame Relay. Figure 3-8 reflects the fact that Frame Relay uses the same Layer 1 features as a point-to-point leased line. For a Frame Relay service, a leased line is installed between each router and a nearby Frame Relay switch; these links are called *access links*. The access links run at the same speed and use the same signaling standards as do point-to-point leased lines. However, instead of extending from one router to the other, each leased line runs from one router to a Frame Relay switch.

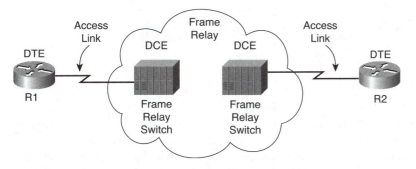

Figure 3-8 *Frame Relay Components*

The difference between Frame Relay and point-to-point links is that the equipment in the telco actually examines the data frames sent by the router. Frame Relay defines its own data-link header and trailer. Each Frame Relay header holds an address field called a data-link connection identifier (DLCI). The WAN switch forwards the frame based on the DLCI, sending the frame through the provider's network until it gets to the remote-site router on the other side of the Frame Relay cloud.

> **Note:**   The Frame Relay header and trailer are defined by a protocol called Link Access Procedure – Frame (LAPF).

Because the equipment in the telco can forward one frame to one remote site and another frame to another remote site, Frame Relay is considered to be a form of *packet switching*. This term means that the service provider actually chooses where to send each data packet sent into the provider's network, switching one packet to one device, and the next packet to another. However, Frame Relay protocols most closely resemble OSI Layer 2 protocols; the term usually used for the bits sent by a Layer 2 device is *frame*. So, Frame Relay is also called a *frame-switching service*, whereas the term packet switching is a more general term.

The terms *DCE* and *DTE* actually have a second set of meanings in the context of any packet-switching or frame-switching service. With Frame Relay, the Frame Relay switches are called DCE, and the customer equipment—routers, in this case—are called DTE. In this case, DCE refers to the device providing the service, and the term DTE refers to the device needing the frame-switching service. At the same time, the CSU/DSU provides clocking to the router, so from a Layer 1 perspective, the CSU/DSU is still the DCE and the router is still the DTE. It is just two different uses of the same terms.

Figure 3-8 depicted the physical and logical connectivity at each connection to the Frame Relay network. In contrast, Figure 3-9 shows the end-to-end connectivity associated with a virtual circuit (VC).

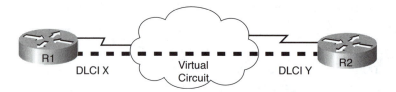

Figure 3-9   *Frame Relay VC Concepts*

The logical path that a frame travels between each pair of routers is called a Frame Relay VC. In Figure 3-9, a single VC is represented by the dashed line between the routers. Typically, the service provider preconfigures all the required details of a VC; these VCs are called permanent virtual circuits (PVC). When R1 needs to forward a packet to R2, it encapsulates the Layer 3 packet into a Frame Relay header and trailer and then sends the frame. R1 uses a Frame Relay address called a DLCI in the Frame Relay header, with the DLCI identifying the correct VC to the provider. This allows the switches to deliver the frame to R2, ignoring the details of the Layer 3 packet and looking at only the Frame Relay header and trailer. Recall that on a point-to-point serial link, the service provider forwards the frame over a physical circuit between R1 and R2. This transaction is similar in Frame Relay, where the provider forwards the frame over a logical VC from R1 to R2.

Frame Relay provides significant advantages over simply using point-to-point leased lines. The primary advantage has to do with VCs. Consider Figure 3-10 with Frame Relay instead of three point-to-point leased lines. Frame Relay creates a logical path (a VC) between two Frame Relay DTE devices. A VC acts like a point-to-point circuit, but physically it is not—it is virtual. For example, R1 terminates two VCs—one whose other endpoint is R2 and one whose other endpoint is R3. R1 can send traffic directly to either of the other two routers by sending it over the appropriate VC, although R1 has only one physical access link to the Frame Relay network.

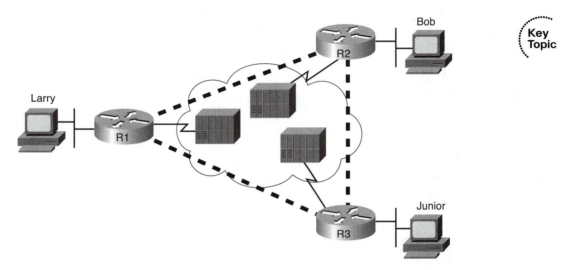

Figure 3-10 *Typical Frame Relay Network with Three Sites*

VCs share the access link and the Frame Relay network. For example, both VCs terminating at R1 use the same access link. So, with large networks with many WAN sites that need to connect to a central location, only one physical access link is required from the main site router to the Frame Relay network. By contrast, using point-to-point links would require a physical circuit, a separate CSU/DSU, and a separate physical interface on the router for each point-to-point link. So, Frame Relay enables you to expand the WAN but add less hardware to do so.

Many customers of a single Frame Relay service provider share that provider's Frame Relay network. Originally, people with leased-line networks were reluctant to migrate to Frame Relay because they would be competing with other customers for the provider's capacity inside the service provider's network. To address these fears, Frame Relay is designed with the concept of a committed information rate (CIR). Each VC has a CIR, which is a guarantee by the provider that a particular VC gets at least that much bandwidth. You can think of the CIR of a VC like the bandwidth or clock rate of a point-to-point circuit, except that it is the minimum value—you can actually send more, in most cases.

Even in this three-site network, it is probably less expensive to use Frame Relay than to use point-to-point links. Now imagine a much larger network, with 100 sites, that needs any-to-any connectivity. A point-to-point link design would require 4950 leased lines! In addition, you would need 99 serial interfaces per router. By contrast, with a Frame Relay design, you could have 100 access links to local Frame Relay switches (1 per router) with 4,950 VCs running over the access links. Also, you would need only one serial interface on each router. As a result, the Frame Relay topology is easier for the service provider to implement, costs the provider less, and makes better use of the core of the provider's network. As you would expect, that makes it less expensive to the Frame Relay customer as well. For connecting many WAN sites, Frame Relay is simply more cost-effective than leased lines.

Chapter Review

Review Key Topics

Review the most important topics from inside the chapter, noted with the key topics icon in the outer margin of the page. Table 3-3 lists a reference of these key topics and the page numbers on which each is found.

Table 3-3   *Key Topics for Chapter 3*

Key Topic Element	Description	Page Number
Figure 3-3	Shows typical cabling diagram of CPE for a leased line	60
Table 3-1	Typical speeds for WAN leased lines	65
Figure 3-6	HDLC framing	66
Table 3-2	List of key WAN terminology	67
Paragraph	List of synonyms for "point-to-point leased line"	67
Figure 3-10	Diagram of Frame Relay virtual circuits	71

Key Topic

Define Key Terms

Define the following key terms from this chapter, and check your answers in the glossary:

access link, back-to-back link, clocking, DTE (Layer 1), CSU/DSU, DCE (Layer 1), DS0, DS1, Frame Relay, HDLC, leased line, packet switching, PPP, serial cable, synchronous, T1, virtual circuit

Answer Review Questions

Answer the following review questions:

1. Which of the following best describes the main function of OSI Layer 1 protocols?

   a. Framing

   b. Delivery of bits from one device to another

   c. Addressing

   d. Local Management Interface (LMI)

   e. DLCI

2. Which of the following typically connects to a four-wire line provided by a telco?

a. Router serial interface

b. CSU/DSU

c. Transceiver

d. Switch serial interface

3. Which of the following typically connects to a V.35 or RS-232 end of a cable when cabling a leased line?

a. Router serial interface

b. CSU/DSU

c. Transceiver

d. Switch serial interface

4. On a point-to-point WAN link using a leased line between two routers located hundreds of miles apart, what devices are considered to be the DTE devices?

a. Routers

b. CSU/DSU

c. The central office equipment

d. A chip on the processor of each router

e. None of these answers are correct.

5. Which of the following functions of OSI Layer 2 is specified by the protocol standard for PPP, but is implemented with a Cisco proprietary header field for HDLC?

a. Framing

b. Arbitration

c. Addressing

d. Error detection

e. Identifying the type of protocol that is inside the frame

6. Imagine that Router1 has three point-to-point serial links, one link each to three remote routers. Which of the following is true about the required HDLC addressing at Router1?

a. Router1 must use HDLC addresses 1, 2, and 3.

b. Router1 must use any three unique addresses between 1 and 1023.

c. Router1 must use any three unique addresses between 16 and 1000.

d. Router1 must use three sequential unique addresses between 1 and 1023.

e. None of these answers are correct.

7. What is the name of the Frame Relay field used to identify Frame Relay virtual circuits?

    a. Data-link connection identifier

    b. Data-link circuit identifier

    c. Data-link connection indicator

    d. Data-link circuit indicator

    e. None of these answers are correct.

8. Which of the following is true about Frame Relay virtual circuits (VCs)?

    a. Each VC requires a separate access link.

    b. Multiple VCs can share the same access link.

    c. All VCs sharing the same access link must connect to the same router on the other side of the VC.

    d. All VCs on the same access link must use the same DLCI.

This chapter covers the following subjects:

- **Classful Network Concepts:** This section examines the ideas related to class A, class B, and class C networks—in other words, classful IP networks.

- **Practice with Classful Networks:** This section helps readers prepare by listing practice problems, tips, and suggestions for how to better review the math and logic used to analyze classful networks.

CHAPTER 4

Class A, B, and C Networks

When operating a network, you often start investigating a problem based on an IP address and mask. Based on the IP address alone, you should be able to determine several facts about the class A, B, or C network in which the IP address resides. These facts can be useful when troubleshooting some networking problems.

This chapter lists the key facts about classful IP networks and explains how to discover these facts. Following that, the chapter lists some practice problems. Before moving on to the next chapter, you should practice until you can consistently determine all these facts, quickly and confidently, based on an IP address.

Classful Network Concepts

Imagine that you have a job interview for your first IT job. As part of the interview, you're given an IPv4 address and mask: 10.4.5.99, 255.255.255.0. What can you tell the interviewer about the classful network (in this case, the class A network), in which the IP address resides?

The following sections review the concepts about *classful IP networks*—in other words, class A, B, and C networks. In particular, this chapter examines how to begin with a single IP address and then determine the following facts:

■ Class (A, B, or C)

■ Default mask

■ Number of network octets/bits

■ Number of host octets/bits

■ Number of host addresses in the network

■ Network ID

■ Network broadcast address

■ First and last usable address in the network

IPv4 Network Classes and Related Facts

IP version 4 (IPv4) defines five address classes. Three of the classes—class A, B, and C—consist of unicast IP addresses. Unicast addresses identify a single host or interface so that the address uniquely identifies the device. Class D addresses serve as multicast addresses, so that one packet sent to a class D multicast IPv4 address might actually be delivered to multiple hosts. Finally, class E addresses are experimental.

The class can be identified based on the value of the first octet of the address, as listed in Table 4-1.

Table 4-1   *IPv4 Address Classes Based on First Octet Values*

First Octet Values	Class	Purpose
1–126	A	Unicast (large networks)
128–191	B	Unicast (medium-sized networks)
192–223	C	Unicast (smaller networks)
224–239	D	Multicast
240–255	E	Experimental

This books focuses mostly on the unicast classes (A, B, and C) rather than classes D and E. After you identify the class as either A, B, or C, many of the other related facts can be derived just through memorization. Table 4-2 lists that information for reference and later study; each of these concepts will be described in this chapter.

Table 4-2   *Key Facts for Classes A, B, and C*

	Class A	Class B	Class C
First octet range	1–126	128–191	192–223
Valid network numbers	1.0.0.0–126.0.0.0	128.0.0.0–191.255.0.0	192.0.0.0–223.255.255.0
Total networks	$2^7 - 2 = 126$	$2^{14} = 16,384$	$2^{21} = 2,097,152$
Hosts per network	$2^{24} - 2$	$2^{16} - 2$	$2^8 - 2$
Octets (bits) in network part	1 (8)	2 (16)	3 (24)
Octets (bits) in host part	3 (24)	2 (16)	1 (8)
Default mask	255.0.0.0	255.255.0.0	255.255.255.0

Actual Class A, B, and C Networks

Table 4-2 lists the range of class A, B, and C network numbers. However, some of the key points can be lost just referencing a table of information. This section examines the class A, B, and C network numbers, focusing on the more important points and the exceptions and unusual cases.

First, the number of networks from each class differs significantly. Only 126 class A networks exist: network 1.0.0.0, 2.0.0.0, 3.0.0.0, and so on, up through network 126.0.0.0. However, 16,384 class B networks exist, with over 2 million class C networks.

Next, note that the size of the networks from each class differs significantly as well. Each class A network is relatively large—over 16 million host IP addresses per network—so they were originally intended to be used by the largest companies and organizations. Class B networks are smaller, with over 65,000 hosts per network. Finally, class C networks, intended for smaller organizations, have 254 hosts in each network. Figure 4-1 summarizes those facts.

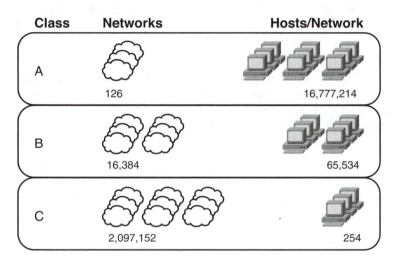

Figure 4-1   *Numbers of and Sizes of Class A, B, and C Networks*

Address Formats

In some cases, an engineer might need to think about a class A, B, or C network as if the network has not been subdivided through the subnetting process. In such a case, the addresses in the classful network have a structure with two parts: the *network part* (sometimes called the *prefix*) and the *host part*. Then, comparing any two IP addresses in one network, the following observations can be made:

> The addresses in the same network have the same values in the network part.
>
> The addresses in the same network have different values in the host part.

Key Topic

For example, in class A network 10.0.0.0, by definition, the network part consists of the first octet. As a result, all addresses have an equal value in the network part, namely a 10 in the first octet. If you then compare any two addresses in the network, the addresses have a different value in the last three octets (the host octets). For example, IP addresses 10.1.1.1 and 10.1.1.2 have the same value (10) in the network part, but different values in the host part.

Figure 4-2 shows the format and sizes (in number of bits) of the network and host parts of IP addresses in class A, B, and C networks, before any subnetting has been applied.

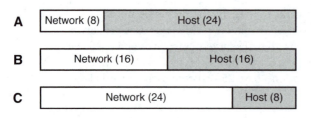

Figure 4-2   *Sizes (Bits) of the Network and Host Parts of Unsubnetted Classful Networks*

Default Masks

Although we humans can easily understand the concepts behind the drawing in Figure 4-2, computers prefer numbers. To communicate those same ideas to computers, each network class has an associated *default mask* that defines the size of the network and host parts of an unsubnetted class A, B, and C network. To do so, the mask lists binary 1s for the bits considered to be in the network part and binary 0s for the bits considered to be in the host part.

For example, class A network 10.0.0.0 has a network part of the first single octet (8 bits) and a host part of the last three octets (24 bits). As a result, the class A default mask is 255.0.0.0, which in binary is as follows:

11111111 00000000 00000000 00000000

Figure 4-3 shows default masks for each network class, both in binary and dotted decimal format.

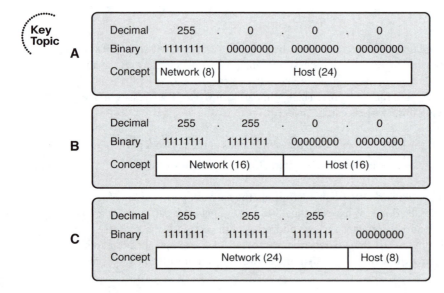

Figure 4-3   *Default Masks for Classes A, B, and C*

Note: Decimal 255 converts to the binary value 11111111. Decimal 0, converted to 8-bit binary, is 00000000. See Appendix B, "IP Access Control Lists," for a conversion table.

Number of Hosts per Network

Calculating the number of hosts per network requires some basic binary math. First, consider a case where you have a single binary digit. How many unique values are there? There are, of course, two values: 0 and 1. With 2 bits, you can make four combinations: 00, 01, 10, and 11. As it turns out, the total combination of unique values you can make with N bits is 2^N.

Host addresses—the IP addresses assigned to hosts—must be unique. The host bits exist for the purpose of giving each host a unique IP address, by virtue of having a different value in the host part of the addresses. So, with H host bits, 2^H unique combinations exist.

However, the number of hosts in a network is not 2^H; instead, it is $2^H - 2$. Each network reserves two numbers: one for the network ID and one for the network broadcast address. As a result, the formula to calculate the number of hosts per class A, B, or C network is

$$2^H - 2$$

where H is the number of host bits.

Deriving the Network ID and Related Numbers

Each classful network has four key numbers that describe the network. You can derive these four numbers if you start with just one IP address in the network. The numbers are

- Network number

- First usable address

- Last usable address

- Network broadcast address

First, consider both the network number and first usable IP address. The *network number*, also called the *network ID* or *network address*, identifies the network. By definition, the network number is the numerically lowest number in the network. However, to prevent any ambiguity, the people that made up IP addressing added the restriction that the network number cannot be assigned by a host as an IP address. So, the lowest number in the network is the network ID, and the first (numerically lowest) number usable as an IP address is *one larger than* the network number.

Next, consider the network broadcast address along with the last (numerically highest) usable IP address. The TCP/IP RFCs define a network broadcast address as a special address in each network. This broadcast address could be used as the destination address in a packet, and the routers would forward a copy of that one packet to all hosts in that classful network. Numerically, a network broadcast address is always the highest (last) number in the network. As a result, the highest (last) number usable as an IP address is the address that is simply *one less than* the network broadcast address.

Simply put, if you can find the network number and network broadcast address, finding the first and last IP address in the network is easy. You should practice until you can find all four values with ease; the process is as follows:

Step 1.   Determine the class (A, B, or C) based on the first octet.

Step 2.   Remember the number of network and host octets based on the class.

Step 3.   To find the network number, change the IP address's host octets to 0.

Step 4.   To find the first address, add 1 to the fourth octet of the network ID.

Step 5.   To find the broadcast address, change the network ID's host octets to 255.

Step 6.   To find the last address, subtract 1 from the fourth octet of the network broadcast address.

The written process actually looks harder than it really is. Figure 4-4 shows an example of the process, using class A IP address 10.1.2.3, with the circled numbers matching the process.

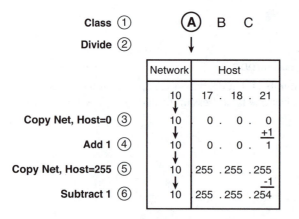

Figure 4-4   *Example of Deriving the Network ID and Other Values from 10.17.18.21*

The figure shows the identification of the class as class A (Step 1) and the number of network/host octets as 1 and 3, respectively. So, to find the network ID at Step 3, the figure copies only the first octet and sets the last three (host) octets to 0. At Step 4, just copy the network ID and add 1 to the fourth octet. Similarly, to find the broadcast address at Step 5, copy the network octets, but set the host octets to 255. Then, at Step 6, just subtract 1 from the fourth octet to find the last usable IP address.

Just to show an alternative example, consider IP address 172.16.8.9. Figure 4-5 shows the process applied to this IP address.

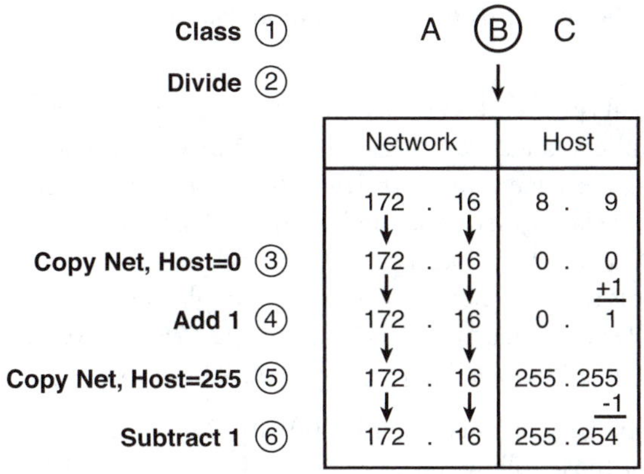

Figure 4-5 *Example Deriving the Network ID and Other Values from 172.16.8.9*

The figure shows the identification of the class as class B (Step 1) and the number of network/host octets as 2 and 2, respectively. So, to find the network ID at Step 3, the figure copies only the first two octets, setting the last two (host) octets to 0. Similarly, Step 5 shows the same action, but with the last two (host) octets being set to 255.

Unusual Network IDs and Network Broadcast Addresses

Some of the more unusual numbers in and around the range of class A, B, and C network numbers can cause some confusion. This short section lists some of these examples of unusual-looking valid numbers and normal-looking valid numbers.

For class A, the first odd fact is that the range of values in the first octet omits the numbers 0 and 127. As it turns out, what would be class A network 0.0.0.0 was originally reserved for some broadcasting requirements, so all addresses that begin with 0 in the first octet are reserved. What would be class A network 127.0.0.0 is still reserved because of a special address used in software testing, called the loopback address (127.0.0.1).

For class B (and C), some of the network numbers can look a little odd, particularly if you fall into a habit of thinking that 0s at the end means that the number is a network ID, and 255s at the end means that it's a network broadcast address. First, the network numbers themselves range from 128.0.0.0 to 191.255.0.0, for a total of 2^{14} class B networks. However, even the very first (lowest number) class B network number (128.0.0.0) looks a little like a class A network number, because it ends with three 0s. However, the first octet is 128, making it a class B network with a two-octet network part (128.0).

For another class B example, the high end of the class B range also might look strange at first glance (191.255.0.0), but this is indeed the numerically highest of the valid class B network numbers. And this network's broadcast address, 199.255.255.255, might look a little like a class A broadcast address because of the three 255s at the end, but it is indeed the broadcast address of a class B network.

Other valid class B network IDs that look a bit unusual include 130.0.0.0, 150.0.0.0, 155.255.0.0, and 190.0.0.0. All of these follow the convention of a value from 128 to 191 in the first octet, a value from 0 to 255 in the second octet, and two more 0s, so they are indeed valid class B network IDs.

Class C networks follow the same general rules as class B, but with the first three octets defining the network. The network numbers range from 192.0.0.0 to 223.255.255.0, with all addresses in a single network sharing the same value in the first three octets. And similar to class B networks, some of the valid class C network numbers do look a little strange. For example, class C network 192.0.0.0 looks a little like a class A network because of the last three octets being 0, but because it is a class C network, it consists of all addresses that begin with three octets equal to 192.0.0. Similarly, class C network 223.255.255.0, another valid class C network, consists of all addresses that begin with 223.255.255.

Other valid class C network IDs that look a bit unusual include 200.0.0.0, 220.0.0.0, 205.255.255.0, and 199.255.255.0. All of these follow the convention of a value from 192 to 223 in the first octet, a value from 0 to 255 in both the second and third octets, and a 0 in the fourth octet.

Practice with Classful Networks

IP addressing and subnetting includes many procedures and calculations akin to what you might learn in math classes. To be a well-prepared network engineer, you should master these processes and calculations by the time you finish this course. Most any technical interview for a job working with IP networking will include some assessment of how well you understand the concepts and how quickly you can calculate various facts about addresses and subnets.

However, you do not need to completely master everything in this chapter right now. You should practice some now, to make sure that you understand the processes, but for now, you can use your notes, the book, or whatever. After you practice enough to confirm that you can get the right answers using any help available, you understand the topics in this chapter well enough to move to the next chapter.

Then, before the midterm and final exams, practice until you master the topics in this chapter. Table 4-3 summarizes the key concepts and suggestions for this two-phase approach.

Table 4-3 *Practice Goals for This Chapter's Topics*

Time Frame	After Reading This Chapter	Before Any Tests
Focus on...	Learning how	Being correct and fast
Tools Allowed	All	Your brain and a notepad
Goal: Accuracy	90% correct	100% correct

Practice Deriving Key Facts Based on an IP Address

Practice finding the various facts that can be derived from an IP address, as discussed throughout this chapter. To do so, complete Table 4-4.

Table 4-4   *Practice Problems: Find the Network ID and Network Broadcast*

	IP Address	Class	Number of Network Octets	Number of Host Octets	Network ID	Network Broadcast Address
1	1.1.1.1					
2	128.1.6.5					
3	200.1.2.3					
4	192.192.1.1					
5	126.5.4.3					
6	200.1.9.8					
7	192.0.0.1					
8	191.255.1.47					
9	223.223.0.1					

The answers are listed in the section "Review Answers to Earlier Practice Problems," later in this chapter.

Practice Remembering the Details of Address Classes

Tables 4-1 and 4-2, earlier in this chapter, summarized some key information about IPv4 address classes. Tables 4-5 and 4-6 show sparse versions of these same tables. To practice recalling those key facts, particularly the range of values in the first octet that identifies the address class, complete these tables. Then refer to Tables 4-1 and 4-2 to check your answers. Repeat this process until you can recall all the information in the tables.

Table 4-5   *Sparse Study Table Version of Table 4-1*

First Octet Values	Class	Purpose
	A	
	B	
	C	
	D	
	E	

Table 4-6   *Sparse Study Table Version of Table 4-2*

	Class A	Class B	Class C
First octet range			
Valid network numbers			
Total networks			
Hosts per network			
Octets (bits) in network part			
Octets (bits) in host part			
Default mask			

Additional Practice

For additional practice with classful networks, consider the following:

- Create your own problems. You can randomly choose any IP address and try and find the same information asked for by the practice problems in this section. Then, to check your work, use any subnet calculator. Most subnet calculators list the class and network ID. (Check the author's reference page for this book [http://www.certskills.com/IPNetworking], as listed in the introduction, for some suggested calculators.)

- The Subnet Prep App "Analyze Networks" iPhone app provides review videos and almost limitless practice problems. It's a great way to review and improve your speed when you have some spare time.

Chapter Review

Review Key Topics

This chapter contains just a few key topics—mainly facts about classes of IPv4 addresses and classful networks, plus a process to determine the network ID and associated values for a classful network. Table 4-7 lists an index to these topics.

Table 4-7 *Key Topics for Chapter 4*

Key Topic Element	Description	Page Number
Table 4-1	Address classes	78
Table 4-2	Key facts about class A, B, and C	78
List	Comparisons of network and host parts of addresses in the same classful network	79
Figure 4-3	Default masks	80
List	Steps to find information about a classful network	82

Key Topic

Define Key Terms

Define the following key terms from this chapter, and check your answers in the glossary.

network, classful network, network number, network ID, network address, network broadcast address, first address, last address, network part, host part, default mask

Practice

If you have not done so already, practice discovering the details of a classful network, as discussed in this chapter. Refer to the earlier section "Practice with Classful Networks" for suggestions.

Review Answers to Earlier Practice Problems

Table 4-4, earlier in this chapter, listed several practice problems. Table 4-8 lists the answers.

Table 4-8 *Practice Problems: Find the Network ID and Network Broadcast*

	IP Address	Class	Number of Network Octets	Number of Host Octets	Network ID	Network Broadcast
1	1.1.1.1	A	1	3	1.0.0.0	1.255.255.255
2	128.1.6.5	B	2	2	128.1.0.0	128.1.255.255

Table 4-8   *Practice Problems: Find the Network ID and Network Broadcast*

	IP Address	Class	Number of Network Octets	Number of Host Octets	Network ID	Network Broadcast
3	200.1.2.3	C	3	1	200.1.2.0	200.1.2.255
4	192.192.1.1	C	3	1	192.192.1.0	192.192.1.255
5	126.5.4.3	A	1	3	126.0.0.0	126.255.255.255
6	200.1.9.8	C	3	1	200.1.9.0	200.1.9.255
7	192.0.0.1	C	3	1	192.0.0.0	192.0.0.255
8	191.255.1.47	B	2	2	191.255.0.0	191.255.255.255
9	223.223.0.1	C	3	1	223.223.0.0	223.223.0.255

The class, number of network octets, and number of host octets all require that you look at the first octet of the IP address to determine the class. If a value is between 1 and 126 inclusive, the address is a class A address, with one network and three host octets. If a value is between 128 and 191 inclusive, the address is a class B address, with two network and two host octets. If a value is between 192 and 223 inclusive, it is a class C address, with three network and one host octet.

The last two columns can be found based on Table 4-2, specifically the number of network and host octets along with the IP address. To find the network ID, copy the IP address, but change the host octets to 0. Similarly, to find the network broadcast address, copy the IP address, but change the host octets to 255.

The last three problems can be confusing and were included on purpose so that you could see an example of these unusual cases. These cases are discussed in the following sections.

Answers to Practice Problem 7

Consider IP address 192.0.0.1. First, 192 is on the lower edge of the first octet range for class C; as such, this address has three network and one host octets. To find the network ID, copy the address, but change the single host octet (the fourth octet) to 0, for a network ID of 192.0.0.0. It looks strange, but it is indeed the network ID.

The network broadcast address choice for problem 7 can also look strange. To find the broadcast address, copy the IP address (192.0.0.1), but change the last octet (the only host octet) to 255, for a broadcast address of 192.0.0.255. In particular, if you decided that the broadcast should be 192.255.255.255, you might have fallen into the trap of logic like "change all 0s in the network ID to 255s," which is not the correct logic. Instead, change all host octets in the IP address (or network ID) to 255s.

Answers to Practice Problem 8

The first octet of problem 8 (191.255.1.47) sits on the upper edge of the class B range for the first octet (128–191). As such, to find the network ID, change the last two octets (host octets) to 0, for a network ID of 191.255.0.0. This value sometimes gives people some problems, because they are used to thinking that 255 somehow means that the number is a broadcast address.

The broadcast address, found by changing the two host octets to 255, means that the broadcast address is 191.255.255.255. It looks more like a broadcast address for a class A network, but in reality, it is the broadcast address for class B network 191.255.0.0.

Answers to Practice Problem 9

The last problem, with IP address 223.223.0.1, is near the high end of the class C range. As a result, only the last (host) octet is changed to 0 to form the network ID of 223.223.0.0. It looks a little like a class B network number at first glance, because it ends in two octets of 0. However, it is indeed a class C network ID (based on the value in the first octet).

Answer Review Questions

Answer the following review questions:

1. Which of the following are not valid class A network IDs? (Choose two.)

    a.   1.0.0.0

    b.   130.0.0.0

    c.   127.0.0.0

    d.   9.0.0.0

2. Which of the following are not valid class B network IDs?

    a.   130.0.0.0

    b.   191.255.0.0

    c.   128.0.0.0

    d.   150.255.0.0

    e.   All are valid class B network IDs.

3. Which of the following is true about IP address 172.16.99.45's IP network? (Choose two.)

    a.   The network ID is 172.0.0.0.

    b.   The network is a class B network.

    c.   The default mask for the network is 255.255.255.0.

    d.   The number of host bits in the unsubnetted network is 16.

4. Which of the following is true about IP address 192.168.6.7's IP network? (Choose two.)

    a. The network ID is 192.168.6.0.

    b. The network is a class B network.

    c. The default mask for the network is 255.255.255.0.

    d. The number of host bits in the unsubnetted network is 16.

5. Which of the following is a network broadcast address?

    a. 10.1.255.255

    b. 192.168.255.1

    c. 224.1.1.255

    d. 172.30.255.255

6. Which of the following is a class A, B, or C network ID?

    a. 10.1.0.0

    b. 192.168.1.0

    c. 127.0.0.0

    d. 172.20.0.1

This chapter covers the following subjects:

- **Overview of Network Layer Functions:** The first section introduces the concepts of routing, logical addressing, and routing protocols.

- **IP Addressing:** Next, the basics of 32-bit IP addresses are explained, with emphasis on how the organization aids the routing process.

- **IP Routing:** This section explains how hosts and routers decide how to forward a packet.

- **IP Routing Protocols:** This brief section explains the basics of how routing protocols populate each router's routing tables.

- **Network Layer Utilities:** This section introduces several other functions useful to the overall process of packet delivery.

CHAPTER 5

Fundamentals of IP Addressing and Routing

This chapter begins the second unit of the textbook by taking a closer look at the most important TCP/IP layer in this course: the TCP/IP internetwork layer. This chapter reviews some details of how Internet Protocol (IP) and the rest of TCP/IP's network layer implement routing and addressing. This unit's Chapter 7, "Operating Cisco Routers," introduces you to the specifics of how to access, configure, and monitor IP routers from Cisco Systems. This text uses Cisco routers in the examples of how to implement IP routing throughout the book. This unit also includes a chapter (Chapter 6, "Fundamentals of TCP/IP Transport, Applications, and Security") that completes this book's review of the various layers of the TCP/IP model so that later units can focus mostly on the network and data link layers.

OSI Layer 3–equivalent protocols define how packets can be delivered from the computer that creates the packet all the way to the computer that needs to receive the packet. To reach that goal, an OSI network layer protocol defines the following features:

Routing: The process of forwarding packets (Layer 3 PDUs).

Logical addressing: Addresses that can be used regardless of the type of physical networks used, providing each device (at least) one address. Logical addressing enables the routing process to identify a packet's source and destination.

Routing protocol: A protocol that aids routers by dynamically learning about the groups of addresses in the network, which in turn allows the routing (forwarding) process to work well.

Other utilities: The network layer also relies on other utilities. For TCP/IP, these utilities include Domain Name System (DNS), Dynamic Host Configuration Protocol (DHCP), Address Resolution Protocol (ARP), and ping.

Note: The term *path selection* sometimes is used to mean the same thing as routing protocol, sometimes is used to refer to the routing (forwarding) of packets, and sometimes is used for both functions.

This chapter begins with an overview of routing, logical addressing, and routing proto-cols. Following that, the text moves on to more details about the specifics of the TCP/IP network layer (called the internetwork layer in the TCP/IP model). In particular, the topics of IP addressing, routing, routing protocols, and network layer utilities are covered.

Overview of Network Layer Functions

A protocol that defines routing and logical addressing is considered to be a network layer, or Layer 3, protocol. OSI does define a unique Layer 3 protocol called Connectionless Network Services (CLNS), but, as usual with OSI protocols, you rarely see it in networks today. In the recent past, you might have seen many other network layer protocols, such as Internet Protocol (IP), Novell Internetwork Packet Exchange (IPX), or AppleTalk Data-gram Delivery Protocol (DDP). Today, the only Layer 3 protocol that is used widely is the TCP/IP network layer protocol—specifically, IP.

The main job of IP is to route data (packets) from the source host to the destination host. Because a network might need to forward large numbers of packets, the IP routing process is very simple. IP does not require any overhead agreements or messages before sending a packet, making IP a connectionless protocol. IP tries to deliver each packet, but if a router or host's IP process cannot deliver the packet, it is discarded—with no error re-covery. The goal with IP is to deliver packets with as little per-packet work as possible, which allows for large packet volumes. Other protocols perform some of the other useful networking functions. For example, Transmission Control Protocol (TCP), which is de-scribed in detail in Chapter 6, provides error recovery, resending lost data, but IP does not.

IP routing relies on the structure and meaning of IP addresses, and IP addressing was de-signed with IP routing in mind. This first major section of this chapter begins by introduc-ing IP routing, with some IP addressing concepts introduced along the way. Then, the text examines IP addressing fundamentals.

Routing (Forwarding)

Routing focuses on the end-to-end logic of forwarding data. Figure 5-1 shows a simple ex-ample of how routing works. The logic illustrated by the figure is relatively simple. For PC1 to send data to PC2, it must send something to router R1, which sends it to router R2, and then to router R3, and finally to PC2. However, the logic used by each device along the path varies slightly.

PC1's Logic: Sending Data to a Nearby Router

In this example, illustrated in Figure 5-1, PC1 has some data to send to PC2. Because PC2 is not on the same Ethernet as PC1, PC1 needs to send the packet to a router that is at-tached to the same Ethernet as PC1. The sender sends a data-link frame across the medium to the nearby router; this frame includes the packet in the data portion of the frame. That frame uses data link layer (Layer 2) addressing in the data-link header to ensure that the nearby router receives the frame.

The main point here is that the computer that created the data does not know much about the network—just how to get the data to some nearby router. Using a post office analogy, it's like knowing how to get to the local post office, but nothing more. Likewise, PC1 needs to know only how to get the packet to R1, not the rest of the path used to send the packet to PC2.

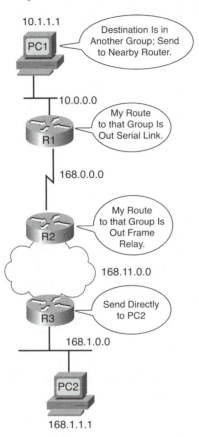

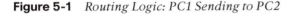

Figure 5-1   *Routing Logic: PC1 Sending to PC2*

R1's and R2's Logic: Routing Data Across the Network

R1 and R2 both use the same general process to route the packet. The *routing table* for any particular network layer protocol contains a list of network layer address *groupings*. Instead of a single entry in the routing table per individual destination network layer address, there is one routing table entry per group. The router compares the destination network layer address in the packet to the entries in the routing table and makes a match. This matching entry in the routing table tells this router where to forward the packet next. The words in the bubbles in Figure 5-1 point out this basic logic.

The concept of network layer address grouping is similar to the U.S. zip code system. Everyone living in the same vicinity is in the same zip code, and the postal sorters just look for the zip codes, ignoring the rest of the address. Likewise, in Figure 5-1, everyone in this network whose IP address starts with 168.1 is on the Ethernet on which PC2 resides, so the routers can have just one routing table entry that means "all addresses that start with 168.1."

Any intervening routers repeat the same process: the router compares the packet's destination network layer (Layer 3) address to the groups listed in its routing table, and the matched routing table entry tells this router where to forward the packet next. Eventually, the packet is delivered to the router connected to the network or subnet of the destination host (R3), as shown in Figure 5-1.

R3's Logic: Delivering Data to the End Destination

The final router in the path, R3, uses almost the exact same logic as R1 and R2, but with one minor difference. R3 needs to forward the packet directly to PC2, not to some other router. On the surface, that difference seems insignificant. In the next section, when you read about how the network layer uses the data link layer, the significance of the difference will become obvious.

Network Layer Interaction with the Data Link Layer

When the network layer protocol is processing the packet, it decides to send the packet out the appropriate network interface. Before the actual bits can be placed onto that physical interface, the network layer must hand off the packet to the data link layer protocols, which, in turn, ask the physical layer to actually send the data. And as was described in Chapter 2, "LAN Fundamentals," the data link layer adds the appropriate header and trailer to the packet, creating a frame, before sending the frames over each physical network. The routing process forwards the packet, and only the packet, end-to-end through the network, *discarding data-link headers and trailers along the way*. The network layer processes deliver the packet end-to-end, using successive data-link headers and trailers just to get the packet to the next router or host in the path. Each successive data link layer just gets the packet from one device to the next. Figure 5-2 points out the key encapsulation logic on each device, using the same examples as in Figure 5-1.

Because the routers build new data-link headers and trailers (trailers not shown in the figure), and because the new headers contain data-link addresses, the PCs and routers must have some way to decide what data-link addresses to use. An example of how the router determines which data-link address to use is the IP Address Resolution Protocol (ARP). *ARP is used to dynamically learn the data-link address of an IP host connected to a LAN.* You will read more about ARP later in this chapter.

Routing as covered so far has two main concepts:

■   The process of routing forwards Layer 3 packets, also called *Layer 3 protocol data units (L3 PDU)*, based on the destination Layer 3 address in the packet.

■   The routing process uses the data link layer to encapsulate the Layer 3 packets into Layer 2 frames for transmission across each successive data link.

IP Packets and the IP Header

The IP packets encapsulated in the data-link frames shown in Figure 5-2 have an IP header, followed by additional headers and data. For reference, Figure 5-3 shows the fields inside the standard 20-byte IPv4 header, with no optional IP header fields, as is typically seen in most networks today.

10.1.1.1
PC1
Encapsulate IP Packet in Ethernet
Eth.
IP Packet
10.0.0.0
R1
Extract IP Packet and Encapsulate in HDLC
HDLC
IP Packet
168.10.0.0
R2
Extract IP Packet, and Encapsulate in Frame Relay
FR
IP Packet
168.11.0.0
R3
Extract IP Packet, and Encapsulate in Ethernet
Eth
IP Packet
168.1.0.0
PC2
168.1.1.1

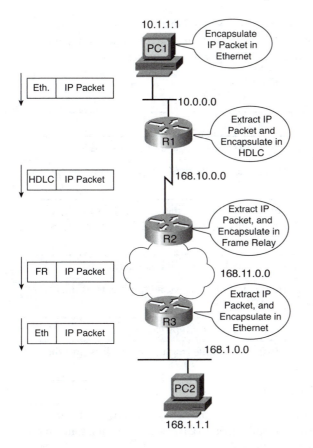

Figure 5-2 *Network Layer and Data Link Layer Encapsulation*

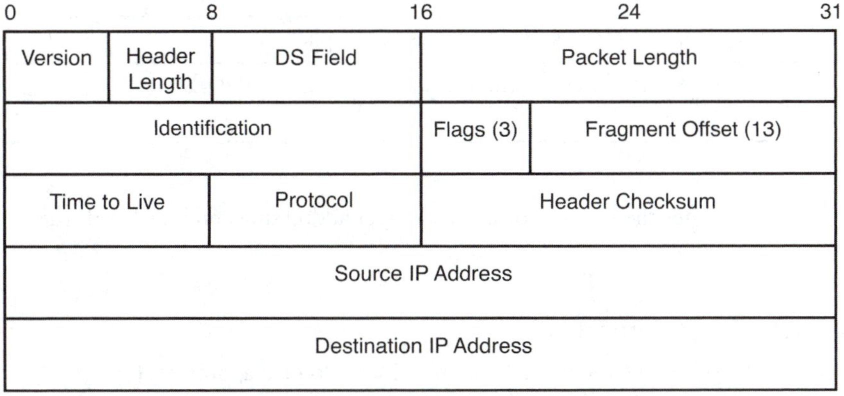

0
8
16
24
31
Version
Header Length
DS Field
Packet Length
Identification
Flags (3)
Fragment Offset (13)
Time to Live
Protocol
Header Checksum
Source IP Address
Destination IP Address

Figure 5-3 *IPv4 Header*

Of the different fields inside the IPv4 header, for the depth that this book discusses IP, the most important fields are Time-To-Live (TTL), protocol, and the source and destination IP address fields. However, for reference, Table 5-1 briefly describes each field.

Table 5-1   *IPv4 Header Fields*

Field	Meaning
Version	Version of the IP protocol. Most networks use version 4 today.
IHL	IP Header Length. Defines the length of the IP header, including optional fields.
DS Field	Differentiated Services Field. It is used for marking packets for the purpose of applying different quality-of-service (QoS) levels to different packets.
Packet length	Identifies the entire length of the IP packet, including the data.
Identification	Used by the IP packet fragmentation process; all fragments of the original packet contain the same identifier.
Flags	3 bits used by the IP packet fragmentation process.
Fragment offset	A number used to help hosts reassemble fragmented packets into the original larger packet.
TTL	Time to live. A value used to prevent routing loops.
Protocol	A field that identifies the contents of the data portion of the IP packet. For example, protocol 6 implies that a TCP header is the first thing in the IP packet data field.
Header Checksum	A value used to store an FCS value, whose purpose is to determine if any bit errors occurred in the IP header.
Source IP address	The 32-bit IP address of the sender of the packet.
Destination IP address	The 32-bit IP address of the intended recipient of the packet.

This section next examines the concept of network layer addressing and how it aids the routing process.

Network Layer (Layer 3) Addressing

Network layer protocols define the format and meaning of logical addresses. (The term *logical address* does not really refer to whether the addresses make sense, but rather to contrast these addresses with physical addresses.) Each computer that needs to communicate will have (at least) one network layer address so that other computers can send data packets to that address, expecting the network to deliver the data packet to the correct computer.

One key feature of network layer addresses is that they were designed to allow logical grouping of addresses. In other words, something about the numeric value of an address implies a group or set of addresses, all of which are considered to be in the same grouping. With IP addresses, this group is called a *network* or a *subnet*. These groupings work just like USPS zip (postal) codes, allowing the routers (mail sorters) to speedily route (sort) lots of packets (letters).

Just like postal street addresses, network layer addresses are grouped based on physical location in a network. The rules differ for some network layer protocols, but with IP addressing, the first part of the IP address is the same for all the addresses in one grouping. For example, in Figures 5-1 and 5-2, the following IP addressing conventions define the groups of IP addresses (IP networks) for all hosts on that internetwork:

■   Hosts on the top Ethernet: Addresses start with 10

■   Hosts on the R1-R2 serial link: Addresses start with 168.10

■   Hosts on the R2-R3 Frame Relay network: Addresses start with 168.11

■   Hosts on the bottom Ethernet: Addresses start with 168.1

Note: To avoid confusion when writing about IP networks, many resources (including this one) use the term *internetwork* to refer more generally to a network made up of routers, switches, cables, and other equipment, and the word *network* to refer to the more specific concept of an IP network.

Routing relies on the fact that Layer 3 addresses are grouped. The routing tables for each network layer protocol can have one entry for the group, not one entry for each individual address. Imagine an Ethernet with 100 TCP/IP hosts. A router that needs to forward packets to any of those hosts needs only one entry in its IP routing table, with that one routing table entry representing the entire group of hosts on the Ethernet. This basic fact is one of the key reasons that routers can scale to allow hundreds of thousands of devices. It's very similar to the USPS zip code system. It would be ridiculous to have people in the same zip code live far from each other, or to have next-door neighbors be in different zip codes. The poor postman would spend all his time driving and flying around the country! Similarly, to make routing more efficient, network layer protocols group addresses.

Routing Protocols

Conveniently, the routers in Figures 5-1 and 5-2 somehow know the correct steps to take to forward the packet from PC1 to PC2. To make the correct choices, each router needs a routing table, with a route that matches the packet sent to PC2. The routes tell the router where to send the packet next.

In most cases, routers build their routing table entries dynamically using a routing protocol. Routing protocols learn about all the locations of the network layer "groups" in a network and advertise the groups' locations. As a result, each router can build a good routing table dynamically. Routing protocols define message formats and procedures, just like any other protocol. The end goal of each routing protocol is to fill the routing table with all known destination groups and with the best route to reach each group.

The terminology relating to routing protocols sometimes can get in the way. A *routing protocol* learns routes and puts those routes in a routing table. A *routed protocol* defines the type of packet forwarded, or routed, through a network. In Figures 5-1 and 5-2, the figures represent how IP packets are routed, so IP would be the *routed protocol*. If the routers used Routing Information Protocol (RIP) to learn the routes, RIP would be the *routing protocol*. Later in this chapter, the section "IP Routing Protocols" shows a detailed example of how routing protocols learn routes.

Now that you have seen the basic function of the OSI network layer at work, the rest of this chapter examines the key components of the end-to-end routing process for TCP/IP.

IP Addressing

By the time you have completed this course, you should be comfortable and confident in your understanding of IP addresses, their formats, the grouping concepts, how to subdivide groups into subnets, how to interpret the documentation for existing networks' IP addressing, and so on. Simply put, you had better know addressing and subnetting!

This section introduces IP addressing and subnetting and also covers the concepts behind the structure of an IP address, including how it relates to IP routing.

IP Addressing Definitions

If a device wants to communicate using TCP/IP, it needs an IP address. When the device has an IP address and the appropriate software and hardware, it can send and receive IP packets. Any device that can send and receive IP packets is called an *IP host*.

Note: IP Version 4 (IPv4) is the most widely used version of IP. Chapter 23, "IP Version 6," discusses the newer version of the IP protocol. Most companies continue to use IPv4, but a migration to use networks that support both IPv4 and IPv6 is under way. In this chapter, and all chapters before Chapter 23, all references to IP addresses in this book should be taken to mean "IP version 4" addresses.

IP addresses consist of a 32-bit number, usually written in *dotted-decimal notation*. The "decimal" part of the term comes from the fact that each byte (8 bits) of the 32-bit IP address is shown as its decimal equivalent. The four resulting decimal numbers are written in sequence, with "dots," or decimal points, separating the numbers—hence the name *dotted decimal*. For instance, 168.1.1.1 is an IP address written in dotted-decimal form; the actual binary version is 10101000 00000001 00000001 00000001. (You almost never need to write down the binary version.)

Each decimal number in an IP address is called an *octet*. The term *octet* is just a vendor-neutral term for *byte*. So, for an IP address of 168.1.1.1, the first octet is 168, the second octet is 1, and so on. The range of decimal numbers in each octet is between 0 and 255, inclusive.

Finally, note that each network interface uses a unique IP address. Most people tend to think that their computer has an IP address, but actually their computer's network card has an IP address. If you put two Ethernet cards in a PC to forward IP packets through both cards, they both would need unique IP addresses. Also, if your laptop has both an Ethernet NIC and a wireless NIC working at the same time, your laptop will have an IP address for each NIC. Similarly, routers, which typically have many network interfaces that forward IP packets, have an IP address for each interface.

Now that you have some idea of the basic terminology, the next section relates IP addressing to the routing concepts of OSI Layer 3.

How IP Addresses Are Grouped

The original specifications for TCP/IP grouped IP addresses into sets of consecutive addresses called *IP networks*. The addresses in a single network have the same numeric value in the first part of all addresses in the network. Figure 5-4 shows a simple internetwork that has three separate IP networks.

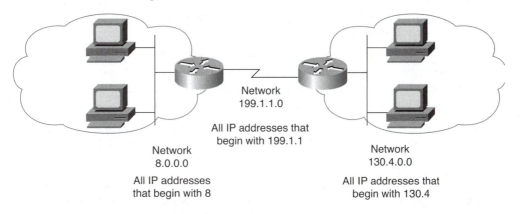

Figure 5-4 *Sample Network Using Class A, B, and C Network Numbers*

The conventions of IP addressing and IP address grouping make routing easy. For example, all IP addresses that begin with 8 are in the IP network that contains all the hosts on the Ethernet on the left. Likewise, all IP addresses that begin with 130.4 are in another IP network that consists of all the hosts on the Ethernet on the right. Along the same lines, 199.1.1 is the prefix for all IP addresses on the network that includes the addresses on the serial link. (The only two IP addresses in this last grouping will be the IP addresses on each of the two routers.) By following this convention, the routers build a routing table with three entries—one for each prefix, or network number. For example, the router on the left can have one route that refers to all addresses that begin with 130.4, with that route directing the router to forward packets to the router on the right.

The example indirectly points out a couple of key points about how IP addresses are organized. To be a little more explicit, the following two rules summarize the facts about which IP addresses need to be in the same grouping:

■ All IP addresses in the same group must not be separated by a router.

■ IP addresses separated by a router must be in different groups.

Key
Topic

As mentioned earlier in this chapter, IP addressing behaves similarly to zip codes. Everyone in my zip code lives in a little town in Ohio. If some members of my zip code were in California, some of my mail might be sent to California by mistake. Likewise, IP routing relies on the fact that all IP addresses in the same group (called either a network or a subnet) are in the same general location. If some of the IP addresses in my network or subnet were allowed to be on the other side of the internetwork compared to my computer, the routers in the network might incorrectly send some of the packets sent to my computer to the other side of the network.

Classes of Networks

Figure 5-4 and the surrounding text claim that the IP addresses of devices attached to the Ethernet on the left all start with 8 and that the IP addresses of devices attached to the Ethernet on the right all start with 130.4. Why only one number (8) for the "prefix" on the Ethernet on the left and two numbers (130 and 4) on the Ethernet on the right? Well, it all has to do with IP address classes.

RFC 791 defines the IP protocol, including several different classes of networks. IP defines three different network classes for addresses used by individual hosts—addresses called unicast IP addresses. These three network classes are called A, B, and C. TCP/IP defines Class D (multicast) addresses and Class E (experimental) addresses as well.

By definition, all addresses in the same Class A, B, or C network have the same numeric value *network* portion of the addresses. The rest of the address is called the *host* portion of the address.

Using the post office example, the network part of an IP address acts like the zip (postal) code, and the host part acts like the street address. Just as a letter-sorting machine three states away from you cares only about the zip code on a letter addressed to you, a router three hops away from you cares only about the network number that your address resides in.

Class A, B, and C networks each have a different length for the part that identifies the network:

- Class A networks have a 1-byte-long network part. That leaves 3 bytes for the rest of the address, called the host part.

- Class B networks have a 2-byte-long network part, leaving 2 bytes for the host portion of the address.

- Class C networks have a 3-byte-long network part, leaving only 1 byte for the host part.

For example, Figure 5-4 lists network 8.0.0.0 next to the Ethernet on the left. Network 8.0.0.0 is a Class A network, which means that only 1 octet (byte) is used for the network part of the address. So, all hosts in network 8.0.0.0 begin with 8. Similarly, Class B network 130.4.0.0 is listed next to the Ethernet on the right. Because it is a Class B network, 2 octets define the network part, and all addresses begin with 130.4 as the first 2 octets.

When listing network numbers, the convention is to write down the network part of the number, with all decimal 0s in the host part of the number. So, Class A network "8," which consists of all IP addresses that begin with 8, is written as 8.0.0.0. Similarly, Class B network "130.4," which consists of all IP addresses that begin with 130.4, is written as 130.4.0.0, and so on.

Now consider the size of each class of network. Class A networks need 1 byte for the network part, leaving 3 bytes, or 24 bits, for the host part. There are 2^{24} different possible values in the host part of a Class A IP address. So, each Class A network can have 2^{24} IP addresses—except for two reserved host addresses in each network, as shown in the last column of Table 5-2. The table summarizes the characteristics of Class A, B, and C networks.

Table 5-2 *Sizes of Network and Host Parts of IP Addresses with No Subnetting*

Key Topic

Any Network of This Class	Number of Network Bytes (Bits)	Number of Host Bytes (Bits)	Number of Addresses Per Network*
A	1 (8)	3 (24)	$2^{24} - 2$
B	2 (16)	2 (16)	$2^{16} - 2$
C	3 (24)	1 (8)	$2^{8} - 2$

* There are two reserved host addresses per network.

Based on the three examples from Figure 5-4, Table 5-3 provides a closer look at the numeric version of the three network numbers: 8.0.0.0, 130.4.0.0, and 199.1.1.0.

Table 5-3 *Sample Network Numbers, Decimal and Binary*

Network Number	Binary Representation, with the Host Part in Bold
8.0.0.0	00001000 **00000000 00000000 00000000**
130.4.0.0	10000010 00000100 **00000000 00000000**
199.1.1.0	11000111 00000001 00000001 **00000000**

Even though the network numbers look like addresses because of their dotted-decimal format, network numbers cannot be assigned to an interface to be used as an IP address. Conceptually, network numbers represent the group of all IP addresses in the network, much like a zip code represents the group of all addresses in a community. It would be confusing to have a single number represent a whole group of addresses and then also use that same number as an IP address for a single device. So, the network numbers themselves are reserved and cannot be used as an IP address for a device.

Besides the network number, a second dotted-decimal value in each network is reserved. Note that the first reserved value, the network number, has all binary 0s in the host part of the number (see Table 5-3). The other reserved value is the one with all binary 1s in the host part of the number. This number is called the *network broadcast* or *directed broadcast* address. This reserved number cannot be assigned to a host for use as an IP address. However, packets sent to a network broadcast address are forwarded to all devices in the network.

Also, because the network number is the lowest numeric value inside that network and the broadcast address is the highest numeric value, all the numbers between the network number and the broadcast address are the valid, useful IP addresses that can be used to address interfaces in the network.

The Actual Class A, B, and C Network Numbers

The Internet is a collection of almost every IP-based network and almost every TCP/IP host computer in the world. The original design of the Internet required several cooperating features that made it technically possible as well as administratively manageable:

■   Each computer connected to the Internet needs a unique, nonduplicated IP address.

■   Administratively, a central authority assigned Class A, B, or C networks to companies, governments, school systems, and ISPs based on the size of their IP network (Class A for large networks, Class B for medium networks, and Class C for small networks).

■   The central authority assigned each network number to only one organization, helping ensure unique address assignment worldwide.

■   Each organization with an assigned Class A, B, or C network then assigned individual IP addresses inside its own network.

By following these guidelines, as long as each organization assigns each IP address to only one computer, every computer in the Internet has a globally unique IP address.

Note: The details of address assignment have changed over time, but the general idea described here is enough detail to help you understand the concept of different Class A, B, and C networks.

The organization in charge of universal IP address assignment is the Internet Corporation for Assigned Names and Numbers (ICANN, www.icann.org). (The Internet Assigned Numbers Authority (IANA) formerly owned the IP address assignment process.) ICANN, in turn, assigns regional authority to other cooperating organizations. For example, the American Registry for Internet Numbers (ARIN, www.arin.org) owns the address assignment process for North America.

Table 5-4 summarizes the possible network numbers that ICANN and other agencies could have assigned over time. Note the total number for each network class and the number of hosts in each Class A, B, and C network.

Table 5-4 *All Possible Valid Network Numbers*

Class	First Octet Range	Valid Network Numbers*	Total Number for This Class of Network	Number of Hosts Per Network
A	1 to 126	1.0.0.0 to 126.0.0.0	$2^7 - 2$ (126)	$2^{24} - 2$ (16,777,214)
B	128 to 191	128.0.0.0 to 191.255.0.0	2^{14} (16,384)	$2^{16} - 2$ (65,534)
C	192 to 223	192.0.0.0 to 223.255.255.0	2^{21} (2,097,152)	$2^8 - 2$ (254)

* The Valid Network Numbers column shows actual network numbers. Networks 0.0.0.0 (originally defined for use as a broadcast address) and 127.0.0.0 (still available for use as the loopback address) are reserved.

Many hiring managers look for strong IP addressing skills when interviewing job candidates. To be better prepared for interviews, students should be able to categorize a network as Class A, B, or C with ease. Also, memorize the number of octets in the network part of Class A, B, and C addresses, as shown in Table 5-2.

IP Subnetting

Although the whole topic of IP subnetting can be a little scary, particularly due to the related math, subnetting concepts remain relatively simple. The IP subnetting process takes a single Class A, B, or C network and subdivides it into a number of smaller groups of IP addresses. The Class A, B, and C rules still exist, but now, a single Class A, B, or C network can be subdivided into many smaller groups. Routers and hosts treat a subdivision of a single Class A, B, or C network as if it were a network itself. In fact, the name "subnet" is just shorthand for "subdivided network."

You can easily discern the concepts behind subnetting by comparing one network topology that does not use subnetting with the same topology but with subnetting implemented. Figure 5-5 shows such a network, without subnetting.

The design in Figure 5-5 requires six groups of IP addresses, each of which is a Class B network in this example. The four LANs each use a single Class B network. In other words, each of the LANs attached to routers A, B, C, and D is in a separate IP network. Additionally, the two serial interfaces composing the point-to-point serial link between routers C and D use one IP network because these two interfaces are not separated by a router. Finally, the three router interfaces composing the Frame Relay network with routers A, B, and C are not separated by an IP router and would use a sixth IP network.

Each Class B network has $2^{16} - 2$ host addresses—far more than you will ever need for each LAN and WAN link. For example, the upper-left Ethernet should contain all addresses that begin with 150.1. Therefore, addresses that begin with 150.1 cannot be assigned anywhere else in the network, except on the upper-left Ethernet. So, if you ran out of IP addresses somewhere else, you could not use the large number of unused addresses that begin with 150.1. As a result, the addressing design shown in Figure 5-5 wastes a lot of addresses.

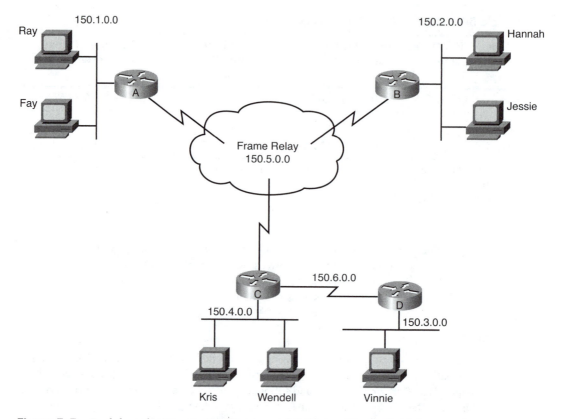

Figure 5-5   *Backdrop for Discussing Numbers of Different Networks/Subnetworks*

In fact, this design would not be allowed if it were connected to the Internet. The ICANN member organization would not assign six separate registered Class B network numbers.

In fact, you probably would not get even one Class B network, because most of the Class B addresses are already assigned. You more likely would get a couple of Class C networks with the expectation that you would use subnetting. Figure 5-6 illustrates a more realistic example that uses basic subnetting.

As in Figure 5-5, the design in Figure 5-6 requires six groups. Unlike Figure 5-5, this figure uses six subnets, each of which is a subnet of a single Class B network. This design subdivides the Class B network 150.150.0.0 into six subnets. To perform subnetting, the third octet (in this example) is used to identify unique subnets of network 150.150.0.0. Notice that each subnet number in the figure shows a different value in the third octet, representing each different subnet number. In other words, this design numbers or identifies each different subnet using the third octet.

When subnetting, a third part of an IP address appears between the network and host parts of the address—namely, the *subnet part* of the address. This field is created by "stealing" or "borrowing" bits from the host part of the address. The size of the network part of the address never shrinks. In other words, Class A, B, and C rules still apply when defining the size of the network part of an address. The host part of the address shrinks to make room for the subnet part of the address. Figure 5-7 shows the format of addresses when subnetting, representing the number of bits in each of the three parts of an IP address.

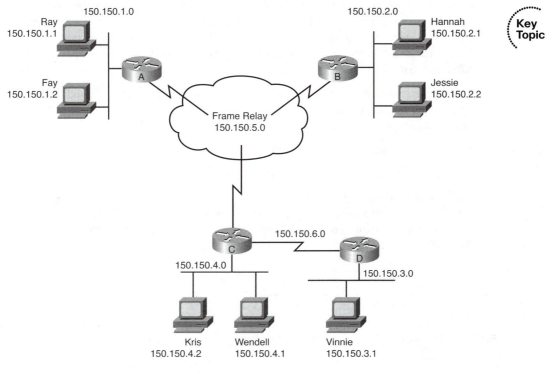

Key
Topic

Figure 5-6   *Using Subnets*

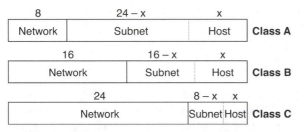

Key
Topic

Figure 5-7   *Address Formats When Subnetting Is Used (Classful)*

Now, instead of routing based on the network part of an address, routers can route based on the combined network and subnet parts. For example, when Kris (150.150.4.2) sends a packet to Hannah (150.150.2.1), router C has an IP route that lists information that means "all addresses that begin with 150.150.2." That same route tells router C to forward the packet to router B next. Note that the information in the routing table includes both the network and subnet part of the address, because both parts together identify the group.

Note that the concepts shown in Figure 5-7, with three parts of an IP address (network, subnet, and host), are called *classful addressing*. The term *classful addressing* refers to how you can think about IP addresses—specifically, that they have three parts. In particular, classful addressing means that you view the address as having a network part that is determined based on the rules about Class A, B, and C addressing—hence the word "classful" in the term.

Because the routing process considers the network and subnet parts of the address together, you can take an alternative view of IP addresses called *classless addressing*. Instead of three parts, each address has two parts:

■   The part on which routing is based

■   The host part

This first part—the part on which routing is based—is the combination of the network and subnet parts from the classful addressing view. This first part is often simply called the subnet part, or sometimes the *prefix*. Figure 5-8 shows the concepts and terms behind classless IP addressing.

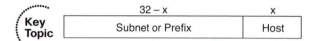

Figure 5-8 *Address Formats When Subnetting Is Used (Classless)*

Finally, IP addressing with subnetting uses a concept called a *subnet mask*. A subnet mask helps define the structure of an IP address, as shown in Figures 5-7 and 5-8. Chapter 8, "IP Subnetting," Chapter 9, "Subnet Mask Conversion," and Chapter 10, "Analyzing Existing Subnet Masks," explain the details of subnet masks.

IP Routing

In the first section of this chapter, you read about the basics of routing using a network with three routers and two PCs. Armed with more knowledge of IP addressing, you now can take a closer look at the process of routing IP. This section focuses on how the originating host chooses where to send the packet, as well as how routers choose where to route or forward packets to the final destination.

Host Routing

Hosts actually use some simple routing logic when choosing where to send a packet. This two-step logic is as follows:

Step 1.   If the destination IP address is in the same subnet as I am, send the packet directly to that destination host.

Step 2.   If the destination IP address is not in the same subnet as I am, send the packet to my *default gateway* (a router's Ethernet interface on the subnet).

For example, consider Figure 5-9, and focus on the Ethernet LAN at the top of the figure. The top Ethernet has two PCs, labeled PC1 and PC11, plus router R1. When PC1 sends a packet to 150.150.1.11 (PC11's IP address), PC1 sends the packet over the Ethernet to PC11—there's no need to bother the router.

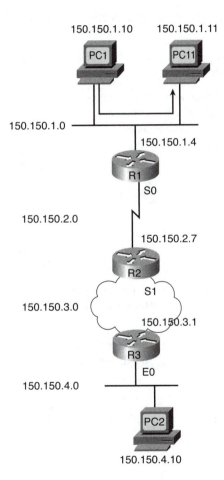

Figure 5-9   *Host Routing Alternatives*

Alternatively, when PC1 sends a packet to PC2 (150.150.4.10), PC1 forwards the packet to its default gateway of 150.150.1.4, which is R1's Ethernet interface IP address according to Step 2 in the host routing logic. The next section describes an example in which PC1 uses its default gateway.

Router Forwarding Decisions and the IP Routing Table

Earlier in this chapter, Figures 5-1 and 5-2 (and the associated text) described generally how routers forward packets, making use of each successive physical network to forward packets to the next device. To better appreciate a router's forwarding decision, this section uses an example that includes three different routers forwarding a packet.

Key Topic

A router uses the following logic when receiving a data-link frame—a frame that has an IP packet encapsulated in it:

Step 1.   Use the data-link FCS field to ensure that the frame had no errors; if errors occurred, discard the frame.

Step 2.   Assuming the frame was not discarded at step 1, discard the old data-link header and trailer, leaving the IP packet.

Step 3.   Compare the IP packet's destination IP address to the routing table, and find the route that matches the destination address. This route identifies the outgoing interface of the router, and possibly the next-hop router.

Step 4.   Encapsulate the IP packet inside a new data-link header and trailer, appropriate for the outgoing interface, and forward the frame.

With these steps, each router sends the packet to the next location until the packet reaches its final destination.

Next, focus on the routing table and the matching process that occurs at Step 3. The packet has a destination IP address in the header, whereas the routing table typically has a list of networks and subnets. To match a routing table entry, the router thinks like this:

> Network numbers and subnet numbers represent a group of addresses that begin with the same prefix. In which of the groups in my routing table does this packet's destination address reside?

As you might guess, routers actually turn that logic into a math problem, but the text indeed shows what occurs. For example, Figure 5-10 shows the same network topology as Figure 5-9, but now with PC1 sending a packet to PC2.

Note: Note that the routers all know in this case that "subnet 150.150.4.0" means "all addresses that begin with 150.150.4."

The following list explains the forwarding logic at each step in the figure. (Note that all references to Steps 1, 2, 3, and 4 refer to the previous list of routing logic.)

Step A.   **PC1 sends the packet to its default gateway.** PC1 first builds the IP packet, with a destination address of PC2's IP address (150.150.4.10). PC1 needs to send the packet to R1 (PC1's default gateway) because the destination address is on a different subnet. PC1 places the IP packet into an Ethernet frame, with a destination Ethernet address of R1's Ethernet address. PC1 sends the frame onto the Ethernet.

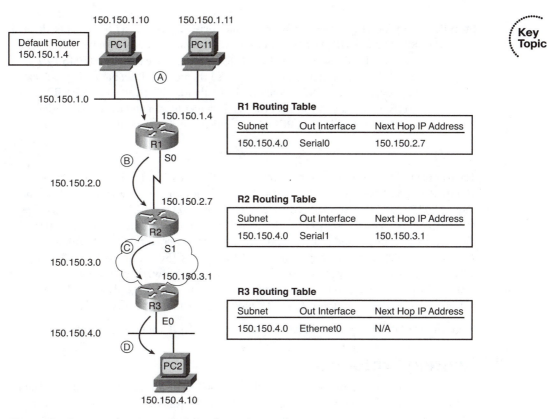

Figure 5-10   *Simple Routing Example, with IP Subnets*

Step B.   **R1 processes the incoming frame and forwards the packet to R2.** Because the incoming Ethernet frame has a destination MAC of R1's Ethernet MAC, R1 copies the frame off the Ethernet for processing. R1 checks the frame's FCS, and no errors have occurred (Step 1). R1 then discards the Ethernet header and trailer (Step 2). Next, R1 compares the packet's destination address (150.150.4.10) to the routing table and finds the entry for subnet 150.150.4.0—which includes addresses 150.150.4.0 through 150.150.4.255 (Step 3). Because the destination address is in this group, R1 forwards the packet out interface Serial0 to next-hop router R2 (150.150.2.7) after encapsulating the packet in an HDLC frame (step 4).

Step C.   **R2 processes the incoming frame and forwards the packet to R3.** R2 repeats the same general process as R1 when R2 receives the HDLC frame. R2 checks the FCS field and finds that no errors occurred (Step 1). R2 then discards the HDLC header and trailer (Step 2). Next, R2 finds its route for subnet 150.150.4.0—which includes the address range 150.150.4.0–150.150.4.255—and realizes that the packet's destination address 150.150.4.10 matches that route (Step 3). Finally, R2 sends the packet out interface serial1 to next-hop router 150.150.3.1 (R3) after encapsulating the packet in a Frame Relay header (Step 4).

Step D.   **R3 processes the incoming frame and forwards the packet to PC2.** Like R1 and R2, R3 checks the FCS, discards the old data-link header and trailer, and matches its own route for subnet 150.150.4.0. R3's routing table entry for 150.150.4.0 shows that the outgoing interface is R3's Ethernet interface, but there is no next-hop router, because R3 is connected directly to subnet 150.150.4.0. All R3 has to do is encapsulate the packet inside an Ethernet header and trailer, with a destination Ethernet address of PC2's MAC address, and forward the frame.

The routing process relies on the rules relating to IP addressing. For instance, why does 150.150.1.10 (PC1) assume that 150.150.4.10 (PC2) is not on the same Ethernet? Well, because 150.150.4.0, PC2's subnet, is different from 150.150.1.0, which is PC1's subnet. Because IP addresses in different subnets must be separated by a router, PC1 needs to send the packet to a router—and it does. Similarly, all three routers list a route to subnet 150.150.4.0, which, in this example, includes IP addresses 150.150.4.1 to 150.150.4.254. What if someone tried to put PC2 somewhere else in the network, still using 150.150.4.10? The routers then would forward packets to the wrong place. So, Layer 3 routing relies on the structure of Layer 3 addressing to route more efficiently.

Next, this chapter briefly introduces the concepts behind IP routing protocols.

IP Routing Protocols

The routing (forwarding) process depends heavily on having an accurate and up-to-date IP routing table on each router. IP routing protocols fill the routers' IP routing tables with valid, loop-free routes. Each route includes a subnet number, the interface out which to forward packets so that they are delivered to that subnet, and the IP address of the next router that should receive packets destined for that subnet (if needed) (as shown in the example surrounding Figure 5-10).

Before examining the underlying logic used by routing protocols, you need to consider the goals of a routing protocol. The goals described in the following list are common for any IP routing protocol, regardless of its underlying logic type:

- To dynamically learn and fill the routing table with a route to all subnets in the network.

- If more than one route to a subnet is available, to place the best route in the routing table.

- To notice when routes in the table are no longer valid, and to remove them from the routing table.

- If a route is removed from the routing table and another route through another neighboring router is available, to add the route to the routing table. (Many people view this goal and the preceding one as a single goal.)

■   To add new routes, or to replace lost routes, with the best currently available route as quickly as possible. The time between losing the route and finding a working replacement route is called *convergence* time.

■   To prevent routing loops.

Routing protocols can become rather complicated, but the basic logic that they use is relatively simple. Routers follow these general steps for advertising routes in a network:

Step 1.   Each router adds a route to its routing table for each subnet directly connected to the router.

Step 2.   Each router's routing protocol tells its neighbors about all the routes in its routing table, including the directly connected routes and routes learned from other routers.

Step 3.   After learning a new route from a neighbor, the router's routing protocol adds a route to its routing table, with the next-hop router typically being the neighbor from which the route was learned.

For example, Figure 5-11 shows the same sample network as in Figures 5-9 and 5-10, but now with focus on how the three routers each learned about subnet 150.150.4.0. Note that routing protocols do more work than is implied in the figure; this figure just focuses on how the routers learn about subnet 150.150.4.0.

Again, follow the items A, B, C, and D shown in the figure to see how each router learns its route to 150.150.4.0. All references to Steps 1, 2, and 3 refer to the list just before Figure 5-11.

Step A.   R3 learns a route that refers to its own E0 interface because subnet 150.150.4.0 is directly connected (Step 1).

Step B.   R3 sends a routing protocol message, called a *routing update*, to R2, causing R2 to learn about subnet 150.150.4.0 (Step 2).

Step C.   R2 sends a similar routing update to R1, causing R1 to learn about subnet 150.150.4.0 (Step 2).

Step D.   R1's route to 150.150.4.0 lists 150.150.2.7 (R2's IP address) as the next-hop address because R1 learned about the route from R2. The route also lists R1's outgoing interface as Serial0, because R1 learned about the route from the update that came in serial0 (at Step C in the figure).

Note: Routes do not always refer to the neighboring router's IP address as the next-hop IP address, but for protocols and processes covered in this book, the routes typically refer to a neighboring router as the next hop.

Chapter 14, "Routing Protocol Concepts and RIP-2 Configuration," covers routing protocols in more detail. Next, the final major section of this chapter introduces several additional functions related to how the network layer forwards packets from source to destination through an internetwork.

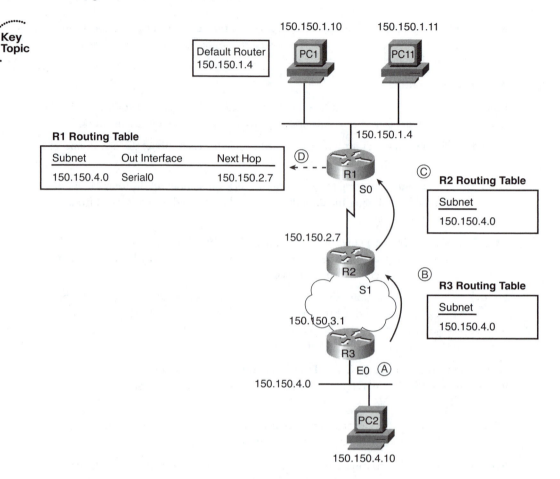

Figure 5-11   *Router R1 Learning About Subnet 150.150.4.0*

Network Layer Utilities

So far, this chapter has described the main features of the OSI network layer—in particular, the TCP/IP internetwork layer, which defines the same general features as OSI Layer 3. To close the chapter, this section covers four tools used almost every day in almost every TCP/IP network in the world to help the network layer with its task of routing packets from end to end through an internetwork:

- Address Resolution Protocol (ARP)

- Domain Name System (DNS)

- Dynamic Host Configuration Protocol (DHCP)

- Ping

Address Resolution Protocol and the Domain Name System

Network designers should try to make using the network as simple as possible. At most, users might want to remember the name of another computer with which they want to communicate, such as remembering the name of a website. They certainly do not want to remember the IP address, nor do they want to try to remember any MAC addresses! So, TCP/IP needs protocols that dynamically discover all the necessary information to allow communications, without the user knowing more than a name.

You might not even think that you need to know the name of another computer. For instance, when you open your browser, you probably have a default home page configured that the browser immediately downloads. You might not think of that universal resource locator (URL) string as a name, but the URL for the home page has a name embedded in it. For example, in a URL such as http://www.certskills.com/blog, the www.certskills.com part is the name of the textbook author's web server. So, whether you enter the name of another networked computer or it is implied by what you see on the screen, the user typically identifies a remote computer by using a name.

So, TCP/IP needs a way to let a computer find the IP address of another computer based on its name. TCP/IP also needs a way to find MAC addresses associated with other computers on the same LAN subnet. Figure 5-12 outlines the problem.

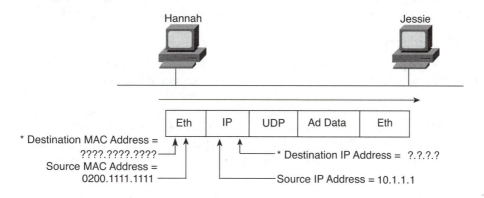

Figure 5-12   *Hannah Knows Jessie's Name, Needs IP Address and MAC Address*

In this example, Hannah needs to communicate with a server on PC Jessie. Hannah knows her own name, IP address, and MAC address. *What Hannah does not know are Jessie's IP and MAC addresses.* To find the two missing facts, Hannah uses DNS to find Jessie's IP address and ARP to find Jessie's MAC address.

DNS Name Resolution

Hannah knows the IP address of a DNS server because the address was either preconfigured on Hannah's machine or was learned with DHCP, as covered later in this chapter. As soon as Hannah somehow identifies the name of the other computer (for example, jessie.example.com), she sends a *DNS request* to the DNS, asking for Jessie's IP address. The DNS replies with the address, 10.1.1.2. Figure 5-13 shows the simple process.

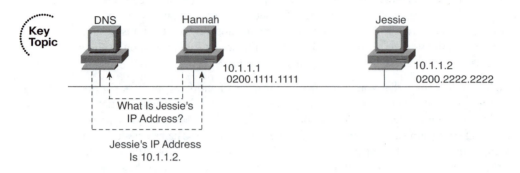

Figure 5-13   *DNS Request and Reply*

Hannah simply sends a DNS request to the server, supplying the name jessie, or jessie.example.com, and the DNS replies with the IP address (10.1.1.2 in this case). Effectively, the same thing happens when you surf the Internet and connect to any website. Your PC sends a request, just like Hannah's request for Jessie, asking the DNS to resolve the name into an IP address. After that happens, your PC can start requesting that the web page be sent.

The ARP Process

As soon as a host knows the IP address of the other host, the sending host might need to know the MAC address used by the other computer. For example, Hannah still needs to know the Ethernet MAC address used by 10.1.1.2, so Hannah issues something called an *ARP broadcast*. An ARP broadcast is sent to a broadcast Ethernet address, so everyone on the LAN receives it. Because Jessie is on the same LAN, she receives the ARP broadcast. Because Jessie's IP address is 10.1.1.2 and the ARP broadcast is looking for the MAC address associated with 10.1.1.2, Jessie replies with her own MAC address. Figure 5-14 outlines the process.

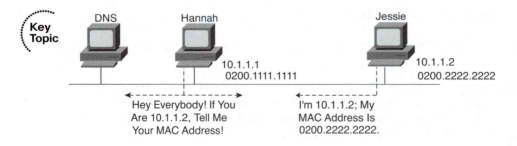

Figure 5-14   *Sample ARP Process*

Now Hannah knows the destination IP and Ethernet addresses that she should use when sending frames to Jessie, and the packet shown in Figure 5-12 can be sent successfully.

Hosts might or might not need to ARP to find the destination host's MAC address based on the two-step routing logic used by a host. If the destination host is on the same subnet, the sending host sends an ARP looking for the destination host's MAC address, as shown in Figure 5-14. However, if the sending host is on a different subnet than the destination host, the sending host's routing logic results in the sending host needing to forward the packet to its default gateway. For example, if Hannah and Jessie had been in different subnets in Figures 5-12 through 5-14, Hannah's routing logic would have caused Hannah to want to send the packet to Hannah's default gateway (router). In that case, Hannah would have used ARP to find the router's MAC address instead of Jessie's MAC address.

Additionally, hosts need to use ARP to find MAC addresses only once in a while. Any device that uses IP should retain, or cache, the information learned with ARP, placing the information in its *ARP cache*. Each time a host needs to send a packet encapsulated in an Ethernet frame, it first checks its ARP cache and uses the MAC address found there. If the correct information is not listed in the ARP cache, the host then can use ARP to discover the MAC address used by a particular IP address. Also, a host learns ARP information when receiving an ARP as well. For example, the ARP process shown in Figure 5-14 results in both Hannah and Jessie learning the other host's MAC address.

Note: You can see the contents of the ARP cache on most PC operating systems by using the **arp -a** command from a command prompt.

Address Assignment and DHCP

Every device that uses TCP/IP—in fact, every interface on every device that uses TCP/IP—needs a valid IP address. For some devices, the address can and should be statically assigned by configuring the device. For example, all commonly used computer operating systems that support TCP/IP allow the user to statically configure the IP address on each interface. Routers and switches typically use statically configured IP addresses as well.

Servers also typically use statically configured IP addresses. Using a statically configured and seldom-changed IP address helps because all references to that server can stay the same over time. This is the same concept that it's good that the location of your favorite grocery store never changes. You know where to go to buy food, and you can get there from home, on the way home from work, or from somewhere else. Likewise, if servers have a static, unchanging IP address, the users of that server know how to reach the server, from anywhere, consistently.

However, the average end-user host computer does not need to use the same IP address every day. Again thinking about your favorite grocery store, you could move to a new apartment every week, but you'd still know where the grocery store is. The workers at the grocery store don't need to know where you live. Likewise, servers typically don't care that your PC has a different IP address today as compared to yesterday. End-user hosts can have their IP addresses dynamically assigned, and even change their IP addresses over time, because it does not matter if the IP address changes.

DHCP defines the protocols used to allow computers to request a lease of an IP address. DHCP uses a server, with the server keeping a list of pools of IP addresses available in each subnet. DHCP clients can send the DHCP server a message, asking to borrow or lease an IP address. The server then suggests an IP address. If accepted, the server notes that the address is no longer available for assignment to any other hosts, and the client has an IP address to use.

DHCP supplies IP addresses to clients, and it also supplies other information. For example, hosts need to know their IP address, plus the subnet mask to use, plus what default gateway to use, as well as the IP address(es) of any DNS servers. In most networks today, DHCP supplies all these facts to a typical end-user host.

Figure 5-15 shows a typical set of four messages used between a DHCP server to assign an IP address, as well as other information. Note that the first two messages are both IP broadcast messages in this particular topology.

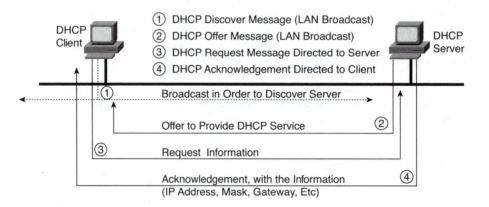

Figure 5-15   *DHCP Messages to Acquire an IP Address*

Figure 5-15 shows the DHCP server as a PC, which is typical in an Enterprise network. Routers can and do provide DHCP services as well. In fact, most home-based routers provide a DHCP server function, dynamically assigning IP addresses to the computers in a small or home office, using DHCP client functions to dynamically lease IP addresses from an Internet service provider (ISP).

DHCP has become a prolific protocol. Most end-user hosts on LANs in corporate networks get their IP addresses and other basic configuration via DHCP.

ICMP Echo and the ping Command

After you have implemented a network, you need a way to test basic IP connectivity with-out relying on any applications to be working. The primary tool for testing basic network connectivity is the **ping** command. **ping** (Packet Internet Groper) uses the *Internet Control Message Protocol (ICMP)*, sending a message called an *ICMP echo request* to an-other IP address. The computer with that IP address should reply with an *ICMP echo reply*. If that works, you successfully have tested the IP network. In other words, you know that the network can deliver a packet from one host to the other, and back. ICMP does not rely on any application, so it really just tests basic IP connectivity—Layers 1, 2, and 3 of the OSI model. Figure 5-16 outlines the basic process.

Chapter 15, "Troubleshooting IP Routing," gives you more information about and exam-ples of ping and ICMP.

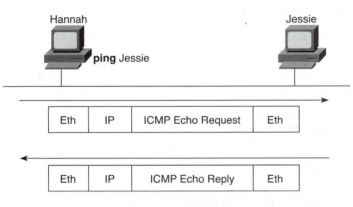

Figure 5-16 *Sample Network,* ping *Command*

Chapter Review

Review Key Topics

Review the most important topics from this chapter, noted with the key topics icon. Table 5-5 lists these key topics and where each is discussed.

Table 5-5   *Key Topics for Chapter 5*

Key Topic Element	Description	Page Number
List	Two statements about how IP expects IP addresses to be grouped into networks or subnets	101
Table 5-2	List of the three types of unicast IP networks and the size of the network and host parts of each type of network	103
Paragraph	Explanation of the concept of a network broadcast or directed broadcast address	104
Table 5-4	Details about the actual Class A, B, and C networks	105
Figure 5-6	Conceptual view of how subnetting works	107
Figure 5-7	Structure of subnetted Class A, B, and C IP addresses, classful view	107
Figure 5-8	Structure of a subnetted unicast IP address, classless view	108
List	Two-step process of how hosts route (forward) packets	108
List	Four-step process of how routers route (forward) packets	110
Figure 5-10	Example of the IP routing process	111
Figure 5-11	Example that shows generally how a routing protocol can cause routers to learn new routes	114
Figure 5-13	Example that shows the purpose and process of DNS name resolution	116
Figure 5-14	Example of the purpose and process of ARP	116
Paragraph	The most important information learned by a host acting as a DHCP client	118

Define Key Terms

Define the following key terms from this chapter, and check your answers in the glossary:

ARP, default gateway/default router, DHCP, DNS, host part, IP address, logical address, network broadcast address, network number/network address, network part, routing table, subnet broadcast address, subnet number/subnet address, subnet part

Answer Review Questions

Answer the following review questions:

1. Which of the following are functions of OSI Layer 3 protocols?

   a. Logical addressing

   b. Physical addressing

   c. Path selection

   d. Arbitration

   e. Error recovery

2. Imagine that PC1 needs to send some data to PC2, and PC1 and PC2 are separated by several routers. What are the largest entities that make it from PC1 to PC2?

   a. Frame

   b. Segment

   c. Packet

   d. L5 PDU

   e. L3 PDU

   f. L1 PDU

3. Imagine a network with two routers that are connected with a point-to-point HDLC serial link. Each router has an Ethernet, with PC1 sharing the Ethernet with Router1, and PC2 sharing the Ethernet with Router2. When PC1 sends data to PC2, which of the following is true?

   a. Router1 strips the Ethernet header and trailer off the frame received from PC1, never to be used again.

   b. Router1 encapsulates the Ethernet frame inside an HDLC header and sends the frame to Router2, which extracts the Ethernet frame for forwarding to PC2.

   c. Router1 strips the Ethernet header and trailer off the frame received from PC1, which is exactly re-created by R2 before forwarding data to PC2.

   d. Router1 removes the Ethernet, IP, and TCP headers and rebuilds the appropriate headers before forwarding the packet to Router2.

4. Which of the following are valid Class C IP addresses that can be assigned to hosts?

   a.   1.1.1.1

   b.   200.1.1.1

   c.   128.128.128.128

   d.   224.1.1.1

   e.   223.223.223.255

5. What is the range of values for the first octet for Class A IP networks?

   a.   0 to 127

   b.   0 to 126

   c.   1 to 127

   d.   1 to 126

   e.   128 to 191

   f.   128 to 192

6. PC1 and PC2 are on two different Ethernets that are separated by an IP router. PC1's IP address is 10.1.1.1, and no subnetting is used. Which of the following addresses could be used for PC2?

   a.   10.1.1.2

   b.   10.2.2.2

   c.   10.200.200.1

   d.   9.1.1.1

   e.   225.1.1.1

   f.   1.1.1.1

7. Each Class B network contains how many IP addresses that can be assigned to hosts?

   a.   16,777,214

   b.   16,777,216

   c.   65,536

   d.   65,534

   e.   65,532

   f.   32,768

   g.   32,766

8. Each Class C network contains how many IP addresses that can be assigned to hosts?

    a.   65,534

    b.   65,532

    c.   32,768

    d.   32,766

    e.   256

    f.   254

9. Which of the following does a router normally use when making a decision about routing TCP/IP packets?

    a.   Destination MAC address

    b.   Source MAC address

    c.   Destination IP address

    d.   Source IP address

    e.   Destination MAC and IP address

10. Which of the following are true about a LAN-connected TCP/IP host and its IP routing (forwarding) choices?

    a.   The host always sends packets to its default gateway.

    b.   The host sends packets to its default gateway if the destination IP address is in a different class of IP network than the host.

    c.   The host sends packets to its default gateway if the destination IP address is in a different subnet than the host.

    d.   The host sends packets to its default gateway if the destination IP address is in the same subnet as the host.

11. Which of the following are functions of a routing protocol?

    a.   Advertising known routes to neighboring routers.

    b.   Learning routes for subnets directly connected to the router.

    c.   Learning routes, and putting those routes into the routing table, for routes advertised to the router by its neighboring routers.

    d.   To forward IP packets based on a packet's destination IP address.

12. Which of the following protocols allows a client PC to discover the IP address of another computer based on that other computer's name?

    a. ARP

    b. RARP

    c. DNS

    d. DHCP

13. Which of the following protocols allows a client PC to request assignment of an IP address as well as learn its default gateway?

    a. ARP

    b. RARP

    c. DNS

    d. DHCP

This chapter covers the following subjects:

- **TCP/IP Layer 4 Protocols: TCP and UDP:** This section explains the functions and mechanisms used by TCP and UDP, including error recovery and port numbers.

- **TCP/IP Applications:** This section explains the purpose of TCP/IP application layer protocols, focusing on HTTP as an example.

- **Network Security:** This section provides some perspectives on the security threats faced by networks today, introducing some of the key tools used to help prevent and reduce the impact of those threats.

CHAPTER 6

Fundamentals of TCP/IP Transport, Applications, and Security

This chapter examines several topics that receive little focus in this text. The first section examines the two most commonly-used TCP/IP transport layer protocols, Transmission Control Protocol (TCP) and User Datagram Protocol (UDP). The second major section of the chapter examines the TCP/IP application layer, including some discussion of how DNS name resolution works. Finally, the third major section examines the importance and concepts of network security, introducing some of the core concepts, terminology, and functions important for security today.

Note that although this book does not examine the topics in this chapter later in this book, the topics still play an important role in modern networks, particularly with network security. However, this text focuses on IP routing, and therefore focuses on functions that match the lower three OSI layers.

TCP/IP Layer 4 Protocols: TCP and UDP

The OSI transport layer (Layer 4) defines several functions, the most important of which are error recovery and flow control. Likewise, the TCP/IP transport layer protocols also implement these same types of features. Note that both the OSI model and TCP/IP model call this layer the transport layer. But as usual, when referring to the TCP/IP model, the layer name and number are based on OSI, so any TCP/IP transport layer protocols are considered Layer 4 protocols.

The key difference between TCP and UDP is that TCP provides a wide variety of services to applications, whereas UDP does not. For example, routers discard packets for many reasons, including bit errors, congestion, and instances in which no correct routes are known. As you have read already, most data-link protocols notice errors (a process called *error detection*) but then discard frames that have errors. TCP provides for retransmission (error recovery) and help to avoid congestion (flow control), whereas UDP does not. As a result, many application protocols choose to use TCP.

However, do not let UDP's lack of services make you think that UDP is worse than TCP. By providing few services, UDP needs fewer bytes in its header compared to TCP, resulting in fewer bytes of overhead in the network. UDP software does not slow down data transfer in cases where TCP might purposefully slow down. Also, some applications, notably today voice over IP (VoIP) and video over IP, do not need error recovery, so they use UDP. So, UDP also has an important place in TCP/IP networks today.

Table 6-1 lists the main features supported by TCP and/or UDP. Note that only the first item listed in the table is supported by UDP, whereas all items in the table are supported by TCP.

Table 6-1   *TCP/IP Transport Layer Features*

Function	Description
Multiplexing using ports	Function that allows receiving hosts to choose the correct application for which the data is destined, based on the port number.
Error recovery (reliability)	Process of numbering and acknowledging data with Sequence and Acknowledgment header fields.
Flow control using windowing	Process that uses window sizes to protect buffer space and routing devices.
Connection establishment and termination	Process used to initialize port numbers and Sequence and Acknowledgment fields.
Ordered data transfer and data segmentation	Continuous stream of bytes from an upper-layer process that is "segmented" for transmission and delivered to upper-layer processes at the receiving device, with the bytes in the same order.

Next, this section describes the features of TCP, followed by a brief comparison to UDP.

Transmission Control Protocol

Each TCP/IP application typically chooses to use either TCP or UDP based on the application's requirements. For instance, TCP provides error recovery, but to do so, it consumes more bandwidth and uses more processing cycles. UDP does not perform error recovery, but it takes less bandwidth and uses fewer processing cycles. Regardless of which of the two TCP/IP transport layer protocols the application chooses to use, you should understand the basics of how each of these transport layer protocols works.

TCP, as defined in RFC 793, accomplishes the functions listed in Table 6-1 through mechanisms at the endpoint computers. TCP relies on IP for end-to-end delivery of the data, including routing issues. In other words, TCP performs only part of the functions necessary to deliver the data between applications. Also, the role that it plays is directed toward providing services for the applications that sit at the endpoint computers. Regardless of whether two computers are on the same Ethernet or are separated by the entire Internet, TCP performs its functions the same way.

Figure 6-1 shows the fields in the TCP header. Although you don't need to memorize the names of the fields or their locations, the rest of this section refers to several of the fields, so the entire header is included here for reference.

Multiplexing Using TCP Port Numbers

TCP provides a lot of features to applications, at the expense of requiring slightly more processing and overhead, as compared to UDP. However, TCP and UDP both use a concept called *multiplexing*. Therefore, this section begins with an explanation of multiplexing with TCP and UDP. Afterward, the unique features of TCP are explored.

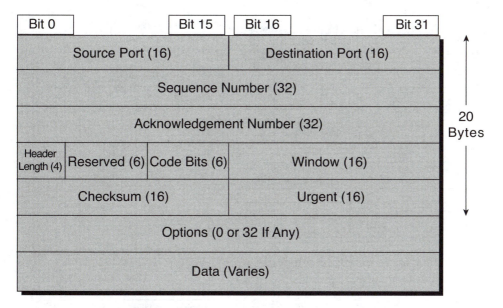

Figure 6-1   *TCP Header Fields*

Multiplexing by TCP and UDP involves the process of how a computer thinks when receiving data. The computer might be running many applications, such as a web browser, an e-mail package, or an Internet VoIP application (for example, Skype). TCP and UDP multiplexing enables the receiving computer to know which application to give the data to.

Some examples will help make the need for multiplexing obvious. The sample network consists of two PCs, labeled Hannah and Jessie. Hannah uses an application that she wrote to send advertisements that appear on Jessie's screen. The application sends a new ad to Jessie every 10 seconds. Hannah uses a second application, a wire-transfer application, to send Jessie some money. Finally, Hannah uses a web browser to access the web server that runs on Jessie's PC. The ad application and wire-transfer application are imaginary, just for this example. The web application works just like it would in real life.

Figure 6-2 shows the sample network, with Jessie running three applications:

■   A UDP-based ad application

■   A TCP-based wire-transfer application

■   A TCP web server application

Jessie needs to know which application to give the data to, but *all three packets are from the same Ethernet and IP address*. You might think that Jessie could look at whether the packet contains a UDP or TCP header, but, as you see in the figure, two applications (wire transfer and web) are using TCP.

TCP and UDP solve this problem by using a port number field in the TCP or UDP header, respectively. Each of Hannah's TCP and UDP segments uses a different *destination port number* so that Jessie knows which application to give the data to. Figure 6-3 shows an example.

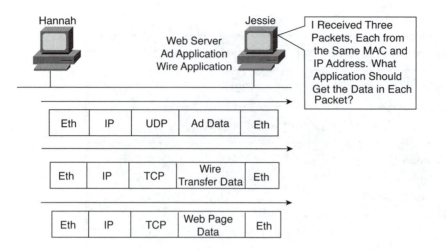

Figure 6-2   *Hannah Sending Packets to Jessie, with Three Applications*

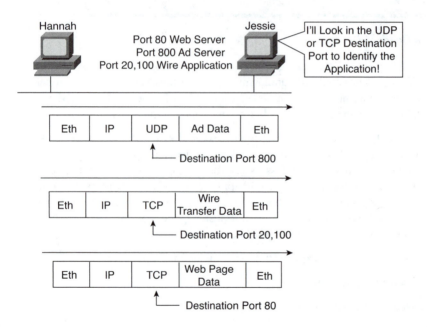

Figure 6-3   *Hannah Sending Packets to Jessie, with Three Applications Using Port Numbers to Multiplex*

Multiplexing relies on a concept called a *socket*. A socket consists of three things:

■   An IP address

■   A transport protocol

■   A port number

So, for a web server application on Jessie, the socket would be (10.1.1.2, TCP, port 80) because, by default, web servers use the well-known port 80. When Hannah's web browser connects to the web server, Hannah uses a socket as well—possibly one like this: (10.1.1.1, TCP, 1030). Why 1030? Well, Hannah just needs a port number that is unique on Hannah, so Hannah sees that port 1030 is available and uses it. In fact, hosts typically allocate *dynamic port numbers* starting at 1024 because the ports below 1024 are reserved for well-known applications, such as web services.

In Figure 6-3, Hannah and Jessie use three applications at the same time—hence, three socket connections are open. Because a socket on a single computer should be unique, a connection between two sockets should identify a unique connection between two computers. This uniqueness means that you can use multiple applications at the same time, talking to applications running on the same or different computers. Multiplexing, based on sockets, ensures that the data is delivered to the correct applications. Figure 6-4 shows the three socket connections between Hannah and Jessie.

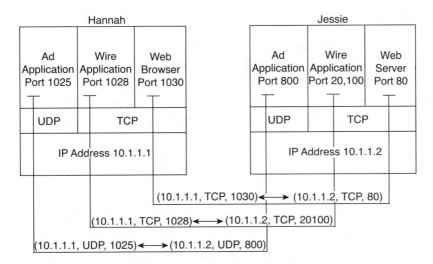

Figure 6-4 *Connections Between Sockets*

Port numbers are a vital part of the socket concept. Well-known port numbers are used by servers; other port numbers are used by clients. Applications that provide a service, such as FTP, Telnet, and web servers, open a socket using a well-known port and listen for connection requests. Because these connection requests from clients are required to include both the source and destination port numbers, the port numbers used by the servers must be well-known. Therefore, each server has a hard-coded, well-known port number. The well-known ports are listed at http://www.iana.org/assignments/port-numbers.

On client machines, where the requests originate, any unused port number can be allocated. The result is that each client on the same host uses a different port number, but a server uses the same port number for all connections. For example, 100 web browsers on the same host computer could each connect to a web server, but the web server with 100 clients connected to it would have only one socket and, therefore, only one port number (port 80 in this case). The server can tell which packets are sent from which of the 100 clients by looking at the source port of received TCP segments. The server can send data to the correct web client (browser) by sending data to that same port number listed as a destination port. The combination of source and destination sockets allows all participating hosts to distinguish between the data's source and destination. Although the example explains the concept using 100 TCP connections, the same port numbering concept applies to UDP sessions in the same way.

Note: You can find all RFCs online at http://www.isi.edu/in-notes/rfcxxxx.txt, where *xxxx* is the number of the RFC. If you do not know the number of the RFC, you can try searching by topic at http://www.rfc-editor.org/rfcsearch.html.

Popular TCP/IP Applications and Application Layer Protocols

Many people use TCP/IP applications. Most people do not care that the applications use TCP/IP. Others might know that it uses TCP/IP, or know that the traffic goes over the Internet, which is based on TCP/IP. Fewer still know that these applications use some application layer protocol to actually send and receive the data needed by the application. This section introduces a few applications and application layer protocols.

The World Wide Web (WWW) application exists through web browsers accessing the content available on web servers. Although it is often thought of as an end-user application, you can actually use WWW to manage a router or switch. You enable a web server function in the router or switch and use a browser to access the router or switch. And as mentioned back in Chapter 1, WWW uses Hyper Text Transport Protocol (HTTP) as its application layer protocol.

The Domain Name System (DNS) allows users to use names to refer to computers, with DNS being used to find the corresponding IP addresses. DNS also uses a client/server model, with DNS servers being controlled by networking personnel, and DNS client functions being part of most any device that uses TCP/IP today. The client simply asks the DNS server to supply the IP address that corresponds to a given name.

Simple Network Management Protocol (SNMP) is an application layer protocol used specifically for network device management. For instance, Cisco supplies a large variety of network management products, many of them in the CiscoWorks network management software product family. They can be used to query, compile, store, and display information about a network's operation. To query the network devices, CiscoWorks software mainly uses SNMP protocols.

Traditionally, to move files to and from a router or switch, Cisco used Trivial File Transfer Protocol (TFTP). TFTP defines a protocol for basic file transfer—hence the word "trivial." Alternatively, routers and switches can use File Transfer Protocol (FTP), which is a much more functional protocol, to transfer files. Both work well for moving files into and out of Cisco devices. FTP allows many more features, making it a good choice for the general end-user population. TFTP client and server applications are very simple, making them good tools as embedded parts of networking devices.

Some of these applications use TCP, and some use UDP. As you will read later, TCP performs error recovery, whereas UDP does not. For instance, Simple Mail Transport Protocol (SMTP) and Post Office Protocol version 3 (POP3), both used for transferring mail, require guaranteed delivery, so they use TCP. Regardless of which transport layer protocol is used, applications use a well-known port number so that clients know which port to attempt to connect to. Table 6-2 lists several popular applications and their well-known port numbers.

Table 6-2 *Popular Applications and Their Well-Known Port Numbers*

Port Number	Protocol	Application
20	TCP	FTP data
21	TCP	FTP control
22	TCP	SSH
23	TCP	Telnet
25	TCP	SMTP
53	UDP, TCP	DNS
67, 68	UDP	DHCP
69	UDP	TFTP
80	TCP	HTTP (WWW)
110	TCP	POP3
161	UDP	SNMP
443	TCP	SSL
16, 384–32, 767	UDP	RTP-based Voice (VoIP) and Video

Key Topic

Error Recovery (Reliability)

TCP provides for reliable data transfer, which is also called *reliability* or *error recovery*, depending on what document you read. To accomplish reliability, TCP numbers data bytes using the Sequence and Acknowledgment fields in the TCP header. TCP achieves reliability in both directions, using the Sequence Number field of one direction combined with the Acknowledgment field in the opposite direction. Figure 6-5 shows the basic operation.

In Figure 6-5, the Acknowledgment field in the TCP header sent by the web client (4000) implies the next byte to be received; this is called *forward acknowledgment*. The sequence number reflects the number of the first byte in the segment. In this case, each TCP segment is 1000 bytes long; the Sequence and Acknowledgment fields count the number of bytes.

Figure 6-6 depicts the same scenario, but the second TCP segment was lost or is in error. The web client's reply has an ACK field equal to 2000, implying that the web client is expecting byte number 2000 next. The TCP function at the web server then could recover lost data by resending the second TCP segment. The TCP protocol allows for resending just that segment and then waiting, hoping that the web client will reply with an acknowledgment that equals 4000.

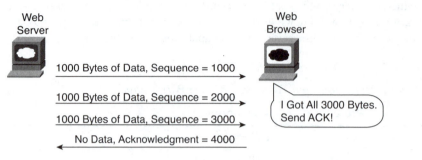

Figure 6-5   *TCP Acknowledgment Without Errors*

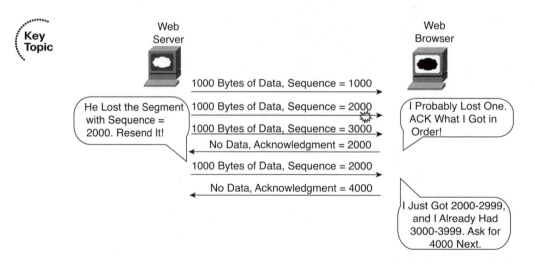

Figure 6-6   *TCP Acknowledgment with Errors*

Although not shown, the sender also sets a retransmission timer per segment, awaiting acknowledgment, just in case the acknowledgment is lost or all transmitted segments are lost. If that timer expires, the TCP sender sends the segment again.

Flow Control Using Windowing

TCP implements flow control by taking advantage of the Sequence and Acknowledgment fields in the TCP header, along with another field called the Window field. This Window field implies the maximum number of unacknowledged bytes that are allowed to be outstanding at any instant in time. The window starts small and then grows until errors occur. The size of the window changes over time, so it is sometimes called a *dynamic window*. Additionally, because the actual sequence and acknowledgment numbers grow over time, the window is sometimes called a *sliding window*, with the numbers sliding (moving) upward. When the window is full, the sender does not send, which controls the flow of data. Figure 6-7 shows windowing with a current window size of 3000. Each TCP segment has 1000 bytes of data.

Key
Topic

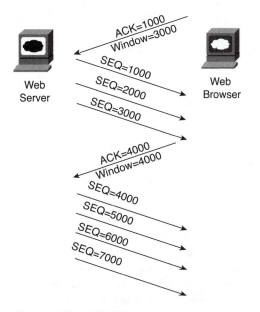

Figure 6-7 *TCP Windowing*

Notice that the web server must wait after sending the third segment because the window is exhausted. When the acknowledgment has been received, another window can be sent. Because no errors have occurred, the web client grants a larger window to the server, so now 4000 bytes can be sent before the server receives an acknowledgment. In other words, the receiver uses the Window field to tell the sender how much data it can send before it must stop and wait for the next acknowledgment. As with other TCP features, windowing is symmetrical. Both sides send and receive, and, in each case, the receiver grants a window to the sender using the Window field.

Windowing does not require that the sender stop sending in all cases. If an acknowledgment is received before the window is exhausted, a new window begins, and the sender continues sending data until the current window is exhausted. (The term *Positive Acknowledgment and Retransmission [PAR]* is sometimes used to describe the error recovery and windowing processes that TCP uses.)

Connection Establishment and Termination

TCP connection establishment occurs before any of the other TCP features can begin their work. Connection establishment refers to the process of initializing sequence and acknowledgment fields and agreeing on the port numbers used. Figure 6-8 shows an example of connection establishment flow.

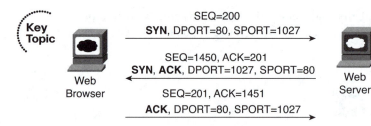

Figure 6-8 *TCP Connection Establishment*

This three-way connection establishment flow must end before data transfer can begin. The connection exists between the two sockets, although the TCP header has no single socket field. Of the three parts of a socket, the IP addresses are implied based on the source and destination IP addresses in the IP header. TCP is implied because a TCP header is in use, as specified by the protocol field value in the IP header. Therefore, the only parts of the socket that need to be encoded in the TCP header are the port numbers.

TCP signals connection establishment using 2 bits inside the flag fields of the TCP header. Called the SYN and ACK flags, these bits have a particularly interesting meaning. SYN means "Synchronize the sequence numbers," which is one necessary component in initialization for TCP. The ACK field means "The Acknowledgment field is valid in this header." Until the sequence numbers are initialized, the Acknowledgment field cannot be very useful. Also notice that in the initial TCP segment in Figure 6-8, no acknowledgment number is shown; this is because that number is not valid yet. Because the ACK field must be present in all the ensuing segments, the ACK bit continues to be set until the connection is terminated.

TCP initializes the Sequence Number and Acknowledgment Number fields to any number that fits into the 4-byte fields; the actual values shown in Figure 6-8 are simply sample values. The initialization flows are each considered to have a single byte of data, as reflected in the Acknowledgment Number fields in the example.

Figure 6-9 shows TCP connection termination. This four-way termination sequence is straightforward and uses an additional flag, called the *FIN bit*. (FIN is short for "finished," as you might guess.) One interesting note: Before the device on the right sends the third TCP segment in the sequence, it notifies the application that the connection is coming down. It then waits on an acknowledgment from the application before sending the third segment in the figure. Just in case the application takes some time to reply, the PC on the right sends the second flow in the figure, acknowledging that the other PC wants to take down the connection. Otherwise, the PC on the left might resend the first segment repeatedly.

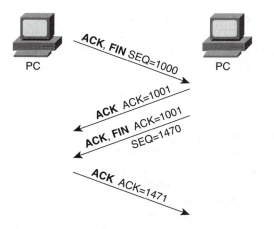

Figure 6-9 *TCP Connection Termination*

TCP establishes and terminates connections between the endpoints, whereas UDP does not. Many protocols operate under these same concepts, so the terms *connection-oriented* and *connectionless* are used to refer to the general idea of each. More formally, these terms can be defined as follows:

■ **Connection-oriented protocol:** A protocol that requires an exchange of messages before data transfer begins or that has a required preestablished correlation between two endpoints.

■ **Connectionless protocol:** A protocol that does not require an exchange of messages and that does not require a preestablished correlation between two endpoints.

Data Segmentation and Ordered Data Transfer

Applications need to send data. Sometimes the data is small—in some cases, a single byte. In other cases, such as with a file transfer, the data might be millions of bytes.

Each different type of data-link protocol typically has a limit on the *maximum transmission unit (MTU)* that can be sent inside a data link layer frame. In other words, the MTU is the size of the largest Layer 3 packet that can sit inside a frame's data field. For many data-link protocols, Ethernet included, the MTU is 1500 bytes.

TCP handles the fact that an application might give it millions of bytes to send by *segmenting* the data into smaller pieces, called *segments*. Because an IP packet can often be no more than 1500 bytes because of the MTU restrictions, and because IP and TCP headers are 20 bytes each, TCP typically segments large data into 1460-byte chunks.

The TCP receiver performs reassembly when it receives the segments. To reassemble the data, TCP must recover lost segments, as discussed previously. However, the TCP receiver must also reorder segments that arrive out of sequence. Because IP routing can choose to balance traffic across multiple links, the actual segments can be delivered out of order. So, the TCP receiver also must perform *ordered data transfer* by reassembling the data into the original order. The process is not hard to imagine: If segments arrive with the sequence numbers 1000, 3000, and 2000, each with 1000 bytes of data, the receiver can reorder them, and no retransmissions are required.

You should also be aware of some terminology related to TCP segmentation. The TCP header and the data field together are called a *TCP segment*. This term is similar to a data-link frame and an IP packet in that the terms refer to the headers and trailers for the respective layers, plus the encapsulated data. The term *L4PDU* also can be used instead of the term *TCP segment* because TCP is a Layer 4 protocol.

User Datagram Protocol

UDP provides a service for applications to exchange messages. Unlike TCP, UDP is connectionless and provides no reliability, no windowing, no reordering of the received data, and no segmentation of large chunks of data into the right size for transmission. However, UDP provides some functions of TCP, such as data transfer and multiplexing using port numbers, and it does so with fewer bytes of overhead and less processing required than TCP.

UDP data transfer differs from TCP data transfer in that no reordering or recovery is accomplished. Applications that use UDP are tolerant of the lost data, or they have some application mechanism to recover lost data. For example, VoIP uses UDP because if a voice packet is lost, by the time the loss could be noticed and the packet retransmitted, too much delay would have occurred, and the voice would be unintelligible. Also, DNS requests use UDP because the user will retry an operation if the DNS resolution fails. As another example, the Network File System (NFS), a remote file system application, performs recovery with application layer code, so UDP features are acceptable to NFS.

Figure 6-10 shows TCP and UDP header formats. Note the existence of both Source Port and Destination Port fields in the TCP and UDP headers, but the absence of Sequence Number and Acknowledgment Number fields in the UDP header. UDP does not need these fields because it makes no attempt to number the data for acknowledgments or resequencing.

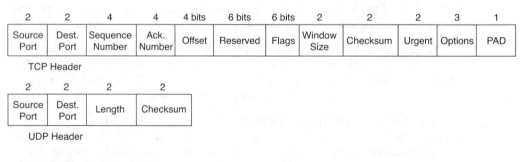

Figure 6-10   *TCP and UDP Headers*

UDP gains some advantages over TCP by not using the Sequence and Acknowledgment fields. The most obvious advantage of UDP over TCP is that there are fewer bytes of overhead. Not as obvious is the fact that UDP does not require waiting on acknowledgments or holding the data in memory until it is acknowledged. This means that UDP applications are not artificially slowed by the acknowledgment process, and memory is freed more quickly.

TCP/IP Applications

The whole goal of building an Enterprise network, or connecting a small home or office network to the Internet, is to use applications—applications such as web browsing, text messaging, e-mail, file downloads, voice, and video. This section examines a few issues related to network design in light of the applications expected in an internetwork. This is followed by a much deeper look at one particular application—web browsing using Hypertext Transfer Protocol (HTTP).

QoS Needs and the Impact of TCP/IP Applications

The needs of networked applications have changed and grown significantly over the years. When networks first became popular in Enterprises in the 1970s, the network typically supported only data applications, mainly text-only terminals and text-only printers. A single user might generate a few hundred bytes of data for the network every time he or she pressed the Enter key, maybe every 10 seconds or so.

The term *quality of service (QoS)* refers to the entire topic of what an application needs from the network service. Each type of application can be analyzed in terms of its QoS requirements on the network, so if the network meets those requirements, the application will work well. For example, the older text-based interactive applications required only a small amount of bandwidth, but they did like low delay. If those early networks supported a round-trip delay of less than 1 second, users were generally happy, because they had to wait less than 1 second for a response.

The QoS needs of data applications have changed over the years. Generally speaking, applications have tended to need more bandwidth, with lower delay as well. From those early days of networking to the present, here are some of the types of data applications that entered the marketplace, and their impact on the network:

■ Graphics-capable terminals and printers, which increased the required bytes for the same interaction as the old text-based terminals and printers

■ File transfers, which introduced much larger volumes of data, but with no significant response time requirements

■ File servers, which allow users to store files on a server—which might require a large volume of data transfer, but with a much smaller end-user response time requirement

■ The maturation of database technology, making vast amounts of data available to casual users, vastly increasing the number of users wanting access to data

■ The migration of common applications to web browsers, which encourages more users to access data

■ The general acceptance of e-mail as both a personal and business communications service, both inside companies and with other companies

■ The rapid commercialization of the Internet, enabling companies to offer data directly to their customers via the data network rather than via phone calls

Besides these and many other trends in the progression of data applications over the years, voice and video are in the middle of a migration onto the data network. Before the mid-to-late 1990s, voice and video typically used totally separate networking facilities. The migration of voice and video to the data network puts even more pressure on the data network to deliver the required quality of network service. Most companies today have either begun or plan on a migration to use IP phones, which pass voice traffic over the data network inside IP packets using application protocols generally referred to as voice over IP (VoIP). Additionally, several companies sell Internet phone service, which sends voice traffic over the Internet, again using VoIP packets. Figure 6-11 shows a few of the details of how VoIP works from a home high-speed Internet connection, with a generic voice adapter (VA) converting the analog voice signal from the normal telephone to an IP packet.

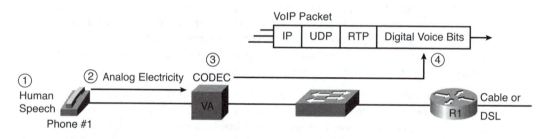

Figure 6-11   *Converting from Sound to Packets with a VA*

A single VoIP call that passes over a WAN typically takes less than 30 kbps of bandwidth, which is not a lot compared with many data applications today. In fact, most data applications consume as much bandwidth as they can grab. However, VoIP traffic has several other QoS demands on the network before the VoIP traffic will sound good:

Key Topic

■ **Low delay:** VoIP requires a very low delay between the sending phone and the receiving phone—typically less than 200 milliseconds (.2 seconds). This is a much lower delay than what is required by typical data applications.

■ **Low jitter:** Jitter is the variation in delay. VoIP requires very low jitter as well, whereas data applications can tolerate much higher jitter. For example, the jitter for consecutive VoIP packets should not exceed 30 milliseconds (.03 seconds), or the quality degrades.

■ **Loss:** If a VoIP packet is lost in transit because of errors or because a router doesn't have room to store the packet while waiting to send it, the VoIP packet is not delivered across the network. Because of the delay and jitter issues, there is no need to try to recover the lost packet. It would be useless by the time it was recovered. Lost packets can sound like a break in the sound of the VoIP call.

Video over IP has the same performance issues, except that video requires either more bandwidth (often 300 to 400 kbps) or a lot more bandwidth (3 to 10 Mbps per video). The world of video over IP is also going through a bit of transformation with the advent of high-definition video over IP, again increasing demands on the bandwidth in the network.

For perspective, Table 6-3 summarizes some thoughts about the needs of various types of applications for the four main QoS requirements—bandwidth, delay, jitter, and packet loss. Memorizing the table is not important, but it is important to note that although VoIP requires relatively little bandwidth, it also requires low delay/jitter/loss for high quality. It is also important to note that video over IP has the same requirements, except for medium to large amounts of bandwidth.

Table 6-3   *Comparing Applications' Minimum Needs*

Type of Application	Bandwidth	Delay	Jitter	Loss
VoIP	Low	Low	Low	Low
Two-way video over IP (such as videoconferencing)	Medium/high	Low	Low	Low
One-way video over IP (such as security cameras)	Medium	Medium	Medium	Low
Interactive mission-critical data (such as web-based payroll)	Medium	Medium	High	High
Interactive business data (such as online chat with a coworker)	Low/medium	Medium	High	High
File transfer (such as backing up disk drives)	High	High	High	High
Nonbusiness (such as checking the latest sports scores)	Medium	High	High	High

To support the QoS requirements of the various applications, routers and switches can be configured with a wide variety of QoS tools that do not happen to be discussed in this book. However, the QoS tools must be used for a modern network to be able to support high-quality VoIP and video over IP.

Next we examine the most popular application layer protocol for interactive data applications today—HTTP and the World Wide Web (WWW). The goal is to show one example of how application layer protocols work.

The World Wide Web, HTTP, and SSL

The *World Wide Web (WWW)* consists of all the Internet-connected web servers in the world, plus all Internet-connected hosts with web browsers. *Web servers*, which consist of web server software running on a computer, store information (in the form of *web pages*) that might be useful to different people. *Web browsers*, which is software installed on an end user's computer, provide the means to connect to a web server and display the web pages stored on the web server.

> **Note:**   Although most people use the term *web browser*, or simply *browser*, web browsers are also called *web clients*, because they obtain a service from a web server.

For this process to work, several specific application-layer functions must occur. The user must somehow identify the server, the specific web page, and the protocol used to get the data from the server. The client must find the server's IP address, based on the server's name, typically using DNS. The client must request the web page, which actually consists of multiple separate files, and the server must send the files to the web browser. Finally, for electronic commerce (e-commerce) applications, the transfer of data, particularly sensitive financial data, needs to be secure, again using application layer features. The following sections address each of these functions.

Universal Resource Locators

For a browser to display a web page, the browser must identify the server that has the web page, plus other information that identifies the particular web page. Most web servers have many web pages. For example, if you use a web browser to browse http://www.cisco.com, and you click around that web page, you'll see another web page. Click again, and you'll see another web page. In each case, the clicking action identifies the server's IP address and the specific web page, with the details mostly hidden from you. (These clickable items on a web page, which in turn bring you to another web page, are called *links*.)

The browser user can identify a web page when you click something on a web page or when you enter a *Universal Resource Locator (URL)* (often called a *web address*) in the browser's address area. Both options—clicking a link and entering a URL—refer to a URL, because when you click a link on a web page, that link actually refers to a URL.

> **Note:**   To see the hidden URL referenced by a link, open a browser to a web page, hover the mouse pointer over a link, right-click, and select **Properties**. The pop-up window should display the URL to which the browser would be directed if you clicked that link.

Each URL defines the protocol used to transfer data, the name of the server, and the particular web page on that server. The URL can be broken into three parts:

- The protocol is listed before the //.

- The hostname is listed between the // and the /.

- The name of the web page is listed after the /.

For example:

> http://www.certskills.com/Blog.aspx

In this case, the protocol is *Hypertext Transfer Protocol (HTTP)*, the hostname is www.certskills.com, and the name of the web page is Blog.aspx.

Finding the Web Server Using DNS

As mentioned in Chapter 5, "Fundamentals of IP Addressing and Routing," a host can use DNS to discover the IP address that corresponds to a particular hostname. Although

URLs can include the IP address of the web server instead of the name of the web server, URLs typically list the hostname. So, before the browser can send a packet to the web server, the browser typically needs to resolve the name in the URL to that name's corresponding IP address.

To pull together several concepts, Figure 6-12 shows the DNS process as initiated by a web browser, as well as some other related information. From a basic perspective, the user enters the URL (http://www.certskills.com/Blog.aspx), resolves the www.certskills.com name into the correct IP address, and starts sending packets to the web server.

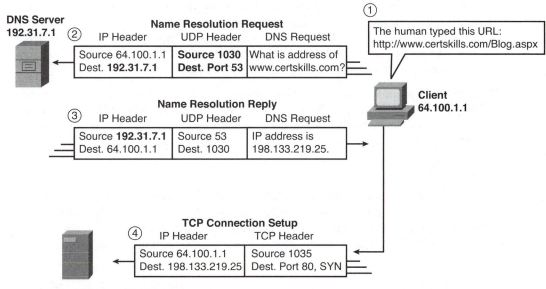

Figure 6-12 *DNS Resolution and Requesting a Web Page*

The steps shown in the figure are as follows:

1. The user enters the URL, http://www.ccertskills.com/Blog.aspx, into the browser's address area.

2. The client sends a DNS request to the DNS server. Typically, the client learns the DNS server's IP address via DHCP. Note that the DNS request uses a UDP header, with a destination port of the DNS well-known port of 53. (See Table 6-2, earlier in this chapter, for a list of popular well-known ports.)

3. The DNS server sends a reply, listing IP address 198.133.219.25 as www.certskills.com's IP address. Note also that the reply shows a destination IP address of 64.100.1.1, the client's IP address. It also shows a UDP header, with source port 53; the source port is 53 because the data is sourced, or sent by, the DNS server.

4. The client begins the process of establishing a new TCP connection to the web server. Note that the destination IP address is the just-learned IP address of the web server.

The packet includes a TCP header, because HTTP uses TCP. Also note the destination TCP port is 80, the well-known port for HTTP. Finally, the SYN bit is shown, as a reminder that the TCP connection establishment process begins with a TCP segment with the SYN bit turned on (binary 1).

At this point in the process, the web browser is almost finished setting up a TCP connection to the web server. The next section picks up the story at that point, examining how the web browser then gets the files that comprise the desired web page.

Transferring Files with HTTP

After a web client (browser) has created a TCP connection to a web server, the client can begin requesting the web page from the server. Most often, the protocol used to transfer the web page is HTTP. The HTTP application-layer protocol, defined in RFC 2616, defines how files can be transferred between two computers. HTTP was specifically created for the purpose of transferring files between web servers and web clients.

HTTP defines several commands and responses, with the most frequently used being the HTTP GET request. To get a file from a web server, the client sends an HTTP GET request to the server, listing the filename. If the server decides to send the file, the server sends an HTTP GET response, with a return code of 200 (meaning "OK"), along with the file's contents.

Note: Many return codes exist for HTTP requests. For instance, when the server does not have the requested file, it issues a return code of 404, which means "file not found." Most web browsers do not show the specific numeric HTTP return codes, instead displaying a response such as "page not found" in reaction to receiving a return code of 404.

Web pages typically consist of multiple files, called *objects*. Most web pages contain text as well as several graphical images, animated advertisements, and possibly voice or video. Each of these components is stored as a different object (file) on the web server. To get them all, the web browser gets the first file. This file can (and typically does) include references to other URLs, so the browser then also requests the other objects. Figure 6-13 shows the general idea, with the browser getting the first file and then two others.

In this case, after the web browser gets the first file—the one called "/go/ccna" in the URL—the browser reads and interprets that file. Besides containing parts of the web page, the file refers to two other files, so the browser issues two additional HTTP get requests. Note that, even though it isn't shown in the figure, all these commands flow over one (or possibly more) TCP connections between the client and the server. This means that TCP would provide error recovery, ensuring that the data was delivered.

This chapter ends with an introduction to network security.

Network Security

In years past, security threats came from geniuses or nerdy students with lots of time. The numbers of these people were relatively small. Their main motivation was to prove that they could break into another network. Since then, the number of potential attackers and the sophistication of the attacks have increased exponentially. Attacks that once required attackers to have an advanced degree in computing now can be done with easily downloaded and freely available tools that the average junior-high student can figure out how to use. Every company and almost every person connects to the Internet, making essentially the whole world vulnerable to attack.

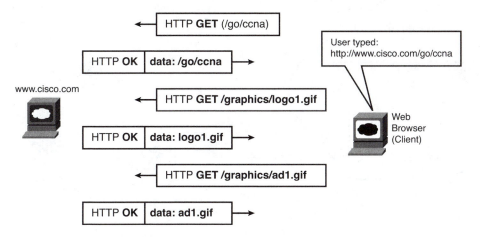

Figure 6-13   *Multiple HTTP Get Requests/Responses*

The biggest danger today might be the changes in attackers' motivation. Instead of looking for a challenge, or to steal millions, today's attackers can be much more organized and motivated. Organized crime tries to steal billions by extorting companies by threatening a denial of service (DoS) attack on the companies' public web servers. Or they steal identity and credit card information for sometimes hundreds of thousands of people with one sophisticated attack. Attacks might come from nation-states or terrorists. Not only might they attack military and government networks, but they might try to disrupt infrastructure services for utilities and transportation and cripple economies.

Security is clearly a big issue, and one that requires serious attention. For the purposes of this book, the goal is to know some of the basic terminology, types of security issues, and some of the common tools used to mitigate security risks. To that end, this final section of the chapter gives you some perspectives on attacks, and then it introduces four classes of security tools.

Perspectives on the Sources and Types of Threats

Figure 6-14 shows a common network topology with a firewall. Firewalls are probably the best-known security appliance, sitting between the Enterprise network and the dark, cold, unsecure Internet. The firewall's role is to stop packets that the network or security engineer has deemed unsafe. The firewall mainly looks at the transport layer port numbers and the application layer headers to prevent certain ports and applications from getting packets into the Enterprise.

Figure 6-14 might give an average employee of the Enterprise a false sense of security. He or she might think the firewall provides protection from all the dangers of connecting to the Internet. However, a perimeter firewall (a firewall on the edge, or perimeter, of the network) does not protect the Enterprise from all the dangers possible through the Internet connection. Not only that, a higher percentage of security attacks actually come from inside the Enterprise network, and the firewall does not even see those packets.

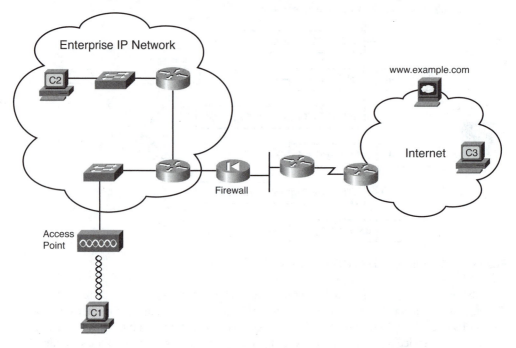

Figure 6-14   *Typical Enterprise Internet Connection with a Firewall*

To appreciate a bit more about the dangers inside the Enterprise network, it helps to understand a bit more about the kinds of attacks that might occur:

Key Topic

- **Denial of service (DoS) attacks:** An attack whose purpose is to break things. DoS attacks called *destroyers* try to harm the hosts, erasing data and software. DoS attacks called *crashers* cause harm by causing hosts to fail or causing the machine to no longer be able to connect to the network. Also, DoS attacks called *flooders* flood the network with packets to make the network unusable, preventing any useful communications with the servers.

- **Reconnaissance attacks:** This kind of attack can be disruptive as a side effect, but its goal is gathering information to perform an access attack. An example is learning IP addresses and then trying to discover servers that do not appear to require encryption to connect to the server.

- **Access attacks:** An attempt to steal data, typically data for some financial advantage, for a competitive advantage with another company, or even for international espionage.

Computer viruses are just one tool that can be used to carry out any of these attacks. A virus is a program that is somehow transferred onto an unsuspecting computer, possibly through an e-mail attachment or website download. A virus could just cause problems on the computer, or it could steal information and send it back to the attacker.

Today, most computers use some type of anti-virus software to watch for known viruses and prevent them from infecting the computer. Among other activities, the anti-virus software loads a list of known characteristics of all viruses, with these characteristics being known as *virus signatures*. By periodically downloading the latest virus signatures, the anti-virus software knows about all the latest viruses. By watching all packets entering the computer, the anti-virus software can recognize known viruses and prevent the computer from being infected. These programs also typically run an automatic periodic scan of the entire contents of the computer disk drives, looking for any known viruses.

To appreciate some of the security risks inherent in an Enterprise network that already has a quality perimeter firewall, consider Figure 6-15. The list following the figure explains three ways in which the Enterprise network is exposed to the possibility of an attack from within.

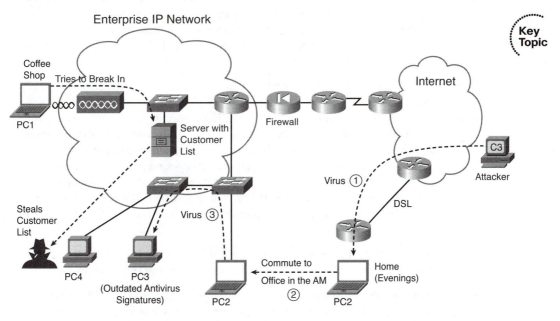

Figure 6-15   *Common Security Issues in an Enterprise*

The following types of problems could commonly occur in this Enterprise:

- **Access from the wireless LAN:** Wireless LANs allow users to access the rest of the devices in the Enterprise. The wireless radio signals might leave the building, so an unsecured wireless LAN allows the user across the street in a coffee shop to access the Enterprise network, letting the attacker (PC1) begin the next phase of trying to gain access to the computers in the Enterprise.

■ **Infected mobile laptops:** When an employee brings his or her laptop (PC2) home, with no firewall or other security, the laptop can become infected with a virus. When the user returns to the office in the morning, the laptop connects to the Enterprise network, with the virus spreading to other PCs, such as PC3. PC3 might be vulnerable in part because the users might have avoided running the daily anti-virus software scans that, although useful, can annoy the user.

■ **Disgruntled employees:** The user at PC4 is planning to move to a new company. He steals information from the network and loads it onto an MP3 player or USB flash drive. This allows him to carry the entire customer database in a device that can be easily concealed and removed from the building.

These attacks are just a few examples; a large number of variations and methods exist. To prevent such problems, Cisco suggests a security model that uses tools that automatically work to defend the network, with security features located throughout the network. Cisco uses the term *security in depth* to refer to a security design that includes security tools throughout the network, including features in routers and switches. Cisco also uses the term "self-defending network" to refer to automation in which the network devices automatically react to network problems.

For example, Network Admission Control (NAC) is one security tool to help prevent two of the attacks just described. Among other things, NAC can monitor when devices first connect to a LAN, be they wireless or wired. The NAC feature, partly implemented by features in the LAN switches, would prevent a computer from connecting to the LAN until its virus definitions were updated, with a requirement for a recent full virus scan. NAC also includes a requirement that the user supply a username and password before being able to send other data into the LAN, helping prevent the guy at the coffee shop from gaining access. However, NAC does not prevent a disgruntled employee from causing harm, because the employee typically has a working username/password to be authenticated with NAC.

Besides viruses, many other tools can be used to form an attack. The following list summarizes some of the more common terms for the tools in an attacker's toolkit:

■ **Scanner:** A tool that sends connection requests to different TCP and UDP ports, for different applications, in an attempt to discover which hosts run which IP services, and possibly the operating system used on each host.

■ **Spyware:** A virus that looks for private or sensitive information, tracking what the user does with the computer, and passing the information back to the attacker in the Internet.

■ **Worm:** A self-propagating program that can quickly replicate itself around Enterprise networks and the Internet, often performing DoS attacks, particularly on servers.

■ **Keystroke logger:** A virus that logs all keystrokes, or possibly just keystrokes from when secure sites are accessed, reporting the information to the attacker. Loggers can actually capture your username and password to secure sites before the information leaves the computer, which could give the attacker access to your favorite financial websites.

■ **Phishing:** The attacker sets up a website that outwardly looks like a legitimate website, often for a bank or credit card company. The phisher sends e-mails listing the illegitimate website's URL but making it look like the real company (for example, "Click here to update the records for your credit card to make it more secure."). The phisher hopes that a few people will take the bait, connect to the illegitimate website, and enter information such as their name, address, credit card number, social security number (in the U.S.), or other national government ID number. The best defense for phishing attacks might well be better user training and more awareness about the exposure.

■ **Malware:** This refers to a broad class of malicious viruses, including spyware.

The solution to these and the many other security issues not mentioned here is to provide security in depth throughout the network. The rest of this section introduces a few of the tools that can be used to provide that in-depth security.

Firewalls and the Cisco Adaptive Security Appliance (ASA)

Firewalls examine all packets entering and exiting a network for the purpose of filtering unwanted traffic. Firewalls determine the allowed traffic versus the disallowed traffic based on many characteristics of the packets, including their destination and source IP addresses and the TCP and UDP port numbers (which imply the application protocol). Firewalls also examine the application layer headers.

The term *firewall* is taken from the world of building and architecture. A firewall in a building has two basic requirements. It must be made of fire-resistant materials, and the architect limits the number of openings in the wall (doors, conduits for wires and plumbing), limiting the paths through which the fire can spread. Similarly, a network firewall must itself be hardened against security attacks. It must disallow all packets unless the engineer has configured a firewall rule that allows the traffic—a process often called "opening a hole," again with analogies to a firewall in a building.

Firewalls sit in the packet-forwarding path between two networks, often with one LAN interface connecting to the secure local network, and one to the other, less-secure network (often the Internet). Additionally, because some hosts in the Enterprise need to be accessible from the Internet—an inherently less secure practice—the firewall typically also has an interface connected to another small part of the Enterprise network, called the demilitarized zone (DMZ). The DMZ LAN is a place to put devices that need to be accessible, but that access puts them at higher risk. Figure 6-16 shows a sample design, with a firewall that has three interfaces.

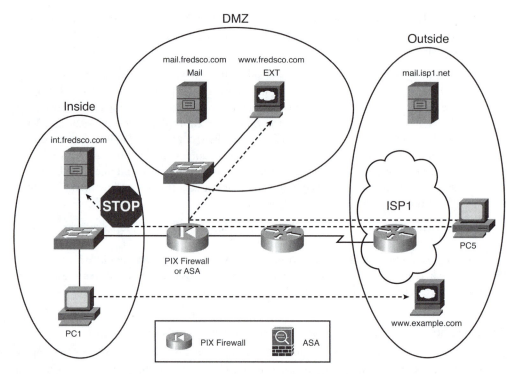

Figure 6-16 *Common Internet Design Using a Firewall*

To do its job, the firewall needs to be configured to know which interfaces are connected to the inside, outside, and DMZ parts of the network. Then, a series of rules can be configured that tell the firewall which traffic patterns are allowed and which are not. The figure shows two typically allowed flows and one typical disallowed flow, shown with dashed lines:

■ Allow web clients on the inside network (such as PC1) to send packets to web servers (such as the www.example.com web server)

■ Prevent web clients in the outside network (such as PC5) from sending packets to web servers in the inside network (such as the internal web server int.fredsco.com)

■ Allow web clients in the outside network (such as PC5) to connect to DMZ web servers (such as the www.fredsco.com web server)

In years past, Cisco sold firewalls with the trade name PIX firewall. A few years ago, Cisco introduced a whole new generation of network security hardware using the trade name Adaptive Security Appliance (ASA). ASA hardware can act as a firewall, in other security roles, and in a combination of roles. So, when speaking about security, the term firewall still refers to the functions, but today the Cisco product might be an older still-installed PIX firewall or a newer ASA. (Figure 6-16 shows the ASA icon at the bottom.)

Anti-x

A comprehensive security plan requires several functions that prevent different known types of problems. For example, host-based anti-virus software helps prevent the spread of viruses. Cisco ASA appliances can provide or assist in the overall in-depth security design with a variety of tools that prevent problems such as viruses. Because the names of several of the individual tools start with "anti-," Cisco uses the term *anti-x* to refer to the whole class of security tools that prevent these various problems, including the following:

- **Anti-virus:** Scans network traffic to prevent the transmission of known viruses based on virus signatures.

- **Anti-spyware:** Scans network traffic to prevent the transmission of spyware programs.

- **Anti-spam:** Examines e-mail before it reaches the users, deleting or segregating junk e-mail.

- **Anti-phishing:** Monitors URLs sent in messages through the network, looking for the fake URLs inherent in phishing attacks, preventing the attack from reaching the users.

- **URL filtering:** Filters web traffic based on URL to prevent users from connecting to inappropriate sites.

- **E-mail filtering:** Provides anti-spam tools. Also filters e-mails containing offensive materials, potentially protecting the Enterprise from lawsuits.

The Cisco ASA appliance can be used to perform the network-based role for all these anti-x functions.

Intrusion Detection and Prevention

Some types of attacks cannot be easily found with anti-x tools. For example, if a known virus infects a computer solely through an e-mail attachment of a file called this-is-a-virus.exe, the anti-virus software on the ASA or the end-user computer can easily identify and delete the virus. However, some forms of attacks can be more sophisticated. The attacks might not even include the transfer of a file, instead using a myriad of other, more-challenging methods, often taking advantage of new bugs in the operating system.

The world of network security includes a couple of types of tools that can be used to help prevent the more sophisticated kinds of attacks: Intrusion Detection Systems (IDS) and Intrusion Prevention Systems (IPS). IDS and IPS tools detect these threats by watching for trends, looking for attacks that use particular patterns of messages, and other factors. For instance, an IDS or IPS can track sequences of packets between hosts to look for a file being sent to more and more hosts, as might be done by a worm trying to spread inside a network.

IDS and IPS systems differ mainly in how they monitor the traffic and how they can respond to a perceived threat. IDS tools typically receive a copy of packets via a monitoring port, rather than being part of the packets' forwarding path. The IDS can then rate and report on each potential threat, and potentially ask other devices, such as firewalls and routers, to help prevent the attack (if they can). IPS tools often sit in the packets' forwarding path, giving the IPS the capability to perform the same functions as the IDS, but also to react and filter the traffic. The ability to react is important with some threats, such as the Slammer worm in 2003, which doubled the number of infected hosts every 9 seconds or so, infecting 75,000 hosts in the first 10 minutes of the attack. This kind of speed requires the use of reactive tools, rather than waiting on an engineer to see a report and take action.

Virtual Private Networks (VPN)

The last class of security tool introduced in this chapter is the virtual private network (VPN), which might be better termed a virtual private WAN. A leased line is inherently secure, effectively acting like an electrical circuit between the two routers. VPNs send packets through the Internet, which is a public network. However, VPNs make the communication secure, like a private leased line.

Without VPN technology, the packets sent between two devices over the Internet are inherently unsecure. The packets flowing through the Internet could be intercepted by attackers in the Internet. In fact, along with the growth of the Internet, attackers found ways to redirect packets and examine the contents, both to see the data and to find additional information (such as usernames and passwords) as part of a reconnaissance attack. Additionally, users and servers might not be able to tell the difference between a legitimate packet from an authentic user and a packet from an attacker who is trying to gain even more information and access.

VPNs provide a solution to allow the use of the Internet without the risks of unknowingly accepting data from attacking hosts and without the risk of others reading the data in transit. VPNs authenticate the VPN's endpoints, meaning that both endpoints can be sure that the other endpoint of the VPN connection is legitimate. Additionally, VPNs encrypt the original IP packets so that even if an attacker managed to get a copy of the packets as they pass through the Internet, he or she cannot read the data. Figure 6-17 shows the general idea, with an intranet VPN and an access VPN.

The figure shows an example of two types of VPNs: an *access VPN* and a *site-to-site intranet VPN*. An access VPN supports a home or small-office user, with the remote office's PC typically encrypting the packets. A site-to-site intranet VPN typically connects two sites of the same Enterprise, effectively creating a secure connection between two different parts inside (intra) the same Enterprise network. For intranet VPNs, the encryption could be done for all devices using different kinds of hardware, including routers, firewalls, purpose-built VPN concentrator hardware, or ASAs, as shown in the main site of the Enterprise.

Figure 6-17 shows how VPNs can use end-to-end encryption, in which the data remains encrypted while being forwarded through one or more routers. Additionally, link encryption can be used to encrypt data at the data link layer, so the data is encrypted only as it passes over one data link.

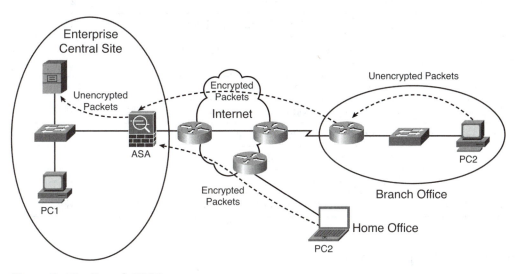

Figure 6-17   *Sample VPNs*

Chapter Review

Review Key Topics

Review the most important topics from this chapter, noted with the key topics icon. Table 6-4 lists these key topics and where each is discussed.

Key Topic

Table 6-4 *Key Topics for Chapter 6*

Key Topic Element	Description	Page Number
Table 6-1	Functions of TCP and UDP	128
Table 6-2	Well-known TCP and UDP port numbers	133
Figure 6-6	Example of TCP error recovery using forward acknowledgments	134
Figure 6-7	Example of TCP sliding windows	135
Figure 6-8	Example of TCP connection establishment	136
List	Definitions of connection-oriented and connectionless	137
List	QoS requirements for VoIP	140
List	Three types of attacks	146
Figure 6-15	Examples of common security exposures in an Enterprise	147

Define Key Terms

Define the following key terms from this chapter and check your answers in the glossary:

Anti-x, connection establishment, DoS, error detection, error recovery, firewall, flow control, forward acknowledgment, HTTP, Intrusion Detection System, Intrusion Prevention System, ordered data transfer, port, Positive Acknowledgment and Retransmission (PAR), segment, sliding windows, URL, virtual private network, VoIP, web server

Answer Review Questions

Answer the following review questions:

1. PC1 is using TCP and has a window size of 4000. PC1 sends four segments to PC2 with 1000 bytes of data each, with sequence numbers 2000, 3000, 4000, and 5000. PC1 does not receive an acknowledgment within its current timeout value for this connection. What should PC1 do next?

   a. Increase its window to 5000 or more segments

   b. Send the next segment, with sequence number 6000

   c. Resend the segment whose sequence number was 5000

   d. Resend all four previously sent segments

2. Which of the following are not features of a protocol that is considered to match OSI Layer 4?

   a. Error recovery

   b. Flow control

   c. Segmenting of application data

   d. Conversion from binary to ASCII

3. Which of the following header fields identify which TCP/IP application gets data received by the computer?

   a. Ethernet Type

   b. SNAP Protocol Type

   c. IP Protocol Field

   d. TCP Port Number

   e. UDP Port Number

   f. Application ID

4. Which of the following are not typical functions of TCP?

   a. Windowing

   b. Error recovery

   c. Multiplexing using port numbers

   d. Routing

   e. Encryption

   f. Ordered data transfer

5. Which of the following functions is performed by both TCP and UDP?

   a. Windowing

   b. Error recovery

   c. Multiplexing using port numbers

   d. Routing

   e. Encryption

   f. Ordered data transfer

6. What do you call data that includes the Layer 4 protocol header, and data given to Layer 4 by the upper layers, not including any headers and trailers from Layers 1 to 3?

   a. Bits

   b. Chunk

   c. Segment

   d. Packet

   e. Frame

   f. L4PDU

   g. L3PDU

7. In the URL http://www.fredsco.com/name.html, which part identifies the web server?

   a. http

   b. www.fredsco.com

   c. fredsco.com

   d. http://www.fredsco.com

   e. The file name.html includes the hostname.

8. When comparing VoIP with an HTTP-based mission-critical business application, which of the following statements are accurate about the quality of service needed from the network?

   a. VoIP needs better (lower) packet loss.

   b. HTTP needs less bandwidth.

   c. HTTP needs better (lower) jitter.

   d. VoIP needs better (lower) delay.

9. Which of the following is a device or function whose most notable feature is to examine trends over time to recognize different known attacks as compared to a list of common attack signatures?

   a. VPN

   b. Firewall

   c. IDS

   d. NAC

10. Which of the following is a device or function whose most notable feature is to encrypt packets before they pass through the Internet?

   a. VPN

   b. Firewall

   c. IDS

   d. NAC

This chapter covers the following subjects:

- **Installing Cisco Routers:** This section gives some perspective of the purpose of enterprise-class routers and consumer-class routers, and how the routers connect users to a network.

- **Accessing and Using the Cisco Router CLI:** This section shows you how to access the command-line interface (CLI) of Cisco routers from which you can issue commands to a router.

- **Configuring Cisco IOS Software:** This section shows you how to tell the router different operational parameters using the CLI.

CHAPTER 7

Operating Cisco Routers

Cisco routers need to know several pieces of information before they can start routing IP packets. First, they need to know which of their physical interfaces currently connect to real LANs and WANs. Next, the router needs to know its IP address and mask for each of these interfaces. The router can then use each interface's IP address/mask pair to calculate the subnet ID of the subnet connected to that interface. Finally, the routers need to advertise information about the subnets so that all routers learn about all subnets and can then choose the best route with which to forward packets to reach each subnet.

The kind of information the router needs to know—the interfaces it should use, the IP address/mask on each interface, and what protocols to use to dynamically learn routes—must be configured using a router's user interface. In other words, an engineer must access the user interface of the router and type commands that provide all these details. Cisco calls this user interface the command-line interface (CLI), in part because the interface provides the user with a command prompt, and the user types a command, asking the router to do something. These commands include configuration commands, which tell the router what to do, and verification commands, which list information that can be used to monitor and troubleshoot various router features.

This chapter explains the details of how to access a Cisco router's user interface, how to use commands to find out how the router is currently working, and how to configure the router to tell it what to do. This chapter focuses on the processes, as opposed to examining a particular set of commands. Many other chapters throughout this book will discuss router features and the associated CLI commands that you can use to configure and monitor that feature.

Installing Cisco Routers

Routers collectively provide the main feature of the network layer—the capability to forward packets end-to-end through a network. As introduced in Chapter 5, "Fundamentals of IP Addressing and Routing," routers forward packets by connecting to various physical network links, like Ethernet, serial links, and Frame Relay, and then using Layer 3 routing logic to choose where to forward each packet. As a reminder, Chapter 2, "LAN Fundamentals," covered the details of making those physical connections to Ethernet networks, while Chapter 3, "WAN Fundamentals," covered the basics of cabling with WAN links.

This section examines some of the details of router installation and cabling, first from the enterprise perspective, and then from the perspective of connecting a typical small office/home office (SOHO) to an ISP using high-speed Internet.

Installing Enterprise Routers

A typical enterprise network has a few centralized sites as well as lots of smaller remote sites. To support devices at each site (the computers, IP phones, printers, and other devices), the network includes at least one LAN switch at each site. Additionally, each site has a router, which connects to the LAN switch and to some WAN link. The WAN link provides connectivity from each remote site, back to the central site, and to other sites via the connection to the central site.

Figure 7-1 shows one way to draw part of an enterprise network. The figure shows a typical branch office on the left, with a router, some end-user PCs, and a nondescript generic drawing of an Ethernet. The central site, on the right, has basically the same components, with a point-to-point serial link connecting the two routers. The central site includes a server farm with two servers, with one of the main purposes of this internetwork being to provide remote offices with access to the data stored on these servers.

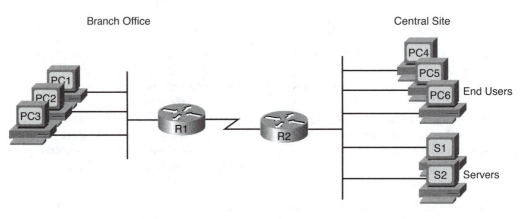

Figure 7-1   *Generic Enterprise Network Diagram*

Figure 7-1 purposefully omits several details to show the basic concepts. Figure 7-2 shows the same network, but now with more detail about the cabling used at each site.

Figure 7-2 shows the types of LAN cables (UTP), with a couple of different WAN cables. The LAN connections all use UTP straight-through cabling pinouts, except for the UTP cable between the two switches, which is a crossover cable.

The serial link in the figure shows the two main options for where the channel service unit/digital service unit (CSU/DSU) hardware resides: either outside the router (as shown at the branch office in this case) or integrated into the router's serial interface (as shown at the central site). Most new installations today include the CSU/DSU in the router's serial interface. The WAN cable installed by the telco typically has an RJ-48 connector, which is the same size and shape as an RJ-45 connector. The telco cable with the RJ-48 connector inserts into the CSU/DSU, meaning it connects directly into the central site router in this case, but into the external CSU/DSU at the branch office router. At the branch, the external CSU/DSU would then be cabled, using a serial cable, to the branch router's serial port. (See Figure 3-4 in Chapter 3 for a reminder of WAN serial cables.)

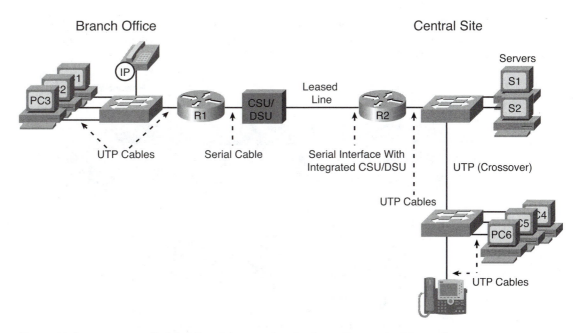

Figure 7-2 *More Detailed Cabling Diagram for the Same Enterprise Network*

Cisco Integrated Services Routers

Product vendors, including Cisco, typically provide several different types of router hardware, including some routers that just do routing, with other routers that serve other functions in addition to routing. A typical enterprise branch office needs a router for WAN/LAN connectivity, and a LAN switch to provide a high-performance local network and connectivity into the router and WAN. Many branches also need Voice over IP (VoIP) services, and several security services as well. Rather than require multiple separate devices at one site, as shown in Figure 7-2, Cisco offers single devices that act as both router and switch, and provide other functions as well.

Following that concept further, Cisco offers several router model series in which the routers support many other functions. In fact, Cisco has several router product series called Integrated Services Routers (ISR), with the name emphasizing the fact that many functions are integrated into a single device. If you have not seen Cisco routers before, go to the book page for this book (http://www.certskills.com/IPNetworking) and look for the links to Cisco's 3D Product Demonstrations, which show interactive views of a variety of Cisco ISR routers. However, for the sake of learning and understanding the different functions, this book focuses on using a separate switch and separate router, which provides a much cleaner path for learning the basics.

Figure 7-3 shows a couple of pictures taken from the interactive demo of the Cisco 1841 ISR, with some of the more important features highlighted. The top part of the figure shows a full view of the back of the router. It also shows a magnified view of the back of the router, with a clearer view of the two FastEthernet interfaces, the console and auxiliary ports, and a serial card with an internal CSU/DSU. (You can find the interactive demo from which these photos were taken at the same ISR web page mentioned in the previous paragraph.)

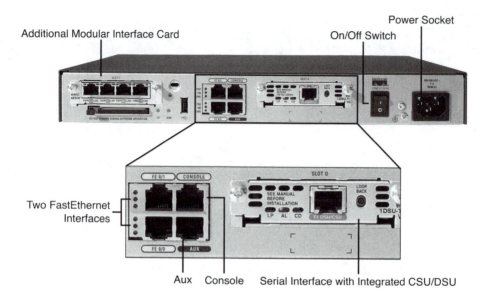

Figure 7-3   *Photos of a Model 1841 Cisco Integrated Services Router (ISR)*

Physical Installation

Armed with the planning information shown in Figure 7-2, and the perspectives shown in Figure 7-3, you can physically install a router. To install a router, follow these steps:

Step 1.   Connect any LAN cables to the LAN ports.

Step 2.   If using an external CSU/DSU, connect the router's serial interface to the CSU/DSU, and the CSU/DSU to the line from the telco.

Step 3.   If using an internal CSU/DSU, connect the router's serial interface to the line from the telco.

Step 4.   Connect the router's console port to a PC (using a rollover cable), as needed, to configure the router.

Step 5.   Connect a power cable from a power outlet to the power port on the router.

Step 6.   Turn on the router.

Note that the steps generally follow the same steps used for installation of LAN switches—install the cables for the interfaces, connect the console (as needed), and connect the power. However, note that most of the Cisco Catalyst LAN switches do not have a power on/off switch—once the switch is connected to power, the switch is on. However, most Cisco routers do have on/off switches.

Installing Internet Access Routers

Routers play a key role in SOHO networks, connecting the LAN-attached end-user devices to a high-speed Internet access service. Once connected to the Internet, SOHO users can send packets to and from their enterprise network at their company or school.

As in the enterprise networking market, product vendors tend to sell integrated networking devices that perform many functions. However, in keeping with the book's strategy of understanding each function separately, this section first examines the various networking functions needed at a typical SOHO network, using a separate device for each function. Following that, a more realistic example is shown, with the functions combined into a single device.

A SOHO Installation with a Separate Switch, Router, and Cable Modem

Figure 7-4 shows an example of the devices and cables used in a SOHO network to connect to the Internet using cable TV (CATV) as the high-speed Internet service. For now, keep in mind that the figure shows one alternative for the devices and cables, whereas many variations are possible.

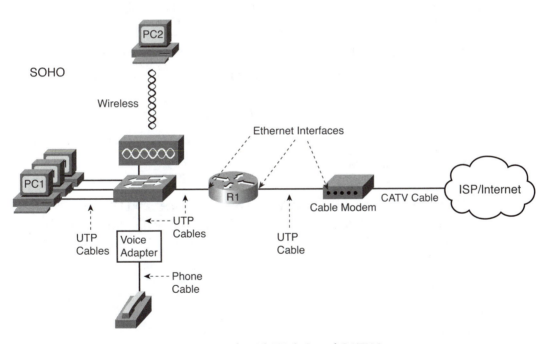

Figure 7-4   *Devices in a SOHO Network with High-Speed CATV Internet*

This figure has many similarities to Figure 7-2, which shows a typical enterprise branch office. The end-user PCs still connect to a switch, and the switch still connects to a router's Ethernet interface. The router still provides routing services, forwarding IP packets. The voice details differ slightly between Figure 7-2 and Figure 7-4, mainly because Figure 7-4 shows a typical home-based Internet phone service, which uses a normal analog phone and a voice adapter to convert from analog voice to IP.

The main differences between the SOHO connection in Figure 7-4 and the enterprise branch in Figure 7-2 relate to the connection into the Internet. An Internet connection that uses CATV or DSL needs a device that converts between the Layer 1 and 2 standards used on the CATV cable or DSL line, and the Ethernet used by the router. These devices, commonly called *cable modems* and *DSL modems*, respectively, convert electrical signals between an Ethernet cable and either CATV or DSL.

In fact, while the details differ greatly, the purpose of the cable modem and DSL modem is similar to a CSU/DSU on a serial link. A CSU/DSU converts between the Layer 1 standards used on a telco's WAN circuit and a serial cable's Layer 1 standards—and routers can use serial cables. Similarly, a cable modem converts between CATV signals and a Layer 1 (and Layer 2) standard usable by a router—namely, Ethernet. Similarly, DSL modems convert between the DSL signals over a home telephone line and Ethernet.

To physically install a SOHO network with the devices shown in Figure 7-4, you basically need the correct UTP cables for the Ethernet connections, and either the CATV cable (for cable Internet services) or a phone line (for DSL services). Note that the router used in Figure 7-4 simply needs to have two Ethernet interfaces—one to connect to the LAN switch, and one to connect to the cable modem. Thinking specifically just about the router installation, you would need to use the following steps to install this SOHO router:

Step 1.   Connect a UTP straight-through cable from the router to the switch.

Step 2.   Connect a UTP straight-through cable from the router to the cable modem.

Step 3.   Connect the router's console port to a PC (using a rollover cable), as needed, to configure the router.

Step 4.   Connect a power cable from a power outlet to the power port on the router.

Step 5.   Turn on the router.

A SOHO Installation with an Integrated Switch, Router, and DSL Modem

Today, most new SOHO installations use an integrated device rather than the separate devices shown in Figure 7-4. In fact, you can buy SOHO devices today that include all of these functions:

■   Router

■   Switch

■   Cable or DSL modem

■   Voice Adapter

■   Wireless AP

■   Hardware-enabled encryption

As mentioned earlier, this book focuses on devices that do one job to help make the details easier to learn. However, a newly installed high-speed SOHO Internet connection today probably looks more like Figure 7-5, with a single integrated device.

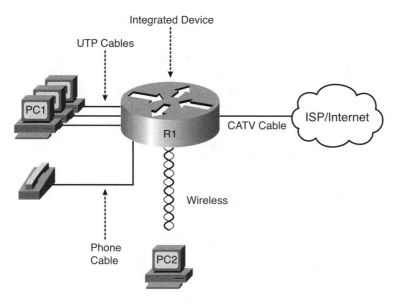

Figure 7-5   *SOHO Network, Using Cable Internet and an Integrated Device*

Regarding the SOHO Devices Used in This Book

Cisco sells products to both enterprise customers and consumers. Cisco sells its consumer products using the Linksys brand. These products are easily found online and in office supply stores. Cisco mainly sells enterprise products either directly to its customers or through Cisco Channel Partners (resellers). This book focuses on the enterprise-class products, which have a command-line interface.

Accessing and Using the Cisco Router CLI

Cisco uses the same concept of a *command-line interface (CLI)* with its router products and most of its Catalyst LAN switch products. The CLI is a text-based interface in which the user, typically a network engineer, enters a text command and presses Enter. Pressing Enter sends the command to the router, which tells the device to do something. The router does what the command says, and in some cases, the switch replies with some messages stating the results of the command.

This section explains the processes of how a network engineer can get access to the CLI to issue commands.

Accessing the CLI

Cisco IOS Software, the operating system (OS) that runs on Cisco enterprise-class routers, implements and controls logic and functions performed by a Cisco router. Besides controlling the router's performance and behavior, Cisco IOS also defines an interface for humans called the CLI. The Cisco IOS CLI allows the user to use a terminal emulation program, which accepts text entered by the user. When the user presses Enter, the terminal emulator sends that text to the router. The router processes the text as if it is a command, does what the command says, and sends text back to the terminal emulator.

The router CLI can be accessed through three popular methods—the console, Telnet, and Secure Shell (SSH). Two of these methods (Telnet and SSH) use the IP network in which the router resides to reach the router. The console is a physical port built specifically to allow access to the CLI. Figure 7-6 depicts the options.

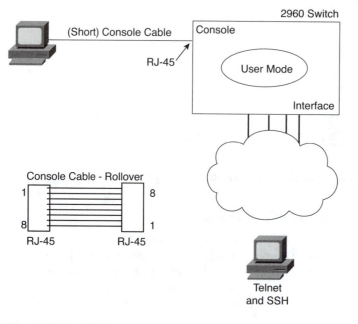

Figure 7-6 *CLI Access*

Next, this section examines each of these three access methods in more detail.

CLI Access from the Console

The console port provides a way to connect to a router CLI even if the router has not been connected to a network yet. Every Cisco router has a console port, which is physically an RJ-45 port. A PC connects to the console port using a UTP rollover cable, which is also connected to the PC's serial port.

The UTP rollover cable has RJ-45 connectors on each end, with pin 1 on one end connected to pin 8 on the other, pin 2 to pin 7, pin 3 to pin 6, and pin 4 to pin 5. In some cases, a PC's serial interface does not use an RJ-45 connector, an adapter must be used to convert from the PC's physical interface—typically either a nine-pin connector or a USB connector—to an RJ-45. Figure 7-7 shows the RJ-45 end of the console cable connected to a router and the DB-9 end connected to a laptop PC.

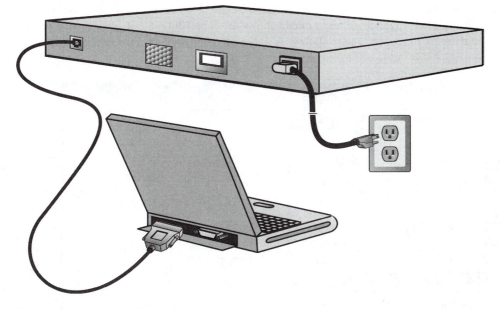

Figure 7-7   *Console Connection to a Router*

As soon as the PC is physically connected to the console port, a terminal emulator software package must be installed and configured on the PC. Today, terminal emulator software includes support for Telnet and Secure Shell (SSH), which can be used to access the router CLI via the network, but not through the console.

Figure 7-8 shows the window created by the Tera Term Pro software package (available for free from http://www.ayera.com). The emulator must be configured to use the PC's serial port, matching the router's console port settings. The default console port settings on a router are as follows:

- 9600 bits/second

- No hardware flow control

- 8-bit ASCII

- No parity bits

- 1 stop bit

Key Topic

Note that the last three parameters are referred to collectively as "8N1."

Figure 7-8 shows a terminal emulator window with some command output. It also shows the configuration window for the settings just listed.

The figure shows the window created by the emulator software. Note that the first highlighted portion shows the text **Emma#show mac address-table dynamic**. The **Emma#**

part is the command prompt, which typically shows the hostname of the router (Emma in this case). The prompt is text created by the router and sent to the emulator. The **show mac address-table dynamic** part is the command that the user entered. The text shown beneath the command is the output generated by the router and sent to the emulator. Finally, the lower highlighted text **Emma#** shows the command prompt again, as sent to the emulator by the router. The window would remain in this state until the user entered something else at the command line.

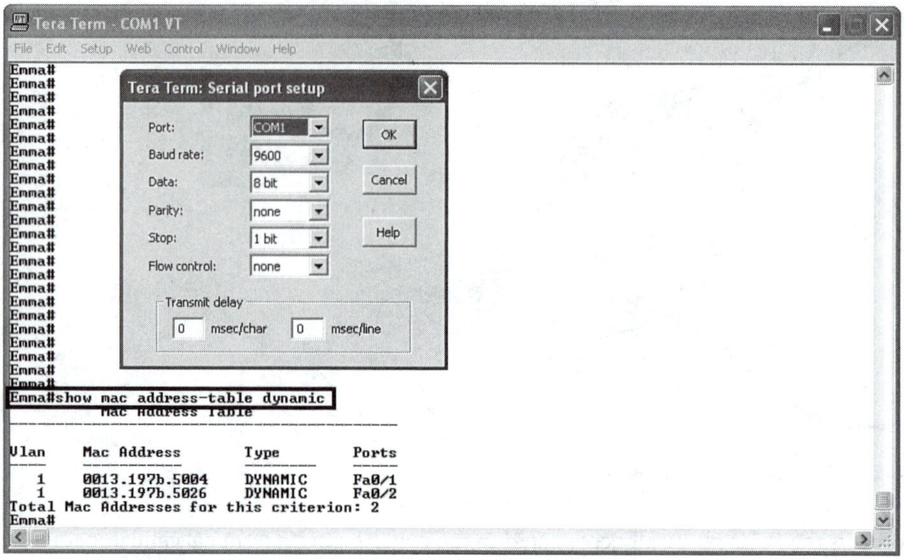

Figure 7-8   *Terminal Settings for Console Access*

Accessing the CLI with Telnet and SSH

The TCP/IP Telnet application allows a terminal emulator to communicate with a device, much like what happens with an emulator on a PC connected to the console. However, Telnet uses an IP network to send and receive the data, rather than a specialized cable and physical port on the device. The Telnet application protocols call the terminal emulator a *Telnet client* and the device that listens for commands and replies to them a *Telnet server*. Telnet is a TCP-based application layer protocol that uses well-known port 23.

To use Telnet, the user must install a Telnet client software package on his or her PC. (As mentioned earlier, most terminal emulator software packages today include both Telnet and SSH client functions.) The router runs Telnet server software by default, but the router does need to have an IP address configured so that it can send and receive IP packets. (Chapter 11, "Cisco Router Configuration," covers router IP address configuration in greater detail.) Additionally, the network between the PC and router needs to be up and working so that the PC and router can exchange IP packets.

Many network engineers habitually use a Telnet client to monitor routers. The engineer can sit at his or her desk without having to walk to another part of the building—or go to another state or country—and still get into the CLI of that device. Telnet sends all data (including any username and password for login to the router) as clear-text data, which presents a potential security risk.

Secure Shell (SSH) does the same basic things as Telnet, but in a more secure manner by using encryption. Like the Telnet model, the SSH client software includes a terminal emulator and the capability to send and receive the data using IP. Like Telnet, SSH uses TCP, while using well-known port 22 instead of Telnet's 23. As with Telnet, the SSH server (on the router) receives the text from each SSH client, processes the text as a command, and sends messages back to the client. The key difference between Telnet and SSH lies in the fact that all the communications are encrypted and therefore are private and less prone to security risk.

Password Security for CLI Access

By default, a Cisco router is very secure as long as the router is locked inside a room. By default, a router allows only console access, but no Telnet or SSH access. From the console, you can gain full access to all router commands, and if so inclined, you can stop all functions of the router. However, console access requires physical access to the router, so allowing console access for routers just removed from the shipping boxes is reasonable.

Regardless of the defaults, it makes sense to password-protect console access, as well as Telnet and SSH access. To add basic password checking for the console and for Telnet, the engineer needs to configure a couple of basic commands. The configuration process is covered a little later in this chapter, but you can get a general idea of the commands by looking in the last column of Table 7-1. The table lists the two commands that configure the console and vty passwords. After it is configured, the router supplies a simple password prompt (as a result of the **login** command), and the router expects the user to enter the password listed in the **password** command.

Table 7-1 *CLI Password Configuration: Console and Telnet*

Access From	Password Type	Sample Configuration
Console	Console password	**line console 0** **login** **password faith**
Telnet	vty password	**line vty 0 15** **login** **password love**

Cisco routers refer to the console as a console line—specifically, console line 0. Similarly, routers support 16 concurrent Telnet sessions, referenced as virtual terminal (vty) lines 0 through 15. (The term vty refers to an old name for terminal emulators.) The **line vty 0 15** configuration command tells the router that the commands that follow apply to all 16 possible concurrent virtual terminal connections to the router, which includes Telnet as well as SSH access.

Note: Some older versions of switch software supported only five vty lines, 0 through 4.

After adding the configuration shown in Table 7-1, a user connecting to the console would be prompted for a password, and he or she would have to supply the word **faith** in this case. New Telnet users would also be prompted for a password, with **love** being the required password. Also, with this configuration, no username is required—just a simple password.

Configuring SSH requires a little more effort than the console and Telnet password configuration examples shown in Table 7-1. SSH uses public key cryptography to exchange a shared session key, which in turn is used for encryption. Additionally, SSH requires slightly better login security, requiring at least a password and a username. The section "Configuring Usernames and Secure Shell (SSH)" in Chapter 11 shows the configuration steps and a sample configuration to support SSH.

User and Enable (Privileged) Modes

All three CLI access methods covered so far (console, Telnet, and SSH) place the user in an area of the CLI called *user EXEC mode*. User EXEC mode, sometimes also called *user mode*, allows the user to look around but not break anything. The "EXEC mode" part of the name refers to the fact that in this mode, when you enter a command, the router executes the command and then displays messages that describe the command's results.

Cisco IOS supports a more powerful EXEC mode called *enable* mode (also known as *privileged* mode or *privileged EXEC* mode). Enable mode is so named because the **enable** command is used to reach this mode, as shown in Figure 7-9. Privileged mode earns its name because powerful, or privileged, commands can be executed there. For example, you can use the **reload** command, which tells the router to reinitialize or reboot Cisco IOS, only from enable mode.

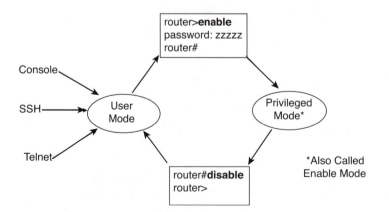

Figure 7-9   *User and Privileged Modes*

Note: If the command prompt lists the hostname followed by a >, the user is in user mode; if it is the hostname followed by the #, the user is in enable mode.

The preferred configuration command for configuring the password for reaching enable mode is the **enable secret** *password* command, where *password* is the text of the password. Note that if the enable password is not configured (the default), Cisco IOS prevents Telnet and SSH users from getting into enable mode, but Cisco IOS does allow a console user to reach enable mode. This default action is consistent with the idea that, by default, users outside the locked room where the router sits cannot get access without additional configuration by the engineer.

Note: The commands that can be used in either user (EXEC) mode or enable (EXEC) mode are called EXEC commands.

So far, this chapter has pointed out some of the first things you should know when unpacking and installing a router. The router will work without any configuration—just plug in the power and Ethernet cables, and it works. However, you should at least connect to the router console port and configure passwords for the console, Telnet, SSH, and the enable secret password.

Next, this chapter examines some of the CLI features that exist regardless of how you access the CLI.

CLI Help Features

If you printed the Cisco IOS Command Reference documents, you would end up with a stack of paper several feet tall. No one should expect to memorize all the commands—and no one does. However, you should know the methods of getting command help.

Table 7-2 summarizes command-recall help options available at the CLI. Note that, in the first column, *command* represents any command. Likewise, *parm* represents a command's parameter. For instance, the third row lists *command* **?**, which means that commands such as **show ?** and **copy ?** would list help for the **show** and **copy** commands, respectively.

Table 7-2 *Cisco IOS Software Command Help*

What You Enter	What Help You Get
?	Help for all commands available in this mode.
help	Text describing how to get help. No actual command help is given.
command **?**	Text help describing all the first parameter options for the command.
com?	A list of commands that start with com.
command parm?	This style of help lists all parameters beginning with **parm**. (Notice that there is no space between *parm* and the **?**.)

Table 7-2   *Cisco IOS Software Command Help*

What You Enter	What Help You Get
command parm<Tab>	If you press the Tab key midword, the CLI either spells the rest of this parameter at the command line or does nothing. If the CLI does nothing, it means that this string of characters represents more than one possible next parameter, so the CLI does not know which one to spell out.
command parm1 ?	If a space is inserted before the question mark, the CLI lists all the next parameters and gives a brief explanation of each.

When you enter the ?, the Cisco IOS CLI reacts immediately; that is, you don't need to press the Enter key or any other keys. The device running Cisco IOS also redisplays what you entered before the ? to save you some keystrokes. If you press Enter immediately after the ?, Cisco IOS tries to execute the command with only the parameters you have entered so far.

command represents any command, not the word *command*. Likewise, *parm* represents a command's parameter, not the word *parameter*.

The information supplied by using help depends on the CLI mode. For example, when ? is entered in user mode, the commands allowed in user mode are displayed, but commands available only in enable mode (not in user mode) are not displayed. Also, help is available in configuration mode, which is the mode used to configure the router. In fact, configuration mode has many different subconfiguration modes, as explained in the section "Configuration Submodes and Contexts." So, you can get help for the commands available in each configuration submode as well.

Cisco IOS stores the commands that you enter in a history buffer, storing ten commands by default. The CLI allows you to move backward and forward in the historical list of commands and then edit the command before reissuing it. These key sequences can help you use the CLI more quickly on the exams. Table 7-3 lists the commands used to manipulate previously entered commands.

Table 7-3   *Key Sequences for Command Edit and Recall*

Keyboard Command	What Happens
Up arrow or Ctrl-p	This displays the most recently used command. If you press it again, the next most recent command appears, until the history buffer is exhausted. (The p stands for previous.)
Down arrow or Ctrl-n	If you have gone too far back into the history buffer, these keys take you forward to the more recently entered commands. (The n stands for next.)
Left arrow or Ctrl-b	This moves the cursor backward in the currently displayed command without deleting characters. (The b stands for back.)

Table 7-3   *Key Sequences for Command Edit and Recall*

Keyboard Command	What Happens
Right arrow or Ctrl-f	This moves the cursor forward in the currently displayed command without deleting characters. (The f stands for forward.)
Backspace	This moves the cursor backward in the currently displayed command, deleting characters.
Ctrl-a	This moves the cursor directly to the first character of the currently displayed command.
Ctrl-e	This moves the cursor directly to the end of the currently displayed command.
Ctrl-r	This redisplays the command line with all characters. It's useful when messages clutter the screen.
Ctrl-d	This deletes a single character.
Esc-b	This moves back one word.
Esc-f	This moves forward one word.

The debug and show Commands

By far, the single most popular Cisco IOS command is the **show** command. The **show** command has a large variety of options, and with those options, you can find the status of almost every feature of Cisco IOS. Essentially, the **show** command lists the currently known facts about the router's operational status. The only work the router does in reaction to **show** commands is to find the current status and list the information in messages sent to the user.

A less popular command is the **debug** command. Like the **show** command, **debug** has many options. However, instead of just listing messages about the current status, the **debug** command asks the router to continue monitoring different processes in the router. The router then sends ongoing messages to the user when different events occur.

The effects of the **show** and **debug** commands can be compared to a photograph and a movie. Like a photo, a **show** command shows what's true at a single point in time, and it takes little effort. The **debug** command shows what's true over time, but it requires more effort. As a result, the **debug** command requires more CPU cycles, but it lets you watch what is happening in a router while it is happening.

Cisco IOS handles the messages created with the **debug** command much differently than with the **show** command. When any user issues a **debug** command, the debug options in the command are enabled. The messages Cisco IOS creates in response to all **debug** commands, regardless of which user(s) issued the **debug** commands, are treated as a special type of message called a *log message*. Any remote user can view log messages by simply using the **terminal monitor** command. Additionally, these log messages also appear at the console automatically. So, whereas the **show** command lists a set of messages for that single user, the **debug** command lists messages for all interested users to see, requiring remote users to ask to view the **debug** and other log messages.

The options enabled by a single **debug** command are not disabled until the user takes action or until the router is reloaded. A **reload** of the router disables all currently enabled debug options. To disable a single debug option, repeat the same **debug** command with those options, prefaced by the word **no**. For example, if the **debug spanning-tree** command was been issued earlier, issue the **no debug spanning-tree** command to disable that same debug. Also, the **no debug all** and **undebug all** commands disable all currently enabled debugs.

Be aware that some **debug** options create so many messages that Cisco IOS cannot process them all, possibly resulting in a crash of Cisco IOS. You might want to check the current router CPU utilization with the **show process** command before issuing any **debug** command. To be more careful, before enabling an unfamiliar **debug** command option, issue a **no debug all** command, and then issue the **debug** that you want to use. Then quickly retrieve the **no debug all** command using the up arrow or Ctrl-p key sequence twice. If the debug quickly degrades router performance, the router might be too busy to listen to what you are typing. The process described in this paragraph saves a bit of typing and can be the difference between preventing the router from failing, or not.

Configuring Cisco IOS Software

This section discusses the basic configuration processes, including the concept of a configuration file and the locations in which the configuration files can be stored. Although this section focuses on the configuration process, and not on the configuration commands themselves, you should know all the commands covered in this chapter, in addition to the configuration processes.

Configuration mode is another mode for the Cisco CLI, similar to user mode and privileged mode. User mode lets you issue nondisruptive commands and displays some information. Privileged mode supports a superset of commands compared to user mode, including commands that might harm the router. However, none of the commands in user or privileged mode changes the router's configuration. Configuration mode accepts *configuration commands*—commands that tell the router the details of what to do, and how to do it. Figure 7-10 illustrates the relationships among configuration mode, user EXEC mode, and privileged EXEC mode.

Commands entered in configuration mode update the active configuration file. *These changes to the configuration occur immediately each time you press the Enter key at the end of a command.* Be careful when you enter a configuration command!

Configuration Submodes and Contexts

Configuration mode itself contains a multitude of subcommand modes. *Context-setting commands* move you from one configuration subcommand mode, or context, to another. These context-setting commands tell the router the topic about which you will enter the next few configuration commands. More importantly, the context tells the router the topic you care about right now, so when you use the **?** to get help, the router gives you help about that topic only.

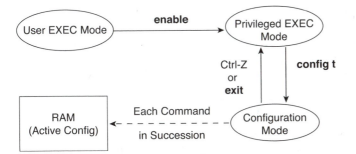

Figure 7-10   *CLI Configuration Mode Versus Exec Modes*

Note: Context setting is not a Cisco term—it's just a term used here to help make sense of configuration mode.

The **interface** command is one of the most commonly used context-setting configuration commands. For example, the CLI user could enter interface configuration mode by entering the **interface FastEthernet 0/1** configuration command. Asking for help in interface configuration mode displays only commands that are useful when configuring Ethernet interfaces. Commands used in this context are called *subcommands*—or, in this specific case, *interface subcommands*. When you begin practicing with the CLI with real equipment, the navigation between modes can become natural. For now, consider Example 7-1, which shows the following:

- Movement from enable mode to global configuration mode by using the **configure terminal** EXEC command

- Using a **hostname Fred** global configuration command to configure the router's name

- Movement from global configuration mode to console line configuration mode (using the **line console 0** command)

- Setting the console's simple password to **hope** (using the **password hope** line subcommand)

- Movement from console configuration mode to interface configuration mode (using the **interface** command)

- Setting the speed to 100 Mbps for interface Fa0/1 (using the **speed 100** interface subcommand)

- Movement interface configuration mode back to global configuration mode (using the **exit** command)

Example 7-1   *Navigating Between Different Configuration Modes*

```
Router# configure terminal
Router(config)# hostname Fred
Fred(config)# line console 0
Fred(config-line)# password hope
Fred(config-line)# interface FastEthernet 0/1
Fred(config-if)# speed 100
Fred(config-if)# exit
Fred(config)#
```

The text inside parentheses in the command prompt identifies the configuration mode. For example, the first command prompt after you enter configuration mode lists (config), meaning global configuration mode. After the **line console 0** command, the text expands to (config-line), meaning line configuration mode. Table 7-4 shows the most common command prompts in configuration mode, the names of those modes, and the context setting commands used to reach those modes.

Table 7-4   *Common Router Configuration Modes*

Prompt	Name of Mode	Context-setting Command(s) to Reach This Mode
hostname(config)#	Global	None—first mode after **configure terminal**
hostname(config-line)#	Line	**line console 0** **line vty 0 15**
hostname(config-if)#	Interface	**interface** *type number*

No set rules exist for what commands are global commands or subcommands. Generally, however, when multiple instances of a parameter can be set in a single router, the command used to set the parameter is likely a configuration subcommand. Items that are set once for the entire router are likely global commands. For example, the **hostname** command is a global command because there is only one hostname per router. Conversely, the **duplex** command is an interface subcommand to allow the router to use a different setting on the different interfaces.

Both the Ctrl-z key sequence and the **end** command exit the user from any part of configuration mode and go back to privileged EXEC mode. Alternatively, the **exit** command backs you out of configuration mode one subconfiguration mode at a time.

Storing Router Configuration Files

When you configure a router, it needs to use the configuration. It also needs to be able to retain the configuration in case the router loses power. Cisco routers contain Random Access Memory (RAM) to store data while Cisco IOS is using it, but RAM loses its contents when the router loses power. To store information that must be retained when the router loses power, Cisco routers use several types of more permanent memory, none of which has any moving parts. By avoiding components with moving parts (such as traditional disk drives), routers can maintain better uptime and availability.

The following list details the four main types of memory found in Cisco routers, as well as the most common use of each type:

- **RAM:** Sometimes called DRAM for Dynamic Random-Access Memory, RAM is used by the router just as it is used by any other computer: for working storage. The running (active) configuration file is stored here.

- **ROM:** Read-Only Memory (ROM) stores a bootstrap (or boothelper) program that is loaded when the router first powers on. This bootstrap program then finds the full Cisco IOS image and manages the process of loading Cisco IOS into RAM, at which point Cisco IOS takes over operation of the router.

- **Flash memory:** Either a chip inside the router or a removable memory card, Flash memory stores fully functional Cisco IOS images and is the default location where the router gets its Cisco IOS at boot time. Flash memory also can be used to store any other files, including backup copies of configuration files.

- **NVRAM:** Nonvolatile RAM (NVRAM) stores the initial or startup configuration file that is used when the router is first powered on and when the router is reloaded.

Figure 7-11 summarizes this same information in a briefer and more convenient form for memorization and study.

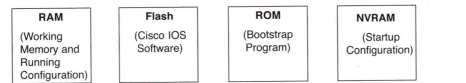

Figure 7-11 *Cisco Router Memory Types*

Cisco IOS stores the collection of configuration commands in a *configuration file*. In fact, routers use multiple configuration files—one file for the initial configuration used when powering on, and another configuration file for the active, currently used running configuration as stored in RAM. Table 7-5 lists the names of these two files, their purpose, and their storage location.

Table 7-5 *Names and Purposes of the Two Main Cisco IOS Configuration Files*

Configuration Filename	Purpose	Where It Is Stored
Startup-config	Stores the initial configuration used any time the router reloads Cisco IOS.	NVRAM
Running-config	Stores the currently used configuration commands. This file changes dynamically when someone enters commands in configuration mode.	RAM

Essentially, when you use configuration mode, you change only the running-config file. This means that the configuration example earlier in this chapter (refer to Example 7-1) updates only the running-config file. However, if the router lost power right after that example, all that configuration would be lost. If you want to keep that configuration, you have to copy the running-config file into NVRAM, overwriting the old startup-config file.

Example 7-2 demonstrates that commands used in configuration mode change only the running configuration in RAM. The example shows the following concepts and steps:

Step 1.   The original **hostname** command on the router, with the startup-config file matching the running-config file.

Step 2.   The **hostname** command changes the hostname, but only in the running-config file.

Step 3.   The **show running-config** and **show startup-config** commands are shown, with only the hostname commands displayed for brevity, to make the point that the two configuration files are now different.

Example 7-2   *How Configuration Mode Commands Change the Running-config File, Not the Startup-config File*

```
! Step 1 next (two commands)
!
hannah# show running-config
! (lines omitted)
hostname hannah
! (rest of lines omitted)


hannah# show startup-config
! (lines omitted)
hostname hannah
! (rest of lines omitted)
! Step 2 next. Notice that the command prompt changes immediately after
! the hostname command.
!hannah# configure terminal
hannah(config)# hostname jessie
jessie(config)# exit
! Step 3 next (two commands)
```

```
!
jessie# show running-config
! (lines omitted)
hostname jessie
! (rest of lines omitted - notice that the running configuration reflects the
!  changed hostname)
jessie# show startup-config
! (lines omitted)
hostname hannah
! (rest of lines omitted - notice that the changed configuration is not
! shown in the startup config)
```

Note: Cisco uses the term *reload* to refer to what most PC operating systems call rebooting or restarting. In each case, it is a reinitialization of the software. The **reload** exec command causes a switch to reload.

Copying and Erasing Configuration Files

If you reload the router at the end of Example 7-2, the hostname reverts to Hannah, because the running-config file has not been copied into the startup-config file. However, if you want to keep the new hostname of jessie, you would use the command **copy running-config startup-config**, which overwrites the current startup-config file with what is currently in the running configuration file. The **copy** command can be used to copy files in a router, most typically a configuration file or a new version of Cisco IOS Software. The most basic method for moving configuration files in and out of a router is to use the **copy** command to copy files between RAM or NVRAM on a router and a TFTP server. The files can be copied between any pair, as shown in Figure 7-12.

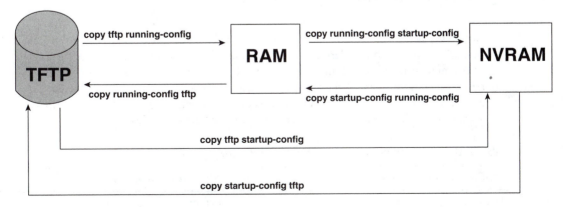

Figure 7-12 *Locations for Copying and Results from Copy Operations*

The commands for copying Cisco IOS configurations can be summarized as follows:

```
copy {tftp | running-config | startup-config} {tftp | running-config |
    startup-config}
```

The first set of parameters enclosed in braces ({}) is the "from" location; the next set of parameters is the "to" location.

The **copy** command always replaces the existing file when the file is copied into NVRAM or into a TFTP server. In other words, it acts as if the destination file was erased and the new file completely replaced the old one. However, when the **copy** command copies a configuration file into the running-config file in RAM, the configuration file in RAM is not replaced, but is merged instead. Effectively, any **copy** into RAM works just as if you entered the commands in the "from" configuration file in the order listed in the config file.

Who cares? Well, we do. If you change the running config and then decide that you want to revert to what's in the startup-config file, the result of the **copy startup-config running-config** command might not cause the two files to actually match. The only way to guarantee that the two configuration files match is to issue the **reload** command, which reloads, or reboots, the router, which erases RAM and then copies the startup-config into RAM as part of the reload process.

You can use three different commands to erase the contents of NVRAM. The **write erase** and **erase startup-config** commands are older, whereas the **erase nvram:** command is the more recent, and recommended, command. All three commands simply erase the contents of the NVRAM configuration file. Of course, if the router is reloaded at this point, there is no initial configuration. Note that Cisco IOS does not have a command that erases the contents of the running-config file. To clear out the running-config file, simply erase the startup-config file, and then **reload** the router.

Note: Making a copy of all current switch and router configurations should be part of any network's overall security strategy, mainly so that you can replace a device's configuration if an attack changes the configuration.

Although startup-config and running-config are the most common names for the two configuration files, Cisco IOS defines a few other more formalized names for these files. These more formalized filenames use a format defined by the *Cisco IOS File System (IFS)*, which is the name of the file system created by Cisco IOS to manage files. For example, the **copy** command can refer to the startup-config file as nvram:startup-config. Table 7-6 lists the alternative names for these two configuration files.

Table 7-6 *IFS Filenames for the Startup and Running Config Files*

Config File Common Name	Alternative Names
startup-config	nvram:
	nvram:startup-config
running-config	system:running-config

Chapter Review

Review Key Topics

Review the most important topics from this chapter, noted with the key topics icon. Table 7-7 lists these key topics and where each is discussed.

Table 7-7   *Key Topics for Chapter 7*

Key Topic Element	Description	Page Number
List	List of installation steps for a router	162
List	A Cisco router's default console port settings	167
Table 7-4	A list of configuration mode prompts, the name of the configuration mode, and the command used to reach each mode	176
Figure 7-11	Types of memory in a router	177
Table 7-5	The names and purposes of the two configuration files in a router or router	177

Define Key Terms

Define the following key terms from this chapter and check your answers in the glossary:

Command-line interface (CLI), Secure Shell (SSH), enable mode, user mode, configuration mode, startup-config file, running-config file, setup mode

Review Command References

Table 7-8 lists and briefly describes the configuration commands used in this chapter.

Table 7-8   *Chapter 7 Configuration Commands*

Command	Mode and Purpose
line console 0	Global command that changes the context to console configuration mode.
line vty 1st-vty 2nd-vty	Global command that changes the context to vty configuration mode for the range of vty lines listed in the command.
login	Line (console and vty) configuration mode. Tells IOS to prompt for a password (no username).

Table 7-8 *Chapter 7 Configuration Commands*

Command	Mode and Purpose
password pass-value	Line (console and vty) configuration mode. Lists the password required if the login command (with no other parameters) is configured.
interface type port-number	Global command that changes the context to interface mode—for example, **interface Fastethernet 0/1**.
shutdown no shutdown	Interface subcommand that disables or enables the interface, respectively.
hostname name	Global command that sets this router's hostname, which is also used as the first part of the router's command prompt.
enable secret pass-value	Global command that sets the automatically encrypted enable secret password. The password is used for any user to reach enable mode.
enable password pass-value	Global command that sets the clear-text enable password, which is used only when the enable secret password is not configured.
exit	Moves back to the next higher mode in configuration mode.
end	Exits configuration mode and goes back to enable mode from any of the configuration submodes.
Ctrl-Z	This is not a command, but rather a two-key combination (the Ctrl key and the letter z) that together do the same thing as the **end** command.

Table 7-9 lists and briefly describes the EXEC commands used in this chapter.

Table 7-9 *Chapter 7 EXEC Command Reference*

Command	Purpose
no debug all undebug all	Enable mode EXEC command to disable all currently enabled debugs.
show process	EXEC command that lists statistics about CPU utilization.
terminal monitor	EXEC command that tells Cisco IOS to send a copy of all syslog messages, including debug messages, to the Telnet or SSH user who issues this command.
reload	Enable mode EXEC command that reboots the router or switch.
copy from-location to-location	Enable mode EXEC command that copies files from one file location to another. Locations include the startup-config and running-config files, files on TFTP and RPC servers, and flash memory.
copy running-config startup-config	Enable mode EXEC command that saves the active config, replacing the startup-config file used when the router initializes.

Table 7-9 *Chapter 7 EXEC Command Reference*

Command	Purpose
copy startup-config running-config	Enable mode EXEC command that merges the startup config file with the currently active config file in RAM.
show running-config	Lists the contents of the running-config file.
write erase erase startup-config erase nvram:	All three enable mode EXEC commands erase the startup-config file.
setup	Enable mode EXEC command that places the user in setup mode, in which Cisco IOS asks the user for input on simple router configurations.
quit	EXEC command that disconnects the user from the CLI session.
show system: running-config	Same as the **show running-config** command.
show startup-config	Lists the contents of the startup-config (initial config) file.
show nvram: startup-config show nvram:	Same as the **show startup-config** command.
enable	Moves the user from user mode to enable (privileged) mode and prompts for an enable password if configured.
disable	Moves the user from enable mode to user mode.
configure terminal	Enable mode command that moves the user into configuration mode.

Answer Review Questions

Answer the following review questions:

1. Which of the following installation steps are typically required on a Cisco router, but not typically required on a Cisco switch?

   a. Connect Ethernet cables

   b. Connect serial cables

   c. Connect to the console port

   d. Connect the power cable

   e. Turn the on/off switch to "on"

2. Which of the following roles does a SOHO router typically play with regard to IP address assignment?

   a.   DHCP server on the interface connected to the ISP

   b.   DHCP server on the interface connected to the PCs at the home/office

   c.   DHCP client on the interface connected to the ISP

   d.   DHCP client on the interface connected to the PCs at the home/office

3. In what modes can you execute the **show mac-address-table** command?

   a.   User mode

   b.   Enable mode

   c.   Global configuration mode

   d.   Setup mode

   e.   Interface configuration mode

4. In which of the following modes of the CLI could you issue a command to reboot the switch?

   a.   User mode

   b.   Enable mode

   c.   Global configuration mode

   d.   Interface configuration mode

5. Which of the following is a difference between Telnet and SSH as supported by a Cisco switch?

   a.   SSH encrypts the passwords used at login, but not other traffic; Telnet encrypts nothing.

   b.   SSH encrypts all data exchange, including login passwords; Telnet encrypts nothing.

   c.   Telnet is used from Microsoft operating systems, and SSH is used from UNIX and Linux operating systems.

   d.   Telnet encrypts only password exchanges; SSH encrypts all data exchanges.

6. What type of switch memory is used to store the configuration used by the switch when it is up and working?

   a.   RAM

   b.   ROM

   c.   Flash

   d.   NVRAM

   e.   Bubble

7. What command copies the configuration from RAM into NVRAM?

   a. copy running-config tftp

   b. copy tftp running-config

   c. copy running-config start-up-config

   d. copy start-up-config running-config

   e. copy startup-config running-config

   f. copy running-config startup-config

8. A switch user is currently in console line configuration mode. Which of the following would place the user in enable mode?

   a. Using the **exit** command once

   b. Using the **exit** command twice in a row

   c. Pressing the Ctrl-z key sequence

   d. Using the **quit** command

This chapter covers the following subjects:

- **Analyze Needs:** This section looks at the first major step in creating a plan to implement IPv4 subnetting in an enterprise. In particular, this step examines the rules used to determine the required number of subnets and hosts/subnet, and the decision of whether to use one mask or many.

- **Make Design Choices:** This section explains the major subnet design choices: the classful network to use and the subnet mask to use. It also looks at the concept of then using that information to calculate a list of subnet numbers.

- **Plan the Implementation:** This short section lists some of the items you need to consider before you can implement the design.

CHAPTER 8

IP Subnetting

Even if you did not design the network that you work with, the better you understand the design of the network, the better you can operate the network. The process of monitoring any network requires that you continually answer the question: "Is the network working as designed?" If a problem exists, you must consider questions like "What happens when the network works normally—and what is different right now?" Both questions require you to understand the intended design of the network, including details of the IP addressing and subnetting design.

Today, a network engineer practically never has the opportunity to design a new internetwork from scratch. Instead, an engineer might make design changes to an existing internetwork and then implement those changes. However, to fully understand IP addressing and subnetting, you need to think about how to design the IP addressing and subnetting conventions for a completely new enterprise internetwork.

This chapter examines the design process and concepts as if you were designing a new network with no preexisting network. This chapter focuses on planning and design, with a brief mention of implementation tasks, as shown in Figure 8-1.

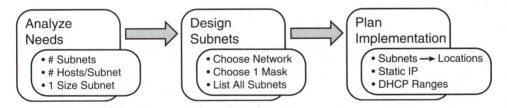

Figure 8-1 *Subnet Planning, Design, and Implementation Tasks*

Note: This chapter shows a subset of the functions included in the Cisco formal design process called PPDIOO: Prepare, Plan, Design, Implement, Operate, and Optimize.

The three main sections of this chapter examine each of the steps listed in Figure 8-1, in sequence, followed by some comments relative to the operational view of these same topics.

Analyze Needs

The following sections discuss the meaning of four basic questions that can be used to analyze the addressing and subnetting needs for any new or changing enterprise network:

1. Which hosts should be grouped together into a subnet?

2. How many subnets does this network require?

3. How many host IP addresses does each subnet require?

4. Will you use a single subnet size for simplicity, or not?

Rules About Which Hosts Are in Which Subnet

Every device that connects to an IP internetwork needs to have an IP address. These devices include computers used by end users, servers, mobile phones, laptops, IP phones, tablets, and networking devices like routers, switches, and firewalls. In short, any device that uses IP to send and receive packets needs an IP address.

> **Note:**   When discussing IP addressing, the term *network* has a specific meaning: a class A, B, or C IP network. To avoid confusion, in cases where the discussion includes references to class A, B, and C networks, this book uses the terms *internetwork* and *enterprise network* when referring to a collection of hosts, routers, switches, and so on.

The IP addresses must be assigned according to some basic rules, and for good reasons. To make routing work efficiently, IP addressing rules group addresses into groups called *subnets*. The rules are as follows:

Key Topic

■ Addresses in the same subnet are not separated by a router.

■ Addresses in different subnets are separated by at least one router.

Figure 8-2 shows the general concept, with hosts A and B in one subnet and host C in another. In particular, note that hosts A and B are not separated from each other by any routers. However, host C, separated from A and B by at least one router, must be in a different subnet.

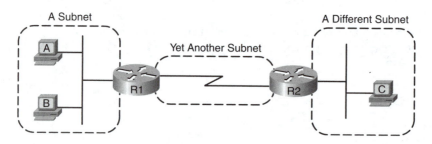

Figure 8-2   *PC A and B in One Subnet, and PC C in a Different Subnet*

The idea that hosts on the same link must be in the same subnet is much like the postal code concept. All mailing addresses in the same town use the same postal code, like the zip code in the United States. Addresses in another town, whether relatively nearby or on the other side of the country, have a different postal code. The postal code gives the postal service a better ability to automatically sort the mail to deliver it to the right location. For the same general reasons, hosts on the same LAN are in the same subnet, and hosts in different LANs are in different subnets.

Note that the point-to-point WAN link in the figure also needs a subnet. Figure 8-2 shows Router R1 connected to the LAN subnet on the left and to a WAN subnet on the right. Router R2 connects to that same WAN subnet. To do so, both R1 and R2 will have IP addresses on their WAN interfaces in this small internetwork, and the addresses will be in the same subnet.

Finally, because the routers' main job is to forward packets from one subnet to another, routers typically connect to multiple subnets. For example, in this case, Router R1 connects to one LAN subnet on the left and one WAN subnet on the right. To do so, R1 will be configured with two different IP addresses, one per interface. These addresses will be in different subnets, because the interfaces connect the router to different subnets.

Determining the Number of Subnets

To determine the number of subnets required, the engineer must think about the internetwork as documented and apply the following rules. To do so, the engineer requires access to network diagrams, VLAN configuration details, and if you use Frame Relay WANs, details about the Permanent Virtual Circuits (PVC). Based on this info, you should use these rules and plan for one subnet for every

■   VLAN

■   Point-to-point serial link

■   Frame Relay PVC

Note: Frame Relay allows other options for subnetting besides one subnet per PVC, but to keep the focus on subnetting in this chapter, assume one subnet per PVC.

For example, imagine that the network planner has only a single diagram on which to base the subnet design (see Figure 8-3).

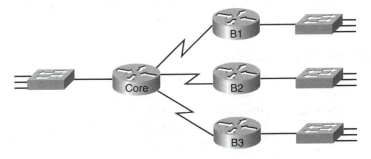

Figure 8-3   *Four-Site Internetwork with Small Central Site*

The number of subnets required cannot be fully predicted with only this figure. Certainly, three subnets will be needed for the WAN links, one per link. However, each LAN switch can be configured with a single VLAN or with multiple VLANs. You can be certain that you need at least one subnet for the LAN at each site, but you might need more.

Next, consider the more detailed version of the same figure shown in Figure 8-4. In this case, the figure still shows VLAN counts in addition to the same Layer 3 topology (the routers and the links connected to the routers). It also shows that the central site has many more switches, but the key fact on the left, regardless of how many switches exist, is that the central site has a total of 12 VLANs. Similarly, the figure lists each branch as having two VLANs. Along with the same three WAN subnets, this internetwork requires 21 subnets.

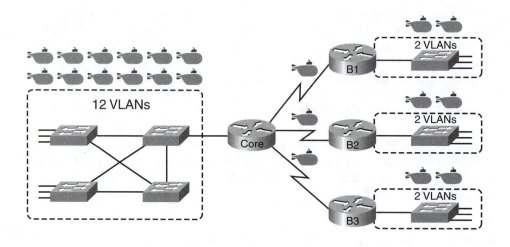

Legend:

 - Subnet

Figure 8-4   *Four-Site Internetwork with Larger Central Site*

Finally, in a real job, you would consider the needs today as well as how much growth you expect in the internetwork over time. Any subnetting plan should include a reasonable estimate of the number of subnets you need to meet future needs.

Determining the Number of Hosts per Subnet

Determining the number of hosts per subnet requires knowing a few simple concepts and then doing a lot of research and questioning. Every device that connects to a subnet needs an IP address. For a totally new network, you can look at business plans—numbers of people at the site, devices on order, and so on—to get some idea of the possible devices.

When expanding an existing network to add new sites, you can use existing sites as a point of comparison and then find out which sites will get bigger or smaller. And don't forget to count the router interface IP address in each subnet and the switch IP address used to remotely manage the switch.

Instead of gathering data for every site, planners often just use a few typical sites for planning purposes. For example, maybe you have some large sales offices and some small sales offices. You might dig in and learn a lot about only one large sales office and only one small sales office. Add that analysis to the fact that point-to-point links need a subnet with just two addresses, plus any analysis of more one-of-a-kind subnets, like some at the main site for the network, and you have enough information to plan the addressing and subnetting design.

For example, in Figure 8-5, the engineer has built a diagram that shows the number of hosts per LAN subnet in the largest branch, B1. For the two other branches, the engineer did not bother to dig to find out the number of required hosts. As long as the number of required IP addresses at sites B2 and B3 stays below the estimate of 50, based on site B1, the engineer can plan for 50 hosts in each branch LAN subnet and have plenty of addresses per subnet.

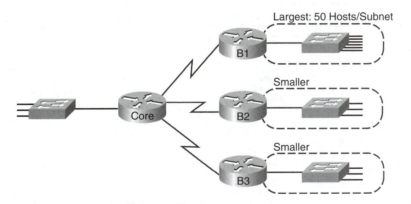

Figure 8-5 *Large Branch B1 with 50 Hosts/Subnet*

One Size Subnet Fits All—or Not

The final choice in the initial planning step is to decide whether you will use a simpler design by using a one-size-subnet-fits-all philosophy. A subnet's size, or length, is simply the number of usable IP addresses in the subnet. A subnetting design can either use one size subnet, or varied sizes of subnets, with pros and cons for each choice.

Defining the Size of a Subnet

The subnet mask used for a subnet defines the size of that subnet. The subnet mask, along with the class of the network, defines the number of network, subnet, and host bits in the design of that one subnet.

The size of a subnet is defined by the number of host bits, which is implied by the mask. The host bits provide binary digits (bits) with which to number different host IP addresses.

Because you can number 2^x things with x binary digits, each subnet contains 2^H different numeric values in the host bits of the addresses (H = the number of host bits).

However, the exact size of every subnet, no matter the mask or network, is a power of 2, *minus 2*. Each subnet includes 2^H numbers, with H being the number of host bits in the mask. Of those 2^H numbers, each subnet reserves the numerically lowest value for the *subnet number* and the numerically highest value as the *subnet broadcast address*. As a result, the number of usable IP addresses per subnet is $2^H - 2$.

Note: The terms *subnet number*, *subnet ID*, and *subnet address* all refer to the number that represents or identifies a subnet.

Figure 8-6 shows the concept behind the host bits in a subnet mask, the size of a subnet, and the reserved values in a subnet.

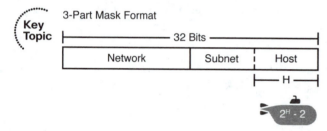

Figure 8-6   *Subnet Size Concepts*

One Size Subnet Fits All

To choose to use a single-size subnet in a network, you must use the same mask for all subnets, because the mask defines the size of the subnet. But which mask?

One requirement to consider when choosing that one mask is the following: That one mask must provide enough host IP addresses to support the largest subnet. To do so, the number of host bits (H) defined by the mask must be large enough so that $2^H - 2$ is larger than (or equal to) the number of host IP addresses required in the largest subnet.

For example, consider Figure 8-7. It shows the required number of hosts per LAN subnet, ignoring the serial links. The branch subnets require only 50 host addresses, but the main site subnet requires 200 host addresses. To accommodate the largest subnet, you need at least 8 host bits. Seven host bits would not be enough, because $2^7 = 126$. Eight host bits would be enough, because $2^8 - 2 = 254$, which is more than enough to support 200 hosts in a subnet.

Note: A binary mask with 8 binary 0s at the end defines the concept that 8 host bits exist, which in turn supplies $2^8 - 2 = 254$ hosts per subnet. The upcoming section "Choosing Enough Subnet and Host Bits" defines more details about this concept.

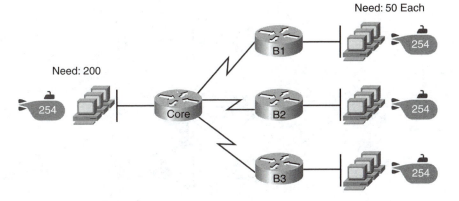

Figure 8-7   *Network Using One Subnet Size*

What is the big advantage when using a single-size subnet? Operational simplicity—in other words, keeping it simple. Everyone on the IT staff who has to work with networking can get used to working with one mask and one mask only. The staff will be able to answer all the subnetting questions discussed in this book—finding the subnet ID, finding the range of addresses in a subnet, determining the number of hosts in a subnet, and so on—much more consistently than if the masks varied from subnet to subnet.

The big disadvantage for using a single-size subnet is that it wastes IP addresses. For example, in Figure 8-7, all the branch LAN subnets support 254 addresses, whereas the largest branch subnet needs only 50 addresses. The WAN subnets need only two IP addresses, but each supports 254 addresses, again wasting more IP addresses.

The wasted IP addresses do not actually cause a problem in most cases, however. Most organizations use private IP networks in their enterprise internetworks, and a single class A or class B private network can supply plenty of IP addresses, even with the waste.

Multiple Subnet Sizes (Variable-Length Subnet Masks)

To create multiple sizes of subnets in one class A, B, or C network, the engineer must create some subnets using one mask, some with another, and so on. Different masks means different numbers of host bits, making the $2^H - 2$ formula create a different number of hosts in each subnet.

For example, consider the requirements listed earlier in Figure 8-7. It showed one LAN subnet on the left that needs 200 host addresses, three branch subnets that need 50 addresses, and three serial links that need two addresses. To meet those needs, but waste fewer IP addresses, three subnet masks could be used, creating subnets of three different sizes, as shown in Figure 8-8.

The smaller subnets now waste fewer IP addresses compared to the design seen earlier in Figure 8-7. The subnets on the right that need 50 IP addresses have subnets with six host bits, for $2^6 - 2 = 62$ available addresses per subnet. The WAN links use masks with two host bits, for $2^2 - 2 = 2$ available addresses per subnet.

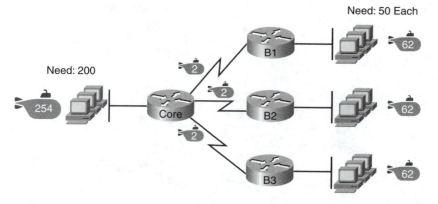

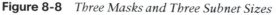

Figure 8-8   *Three Masks and Three Subnet Sizes*

However, some are still wasted, because you cannot set the size of the subnet as some arbitrary size. All subnets will be a size based on the $2^H – 2$ formula, with H being the number of host bits defined by the mask for each subnet.

This Book: One Size Subnet Fits All

Most of this book explains subnetting with the understanding that inside a single classful IP network, the designer chooses to use a single mask, creating a single subnet size for all subnets. Why? First, it makes the process of learning subnetting easier. Second, some types of analysis that you can do about a network—specifically, calculating the number of subnets in the classful network—only make sense when a single mask is used. So most of this book focuses on examples and descriptions using the assumption of a single mask in each classful IP network.

Later in this book, Chapter 19, "VLSM and Route Summarization," examines the use of *variable-length subnet masks (VLSM)*. VLSM refers to the practice of using different masks for different subnets in the same classful IP network.

Make Design Choices

Now that you know how to analyze the IP addressing and subnetting needs, the next major step examines how to apply the rules of IP addressing and subnetting to those needs and make some choices. In other words, now that you know how many subnets you need, and how many host addresses you need in the largest subnet, how do you create a useful subnetting design that meets those requirements? The short answer is that you need to do the three tasks shown on the right side of Figure 8-9.

Choose a Classful Network

In the original design for what we know of today as the Internet, companies used registered *public classful IP networks* when implementing TCP/IP inside the company. By the mid-1990s, an alternative became more popular: *private IP networks*. The following sections discuss the background behind these two choices, because they impact the choice of what IP network that a company will then subnet and implement in its enterprise internetwork.

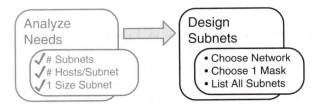

Figure 8-9   *Input to the Design Phase and Design Questions to Answer*

Public IP Networks

The original design of the Internet required that any company that connected to the Internet had to use a *registered public IP network*. To do so, the company would complete some paperwork describing the enterprise's internetwork and the number of hosts existing, plus plans for growth. After submitting the paperwork, the company would receive assignment of either a class A, B, or C network that only that one company was allowed to use.

Public IP networks, and the administrative processes surrounding them, ensure that all the companies that connect to the Internet all use unique IP addresses. In particular, after a public IP network has been assigned to a company, only that company should use the addresses in that network. That guarantee of uniqueness means that Internet routing can work well, because there are no duplicate public IP addresses.

For example, consider the example shown in Figure 8-10. Company 1 has been assigned public class A network 1.0.0.0, and Company 2 has been assigned public class A network 2.0.0.0. Per the original intent for public addressing in the Internet, after these public network assignments have been made, no other companies can use addresses in class A networks 1.0.0.0 or 2.0.0.0.

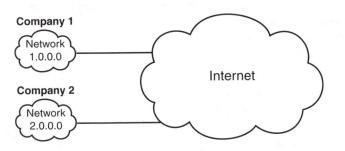

Figure 8-10   *Two Companies with Unique Public IP Networks*

This original address assignment process ensured unique IP addresses across the entire planet. The idea is much like the fact that your telephone number should be unique in the universe, your postal mailing address should also be unique, and your email address should be unique as well. If someone calls you, your phone rings—but no one else's phone rings. Similarly, if Company 1 is assigned class A network 1.0.0.0, and it assigns address 1.1.1.1 to a particular PC, that address should be unique in the universe. A packet sent through the Internet, to destination 1.1.1.1, should arrive only at this one PC inside Company 1, instead of being delivered to some other host.

Growth Exhausts the Public IP Address Space

By the early 1990s, the world was running out of public IP networks that could be assigned. During most of the 1990s, the number of hosts newly connected to the Internet was growing at a double-digit pace, *per month*. Companies kept following the rules, asking for public IP networks, and it was clear that the current address assignment scheme could not continue without some changes. Simply put, the number of class A, B, and C networks supported by the 32-bit addresses in IP version 4 (IPv4) was not enough to support one public classful network per organization, while also providing enough IP addresses in each company.

From one perspective, the universe ran out of IPv4 addresses in early 2011. The Internet Assigned Numbers Authority (IANA), which assigns address blocks to the five Internet registries around the globe, assigned the last of the IPv4 address spaces in early 2011.

The Internet community worked hard during the 1990s to solve this problem, coming up with several solutions, including

■   A new version of IP (IP version 6, or IPv6), with much larger addresses (128-bit)

■   Assigning a subset of a public IP network to each company, instead of an entire public IP network, to reduce waste

■   Network Address Translation (NAT), which allows the use of private IP networks

All of these three solutions matter to real networks today. However, to stay focused on the topic of subnet design, this chapter focuses on the third option, and in particular, the private IP networks that can be used by an enterprise when also using NAT.

NAT allows multiple companies to use the same *private IP networks*, using the same IP addresses as other companies, while still connecting to the Internet. For example, Figure 8-11 shows the same two companies connecting to the Internet as in Figure 8-10, but now with both using the same private class A network of 10.0.0.0.

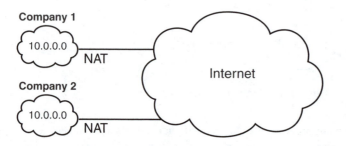

Figure 8-11   *Reusing the Same Private Network 10.0.0.0 with NAT*

Both companies use the same classful IP network (10.0.0.0). Both companies can implement their subnet design internal to their respective networks, without talking to each other. The two companies can even using the same IP addresses inside network 10.0.0.0.

And amazingly, at the same time, both companies can even communicate with each other through the Internet.

The technology called Network Address Translation (NAT) makes it possible for companies to reuse the same IP networks, as shown in Figure 8-11. NAT does this by translating the IP addresses inside the packets as they go from the enterprise to the Internet, using a small number of public IP addresses to support tens of thousands of private IP addresses.

That one bit of information is not enough to understand how NAT works. However, this chapter keeps the focus on IP addressing and subnetting inside the enterprise, with NAT being left outside the scope of the book. For now, accept that most companies use NAT and therefore can use private IP networks for their internetworks.

Private IP Networks

RFC 1918 defines the set of private IP networks, as listed in Table 8-1. By definition, these private IP networks

■   Will never be assigned to an organization as a public IP network

■   Can be used by organizations that will use NAT when sending packets into the Internet

■   Can also be used by organizations that never need to send packets into the Internet

So, when using NAT—and almost every organization that connects to the Internet uses NAT—the company can simple pick one or more of the private IP networks from the list of reserved private IP network numbers. RFC 1918 defines the list, as summarized in Table 8-1.

Table 8-1   *RFC 1918 Private Address Space*

Private IP Networks	Class of Networks	Number of Networks
10.0.0.0	A	1
172.16.0.0 through 172.31.0.0	B	16
192.168.0.0 through 192.168.255.0	C	256

Note: According to an informal survey I ran in my blog back in late 2010, about half of the respondents said that their networks use private class A network 10.0.0.0, as opposed to other private networks or public networks.

Choosing an IP Network During the Design Phase

Today, some organizations use private IP networks along with NAT, and some use public IP networks. Most new enterprise internetworks use private IP addresses throughout the network along with NAT as part of the connection to the Internet. Those organizations that already have a registered public IP network—often obtained before the addresses started running short in the early 1990s—can continue to use those public addresses throughout their enterprise networks.

After the choice to use a private IP network has been made, just pick one that has enough IP addresses. You can have a small internetwork and still choose to use private class A network 10.0.0.0. It might seem wasteful to choose a class A network that has over 16 million IP addresses, especially if you need only a few hundred. However, there's no penalty or problem with using a private network that is too large for your current or future needs.

For the purposes of this book, most examples use private IP network numbers. For the design step to choose a network number, just choose a private class A, B, or C network from the list of RFC 1918 private networks.

Regardless, from a math and concept perspective, the methods to subnet a public IP network versus a private IP network are the same.

Choose the Mask

If a design engineer followed the topics in this chapter so far, in order, he or she would know

- The number of subnets required

- The number of hosts/subnet required

- That a choice was made to use only one mask for all subnets so that all subnets are the same size (same number of hosts/subnet)

- The classful IP network number that will be subnetted

The following sections complete the design process, at least the parts described in this chapter, by discussing how to choose that one mask to use for all subnets. First, these sections examine default masks, used when a network is not subnetted, as a point of comparison. Next, the concept of borrowing host bits to create subnet bits is explored. Finally, these sections end with an example of how to create a subnet mask based on the analysis of the requirements.

IP Networks Before Subnetting

Before an engineer subnets a classful network, the network is a single group of addresses. In other words, the engineer has not yet subdivided the network into many smaller subsets called *subnets*.

When thinking about an unsubnetted classful network, the addresses in a network have only two parts: the network part and host part. Comparing any two addresses in the classful network

- The addresses have the same value in the network part.

- The addresses have different values in the host part.

The actual sizes of the network and host part of the addresses in a network can be easily predicted, as shown in Figure 8-12.

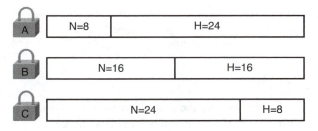

Figure 8-12 *Format of Unsubnetted Class A, B, and C Networks*

In the figure, N and H represent the number of network and host bits, respectively. Class rules define the number of network octets (1, 2, or 3) for classes A, B, and C, respectively. The number of host octets is 3, 2, or 1, respectively.

Continuing the analysis of classful network before subnetting, the number of addresses in the network can be calculated with the same $2^H - 2$ formula discussed earlier in this chapter. In particular, the size of an unsubnetted class A, B, or C network is as follows:

- Class A: $2^{24} - 2 = 16,777,214$

- Class B: $2^{16} - 2 = 65,534$

- Class C: $2^8 - 2 = 254$

Borrowing Host Bits to Create Subnet Bits

To subnet a network, the designer thinks about the network and host parts, as shown in Figure 8-12, and then the engineer adds a third part in the middle: the subnet part. However, the designer cannot change the size of the network part or the size of the entire address (32 bits). To create a subnet part of the address structure, the engineer borrows bits from the host part. Figure 8-13 shows the general idea.

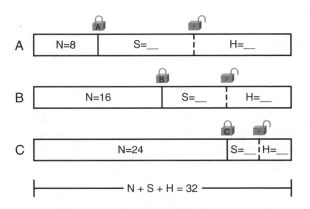

Figure 8-13 *Concept of Borrowing Host Bits*

The figure shows a rectangle that represents the subnet mask. N, representing the number of network bits, remains locked at 8, 16, or 24, depending on the class. Conceptually, the designer moves a (dashed) dividing line into the host field, with subnet bits (S) between the network and host parts, and the remaining host bits (H) on the right. The three parts must add up to 32, because IPv4 addresses consist of 32 bits.

Choosing Enough Subnet and Host Bits

The design process requires a choice of where to place the dashed line shown in Figure 8-13. But what is the right choice? How many subnet and host bits should the designer choose? The answers hinge on the requirements gathered in the early stages of the planning process:

- The number of subnets required

- The number of hosts/subnet

The bits in the subnet part create a way to uniquely number the different subnets that the design engineer wants to create. With 1 subnet bit, you can number 2^1 or 2 subnets. With 2 bits, 2^2 or 4 subnets, with 3 bits, 2^3 or 8 subnets, and so on. The number of subnet bits must be large enough to uniquely number all the subnets, as determined during the planning process.

At the same time, the remaining number of host bits must also be large enough to number the host IP addresses in the largest subnet. Remember, in this chapter, I assume the use of a single mask for all subnets. This single mask must support both the required number of subnets and the required number of hosts in the largest subnet. Figure 8-14 shows the concept.

Key Topic

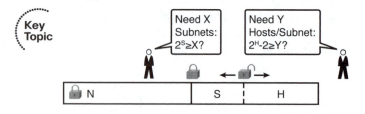

Figure 8-14   *Borrowing Enough Subnet and Host Bits*

The figure shows the idea of the designer choosing a number of subnet (S) and host (H) bits, and then checking the math. 2^S must be more than the number of required subnets, or the mask will not supply enough subnets in this IP network. Also, $2^H - 2$ must be more than the required number of hosts/subnet.

Note: The idea of calculating the number of subnets as 2^S applies only in cases where a single mask is used for all subnets of a single classful network, as is being assumed in this chapter.

To effectively design masks, or to interpret masks that were chosen by someone else, you need a good working memory of the powers of 2. Table 8-2 lists the powers of 2 up through 2^{12}, along with a column with $2^H - 2$, for perspective when calculating the number of hosts/subnet. Appendix B, "IP Access Control Lists," lists a table with powers of 2 up through 2^{24} for reference.

Table 8-2 *Powers of 2 Reference for Designing Masks*

Number of Bits	2^x	$2^H - 2$
1	2	0
2	4	2
3	8	6
4	16	14
5	32	30
6	64	62
7	128	126
8	256	254
9	512	510
10	1024	1022
11	2048	2046
12	4096	4094

Example Design: 172.16.0.0, 200 Subnets, and 200 Hosts

To help make sense of the theoretical discussion so far, next consider an example that focuses on the design choice for the subnet mask. In this case, the planning and design choices so far tell us to

■ Use a single mask for all subnets.

■ Plan for 200 subnets.

■ Plan for 200 host IP addresses/subnet.

■ Use a private class B network 172.16.0.0.

To choose the mask, the designer then asks this question:

How many subnet (S) bits do I need to number 200 subnets?

From Table 8-2, you can see that S=7 is not large enough (2^7 = 128), but S=8 is enough (2^8 = 256). So, you need at least 8 subnet bits.

Next, the designer asks a similar question, based on the number of hosts per subnet:

How many host (H) bits do I need to number 200 hosts/subnet?

The math is basically the same, but the formula subtracts 2 when counting the number of hosts/subnet. From Table 8-2, you can see that H=7 is not large enough ($2^7 - 2 = 126$), but H=8 is enough ($2^8 - 2 = 254$). Figure 8-15 shows the resulting mask.

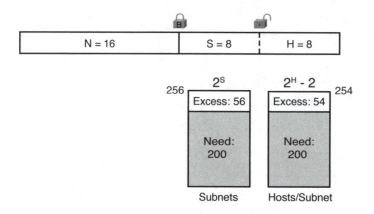

Figure 8-15 *Example Mask Choice: S=8, H=8*

Masks and Mask Formats

Although engineers think about IP addresses in three parts (network, subnet, and host), when making design choices, the subnet mask gives the engineer a way to communicate those design choices to all the devices in the network.

The subnet mask is a 32-bit binary number with a number of binary 1s on the left and with binary 0s on the right. By definition, the number of binary 0s equals the number of host bits. In fact, that is exactly how the mask communicates the idea of the size of the host part of the addresses in a subnet. The beginning bits in the mask equal binary 1, with those bit positions representing the combined network and subnet parts of the addresses in the subnet.

Because the network part always comes first, then the subnet part, and then the host part, the subnet mask, in binary form, cannot have interleaved 1s and 0s. Each subnet mask has one unbroken string of binary 1s on the left, with the rest of the bits as binary 0s.

After the engineer has chosen the classful network and has chosen the number of subnet and host bits in a subnet, creating the binary subnet mask is easy. Just write down N 1s, S 1s, and then H 0s (assuming that N, S, and H represent the number of network, subnet, and host bits). Figure 8-16 shows the mask based on the previous example, which subnets a class B network by creating 8 subnet bits, leaving 8 host bits.

In addition to the binary mask shown in Figure 8-16, masks can also be written in two other formats: the familiar *dotted decimal notation (DDN)* seen in IP addresses and an even briefer *prefix* notation. Chapter 9, "Subnet Mask Conversion," discusses these formats, and more importantly, how to convert between the different formats.

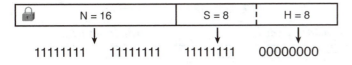

Figure 8-16 *Creating the Subnet Mask—Binary—Class B Network*

Build a List of All Subnets

This final task of the subnet design step determines the actual subnets that can be used, based on all the earlier choices. The earlier design work determined the class A, B, or C network to use, and the (one) subnet mask to use that supplies enough subnets and enough host IP addresses per subnet. But what are those subnets? How do you identify or describe a subnet? This section answers these questions.

A subnet consists of a group of consecutive numbers. Most of these numbers can be used as IP addresses by hosts. However, each subnet reserves the first and last numbers in the group, so these two numbers cannot be used as IP addresses. In particular, each subnet contains the following:

- **Subnet number:** Also called the *subnet ID*, or *subnet address*, this number is used to identify the subnet. It is the numerically smallest number in the subnet. It cannot be used as an IP address by a host.

- **Subnet broadcast:** Also called the *subnet broadcast address*, or *directed broadcast address*, this is the last (numerically highest) number in the subnet. It also cannot be used as an IP address by a host.

- **IP addresses:** All the numbers between the subnet ID and the subnet broadcast address can be used as a host IP address.

For example, consider the earlier case in which the design results were as follows:

Network: 172.16.0.0 (Class B)

Mask: 255.255.255.0 (for all subnets)

With some math, the four facts about each subnet that exists in this network can be calculated. In this case, Table 8-3 shows the first ten such subnets. It then skips many subnets and shows the last two (numerically largest) subnets.

Table 8-3 *Subnets of Network 172.16.0.0, Mask 255.255.255.0, Abbreviated*

Subnet Number	IP Addresses	Broadcast Address
172.16.0.0	172.16.0.1–172.16.0.254	172.16.0.255
172.16.1.0	172.16.1.1–172.16.1.254	172.16.1.255
172.16.2.0	172.16.2.1–172.16.2.254	172.16.2.255
172.16.3.0	172.16.3.1–172.16.3.254	172.16.3.255
172.16.4.0	172.16.4.1–172.16.4.254	172.16.4.255
172.16.5.0	172.16.5.1–172.16.5.254	172.16.5.255

Table 8-3   *Subnets of Network 172.16.0.0, Mask 255.255.255.0, Abbreviated*

Subnet Number	IP Addresses	Broadcast Address
172.16.6.0	172.16.6.1–172.16.6.254	172.16.6.255
172.16.7.0	172.16.7.1–172.16.7.254	172.16.7.255
172.16.8.0	172.16.8.1–172.16.8.254	172.16.8.255
172.16.9.0	172.16.9.1–172.16.9.254	172.16.9.255
Skipping many...		
172.16.254.0	172.16.254.1–172.16.254.254	172.16.254.255
172.16.255.0	172.16.255.1–172.16.255.254	172.16.255.255

Calculating the subnet IDs and other details for all subnets, after you have the network number and the mask, requires some math. In real life, most people use subnet calculators or subnet planning tools. Even if you use a calculator, you should be able to make the calculations yourself. Chapter 13, "Analyze Existing Subnets," shows how to find all subnets of a given network.

Plan the Implementation

The next step, planning the implementation, is the last step before actually configuring the devices to create a subnet. The engineer first needs to choose where to use each subnet. For example, at a branch office in a particular city, which subnet from the subnet planning chart, as seen in Table 8-3, should be used for each VLAN at that site? Also, for any IP addresses that require static IP addresses, which addresses should be used in each case? Finally, what range from inside each subnet should be configured in the DHCP server to be dynamically leased to hosts for use as their IP address? Figure 8-17 summarizes the list of implementation planning tasks.

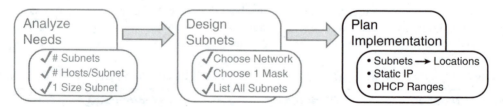

Figure 8-17   *Facts Supplied to the Plan Implementation Step*

The implementation planning document details these and other specific choices. After they are completed, the engineer has enough information to configure IP addresses on all devices with static IP addresses, DHCP address ranges on all DHCP servers, and to complete the implementation of IP addresses in the internetwork. This chapter does not examine this step any further, deferring these discussions for later chapters in which the commands used to configure IP addresses and DHCP services are discussed.

Chapter Review

Review Key Topics

Review the most important topics from this chapter, noted with the Key Topic icon. Table 8-4 lists these key topics and indicates where each is discussed.

Table 8-4   *Key Topics for Chapter 8*

Key Topic Element	Description	Page Number
List	Key facts about subnets	188
List	Rules about what places in a network topology need a subnet	189
Figure 8-6	Locations of the network, subnet, and host parts of an IPv4 address	192
List	Features that extended the life of IPv4	196
Figure 8-13	Formats of class A, B, and C addresses when subnetted	199
Figure 8-14	General logic when choosing the size of the subnet and host parts of addresses in a subnet	200
List	Items that together define a subnet	203

Define Key Terms

Define the following key terms from this chapter, and check your answers in the glossary:

Subnet, network, classful network, variable-length subnet masks, network part, subnet part, host part, public IP network, private IP network, subnet mask

Answer Review Questions

Answer the following review questions:

1. Host A is a PC, connected to switch SW1, and assigned to VLAN 1. Which of the following are typically assigned an IP address in the same subnet as host A? (Select two.)

   a. The local router's WAN interface

   b. The local router's LAN interface

   c. All other hosts attached to the same switch

   d. Other hosts attached to the same switch and also in VLAN 1

2. Why does the formula for the number of hosts per subnet ($2^H - 2$) require the subtraction of two hosts?

   a. To reserve two addresses for redundant default gateways (routers)

   b. To reserve the two addresses required for DHCP operation

   c. To reserve addresses for the subnet ID and default gateway (router)

   d. To reserve addresses for the subnet broadcast address and subnet ID

3. A class B network needs to be subnetted so that it supports 100 subnets and 100 hosts/subnet. Which of the following answers list a workable combination for the number of networks, subnets, and host bits? (Select two.)

   a. Network = 16, subnet = 7, host = 7

   b. Network = 16, subnet = 8, host = 8

   c. Network = 16, subnet = 9, host = 7

   d. Network = 8, subnet = 7, host = 17

4. Which of the following are private IP networks? (Select two.)

   a. 172.31.0.0

   b. 172.32.0.0

   c. 192.168.255.0

   d. 192.1.168.0

   e. 11.0.0.0

5. Which of the following are public IP networks? (Select three.)

   a. 9.0.0.0

   b. 172.30.0.0

   c. 192.168.255.0

   d. 192.1.168.0

   e. 11.0.0.0

6. Before class B network 172.16.0.0 is subnetted by a network engineer, what parts of the structure of the IP addresses in this network already exist, with a specific size? (Select two.)

   a. Network

   b. Subnet

   c. Host

   d. Broadcast

7. A network engineer spends time thinking about the entire class B network 172.16.0.0 and how to subnet that network. He then chooses how to subnet this class B network and creates an addressing and subnetting plan, on paper, showing his choices. If you compare his thoughts about this network before subnetting the network to his thoughts about this network after mentally subnetting the network, which of the following occurred to the parts of the structure of addresses in this network?

    a. The subnet part got smaller.

    b. The host part got smaller.

    c. The network part got smaller.

    d. The host part was removed.

    e. The network part was removed.

8. Which of the following terms is *not* used to reference the one number in each subnet used to uniquely identify the subnet? (Select two.)

    a. Subnet ID

    b. Subnet number

    c. Subnet broadcast

    d. Subnet name

    e. Subnet address

This chapter covers the following subjects:

- **Subnet Mask Conversion:** This section explains how to convert subnet masks between the three formats: binary, dotted decimal, and prefix.

- **Practice Converting Subnet Masks:** This section provides practices problems and tips for converting between the three subnet mask formats.

CHAPTER 9

Subnet Mask Conversion

Subnet masks serve many very important roles in the world of IPv4 addressing and subnetting. However, this chapter ignores those roles. Instead, this chapter focuses on the numbers used as subnet masks, with the focus on the three different formats for subnet masks:

■ Binary

■ Dotted decimal notation (DDN)

■ Prefix (also called classless interdomain routing [CIDR])

This chapter focuses on the numbers, and converting between the three different numbering formats, so that in later chapters, you can work with the masks without the math getting in the way.

Subnet Mask Conversion

The following sections describe how to convert between different formats for the subnet mask. You can then use these processes when you practice. If you already know how to convert from one format to the other, move ahead to the section "Practice Converting Subnet Masks."

The Three Mask Formats

Subnet masks can be written as 32-bit binary numbers—but not just any binary number. In particular, the binary subnet mask must follow these rules:

■ The value must not interleave 1s and 0s.

Key Topic

■ If 1s exist, they are on the left.

■ If 0s exist, they are on the right.

For example, the following values would be illegal. The first is illegal because the value interleaves 0s and 1s, and the second is illegal because it lists 0s on the left and 1s on the right:

    10101010 01010101 11110000 00001111
    00000000 00000000 00000000 11111111

The following two binary values meet the requirements, in that they have all 1s on the left, followed by all 0s, with no interleaving of 1s and 0s:

    11111111 00000000 00000000 00000000
    11111111 11111111 11111111 00000000

Two alternate subnet mask formats exist so that we humans do not have to work with 32-bit binary numbers. One format, *dotted decimal notation (DDN)*, converts each set of 8 bits into the decimal equivalent. For example, the two previous sample valid binary masks would convert to the following DDN subnet masks, because binary 11111111 converts to decimal 255 and binary 00000000 converts to decimal 0:

255.0.0.0

255.255.255.0

Although the DDN format has been around since the beginning of IPv4 addressing, the third mask format was added later, in the early 1990s: the *prefix* format. The prefix format takes advantage of the rule that the subnet mask starts with some number of 1s, and then the rest of the digits are 0s. Prefix format lists a slash (/) followed by the number of binary 1s in the binary mask. Using the same two examples as shown earlier in this section, the prefix format equivalent masks are as follows:

/8

/24

Note that while the terms *prefix* or *prefix mask* can be used, the terms *CIDR mask* or *slash mask* can also be used. This newer prefix style mask was created around the same time as the *classless interdomain routing (CIDR)* specification back in the early 1990s, and the acronym CIDR grew to be used for anything related to CIDR, including prefix-style masks. Additionally, the term *slash mask* is sometimes used because the value includes a slash mark (/).

The rest of these sections examine how to convert between the three formats.

Converting Between Binary and Prefix Masks

Converting between binary and prefix masks should be relatively intuitive after you know that the prefix value is simply the number of binary 1s in the binary mask. For the sake of completeness, the processes to convert in each direction are as follows:

Key Topic

- **Binary to prefix:** Count the number of binary 1s in the binary mask, and write the total, in decimal, after a slash (/).

- **Prefix to binary:** Write P binary 1s, where P is the prefix value, followed by as many binary 0s as required to create a 32-bit number.

Tables 9-1 and 9-2 show some examples.

Table 9-1   *Example Conversions—Binary to Prefix*

Binary Mask	Logic	Prefix Mask
11111111 11111111 11000000 00000000	Count 8 + 8 + 2 = 18 binary 1s	/18
11111111 11111111 11111111 11110000	Count 8 + 8 + 8 + 4 = 28 binary 1s	/28
11111111 11111000 00000000 00000000	Count 8 + 5 = 13 binary 1s	/13

Table 9-2 *Example Conversions—Prefix to Binary*

Prefix Mask	Logic	Binary Mask
/18	Write 18 1s, then 14 0s, total 32	11111111 11111111 11000000 00000000
/28	Write 28 1s, then 4 0s, total 32	11111111 11111111 11111111 11110000
/13	Write 13 1s, then 19 0s, total 32	11111111 11111000 00000000 00000000

Converting Between Binary and DDN Masks

By definition, a *dotted decimal number (DDN)* used with IPv4 addressing contains four decimal numbers, separated by dots. Each decimal number represents 8 bits. So, a single DDN shows four decimal numbers that together represent a 32-bit binary number.

Conversion from a DDN mask to the binary equivalent is relatively simple to describe but can be laborious to perform. First, to do the conversion, the process is as follows:

For each octet, perform a decimal-to-binary conversion.

However, depending on your comfort with doing decimal-to-binary conversions, that process can be difficult or time-consuming. If you want to think about masks in binary for the exam, consider picking one of the following methods to do the conversion and practicing until you can do it quickly and accurately:

- Do the decimal-binary conversions, but practice your decimal-binary conversions to get fast. If you choose this path, consider using the Cisco Binary Game, which you can find by searching on its name at the CLN (Cisco Learning Network), at https://learningnetwork.cisco.com.

- Use the decimal-binary conversion chart in Appendix A, "Numeric Reference Tables." This lets you find the answer more quickly now, but you might not be allowed to refer to any such tables during tests.

- Memorize the nine possible decimal values that can be in a decimal mask, and practice using a reference table with those values.

The third method—which is the method recommended in this book—takes advantage of the fact that any and every decimal mask octet must be one of only nine values. Why?

Key Topic

Well, remember how a binary mask cannot interleave 1s and 0s, and the 0s must be on the right? It turns out that only nine different 8-bit binary numbers conform to these rules. Table 9-3 lists the values, along with other relevant information.

Table 9-3   *Nine Possible Values in One Octet of a Subnet Mask*

Binary Mask Octet	Decimal Equivalent	Number of Binary 1s
00000000	0	0
10000000	128	1
11000000	192	2
11100000	224	3
11110000	240	4
11111000	248	5
11111100	252	6
11111110	254	7
11111111	255	8

Many subnetting processes that are done using binary math can also be done without the binary math. Some of those processes, mask conversion included, use the information in Table 9-3. You should plan to memorize the information in the table. I would recommend making a copy of the table to keep handy while practicing. (You will likely memorize the contents of this table simply by practicing the conversion process enough to get both good and fast at the conversion.)

Using the table, the conversion processes in each direction with binary and decimal masks are as follows:

Key Topic

- **Binary to decimal:** For each octet, find the binary value in the table, and write down the corresponding decimal value.

- **Decimal to binary:** For each octet, find the decimal value in the table, and write down the corresponding binary value.

Tables 9-4 and 9-5 show some examples.

Table 9-4   *Example Conversions—Binary to Decimal*

Binary Mask	Logic	Decimal Mask
11111111 11111111 11000000 00000000	11111111 maps to 255 11000000 maps to 192 00000000 maps to 0	255.255.192.0

Table 9-4 *Example Conversions—Binary to Decimal*

Binary Mask	Logic	Decimal Mask
11111111 11111111 11111111 11110000	11111111 maps to 255 11110000 maps to 240	255.255.255.240
11111111 11111000 00000000 00000000	11111111 maps to 255 11111000 maps to 248 00000000 maps to 0	255.248.0.0

Table 9-5 *Example Conversions—Decimal to Binary*

Decimal Mask	Logic	Binary Mask
255.255.192.0	255 maps to 11111111 192 maps to 11000000 0 maps to 00000000	11111111 11111111 11000000 00000000
255.255.255.240	255 maps to 11111111 240 maps to 11110000	11111111 11111111 11111111 11110000
255.248.0.0	255 maps to 11111111 248 maps to 11111000 0 maps to 00000000	11111111 11111000 00000000 00000000

Converting Between Prefix and DDN Masks

When learning, the best way to convert between the prefix and decimal formats is to first convert to binary. For example, to move from decimal to prefix, first convert from decimal to binary and then from binary to prefix.

Set a goal to master these conversions doing the math in your head. While learning, you will likely want to use paper. To train yourself to do all this without writing it down, instead of writing each octet of binary, just write down the number of binary 1s in that octet.

Figure 9-1 shows an example with a prefix-to-decimal conversion. The left side shows the conversion to binary as an interim step. For comparison, the right side shows the binary interim step in shorthand that just lists the number of binary 1s in each octet of the binary mask.

Similarly, when converting from decimal to prefix, mentally convert to binary along the way, and as you improve, just think of the binary as the number of 1s in each octet. Figure 9-2 shows an example of such a conversion.

Note that Appendix B, "IP Access Control Lists," has a table that lists all 33 legal subnet masks, with all three formats shown.

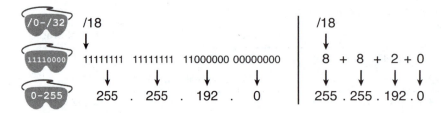

Figure 9-1 *Conversion from Prefix to Decimal: Full Binary Versus Shorthand*

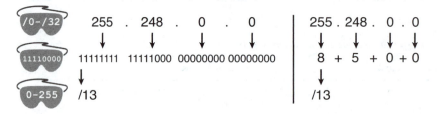

Figure 9-2 *Conversion from Decimal to Prefix: Full Binary Versus Shorthand*

Practice Converting Subnet Masks

To be a well-prepared network engineer, you should master any and all IP addressing processes and calculations by the time you finish this course. Most any technical interview for a job working with IP networking will include some assessment of how well you understand the concepts and how quickly you can calculate various facts about addresses and subnets.

However, you do not need to completely master everything in this chapter right now. Practice now to make sure that you understand the processes, using your notes, the book, and whatever helps. Then you can move on to the next chapter. However, before the midterm and final exams, practice until you master the topics in this chapter. Table 9-6 summarizes the key concepts and suggestions for this two-phase approach.

Table 9-6 *Practice Goals for This Chapter's Topics*

Time Frame	Before Moving to the Next Chapter	Before Taking the Exam
Focus on...	Learning how	Being correct and fast
Tools Allowed	All	Your brain and a notepad
Goal: Accuracy	90% correct	100% correct

Practice Problems for This Chapter

Table 9-7 lists three headings: Prefix, Binary Mask, and Decimal. Each row lists a mask in one of the three formats. Your job is to find the mask's value in the other two formats for each row. Table 9-8, located later in the "Chapter Review" section, lists the answers.

Table 9-7   *Practice Problems: Find the Mask Values in the Other Two Formats*

Prefix	Binary Mask	Decimal
	11111111 11111111 11000000 00000000	
		255.255.255.252
/25		
/16		
		255.0.0.0
	11111111 11111111 11111100 00000000	
		255.254.0.0
/27		

Additional Practice

For additional practice converting subnet masks, consider the following

- Create your own problems. Only 33 legal subnet masks exist, so pick one and convert that mask to the other two formats. Then check your work based on Appendix A; this appendix lists all mask values in all three formats. (Recommendation: Think of a prefix, and then convert to binary and then decimal. Then think of a DDN mask, and convert it to binary and prefix formats.)

- The Subnet Prep iPhone App "Convert Masks" provides review videos and practice problems (subnetprep.com). It's a great way to review and improve your speed when you have the time.

Note that many other subnetting problems will require you to do these conversions, so you will get extra practice as well.

Chapter Review

Review Key Topics

The narrow focus of this chapter means that all the key topics have something to do with the three mask formats and converting between the formats. Review the key topics as part of your study, but know that you will likely come to know all the information in these key topics through practice and repetition.

Table 9-8 *Key Topics for Chapter 9*

Key Topic Element	Description	Page Number
List	Rules for binary subnet mask values	209
List	Rules to convert between binary and prefix masks	210
List	Rules to convert between binary and DDN masks	211
List	Rules to convert between DDN and prefix masks	212

Define Key Terms

Define the following key terms from this chapter, and check your answers in the glossary:

binary mask, dotted decimal notation, decimal mask, prefix mask, slash mask, CIDR mask

Practice

If you have not done so already, practice converting subnet masks as discussed in this chapter. Refer to the earlier section "Practice Converting Subnet Masks" for suggestions.

Review Answers to Earlier Practice Problems

Table 9-7, earlier in this chapter, listed several practice problems. Table 9-9 lists the answers.

Table 9-9 *Answers to Problems in Table 9-7*

Prefix	Binary Mask	Decimal
/18	11111111 11111111 11000000 00000000	255.255.192.0
/30	11111111 11111111 11111111 11111100	255.255.255.252
/25	11111111 11111111 11111111 10000000	255.255.255.128
/16	11111111 11111111 00000000 00000000	255.255.0.0
/8	11111111 00000000 00000000 00000000	255.0.0.0
/22	11111111 11111111 11111100 00000000	255.255.252.0
/15	11111111 11111110 00000000 00000000	255.254.0.0
/27	11111111 11111111 11111111 11100000	255.255.255.224

Answer Review Questions

Answer the following review questions:

1. Which of the following answers lists the prefix (CIDR) format equivalent of 255.255.254.0?

    a. /19

    b. /20

    c. /23

    d. /24

    e. /25

2. Which of the following answers lists the prefix (CIDR) format equivalent of 255.255.255.240?

    a. /26

    b. /28

    c. /27

    d. /30

    e. /29

3. Which of the following answers lists the prefix (CIDR) format equivalent of 255.255.192.0?

    a. /18

    b. /19

    c. /20

    d. /21

    e. /22

4. Which of the following answers lists the dotted decimal notation (DDN) equivalent of /24?

    a. 255.255.240.0

    b. 255.255.252.0

    c. 255.255.255.0

    d. 255.255.255.192

    e. 255.255.255.240

5. Which of the following answers lists the dotted decimal notation (DDN) equivalent of /30?

   a.   255.255.255.192

   b.   255.255.255.252

   c.   255.255.255.240

   d.   255.255.254.0

   e.   255.255.255.0

6. Which of the following answers lists the dotted decimal notation (DDN) equivalent of /21?

   a.   255.255.240.0

   b.   255.255.248.0

   c.   255.255.252.0

   d.   255.255.254.0

   e.   255.255.255.0

This chapter covers the following subjects:

■ **Defining the Format of IPv4 Addresses:** This section explains how subnet masks and address class separate IP addresses into parts called network, subnet, and host.

■ **Practice Analyzing Subnet Masks:** This section supplies suggestions for how to practice the math related to this chapter.

CHAPTER 10

Analyzing Existing Subnet Masks

Some basic analysis of an IP address and its subnet mask can tell you the size of three parts of the IP addresses in that subnet. First, the mask divides addresses into two parts: prefix and host. Then, the network class further subdivides the addresses, breaking the prefix part into the network and subnet parts.

After you know the size of the three parts of an IP address, you can make some generalizations about the subnet and about the entire classful network. This chapter examines the process of breaking the subnet addresses into the three parts (network, subnet, and host), based on the class and the subnet mask, along with the additional facts that can then be calculated based on that information.

Defining the Format of IPv4 Addresses

Subnet masks have many purposes. Subnet masks define some fundamental concepts about a subnet, plus they can be used in different math operations related to addressing and subnetting. In fact, the subnet mask used in a given subnet:

Key Topic

1. Defines the size of the prefix (combined network and subnet) part of the addresses in a subnet.
2. Defines the size of the host part of the addresses in the subnet.
3. Can be used to help calculate the number of hosts in the subnet.
4. Provides a means for the network designer to communicate the design details—the number of subnet and host bits—to the devices in the network.
5. Under certain assumptions, can be used to help calculate the number of subnets in the entire classful network.
6. Can be used in binary calculations of both the subnet ID and the subnet broadcast address.

This chapter examines the first four items in the list. Chapter 13, "Analyzing Existing Subnets," and Chapter 17, "Subnet Mask Design," discuss the remaining roles for the subnet mask.

Masks Divide the Subnet's Addresses into Two Parts

The subnet mask subdivides the IP addresses in a subnet into two parts: the *prefix* or *subnet part* and the *host part*.

The prefix part identifies the addresses that reside in the same subnet, because all IP addresses in the same subnet have the same value in the prefix part of their addresses. The idea is much like postal codes (zip codes in the United States) in postal addresses: All postal addresses in the same town have the same postal code. Likewise, all IP addresses with identical values in the prefix part of their addresses are in the same subnet.

The host part of an address identifies the host uniquely inside the subnet. If you compare any two IP addresses in the same subnet, their host parts will differ, even though the prefix parts of their addresses have the same value. Summarizing these key comparisons:

- **Prefix (subnet) part:** Equal in all addresses in the same subnet.

- **Host part:** Different in all addresses in the same subnet.

For example, imagine a subnet that in concept includes all addresses whose first three octets are 10.1.1. So, the following list shows several addresses in this subnet:

10.1.1.**1**

10.1.1.**2**

10.1.1.**3**

In this list, the prefix or subnet parts—the first three octets of 10.1.1—are equal. The host parts—the last octet (in bold)—are different. So, the prefix or subnet part of the address identifies the group, and the host part identifies the specific member of the group.

The subnet mask defines the dividing line between the prefix and the host part. To do so, the mask creates a conceptual line between the binary 1s in the binary mask and the binary 0s in the mask. In short, if a mask has P binary 1s, the prefix part is P bits long, and the rest of the bits are host bits. Figure 10-1 shows the general concept.

Mask 1s		Mask 0s
Prefix (P)		Host (H)
	32 Bits	

Figure 10-1   *Prefix (Subnet) and Host Parts Defined by Masks 1s and 0s*

While Figure 10-1 shows the general concept, Figure 10-2 then shows the same concept, but specifically with mask 255.255.255.0. As shown in the figure, mask 255.255.255.0 (/24) has 24 binary 1s, meaning that the first three octets of each IP address must have the same value—just like the example earlier in this section.

Masks and Class Divide Addresses into Three Parts

In addition to the two-part view of IPv4 addresses, you can also think about IPv4 addresses as having three parts. To do so, just apply class A, B, and C rules to the address format to define the network part at the beginning of the address. This added logic divides the prefix into two parts: the network part and the subnet part. The class defines the length of the network part, with the subnet part simply being the rest of the prefix. Figure 10-3 shows the idea.

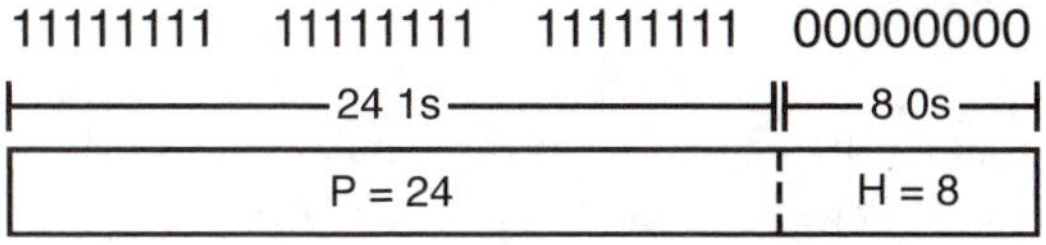

11111111   11111111   11111111   00000000

|———————————— 24 1s ————————————||——— 8 0s ———|

| P = 24 | H = 8 |

Figure 10-2   *Mask 255.255.255.0: P=24, H=8*

|———— Mask 1s ————||———— Mask 0s ————|

| Network | Subnet | Host |

↑

Size: 8, 16, 24 (A, B, C)

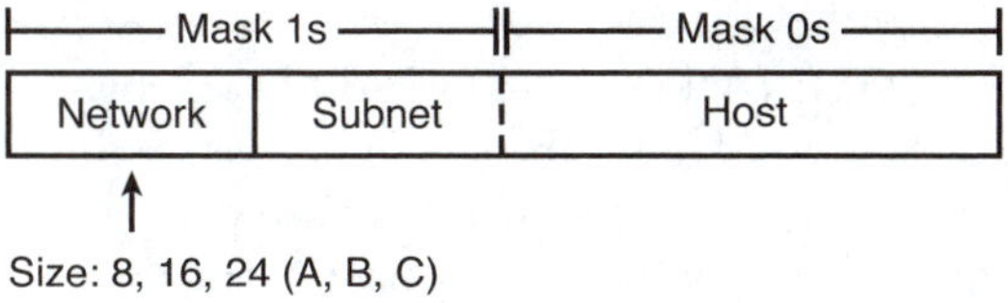

Figure 10-3   *Class Concepts Applied to Create Three Parts*

The combined network and subnet parts act like the prefix, in that all addresses in the same subnet must have identical values in the network and subnet parts. The host part remains the same size and uses the same concept as well, with each host in the same subnet having a unique value in the host part of the address.

To be complete, Figure 10-4 shows the same example as in the previous section, with the subnet of "all addresses that begin with 10.1.1." In that example, the subnet uses mask 255.255.255.0 and the addresses are all in class A network 10.0.0.0. The class defines 8 network bits, and the mask defines 24 prefix bits, meaning that 24 – 8 = 16 subnet bits exist. The host part remains as 8 bits per the mask.

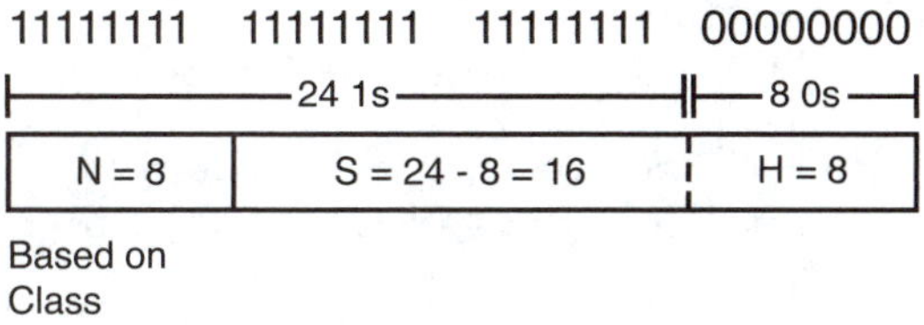

11111111   11111111   11111111   00000000

|———————————— 24 1s ————————————||——— 8 0s ———|

| N = 8 | S = 24 - 8 = 16 | H = 8 |

Based on
Class

Figure 10-4   *Subnet 10.1.1.0, Mask 255.255.255.0: N=8, S=16, H=8*

Classless and Classful Addressing

The terms *classless addressing* and *classful addressing* refer to the two different ways to think about IPv4 addresses as described so far in this chapter. Classful addressing means that you think about class A, B, and C rules, so the prefix is separated into the network and subnet parts, as shown in Figures 10-3 and 10-4. Classless addressing means that you ignore the class A, B, and C rules and treat the prefix part as one part, as shown in Figures 10-1 and 10-2. The following more formal definitions are listed for reference and study:

Key Topic

- **Classless addressing:** The concept that an IPv4 address has two parts—the prefix or subnet part plus the host part—as defined by the mask, with *no consideration of the class* (A, B, or C)

- **Classful addressing:** The concept that an IPv4 address has three parts—network, subnet, and host—as defined by the mask *as well as class A, B, and C rules*

Note: The networking industry uses two other related topics that are (unfortunately) also referenced as *classless* and *classful*. In addition to the classless and classful addressing described here, the terms *classless routing* and *classful routing* refer to some details of how Cisco routers forward (route) packets using the default route. Additionally, each routing protocol can be categorized as either a *classless routing protocol* or a *classful routing protocol*. As a result, these terms can be easily confused and misused. So, when you see the words *classless* and *classful*, be careful to note the context: addressing, routing, or routing protocols.

Calculations Based on the IPv4 Address Format

After you know how to break down an address using both classless and classful addressing rules, you can easily calculate a couple of important facts using some basic math formulas.

First, for any subnet, after you know the number of host bits, you can calculate the number of host IP addresses in the subnet. Next, if you know the number of subnet bits (using classful addressing concepts) and you know that only one subnet mask is used throughout the network, you can also calculate the number of subnets in the network. The formulas just require that you know the powers of 2:

- **Hosts in the subnet:** $2^H - 2$, where H is the number of host bits.

- **Subnets in the network:** 2^S, where S is the number of subnet bits. Use this formula only if just one mask is used throughout the network.

Note: Chapter 8's section "Choose the Mask" details many concepts related to masks, including comments about this assumption of one mask throughout a single class A, B, or C network.

The sizes of the parts of IPv4 addresses can also be calculated. The math is very basic, but the concepts are very important. Keep in mind that IPv4 addresses are 32 bits long, the two parts with classless addressing must add up to 32 (P + H = 32), and with classful addressing, the three parts must add up to 32 (N + S + H = 32). Figure 10-5 shows the relationships.

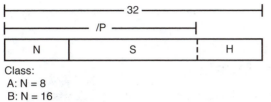

Class:
A: N = 8
B: N = 16
C: N = 24

Figure 10-5   *Relationship Between /P, N, S, and H*

You often begin with an IP address and mask when examining problems that occur in real networks. Based on the information in this chapter and earlier chapters, you should be able to find all the information in Figure 10-5 and then calculate the number of hosts/subnet and the number of subnets in the network. For reference, the following process spells out the steps:

Step 1.   Convert the mask to prefix format (/P) as needed (see Chapter 9, "Subnet Mask Conversion," for review).

Step 2.   Determine N based on the class (see Chapter 4, "Class A, B, and C Networks," for review).

Step 3.   Calculate $S = P - N$

Step 4.   Calculate $H = 32 - P$

Step 5.   Calculate hosts/subnet: $2^H - 2$

Step 6.   Calculate the number of subnets: 2^S

For example, consider the case of IP address 8.1.4.5 with mask 255.255.0.0. Following the process:

Step 1.   255.255.0.0 = /16, so P=16

Step 2.   8.1.4.5 is in the range 1–126 in the first octet, so it is class A and N=8

Step 3. $S = P - N = 16 - 8 = 8$

Step 4. $H = 32 - P = 32 - 16 = 16$

Step 5. $2^{16} - 2 = 65,534$ hosts/subnet

Step 6. $2^8 = 256$ subnets

For another example, consider address 200.1.1.1, mask 255.255.255.252. Following the process:

Step 1.   255.255.255.252 = /30, so P=30

Step 2.   200.1.1.1 is in the range 192–223 in the first octet, so it is class C and N=24

Step 3. $S = P - N = 30 - 24 = 6$

Step 4. $H = 32 - P = 32 - 30 = 2$

Step 5. $2^2 - 2 = 2$ hosts/subnet

Step 6. $2^6 = 64$ subnets

Note that this example uses a popular mask for serial links, because serial links only require two host addresses and the mask supports only two host addresses.

Practice Analyzing Subnet Masks

To be a well-prepared network engineer, you should master any and all IP addressing processes and calculations by the time you finish this course. Most any technical interview for a job working with IP networking will include some assessment of how well you understand the concepts and how quickly you can calculate various facts about addresses and subnets.

However, you do not need to completely master everything in this chapter right now. Practice now to make sure that you understand the processes, using your notes, the book, and whatever helps. Then you can move on to the next chapter. However, before the midterm and final exams, practice until you master the topics in this chapter. Table 10-1 summarizes the key concepts and suggestions for this two-phase approach.

Table 10-1   *Practice Goals for This Chapter's Topics*

Time Frame	Before Moving to the Next Chapter	Before Taking the Exam
Focus on...	Learning how	Being correct and fast
Tools Allowed	All	Your brain and a notepad
Goal: Accuracy	90% correct	100% correct

Practice Problems for This Chapter

On a piece of scratch paper, answer the following questions. In each case:

- Determine the structure of the addresses in each subnet based on the class and mask, using classful IP addressing concepts. In other words, find the size of the network, subnet, and host parts of the addresses.

- Calculate the number of hosts in the subnet.

- Calculate the number of subnets in the network, assuming that the same mask is used throughout.

The answers are listed at the end of the "Chapter Review" section, later in this chapter.

1. 8.1.4.5, 255.255.254.0
2. 130.4.102.1, 255.255.255.0
3. 199.1.1.100, 255.255.255.0
4. 130.4.102.1, 255.255.252.0
5. 199.1.1.100, 255.255.255.224

Additional Practice

For additional practice analyzing subnet masks, consider the following:

■ Your instructor might have access to practice problems that he or she can share; ask if you want more practice.

■ The book's author lists some subnetting practice in one of his blogs (http://ccentskills.certskills.com); in particular, look for the subnetting speed practice problems.

■ Create your own problems. Many subnet calculators show the number of network, subnet, and host bits when you type in an IP address and mask, so make up an IP address and mask on paper and find N, S, and H. Then, to check your work, use any subnet calculator. Most subnet calculators list the class and network ID. (Check the author's web pages for this book, as listed in the introduction, for some suggested calculators.)

Chapter Review

Review Key Topics

The narrow focus of this chapter means that all the key topics have something to do with the three mask formats and converting between the formats. Review the key topics as part of your study, but know that you will likely come to know all the information in these key topics through practice and repetition.

Key Topic

Table 10-2 *Key Topics for Chapter 10*

Key Topic Element	Description	Page Number
List	Some functions of a subnet mask	221
List	Comparisons of IP addresses in the same subnet	222
Figure 10-1	Two-part classless view of an IP address	222
Figure 10-3	Three-part classful view of an IP address	223
List	Definitions of classful addressing and classless addressing	224
List	Formal steps to analyze and calculate values discussed in this chapter	225

Define Key Terms

Define the following key terms from this chapter, and check your answers in the glossary:

Classful addressing, classless addressing

Practice

If you have not done so already, practice analyzing subnet masks as discussed in this chapter. Refer to the earlier section "Practice Analyzing Subnet Masks" for suggestions.

Review Answers to Earlier Practice Problems

The earlier section "Practice Problems for This Chapter" listed several practice problems. The answers are listed here so that the answers are nearby, but not visible from the list of problems. Table 10-3 lists the answers.

Table 10-3 *Answers to Problems from Earlier in the Chapter*

	Problem	/P	Class	N	S	H	2^s	$2^H - 2$
1	8.1.4.5 255.255.254.0	23	A	8	15	9	32,768	510
2	130.4.102.1 255.255.255.0	24	B	16	8	8	256	254
3	199.1.1.100 255.255.255.0	24	C	24	0	8	—	254
4	130.4.102.1 255.255.252.0	22	B	16	6	10	64	1022
5	199.1.1.100 255.255.255.224	27	C	24	3	5	8	30

The following list reviews the problems:

1. 8.1.4.5, the first octet (8) is in the 1–126 range, so it is a class A address, with 8 network bits. Mask 255.255.254.0 converts to /23, so P – N = 15, for 15 subnet bits. H can be found by subtracting /P (23) from 32, for 9 host bits.

2. 130.4.102.1 is in the 128–191 range in the first octet, making it a class B address, with N = 16 bits. 255.255.255.0 converts to /24, so the number of subnet bits is 24 – 16 = 8. With 24 prefix bits, the number of host bits is 32 – 24 = 8.

3. The third problem purposefully shows a case where the mask does not create a subnet part of the address. The address, 199.1.1.100, has a first octet in the range 192–223, making it a class C address, with 24 network bits. The prefix version of the mask is /24, so the number of subnet bits is 24 – 24 = 0. The number of host bits is 32 minus the prefix length (24), for a total of 8 host bits. So, in this case, the mask shows that the network engineer is using the default mask, which creates no subnet bits and no subnets.

4. With the same address as the second problem, 130.4.102.1 is a class B address with N = 16 bits. This problem uses a different mask, 255.255.252.0, which converts to /22. This makes the number of subnet bits 22 – 16 = 6. With 22 prefix bits, the number of host bits is 32 – 22 = 10.

5. With the same address as the third problem, 199.1.1.100 is a class C address with N = 24 bits. This problem uses a different mask, 255.255.255.224, which converts to /27. This makes the number of subnet bits 27 – 24 = 3. With 27 prefix bits, the number of host bits is 32 – 27 = 5.

Answer Review Questions

Answer the following review questions:

1. Working at the help desk, you receive a call and learn a user's PC IP address (10.55.66.77, mask 255.255.255.0). When thinking about this using classful logic, you determine the number of network (N), subnet (S), and host (H) bits. Which of the following is true in this case?

   a.   N = 12

   b.   S = 12

   c.   H = 8

   d.   S = 8

   e.   N = 24

2. Working at the help desk, you receive a call and learn a user's PC IP address and mask (192.168.9.0/27). When thinking about this using classful logic, you determine the number of network (N), subnet (S), and host (H) bits. Which of the following is true in this case?

   a.   N = 24

   b.   S = 24

   c.   H = 8

   d.   H = 7

3. Working at the help desk, you receive a call and learn a user's PC IP address (172.28.99.101, mask 255.255.255.128). When thinking about this using classful logic, you determine the number of network (N), subnet (S), and host (H) bits. Which of the following is true in this case?

   a.   N = 12

   b.   S = 12

   c.   H = 8

   d.   S = 8

   e.   N = 16

4. An engineer is thinking about the following IP address and mask using classless IP addressing logic: 10.55.66.77, 255.255.255.0. Which of the following statements are true when using classless addressing logic? (Choose two.)

a. The network part's size is 8 bits.

b. The prefix length is 24 bits.

c. The prefix length is 16 bits.

d. The host part's size is 8 bits.

5. Which of the following statements is true about classless IP addressing concepts?

a. Uses a 128-bit IP address

b. Applies only for class A and B networks

c. Separates IP addresses into network, subnet, and host parts

d. Ignores class A, B, and C network rules

6. Which of the following masks, when used as the only mask within a class B network, would supply enough subnet bits to support 100 subnets? (Choose two.)

a. /24

b. 255.255.255.252

c. /20

d. 255.255.252.0

This chapter covers the following subjects:

- **Configuration Features in Common with Switches:** This section gives some perspectives on the purpose of enterprise-class routers and consumer-grade routers, and how the routers connect users to a network.

- **Configuration Features Specific to Routers:** This section examines a few of the many features that are unique to routers.

- **Upgrading Cisco IOS Software and the Cisco IOS Software Boot Process:** This section examines how a router boots, including how a router chooses which Cisco IOS Software image to load.

CHAPTER 11

Cisco Router Configuration

Chapter 7, "Operating Cisco Routers," previously showed how to access a router's command-line interface (CLI). It also showed how to enter configuration mode in the CLI, for the purpose of adding configuration commands. These commands tell the router what to do. However, Chapter 7 discussed the process of getting into the CLI, and moving to configuration mode, but was focused on the process only. That chapter did not focus on the specific items that can be configured on a router.

This chapter examines a variety of configuration settings that can be done on a router. To help you later learn about Cisco switches, the first section examines configuration settings that happen to use commands common to both Cisco routers and switches. The second section then moves on to router-specific configuration settings. The final section of this chapter examines how to perform software upgrades, as well as describes the process by which a Cisco router boots its operating system.

Configuration Features in Common with Switches

As you might imagine, both routers and switches need some of the same configuration settings. For example, both need a name. Both need some passwords to secure access to the CLI. The first major sections of this chapter examine these settings, and groups them into one section so that when you start working with switches, you can find the commands in this chapter that also happen to apply to switches.

Securing the Router CLI

To reach a router's enable mode, a user must reach user mode either from the console or from a Telnet or SSH session, and then use the **enable** command. With default configuration settings, a user at the console does not need to supply a password to reach user mode or enable mode. The reason is that anyone with physical access to the switch or router console could reset the passwords in less than 5 minutes by using the password recovery procedures that Cisco publishes. So, routers and switches default to allow the console user access to enable mode.

Note: To see the password recovery/reset procedures, go to Cisco.com and search on the phrase "password recovery." The first listed item probably will be a web page with password recovery details for most every product made by Cisco.

To reach enable mode from a vty (Telnet or SSH), the router must be configured with several items:

- An IP address

- Login security on the vty lines

- An enable password

Most network engineers will want to be able to establish a Telnet or SSH connection to each router, so it makes sense to configure the routers to allow secure access. Additionally, although someone with physical access to the router can use the password recovery process to get access to the router, it still makes sense to configure security even for access from the console.

This section examines most of the configuration details related to accessing enable mode on a switch or router. The one key topic not covered here is the IP address configuration, which is covered later in this chapter in the section "Router Interface IP Addresses." In particular, this section covers the following topics:

- Simple password security for the console and Telnet access

- Secure Shell (SSH)

- Password encryption

- Enable mode passwords

Configuring Simple Password Security

An engineer can reach user mode in a Cisco switch or router from the console or via either Telnet or SSH. By default, switches and routers allow a console user to immediately access user mode after logging in, with no password required. With default settings, Telnet users are rejected when they try to access the router, because a vty password has not yet been configured. Regardless of these defaults, it makes sense to password protect user mode for console, Telnet, and SSH users.

A user in user mode can gain access to enable mode by using the enable command, but with different defaults depending on whether the user is at the console or has logged in remotely using Telnet or SSH. By default, the **enable** command allows console users into enable mode without requiring a password, but Telnet users are rejected without even a chance to supply a password. Regardless of these defaults, it makes sense to password protect enable mode using the **enable secret** global configuration command.

Note: The later section "The Two Enable Mode Passwords" explains two options for configuring the password required by the **enable** command, as configured with the **enable secret** and **enable password** commands, and why the **enable secret** command is preferred.

Example 11-1 shows a sample configuration process that sets the console password, the vty (Telnet) password, the enable secret password, and a hostname for the router. The example shows the entire process, including command prompts, which provide some reminders of the different configuration modes explained in Chapter 7, "Operating Cisco Routers."

Example 11-1 *Configuring Basic Passwords and a Hostname*

```
Router> enable
Router# configure terminal
Router(config)# enable secret cisco
Router(config)# hostname Emma
Emma(config)# line console 0
Emma(config-line)# password faith
Emma(config-line)# login
Emma(config-line)# exit
Emma(config)# line vty 0 15
Emma(config-line)# password love
Emma(config-line)# login
Emma(config-line)# exit
Emma(config)# exit
Emma#
! The next command lists the router's current configuration (running-config)
Emma# show running-config
!
Building configuration...
Current configuration : 1333 bytes
!
version 12.2
no service pad
service timestamps debug uptime
service timestamps log uptime
!
hostname Emma
!
enable secret 5 $1$YXRN$11zOe1Lb0Lv/nHyTquobd.
!
spanning-tree mode pvst
spanning-tree extend system-id
!
interface FastEthernet0/1
!
interface FastEthernet0/2
!
! Several lines have been omitted here - in particular, lines for FastEthernet
! interfaces 0/3 through 0/23.
!
interface FastEthernet0/24
!
interface GigabitEthernet0/1
```

Key Topic

```
!
interface GigabitEthernet0/2
!
interface Vlan1
 no ip address
 no ip route-cache
!
ip http server
ip http secure-server
!
control-plane
!
!
line con 0
 password faith
 login
line vty 0 4
 password love
 login
line vty 5 15
 password love
 login
```

Example 11-1 begins by showing the user moving from enable mode to configuration mode by using the **configure terminal** EXEC command. As soon as the user is in global configuration mode, he enters two global configuration commands (**enable secret** and **hostname**) that add the configuration that applies to the whole router.

For instance, the **hostname** global configuration command simply sets the one and only name for this router (in addition to changing the router's command prompt). The **enable secret** command sets the only password used to reach enable mode, so it is also a global command. However, the **login** command (which tells the router to ask for a text password, but no username) and the **password** command (which defines the required password) are shown in both console and vty line configuration submodes. So, these commands are subcommands in these two different configuration modes. These subcommands define different console and vty passwords based on the configuration submodes in which the commands were used, as shown in the example.

Pressing the Ctrl-z key sequence from any part of configuration mode takes you all the way back to enable mode. However, the example shows how to repeatedly use the **exit** command to move back from a configuration submode to global configuration mode, with another **exit** command to exit back to enable mode. The **end** configuration mode command performs the same action as the Ctrl-z key sequence, moving the user from any part of configuration mode back to privileged EXEC mode.

The second half of Example 11-1 lists the output of the **show running-config** command. This command shows the currently used configuration in the router, which includes the changes made earlier in the example. The output highlights in gray the configuration commands added due to the earlier configuration commands.

Note: The output of the **show running-config** command lists five vty lines (0 through 4) in a different location than the rest (5 through 15). In earlier IOS releases, Cisco IOS routers and switches had five vty lines, numbered 0 through 4, which allowed five concurrent Telnet connects to a switch or router. Later, Cisco added more vty lines (5 through 15), allowing 16 concurrent Telnet connections into each switch and router. That's why the command output lists the two vty line ranges separately.

Configuring Usernames and Secure Shell (SSH)

Telnet sends all data, including all passwords entered by the user, as clear text. The Secure Shell (SSH) application provides the same function as Telnet, displaying a terminal emulator window and allowing the user to remotely connect to another host's CLI. However, SSH encrypts the data sent between the SSH client and the SSH server, making SSH the preferred method for remote login to switches and routers today.

To add support for SSH login to a Cisco switch or router, the switch needs several configuration commands. For example, SSH requires that the user supply both a username and password instead of just a password. So, the router must be reconfigured to use one of two user authentication methods that require both a username and password: one method with the usernames and passwords configured on the router, and the other with the usernames and passwords configured on an external server called an Authentication, Authorization, and Accounting (AAA) server. (This book covers the configuration using locally configured usernames/passwords.) Figure 11-1 shows a diagram of the configuration and process required to support SSH.

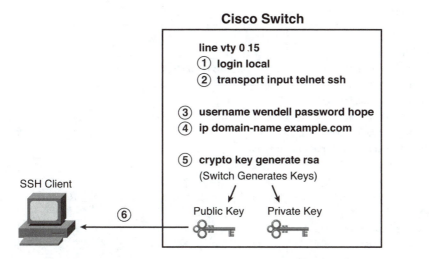

Figure 11-1 *SSH Configuration Concepts*

The steps in the figure, explained with the matching numbered list that follows, detail the required transactions before an SSH user can connect to the router using SSH:

Key Topic

Step 1. Change the vty lines to use usernames, with either locally configured usernames or an AAA server. In this case, the **login local** subcommand defines the use of local usernames, replacing the **login** subcommand in vty configuration mode.

Step 2. Tell the router to accept both Telnet and SSH with the **transport input telnet ssh** vty subcommand. (The default is **transport input telnet**, omitting the **ssh** parameter.)

Step 3. Add one or more **username** *name* **password** *pass-value* global configuration commands to configure username/password pairs.

Step 4. Configure a DNS domain name with the **ip domain-name** *name* global configuration command.

Step 5. Configure the router to generate a matched public and private key pair, as well as a shared encryption key, using the **crypto key generate rsa** global configuration command.

Step 6. Although no router commands are required, each SSH client needs a copy of the router's public key before the client can connect.

Note: This book contains several step lists that refer to specific configuration steps, such as the one shown here for SSH. These lists use step numbers to help you study, but the specific step number for a specific command is not important.

Example 11-2 shows the same router commands shown in Figure 11-1, entered in configuration mode.

Example 11-2 *SSH Configuration Process*

```
Emma#
Emma# configure terminal
Enter configuration commands, one per line.  End with CNTL/Z.
Emma(config)# line vty 0 15
! Step 1's command happens next
Emma(config-line)# login local
! Step 2's command happens next
Emma(config-line)# transport input telnet ssh
Emma(config-line)# exit
! Step 3's command happens next
Emma(config)# username wendell password hope
! Step 4's command happens next
Emma(config)# ip domain-name example.com
! Step 5's command happens next
Emma(config)# crypto key generate rsa
```

```
The name for the keys will be: Emma.example.com
Choose the size of the key modulus in the range of 360 to 2048 for your
  General Purpose Keys. Choosing a key modulus greater than 512 may take
  a few minutes.
How many bits in the modulus [512]: 1024
% Generating 1024 bit RSA keys ...[OK]
00:03:58: %SSH-5-ENABLED: SSH 1.99 has been enabled
Emma(config)# ^Z
! Next, the contents of the public key are listed; the key will be needed by the
SSH client.
Emma# show crypto key mypubkey rsa
% Key pair was generated at: 00:03:58 UTC Mar 1 1993
Key name: Emma.example.com
 Usage: General Purpose Key
 Key is not exportable.
 Key Data:
  30819F30 0D06092A 864886F7 0D010101 05000381 8D003081 89028181 00DB43DC
  49C258FA 8E0B8EB2 0A6C8888 A00D29CE EAEE615B 456B68FD 491A9B63 B39A4334
  86F64E02 1B320256 01941831 7B7304A2 720A57DA FBB3E75A 94517901 7764C332
  A3A482B1 DB4F154E A84773B5 5337CE8C B1F5E832 8213EE6B 73B77006 BA8782DE
  180966D9 9A6476D7 C9164ECE 1DC752BB 955F5BDE F82BFCB2 A273C58C 8B020301 0001
% Key pair was generated at: 00:04:01 UTC Mar 1 1993
Key name: Emma.example.com.server
 Usage: Encryption Key
 Key is not exportable.
Key Data:
  307C300D 06092A86 4886F70D 01010105 00036B00 30680261 00AC339C D4916728
  6ACB627E A5EE26A5 00946AF9 E63FF322 A2DB4994 9E37BFDA AB1C503E AAF69FB3
  2A22A5F3 0AA94454 B8242D72 A8582E7B 0642CF2B C06E0710 B0A06048 D90CBE9E
  F0B88179 EC1C5EAC D551109D 69E39160 86C50122 9A37E954 85020301 0001
```

The example shows a gray highlighted comment just before the configuration commands at each step. Also, note the public key created by the router, listed in the highlighted portion of the output of the **show crypto key mypubkey rsa** command. Each SSH client needs a copy of this key, either by adding this key to the SSH client's configuration beforehand, or by letting the router send this public key to the client when the SSH client first connects to the router.

For even tighter security, you might want to disable Telnet access completely, requiring all the engineers to use SSH to remotely log in to the router. To prevent Telnet access, use the **transport input ssh** line subcommand in vty configuration mode. If the command is given only the SSH option, the router will no longer accept Telnet connections.

Password Encryption

Several of the configuration commands used to configure passwords store the passwords in clear text in the running-config file, at least by default. In particular, the simple passwords configured on the console and vty lines, with the **password** command, plus the password in the **username** command, are all stored in clear text by default. (The **enable secret** command automatically hides the password value.)

To prevent password vulnerability in a printed version of the configuration file, or in a backup copy of the configuration file stored on a server, you can encrypt or encode the passwords using the **service password-encryption** global configuration command. The presence or absence of the **service password-encryption** global configuration command dictates whether the passwords are encrypted as follows:

■   When the **service password-encryption** command is configured, all existing console, vty, and **username** command passwords are immediately encrypted.

■   If the **service password-encryption** command has already been configured, any future changes to these passwords are encrypted.

■   If the **no service password-encryption** command is used later, the passwords remain encrypted, until they are changed—at which point they show up in clear text.

Example 11-3 shows an example of these details.

Note: The **show running-config | begin line vty command**, as used in Example 11-3, lists the running configuration, beginning with the first line, which contains the text line vty. This is just a shorthand way to see a smaller part of the running configuration.

Example 11-3   *Encryption and the* service password-encryption *Command*

```
Router3# show running-config | begin line vty
line vty 0 4
 password cisco
 login
Router3# configure terminal
Enter configuration commands, one per line.  End with CNTL/Z.
Router3(config) # service password-encryption
Router3(config)# ^Z
Router3# show running-config | begin line vty
line vty 0 4
```

```
   password 7 070C285F4D06
  login
 end
Router3# configure terminal
Enter configuration commands, one per line.  End with CNTL/Z.
Router3(config)# no service password-encryption
Router3(config)# ^Z
Router3# show running-config | begin line vty
line vty 0 4
  password 7 070C285F4D06
  login
 end
Router3# configure terminal
Enter configuration commands, one per line.  End with CNTL/Z.
Router3(config)# line vty 0 4
Router3(config-line)# password cisco
Router3(config-line)# ^Z
Router3# show running-config | begin line vty
line vty 0 4
  password cisco
  login
```

Note: The encryption type used by the **service password-encryption** command, as noted with the "7" in the **password** commands, refers to one of several underlying password encryption algorithms. Type 7, the only type used by the **service password-encryption** command, is a weak encryption algorithm, and the passwords can be easily decrypted.

The Two Enable Mode Passwords

The **enable** command moves you from user EXEC mode (with a prompt of hostname>) to privileged EXEC mode (with a prompt of hostname#). A router or switch can be configured to require a password to reach enable mode according to the following rules:

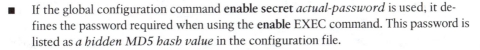

■   If the global configuration command **enable password** *actual-password* is used, it defines the password required when using the **enable** EXEC command. This password is listed as *clear text* in the configuration file by default.

■   If the global configuration command **enable secret** *actual-password* is used, it defines the password required when using the **enable** EXEC command. This password is listed as *a hidden MD5 hash value* in the configuration file.

■   If *both commands* are used, the password set in the **enable secret** command defines which password is required.

When the **enable secret** command is configured, the router or switch automatically hides the password. While it is sometimes referenced as being encrypted, the enable secret password is not actually encrypted. Instead, IOS applies a mathematical function to the password, called a Message Digest 5 (MD5) hash, storing the results of the formula in the configuration file. IOS references this style of encoding the password as type 5 in the output in Example 11-4. Note that the MD5 encoding is much more secure than the encryption used for other passwords with the **service password-encryption** command. The example shows the creation of the **enable secret** command, its format, and its deletion.

Example 11-4   *Encryption and the* **enable secret** *Command*

```
Router3(config)# enable secret ?
  0       Specifies an UNENCRYPTED password will follow
  5       Specifies an ENCRYPTED secret will follow
  LINE    The UNENCRYPTED (cleartext) 'enable' secret
  level   Set exec level password
Router3(config)# enable secret fred
Router3(config)# ^Z
Router3# show running-config
! all except the pertinent line has been omitted!
enable secret 5 $1$ZGMA$e8cmvkz4UjiJhVp7.maLE1
Router3# configure terminal
Enter configuration commands, one per line.  End with CNTL/Z.
Router3(config)# no enable secret
Router3(config)# ^Z
```

When you use the (recommended) **enable secret** command, rather than the **enable password** command, the password is automatically encrypted. Example 11-4 uses the **enable secret fred** command, setting the password text to **fred**. However, the syntax **enable secret 0 fred** could have been used, with the **0** implying that the password that followed was clear text. IOS then takes the command, applies the encryption type used by the **enable secret** command (type 5 in this case, which uses an MD5 hash), and stores the encrypted or encoded value in the running configuration. The **show running-configuration** command shows the resulting configuration command, listing encryption type 5, with the gobbledygook long text string being the encrypted/encoded password.

Thankfully, to delete the enable secret password, you can simply use the **no enable secret** command, without even having to enter the password value. For instance, in Example 11-4, the command **no enable secret** deletes the enable secret password. Although you can delete the enable secret password, more typically, you will want to change it to a new value, which can be done with the **enable secret** *another-password* command, with *another-password* simply meaning that you put in a new text string for the new password.

Console and vty Settings

This section covers a few small configuration settings that affect the behavior of the CLI connection from the console and/or vty (Telnet and SSH).

Banners

Cisco routers and switches can display a variety of banners depending on what a router or switch administrator is doing. A banner is simply some text that appears on the screen for the user. You can configure a router or switch to display multiple banners, some before login and some after. Table 11-1 lists the three most popular banners and their typical use.

Table 11-1   *Banners and Their Use*

Banner	Typical Use
Message of the Day (MOTD)	Shown before the login prompt. For temporary messages that can change from time to time, such as "Router1 down for maintenance at midnight."
Login	Shown before the login prompt but after the MOTD banner. For permanent messages such as "Unauthorized Access Prohibited."
Exec	Shown after the login prompt. Used to supply information that should be hidden from unauthorized users.

The **banner** global configuration command can be used to configure all three types of these banners. In each case, the type of banner is listed as the first parameter, with MOTD being the default option. The first nonblank character after the banner type is called a beginning delimiter character. The banner text can span several lines, with the CLI user pressing Enter at the end of each line. The CLI knows that the banner has been configured as soon as the user enters the same delimiter character again.

Example 11-5 shows all three types of banners from Table 11-1, with a user login that shows the banners in use. The first banner in the example, the MOTD banner, omits the banner type in the **banner** command as a reminder that **motd** is the default banner type. The first two **banner** commands use a # as the delimiter character. The third **banner** command uses a Z as the delimiter, just to show that any character can be used. Also, the last **banner** command shows multiple lines of banner text.

Example 11-5   *Banner Configuration*

```
! Below, the three banners are created in configuration mode. Note that any
! delimiter can be used, as long as the character is not part of the message
! text.
R1(config)# banner #
Enter TEXT message.  End with the character '#'.
Router down for maintenance at 11PM Today #
R1(config)# banner login #
Enter TEXT message.  End with the character '#'.
Unauthorized Access Prohibited!!!!
#
R1(config)# banner exec Z
Enter TEXT message.  End with the character 'Z'.
```

```
Company picnic at the park on Saturday
 Don't tell outsiders!
Z
R1(config)# ^Z
! Below, the user of this router quits the console connection, and logs back in,
! seeing the motd and login banners, then the password prompt, and then the
! exec banner.
R1# quit
R1 con0 is now available
Press RETURN to get started.
Router down for maintenance at 11PM Today
Unauthorized Access Prohibited!!!!
User Access Verification
Username: fred
Password:
Company picnic at the park on Saturday
don't tell outsiders!
R1>
```

History Buffer Commands

When you enter commands from the CLI, the last several commands are saved in the history buffer. As mentioned in Chapter 7, you can use the up-arrow key, or Ctrl-p, to move back in the history buffer stack to retrieve a command you entered a few commands ago. This feature makes it very easy and fast to use a set of commands repeatedly. Table 11-2 lists some of the key commands related to the history buffer.

Key Topic

Table 11-2 *Commands Related to the History Buffer*

Command	Description
show history	Lists the commands currently held in the history buffer.
history size x	From console or vty line configuration mode, sets the default number of commands saved in the history buffer for the user(s) of the console or vty lines, respectively.
terminal history size x	From EXEC mode, this command allows a single user to set, just for this one connection, the size of his or her history buffer.

The logging synchronous and exec-timeout Commands

The console automatically receives copies of all unsolicited syslog messages on a switch or router; that feature cannot be disabled. The idea is that if the switch or router needs to tell the network administrator some important and possibly urgent information, the administrator can be at the console and can notice the message. Normally a switch or router puts these syslog messages on the console's screen at any time—including right in the middle of a command you are entering, or in the middle of the output of a **show** command.

To make using the console a little easier, you can tell the router to display syslog messages only at more convenient times, such as at the end of output from a **show** command or to prevent the interruption of a command text input. To do so, just configure the **logging synchronous** console line subcommand.

You can also make using the console or vty lines more convenient by setting a different inactivity timeout on the console or vty. By default, the switch or router automatically disconnects users after 5 minutes of inactivity, for both console users and users who connect to vty lines using Telnet or SSH. When you configure the **exec-timeout** *minutes seconds* line subcommand, the switch or router can be told a different inactivity timer. Also, if you set the timeout to 0 minutes and 0 seconds, the router never times out the console connection. Example 11-6 shows the syntax for these two commands.

Example 11-6 *Defining Console Inactivity Timeouts and When to Display Log Messages*

```
line console 0
 login
 password cisco
 exec-timeout 0 0
 logging synchronous
```

Configuring Features Specific to Cisco Routers

Cisco routers support a large number of features specific to the Layer 3 functions related to IP routing. This section introduces a few of these features, including how to configure IP addresses on router interfaces.

Router Interfaces

The two most commonly-used router interfaces are Ethernet interfaces and serial interfaces. The term *Ethernet interface* refers to any type of Ethernet interface. However, on Cisco routers, the name referenced by the CLI refers to the fastest speed possible on the interface. For example, some Cisco routers have an Ethernet interface capable of only 10 Mbps, so to configure that type of interface, you would use the **interface ethernet** *number* configuration command. However, other routers have interfaces capable of 100 Mbps, or even of auto-negotiating to use 10 Mbps or 100 Mbps, so routers refer to these interfaces by the fastest speed, with the **interface fastethernet** *number* command. Similarly, interfaces capable of Gigabit Ethernet speeds are referenced with the **interface gigabitethernet** *number* command.

Serial interfaces are the second major type of physical interface on routers. As you might recall from Chapter 3, "WAN Fundamentals," point-to-point leased lines and Frame Relay access links both use the same underlying Layer 1 standards. To support those same standards, Cisco routers use serial interfaces. The network engineer then chooses which data link layer protocol to use, such as High-Level Data Link Control (HDLC) or Point-to-Point Protocol (PPP) for leased lines or Frame Relay for Frame Relay connections, and configures the router to use the correct data link layer protocol. (Serial interfaces default to use HDLC as the data link layer protocol.)

Routers use numbers to distinguish between the different interfaces of the same type. On routers, the interface numbers might be a single number, or two numbers separated by a slash, or three numbers separated by slashes. For example, all three of the following configuration commands are correct on at least one model of Cisco router:

```
interface ethernet 0
interface fastEthernet 0/1
interface serial 1/0/1
```

You can view information about interfaces by using several commands. To see a brief list of interfaces, use the **show ip interface brief** command. To see brief details about a particular interface, use the **show protocols** *type number* command. (Note that the **show protocols** command is not available in all versions of Cisco IOS Software.) You can also see a lot of detail about each interface, including statistics about the packets flowing in and out of the interface, by using the **show interfaces** command. Optionally, you can include the interface type and number on many commands, for example, **show interfaces** *type number*, to see details for just that interface. Example 11-7 shows sample output from these three commands.

Example 11-7   *Listing the Interfaces in a Router*

```
Albuquerque# show ip interface brief
Interface            IP-Address     OK? Method Status                Protocol
FastEthernet0/0      unassigned     YES unset  up                    up
FastEthernet0/1      unassigned     YES unset  administratively down down
Serial0/0/0          unassigned     YES unset  administratively down down
Serial0/0/1          unassigned     YES unset  up                    up
Serial0/1/0          unassigned     YES unset  up                    up
Serial0/1/1          unassigned     YES unset  administratively down down
Albuquerque# show protocols fa0/0
FastEthernet0/0 is up, line protocol is up
Albuquerque# show interfaces s0/1/0
Serial0/1/0 is up, line protocol is up
  Hardware is GT96K Serial
  MTU 1500 bytes, BW 1544 Kbit, DLY 20000 usec,
     reliability 255/255, txload 1/255, rxload 1/255
  Encapsulation HDLC, loopback not set
  Keepalive set (10 sec)
  CRC checking enabled
  Last input 00:00:03, output 00:00:01, output hang never
  Last clearing of "show interface" counters never
  Input queue: 0/75/0/0 (size/max/drops/flushes); Total output drops: 0
  Queueing strategy: weighted fair
```

```
    Output queue: 0/1000/64/0 (size/max total/threshold/drops)
       Conversations  0/1/256 (active/max active/max total)
       Reserved Conversations 0/0 (allocated/max allocated)
       Available Bandwidth 1158 kilobits/sec
  5 minute input rate 0 bits/sec, 0 packets/sec
  5 minute output rate 0 bits/sec, 0 packets/sec
       70 packets input, 6979 bytes, 0 no buffer
       Received 70 broadcasts, 0 runts, 0 giants, 0 throttles
       0 input errors, 0 CRC, 0 frame, 0 overrun, 0 ignored, 0 abort
       36 packets output, 4557 bytes, 0 underruns
       0 output errors, 0 collisions, 8 interface resets
       0 output buffer failures, 0 output buffers swapped out
       13 carrier transitions
       DCD=up  DSR=up  DTR=up  RTS=up  CTS=up
```

Note: Commands that refer to router interfaces can be significantly shortened by truncating the words. For example, **sh int fa0/0** can be used instead of **show interfaces fastethernet 0/0**. In fact, many network engineers, when looking over someone's shoulder, would say something like, "just do a show int F-A-oh-oh command" in this case, rather than speaking the long version of the command.

Interface Status Codes

Each of the commands in Example 11-7 lists two *interface status codes*. For a router to use an interface, the two interface status codes on the interface must be in an "up" state. The first status code refers essentially to whether Layer 1 is working, and the second status code mainly (but not always) refers to whether the data link layer protocol is working. Table 11-3 summarizes these two status codes.

Table 11-3 *Interface Status Codes and Their Meanings*

Name	Location	General Meaning
Line status	First status code	Refers to the Layer 1 status—for example, is the cable installed, is it the right/wrong cable, is the device on the other end powered on?
Protocol status	Second status code	Refers generally to the Layer 2 status. It is always down if the line status is down. If the line status is up, a protocol status of down usually is caused by mismatched data link layer configuration.

Four combinations of settings exist for the status codes when troubleshooting a network. Table 11-4 lists the four combinations, along with an explanation of the typical reasons why an interface would be in that state. As you review the list, note that if the line status (the first status code) is not "up," the second will always be "down," because the data link layer functions cannot work if the physical layer has a problem.

Key
Topic
Table 11-4   *Typical Combinations of Interface Status Codes*

Line and Protocol Status	Typical Reasons
Administratively down, down	The interface has a **shutdown** command configured on it.
down, down	The interface has a **no shutdown** command configured, but the physical layer has a problem. For example, no cable has been attached to the interface, or with Ethernet, the interface on the other end of the cable is shut down, or the switch is powered off.
up, down	Almost always refers to data link layer problems, most often configuration problems. For example, serial links have this combination when one router was configured to use PPP, and the other defaults to use HDLC.
up, up	All is well, interface is functioning.

Router Interface IP Addresses

As has been mentioned many times throughout this book, routers need an IP address on each interface. If no IP address is configured, even if the interface is in an up/up state, the router will not attempt to send and receive IP packets on the interface. For proper operation, for every interface a router should use for forwarding IP packets, the router needs an IP address.

The configuration of an IP address on an interface is relatively simple. To configure the address and mask, simply use the **ip address** *address mask* interface subcommand. Example 11-8 shows an example configuration of IP addresses on two router interfaces, and the resulting differences in the **show ip interface brief** and **show interfaces** commands from Example 11-7. (No IP addresses were configured when the output in Example 11-7 was gathered.)

Example 11-8   *Configuring IP Addresses on Cisco Routers*

```
Albuquerque# configure terminal
Enter configuration commands, one per line.  End with CNTL/Z.
Albuquerque (config)# interface Fa0/0
Albuquerque (config-if)# ip address 10.1.1.1 255.255.255.0
Albuquerque (config-if)# interface S0/0/1
Albuquerque (config-if)# ip address 10.1.2.1 255.255.255.0
Albuquerque (config-if)# ^Z
Albuquerque# show ip interface brief
```

```
Interface                 IP-Address    OK? Method Status                  Protocol
FastEthernet0/0           10.1.1.1      YES manual up                      up
FastEthernet0/1           unassigned    YES NVRAM  administratively down   down
Serial0/0/0               unassigned    YES NVRAM  administratively down   down
Serial0/0/1               10.1.2.1      YES manual up                      up
Serial0/1/0               unassigned    YES NVRAM  up                      up
Serial0/1/1               unassigned    YES NVRAM  administratively down   down
Albuquerque# show interfaces fa0/0
FastEthernet0/0 is up, line protocol is up
  Hardware is Gt96k FE, address is 0013.197b.5004 (bia 0013.197b.5004)
  Internet address is 10.1.1.1/24
! lines omitted for brevity
```

Bandwidth and Clock Rate on Serial Interfaces

Ethernet interfaces use either a single speed or one of a few speeds that can be auto-negotiated. However, as mentioned in Chapter 3, WAN links can run at a wide variety of speeds. To deal with the wide range of speeds, routers physically slave themselves to the speed as dictated by the CSU/DSU through a process called *clocking*. As a result, routers can use serial links without the need for additional configuration or autonegotiation to sense the serial link's speed. The CSU/DSU knows the speed, the CSU/DSU sends clock pulses over the cable to the router, and the router reacts to the clocking signal. In effect, the CSU/DSU tells the router when to send the next bit over the cable, and when to receive the next bit, with the router just blindly reacting to the CSU/DSU for that timing.

The physical details of how clocking works prevent routers from sensing and measuring the speed used on a link with CSU/DSUs. So, routers use two different interface configuration commands that specify the speed of the WAN link connected to a serial interface, namely the **clock rate** and **bandwidth** interface subcommands.

The **clock rate** command dictates the actual speed used to transmit bits on a serial link, but only when the physical serial link is actually created with cabling in a lab. The lab networks used to build the examples in this book, and probably in any labs engineers use to do proof-of-concept testing, or even labs you use when taking an on-site class, use *back-to-back serial cables* (see the Chapter 3 section "Building a WAN Link in a Lab" for a reminder). Back-to-back WAN connections do not use a CSU/DSU, so one router must supply the clocking, which defines the speed at which bits are transmitted. The other router works as usual when CSU/DSUs are used, slaving itself to the clocking signals received from the other router. Example 11-9 shows an example configuration for a router named Albuquerque, with a couple of important commands related to WAN links.

Note: Example 11-9 omits some of the output of the **show running-config** command, specifically the parts that do not matter to the information covered here.

Example 11-9   *Albuquerque Router Configuration with* clock rate *Command*

```
Albuquerque# show running-config
! lines omitted for brevity
interface Serial0/0/1
 clock rate 128000
!
interface Serial0/1/0
 clock rate 128000
 bandwidth 128
!
interface FastEthernet0/0
! lines omitted for brevity
Albuquerque# show controllers serial 0/0/1
Interface Serial0
Hardware is PowerQUICC MPC860
DCE V.35, clock rate 128000
idb at 0x8169BB20, driver data structure at 0x816A35E4
! Lines omitted for brevity
```

The **clock rate** *speed* interface subcommand sets the rate in bits per second on the router that has the DCE cable plugged into it. If you do not know which router has the DCE cable in it, you can find out by using the **show controllers** command, which lists whether the attached cable is DCE (as shown in Example 11-9) or DTE. Interestingly, IOS accepts the **clock rate** command on an interface only if the interface already has a DCE cable installed, or if no cable is installed. If a DTE cable has been plugged in, IOS silently rejects the command, meaning that IOS does not give you an error message, but IOS ignores the command.

The second interface subcommand that relates to the speed of the serial link is the **bandwidth** *speed* command, as shown on interface serial 0/1/0 in Example 11-9. The **bandwidth** command tells IOS the speed of the link, in kilobits per second, regardless of whether the router is supplying clocking. However, the **bandwidth** setting does not change the speed at which bits are sent and received on the link. Instead, the router uses it for documentation purposes, in calculations related to the utilization rates of the link, and for many other purposes. In particular, the EIGRP and OSPF routing protocols use the interface **bandwidth** settings to set their default metrics, with the metrics impacting a router's choice of the best IP route to reach each subnet. (Later chapters in this book examine the EIGRP and OSPF routing protocols, and describe how the **bandwidth** command impacts how these protocols choose the best route.)

Every router interface has a default setting of the **bandwidth** command that is used when there is no **bandwidth** command configured on the interface. For serial links, the default bandwidth is 1544, meaning 1544 kbps, or 1.544 Mbps—in other words, the speed of a T1 line. Router Ethernet interfaces default to a bandwidth setting that reflects the current speed of the interface. For example, if a router's FastEthernet interface is running at 100 Mbps, the bandwidth is 100,000 (kbps); if the interface is currently running at 10 Mbps, the router automatically changes the bandwidth to 10,000 kbps. Note that the configuration of the **bandwidth** command on an interface overrides these defaults.

> **Note:**   The **clock rate** command uses a unit of bps, whereas the **bandwidth** command uses a unit of kbps. In other words, a **show** command that lists bandwidth as 10,000 means 10,000 kbps, or 10 Mbps.

Router Auxiliary (Aux) Port

Routers have an auxiliary (Aux) port that allows access to the CLI by using a terminal emulator. Normally, the Aux port is connected via a cable (RJ-45, 4 pair, with straight-through pinouts) to an external analog modem. The modem connects to a phone line. Then, the engineer uses a PC, terminal emulator, and modem to call the remote router. Once connected, the engineer can use the terminal emulator to access the router CLI, starting in user mode as usual.

Aux ports can be configured beginning with the **line aux 0** command to reach aux line configuration mode. From there, all the commands for the console line, covered mostly in Chapter 7, can be used. For example, the **login** and **password** *passvalue* commands could be used to set up simple password checking when a user dials in.

Cisco switches do not have an Aux port.

Initial Configuration (Setup Mode)

The processes related to setup mode in routers follow the same rules as for switches. You can refer to the Chapter 7 section "Initial Configuration Using Setup Mode" for more details, but the following statements summarize some of the key points, all of which are true on both switches and routers:

- Setup mode is intended to allow basic configuration by prompting the CLI user via a series of questions.

- You can reach setup mode either by booting a router after erasing the startup-config file or by using the **setup** enable-mode EXEC command.

- At the end of the process, you get three choices (0, 1, or 2), to either ignore the answers and go back to the CLI (0); ignore the answers but begin again in setup mode (1); or to use the resulting configuration (2).

- If you tire of the process, the Ctrl-C key combination will eject the user out of setup mode and back to the previous CLI mode.

- If you select to use the resulting configuration, the router writes the configuration to the startup-config file, as well as the running-config file.

The main difference between the setup mode on switches and routers relates to the information requested while in setup mode. For example, routers need to know the IP address and mask for each interface on which you want to configure IP, whereas switches have only one IP address. To be complete, Example 11-10 demonstrates the use of setup mode. If you do not have a router with which to practice setup mode, take the time to review the example, and see the kinds of information requested in the various questions.

Note: The questions asked, and the default answers, differ on some routers in part due to the IOS revision, feature set, and router model.

Example 11-10 *Router Setup Configuration Mode*

```
--- System Configuration Dialog ---


Would you like to enter the initial configuration dialog? [yes/no]: yes
At any point you may enter a question mark '?' for help.
Use ctrl-c to abort configuration dialog at any prompt.
Default settings are in square brackets '[]'.Basic management setup configures
only enough connectivity
for management of the system, extended setup will ask you
to configure each interface on the system



Would you like to enter basic management setup? [yes/no]: no
First, would you like to see the current interface summary? [yes]:
Any interface listed with OK? value "NO" does not have a valid configuration
Interface              IP-Address      OK? Method Status              Protocol
Ethernet0              unassigned      NO  unset  up                  down
Serial0                unassigned      NO  unset  down                down
Serial1                unassigned      NO  unset  down                down
Configuring global parameters:
  Enter host name [Router]: R1
      The enable secret is a password used to protect access to
      privileged EXEC and configuration modes. This password, after
      entered, becomes encrypted in the configuration.
      Enter enable secret: cisco
    The enable password is used when you do not specify an
      enable secret password, with some older software versions, and
      some boot images.
      Enter enable password: fred
    The virtual terminal password is used to protect
      access to the router over a network interface.
      Enter virtual terminal password: barney
    Configure SNMP Network Management? [yes]: no
```

```
    Configure bridging? [no]:
    Configure DECnet? [no]:
    Configure AppleTalk? [no]:
    Configure IPX? [no]:
    Configure IP? [yes]:
    Configure RIP routing? [yes]:
Configure CLNS? [no]:
  Configure bridging? [no]:


Configuring interface parameters:
    Do you want to configure Ethernet0  interface? [yes]:
    Configure IP on this interface? [yes]:
    IP address for this interface: 172.16.1.1
    Subnet mask for this interface [255.255.0.0] : 255.255.255.0
    Class B network is 172.16.0.0, 24 subnet bits; mask is /24
    Do you want to configure Serial0  interface? [yes]:
      Configure IP on this interface? [yes]:
    Configure IP unnumbered on this interface? [no]:
    IP address for this interface: 172.16.12.1
    Subnet mask for this interface [255.255.0.0] : 255.255.255.0
    Class B network is 172.16.0.0, 24 subnet bits; mask is /24
    Do you want to configure Serial1  interface? [yes]:
    Configure IP on this interface? [yes]:
    Configure IP unnumbered on this interface? [no]:
    IP address for this interface: 172.16.13.1
    Subnet mask for this interface [255.255.0.0] : 255.255.255.0
    Class B network is 172.16.0.0, 24 subnet bits; mask is /24


    The following configuration command script was created:


    hostname R1
    enable secret 5 $1$VOLh$pkIe0Xjx2sgjgZ/Y6Gt1s.
    enable password fred
    line vty 0 4
    password barney
    no snmp-server
    !
    ip routing
     !
    interface Ethernet0
    ip address 172.16.1.1 255.255.255.0
    !
    interface Serial0
    ip address 172.16.12.1 255.255.255.0
    !
```

```
      interface Serial1
      ip address 172.16.13.1 255.255.255.0
      !
      router rip
      network 172.16.0.0
      !
      end


      [0] Go to the IOS command prompt without saving this config.
      [1] Return back to the setup without saving this config.
      [2] Save this configuration to nvram and exit.


      Enter your selection [2]: 2
      Building configuration...
      [OK]Use the enabled mode 'configure' command to modify this configuration.
      Press RETURN to get started!
```

Note: Although not shown in this example, routers that use an IOS feature set that includes additional security features will also ask the user if they want to configure *Cisco Auto Secure*. This feature automatically configures many router security best practice settings, for example, disabling CDP.

Upgrading Cisco IOS Software and the Cisco IOS Software Boot Process

Engineers need to know how to upgrade IOS to move to a later release or version of IOS. Typically, a router has one IOS image in Flash memory, and that is the IOS image that is used. (The term *IOS image* simply refers to a file containing IOS.) The upgrade process might include steps such as copying a newer IOS image into Flash memory, configuring the router to tell it which IOS image to use, and deleting the old one when you are confident that the new release works well. Alternately, you could copy a new image to a TFTP server, with some additional configuration on the router to tell it to get the new IOS from the TFTP server the next time the router is reloaded.

This section shows how to upgrade IOS by copying a new IOS file into Flash memory and telling the router to use the new IOS. Because the router decides which IOS to use when the router boots, this is also a good place to review the process by which routers boot (initialize). Switches follow the same basic process as described here, with some minor differences, as specifically noted.

Upgrading a Cisco IOS Software Image into Flash Memory

Routers and switches typically store IOS images in Flash memory. Flash memory is rewriteable, permanent storage, which is ideal for storing files that need to be retained when the router loses power. Cisco purposefully uses Flash memory instead of disk drives in its products because there are no moving parts in Flash memory, so there is a smaller chance of failure as compared with disk drives. Additionally, the IOS image can be placed on an external TFTP server, but using an external server typically is done for testing; in production, practically every Cisco router loads an IOS image stored in the only type of large, permanent memory in a Cisco router—Flash memory.

Figure 11-2 illustrates the process to upgrade an IOS image into Flash memory:

Step 1.   Obtain the IOS image from Cisco, typically by downloading the IOS image from Cisco.com using HTTP or FTP.

Step 2.   Place the IOS image into the default directory of a TFTP server that is accessible from the router.

Step 3.   Issue the **copy** command from the router, copying the file into Flash memory.

You also can use an FTP or remote copy (rcp) server, but the TFTP feature has been around a long time and is a more likely topic for the exams.

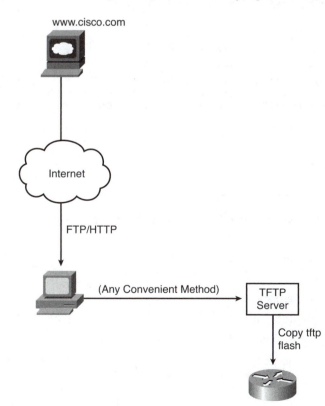

Figure 11-2   *Complete Cisco IOS Software Upgrade Process*

Example 11-11 provides an example of the final step, copying the IOS image into Flash memory. Note that the **copy tftp flash** command shown here works much like the **copy tftp startup-config** command that can be used to restore a backup copy of the configuration file into NVRAM.

Example 11-11   copy tftp flash *Command Copies the IOS Image to Flash Memory*

```
R1# copy tftp flash

System flash directory:
File  Length   Name/status
  1   7530760   c4500-d-mz.120-2.bin
[7530824 bytes used, 857784 available, 8388608 total]
Address or name of remote host [255.255.255.255]? 134.141.3.33
Source file name? c4500-d-mz.120-5.bin
Destination file name [c4500-d-mz.120-5.bin]?
Accessing file c4500-d-mz.120-5.bin ' on 134.141.3.33...
Loading c4500-d-mz.120-5.bin from 134.141.3.33 (via Ethernet0): ! [OK]

Erase flash device before writing? [confirm]
Flash contains files. Are you sure you want to erase? [confirm]

Copy 'c4500-d-mz.120-5.bin' from server
  as 'c4500-d-mz.120-5.bin' into Flash WITH erase? [yes/no]y
Erasing device... eeeeeeeeeeeeeeeeeeeeeeeeeeeeeeeee ...erased
Loading c4500-d-mz.120-5.bin  from 134.141.3.33 (via Ethernet0):
!!!!!!!!!!!!!!!!!!!!!!!!!!!!!!!!!!!!!!!!!!!!!!!!!!!!!!!!!!!!!!!!!!!!!!!!!!!!!!!!!!
!!!!!!!!!!!!!!!!!!!!!!!!!!!!!!!!!!!!!!!!!!!!!!!!!!! (leaving out lots of exclamation
points)
[OK  7530760/8388608 bytes]

Verifying checksum...  OK (0xA93E)
Flash copy took 0:04:26 [hh:mm:ss]
```

During this process of copying the IOS image into Flash memory, the router needs to discover several important facts:

1. What is the IP address or host name of the TFTP server?
2. What is the name of the file?
3. Is space available for this file in Flash memory?
4. Does the server actually have a file by that name?
5. Do you want the router to erase the old files?

The router will prompt you for answers, as necessary. For each question, you should either type an answer or press Enter if the default answer (shown in square brackets at the end of the question) is acceptable. Afterward, the router erases Flash memory if directed, copies the file, and then verifies that the checksum for the file shows that no errors occurred in transmission. You can then use the **show flash** command to verify the contents of Flash memory, as demonstrated in Example 11-12. (The **show flash** output can vary among router families. Example 11-12 is output from a 2500 series router.)

Example 11-12 *Verifying Flash Memory Contents with the* **show flash** *Command*

```
fred# show flash
System flash directory:
File  Length    Name/status
  1   13305352  c2500-ds-1.122-1.bin
[13305416 bytes used, 3471800 available, 16777216 total]
16384K bytes of processor board System flash (Read ONLY)
```

The shaded line in Example 11-12 lists the amount of Flash memory, the amount used, and the amount of free space. When copying a new IOS image into Flash, the **copy** command will ask you if you want to erase Flash, with a default answer of [yes]. If you reply with an answer of **no**, and IOS realizes that not enough available Flash memory exists, the copy will fail. Additionally, even if you answer **yes**, and erase all of the Flash memory, the new Flash IOS image must be of a size that fits into flash memory; if not, the **copy** command will fail.

Once the new IOS has been copied into Flash, the router must be reloaded to use the new IOS image. The next section, which covers the IOS boot sequence, explains the details of how to configure a router so that it loads the right IOS image.

The Cisco IOS Software Boot Sequence

Cisco routers perform the same types of tasks that a typical computer performs when you power it on or reboot (reload) it. Most computers have a single operating system (OS) installed, and that OS boots by default. However, a router can have multiple IOS images available both in Flash memory and on external TFTP servers, so the router needs to know which IOS image to load. This section examines the entire boot process, with extra emphasis on the options that impact a router's choice of what IOS image to load.

Note: The boot sequence details in this section, particularly those regarding the configuration register and the ROMMON OS, differ from Cisco LAN switches, but they do apply to most every model of Cisco router. This book does not cover the equivalent options in Cisco switches.

When a router first powers on, it follows these four steps:

1. The router performs a power-on self-test (POST) to discover the hardware components and verify that all components work properly.

2. The router copies a bootstrap program from ROM into RAM, and runs the bootstrap program.

3. The bootstrap program decides which IOS image (or other OS) to load into RAM, and loads that OS. After loading the IOS image, the bootstrap program hands over control of the router hardware to the newly loaded OS.

4. If the bootstrap program loaded IOS, IOS finds the configuration file (typically the startup-config file in NVRAM) and loads it into RAM as the running-config.

All routers attempt all four steps each time that the router is powered on or reloaded. The first two steps do not have any options to choose; these steps either work or the router initialization fails and you typically need to call the Cisco Technical Assistance Center (TAC) for support. However, Steps 3 and 4 have several configurable options that tell the router what to do next. Figure 11-3 depicts those options, referencing Steps 2 through 4 shown in the earlier boot process.

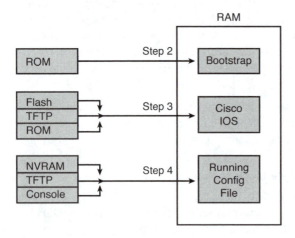

Figure 11-3   *Loading the Cisco IOS*

As you can see, the router can get the IOS image from three locations and can get the initial configuration from three locations as well. Frankly, routers almost always load the configuration from NVRAM (the startup-config file), when it exists. There is no real advantage to storing the initial configuration anywhere else except NVRAM. So, this chapter will not look further into the options of Step 4. However, there are good reasons for putting multiple IOS images in Flash, and keeping images on external servers, so the rest of this section examines Step 3 in more detail. In particular, the next few pages explain a few facts about some alternate router operating systems besides IOS, and a router feature called the *configuration register*, before showing how a router chooses which IOS image to load.

Note: The IOS image is typically a compressed file so that it consumes less space in Flash memory. The router decompresses the IOS image when it is loaded into RAM.

The Three Router Operating Systems

A router typically loads and uses a Cisco IOS image that allows the router to perform its normal function of routing packets. However, Cisco routers can use a different OS to perform some troubleshooting, to recover router passwords, and to copy new IOS files into Flash when Flash has been inadvertently erased or corrupted. In the more recent additions to the Cisco router product line (for example, 1800 and 2800 series routers), Cisco routers use only one other OS, whereas older Cisco routers (for example, 2500 series routers) actually had two different operating systems to perform different subsets of these same functions. Table 11-5 lists the other two router operating systems, and a few details about each.

Table 11-5 *Comparing ROMMON and RxBoot Operating Systems*

Operating Environment	Common Name	Stored In	Used in...
ROM Monitor	ROMMON	ROM	Old and new routers
Boot ROM	RxBoot, boot helper	ROM	Only in older routers

Key Topic

Because the RxBoot OS is only available in older routers and is no longer needed in the newer routers, this chapter will mainly refer to the OS that continues to be available for these special functions, the ROMMON OS.

The Configuration Register

The configuration register is a special 16-bit number that can be set on any Cisco router. The configuration register's bits control different settings for some low-level operating characteristics of the router. For example, the console runs at a speed of 9600 bps by default, but that console speed is based on the default settings of a couple of bits in the configuration register.

You can set the *configuration register* value with the **config-register** global configuration command. Engineers set the configuration register to different values for many reasons, but the most common are to help tell the router what IOS image to load, as explained in the next few pages, and in the password recovery process. For example, the command **config-register 0x2100** sets the value to hexadecimal 2100, which causes the router to load the ROMMON OS instead of IOS. Interestingly, this value is automatically saved when you press Enter at the end of the **config-register** command—you do not need to save the running-config file into the startup-config file after changing the configuration register. However, the configuration register's new value is not used until the next time the router is reloaded.

Tip: The **show version** command, shown near the end of this chapter in Example 11-13, shows the configuration register's current value and, if different, the value that will be used once the router is reloaded.

> **Note:**   On most Cisco routers, the default configuration register setting is hexadecimal 2102.

How a Router Chooses Which OS to Load

A router chooses the OS to load based on the low-order 4 bits in the configuration register and the details configured in any **boot system** global configuration commands found in the startup-config file. The low-order 4 bits (the 4th hex digit) in the configuration register are called the *boot field*, with the value of these bits being the first value a router examines when choosing which OS to try and load. The boot field's value when the router is powered on or reloaded tells the router how to proceed with choosing which OS to load.

> **Note:**   Cisco represents hexadecimal values by preceding the hex digit(s) with 0x—for example, 0xA would mean a single hex digit A.

The process to choose which OS to load, on more modern routers that do not have an Rx-Boot OS, happens as follows (note that "boot" refers to the boot field in the configuration register):

Key Topic

Step 1.   If boot field = 0, use the ROMMON OS.

Step 2.   If boot field = 1, load the first IOS file found in Flash memory.

Step 3.   If boot field = 2-F:

    a.   Try each **boot system** command in the startup-config file, in order, until one works.

    b.   If none of the **boot system** commands work, load the first IOS file found in Flash memory.

> **Note:**   The actual step numbers are not important—the list is just numbered for easier reference.

The first two steps are pretty straightforward, but Step 3 then tells the router to look to the second major method to tell the router which IOS to load: the **boot system** global configuration command. This command can be configured multiple times on one router, with details about files in Flash memory, and filenames and IP addresses of servers, telling the router where to look for an IOS image to load. The router tries to load the IOS images, in the order of the configured **boot system** commands. Once the router succeeds in loading one of the referenced IOS images, the process is complete, and the router can ignore the remaining **boot system** commands. If the router fails to load an IOS based on the **boot system** commands, the router then tries what Step 1 suggests, which is to load the first IOS file found in Flash memory.

Both Step 2 and Step 3b refer to a concept of the "first" IOS file, a concept which needs a little more explanation. Routers number the files stored in Flash memory, with each new file typically getting a higher and higher number. When a router tries Step 2 or Step 3b from the preceding list, the router will look in Flash memory, starting with file number 1, and then file number 2, and so on, until it finds the lowest numbered file that happens to be an IOS image. The router will then load that file.

Interestingly, most routers end up using Step 3b to find their IOS image. From the factory, Cisco routers do not have any **boot system** commands configured; in fact, they do not have any configuration in the startup-config file at all. Cisco loads Flash memory with a single IOS when it builds and tests the router, and the configuration register value is set to 0x2102, meaning a boot field of 0x2. With all these settings, the process tries Step 3 (because boot = 2), finds no **boot system** commands (because the startup-config is empty), and then looks for the first file in Flash memory at Step 3b.

Figure 11-4 shows a diagram that summarizes the key concepts behind how a router chooses the OS to load.

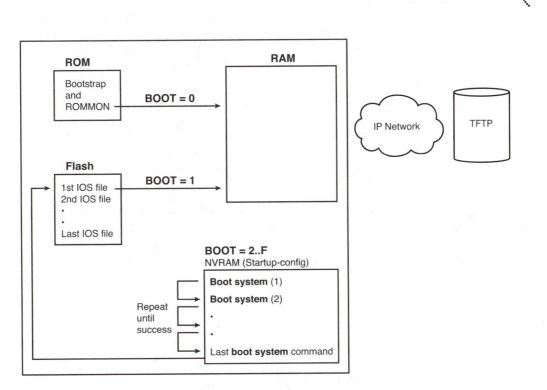

Figure 11-4 *Choices for Choosing the OS at Boot Time: Modern Cisco Router*

The **boot system** commands need to refer to the exact file that the router should load. Table 11-6 shows several examples of the commands.

Table 11-6 *Sample* boot system *Commands*

Boot System Command	Result
boot system flash	The first file from Flash memory is loaded.
boot system flash *filename*	IOS with the name *filename* is loaded from Flash memory.
boot system tftp *filename* **10.1.1.1**	IOS with the name *filename* is loaded from the TFTP server.

In some cases, a router fails to load on OS based on the three-step process listed earlier in this section. For example, someone might accidentally erase all the contents of Flash, including the IOS image. So, routers need more options to help recover from these unexpected but possible scenarios. If no OS is found by the end of Step 3, the router will send broadcasts looking for a TFTP server, guess at a filename for the IOS image, and load an IOS image (assuming that a TFTP server is found). In practice, it is highly unlikely to work. The final step is to simply load ROMMON, which is designed in part to provide tools to recover from these unexpected types of problems. For example, an IOS image can be copied into Flash from a TFTP server while using ROMMON.

For older models of Cisco router that have an RxBoot (boot helper) OS in ROM, the process to choose which OS to load works generally the same, with two differences. When the boot field is 0x1, the router loads the RxBoot OS stored in ROM. Also, in the final efforts to find an OS as described in the previous paragraph, if the effort to find an image from a TFTP server fails, and the router has an RxBoot image, the router first tries to load RxBoot before trying to load the ROM Monitor OS.

The show version Command and Seeing the Configuration Register's Value

The **show version** command supplies a wide variety of information about a router, including both the current value of the configuration register and the expected value at the next reload of the router. The following list summarizes some of the other very interesting information in this command:

Key Topic

1. The IOS version
2. The uptime (the length of time that has passed since the last reload)
3. The reason for the last reload of IOS (**reload** command, power off/on, software failure)
4. The time of the last loading of IOS (if the router's clock has been set)
5. The source from which the router loaded the current IOS
6. The amount of RAM memory
7. The number and types of interfaces
8. The amount of NVRAM memory
9. The amount of Flash memory
10. The configuration register's current and future setting (if different)

Example 11-13 demonstrates output from the **show version** command, highlighting the key pieces of information. Note that the preceding list is in the same order in which the highlighted information appears in the example.

Example 11-13   show version *Command Output*

```
Albuquerque# show version
Cisco IOS Software, 1841 Software (C1841-ADVENTERPRISEK9-M), Version 12.4(9)T,
RELEASE   SOFTWARE (fc1)
Technical Support: http://www.cisco.com/techsupport
Copyright (c) 1986-2006 by Cisco Systems, Inc.
Compiled Fri 16-Jun-06 21:26 by prod_rel_team
ROM: System Bootstrap, Version 12.3(8r)T8, RELEASE SOFTWARE (fc1)


Albuquerque uptime is 5 hours, 20 minutes
System returned to ROM by reload at 13:12:26 UTC Wed Jan 17 2007
System restarted at 13:13:38 UTC Wed Jan 17 2007
System image file is "flash:c1841-adventerprisek9-mz.124-9.T.bin"



This product contains cryptographic features and is subject to United
States and local country laws governing import, export, transfer and
use. Delivery of Cisco cryptographic products does not imply
third-party authority to import, export, distribute or use encryption.
Importers, exporters, distributors and users are responsible for
compliance with U.S. and local country laws. By using this product you
agree to comply with applicable laws and regulations. If you are unable
to comply with U.S. and local laws, return this product immediately.

A summary of U.S. laws governing Cisco cryptographic products may be found at:
http://www.cisco.com/wwl/export/crypto/tool/stqrg.html
If you require further assistance please contact us by sending email to
export@cisco.com.


Cisco 1841 (revision 4.1) with 354304K/38912K bytes of memory.
Processor board ID FTX0906Y03T
2 FastEthernet interfaces
4 Serial(sync/async) interfaces
1 Virtual Private Network (VPN) Module
DRAM configuration is 64 bits wide with parity disabled.
191K bytes of NVRAM.
125440K bytes of ATA CompactFlash (Read/Write)


Configuration register is 0x2102 (will be 0x2101 at next reload)
```

Most of the information highlighted in the example can be easily found in comparison to the list preceding Example 11-13. However, note that the amount of RAM, listed as 354304K/38912K, shows the RAM in two parts. The sum of these two parts is the total amount of available RAM, about 384 MB in this case.

Chapter Review

Review Key Topics

Review the most important topics from inside the chapter, noted with the Key Topic icon in the outer margin of the page. Table 11-7 lists a reference of these key topics and the page numbers on which each is found.

Table 11-7   *Key Topics for Chapter 11*

Key Topic	Description	Page Number
Example 11-1	Configuring Passwords and a Hostname	235
Figure 11-1	SSH Configuration Concepts	237
List	SSH configuration steps	238
List	Comparisons of the two enable passwords	241
Table 11-2	Commands related to the history buffer	244
Table 11-3	Router interface status codes and their meanings	247
Table 11-4	Combinations of the two interface status codes and the likely reasons for each combination	248
List	Summary of important facts about the initial configuration dialog (setup mode)	251
List	The four steps a router performs when booting	258
Table 11-5	Comparison of ROMMON and RxBoot operating systems	259
List	Steps a router uses to choose which IOS image to load	260
Figure 11-4	Diagram of how a router chooses which IOS image to load	261
List	A list of the many important facts that can be seen in the output from the **show version** command	262

Define Key Terms

Define the following key terms from this chapter and check your answers in the glossary:

bandwidth, boot field, clock rate, configuration register, IOS image, power-on self-test (POST), ROMMON, RxBoot

Review Command References to Check Your Memory

Although you should not necessarily memorize the information in the tables in this section, this section does include a reference for the configuration commands (Table 11-8) and EXEC commands (Table 11-9) covered in this chapter. Practically speaking, you should memorize the commands as a complement to reading the chapter and doing all the activities in the "Chapter Review" section. To check to see how well you have memorized the commands, cover the left side of the table with a piece of paper, read the descriptions on the right side, and see whether you remember the command.

Table 11-8 *Chapter 11 Configuration Command Reference*

Command	Mode/Purpose/Description
Basic Password Configuration	
The following four commands are related to basic password configuration.	
line console 0	Changes the context to console configuration mode.
line vty *1st-vty 2nd-vty*	Changes the context to vty configuration mode for the range of vty lines listed in the command.
login	Console and vty configuration mode. Tells IOS to prompt for a password.
password *pass-value*	Console and vty configuration mode. Lists the password required if the **login** command (with no other parameters) is configured.
Username/Password and SSH Configuration	
The following four commands are related to username/password and SSH configuration.	
login local	Console and vty configuration mode. Tells IOS to prompt for a username and password, to be checked against locally configured **username** global configuration commands on this switch or router.
username *name* **password** *pass-value*	Global command. Defines one of possibly multiple usernames and associated passwords, used for user authentication. Used when the **login local** line configuration command has been used.
crypto key generate rsa	Global command. Creates and stores (in a hidden location in flash memory) the keys required by SSH.
**transport input {telnet	ssh}**	vty line configuration mode. Defines whether Telnet and/or SSH access is allowed into this switch. Both values can be configured on one command to allow both Telnet and SSH access (the default).

Table 11-8 *Chapter 11 Configuration Command Reference*

Command	Mode/Purpose/Description
Interface Configuration	
The following commands are related to interface configuration.	
interface *type number*	Changes context to interface mode. The *type* is typically Ethernet, FastEthernet, GigabitEthernet, or Serial. The possible port numbers vary depending on the model of router—for example, Fa0/1, Serial0/1, and so on.
shutdown no shutdown	Interface mode. Disables or enables the interface, respectively.
speed {10	100	1000	auto}	Interface mode. Manually sets the speed to the listed speed on LAN interfaces that support multiple speeds, or, with the **auto** setting, automatically negotiates the speed.
duplex {auto	full	half}	Interface mode. Manually sets the duplex to half or full on LAN interfaces, or to autonegotiate the duplex setting.
description *text*	Interface mode. Lists any information text that the engineer wants to track for the interface, such as the expected device on the other end of the cable.
ip address *address mask*	Configures the IP address and mask to use on the interface.
bandwidth *kbps*	Interface command that sets the router's perception of bandwidth of the interface, in a unit of kbps.
clock rate *rate*	Interface command that sets the speed at which the router supplies a clocking signal on serial interfaces, applicable only when the router has a DCE cable installed. The unit is bits/second.
Miscellaneous	
The following commands are related to miscellaneous configuration topics.	
hostname *name*	Global command. Sets this router's hostname, which is also used as the first part of the router's command prompt.
enable secret *pass-value*	Global command. Sets this router's password that is required for any user to reach enable mode.
history size *length*	Line config mode. Defines the number of commands held in the history buffer, for later recall, for users of those lines.
Boot Commands	
The following commands are related to booting the router.	
config-register *value*	Global command that sets the hexadecimal value of the configuration register.

Table 11-8 *Chapter 11 Configuration Command Reference*

Command	Mode/Purpose/Description
boot system {*file-url* | *filename*}	Global command that identifies an externally located IOS image using a URL.
boot system flash [*flash-fs:*] [*filename*]	Global command that identifies the location of an IOS image in Flash memory.
boot system rom	Global command that tells the router to load the RxBoot OS found in ROM, if one exists.
boot system {**rcp** | **tftp** | **ftp**} *filename* [*ip-address*]	Global command that identifies an external server, protocol, and filename to use to load an IOS from an external server.

Table 11-9 *Chapter 11 EXEC Command Reference*

Command	Purpose
show interfaces [*type number*]	Lists a large set of informational messages about each interface, or about the one specifically listed interface.
show ip interface brief	Lists a single line of information about each interface, including the IP address, line and protocol status, and the method with which the address was configured (manual or DHCP).
show crypto key mypubkey rsa	Lists the public and shared key created for use with SSH using the **crypto key generate rsa** global configuration command.
show protocols *type number*	Lists a single line of information about the listed interface, including the IP address, mask, and line/protocol status.
show controllers [*type number*]	Lists many lines of information per interface, or for one interface, for the hardware controller of the interface. On serial interfaces, this command identifies the cable as either a DCE or DTE cable.
show version	Lists the IOS version, as well as a large set of other useful information (see Example 11-13).
setup	Starts the setup (initial configuration) dialog in which the router prompts the user for basic configuration settings.
copy *source-url destination-url*	Copies a file from the first listed URL to the destination URL.
show flash	Lists the names and size of the files in Flash memory, as well as noting the amount of Flash memory consumed and available.
reload	Enable mode command that reinitializes (reboots) the router.

Answer Review Questions

Answer the following review questions:

1. Imagine that you have configured the **enable secret** command, followed by the **enable password** command, from the console. You log out of the switch and log back in at the console. Which command defines the password that you had to enter to access privileged mode?

   a.   enable password

   b.   enable secret

   c.   Neither

   d.   The **password** command, if it's configured

2. An engineer had formerly configured a Cisco router to allow Telnet access so that the switch expected a password of **mypassword** from the Telnet user. The engineer then changed the configuration to support Secure Shell. Which of the following commands could have been part of the new configuration?

   a.   A **username** *name* **password** *password* command in vty config mode

   b.   A **username** *name* **password** *password* global configuration command

   c.   A **transport input ssh** command in vty config mode

   d.   A **transport input ssh** global configuration command

3. The following command was copied and pasted into configuration mode when a user was telnetted into a Cisco router:

   banner login this is the login banner

   Which of the following are true about what occurs the next time a user logs in from the console?

   a.   No banner text is displayed.

   b.   The banner text "his is" is displayed.

   c.   The banner text "this is the login banner" is displayed.

   d.   The banner text "Login banner configured, no text defined" is displayed.

4. Which of the following features would you typically expect to be associated with the router CLI, but not with the switch CLI?

   a.   The **clock rate** command

   b.   The **ip address** *address mask* command

   c.   The **ip address dhcp** command

   d.   The **interface vlan 1** command

5. You just bought two Cisco routers for use in a lab, connecting each router to a different LAN switch with their Fa0/0 interfaces. You also connected the two routers' serial interfaces using a back-to-back cable. Which of the following steps is not required to be able to forward IP on both routers' interfaces?

   a. Configuring an IP address on each router's FastEthernet and serial interfaces

   b. Configuring the **bandwidth** command on one router's serial interface

   c. Configuring the **clock rate** command on one router's serial interface

   d. Setting the interface **description** on both the FastEthernet and serial interface of each router

6. The output of the **show ip interface brief** command on R1 lists interface status codes of "down" and "down" for interface Serial 0/0. Which of the following could be true?

   a. The **shutdown** command is currently configured for that interface.

   b. R1's serial interface has been configured to use Frame Relay, but the router on the other end of the serial link has been configured to use PPP.

   c. R1's serial interface does not have a serial cable installed.

   d. Both routers have been cabled to a working serial link (CSU/DSUs included), but only one router has been configured with an IP address.

7. Which of the following commands does not list the IP address and mask of at least one interface?

   a. show running-config

   b. show protocols *type number*

   c. show ip interface brief

   d. show interfaces

   e. show version

8. Which of the following is different on the Cisco switch CLI as compared with the Cisco router CLI?

   a. The commands used to configure simple password checking for the console

   b. The number of IP addresses configured

   c. The types of questions asked in setup mode

   d. The configuration of the device's host name

   e. The configuration of an interface description

9. Which of the following could cause a router to change the IOS that is loaded when the router boots?

    a.   reload EXEC command

    b.   boot EXEC command

    c.   reboot EXEC command

    d.   **boot system** configuration command

    e.   **reboot system** configuration command

    f.   configuration register

10. Which of the following hexadecimal values in the last nibble of the configuration register would cause a router to not look in Flash memory for an IOS?

    a.   0

    b.   2

    c.   4

    d.   5

    e.   6

This chapter covers the following subjects:

- **IP Routing and Addressing:** This section reviews the relationship between IP addressing and IP routing, and fills in more of the details of how routing works with multiple overlapping routes.

- **Routes to Directly Connected Subnets:** This section examines how routers add routes for subnets connected to a router's interfaces.

- **Static Routes:** This section describes how to configure static routes, including static default routes.

CHAPTER 12

IP Routing: Static and Connected Routes

This chapter begins Unit 4, "IP Routing with Connected, Static, and RIP-2 Routes." This chapter reviews the IP routing process—also called IP forwarding—by which hosts and routers deliver packets from the source host to the destination host.

The IP routing process on routers uses a routing table built by the router. Each route lists a subnet ID and subnet mask, which together define the set or range of addresses in the subnet. To build these routes, routers must discover routing information from various sources, including the connected routes and static routes discussed in this chapter, and the dynamically learned routes using the RIP-2 routing protocol, as discussed in Chapter 14, "Routing Protocol Concepts and RIP-2 Configuration."

This unit includes three chapters, all related to IP routing, IP routes, and how routers learn and add routes to their routing tables. This chapter explains static routes, including default routes, as well as reviews the basic codependent topics of IP addressing and IP routing. Chapter 13, "Analyzing Existing Subnets," discusses the math related to defining a subnet. Finally, Chapter 14 discusses how routers can dynamically learn routes using the RIP routing protocol.

IP Routing and Addressing

IP routing depends on the rules of IP addressing, with one of the original core design goals for IP addressing being the creation of efficient IP routing. IP routing defines how an IP packet can be delivered from the host at which the packet is created to the destination host. IP addressing conventions group addresses into consecutively numbered sets of addresses called subnets, which then aids the IP forwarding or IP routing process.

Note: This book uses the terms *IP routing* and *IP forwarding* as synonymous terms. The term *IP routing protocols* refers to routing protocols that routers use to dynamically fill the routing tables with the currently best routes. Note that some texts and courses use the term *IP routing* when referring to both the packet-forwarding process and the protocols used to learn routes.

IP Routing

Both hosts and routers participate in the IP routing process. The next list summarizes a host's logic when forwarding a packet, assuming that the host is on an Ethernet LAN or wireless LAN:

1. When sending a packet, compare the destination IP address of the packet to the sending host's perception of the range of addresses in the connected subnet, based on the host's IP address and subnet mask.

   a. If the destination is in the same subnet as the host, send the packet directly to the destination host. Address Resolution Protocol (ARP) is needed to find the destination host's MAC address.

   b. If the destination is not in the same subnet as the host, send the packet directly to the host's default gateway (default router). ARP is needed to find the default gateway's MAC address.

Routers use the following general steps, noting that with routers, the packet must first be received, whereas the sending host (as previously summarized) begins with the IP packet in memory:

1. For each received frame, use the data-link trailer frame check sequence (FCS) field to ensure that the frame had no errors; if errors occurred, discard the frame (and do not continue to the next step).

2. Check the frame's destination data link layer address, and process only if addressed to this router or to a broadcast/multicast address.

3. Discard the incoming frame's old data-link header and trailer, leaving the IP packet.

4. Compare the packet's destination IP address to the routing table, and find the route that matches the destination address. This route identifies the outgoing interface of the router, and possibly the next-hop router.

5. Determine the destination data-link address used for forwarding packets to the next router or destination host (as directed in the routing table).

6. Encapsulate the IP packet inside a new data-link header and trailer, appropriate for the outgoing interface, and forward the frame out that interface.

For example, consider Figure 12-1, which shows a simple network with two routers and three hosts. In this case, PC1 creates a packet to be sent to PC3's IP address, namely 172.16.3.3. The figure shows three major routing steps, labeled A, B, and C: PC1's host routing logic that forwards the packet toward R1, R1's routing logic that forwards the packet toward R2, and R2's routing logic that forwards the packet toward PC3.

First, consider Step A from Figure 12-1. PC1 knows its own IP address of 172.16.1.1, mask 255.255.255.0. (All interfaces use an easy mask of 255.255.255.0 in this example.) PC1 can calculate its subnet number (172.16.1.0/24) and range of addresses (172.16.1.1–172.16.1.254). Destination address 172.16.3.3 is not in PC1's subnet, so PC1 uses Step 1B in the summary of host routing logic—namely, PC1 sends the packet, inside an Ethernet frame, to its default gateway IP address of 172.16.1.251.

This first step (Step A) of PC1 sending the packet to its default gateway also reviews a couple of important concepts. As you can see from the lower part of the figure, PC1 uses its own MAC address as the source MAC address, but it uses R1's LAN MAC address as the destination MAC address. As a result, any LAN switches can deliver the frame correctly to R1's Fa0/0 interface. Also note that PC1 looked for and found 172.16.1.251's MAC address in PC1's ARP cache. If the MAC address had not been found, PC1 would have had to use ARP to dynamically discover the MAC address used by 172.16.1.251 (R1) before being able to send the frame shown in Figure 12-1.

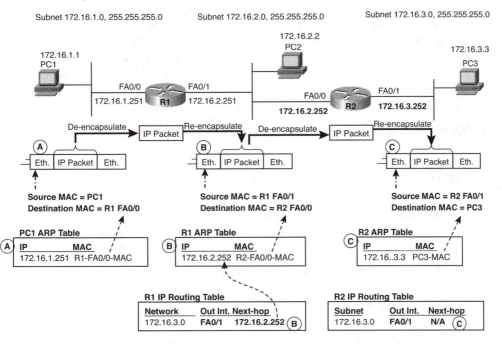

Figure 12-1   *Example of the IP Routing Process*

Next focus on Step B from Figure 12-1, which is the work done by router R1 to forward the packet. Using the router's six summarized routing steps that preceded Figure 12-1, the following occurs at R1. Note that the figure denotes many of the details with letter *B*:

1. R1 checks the FCS, and the frame has no errors.

2. R1 finds its own Fa0/0 interface MAC address in the frame's destination MAC address field, so R1 should process the encapsulated packet.

3. R1 discards the old data-link header and trailer, leaving the IP packet (as shown directly under the R1 icon in Figure 12-1).

4. (In the bottom center of Figure 12-1) R1 compares the destination IP address (172.16.3.3) to R1's routing table, finding the matching route shown in the figure, with outgoing interface Fa0/1 and next-hop router 172.16.2.252.

5. R1 needs to find the next-hop device's MAC address (R2's MAC address), so R1 looks and finds that MAC address in its ARP table.

6. R1 encapsulates the IP packet in a new Ethernet frame, with R1's Fa0/1 MAC address as the source MAC address, and R2's Fa0/0 MAC address (per the ARP table) as the destination MAC address. R2 sends the frame.

Although the steps might seem laborious, you can think of briefer versions of this logic in cases where a question does not require this level of depth. For example, when troubleshooting routing problems, focusing on Step 4—the matching of the packet's destination IP address to a router's routing table—is probably one of the most important steps. So, a briefer summary of the routing process might be: Router receives a packet, matches the packet's destination address with the routing table, and forwards the packet based on that matched route. While this abbreviated version ignores some details, it can make for quicker work when troubleshooting problems or discussing routing issues.

To complete the example, consider the same six-step router forwarding logic as applied on router R2, listed with letter C in Figure 12-1, as follows:

1. R2 checks the FCS, and the frame has no errors.
2. R2 finds its own Fa0/0 interface MAC address in the frame's destination MAC address field, so R2 should process the encapsulated packet.
3. R2 discards the old data-link header and trailer, leaving the IP packet (as shown directly under the R2 icon in Figure 12-1).
4. (In the bottom right of Figure 12-1) R2 compares the destination IP address (172.16.3.3) to R2's routing table, finding the matching route shown in the figure, with outgoing interface Fa0/1 and no next-hop router listed.
5. Because no next-hop router exists, R2 needs to find the true destination host's MAC address (PC3's MAC address), so R2 looks and finds that MAC address in its ARP table.
6. R2 encapsulates the IP packet in a new Ethernet frame, with R2's Fa0/1 MAC address as the source MAC address, and PC3's MAC address (per the ARP table) as the destination MAC address. R1 sends the frame.

Finally, when this frame arrives at PC3, PC3 sees its own MAC address listed as the destination MAC address, so PC3 begins to process the frame.

The same general process works with WAN links as well, with a few different details. On point-to-point links, as shown in Figure 12-2, an ARP table is not needed. Because a point-to-point link can have at most one other router connected to it, you can ignore the data-link addressing. However, with Frame Relay, the routing process does consider the data-link addresses, called data-link connection identifiers (DLCI). The routing details regarding Frame Relay DLCIs are covered later in this book in Chapter 28, "Frame Relay Concepts."

The IP routing process on both the hosts and the routers relies on these devices' abilities to understand IP addressing and predict which IP addresses are in each group or subnet. The next section provides a brief review of IP addresses and subnetting.

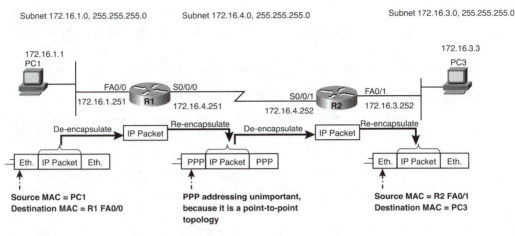

Figure 12-2 *Example of the IP Routing Process*

The Impact of Addressing and Subnetting on Routing

IP addressing rules aid the IP routing processes by requiring that IP addresses be organized into groups of consecutively numbered IP addresses called subnets. To allow a concise way to refer to a subnet, IP addressing defines the concept of a subnet number and subnet mask, which together exactly identify the range of addresses in a subnet.

For example, the routers in Figures 12-1 and 12-2 used routes that listed subnet number 172.16.3.0 when forwarding the packet destined for PC3 (172.16.3.3). The figures omitted the subnet mask to reduce clutter, but any device can look at subnet number 172.16.3.0, with mask 255.255.255.0, and know that these two numbers concisely represent the following subnet:

■ Subnet number 172.16.3.0

■ Range of usable addresses in the subnet: 172.16.3.1–172.16.3.254

■ Subnet broadcast address (not usable for individual hosts): 172.16.3.255

The following list provides a brief review of some of the major IPv4 addressing concepts:

■ Unicast IP addresses are IP addresses that can be assigned to an individual interface for sending and receiving packets.

■ Each unicast IP address resides in a particular Class A, B, or C network, called a classful IP network.

■ If subnetting is used, which is almost always true in real life, each unicast IP address also resides in a specific subset of the classful network called a subnet.

■ The subnet mask, written in either dotted decimal form (for example, 255.255.255.0) or prefix notation form (for example, /24), identifies the structure of unicast IP addresses and allows devices and people to derive the subnet number, range of addresses, and broadcast address for a subnet.

- Devices in the same subnet should all use the same subnet mask; otherwise, they have different opinions about the range of addresses in the subnet, which can break the IP routing process.

- Devices in a single VLAN should be in the same single IP subnet.

- Devices in different VLANs should be in different IP subnets.

- To forward packets between subnets, a device that performs routing must be used. In this book, only routers are shown, but multilayer switches—switches that also perform routing functions—can also be used.

- Point-to-point serial links use a different subnet than the LAN subnets, but these subnets only require two IP addresses, one for each router interface on either end of the link.

- Hosts separated by a router must be in separate subnets.

Figure 12-3 shows an example internetwork that exhibits many of these features. Switch SW1 defaults to put all interfaces into VLAN 1, so all hosts on the left (PC1 included) are in a single subnet. Note that SW1's management IP address, also in VLAN 1, will be from that same subnet. Similarly, SW2 defaults to put all ports in VLAN 1, requiring a second subnet. The point-to-point link requires a third subnet. The figure shows the subnet numbers, masks, and range of addresses. Note that all addresses and subnets are part of the same single classful Class B network 172.16.0.0, and all subnets use a mask of 255.255.255.0.

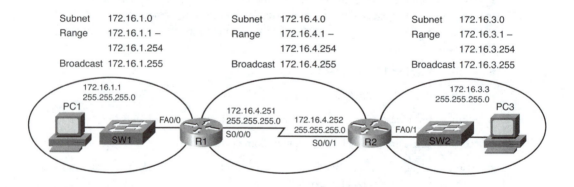

Figure 12-3 *Example IP Addressing Design*

Figure 12-3 lists the subnet numbers, ranges of addresses, and subnet broadcast addresses. However, each device in the figure can find the same information just based on its respective IP address and subnet mask configuration, deriving the subnet number, range of addresses, and broadcast address for each attached subnet.

With these details of subnetting in mind, the next section examines how a router matches the routing table when the subnets listed in the routing table overlap so that one packet's destination matches more than one route.

IP Forwarding by Matching the Most Specific Route

Any router's IP routing process requires that the router compare the destination IP address of each packet with the existing contents of that router's IP routing table. Often, only one route matches a particular destination address. However, in some cases, a particular destination address matches more than one of the router's routes. Some legitimate and normal reasons for the overlapping routes in a routing table include the following:

■ The use of autosummary

■ Manual route summarization

■ The use of static routes

■ Incorrectly designed subnetting so that subnets overlap their address ranges

Chapter 19, "VLSM and Route Summarization," explains more detail about each of these reasons. While some cases of overlapping routes are problems, other cases are normal operation resulting from some other feature. This section focuses on how a router chooses which of the overlapping routes to use, with the features that cause the overlap being covered in Chapter 19.

The following statement summarizes a router's forwarding logic with overlapping routes:

> When a particular destination IP address matches more than one route in a router's routing table, the router uses the most specific route—in other words, the route with the longest prefix length.

To see exactly what that means, the routing table listed in Example 12-1 shows a series of overlapping routes. First, before reading any text beneath the example, try to predict which route would be used for packets sent to the following IP addresses: 172.16.1.1, 172.16.1.2, 172.16.2.3, and 172.16.4.3.

Example 12-1 show ip route *Command with Overlapping Routes*

```
R1# show ip route rip


     172.16.0.0/16 is variably subnetted, 5 subnets, 4 masks
R       172.16.1.1/32 [120/1] via 172.16.25.2, 00:00:04, Serial0/1/1
R       172.16.1.0/24 [120/2] via 172.16.25.129, 00:00:09, Serial0/1/0
R       172.16.0.0/22 [120/1] via 172.16.25.2, 00:00:04, Serial0/1/1
R       172.16.0.0/16 [120/2] via 172.16.25.129, 00:00:09, Serial0/1/0
R       0.0.0.0/0 [120/3] via 172.16.25.129, 00:00:09, Serial0/1/0
R1# show ip route 172.16.4.3
Routing entry for 172.16.0.0/16
  Known via "rip", distance 120, metric 2
  Redistributing via rip
  Last update from 172.16.25.129 on Serial0/1/0, 00:00:19 ago
  Routing Descriptor Blocks:
  * 172.16.25.129, from 172.16.25.129, 00:00:19 ago, via Serial0/1/0
      Route metric is 2, traffic share count is 1
```

Although a diagram of the internetwork might be supplied with the question, you really only need two pieces of information to determine which route will be matched: the destination IP address of the packet and the contents of the router's routing table. By examining each subnet and mask in the routing table, you can then determine the range of IP addresses in each subnet. In this case, the ranges defined by each route, respectively, are as follows:

- 172.16.1.1 (just this one address)
- 172.16.1.0–172.16.1.255
- 172.16.0.0–172.16.3.255
- 172.16.0.0–172.16.255.255
- 0.0.0.0–255.255.255.255 (all addresses)

Note: The route listed as 0.0.0.0/0 is the default route, which matches all IP addresses, and is explained later in this chapter.

As you can see from these ranges, several of the routes' address ranges overlap. When matching more than one route, the route with the longer prefix length is used. For example:

- **172.16.1.1:** Matches all five routes; longest prefix is /32, the route to 172.16.1.1/32.
- **172.16.1.2:** Matches last four routes; longest prefix is /24, the route to 172.16.1.0/24.
- **172.16.2.3:** Matches last three routes; longest prefix is /22, the route to 172.16.0.0/22.
- **172.16.4.3:** Matches the last two routes; longest prefix is /16, the route to 172.16.0.0/16.

Besides just doing the subnetting math on every route in the routing table, the **show ip route** *ip-address* command can also be particularly useful. This command lists detailed information about the route that the router matches for the IP address listed in the command. If multiple routes are matched for the IP address, this command lists the best route: the route with the longest prefix. For example, Example 12-1 lists the output of the **show ip route 172.16.4.3** command. The first line of (highlighted) output lists the matched route: the route to 172.16.0.0/16. The rest of the output lists the details of that particular route.

Routes to Directly Connected Subnets

A router automatically adds a route to its routing table for the subnet connected to each interface, assuming that the following two facts are true:

Key Topic

- The interface is in a working state—in other words, the interface status in the **show interfaces** command lists a line status of up and a protocol status of up.
- The interface has an IP address assigned, either through the **ip address** interface subcommand or by using DHCP client services.

The concept of connected routes is relatively basic. The router of course needs to know the subnet number used on the physical network connected to each of its interfaces, but if the interface is not currently working, the router needs to remove the route from its routing table. The **show ip route** command lists these routes with a *c* as the route code, meaning connected, and the **show ip route connected** command lists only connected routes.

The following sections about connected routes focus on a couple of variations in configuration that affect connected routes, thereby affecting how routers forward packets. The first topic relates to a tool called secondary IP addressing, whereas the second relates to a router's configuration when using VLAN trunking.

Connected Routes

A router adds routes to its routing table for the subnets connected to each of the router's interfaces. For this to occur, the router must have an IP address and mask configured on the interface (statically with the **ip address** command or dynamically using Dynamic Host Configuration Protocol [DHCP]) and both interface status codes must be "up." The concept is simple: If a router has an interface in a subnet, the router has a way to forward packets into that subnet, so the router needs a route in its routing table.

Figure 12-4 illustrates a sample internetwork that will be used in Example 12-2 to show some connected routes and some related **show** commands. Figure 12-4 shows an internetwork with six subnets, with each of the three routers having three interfaces in use. Each of the LANs in this figure could consist of one switch, one hub, or lots of switches and/or hubs together—but for the purposes of this chapter, the size of the LAN does not matter. Once the interfaces have been configured as shown in the figure, and once each interface is up and working, each of the routers should have three connected routes in their routing tables.

Example 12-2 shows the connected routes on Albuquerque after its interfaces have been configured with the addresses shown in Figure 12-4. The example includes several comments, with more detailed comments following the example.

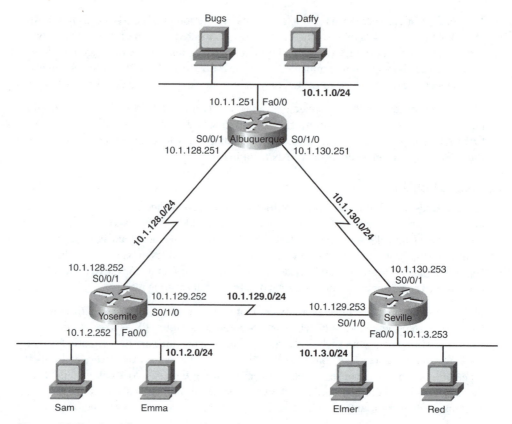

Figure 12-4 *Sample Internetwork Used Throughout Chapter 12*

Example 12-2 *Albuquerque Connected Routes*

```
! The following command just lists the IP address configuration on Albuquerque.
! The output has been edited to show only the three interfaces used in Figure
! 12-1.
!
Albuquerque# show running-config
interface FastEthernet0/0
 ip address 10.1.1.251 255.255.255.0
!
interface Serial 0/0/1
 ip address 10.1.128.251 255.255.255.0
!
interface Serial 0/1/0
 ip address 10.1.130.251 255.255.255.0
! Lines omitted for brevity
! The next command lists the interfaces, and confirms that Albuquerque's three
! interfaces shown in Figure 12-4 are in an "up and up" status.
```

```
!
Albuquerque# show ip interface brief
Interface               IP-Address      OK? Method Status              Protocol
FastEthernet0/0         10.1.1.251      YES manual up                      up
FastEthernet0/1         unassigned      YES manual administratively down down
Serial0/0/0             unassigned      YES NVRAM  administratively down down
Serial0/0/1             10.1.128.251    YES NVRAM  up                      up
Serial0/1/0             10.1.130.251    YES NVRAM  up                      up
Serial0/1/1             unassigned      YES NVRAM  administratively down down
!
! The next command lists the routes known by Albuquerque – all connected routes
!
Albuquerque#show ip route
Codes: C - connected, S - static, I - IGRP, R - RIP, M - mobile, B - BGP
       D - EIGRP, EX - EIGRP external, O - OSPF, IA - OSPF inter area
       N1 - OSPF NSSA external type 1, N2 - OSPF NSSA external type 2
       E1 - OSPF external type 1, E2 - OSPF external type 2, E - EGP
       i - IS-IS, L1 - IS-IS level-1, L2 - IS-IS level-2, ia - IS-IS inter area
       * - candidate default, U - per-user static route, o - ODR
       P - periodic downloaded static route

Gateway of last resort is not set


     10.0.0.0/24 is subnetted, 3 subnets
C       10.1.1.0 is directly connected, FastEthernet0/0
C       10.1.130.0 is directly connected, Serial0/1/0
C       10.1.128.0 is directly connected, Serial0/0/1
!
! The next command changes the mask format used by the show ip route command
!
Albuquerque# terminal ip netmask-format decimal
Albuquerque# show ip route
Codes: C - connected, S - static, I - IGRP, R - RIP, M - mobile, B - BGP
       D - EIGRP, EX - EIGRP external, O - OSPF, IA - OSPF inter area
       N1 - OSPF NSSA external type 1, N2 - OSPF NSSA external type 2
       E1 - OSPF external type 1, E2 - OSPF external type 2, E - EGP
       i - IS-IS, L1 - IS-IS level-1, L2 - IS-IS level-2, ia - IS-IS inter area
       * - candidate default, U - per-user static route, o - ODR
       P - periodic downloaded static route


Gateway of last resort is not set


     10.0.0.0 255.255.255.0 is subnetted, 3 subnets
C       10.1.1.0 is directly connected, FastEthernet0/0
C       10.1.130.0 is directly connected, Serial0/1/0
C       10.1.128.0 is directly connected, Serial0/0/1
```

To begin, the **show ip interface brief** command in Example 12-2 confirms that Albuquerque's three interfaces meet the requirements to have their connected subnets added to the routing table. Note that all three interfaces are in an "up and up" state and have an IP address configured.

The output of the **show ip route** command confirms that Albuquerque indeed added a route to all three subnets to its routing table. The output begins with a single-letter code legend, with "C" meaning "connected." The individual routes begin with a code letter on the far left—in this case, all three routes have the letter C. Also, note that the output lists the mask in prefix notation by default. Additionally, in cases when one mask is used throughout a single classful network—in other words, static-length subnet masking (SLSM) is used—the **show ip route** command output lists the mask on a heading line above the subnets of that classful network. For example, the lines with 10.1.1.0, 10.1.128.0, and 10.1.130.0 do not show the mask, but the line just above those three lines does list classful network 10.0.0.0 and the mask, as highlighted in the example.

Finally, you can change the format of the display of the subnet mask in **show** commands, for the duration of your login session to the router, using the **terminal ip netmask-format decimal** EXEC command, as shown at the end of Example 12-2.

Secondary IP Addressing

Imagine that you planned your IP addressing scheme for a network. Later, a particular subnet grows, and you have used all the valid IP addresses in the subnet. What should you do? Three main options exist:

- Make the existing subnet larger

- Migrate the hosts to use addresses in a different, larger subnet

- Use secondary addressing

All three options are reasonable, but all have some problems.

To make the subnet larger, just change the mask used on that subnet. However, changing the mask could create overlapped subnets. For example, if subnet 10.1.4.0/24 is running out of addresses, and you make a change to mask 255.255.254.0 (9 host bits, 23 network/subnet bits), the new subnet includes addresses 10.1.4.0 to 10.1.5.255. If you have already assigned subnet 10.1.5.0/24, with assignable addresses 10.1.5.1 through 10.1.5.254, you would create an overlap, which is not allowed. However, if the 10.1.5.x addresses are unused, expanding the old subnet might be reasonable.

The second option is to simply pick a new, unused, but larger subnet. All the IP addresses would need to be changed. This is a relatively simple process if most or all hosts use DHCP, but a potentially laborious process if many hosts use statically configured IP addresses.

Note that both of the first two solutions imply a strategy of using different masks in different parts of the network. Use of these different masks is called variable-length subnet masking (VLSM), which introduces more complexity into the network, particularly for people who are monitoring and troubleshooting the network.

The third major option is to use a Cisco router features called *secondary IP addressing*. Secondary addressing uses multiple networks or subnets on the same data link. By using more than one subnet on the same medium, you increase the number of available IP addresses. To make it work, the router needs an IP address in each subnet so that the hosts in each subnet have a usable default gateway IP address in the same subnet. Additionally, packets that need to pass between these subnets must be sent to the router.

For example, Figure 12-5 has subnet 10.1.2.0/24; assume that it has all IP addresses assigned. Assuming secondary addressing to be the chosen solution, subnet 10.1.7.0/24 also could be used on the same Ethernet. Example 12-3 shows the configuration for secondary IP addressing on Yosemite.

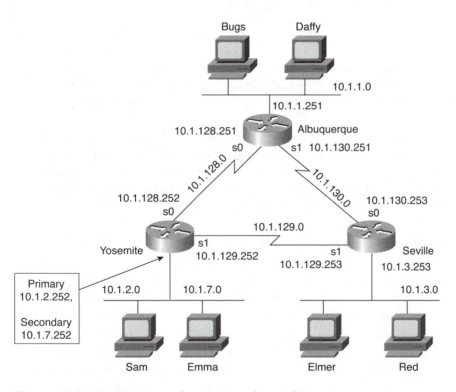

Figure 12-5 *TCP/IP Network with Secondary Addresses*

Example 12-3 *Secondary IP Addressing Configuration and the* show ip route *Command on Yosemite*

```
! Excerpt from show running-config follows...
Hostname Yosemite
ip domain-lookup
```

```
ip name-server 10.1.1.100 10.1.2.100
interface  ethernet    0
ip address 10.1.7.252   255.255.255.0 secondary
ip address 10.1.2.252   255.255.255.0
interface serial 0
 ip address 10.1.128.252  255.255.255.0
interface serial 1
 ip address 10.1.129.252  255.255.255.0


Yosemite# show ip route connected
     10.0.0.0/24 is subnetted, 4 subnets
C       10.1.2.0 is directly connected, Ethernet0
C       10.1.7.0 is directly connected, Ethernet0
C       10.1.129.0 is directly connected, Serial1
C       10.1.128.0 is directly connected, Serial0
```

The router has connected routes to subnets 10.1.2.0/24 and 10.1.7.0/24, so it can forward packets to each subnet. The hosts in each subnet on the same LAN can use either 10.1.2.252 or 10.1.7.252 as their default gateway IP addresses, depending on the subnet in which they reside.

The biggest negative to secondary addressing is that packets sent between hosts on the LAN might be inefficiently routed. For example, when a host in subnet 10.1.2.0 sends a packet to a host in 10.1.7.0, the sending host's logic is to send the packet to its default gateway, because the destination is on a different subnet. So, the sending host sends the packet to the router, which then sends the packet back into the same LAN.

Supporting Connected Routes to Subnet Zero

IOS can restrict a router from configuring an **ip address** command with an address inside the zero subnet. The zero subnet (or subnet zero) is the one subnet in each classful network that has all binary 0s in the subnet part of the binary version of the subnet number. In decimal, the zero subnet happens to be the same number as the classful network number.

With the **ip subnet-zero** command configured, IOS allows the zero subnet to become a connected route as a result of an **ip address** command being configured on an interface. This command has been a default setting since at least IOS version 12.0, which was a relatively old IOS version by the time this book was published. So, if you see the **ip subnet-zero** command configured, or if the question does not specify that the **no ip subnet-zero** command is configured, assume that the zero subnet can be configured.

With the **no ip subnet-zero** command configured on a router, that router rejects any **ip address** command that uses an address/mask combination for the zero subnet. For example, the interface subcommand **ip address 10.0.0.1 255.255.255.0** implies zero subnet 10.0.0.0/24, so the router would reject the command if the **no ip subnet-zero** global configuration command was configured. Note that the error message simply says "bad mask," rather than stating that the problem was because of the zero subnet.

The **no ip subnet-zero** command on one router does not affect other routers, and it does not prevent a router from learning about a zero subnet through a routing protocol. It simply prevents the router from configuring an interface to be in a zero subnet.

The default settings on Cisco routers allow the use of the zero subnet. However, if you see a design that uses a classful routing protocol (as discussed in Chapter 14), or if the router configuration includes the **no ip subnet-zero** command, avoid using the zero and broadcast subnets.

ISL and 802.1Q Configuration on Routers

Later in this book, Chapter 26, "Virtual LANs," discusses a topic related to LAN switches: virtual LANs, or VLANs. Without the concept of virtual LANs, switches consider the devices connected to all ports (interfaces) to be in the same LAN. With VLANs, an engineer can configure a switch to group a subset of ports as one LAN, and another subset of ports as another LAN, with each group being called a VLAN.

When thinking about Layer 3 concepts, the devices in one VLAN should normally also be in the same subnet. That is, if a switch puts ports 1–4 into one VLAN, the devices connected to those ports should be in one VLAN. If the switch configuration puts ports 5–8 in another VLAN, the devices should use IP addresses in a different VLAN.

A router must be used to forward traffic between VLANs. That is, if you have a switch with three VLANs configured, some router needs an IP address in the subnet used in each VLAN, and the router will then route IP packets between those subnets. However, instead of connecting multiple cables from the router to the switch, one per VLAN, a router can connect one cable to the switch and configure that connection to use something called *VLAN trunking*.

Figure 12-6 shows a router with a single Fast Ethernet interface and a single connection to a switch. Either Inter-Switch Link (ISL) or 802.1Q trunking can be used, with only small differences in the configuration for each. For frames that contain packets that the router routes between the two VLANs, the incoming frame is tagged by the switch with one VLAN ID, and the outgoing frame is tagged by the router with the other VLAN ID. Example 12-4 shows the router configuration required to support ISL encapsulation and forwarding between these VLANs.

Example 12-4 *Router Configuration for the ISL Encapsulation Shown in Figure 12-6*

```
interface fastethernet 0/0.1
 ip address 10.1.1.1 255.255.255.0
 encapsulation isl 1
!
interface fastethernet 0/0.2
 ip address 10.1.2.1 255.255.255.0
 encapsulation isl 2
!
interface fastethernet 0/0.3
 ip address 10.1.3.1 255.255.255.0
 encapsulation isl 3
```

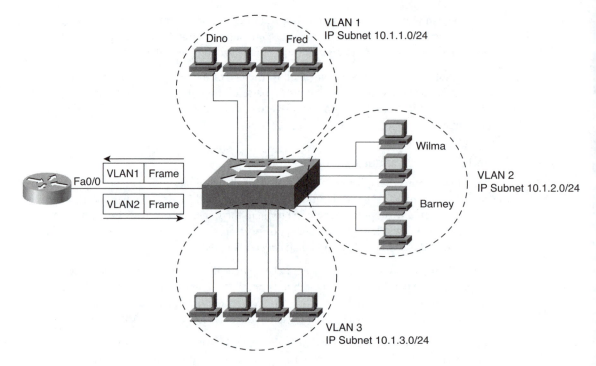

Figure 12-6   *Router Forwarding Between VLANs*

Example 12-4 shows the configuration for three *subinterfaces* of the Fast Ethernet inter-face on the router. A subinterface is a logical subdivision of a physical interface. The router assigns each subinterface an IP address and assigns the subinterface to a single VLAN. So, instead of three physical router interfaces, each attached to a different sub-net/VLAN, the router uses one physical router interface with three logical subinterfaces, each attached to a different subnet/VLAN. The **encapsulation** command numbers the VLANs, which must match the configuration for VLAN IDs in the switch.

This example uses subinterface numbers that match the VLAN ID on each subinterface. There is no requirement that the numbers match, but most people choose to make them match, just to make the configuration more obvious and to make troubleshooting easier. In other words, the VLAN IDs can be 1, 2, and 3, but the subinterface numbers could have been 4, 5, and 6, because the subinterface numbers are just used internally by the router.

Example 12-5 shows the same network, but this time with 802.1Q used instead of ISL. IEEE 802.1Q trunking has a concept called the native VLAN, which is a special VLAN on each trunk for which no 802.1Q headers are added to the frames. By default, VLAN 1 is the native VLAN. Example 12-5 shows the difference in configuration.

Example 12-5   *Router Configuration for the 802.1Q Encapsulation Shown in Figure 12-6*

```
interface fastethernet 0/0
ip address 10.1.1.1 255.255.255.0
!
interface fastethernet 0/0.2
 ip address 10.1.2.1 255.255.255.0
 encapsulation dot1q 2
!
interface fastethernet 0/0.3
 ip address 10.1.3.1 255.255.255.0
 encapsulation dot1q 3
```

The configuration creates three VLANs on the router Fa0/0 interface. Two of the VLANs, VLANs 2 and 3, are configured just like Example 12-4, except that the **encapsulation** command lists 802.1Q as the type of encapsulation.

The native VLAN, VLAN 1 in this case, can be configured with two styles of configuration. Example 12-5 shows one style in which the native VLAN's IP address is configured on the physical interface. As a result, the router does not use VLAN trunking headers in this VLAN, as is intended for the native VLAN. The alternative is to configure the native VLAN's IP address on another subinterface and to use the **encapsulation dot1q 1 native** interface subcommand. This command tells the router that the subinterface is associated with VLAN 1, but the **native** keyword tells the router not to use any 802.1Q headers with that subinterface.

To route IP packets between VLANs, the network needs a device that performs IP routing. That device can be a router, as described in this section. However, in reality, most networks today use devices called Layer 3 switches to route packets between VLANs. A Layer 3 switch performs LAN switching (an OSI Layer 2 function) and IP routing (an OSI Layer 3 function), all on the same device.

Static Routes

Routers use three main methods to add routes to their routing tables: connected routes, static routes, and dynamic routing protocols. Routers always add connected routes when interfaces have IP addresses configured and the interfaces are up and working. In most networks, engineers purposefully use dynamic routing protocols to cause each router to learn the rest of the routes in an internetwork. Using static routes—routes added to a routing table through direct configuration—is the least used of the three options.

Static routing consists of individual **ip route** global configuration commands that define a route to a router. The configuration command includes a reference to the subnet—the subnet number and mask—along with instructions about where to forward packets destined to that subnet. To see the need for static routes, and to see the configuration, look at Example 12-6, which shows two **ping** commands testing IP connectivity from Albuquerque to Yosemite (see Figure 12-7).

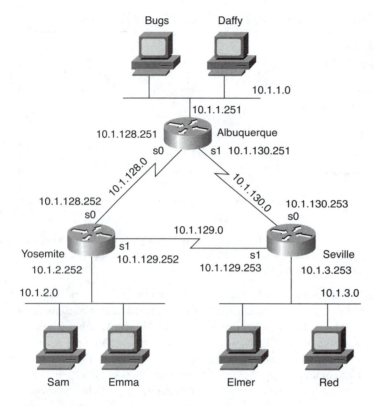

Figure 12-7 *Sample Network Used in Static Route Configuration Examples*

Example 12-6 *Albuquerque Router EXEC Commands with Only Connected Routers*

```
Albuquerque# show ip route
Codes: C - connected, S - static, I - IGRP, R - RIP, M - mobile, B - BGP
       D - EIGRP, EX - EIGRP external, O - OSPF, IA - OSPF inter area
       N1 - OSPF NSSA external type 1, N2 - OSPF NSSA external type 2
       E1 - OSPF external type 1, E2 - OSPF external type 2, E - EGP
       i - IS-IS, L1 - IS-IS level-1, L2 - IS-IS level-2, ia - IS-IS inter area
       * - candidate default, U - per-user static route, o - ODR
       P - periodic downloaded static route

Gateway of last resort is not set

     10.0.0.0/24 is subnetted, 3 subnets

C       10.1.1.0 is directly connected, Ethernet0
C       10.1.130.0 is directly connected, Serial1
C       10.1.128.0 is directly connected, Serial0
Albuquerque# ping 10.1.128.252
Type escape sequence to abort.
```

```
Sending 5, 100-byte ICMP Echos to 10.1.128.252, timeout is 2 seconds:
!!!!!
Success rate is 100 percent (5/5), round-trip min/avg/max = 4/4/8 ms

Albuquerque# ping 10.1.2.252
Type escape sequence to abort.
Sending 5, 100-byte ICMP Echos to 10.1.2.252, timeout is 2 seconds:
.....
Success rate is 0 percent (0/5)
```

The end of the example shows two different **ping** commands on router Albuquerque, one to 10.1.128.252 (Yosemite's S0 IP address) and one to 10.1.2.252 (Yosemite's LAN IP address). The IOS **ping** command sends five ICMP Echo Request packets by default, with the command output listing an exclamation point (!) to mean that an Echo Reply was received, and a period (.) to mean no reply was received. In the example, the first instance, **ping 10.1.128.252**, shows five responses (100%), and the second instance, **ping 10.1.2.252**, shows that no responses were received (0%). The first **ping** command works because Albuquerque has a route to the subnet in which 10.1.128.2 resides (subnet 10.1.128.0/24). However, the ping to 10.1.2.252 does not work because Albuquerque does not have a route that matches address 10.1.2.252. At this point, Albuquerque only has routes for its three connected subnets. So, Albuquerque's **ping 10.1.2.252** command creates the packets, but Albuquerque discards the packets because no routes exist.

Configuring Static Routes

One simple solution to the failure of the **ping 10.1.2.252** command is to enable an IP routing protocol on all three routers. In fact, in a real network, that is the most likely solution. As an alternative, you can configure static routes. Many networks have a few static routes, so you need to configure them occasionally. Example 12-7 shows the **ip route** command on Albuquerque, which adds static routes and makes the failed ping from Example 12-6 work.

Example 12-7   *Static Routes Added to Albuquerque*

```
ip route 10.1.2.0 255.255.255.0 10.1.128.252
ip route 10.1.3.0 255.255.255.0 10.1.130.253
```

The **ip route** command defines the static route by defining the subnet number and the next-hop IP address. One **ip route** command defines a route to 10.1.2.0 (mask 255.255.255.0), which is located off Yosemite, so the next-hop IP address as configured on Albuquerque is 10.1.128.252, which is Yosemite's Serial0 IP address. Similarly, a route to 10.1.3.0, the subnet off Seville, points to Seville's Serial0 IP address, 10.1.130.253. Note that the next-hop IP address is an IP address in a directly connected subnet; the goal is to define the next router to send the packet to. Now Albuquerque can forward packets to these two subnets.

The **ip route** command has two basic formats. The command can refer to a next-hop IP address, as shown in Example 12-7. Alternately, for static routes that use point-to-point serial links, the command can list the outgoing interface instead of the next-hop IP address. For example, Example 12-7 could instead use the **ip route 10.1.2.0 255.255.255.0 serial0** global configuration command instead of the first **ip route** command.

Unfortunately, adding the two static routes in Example 12-7 to Albuquerque does not solve all the network's routing problems. The static routes help Albuquerque deliver packets to these two subnets, but the other two routers don't have enough routing information to forward packets back toward Albuquerque. For example, PC Bugs cannot ping PC Sam in this network, even after the addition of the commands in Example 12-7. The problem is that although Albuquerque has a route to subnet 10.1.2.0, where Sam resides, Yosemite does not have a route to 10.1.1.0, where Bugs resides. The ping request packet goes from Bugs to Sam correctly, but Sam's ping response packet cannot be routed by the Yosemite router back through Albuquerque to Bugs, so the ping fails.

The Extended ping Command

In real life, you might not be able to find a user, like Bugs, to ask to test your network by pinging. Instead, you can use the extended **ping** command on a router to test routing in the same way that a ping from Bugs to Sam tests routing. Example 12-8 shows Albuquerque with the working **ping 10.1.2.252** command, but with an extended **ping 10.1.2.252** command that works similarly to a ping from Bugs to Sam—a ping that fails in this case (only the two static routes from Example 12-7 have been added at this point).

Example 12-8 *Albuquerque: Working Ping After Adding Default Routes, Plus Failing Extended ping Command*

```
Albuquerque# show ip route
Codes: C - connected, S - static, I - IGRP, R - RIP, M - mobile, B - BGP
       D - EIGRP, EX - EIGRP external, O - OSPF, IA - OSPF inter area
       N1 - OSPF NSSA external type 1, N2 - OSPF NSSA external type 2
       E1 - OSPF external type 1, E2 - OSPF external type 2, E - EGP
       i - IS-IS, L1 - IS-IS level-1, L2 - IS-IS level-2, ia - IS-IS inter area
       * - candidate default, U - per-user static route, o - ODR
       P - periodic downloaded static route

Gateway of last resort is not set

     10.0.0.0/24 is subnetted, 5 subnets
S       10.1.3.0 [1/0] via 10.1.130.253
S       10.1.2.0 [1/0] via 10.1.128.252
C       10.1.1.0 is directly connected, Ethernet0
C       10.1.130.0 is directly connected, Serial1
C       10.1.128.0 is directly connected, Serial0
Albuquerque# ping 10.1.2.252

Type escape sequence to abort.
Sending 5, 100-byte ICMP Echos to 10.1.2.252, timeout is 2 seconds:
!!!!!
```

```
Success rate is 100 percent (5/5), round-trip min/avg/max = 4/4/8 ms


Albuquerque# ping
Protocol [ip]:
Target IP address: 10.1.2.252
Repeat count [5]:
Datagram size [100]:
Timeout in seconds [2]:
Extended commands [n]: y
Source address or interface: 10.1.1.251
Type of service [0]:
Set DF bit in IP header? [no]:
Validate reply data? [no]:
Data pattern [0xABCD]:
Loose, Strict, Record, Timestamp, Verbose[none]:
Sweep range of sizes [n]:
Type escape sequence to abort.
Sending 5, 100-byte ICMP Echos to 10.1.2.252, timeout is 2 seconds:
. . . . .
Success rate is 0 percent (0/5)
```

The simple **ping 10.1.2.252** command works for one obvious reason and one not-so-obvious reason. First, Albuquerque can forward a packet to subnet 10.1.2.0 because of the static route. The return packet, sent by Yosemite, is sent to address 10.1.128.251—Albuquerque's Serial0 IP address—and Yosemite has a connected route to reach subnet 10.2.128.0. But why does Yosemite send the Echo Reply to Albuquerque's S0 IP address of 10.1.128.251? Well, the following points are true about the **ping** command on a Cisco router:

- The Cisco **ping** command uses, by default, the output interface's IP address as the packet's source address, unless otherwise specified in an extended ping. The first ping in Example 12-8 uses a source of 10.1.128.251, because the route used to send the packet to 10.1.2.252 sends packets out Albuquerque's Serial0 interface, whose IP address is 10.1.128.251.

- Ping response packets (ICMP Echo Replies) reverse the IP addresses used in the received ping request to which they are responding. So, in this example, Yosemite's Echo Reply, in response to the first ping in Example 12-8, uses 10.1.128.251 as the destination address and 10.1.2.252 as the source IP address.

Because the **ping 10.1.2.252** command on Albuquerque uses 10.1.128.251 as the packet's source address, Yosemite can send back a response to 10.1.128.251, because Yosemite happens to have a (connected) route to 10.1.128.0.

The danger when troubleshooting with the standard **ping** command is that routing problems can still exist, but the **ping 10.1.2.252** command, which worked, gives you a false sense of security. A more thorough alternative is to use the extended **ping** command to act like you issued a ping from a computer on that subnet, without having to call a user and ask to enter a **ping** command for you on the PC. The extended version of the **ping** command can be used to refine the problem's underlying cause by changing several details of what the ping command sends in its request. In fact, when a ping from a router works, but a ping from a host does not, the extended ping could help you re-create the problem without needing to work with the end user on the phone.

For example, in Example 12-8, the extended **ping** command on Albuquerque sends a packet from source IP address 10.1.1.251 (Albuquerque's Ethernet) to 10.1.2.252 (Yosemite's Ethernet). According to the output, Albuquerque did not receive a response. Normally, the **ping** command would be sourced from the IP address of the outgoing interface. With the use of the extended ping source address option, the source IP address of the echo packet is set to Albuquerque's Ethernet IP address, 10.1.1.251. Because the ICMP echo generated by the extended ping is sourced from an address in subnet 10.1.1.0, the packet looks more like a packet from an end user in that subnet. Yosemite builds an Echo Reply, with destination 10.1.1.251, but it does not have a route to that subnet. So Yosemite cannot send the ping reply packet back to Albuquerque.

To solve this problem, all routers could be configured to use a routing protocol. Alternatively, you could simply define static routes on all the routers in the network.

Static Default Routes

A default route is a special route that matches all packet destinations. Default routes can be particularly useful when only one physical path exists from one part of the network to another, and in cases for which one enterprise router provides connectivity to the Internet for that enterprise. For example, in Figure 12-8, R1, R2, and R3 are connected to the rest of the network only through R1's LAN interface. All three routers can forward packets to the rest of the network as long as the packets get to R1, which in turn forwards packets to router Dist1.

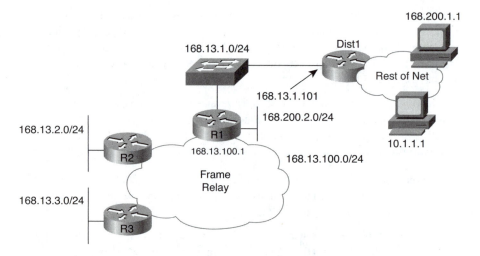

Figure 12-8   *Sample Network Using a Default Route*

The following sections show two options for configuring static default routes: one using the **ip route** command and another using the **ip default-network** command.

Default Routes Using the ip route Command

By configuring a default route on R1, with next-hop router Dist1, and by having R1 advertise the default to R2 and R3, default routing can be accomplished. By using such a default route, R1, R2, and R3 should not need specific routes to the subnets to the right of router Dist1. Example 12-9 begins an examination of this design by showing the definition of a static default route on R1 and the resulting information in R1's IP routing table.

Example 12-9 *R1 Static Default Route Configuration and Routing Table*

```
R1(config)# ip route 0.0.0.0 0.0.0.0 168.13.1.101
R1# show ip route
Codes: C - connected, S - static, I - IGRP, R - RIP, M - mobile, B - BGP
       D - EIGRP, EX - EIGRP external, O - OSPF, IA - OSPF inter area
       N1 - OSPF NSSA external type 1, N2 - OSPF NSSA external type 2
       E1 - OSPF external type 1, E2 - OSPF external type 2, E - EGP
       i - IS-IS, L1 - IS-IS level-1, L2 - IS-IS level-2, ia - IS-IS inter area
       * - candidate default, U - per-user static route, o - ODR
       P - periodic downloaded static route

Gateway of last resort is 168.13.1.101 to network 0.0.0.0

     168.13.0.0/24 is subnetted, 4 subnets
C       168.13.1.0 is directly connected,  FastEthernet0/0
R       168.13.3.0 [120/1] via 168.13.100.3, 00:00:05, Serial0.1
R       168.13.2.0 [120/1] via 168.13.100.2, 00:00:21, Serial0.1
C       168.13.100.0 is directly connected, Serial0.1
S*   0.0.0.0/0 [1/0] via 168.13.1.101
```

R1 defines the default route with a static **ip route** command, with destination 0.0.0.0, mask 0.0.0.0. As a result, R1's **show ip route** command lists a static route to 0.0.0.0, mask 0.0.0.0, with next hop 168.13.1.101—essentially, the same information in the **ip route 0.0.0.0 0.0.0.0 168.13.1.101** global configuration command. A destination of 0.0.0.0, with mask 0.0.0.0, represents all destinations by convention. With just that configuration, R1 has a static route that matches any and all IP packet destinations.

Note also in Example 12-9 that R1's **show ip route** command output lists a "Gateway of last resort" as 168.13.1.101. When a router knows about at least one default route, the router notes that route with an asterisk in the routing table. If a router learns about multiple default routes—either through static configuration or from routing protocols—the router notes each default route with an asterisk in the routing table. Then, the router chooses the best default route, noting that choice as the gateway of last resort. (The administrative distance of the source of the routing information, as defined by the administrative distance setting, has some impact on this choice.)

Although the Routing Information Protocol (RIP) configuration is not shown, R1 also advertises this default route to R2 and R3, as shown in the output of the **show ip route** command on R3 in Example 12-10.

Example 12-10   *R3: Nuances of the Successful Use of the Static Route on R1*

```
R3# show ip route
Codes: C - connected, S - static, I - IGRP, R - RIP, M - mobile, B - BGP
       D - EIGRP, EX - EIGRP external, O - OSPF, IA - OSPF inter area
       N1 - OSPF NSSA external type 1, N2 - OSPF NSSA external type 2
       E1 - OSPF external type 1, E2 - OSPF external type 2, E - EGP
       i - IS-IS, L1 - IS-IS level-1, L2 - IS-IS level-2, ia - IS-IS inter area
       * - candidate default, U - per-user static route, o - ODR
       P - periodic downloaded static route

Gateway of last resort is 168.13.100.1 to network 0.0.0.0

     168.13.0.0/24 is subnetted, 4 subnets
R       168.13.1.0 [120/1] via 168.13.100.1, 00:00:13, Serial0.1
C       168.13.3.0 is directly connected, Ethernet0
R       168.13.2.0 [120/1] via 168.13.100.2, 00:00:06, Serial0.1
C       168.13.100.0 is directly connected, Serial0.1
```

Different routing protocols advertise default routes in a couple of different ways. As an example, when R3 learns a default route from R1 using RIP, R3 lists the destination of the default route (0.0.0.0) and the next-hop router, which is R1 in this case (168.13.100.1), as highlighted in Example 12-10. So, when R3 needs to use its default route, it forwards packets to R1 (168.13.100.1)

Default Routes Using the ip default-network Command

Another style of configuration for the default route uses the **ip default-network** command. This command lists a classful IP network as its parameter, telling the router to use the routing details of the route for that classful network as the forwarding details for a default route.

This command is most useful when the engineer wants to use the default route to reach networks besides the networks used inside that enterprise. For example, in Figure 12-8, imagine that all subnets of the enterprise's 168.13.0.0 Class B network are known; they exist only near routers R1, R2, and R3; and these routes are all in the routing tables of R1, R2, and R3. Also, none of the subnets of 168.13.0.0 are to the right of Router Dist1. If the engineer wants to use a default route for forwarding packets to destinations to the right of Dist1, the **ip default-network** command works well.

To use the **ip default-network** command to configure a default route, the engineer relies on her knowledge that Dist1 is already advertising a route for classful network 10.0.0.0 to R1. R1's route to network 10.0.0.0 points to Dist1's 168.13.1.101 address as the next-hop address. Knowing that, the engineer can configure the **ip default-network 10.0.0.0** command on R1, which tells R1 to build its default route based on its learned route for network 10.0.0.0/8. Example 12-11 shows several details about this scenario on R1.

Example 12-11 *R1's Use of the* **ip default-network** *Command*

```
R1# configure terminal
R1(config)# ip default-network 10.0.0.0
R1(config)# exit
R1# show ip route
Codes: C - connected, S - static, I - IGRP, R - RIP, M - mobile, B - BGP
       D - EIGRP, EX - EIGRP external, O - OSPF, IA - OSPF inter area
       N1 - OSPF NSSA external type 1, N2 - OSPF NSSA external type 2
       E1 - OSPF external type 1, E2 - OSPF external type 2, E - EGP
       i - IS-IS, L1 - IS-IS level-1, L2 - IS-IS level-2, ia - IS-IS inter area
       * - candidate default, U - per-user static route, o - ODR
       P - periodic downloaded static route


Gateway of last resort is 168.13.1.101 to network 10.0.0.0

     168.13.0.0/24 is subnetted, 5 subnets
R       168.13.200.0 [120/1] via 168.13.1.101, 00:00:12, FastEthernet0/0
C       168.13.1.0 is directly connected, FastEthernet0/0
R       168.13.3.0 [120/1] via 168.13.100.3, 00:00:00, Serial0.1
R       168.13.2.0 [120/1] via 168.13.100.2, 00:00:00, Serial0.1
C       168.13.100.0 is directly connected, Serial0.1
R*   10.0.0.0/8 [120/1] via 168.13.1.101, 00:00:12, FastEthernet0/0
```

R1 shows both the result of having normally learned a route to network 10.0.0.0 through RIP, plus the additional results of the **ip default-network 10.0.0.0** global command. R1's RIP route for 10.0.0.0/8 lists a next-hop IP address of 168.13.1.101, Dist1's IP address on their common LAN, as normal. Because of the **ip default-network 10.0.0.0** command, R1 decides to use the details in the route to network 10.0.0.0 as its default route. The last part of the line about the gateway of last resort lists the default network, 10.0.0.0. Also, R1 lists an asterisk beside the route referenced in the **ip default-network** command.

Default Route Summary

Remembering the details of configuring default routes, and in particular the resulting details in the output of the **show ip route** command, can be a challenge. However, make it a point to remember these key points regarding default routes:

- Default static routes can be statically configured using the **ip route 0.0.0.0 0.0.0.0** *next-hop-address* or **the ip default-network** *net-number* command.

Key Topic

- When a router only matches a packet with the default route, that router uses the forwarding details listed in the gateway of last resort line.

Regardless of how the default route shows up—whether it's a gateway of last resort, a route to 0.0.0.0, or a route to some other network with an * beside it in the routing table—it is used according to the rules of classless or classful routing, as is explained in the next section.

Classful and Classless Routing

Cisco routers have two configurable options for how a router uses an existing default route: classless routing and classful routing. Classless routing causes a router to use its default routes for any packet that does not match some other route. Classful routing places one restriction on when a router can use its default route, resulting in cases in which a router has a default route but the router chooses to discard a packet rather than forwarding the packet based on the default route.

The terms *classless* and *classful* also characterize both IP addressing and IP routing protocols, so a fair amount of confusion exists as to the meaning of the terms. Before explaining the details of classful routing and classless routing, the next section summarizes the other use of these terms.

Summary of the Use of the Terms Classless and Classful

The terms *classless addressing* and *classful addressing* refer to two different ways to think about IP addresses. Both terms refer to a perspective on the structure of a subnetted IP address. Classless addressing uses a two-part view of IP addresses, and classful addressing has a three-part view. With classful addressing, the address always has an 8-, 16-, or 24-bit network field, based on the Class A, B, and C addressing rules. The end of the address has a host part that uniquely identifies each host inside a subnet. The bits in between the network and host part comprise the third part, namely the subnet part of the address. With classless addressing, the network and subnet parts from the classful view are combined into a single part, often called the subnet or prefix, with the address ending in the host part.

The terms *classless routing protocol* and *classful routing protocol* refer to features of different IP routing protocols. These features cannot be enabled or disabled; a routing protocol is, by its very nature, either classless or classful. In particular, classless routing protocols advertise mask information for each subnet, giving classless protocols the ability to support both VLSM and route summarization. Classful routing protocols do not advertise mask information, so they do not support VLSM or route summarization.

The third use of the terms *classless* and *classful*—the terms *classful routing* and *classless routing*—have to do with how the IP routing process makes use of the default route. Interestingly, this is the only one of the three uses of the terms that can be changed based on router configuration. Table 12-1 lists the three uses of the classless and classful terms, with a brief explanation. A more complete explanation of classless and classful routing follows the table. Chapter 14 explains more background information about the terms *classless routing protocol* and *classful routing protocol*.

Table 12-1 *Comparing the Use of the Terms Classless and Classful*

As Applied To	Classful	Classless
Addresses	Addresses have three parts: network, subnet, and host.	Addresses have two parts: subnet or prefix, and host.
Routing protocols	Routing protocol does not advertise masks nor support VLSM; RIP-1 and IGRP.	Routing protocol does advertise masks and support VLSM; RIP-2, EIGRP, OSPF.
Routing (forwarding)	IP forwarding process is restricted in how it uses the default route.	IP forwarding process has no restrictions on using the default route.

Key Topic

Classless and Classful Routing Compared

Classless IP routing works just like most people think IP routing would work when a router knows a default route. Compared to classful routing, classless routing's core concepts are straightforward. Classful routing restricts the use of the default route. The following two statements give a general description of each, with an example following the definitions:

■ **Classless routing:** When a packet's destination only matches a router's default route, and does not match any other routes, forward the packet using that default route.

Key Topic

■ **Classful routing:** When a packet's destination only matches a router's default route, and does not match any other routes, only use the default route if this router does not know any routes in the classful network in which the destination IP address resides.

The use of the term *classful* refers to the fact that the logic includes some consideration of classful IP addressing rules—namely, the classful (Class A, B, or C) network of the packet's destination address. To make sense of this concept, Example 12-12 shows a router with a default route, but classful routing allows the use of the default route in one case, but not another. The example uses the same default routes examples from earlier in this chapter, based on Figure 12-8. Both R3 and R1 have a default route that could forward packets to Router Dist1. However, as seen in Example12-12, on R3, the **ping 10.1.1.1** works, but the **ping 168.200.1.1** fails.

Note: This example uses the default route on R1 as defined with the ip route command and as explained in Examples 4-8 and 4-9, but it would have worked the same regardless of how the default route was learned.

Example 12-12 *Classful Routing Causes One Ping on R3 to Fail*

```
R3# show ip route
Codes: C - connected, S - static, I - IGRP, R - RIP, M - mobile, B - BGP
       D - EIGRP, EX - EIGRP external, O - OSPF, IA - OSPF inter area
       N1 - OSPF NSSA external type 1, N2 - OSPF NSSA external type 2
```

```
            E1 - OSPF external type 1, E2 - OSPF external type 2, E - EGP
            i - IS-IS, L1 - IS-IS level-1, L2 - IS-IS level-2, ia - IS-IS inter area
            * - candidate default, U - per-user static route, o - ODR
            P - periodic downloaded static route

Gateway of last resort is 168.13.100.1 to network 0.0.0.0

       168.200.0.0/24 is subnetted, 1 subnet
          168.200.2.0 [120/1] via 168.13.100.1, 00:00:13, Serial0.1
       168.13.0.0/24 is subnetted, 4 subnets
R         168.13.1.0 [120/1] via 168.13.100.1, 00:00:13, Serial0.1
C         168.13.3.0 is directly connected, Ethernet0
R         168.13.2.0 [120/1] via 168.13.100.2, 00:00:06, Serial0.1
C         168.13.100.0 is directly connected, Serial0.1
R3# ping 10.1.1.1

Type escape sequence to abort.
Sending 5, 100-byte ICMP Echos to 10.1.1.1, timeout is 2 seconds:
!!!!!
Success rate is 100 percent (5/5), round-trip min/avg/max = 84/89/114 ms
R3#
R3# ping 168.200.1.1

Type escape sequence to abort.
Sending 5, 100-byte ICMP Echos to 168.200.1.1, timeout is 2 seconds:
.....
Success rate is 0 percent (0/5)
```

First, consider R3's attempt to match both destinations (10.1.1.1 and 168.200.1.1) against the routes in the routing table. R3's routing table does not have any routes that match either destination IP address, other than the default route. So, R3's only option is to use its default route.

R3 is configured to use classful routing. With classful routing, the router first matches the Class A, B, or C network number in which a destination resides. If the Class A, B, or C network is found, Cisco IOS Software then looks for the specific subnet number. If it isn't found, the packet is discarded, as is the case with the ICMP echoes sent with the **ping 168.200.1.1** command. However, with classful routing, if the packet does not match a Class A, B, or C network in the routing table, and a default route exists, the default route is indeed used—which is why R3 can forward the ICMP echoes sent by the successful **ping 10.1.1.1** command.

In short, with classful routing, the only time the default route is used is when the router does not know about any subnets of the packet's destination Class A, B, or C network.

You can toggle between classless and classful routing with the **ip classless** and **no ip classless** global configuration commands, respectively. With classless routing, Cisco IOS Software looks for the best match, ignoring class rules. If a default route exists, with classless routing, the packet always at least matches the default route. If a more specific route matches the packet's destination, that route is used. Example 12-13 shows R3 changed to use classless routing, and the successful ping of 168.200.1.1.

Example 12-13 *Classless Routing Allows Ping 168.200.1.1 to Now Succeed*

```
R3# configure terminal
Enter configuration commands, one per line.  End with CNTL/Z.
R3(config)# ip classless
R3(config)# ^Z
R3# ping 168.200.1.1

Type escape sequence to abort.
Sending 5, 100-byte ICMP Echos to 168.200.1.1, timeout is 2 seconds:
!!!!!
Success rate is 100 percent (5/5), round-trip min/avg/max = 80/88/112 ms
```

Chapter Review

Review Key Topics

Review the most important topics from this chapter, noted with the Key Topic icon in the outer margin of the page. Table 12-2 lists a reference of these key topics and the page numbers on which each is found.

Table 12-2 *Key Topics for Chapter 12*

Key Topic Element	Description	Page Number
List	Steps taken by a host when forwarding IP packets	274
List	Steps taken by a router when forwarding IP packets	274
List	Review of key points about IP addressing	277
Thought	Summary of the logic a router uses when a packet's destination matches more than one route	279
List	Rules regarding when a router creates a connected route	280
List	Rules about the source address used for packets generated by the IOS ping command	293
List	Key facts regarding the definition of static default routes	297
Table 12-1	Summary of the three separate but related uses of the terms *classless* and *classful*	299
List	Definitions of classless routing and classful routing	299

Define Key Terms

Define the following key terms from this chapter, and check your answers in the glossary:

classful addressing, classful routing, classful routing protocol, classless addressing, classless routing, classless routing protocol, extended ping, secondary IP address, zero subnet

Review Command Reference to Check Your Memory

Although you should not necessarily memorize the information in the tables in this section, this section does include a reference for the configuration and EXEC commands covered in this chapter. Practically speaking, you should memorize the commands as a side effect of reading the chapter and doing all the activities in this "Chapter Review" section. To check to see how well you have memorized the commands as a side effect of your other studies, cover the left side of the table with a piece of paper, read the descriptions on the right side, and see whether you remember the command.

Table 12-3 *Chapter 12 Configuration Command Reference*

Command	Description
encapsulation dot1q *vlan-id* [native]	A subinterface subcommand that tells the router to use 802.1Q trunking, for a particular VLAN, and with the **native** keyword, to not encapsulate in a trunking header
encapsulation isl *vlan-identifier*	A subinterface subcommand that tells the router to use ISL trunking, for a particular VLAN
[no] ip classless	Global command that enables (**ip classless**) or disables (**no ip classless**) classless routing
[no] ip subnet-zero	Global command that allows (**ip subnet-zero**) or disallows (**no ip subnet-zero**) the configuration of an interface IP address in a zero subnet
ip address *ip-address mask* [secondary]	Interface subcommand that assigns the interface's IP address, and optionally makes the address a secondary address
ip route *prefix mask* {*ip-address* | *interface-type interface-number*} [*distance*] [permanent]	Global configuration command that creates a static route
ip default-network *network-number*	Global command that creates a default route based on the router's route to reach the classful network listed in the command

Table 12-4 *Chapter 12 EXEC Command Reference*

Command	Description
show ip route	Lists the router's entire routing table
show ip route *ip-address*	Lists detailed information about the route that a router matches for the listed IP address
ping {*host-name* | *ip-address*}	Tests IP routes by sending an ICMP packet to the destination host
traceroute {*host-name* | *ip-address*}	Tests IP routes by discovering the IP addresses of the routes between a router and the listed destination

Answer Review Questions

Answer the following review questions:

1. A PC user turns on her computer, and as soon as the computer is up and working, she opens a web browser to browse http://www.ciscopress.com. Which protocol(s) would definitely not be used by the PC during this process?

   a. DHCP

   b. DNS

   c. ARP

   d. ICMP

2. A PC user turns on her computer, and as soon as the computer is up and working, she opens a command prompt. From there, she issues the **ping 2.2.2.2** command, and the ping shows 100 percent success. The PC's IP address is 1.1.1.1 with mask 255.255.255.0. Which of the following settings would be required on the PC to support the successful ping?

   a. The IP address of a DNS server

   b. The IP address of a default gateway

   c. The IP address of an ARP server

   d. The IP address of a DHCP server

3. Router 1 has a Fast Ethernet interface 0/0 with IP address 10.1.1.1. The interface is connected to a switch. This connection is then migrated to use 802.1Q trunking. Which of the following commands could be part of a valid configuration for Router 1's Fa0/0 interface?

   a. interface fastethernet 0/0.4

   b. dot1q enable

   c. dot1q enable 4

   d. trunking enable

   e. trunking enable 4

   f. encapsulation dot1q

4. A router is configured with the **no ip subnet-zero** global configuration command. Which of the following interface subcommands would not be accepted by this router?

   a. ip address 10.1.1.1 255.255.255.0

   b. ip address 10.0.0.129 255.255.255.128

   c. ip address 10.1.2.2 255.254.0.0

   d. ip address 10.0.0.5 255.255.255.252

5. Which one of the following answers describes an action or event that most directly causes a router's **show ip route** command to list an identifying code of S beside a route?

    a. The IP address must be configured on an interface.

    b. The router must receive a routing update from a neighboring router.

    c. The **ip route** command must be added to the configuration.

    d. The **ip address** command must use the **special** keyword.

    e. The interface must be up and up.

6. Which of the following commands correctly configures a static route?

    a. ip route 10.1.3.0 255.255.255.0 10.1.130.253

    b. ip route 10.1.3.0 serial 0

    c. ip route 10.1.3.0 /24 10.1.130.253

    d. ip route 10.1.3.0 /24 serial 0

7. Which of the following is affected by whether a router is performing classful or classless routing?

    a. When to use a default route

    b. When to use a default route

    c. When to use masks in routing updates

    d. When to use masks in routing updates

    e. When to convert a packet's destination IP address to a network number

    f. When to perform queuing based on the classification of a packet into a particular queue

8. A router has been configured with the **ip classless** global configuration command. The router receives a packet destined to IP address 168.13.4.1. The following text lists the contents of the router's routing table. Which of the following is true about how this router forwards the packet?

```
Gateway of last resort is 168.13.1.101 to network 0.0.0.0

     168.13.0.0/24 is subnetted, 2 subnets
C        168.13.1.0 is directly connected,  FastEthernet0/0
R        168.13.3.0 [120/1] via 168.13.100.3, 00:00:05, Serial0.1
```

    a. It is forwarded to 168.13.100.3.

    b. It is forwarded to 168.13.1.101.

    c. It is forwarded out interface Fa0/0, directly to the destination host.

    d. The router discards the packet.

This chapter covers the following subjects:

■ **Defining a Subnet:** This section discusses the concept of a subnet and the key numbers that define a subnet: the subnet ID, the subnet broadcast address, plus the range of usable IP addresses in the subnet.

■ **Analyzing Existing Subnets—Binary:** This section examines the key numbers that define a subnet by analyzing the binary values.

■ **Analyzing Existing Subnets—Decimal:** This section examines the key numbers that define a subnet by analyzing the decimal values.

■ **Practice Analyzing Existing Subnets:** This brief section gives tips and suggestions for where to find more practice for the topics in this chapter.

CHAPTER 13

Analyzing Existing Subnets

Most networking jobs require you to work with existing IP addresses, masks, and subnets. Often, a networking task begins with the discovery of the IP address and mask used by some host. Then, to understand how the internetwork routes packets to that host, you must find key pieces of information about the subnet, specifically

- The subnet ID
- The subnet broadcast address
- The subnet's range of usable unicast IP addresses

This chapter discusses the concepts and math to take a known IP address and mask and then fully describe a subnet by finding the values in this list. These specific tasks might well be the most important IP skills in the entire IP addressing and subnetting topics in this book, because these task might be the most commonly used tasks when operating and troubleshooting real networks.

Defining a Subnet

An IP subnet is a subset of a classful network, created by choice of some network engineer. However, that engineer cannot pick just any arbitrary subset of addresses; instead, the engineer must follow certain rules, like the following:

- The subnet contains a set of consecutive numbers.
- The subnet holds 2^H numbers, where H is the number of host bits defined by the subnet mask.
- Two special numbers in the range cannot be used as IP addresses:
  - The first (lowest) number acts as an identifier for the subnet (*subnet ID*).
  - The last (highest) number acts as a *subnet broadcast address*.
- The remaining addresses, whose values sit between the subnet ID and subnet broadcast address, are used as *unicast IP addresses*.

The following sections review and expand on the basic concepts of the subnet ID, subnet broadcast address, and range of addresses in a subnet.

An Example with Network 172.16.0.0 and Four Subnets

Imagine that you work at the customer support center, where you receive all initial calls from users who have problems with their computer. You coach the user through finding his or her IP address and mask: 172.16.150.41, mask 255.255.192.0. One of the first and most common tasks you will do based on that information is to find the subnet ID of the subnet in which that address resides. (In fact, this subnet ID is sometimes called the *resident subnet*, because the IP address exists in or resides in that subnet.)

Before getting into the math, examine the mask (255.255.192.0) and classful network (172.16.0.0) for a moment. From the mask, based on what you learned in Chapter 10, "Analyzing Existing Subnet Masks," you can find the structure of the subnet, including the number of host and subnet bits. That analysis tells you that two subnet bits exist, meaning that there should be four (2^2) subnets. (If these concepts are not yet clear, take a few moments to review Chapter 10's section "How Masks Define the Format of Addresses.") Figure 13-1 shows the idea.

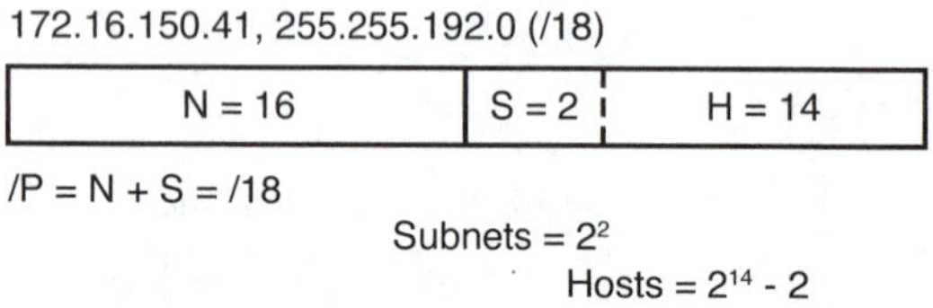

172.16.150.41, 255.255.192.0 (/18)

N = 16	S = 2	H = 14

/P = N + S = /18

Subnets = 2^2

Hosts = 2^{14} - 2

Figure 13-1   *Address Structure: Class B Network, /18 Mask*

So far, this book assumes that only one mask is used throughout a single class A, B, or C network. Continuing with that assumption, all subnets of a single network must be the same size, because all subnets have the same structure. For example, in the example begun in Figure 13-1, all four subnets will have the structure shown in the figure, so all four subnets will have $2^{14} - 2$ host addresses.

Next, focus on two concepts related to this example: that four subnets exist in this network and that they are all the same size. Conceptually, if you represent the entire class B network as a number line, and four equal-sized subnets exist, each subnet contains essentially one-fourth of the network, and each subnet consumes one-fourth of the number line, as shown in Figure 13-2.

The figure also shows the concept of the four subnets on a number line at the top of the figure and the entire class B network 172.16.0.0 on a number line at the bottom. Each subnet has a subnet ID on the far left (the smallest number in that subnet) and a subnet broadcast address on the right (the highest number in the subnet).

As mentioned earlier in this chapter, you often begin a task with an IP address and mask, and you then need to find the subnet in which the address resides. Again, using IP address

172.16.150.41 as an example, Figure 13-3 shows the resident subnet, along with the subnet ID and subnet broadcast address that bracket the subnet.

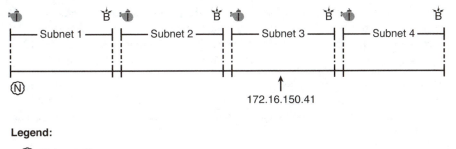

Legend:

(N) Network ID

Subnet ID

B Subnet Broadcast Address

Figure 13-2   *Network 172.16.0.0, Divided into Four Equal Subnets*

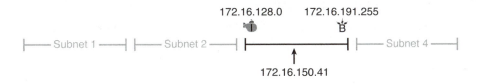

Legend:

Subnet ID

B Subnet Broadcast Address

Figure 13-3   *Resident Subnet for 172.16.150.41, 255.255.192.0*

Subnet ID Concepts

A subnet ID is simply a number used to succinctly represent a subnet. When listed along with its matching subnet mask, the subnet ID identifies the subnet and can be used to derive the subnet broadcast address and range of addresses in the subnet. Rather than having to write down all these details about a subnet, you simply need to write down the subnet ID and mask, and you have enough information to fully describe the subnet.

The subnet ID appears in many places, but it is seen most often in IP routing tables. For example, when an engineer configures a router with its IP address and mask, the router calculates the subnet ID and puts a route into its routing table for that subnet. The router typically then advertises the subnet ID/mask combination to neighboring routers with some IP routing protocol. Eventually, all the routers in an enterprise learn about the subnet—again using the subnet ID and subnet mask combination—and display it in their routing tables. (You can display the contents of a router's IP routing table using the **show ip route** command.)

Unfortunately, the terminology-related subnets can sometimes cause problems. First, the terms *subnet ID*, *subnet number*, and *subnet address* are synonyms. Additionally, people sometimes simply say *subnet* when referring to the idea of a subnet and sometimes when referring to the number used as the *subnet ID*. And when talking about routing, sometimes people use the term *prefix* instead of *subnet*. The term *prefix* refers to the same idea as *subnet*; it just uses terminology from the classless addressing way to describe IP addresses, as discussed in Chapter 10's section "Classless and Classful Addressing."

The biggest terminology confusion arises between the terms *network* and *subnet*. In the real world, people often use these terms synonymously, and that is perfectly reasonable in some cases. In other cases, the specific meaning of these terms, and their differences, matter to what is being discussed.

For example, often people might say "What is the network ID?" when they really want to know the subnet ID. In another case, they might want to know the class A, B, or C network ID. So, when one engineer asks something like "What's the net-ID for 172.16.150.41 slash 18?," use the context to figure out if he wants the literal classful network ID (172.16.0.0 in this case) or the literal subnet ID (172.16.128.0 in this case).

Be ready to notice when the terms *subnet* and *network* are used, and then use the context to figure out the specific meaning of the term in that case.

Table 13-1 summarizes the key facts about the subnet ID, along with the possible synonyms, for easier review and study.

Table 13-1 *Summary of Subnet ID Key Facts*

Definition	A number that represents the subnet
Numeric value	First (smallest) number in the subnet
Literal synonyms	Subnet number, subnet address, prefix, resident subnet
Common-use synonyms	Network, network ID, network number, network address
Typically seen in...	Routing tables, documentation

The Subnet Broadcast Address

The subnet broadcast address has two main roles: to be used as a destination IP address for the purpose of sending packets to all hosts in the subnet, and as a means to find the high end of the range of addresses in a subnet.

The original purpose for the subnet broadcast address was to give hosts a way to send one packet to all hosts in a subnet, and to do so efficiently. For example, a host in subnet A could send a packet with a destination address of subnet B's subnet broadcast address. The routers would forward this one packet just like a packet sent to a host in subnet B. After the packet arrives at the router connected to subnet B, that last router would then forward the packet to all hosts in subnet B, typically by encapsulating the packet in a data link layer broadcast frame. As a result, all hosts in host B's subnet would receive a copy of the packet.

Although the subnet broadcast address has little practical use today, you will probably use it a lot because the broadcast address is the last (highest) number in a subnet's range of addresses. To find the low end of the range, calculate the subnet ID; to find the high end of the range, calculate the subnet broadcast address.

Table 13-2 summarizes the key facts about the subnet broadcast address, along with the possible synonyms, for easier review and study.

Table 13-2 *Summary of Subnet Broadcast Address Key Facts*

Definition	A reserved number in each subnet that, when used as the destination address of a packet, causes the routers to forward the packet to all hosts in that subnet
Numeric value	Last (highest) number in the subnet
Literal synonym	Directed broadcast address
Broader-use synonym	Network broadcast
Typically seen in...	Calculations of the range of addresses in a subnet

Key Topic

The Range of Usable Addresses

The engineers implementing an IP internetwork need to know the range of unicast IP addresses in each subnet. Before you can plan which addresses to use as statically assigned IP addresses, which to configure to be leased by the DHCP server, and which to reserve for later use, you need to know the range of usable addresses.

To find the range of usable IP addresses in a subnet, first find the subnet ID and the subnet broadcast address. Then, just add 1 to the fourth octet of the subnet ID to get the first (lowest) usable address, and subtract one from the fourth octet of the subnet broadcast address to get the last (highest) usable address in the subnet.

For example, the earlier Figure 13-3 showed subnet ID 172.16.128.0, mask /18. The first usable address is simply one more than the subnet ID—in this case, 172.16.128.1. That same figure showed a subnet broadcast address of 172.16.191.255, so the last usable address is 1 less, or 172.16.191.254.

Now that this section has described the concepts behind the numbers that collectively define a subnet, the rest of the chapter focuses on the math used to find these values.

Analyzing Existing Subnets: Binary

What does it mean to "analyze a subnet"? For this book, it means that you should be able to start with an IP address and mask and then define key facts about the subnet in which that address resides. Specifically, that means discovering the subnet ID, subnet broadcast address, and range of addresses. The analysis can also include the calculation of the number of addresses in the subnet, as discussed in Chapter 10, but this chapter does not review those concepts.

Many methods exist to calculate the details about a subnet based on the address/mask. The following sections begin by discussing some calculations that use binary math, with later sections showing alternatives that use only decimal math. While many people prefer the decimal method for going faster, the binary calculations ultimately give you a better understanding of IPv4 addressing.

Finding the Subnet ID—Binary

To start this section that uses binary, first consider a simple decimal math problem: Find the smallest three-digit decimal number that begins with 4. The answer, of course, is 400. And although most people would not have to break down the logic into steps, you know that 0 is the lowest value digit you can use for any digit in a decimal number. You know that the first digit must be a 4 and the number is a three-digit number, so you just use the lowest value (0) for the last two digits and find the answer: 400.

This same concept, applied to binary IP addresses, gives you the subnet ID. You have seen all the related concepts in other chapters, so if you already intuitively know how to find the subnet ID in binary, great! If not, the following key facts should help you see the logic:

■   All numbers in the subnet (subnet ID, subnet broadcast address, and all usable IP addresses) have the same value in the prefix part of the numbers.

■   The subnet ID is the lowest numeric value in the subnet, so its host part, in binary, is all 0s.

To find the subnet ID in binary, you take the IP address in binary and change all host bits to binary 0. To do so, you need to convert the IP address to binary. You also need to identify the prefix and host bits, which can be easily done by converting the mask (as needed) to prefix format. (Note that Appendix B, "IP Access Control Lists," includes a decimal-binary conversion table.) Figure 13-4 shows the idea, using the same address/mask as in the earlier examples in this chapter: 172.16.150.41, mask /18.

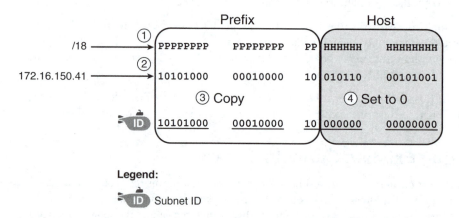

Figure 13-4 *Binary Concept: Convert the IP Address to the Subnet ID*

Starting at the top of the figure, the format of the IP address is represented with 18 prefix (P) and 14 host (H) bits in the mask (Step 1). The second row (Step 2) shows the binary version of the IP address, converted from the dotted decimal notation (DDN) value 172.16.150.41. (If you have not used the conversion table in Appendix B yet, it might be useful to double-check the conversion of all four octets based on the table.)

The next two steps show the action to copy the IP address's prefix bits (Step 3) and to give the host bits a value of binary 0 (Step 4). This resulting number is the subnet ID, in binary.

The last step, not shown in Figure 13-4, is to convert the subnet ID from binary to decimal. This book shows that conversion as a separate step, in Figure 13-5, mainly because many people make a mistake at this step in the process. When converting a 32-bit number (like an IP address or IP subnet ID) back to an IPv4 dotted decimal number, you must follow this rule:

> Convert 8 bits at a time from binary to decimal, regardless of the line between the prefix and host parts of the number.

Figure 13-5 shows this final step. Note that the third octet (the third set of 8 bits) has 2 bits in the prefix and 6 bits in the host part of the number, but the conversion occurs for all 8 bits.

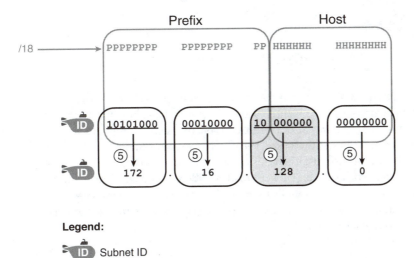

Figure 13-5 *Converting the Subnet ID from Binary to DDN*

Note: You can do the numeric conversions in Figures 13-4 and 13-5 by relying on the conversion table in Appendix B. To convert from DDN to binary, for each octet, find the decimal value in the table and then write down the 8-bit binary equivalent. To convert from binary back to DDN, for each octet of 8 bits, find the matching binary entry in the table and write down the corresponding decimal value. For example, 172 converts to binary 10101100, and 00010000 converts to decimal 16.

Finding the Subnet Broadcast—Binary

Finding the subnet broadcast address uses a very similar process. To find the subnet broadcast address, use the same binary process used to find the subnet ID, but instead of setting all the host bits to the lowest value (all binary 0s), set the host part to the highest value (all binary 1s). Figure 13-6 shows the concept.

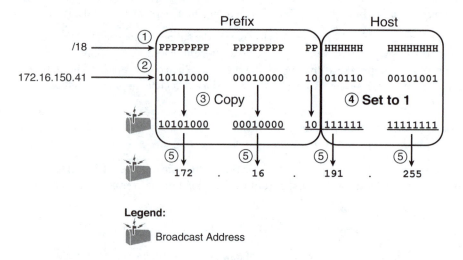

Figure 13-6 *Finding a Subnet Broadcast Address: Binary*

The process in Figure 13-6 demonstrates the same first three steps as shown in Figure 13-4. Specifically, the figure shows the identification of the prefix and host bits (Step 1), the results of converting the IP address 172.16.150.41 to binary (Step 2), and the copying of the prefix bits (the first 18 bits in this case). The difference occurs in the host bits on the right, changing all host bits (the last 14 in this case) to the largest possible value (all binary 1s). The final step converts the 32-bit subnet broadcast address to DDN format. Also, remember that with any conversion from DDN to binary or vice versa, the process always converts using 8 bits at a time. In particular, in this case, the entire third octet of binary 10111111 is converted back to decimal 191.

Binary Practice Problems

Figures 13-4 through 13-6 demonstrate a process to find the subnet ID using binary math. The following written process summarizes those steps in written form for easier reference and practice:

Key Topic

Step 1. Convert the mask to prefix format to find the length of the prefix (/P) and the length of the host part (32 − P).

Step 2. Convert the IP address to its 32-bit binary equivalent.

Step 3. Copy the prefix bits of the IP address.

Step 4. Write down 0s for the host bits.

Step 5.   Convert the resulting 32-bit number, 8 bits at a time, back to decimal.

The process to find the subnet broadcast address is exactly the same, except in Step 4, set the bits to 1s.

Take a few moments and run through the following five practice problems on a scratch piece of paper. In each case, find both the subnet ID and subnet broadcast address. Record the prefix style mask as well:

1. 8.1.4.5, 255.255.0.0
2. 130.4.102.1, 255.255.255.0
3. 199.1.1.100, 255.255.255.0
4. 130.4.102.1, 255.255.252.0
5. 199.1.1.100, 255.255.255.224

Tables 13-3 through 13-7 show the results for the five different examples. The tables show the host bits in bold, and include the binary version of the address and mask and the binary version of the subnet ID and subnet broadcast address.

Table 13-3   *Subnet Analysis for Address 8.1.4.5, Mask 255.255.0.0*

Prefix Length	/16	11111111 11111111 00000000 00000000
Address	8.1.4.5	00001000 00000001 00000100 00000101
Subnet ID	8.1.0.0	00001000 00000001 00000000 00000000
Broadcast Address	8.1.255.255	00001000 00000001 11111111 11111111

Table 13-4   *Subnet Analysis for Subnet with Address 130.4.102.1, Mask 255.255.255.0*

Prefix Length	/24	11111111 11111111 11111111 00000000
Address	130.4.102.1	10000010 00000100 01100110 00000001
Subnet ID	130.4.102.0	10000010 00000100 01100110 00000000
Broadcast Address	130.4.102.255	10000010 00000100 01100110 11111111

Table 13-5   *Subnet Analysis for Subnet with Address 199.1.1.100, Mask 255.255.255.0*

Prefix Length	/24	11111111 11111111 11111111 00000000
Address	199.1.1.100	11000111 00000001 00000001 01100100
Subnet ID	199.1.1.0	11000111 00000001 00000001 00000000
Broadcast Address	199.1.1.255	11000111 00000001 00000001 11111111

Table 13-6   *Subnet Analysis for Subnet with Address 130.4.102.1, Mask 255.255.252.0*

Prefix Length	/22	11111111 11111111 11111100 00000000
Address	130.4.102.1	10000010 00000100 01100110 00000001
Subnet ID	130.4.100.0	10000010 00000100 01100100 00000000
Broadcast Address	130.4.103.255	10000010 00000100 01100111 11111111

Table 13-7   *Subnet Analysis for Subnet with Address 199.1.1.100, Mask 255.255.255.224*

Prefix Length	/27	11111111 11111111 11111111 11100000
Address	199.1.1.100	11000111 00000001 00000001 01100100
Subnet ID	199.1.1.96	11000111 00000001 00000001 01100000
Broadcast Address	199.1.1.127	11000111 00000001 00000001 01111111

A Shortcut for the Binary Process

The binary process described so far requires that all four octets be converted to binary and then back to decimal. However, you can easily predict the results in at least three of the four octets, based on the DDN mask. You can then avoid the binary math in all but one octet and reduce the number of binary conversions you need to do.

First, consider an octet whose DDN mask value is 255 in the first octet. Decimal 255 converts to binary 11111111, which means that all 8 bits in the first octet are prefix bits. Now think through the five-step process listed in this chapter, but just in the first octet. With the binary process to find the subnet ID, you will spend time to convert the first octet of the IP address to binary (Step 2). But what happens to all 8 bits of the first octet of the IP address? You will copy them (Step 3)! And then in Step 4, you will convert the same 8-bit value back to decimal, ending up with the same decimal value you started with!

For example, consider the familiar case of 172.16.150.41, mask 255.255.192.0, as shown in Figures 13-4 through 13-6. In this example, the first two octets of the mask are 255. If you look back at the earlier figures, they show that the first two octets of the subnet ID and the subnet broadcast address are 172.16. In short, because the mask in each of the first two octets was 255, all you have to do is copy the decimal IP address values for those octets.

Another shortcut exists for octets whose DDN mask value is decimal 0. Decimal 0 converts to the 8-bit binary value 00000000. A mask octet with eight binary 0s means that all 8 bits in this octet are host bits. Again, thinking through the five-step process, you will convert the IP address value to binary (Step 2), but at Step 4, you convert all 8 of these bits, whatever they are, to binary 00000000. And at Step 5 in this octet, you convert binary 00000000 back to decimal, for a value of decimal 0. As it turns out, if the DDN mask is decimal 0 in some octet, the subnet ID will be decimal 0 in that octet, and you can avoid the binary math in that octet.

The following revised process steps take these two shortcuts into account. However, when the mask is neither 0 nor 255, the process requires the same conversions. At most, you have to do only one octet of the conversions. To find the subnet ID, apply the logic in these steps, for each of the four octets:

Step 1. If the mask = 255, copy the decimal IP address for that octet.

Step 2. If the mask = 0, write down a decimal 0 for that octet.

Step 3. If the mask is neither 0 nor 255, in this octet, use the same binary logic as seen in the section "Finding the Subnet ID—Binary," earlier in this chapter.

Figure 13-7 shows an example of the process, again using 172.16.150.41, mask 255.255.192.0.

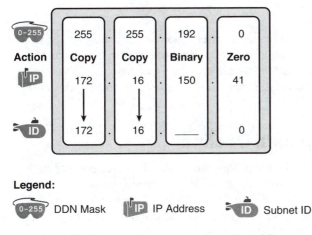

Legend:

0-255 DDN Mask   IP IP Address   ID Subnet ID

Figure 13-7 *Binary Concept: Convert IP Address to Subnet Broadcast Address*

A similar shortcut exists when finding the subnet broadcast address. For DDN mask octets equal to decimal 0, set the decimal subnet broadcast address value to 255 instead of 0, as noted in the following list:

Step 1. If the mask = 255, copy the decimal IP address for that octet.

Step 2. If the mask = 0, write down a decimal 255 for that octet.

Step 3. If the mask is neither 0 nor 255, in this octet, use the same binary logic as seen in the earlier section "Finding the Subnet Broadcast Address—Binary."

Brief Note About Boolean Math

So far, this chapter has described how humans can use binary math to find the subnet ID and subnet broadcast address. However, computers typically use an entirely different binary process to find the same values, using a branch of mathematics called *Boolean algebra*. Computers already store the IP address and mask in binary form, so they do not have to do any conversions to and from decimal. Then, certain Boolean operations allow the computers to calculate the subnet ID and subnet broadcast address with just a few CPU instructions.

You do not need to know Boolean math to have a good understanding of IP subnetting. However, in case you are interested, computers use the following Boolean logic to find the subnet ID and subnet broadcast address respectively:

■ Perform a *Boolean AND* of the IP address and mask. This process converts all host bits to binary 0.

■ Invert the mask, and then perform a *Boolean OR* of the IP address and inverted subnet mask. This process converts all host bits to binary 1s.

Finding the Range of Addresses

Finding the range of usable addresses in a subnet, after you know the subnet ID and subnet broadcast address, requires only simple addition and subtraction. To find the first (lowest) usable IP address in the subnet, simply add 1 to the fourth octet of the subnet ID. To find the last (highest) usable IP address, simply subtract 1 from the fourth octet of the subnet broadcast address.

Analyzing Existing Subnets: Decimal

Analyzing existing subnets using the binary process works well. However, some of the math just takes time for most people, particularly the decimal-binary conversions. If you plan to focus on networking in your career, you should strive to learn subnetting math well enough so that you can take an IP address and mask, and calculate the subnet ID and range of usable addresses within about 15 seconds. When using binary methods, most people require a lot of practice to be able to find these answers, even when using even the abbreviated binary process.

The following sections discuss how to find the subnet ID and subnet broadcast address using only decimal math. Most people can find the answers more quickly using this process, at least after a little practice, as compared with the binary process. However, the decimal process does not tell you anything about the meaning behind the math. So, if you have not read through the previous section "Analyzing Existing Subnets: Binary," it is worthwhile to read for the sake of understanding subnetting. These sections focus on getting the right answer using a method that, after it is practiced, should be faster.

Analysis with Easy Masks

With three easy subnet masks in particular, finding the subnet ID and subnet broadcast address requires only easy logic and literally no math. Three easy masks exist:

255.0.0.0

255.255.0.0

255.255.255.0

These easy masks have only 255 and 0 in decimal. In comparison, difficult masks have one octet that has neither a 255 nor a 0 in the mask, which makes the logic more challenging.

Note: The terms *easy mask* and *difficult mask* are terms created for use in this book to describe the masks and the level of difficulty when working with each.

When the problem uses an easy mask, you can quickly find the subnet ID based on the IP address and mask in DDN format. Just use the following process for each of the four octets to find the subnet ID:

Step 1. If the mask octet = 255, copy the decimal IP address.

Step 2. If the mask octet = 0, write a decimal 0.

A similar simple process exists to find the subnet broadcast address, as follows:

Step 1. If the mask octet = 255, copy the decimal IP address.

Step 2. If the mask octet = 0, *write a decimal 255.*

Before moving to the next section, take some time to fill in the blanks in Table 13-8. Check your answers against Table 13-13 in the "Chapter Review" section, later in this chapter. Complete the table by listing the subnet ID and subnet broadcast address.

Table 13-8 *Practice Problems: Find Subnet ID and Broadcast, Easy Masks*

	IP Address	Mask	Subnet ID	Broadcast Address
1	10.77.55.3	255.255.255.0		
2	172.30.99.4	255.255.255.0		
3	192.168.6.54	255.255.255.0		
4	10.77.3.14	255.255.0.0		
5	172.22.55.77	255.255.0.0		
6	1.99.53.76	255.0.0.0		

Predictability in the Interesting Octet

While three masks are easier to work with (255.0.0.0, 255.255.0.0, and 255.255.255.0), the rest make the decimal math a little more difficult—so we call these masks difficult masks. With difficult masks, one octet is neither a 0 nor a 255. The math in the other three octets is pretty easy and boring, so this book calls the one octet with the more difficult math the interesting octet.

If you take some time to think about different problems and focus on the interesting octet, you will begin to see a pattern. This section takes you through that examination so that you can learn how to predict the pattern, in decimal, and find the subnet ID.

First, the subnet ID value has a predictable decimal value because of the assumption that a single subnet mask is used for all subnets of a single classful network. Remember, most of this book assumes that for a given classful network, the design engineer chooses to use a single subnet mask for all subnets. (Look back to Chapter 8's section "One Size Subnet Fits All—Or Not" for more detail.)

To see that predictability, consider Figure 13-8. The figure shows some ideas considered by a design engineer when subnetting class B network 172.16.0.0. The figure shows some comparisons of using masks 255.255.128.0, 255.255.192.0, 255.255.224.0, and 255.255.240.0. Each of these masks is a difficult mask because of having neither a 255 nor a 0 in the third octet, making the third octet interesting. The figure shows the decimal values in the third octet of all the subnet IDs of this network, and the number of subnets, based on each competing choice for the mask.

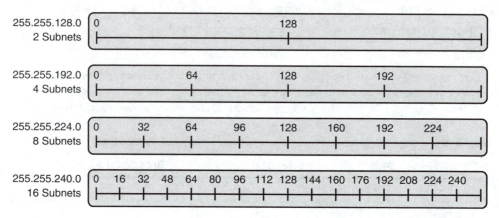

Figure 13-8   *Numeric Patterns in the Interesting Octet*

First, take a closer look at the top of the figure, where the results of using mask 255.255.128.0 are shown. Visually, the original class B network is represented by the entire width of the lines, and with the 255.255.128.0 mask, the network has been broken into two equal halves. Why two subnets? Only one subnet bit exists, so 2^1 or 2 subnets exist. The figure shows only the values in the interesting octet, to emphasize the patterns, but the full subnet IDs are 172.16.0.0 and 172.16.128.0.

Next, move down to the example using mask 255.255.192.0. Using this mask, and only this mask, subnets the class B network into four equal-sized subnets, because two subnet bits exist, meaning that four (2^2) subnets exist. The subnet IDs are 172.16.0.0, 172.16.64.0, 172.16.128.0, and 172.16.192.0.

Finally, for the last two examples, the example with mask 255.255.224.0 has eight subnets, dividing the network into eight equal parts. The example with mask 255.255.240.0 subnets the network into 16 equal parts. The figure shows the interesting octet values (the third octet in this case), with all subnets following the format 172.16.___.0 for this example.

The patterns in the figure are pretty obvious. No matter which subnet mask the design engineer chooses, the subnet ID values follow a pattern. To find the subnet ID, you just need a way to figure out what the pattern is. If you started with an IP address, just find the subnet ID closest to the IP address, without going over, as discussed in the next section.

Finding the Subnet ID: Difficult Masks

The following written process lists all the steps for find the subnet ID, using only decimal math. This process adds to the earlier process used with easy masks. For each octet, follow these steps:

Step 1.   If the mask octet = 255, copy the decimal IP address.

Step 2.   If the mask octet = 0, write a decimal 0.

Step 3.   If the mask is neither, refer to this octet as the *interesting octet*:

   a.   Calculate the *magic number* as 256 – mask.
   b.   Set the subnet ID's value to the multiple of the magic number that is closest to the IP address, without going over.

The process uses two new terms created for this book: *magic number* and *interesting octet*. The term *interesting octet* refers to the octet identified at Step 3 in the process—in other words, the octet with the mask that is neither 255 nor 0. Step 3a then uses the term *magic number*, which is derived from the DDN mask. Conceptually, the magic number is the number you add to one subnet ID to get the next subnet ID in order, as shown in Figure 13-8.

It helps to practice this process using the examples in the next few pages, which show the process being used on paper. Then follow the practice opportunities outlined in the section "Practice Analyzing Existing Subnets," later in this chapter.

Resident Subnet Example 1

For example, consider the requirement to find the resident subnet for IP address 130.4.102.1, mask 255.255.240.0. The process does not require you to think about prefix bits versus host bits, convert the mask, think about the mask in binary, or convert the IP address to and from binary. Instead, for each of the four octets, choose an action based on the value in the mask. Figure 13-9 shows the results. The circled numbers in the figure refer to the step numbers in the written process to find the subnet ID, as listed in the previous few pages.

First, examine the three uninteresting octets (1, 2, and 4). The process keys on the mask, and the first two octets have a mask value of 255, so simply copy the IP address to the place where you intend to write down the subnet ID. The fourth octet has a mask value 0, so write down a 0 for the fourth octet of the subnet ID.

The most challenging work occurs in the interesting octet, the third octet in this example, because of the mask value 240 in that octet. For this octet, Step 3a asks you to calculate the magic number as 256 – mask. That means to take the mask's value in the interesting octet (240 in this case) and subtract it from 256: 256 – 240 = 16. The subnet ID's values in this octet must be a multiple of decimal 16 in this case.

Step 3b then asks you to find the multiples of the magic number (16 in this case) and choose the one that is closest to the IP address without going over. Specifically, that means that you should mentally calculate the multiples of the magic number, starting at 0. (Do not forget to start at 0!) Count, starting at 0: 0, 16, 32, 48, 64, 80, 96, 112, and so on.

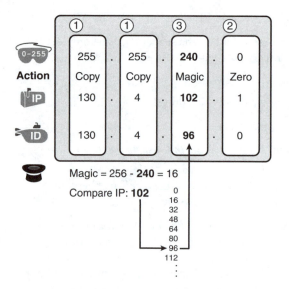

Figure 13-9   *Find the Subnet ID: 130.4.102.1, 255.255.240.0*

Then, find the multiple closest to the IP address value in this octet (102 in this case) without going over 102. So, as shown in the figure, you would make the third octet's value be 96 to complete the subnet ID of 130.4.96.0.

Resident Subnet Example 2

Consider another example: 192.168.5.77, mask 255.255.255.224. In this case, the fourth octet is the interesting octet, with mask value 224. As a result, the magic number is 256 − 224 = 32, and the multiples are 0, 32, 64, 96, and so on. Figure 13-10 shows the results.

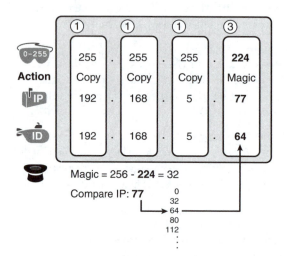

Figure 13-10   *Resident Subnet for 192.168.5.73, 255.255.255.224*

The three uninteresting octets (1, 2, and 3 in this case) require only a little thought. For each of these octets, each with a mask value of 255, just copy the IP address.

For the interesting octet, at Step 3a, the magic number is 256 – 224 = 32. The multiples of the magic number are 0, 32, 64, 96, and so on. Because the IP address value in the fourth octet is 77 in this case, the multiple must be the number closest to 77 without going over, so the subnet ID ends with 64, for a value of 192.168.5.64.

Resident Subnet Practice Problems

Before moving to the next section, take some time to fill in the blanks in Table 13-9. Check your answers against Table 13-14 in the later "Chapter Review" section. Complete the table by listing the subnet ID in each case. The text following the answers table also lists explanations for each problem.

Table 13-9 *Practice Problems: Find Subnet ID, Difficult Masks*

Problem	IP Address	Mask	Subnet ID
1	10.77.55.3	255.248.0.0	
2	172.30.99.4	255.255.192.0	
3	192.168.6.54	255.255.255.252	
4	10.77.3.14	255.255.128.0	
5	172.22.55.77	255.255.254.0	
6	1.99.53.76	255.255.255.248	

Finding the Subnet Broadcast Address: Difficult Masks

To find a subnet's broadcast address, a similar process can be used. For simplicity, this process begins with the subnet ID, rather than the IP address. If you happen to start with an IP address instead, use the processes in this chapter to first find the subnet ID and then use the following process to find the subnet broadcast address for that same subnet. For each octet:

Step 1.   If the mask octet = 255, copy the subnet ID.

Step 2.   If the mask octet = 0, write a 255.

Step 3.   If the mask is neither, identify this octet as the *interesting octet*:

    a.   Calculate the *magic number* as 256 – mask.

    b.   Take the subnet ID's value, add the magic number, and subtract 1 (*ID + magic – 1*).

Key Topic

As with the similar process used to find the subnet ID, look at the examples in this section, which show the process being used on paper. Then follow the practice opportunities outlined in the section "Practice Problems for This Chapter," later in this chapter.

Subnet Broadcast Example 1

The first example continues the first example from the earlier section "Find the Subnet ID Decimal: Difficult Masks," as demonstrated in Figure 13-9. That example started with the IP address/mask of 130.4.102.1, 255.255.240.0 and showed how to find subnet ID 130.4.96.0. Figure 13-11 now begins with that subnet ID and the same mask.

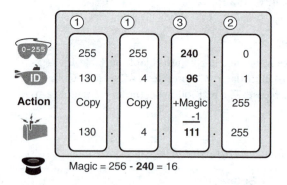

Figure 13-11   *Find the Subnet Broadcast: 130.4.96.0, 255.255.240.0*

First, examine the three uninteresting octets (1, 2, and 4). The process keys on the mask, and the first two octets have a mask value of 255, so simply copy the subnet ID to the place where you intend to write down the subnet broadcast address. The fourth octet has a mask value 0, so write down a 255 for the fourth octet.

The logic related to the interesting octet occurs in the third octet in this example, because of the mask value 240. First, Step 3a asks you to calculate the magic number as 256 – mask. (If you had already calculated the subnet ID using the decimal process in this book, you should already know the magic number.) At Step 3b, you take the subnet ID's value (96), add the magic number (16), and subtract 1, for a total of 111. That makes the subnet broadcast address 130.4.111.255.

Subnet Broadcast Example 2

Again, this example continues an earlier example, from the earlier section "Resident Subnet Example 2," as demonstrated in Figure 13-10. That example started with the IP address/mask of 192.168.5.77, mask 255.255.255.224 and showed how to find subnet ID 192.168.5.64. Figure 13-12 now begins with that subnet ID and the same mask.

First, examine the three uninteresting octets (1, 2, and 3). The process keys on the mask, and the first three octets have a mask value of 255, so simply copy the subnet ID to the place where you intend to write down the subnet broadcast address.

The interesting logic occurs in the interesting octet, the fourth octet in this example, because of the mask value 224. First, Step 3a asks you to calculate the magic number as 256 – mask. (If you had already calculated the subnet ID, it is the same magic number, because the same mask is used.) At Step 3b, you take the subnet ID's value (64), add the magic number (32), and subtract 1, for a total of 95. That makes the subnet broadcast address 192.168.5.95.

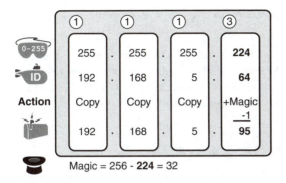

Magic = 256 - **224** = 32

Figure 13-12   *Find the Subnet Broadcast: 192.168.5.64, 255.255.255.224*

Subnet Broadcast Address Practice Problems

Before moving to the next section, take some time to do several practice problems on a scratch piece of paper. Go back to Table 13-9, which lists IP addresses and masks, and practice by finding the subnet broadcast address for all the problems in that table. Then check your answers against Table 13-15 in the "Chapter Review" section, later in this chapter.

Practice Analyzing Existing Subnets

To be a well-prepared network engineer, you should master any and all IP addressing processes and calculations by the time you finish this course. Most technical interviews for a job working with IP networking will include some assessment of how well you understand the concepts and how quickly you can calculate various facts about addresses and subnets.

However, you do not need to completely master everything in this chapter right now. Practice now to make sure that you understand the processes, using your notes, the book, and whatever helps. Then you can move on to the next chapter. However, before the midterm and final exams, practice until you master the topics in this chapter. Table 13-10 summarizes the key concepts and suggestions for this two-phase approach.

Table 13-10   *Practice Goals for This Chapter's Topics*

Time Frame	Before Moving to the Next Chapter	Before Taking the Exam
Focus on...	Learning how	Being correct and fast
Tools Allowed	All	Your brain and a notepad
Goal: Accuracy	90% correct	100% correct

A Choice: To Memorize or to Calculate

As described in this chapter, the decimal processes to find the subnet ID and subnet broadcast address do require some calculation, including the calculation of the magic number (256 – mask). These same processes assume that you start with a DDN mask, so to use the processes listed in this book, you have to take time to convert the mask to DDN format if a question uses a prefix mask.

Over the years, some people have told me that they prefer to memorize a table to find the magic number. These tables could list the magic number for different masks and also list prefix masks as well, so you avoid converting from the prefix mask to DDN. Table 13-11 shows an example of such a table. Feel free to ignore this table, use this one, or make your own.

Table 13-11 *Reference Table: Prefix Lengths with Matching Magic Number and DDN Mask Values*

Prefix, interesting octet 2	/9	/10	/11	/12	/13	/14	/15	/16
Prefix, interesting octet 3	/17	/18	/19	/20	/21	/22	/23	/24
Prefix, interesting octet 4	/25	/26	/27	/28	/29	/30		
Magic number	128	64	32	16	8	4	2	1
DDN mask in the interesting octet	128	192	224	240	248	252	254	255

Practice Problems for This Chapter

Unlike the other subnetting chapters in this book, this chapter spreads the practice problems throughout the chapter, so this section does not list any additional practice. For reference, the practice problems in this chapter are found in the following sections:

■ "Binary Practice Problems"

■ "Resident Subnet Practice Problems"

■ "Subnet Broadcast Address Practice Problems"

Additional Practice

1. Create your own problems. Many subnet calculators list the number of network, subnet, and host bits when you type in an IP address and mask, so make up an IP address and mask on paper and find the subnet ID and range of addresses. Then, to check your work, use any subnet calculator. (Check the author's web pages for this book, as listed in the introduction, for some suggested calculators.)

2. The Subnet Prep apps "Find a Subnet ID" and "Find the Address Range" (subnet-prep.com) each provide review videos and practice problems related to this chapter. The first of these apps focuses on finding the subnet ID, and the second focuses on finding the range of addresses in a subnet.

Chapter Review

Review Key Topics

Review the key topics as part of your study, but know that you will likely come to know all the information in these key topics through practice and repetition (see Table 13-12).

Table 13-12 *Key Topics for Chapter 13*

Key Topic Element	Description	Page Number
Table 13-1	Key facts about the subnet ID	310
Table 13-2	Key facts about the subnet broadcast address	311
List	Steps to use binary math to find the subnet ID	314
List	General steps to use binary and decimal math to find the subnet ID	317
List	Steps to use decimal and binary math to find the Subnet broadcast address	317
List	Steps to use only decimal math to find the subnet ID	321
List	Steps to use only decimal math to find the subnet broadcast address	323

Define Key Terms

Define the following key terms from this chapter, and check your answers in the glossary:

resident subnet, subnet ID, subnet number, subnet address, subnet broadcast address

Practice

If you have not done so already, practice finding the subnet ID, range of addresses, and subnet broadcast address associated with an IP address and mask. Refer to the earlier section "Practice Analyzing Existing Subnets" for suggestions.

Answers to Earlier Practice Problems

This chapter includes practice problems spread around different locations in the chapter. The answers are located in Tables 13-13, 13-14, and 13-15.

Table 13-13   *Answers to Problems in Table 13-8*

	IP Address	Mask	Subnet ID	Broadcast Address
1	10.77.55.3	255.255.255.0	10.77.55.0	10.77.55.255
2	172.30.99.4	255.255.255.0	172.30.99.0	172.30.99.255
3	192.168.6.54	255.255.255.0	192.168.6.0	192.168.6.255
4	10.77.3.14	255.255.0.0	10.77.0.0	10.77.255.255
5	172.22.55.77	255.255.0.0	172.22.0.0	172.22.255.255
6	1.99.53.76	255.0.0.0	1.0.0.0	1.255.255.255

Table 13-14   *Answers to Problems in Table 13-9*

	IP Address	Mask	Subnet ID
1	10.77.55.3	255.248.0.0	10.72.0.0
2	172.30.99.4	255.255.192.0	172.30.64.0
3	192.168.6.54	255.255.255.252	192.168.6.52
4	10.77.3.14	255.255.128.0	10.77.0.0
5	172.22.55.77	255.255.254.0	172.22.54.0
6	1.99.53.76	255.255.255.248	1.99.53.72

Table 13-15   *Answers to Problems in the Section "Subnet Broadcast Address Practice Problems"*

	Subnet ID	Mask	Broadcast Address
1	10.72.0.0	255.248.0.0	10.79.255.255
2	172.30.64.0	255.255.192.0	172.30.127.255
3	192.168.6.52	255.255.255.252	192.168.6.55
4	10.77.0.0	255.255.128.0	10.77.127.255
5	172.22.54.0	255.255.254.0	172.22.55.255
6	1.99.53.72	255.255.255.248	1.99.53.79

The following list explains the answers for Table 13-14:

1. The second octet is the interesting octet, with magic number 256 − 248 = 8. The multiples of 8 include 0, 8, 16, 24 . . . 64, 72, 80. 72 is closest to the IP address value in that same octet (77) without going over, making the subnet ID 10.72.0.0.

2. The third octet is the interesting octet, with magic number 256 − 192 = 64. The multiples of 64 include 0, 64, 128, and 192. 64 is closest to the IP address value in that same octet (99) without going over, making the subnet ID 172.30.64.0.

3. The fourth octet is the interesting octet, with magic number 256 − 252 = 4. The multiples of 4 include 0, 4, 8, 12, 16 . . . 48, 52, 56. 52 is the closest to the IP address value in that same octet (54) without going over, making the subnet ID 192.168.6.52.

4. The third octet is the interesting octet, with magic number 256 − 128 = 128. Only two multiples exist that matter: 0 and 128. 0 is the closest to the IP address value in that same octet (3) without going over, making the subnet ID 10.77.0.0.

5. The third octet is the interesting octet, with magic number 256 − 254 = 2. The multiples of 2 include 0, 2, 4, 6, 8, and so on—essentially all even numbers. 54 is closest to the IP address value in that same octet (55) without going over, making the subnet ID 172.22.54.0.

6. The fourth octet is the interesting octet, with magic number 256 − 248 = 8. The multiples of 8 include 0, 8, 16, 24 . . . 64, 72, 80. 72 is closest to the IP address value in that same octet (76) without going over, making the subnet ID 1.99.53.72.

The following list explains the answers for Table 13-15:

1. The second octet is the interesting octet. Completing the three easy octets means that the broadcast address in the interesting octet will be 10.____.255.255. With a magic number 256 − 248 = 8, the second octet will be 72 (from the subnet ID) plus 8, minus 1, or 79.

2. The third octet is the interesting octet. Completing the three easy octets means that the broadcast address in the interesting octet will be 172.30.____.255. With magic number 256 − 192 = 64, the interesting octet will be 64 (from the subnet ID) plus 64 (the magic number), minus 1, for 127.

3. The fourth octet is the interesting octet. Completing the three easy octets means that the broadcast address in the interesting octet will be 192.168.6.____. With magic number 256 − 252 = 4, the interesting octet will be 52 (the subnet ID value) plus 4 (the magic number), minus 1, or 55.

4. The third octet is the interesting octet. Completing the three easy octets means that the broadcast address will be 10.77.____.255. With magic number 256 − 128 = 128, the interesting octet will be 0 (the subnet ID value) plus 128 (the magic number), minus 1, or 127.

5. The third octet is the interesting octet. Completing the three easy octets means that the broadcast address will be 172.22.____.255. With magic number 256 − 254 = 2, the broadcast address in the interesting octet will be 54 (the subnet ID value) plus 2 (the magic number), minus 1, or 55.

6. The fourth octet is the interesting octet. Completing the three easy octets means that the broadcast address will be 1.99.53.____. With magic number 256 − 248 = 8, the broadcast address in the interesting octet will be 72 (the subnet ID value) plus 8 (the magic number), minus 1, or 79.

Answer Review Questions

Answer the following review questions:

1. An address can have three parts: network, subnet, and host. If you examined all the addresses in one subnet, in binary, which of the following answers correctly states which of the three parts of the addresses will be equal among all addresses? Pick the best answer.

    a. Network part only

    b. Subnet part only

    c. Host part only

    d. Network and subnet parts

    e. Subnet and host parts

2. Which of the following statements are true regarding the binary subnet ID, subnet broadcast address, and host IP address values in any single subnet? (Choose two.)

    a. The host part of the broadcast address is all binary 0s.

    b. The host part of the subnet ID is all binary 0s.

    c. The host part of a usable IP address can have all binary 1s.

    d. The host part of any usable IP address must not be all binary 0s.

3. Which of the following is the resident subnet ID for IP address 10.7.99.133/24?

    a. 10.0.0.0

    b. 10.7.0.0

    c. 10.7.99.0

    d. 10.7.99.128

4. Which of the following is the resident subnet for IP address 192.168.44.97/30?

    a. 192.168.44.0

    b. 192.168.44.64

    c. 192.168.44.96

    d. 192.168.44.128

5. Which of the following is the subnet broadcast address for the subnet in which IP address 172.31.77.201/27 resides?

   a. 172.31.201.255

   b. 172.31.255.255

   c. 172.31.77.223

   d. 172.31.77.207

6. A fellow engineer tells you to configure the DHCP server to lease the last 100 usable IP addresses in subnet 10.1.4.0/23. Which of the following IP addresses could be leased as a result of your new configuration?

   a. 10.1.4.156

   b. 10.1.4.254

   c. 10.1.5.200

   d. 10.1.7.200

   e. 10.1.255.200

7. A fellow engineer tells you to configure the DHCP server to lease the first 20 usable IP addresses in subnet 192.168.9.96/27. Which of the following IP addresses could be leased as a result of your new configuration?

   a. 192.168.9.126

   b. 192.168.9.110

   c. 192.168.9.1

   d. 192.168.9.119

This chapter covers the following subjects:

■ **Routing Protocol Overview:** This section explains the terminology and theory related to routing protocols in general and Routing Information Protocol (RIP) in particular.

■ **Configuring and Verifying RIP-2:** This section explains how to configure RIP version 2 (RIP-2) and how to confirm that RIP-2 is working correctly.

CHAPTER 14

Routing Protocol Concepts and RIP-2 Configuration

The United States Postal Service routes a huge number of letters and packages each day. To do so, the postal sorting machines run fast, sorting lots of letters. Then the letters are placed in the correct container and onto the correct truck or plane to reach the final destination. However, if no one programs the letter-sorting machines to know where letters to each zip code should be sent, the sorter cannot do its job.

Similarly, Cisco routers can route many IP packets. However, if the router does not know any routes—routes that tell the router where to send the packets—the router cannot do its job, and because the routes can change when links fail and recover, the routers need to figure out the best routes right now, and then react to any changes.

This chapter introduces the basic concepts of how routers dynamically fill their routing tables with routes using routing protocols. Routers use these protocols to send messages to neighboring routers so that, collectively, all routers can learn all the possible routes to reach each subnet. Then, each router can choose the best current route to use when forwarding packets to each subnet.

This chapter begins by introducing the terminology, core concepts, and options for dynamic IP routing protocols. The second major section of this chapter examines the concepts and configuration related to one of these dynamic IP routing protocols—namely, the Routing Information Protocol, version 2 (RIP-2).

Routing Protocol Overview

IP routing protocols have one primary goal: to fill the IP routing table with the current best routes it can find. The goal is simple, but the process and options can be complicated.

Routing protocols help routers learn routes by having each router advertise the routes it knows. Each router begins by knowing only connected routes. Then, each router sends messages, defined by the routing protocol, that list the routes. When a router hears a routing update message from another router, the router hearing the update learns about the subnets and adds routes to its routing table. If all the routers participate, all the routers can learn about all subnets in an internetwork.

When learning routes, routing protocols must also prevent loops from occurring. A loop occurs when a packet keeps coming back to the same router due to errors in the routes in the collective routers' routing tables. These loops can occur with routing protocols, unless the routing protocol makes an effort to avoid the loops.

This section starts by explaining how RIP-2 works in a little more detail. Following that, the various IP routing protocols are compared.

RIP-2 Basic Concepts

Routers using RIP-2 advertise a small amount of simple information about each subnet to their neighbors. Their neighbors in turn advertise the information to their neighbors, and so on, until all routers have learned the information. In fact, it works a lot like how rumors spread in a neighborhood, school, or company. You might be out in the yard, stop to talk to your next-door neighbor, and tell your neighbor the latest gossip. Then, that neighbor sees his other next-door neighbor, and tells them the same bit of gossip—and so on, until everyone in the neighborhood knows the latest gossip. Distance vector protocols work the same way, but hopefully, unlike rumors in a real neighborhood, the rumor has not changed by the time everyone has heard about it.

For example, consider what occurs in Figure 14-1. The figure shows RIP-2 advertising a subnet number, mask (shown in prefix notation), and metric to its neighbors.

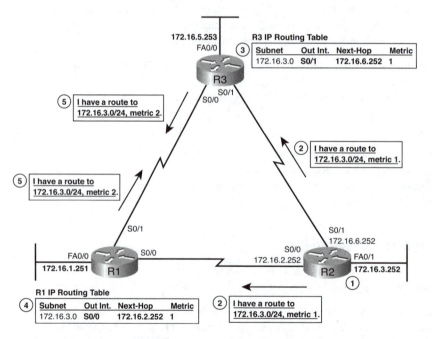

Figure 14-1   *Example of How RIP-2 Advertises Routes*

For the sake of keeping the figure less cluttered, Figure 14-1 only shows how the routers advertise and learn routes for subnet 172.16.3.0/24, even though the routers do advertise about other routes as well. Following the steps in the figure:

1. Router R2 learns a connected route for subnet 172.16.3.0/24.

2. R2 sends a *routing update* to its neighbors, listing a subnet (172.16.3.0), mask (/24), and a distance, or metric (1 in this case).

3. R3 hears the routing update, and adds a route to its routing table for subnet 172.16.3.0/24, referring to R2 as the next-hop router.

4. Around the same time, R1 also hears the routing update sent directly to R1 by R2. R1 then adds a route to its routing table for subnet 172.16.3.0/24, referring to R2 as the next-hop router.

5. R1 and R3 then send a routing update to each other, for subnet 172.16.3.0/24, metric 2.

By the end of this process, both R1 and R3 have heard of two possible routes to reach subnet 172.16.3.0/24—one with metric 1, and one with metric 2. Each router uses its respective lower-metric (metric 1) routes to reach 172.16.3.0.

Interestingly, distance vector protocols such as RIP-2 repeat this process continually on a periodic basis. For example, RIP routers send periodic routing updates about every 30 seconds by default. As long as the routers continue to hear the same routes, with the same metrics, the routers' routing tables do not need to change. However, when something changes, the next routing update will change or simply not occur due to some failure, so the routers will react and converge to use the then-best working routes.

Now that you have seen the basics of one routing protocol, the next section explains a wide variety of features of different routing protocols for the sake of comparison.

Comparing and Contrasting IP Routing Protocols

IP's long history and continued popularity have driven the need for several different competing routing protocols over time. So, it is helpful to make comparisons between the different IP routing protocols to see their relative strengths and weaknesses. This section describes several technical points on which the routing protocols can be compared. The second part of this chapter examines one option, RIP-2, with other chapters in this book explaining OSPF and EIGRP in more detail.

One of the first points of comparison is whether the protocol is defined in RFCs, making it a public standard, or whether it is Cisco proprietary. Another very important consideration is whether the routing protocol supports variable-length subnet masking (VLSM). This section introduces several different terms and concepts used to compare the various IP routing protocols, with Table 14-3 at the end of this section summarizing the comparison points for many of the IP routing protocols.

Interior and Exterior Routing Protocols

IP routing protocols fall into one of two major categories:

■ **Interior Gateway Protocol (IGP):** A routing protocol that was designed and intended for use inside a single autonomous system

Key Topic

■ **Exterior Gateway Protocol (EGP):** A routing protocol that was designed and intended for use between different autonomous systems

Note: The terms IGP and EGP include the word *gateway* because routers used to be called gateways.

These definitions use another new term: *autonomous system.* An autonomous system is an internetwork under the administrative control of a single organization. For instance, an internetwork created and paid for by a single company is probably a single autonomous system, and an internetwork created by a single school system is probably a single autonomous system. Other examples include large divisions of a state or national government, where different government agencies might be able to build their own separate internetworks.

Some routing protocols work best inside a single autonomous system, by design, so these routing protocols are called IGPs. Conversely, only one routing protocol, *Border Gateway Protocol (BGP)*, is used today to exchange routes between routers in different autonomous systems, so it is called an EGP.

Each autonomous system can be assigned a number, called (unsurprisingly) an *autonomous system number (ASN)*. Like public IP addresses, the Internet Corporation for Assigned Network Numbers (ICANN) controls the worldwide rights to assign ASNs, delegating that authority to other organizations around the planet, typically to the same organizations that assign public IP addresses. By assigning each autonomous organization an ASN, BGP can ensure that packets do not loop around the global Internet by making sure that packets do not pass through the same autonomous system twice.

Figure 14-2 shows a small view into the worldwide Internet. Two companies and three ISPs use IGPs (OSPF and EIGRP) inside their own networks, with BGP being used between the ASNs.

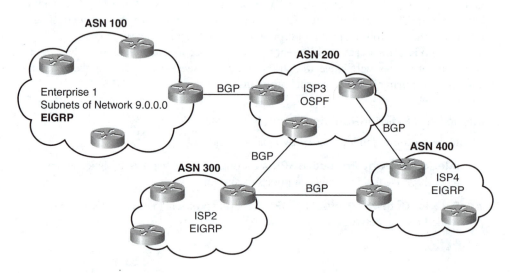

Figure 14-2   *Comparing Locations for Using IGPs and EGPs*

Routing Protocol Types/Algorithms

Each IGP can be classified as using a particular class, or type, of underlying logic. Table 14-1 lists the three options, noting which IGPs use which class of algorithm.

Table 14-1   *Routing Protocol Classes/Algorithms and Protocols That Use Them*

Class/Algorithm	IGPs
Distance vector	RIP-1, RIP-2, IGRP
Link-state	OSPF, Integrated IS-IS
Balanced hybrid (also called advanced distance vector)	EIGRP

Key Topic

Metrics

Routing protocols must have some way to decide which route is best when a router learns of more than one route to reach a subnet. To that end, each routing protocol defines a *metric* that gives an objective numeric value to the "goodness" of each route. The lower the metric, the better the route. For example, earlier, in Figure 14-1, R1 learned a metric 1 route for subnet 172.16.3.0/24 from R2, and a metric 2 route for that same subnet from R3, so R1 chose the lower-metric (1) route through R2.

Some metrics work better than others. To see why, consider Figure 14-3. The figure shows two analyses of the same basic internetwork, focusing on router B's choice of a route to reach subnet 10.1.1.0, which is on the LAN on the left side of router A. In this case, the link between A and B is only a 64-kbps link, whereas the other two links are T1s, running at 1.544 Mbps each. The top part of the figure shows router B's choice of route when using RIP (Version 1 or Version 2), whereas the bottom part of the figure shows router B's choice when the internetwork uses EIGRP.

RIP uses a metric called hop count, which measures the number of routers (hops) between a router and a subnet. With RIP, router B would learn two routes to reach subnet 10.1.1.0: a one-hop route through router A, and a two-hop route first through router C and then to router A. So, router B, using RIP, would add a route for subnet 10.1.1.0 pointing to router A as the next-hop IP address (represented as the dashed line in Figure 14-3).

EIGRP, on the other hand, uses a metric that (by default) considers both the interface bandwidth and interface delay settings as input into a mathematical formula to calculate the metric. If routers A, B, and C were configured with correct **bandwidth** interface subcommands, as listed in Figure 14-3, EIGRP would add a route for subnet 10.1.1.0 to its routing table, but with router C as the next-hop router, again shown with a dashed line.

Note: For a review of the **bandwidth** command, refer to the section "Bandwidth and Clock Rate on Serial Interfaces" in Chapter 11, "Cisco Router Configuration."

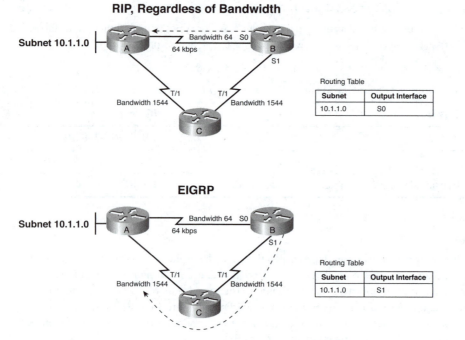

Figure 14-3 *Comparing the Effect of the RIP and EIGRP Metrics*

Autosummarization and Manual Summarization

Routers generally perform routing (forwarding) more quickly with smaller routing tables, and less quickly with larger routing tables. Route summarization helps shorten the routing table while retaining all the needed routes in the network.

Two general types of route summarization can be done, with varying support for these two types depending on the routing protocol. The two types, both of which are introduced in this section, are called *autosummarization* and *manual summarization*. Manual summarization gives the network engineer a great deal of control and flexibility, allowing the engineer to choose what summary routes to advertise, instead of just being able to summarize with a classful network. As a result, support for manual summarization is the more useful feature as compared to autosummarization.

Chapter 19, "VLSM and Route Summarization," explains both autosummarization and manual summarization in great detail.

Classless and Classful Routing Protocols

Some routing protocols must consider the Class A, B, or C network number that a subnet resides in when performing some of its tasks. Other routing protocols can ignore Class A, B, and C rules altogether. Routing protocols that must consider class rules are called *classful routing protocols*; those that do not need to consider class rules are called *classless routing protocols*.

Classless routing protocols and classful routing protocols are identified by the same three criteria, as summarized in Table 14-2.

Table 14-2 *Comparing Classless and Classful Routing Protocols*

Key Topic

Feature	Classless	Classful
Supports VLSM	Yes	No
Sends subnet mask in routing updates	Yes	No
Supports manual route summarization	Yes	No

Convergence

The term *convergence* refers to the overall process that occurs with routing protocols when something changes in a network topology. When a link comes up or fails, or when a router fails or is first turned on, the possible routes in the internetwork change. The processes used by routing protocols to recognize the changes, to figure out the now-best routes to each subnet, and to change all the routers' routing tables, is called convergence.

Some routing protocols converge more quickly than others. As you might imagine, the capability to converge quickly is important, because in some cases, until convergence completes, users might not be able to send their packets to particular subnets. (Table 14-3 in the next section summarizes the relative convergence speed of various IP routing protocols, along with other information.)

Miscellaneous Comparison Points

Two other minor comparison points between the various IGPs are interesting as well. First, the original routing protocol standards defined that routing updates should be sent to the IP all-local-hosts broadcast address of 255.255.255.255. After those original routing protocols were defined, IP multicast emerged, which allowed newer routing protocols to send routing updates only to other interested routers by using various IP multicast IP addresses.

The earlier IGPs did not include any authentication features. As time went on, it became obvious that attackers could form a denial-of-service (DoS) attack by causing problems with routing protocols. For example, an attacker could connect a router to a network and advertise lots of lower-metric routes for many subnets, causing the packets to be routed to the wrong place—and possibly copied by the attacker. The later-defined IGPs typically support some type of authentication, hoping to mitigate the exposure to these types of DoS attacks.

Summary of Interior Routing Protocols

For convenient comparison and study, Table 14-3 summarizes the most important features of interior routing protocols.

**Key
Topic**

Table 14-3 *Interior IP Routing Protocols Compared*

Feature	RIP-1	RIP-2	EIGRP	OSPF	IS-IS
Classless	No	Yes	Yes	Yes	Yes
Supports VLSM	No	Yes	Yes	Yes	Yes
Sends mask in update	No	Yes	Yes	Yes	Yes
Distance vector	Yes	Yes	No[1]	No	No
Link-state	No	No	No[1]	Yes	Yes
Supports autosummarization	Yes	Yes	Yes	No	No
Supports manual summarization	No	Yes	Yes	Yes	Yes
Proprietary	No	No	Yes	No	No
Routing updates sent to a multicast IP address	No	Yes	Yes	Yes	N/A
Supports authentication	No	Yes	Yes	Yes	Yes
Convergence	Slow	Slow	Very fast	Fast	Fast

[1]EIGRP is often described as a balanced hybrid routing protocol, instead of link-state or distance vector. Some documents refer to EIGRP as an advanced distance vector protocol.

Note: For reference, IGRP has the same characteristics as RIP-1 in Table 14-3, with the exception that IGRP is proprietary and RIP-1 is not.

Configuring and Verifying RIP-2

RIP-2 configuration is actually somewhat simple as compared to the concepts related to routing protocols. The configuration process uses three required commands, with only one command, the **network** command, requiring any real thought. You should also know the more-popular **show** commands for helping you analyze and troubleshoot routing protocols.

RIP-2 Configuration

The RIP-2 configuration process takes only the following three required steps, with the possibility that the third step might need to be repeated:

**Key
Topic**

Step 1.   Use the **router rip** configuration command to move into RIP configuration mode.

Step 2.   Use the **version 2** RIP subcommand to tell the router to use RIP Version 2 exclusively.

Step 3.   Use one or more **network** *net-number* RIP subcommands to enable RIP on the correct interfaces.

Step 4.   (Optional) As needed, disable RIP on an interface using the **passive-interface** *type number* RIP subcommand.

Of the required first three steps, only the third step—the RIP **network** command—requires much thought. Each RIP **network** command enables RIP on a set of interfaces. The RIP **network** command only uses a classful network number as its one parameter. For any of the router's interface IP addresses in that entire classful network, the router does the following three things:

■   The router multicasts routing updates to a reserved IP multicast IP address, 224.0.0.9.

■   The router listens for incoming updates on that same interface.

■   The router advertises about the subnet connected to the interface.

Key Topic

Sample RIP Configuration

Keeping these facts in mind, now consider how to configure RIP on a single router. Examine Figure 14-4 for a moment and try to apply the first three configuration steps to this router and anticipate the configuration required on the router to enable RIP on all interfaces.

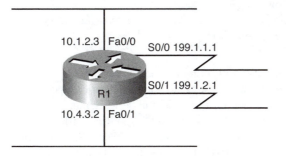

Figure 14-4   *RIP-2 Configuration: Sample Router with Four Interfaces*

The first two configuration commands are easy, **router rip**, followed by **version 2**, with no parameters to choose. Then you need to pick which **network** commands need to be configured at Step 3. To match interface S0/0, you have to figure out that address 199.1.1.1 is in Class C IP network 199.1.1.0, meaning you need a **network 199.1.1.0** RIP subcommand. Similarly, to match interface S0/1, you need a **network 199.1.2.0** command, because IP address 199.1.2.1 is in Class C network 199.1.2.0. Finally, both of the LAN interfaces have an IP address in Class A network 10.0.0.0, so a single **network 10.0.0.0** command matches both interfaces. Example 14-1 shows the entire configuration process, with all five configuration commands.

Example 14-1   *Sample Router Configuration with RIP Enabled*

```
R1# configure terminal
R1(config)# router rip
R1(config-router)# version 2
R1(config-router)# network 199.1.1.0
R1(config-router)# network 199.1.2.0
R1(config-router)# network 10.0.0.0
```

With this configuration, R1 starts using RIP—sending RIP updates, listening for incoming RIP updates, and advertising about the connected subnet—on each of its four interfaces. However, imagine that for some reason, you wanted to enable RIP on R1's Fa0/0 interface, but did not want to enable RIP on Fa0/1's interface. Both interfaces are in network 10.0.0.0, so both are matched by the **network 10.0.0.0** command.

RIP configuration does not provide a way to enable RIP on only some of the interfaces in a single Class A, B, or C network. So, if you needed to enable RIP only on R1's Fa0/0 interface, and not on the Fa0/1 interface, you would actually need to use the **network 10.0.0.0** command to enable RIP on both interfaces, and then disable the sending of RIP updates on Fa0/1 using the **passive-interface** *type number* RIP subcommand. For example, to enable RIP on all interfaces of router R1 in Figure 14-4, except for Fa0/1, you could use the same configuration in Example 14-1, but then also add the **passive-interface fa0/1** subcommand while in RIP configuration mode. This command tells R1 to stop sending RIP updates out its Fa0/1 interface, disabling one of the main functions of RIP.

> **Note:**   The **passive-interface** command only stops the sending of RIP updates on the interface. Other features outside the scope of this book could be used to disable the processing of received updates and the advertisement of the connected subnet.

One final note on the **network** command: IOS will actually accept a parameter besides a classful network number on the command, and IOS does not supply an error message, either. However, IOS, knowing that the parameter must be a classful network number, changes the command. For example, if you typed **network 10.1.2.3** in RIP configuration mode, IOS would accept the command, with no error messages. However, when you look at the configuration, you would see a **network 10.0.0.0** command, and the **network 10.1.2.3** command that you had typed would not be there. The **network 10.0.0.0** command would indeed match all interfaces in network 10.0.0.0.

RIP-2 Verification

IOS includes three primary **show** commands that are helpful to confirm how well RIP-2 is working. Table 14-4 lists the commands and their main purpose.

Table 14-4   *RIP Operational Commands*

Command	Purpose
show ip interface brief	Lists one line per router interface, including the IP address and interface status; an interface must have an IP address, and be in an "up and up" status, before RIP begins to work on the interface.
show ip route [rip]	Lists the routing table, including RIP-learned routes, and optionally just RIP-learned routes.
show ip protocols	Lists information about the RIP configuration, plus the IP addresses of neighboring RIP routers from which the local router has learned routes.

To better understand these commands, this section uses the internetwork shown in Figure 14-5.

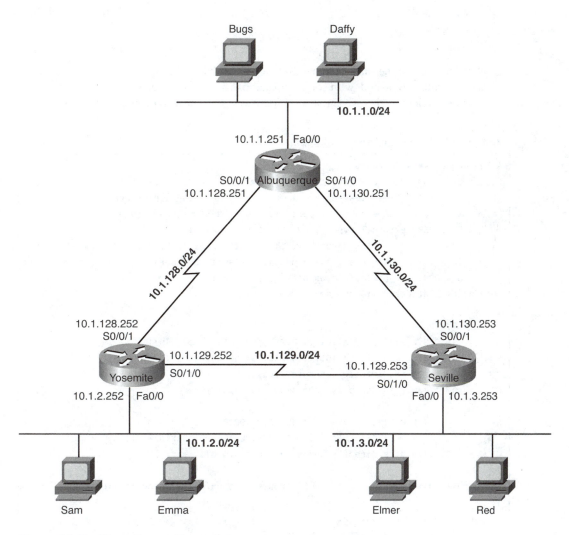

Figure 14-5   *Three-Router Network*

Consider the RIP-2 configuration required on each of the three routers. All three interfaces on all three routers are in classful network 10.0.0.0. So each router needs only one

network command, **network 10.0.0.0**, to match all three of its interfaces. The configuration needs to be the same on all three routers, as follows:

```
router rip
 version 2
 network 10.0.0.0
```

Now, to focus on the **show** commands, Example 14-2 lists a couple of variations of the **show ip route** command, with some explanations in the example, and some following the example. Following that, Example 14-3 focuses on the **show ip protocols** command.

Example 14-2   show ip route *Command*

```
Albuquerque# show ip route
Codes: C - connected, S - static, R - RIP, M - mobile, B - BGP
       D - EIGRP, EX - EIGRP external, O - OSPF, IA - OSPF inter area
       N1 - OSPF NSSA external type 1, N2 - OSPF NSSA external type 2
       E1 - OSPF external type 1, E2 - OSPF external type 2
       i - IS-IS, su - IS-IS summary, L1 - IS-IS level-1, L2 - IS-IS level-2
       ia - IS-IS inter area, * - candidate default, U - per-user static route
       o - ODR, P - periodic downloaded static route
Gateway of last resort is not set


     10.0.0.0/24 is subnetted, 6 subnets
R       10.1.3.0 [120/1] via 10.1.130.253, 00:00:16, Serial0/1/0
R       10.1.2.0 [120/1] via 10.1.128.252, 00:00:09, Serial0/0/1
C       10.1.1.0 is directly connected, FastEthernet0/0
C       10.1.130.0 is directly connected, Serial0/1/0

R       10.1.129.0 [120/1] via 10.1.130.253, 00:00:16, Serial0/1/0
                   [120/1] via 10.1.128.252, 00:00:09, Serial0/0/1
C       10.1.128.0 is directly connected, Serial0/0/1
!
! The next command lists just the RIP routes, so no code legend is listed
!
Albuquerque# show ip route rip
     10.0.0.0/24 is subnetted, 6 subnets
R       10.1.3.0 [120/1] via 10.1.130.253, 00:00:20, Serial0/1/0
R       10.1.2.0 [120/1] via 10.1.128.252, 00:00:13, Serial0/0/1
R       10.1.129.0 [120/1] via 10.1.130.253, 00:00:20, Serial0/1/0
                   [120/1] via 10.1.128.252, 00:00:13, Serial0/0/1
!
! The next command lists the route matched by this router for packets going to the
! listed IP address 10.1.2.1.
!
Albuquerque# show ip route 10.1.2.1
Routing entry for 10.1.2.0/24
```

```
Known via "rip", distance 120, metric 1
  Redistributing via rip
  Last update from 10.1.128.252 on Serial0/0/1, 00:00:18 ago
  Routing Descriptor Blocks:
  * 10.1.128.252, from 10.1.128.252, 00:00:18 ago, via Serial0/0/1
      Route metric is 1, traffic share count is 1
!
! The same command again, but for an address that does not have a matching route in
! the routing table.
Albuquerque# show ip route 10.1.7.1
% Subnet not in table
Albuquerque#
```

Interpreting the Output of the show ip route Command

Example 14-2 shows the **show ip route** command, which lists all IP routes, the **show ip route rip** command, which lists only RIP-learned routes, and the **show ip route** *address* command, which lists details about the route matched for packets sent to the listed IP address. Focusing on the **show ip route** command, note that the legend lists "R," which means that a route has been learned by RIP, and that three of the routes list an R beside them. Next, examine the details in the route for subnet 10.1.3.0/24, highlighted in the example. The important details are as follows:

■   The subnet number is listed, with the mask in the heading line above.

■   The next-hop router's IP address, 10.1.130.253, which is Seville's S0/0/1 IP address.

■   Albuquerque's S0/1/0 interface is the outgoing interface.

■   The length of time since Albuquerque last heard about this route in a periodic RIP update, 20 seconds ago in this case.

■   The RIP metric for this route (1 in this case), listed as the second number in the square brackets. For example, between Albuquerque and subnet 10.1.3.0/24, one other router (Seville) exists.

■   The administrative distance of the route (120 in this case; the first number in brackets).

Take the time now to review the other two RIP routes, noting the values for these various items in those routes. As you can see, the **show ip route rip** command output lists the routes in the exact same format, the difference being that only RIP-learned routes are shown, and the legend is not displayed at the top of the command output. The **show ip route** *address* command lists more detailed output about the route that matches the destination IP address listed in the command, with the command output supplying more detailed information about the route.

Administrative Distance

When an internetwork has redundant links, and uses a single routing protocol, each router can learn multiple routes to reach a particular subnet. As stated earlier in this chapter, the routing protocol then uses a metric to choose the best route, and the router adds that route to its routing table.

In some cases, internetworks use multiple IP routing protocols. In such cases, a router might learn of multiple routes to a particular subnet using different routing protocols. In these cases, the metric does not help the router choose which route is best, because each routing protocol uses a metric unique to that routing protocol. For example, RIP uses the hop count as the metric, but EIGRP uses a math formula with bandwidth and delay as inputs. A route with RIP metric 1 might need to be compared to an EIGRP route, to the same subnet, but with metric 4,132,768. (Yes, EIGRP metrics tend to be large numbers.) Because the numbers have different meanings, there is no real value in comparing the metrics.

The router still needs to choose the best route, so IOS solves this problem by assigning a numeric value to each routing protocol. IOS then chooses the route whose routing protocol has the lower number. This number is called the *administrative distance (AD)*. For example, EIGRP defaults to use an AD of 90, and RIP defaults to use the value of 120, as seen in the routes in Example 14-2. So, an EIGRP route to a subnet would be chosen instead of a competing RIP route. Table 14-5 lists the AD values for the most common sources of routing information.

Table 14-5   *IOS Defaults for Administrative Distance*

Route Source	Administrative Distance
Connected routes	0
Static routes	1
EIGRP	90
IGRP	100
OSPF	110
IS-IS	115
RIP (V1 and V2)	120
Unknown or unbelievable	255

While this might be a brief tangent away from RIP and routing protocols, now that this chapter has explained administrative distance, the concept behind a particular type of static route, called a *backup static route*, can be explained. Static routes have a default AD that is better than all routing protocols, so if a router has a static route defined for a subnet, and the routing protocol learns a route to the same subnet, the static route will be added to the routing table. However, in some cases, the static route is intended to be used only if the routing protocol fails to learn a route. In these cases, an individual static route can be configured with an AD higher than the routing protocol, making the routing protocol more believable.

For example, the **ip route 10.1.1.0 255.255.255.0 10.2.2.2 150** command sets this static route's AD to 150, which is higher than all the default AD settings in Table 14-5. If RIP-2 learned a route to 10.1.1.0/24 on this same router, the router would place the RIP-learned route into the routing table, assuming a default AD of 120, which is better than the static route's AD in this case.

The show ip protocols Command

The final command for examining RIP operations is the **show ip protocols** command. This command identifies some of the details of RIP operation. Example 14-3 lists the output of this command, again on Albuquerque. Due to the variety of information in the command output, the example includes many comments inside the example.

Example 14-3   show ip protocols *Command*

```
Albuquerque# show ip protocols
Routing Protocol is "rip"
  Outgoing update filter list for all interfaces is not set
  Incoming update filter list for all interfaces is not set
!
! The next line identifies the time interval for periodic routing updates, and when
! this
! router will send its next update.
  Sending updates every 30 seconds, next due in 22 seconds
  Invalid after 180 seconds, hold down 180, flushed after 240
  Redistributing: rip
!
! The next few lines result from the version 2 command being configured
  Default version control: send version 2, receive version 2
    Interface          Send  Recv  Triggered RIP  Key-chain
    FastEthernet0/0     2     2
    Serial0/0/1         2     2
    Serial0/1/0         2     2
  Automatic network summarization is in effect
  Maximum path: 4
!
! The next two lines reflect the fact that this router has a single network command,
! namely network 10.0.0.0. If other network commands were configured, these networks
! would also be listed.
  Routing for Networks:
    10.0.0.0
!
! The next section lists the IP addresses of neighboring routers from which
! Albuquerque
! has received routing updates, and the time since this router last heard from the
! neighbors. Note 10.1.130.253 is Seville, and 10.1.128.252 is Yosemite.
  Routing Information Sources:
    Gateway         Distance      Last Update
```

Key Topic

```
      10.1.130.253          120         00:00:25
      10.1.128.252          120         00:00:20
    Distance: (default is 120)
```

Of particular importance for real-life troubleshooting and for the exam, focus on both the version information and the routing information sources. If you forget to configure the **version 2** command on one router, that router will send only RIP-1 updates by default, and the column labeled "Send" would list a 1 instead of a 2. The other routers, only listening for Version 2 updates, could not learn routes from this router.

Also, a quick way to find out if the local router is hearing RIP updates from the correct routers is to look at the list of routing information sources listed at the end of the **show ip protocols** command. For example, given the internetwork in Figure 14-5, you should expect Albuquerque to receive updates from two other routers (Yosemite and Seville). The end of Example 14-3 shows exactly that, with Albuquerque having heard from both routers in the last 30 seconds. If only one router was listed in this command's output, you could figure out which one Albuquerque was hearing from, and then investigate the problem with the missing router.

Examining RIP Messages with debug

The best way to understand whether RIP is doing its job is to use the **debug ip rip** command. This command enables a debug option that tells the router to generate log messages each time the router sends and receives a RIP update. These messages include information about every subnet listed in those advertisements as well, and the meaning of the messages is relatively straightforward.

Example 14-4 shows the output generated by the **debug ip rip** command on the Albuquerque router, based on Figure 14-5. Note that to see these messages, the user needs to be connected to the console of the router, or use the **terminal monitor** privileged mode EXEC command if using Telnet or SSH to connect to the router. The notes inside the example describe some of the meaning of the messages, in five different groups. The first three groups of messages describe Albuquerque's updates sent on each of its three RIP-enabled interfaces; the fourth group includes messages generated when Albuquerque receives an update from Seville; and the last group describes the update received from Yosemite.

Example 14-4   *Example RIP Debug Output*

```
Albuquerque# debug ip rip
RIP protocol debugging is on
Albuquerque#

! Update sent by Albuquerque out Fa0/0:
! The next two messages tell you that the local router is sending a version 2 update
! on Fa0/0, to the 224.0.0.9 multicast IP address. Following that, 5 lines list the
! 5 subnets listed in the advertisement.
```

```
*Jun  9 14:35:08.855: RIP: sending v2 update to 224.0.0.9 via FastEthernet0/0
  (10.1.1.251)
*Jun  9 14:35:08.855: RIP: build update entries
*Jun  9 14:35:08.855:    10.1.2.0/24 via 0.0.0.0, metric 2, tag 0
*Jun  9 14:35:08.855:    10.1.3.0/24 via 0.0.0.0, metric 2, tag 0
*Jun  9 14:35:08.855:    10.1.128.0/24 via 0.0.0.0, metric 1, tag 0
*Jun  9 14:35:08.855:    10.1.129.0/24 via 0.0.0.0, metric 2, tag 0
*Jun  9 14:35:08.855:    10.1.130.0/24 via 0.0.0.0, metric 1, tag 0

! The next 5 debug messages state that this local router is sending an update on its
! S0/1/0 interface, listing 3 subnets/masks
*Jun  9 14:35:10.351: RIP: sending v2 update to 224.0.0.9 via Serial0/1/0
  (10.1.130.251)
*Jun  9 14:35:10.351: RIP: build update entries
*Jun  9 14:35:10.351:    10.1.1.0/24 via 0.0.0.0, metric 1, tag 0
*Jun  9 14:35:10.351:    10.1.2.0/24 via 0.0.0.0, metric 2, tag 0
*Jun  9 14:35:10.351:    10.1.128.0/24 via 0.0.0.0, metric 1, tag 0

! The next 5 debug messages state that this local router is sending an update on its
! S0/0/1 interface, listing 3 subnets/masks
*Jun  9 14:35:12.443: RIP: sending v2 update to 224.0.0.9 via Serial0/0/1
  (10.1.128.251)
*Jun  9 14:35:12.443: RIP: build update entries
*Jun  9 14:35:12.443:    10.1.1.0/24 via 0.0.0.0, metric 1, tag 0
*Jun  9 14:35:12.443:    10.1.3.0/24 via 0.0.0.0, metric 2, tag 0
*Jun  9 14:35:12.443:    10.1.130.0/24 via 0.0.0.0, metric 1, tag 0

! The next 4 messages are about a RIP version 2 (v2) update received by Albuquerque
! from Seville (S0/1/0), listing three subnets. Note the mask is listed as /24.
*Jun  9 14:35:13.819: RIP: received v2 update from 10.1.130.253 on Serial0/1/0
*Jun  9 14:35:13.819:       10.1.2.0/24 via 0.0.0.0 in 2 hops
*Jun  9 14:35:13.819:       10.1.3.0/24 via 0.0.0.0 in 1 hops
*Jun  9 14:35:13.819:       10.1.129.0/24 via 0.0.0.0 in 1 hops

! The next 4 messages are about a RIP version 2 (v2) update received by Albuquerque
! from Yosemite (S0/0/1), listing three subnets. Note the mask is listed as /24.
*Jun  9 14:35:16.911: RIP: received v2 update from 10.1.128.252 on Serial0/0/1
*Jun  9 14:35:16.915:       10.1.2.0/24 via 0.0.0.0 in 1 hops
*Jun  9 14:35:16.915:       10.1.3.0/24 via 0.0.0.0 in 2 hops
*Jun  9 14:35:16.915:       10.1.129.0/24 via 0.0.0.0 in 1 hops

Albuquerque# undebug all
All possible debugging has been turned off
Albuquerque# show process
```

```
CPU utilization for five seconds: 0%/0%; one minute: 0%; five minutes: 0%
  PID QTy       PC Runtime (ms)     Invoked    uSecs    Stacks TTY Process
    1 Cwe 601B2AE8            0           1        0 5608/6000    0 Chunk Manager
```

First, if you take a broader look at the five sets of messages, it helps reinforce the expected updates that Albuquerque should both send and receive. The messages state that Albuquerque is sending updates on Fa0/0, S0/0/1, and S0/1/0, on which RIP should be enabled. Additionally, other messages state that the router received updates on interface S0/1/0, which is the link connected to Seville, and S0/0/1, which is the link connected to Yosemite.

Most of the details in the messages can be easily guessed. Some messages mention "v2," for RIP Version 2, and the fact that the messages are being sent to multicast IP address 224.0.0.9. (RIP-1 sends updates to the 255.255.255.255 broadcast address.) The majority of the messages in the example describe the routing information listed in each update, specifically the subnet and prefix length (mask), and the metric.

A close examination of the number of subnets in each routing update shows that the routers do not advertise all routes in the updates. In Figure 14-5, six subnets exist. However, the updates in the example have either three or five subnets listed. The reason has to do with the theory behind RIP, specifically a feature called split horizon. This loop-avoidance feature limits which subnets are advertised in each update to help avoid some forwarding loops.

Finally, a few comments about the **debug** command itself can be helpful. First, before using the **debug** command, it is helpful to look at the router's CPU utilization with the **show process** command, as shown at the end of Example 14-4. This command lists the router's CPU utilization as a rolling average over three short time periods. On routers with a higher CPU utilization, generally above 30 to 40 percent, be very cautious when enabling debug options, as this can drive the CPU to the point of impacting packet forwarding. Also, you might have noticed the time stamps on the debug messages; to make the router generate time stamps, you need to configure the **service timestamps** global configuration command.

Chapter Review

Review Key Topics

Review the most important topics in the chapter, noted with the Key Topic icon in the outer margin of the page. Table 14-6 lists a reference of these key topics and the page numbers on which each is found.

Table 14-6   *Key Topics for Chapter 14*

Key Topic Element	Description	Page Number
Definitions	IGP and EGP	335
Table 14-1	List of IGP algorithms and the IGPs that use them	337
Table 14-2	Comparison points for classless and classful routing protocols	339
Table 14-3	Summary of comparison points for IGPs	340
List	RIP-2 configuration checklist	340
List	The three things that occur on an interface matched by a RIP network command	341
Table 14-5	List of routing protocols and other routing sources and their default administrative distance settings	346
Example 14-3	Lists the **show ip protocol** command and how it can be used to troubleshoot RIP problems	347

Define Key Terms

Define the following key terms from this chapter and check your answers in the glossary:

administrative distance, autonomous system, backup static route, balanced hybrid, classful routing protocol, classless routing protocol, convergence, default route, distance vector, Exterior Gateway Protocol (EGP), Interior Gateway Protocol (IGP), link state, metric, routing update, variable-length subnet masking (VLSM)

Review Command Reference to Check Your Memory

Although you should not necessarily memorize the information in the tables in this section, this section does include a reference for the configuration commands (Table 14-7) and EXEC commands (Table 14-8) covered in this chapter. Practically speaking, you should memorize the commands as a side effect of reading the chapter and doing all the activities in this Chapter Review section. To check to see how well you have memorized the commands, cover the left side of the table with a piece of paper, read the descriptions in the right side, and see if you remember the command.

Table 14-7 *Chapter 14 Configuration Command Reference*

Command	Description
router rip	Global command that moves the user into RIP configuration mode.
network *network-number*	RIP subcommand that lists a classful network number, enabling RIP on all of that router's interfaces in that classful network.
**version {1	2}**	RIP subcommand that sets the RIP version.
passive-interface [default] {*interface-type interface-number*}	RIP subcommand that tells RIP to no longer advertise RIP updates on the listed interface.
service timestamps	Global command that tells the router to put a timestamp on log messages, including debug messages.

Table 14-8 *Chapter 14 EXEC Command Reference*

Command	Purpose
show ip interface brief	Lists one line per router interface, including the IP address and interface status; an interface must have an IP address, and be in an "up and up" status, before RIP begins to work on the interface.
**show ip route [rip	static	connected]**	Lists the routing table, including RIP-learned routes, and optionally just RIP-learned routes.
show ip route *ip-address*	Lists details about the route the router would match for a packet sent to the listed IP address.
show ip protocols	Lists information about the RIP configuration, plus the IP addresses of neighboring RIP routers from which the local router has learned routes.
show process	Lists information about the various processes running in IOS, and most importantly, overall CPU utilization statistics.
terminal ip netmask-format decimal	For the length of the user's session, causes IOS to display mask information in dotted-decimal format instead of prefix format.
debug ip rip	Tells the router to generate detailed messages for each sent and received RIP update.

Answer Review Questions

Answer the following review questions:

1. Which of the following routing protocols are considered to use distance vector logic?

   a. RIP

   b. IGRP

   c. EIGRP

   d. OSPF

2. Which of the following routing protocols are considered to use link-state logic?

   a. RIP

   b. RIP-2

   c. IGRP

   d. EIGRP

   e. OSPF

   f. Integrated IS-IS

3. Which of the following routing protocols support VLSM?

   a. RIP

   b. RIP-2

   c. IGRP

   d. EIGRP

   e. OSPF

   f. Integrated IS-IS

4. Which of the following routing protocols are considered to be capable of converging quickly?

   a. RIP

   b. RIP-2

   c. IGRP

   d. EIGRP

   e. OSPF

   f. Integrated IS-IS

5. Router1 has interfaces with addresses 9.1.1.1 and 10.1.1.1. Router2, connected to Router1 over a serial link, has interfaces with addresses 10.1.1.2 and 11.1.1.2. Which of the following commands would be part of a complete RIP Version 2 configuration on Router2, with which Router2 advertises out all interfaces, and about all routes?

   a. router rip

   b. router rip 3

   c. network 9.0.0.0

   d. version 2

   e. network 10.0.0.0

   f. network 10.1.1.1

   g. network 10.1.1.2

   h. network 11.0.0.0

   i. network 11.1.1.2

6. Which of the following **network** commands, following a **router rip** command, would cause RIP to send updates out two interfaces whose IP addresses are 10.1.2.1 and 10.1.1.1, mask 255.255.255.0?

   a. network 10.0.0.0

   b. network 10.1.1.0 10.1.2.0

   c. network 10.1.1.1. 10.1.2.1

   d. network 10.1.0.0 255.255.0.0

   e. network 10

   f. You cannot do this with only one **network** command.

7. What command(s) list(s) information identifying the neighboring routers that are sending routing information to a particular router?

   a. show ip

   b. show ip protocol

   c. show ip routing-protocols

   d. show ip route

   e. show ip route neighbor

   f. show ip route received

8. Review the snippet from a **show ip route** command on a router:

```
R        10.1.2.0 [120/1] via 10.1.128.252, 00:00:13, Serial0/0/1
```

Which of the following statements are true regarding this output?

a. The administrative distance is 1.

b. The administrative distance is 120.

c. The metric is 1.

d. The metric is not listed.

e. The router added this route to the routing table 13 seconds ago.

f. The router must wait 13 seconds before advertising this route again.

This chapter covers the following subjects:

- **IP Troubleshooting Tips and Tools:** This section suggests some tips for how to approach host routing issues, routing related to routers, and IP addressing problems, including how to use several additional tools not covered elsewhere in this book.

- **A Routing Troubleshooting Scenario:** This section shows a three-part scenario, with tasks for each part that can be performed before seeing the answers.

CHAPTER 15

Troubleshooting IP Routing

To troubleshoot a network, you need to know several pieces of information. You need to know how IP addressing works, how IP subnetting works, as well as IP routing, RIP-2, and many related protocols, like ARP and Ethernet. In other words, you need to know how all the network components work by themselves and how they relate to each other.

In addition to that core networking knowledge, you also need information about the network on which you are working. What subnets should exist at which sites? Which router WAN interface at the main site connects to the branch office from which the user called with a problem? Did a particular part of the network work correctly yesterday, or has it just not been placed into production yet?

To answer these questions, you need to be able to find documentation, and interpret information in that documentation, to determine a baseline. A baseline defines normal for a particular network. That baseline relies on the core network protocol concepts that apply to any network: IP routing, IP addressing, ARP, Ethernet, and so on. That baseline also includes documentation of the network, what should work, what is not yet finished being installed, and so on.

Before you can troubleshoot any networking problem, you need to know something about how networking protocols work. By this point, you should know a lot about IP addressing, IP routing, IP subnetting, RIP-2, and several related protocols and functions.

Finally, to succeed when troubleshooting a network, you need to practice. Troubleshooting can be taught and it can be learned, but more so than most topics in this book, it is best learned through practice.

This chapter has three main goals. Although the previous chapters have explained a large amount of detail about various networking protocols, some key pieces, including some that are most useful for troubleshooting, have not yet been explained in this book. So, this chapter includes a few more new protocols and concepts. Next, this chapter also lists some hints and tips to consider when troubleshooting a problem related to IP. Finally, the last section of this chapter shows a troubleshooting scenario to begin your journey toward practicing and learning solid IP troubleshooting skills.

IP Troubleshooting Tips and Tools

The primary goal of this chapter is to better prepare you for the more challenging problems that involve potential Layer 3 problems. These problems often require the same thought processes and tools that you would use to troubleshoot networking problems in a real job. The first half of this chapter reviews the main types of problems that can occur, mainly related to addressing, host routing, and a router's routing logic. The second half of the chapter shows a scenario that explains one internetwork that has several problems, giving you a chance to first analyze the problems, and then showing how to solve the problems.

IP Addressing

This section includes some reminders relating to some of the basic features of IP addressing. More importantly, the text includes some tips on how to apply this basic knowledge to a given troubleshooting scenario, helping you know how to attack a particular type of problem.

Avoiding Reserved IP Addresses

One of the first things to check when examining a networking problem is whether the IP addresses are reserved and should not be used as unicast IP addresses. These reserved addresses can be categorized into one of three groups:

■   Addresses that are always reserved

■   Two addresses that are reserved in each subnet

■   Addresses in two special subnets of each classful network, namely the zero subnet and broadcast subnet

The first category of reserved addresses includes two Class A networks that are always reserved, plus all Class D (multicast) and Class E (experimental) IP addresses. You can easily recognize these IP addresses based on the value of their first octet, as follows:

Key Topic

■   0 (because network 0.0.0.0 is always reserved)

■   127 (because network 127.0.0.0 is always reserved)

■   224–239 (all Class D multicast IP addresses)

■   240–255 (all Class E experimental IP addresses)

The second category of reserved IP addresses includes the two reserved addresses inside each subnet. When subnetting, each subnet reserves two numbers—the smallest and largest numbers in the subnet—otherwise known as

■   The subnet number

■   The subnet's broadcast address

So the ability to quickly and confidently determine the subnet number and subnet broadcast address has yet another application, when attempting to confirm that the addresses shown in a question can be legally used.

The third category of reserved IP addresses might or might not apply to a particular internetwork or question. For a given classful network, depending on several factors, the following two subnets might not be allowed to be used:

■   The zero subnet

■   The broadcast subnet

Use of the broadcast subnet does not typically cause any problems, but use of the zero subnet can cause problems. For perspective, Table 15-1 lists some information that you might see in documentation or on a router that tells you whether to reserve these subnets and not use them, or not.

Table 15-1 *Determining Whether a Question Allows the Use of the Zero and Broadcast Subnet*

Key Topic

Clues About the Enterprise Network	Subnets Reserved?
Documentation says nothing about it either way	No
The configuration lists the **ip subnet-zero** command	No
The network uses a classless routing protocol (RIP-2, EIGRP, OSPF)	No
The configuration lists the **no ip subnet-zero** configuration command	Yes
The configuration uses a classful routing protocol (RIP-1)	Yes

One Subnet, One Mask, for Each LAN

The hosts on a single LAN or VLAN (a single broadcast domain) should all be in the same subnet. As a result, each host, each router interface attached to the LAN, and each switch management address in that LAN should also use the same mask.

For an exam, you should check all the details documented in the question to determine the mask used by the various devices on the same LAN. Often, a question that is intended to test your knowledge will not just list all the information in a nice organized figure. Instead, you might have to look at the configuration and diagrams and use **show** commands to gather the information, and then apply subnetting math to discover key facts, like the subnet ID and range of addresses in the subnet.

Figure 15-1 shows an example of a LAN that could be part of a test question. For convenience, the figure lists several details about IP addresses and masks, but for a given question, you might have to gather some of the facts from a figure, a simulator, and from an exhibit that lists command output.

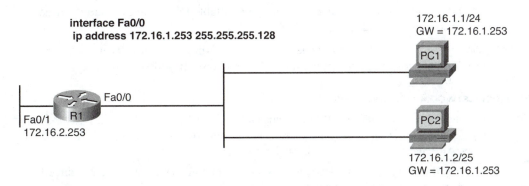

Figure 15-1 *One LAN with Three Different Opinions About the Subnet*

From the information in Figure 15-1, you can quickly tell that the two PCs use different masks (listed in prefix notation). In this case, you would need to know to look in the configuration for the subnet mask in the **ip address** interface subcommand, and then convert that mask to prefix notation to compare it with the other masks in this example. Table 15-2 lists the three differing opinions about the subnet.

Table 15-2 *Different Opinions About the Subnet in Figure 15-1*

	R1 Fa0/0	**PC1**	**PC2**
Mask	255.255.255.128	255.255.255.0	255.255.255.128
Subnet number	172.16.1.128	172.16.1.0	172.16.1.0
Broadcast address	172.16.1.255	172.16.1.255	172.16.1.127

In this case, several problem symptoms occur. For example, PC1 thinks 172.16.1.253 (R1) is in the same subnet, and PC1 thinks that it can forward packets to R1 over the LAN. However, R1 does not think that PC1 (172.16.1.1) is in the same subnet, so R1's connected route on the LAN interface (172.16.1.128/25) will not provide a route that R1 can use to forward packets back to PC1. For the exam, recognizing the fact that the hosts on the same LAN do not have the same opinion about the subnet should be enough to either answer the question, or to know what to fix in a Sim question. Table 15-3, found a little later in this chapter, summarizes the router commands that can be used to find the information required to analyze such problems.

Summary of IP Addressing Tips

Generally, keep the following tips and facts in mind when you approach questions that include details about IP addresses:

1. Check the mask used on each device in the same LAN; if different, the devices cannot have the same view of the range of addresses in the subnet.

2. On point-to-point WAN links, check the IP addresses and masks on both ends of the link, and confirm that the two IP addresses are in the same subnet.

3. When checking to confirm that hosts are in the same subnet, do not just examine the subnet number. Also check the subnet mask, and the implied range of IP addresses.

4. Be ready to use the commands summarized in Table 15-3 to quickly find the IP addresses, masks, and subnet numbers.

The next section, in addition to reviewing a host's routing logic, introduces some commands on Microsoft operating systems that list the host's IP address and mask.

Host Networking Commands

Chapter 5, "Fundamentals of IP Addressing and Routing," explained the simple two-step logic a host uses when forwarding packets, in addition to how a host typically uses DHCP, DNS, ARP, and ICMP. These details can be summarized as follows:

- **Routing:** If the packet's destination is on the same subnet, send the packet directly; if not, send the packet to the default gateway.

- **Address assignment:** Before sending any packets, the host can use DHCP client services to learn its IP address, mask, default gateway, and DNS IP addresses. The host could also be statically configured with these same details.

- **Name resolution:** When the user directly or indirectly references a host name, the host typically uses DNS name resolution requests to ask a DNS to identify that host's IP address unless the host already has that information in its name cache.

- **IP-to-MAC resolution:** The host uses ARP requests to find the other host's MAC address, or the default gateway's IP address, unless the information is already in the host's ARP cache.

Of these four items, note that only the routing (forwarding) process happens for each packet. The address assignment function usually happens once, soon after booting. Name resolution and ARPs occur as needed, typically in reaction to something done by the user.

To analyze how well a host has accomplished these tasks, it is helpful to know a few networking commands on a host. Table 15-3 lists several of the commands on Microsoft Windows XP, but other similar commands exist for other operating systems. Example 15-1 following the table shows the output from some of these commands.

Table 15-3 *Microsoft Windows XP Network Command Reference*

Command	Function
ipconfig /all	Displays detailed IP configuration information for all interfaces, including IP address, mask, default gateway, and DNS IP addresses
ipconfig /release	Releases any DHCP-leased IP addresses
ipconfig /renew	Acquires an IP address and related information using DHCP
nslookup *name*	Sends a DNS request for the listed name
arp –a	Lists the host's ARP cache
ipconfig /displaydns	Lists the host's name cache
ipconfig /flushdns	Removes all DNS-found name cache entries
arp -d	Flushes (empties) the host's ARP cache
netstat -rn	Displays a host's routing table

Example 15-1   *Example Use of Host Networking Commands*

```
C:\> ipconfig /all
! Some lines omitted for brevity
Ethernet adapter Local Area Connection:

        Connection-specific DNS Suffix  . : cinci.rr.com
        Description . . . . . . . . . . . : Broadcom NetXtreme 57xx Gigabit Cont
roller
        Physical Address. . . . . . . . . : 00-11-11-96-B5-13
        Dhcp Enabled. . . . . . . . . . . : Yes
        Autoconfiguration Enabled . . . . : Yes
        IP Address. . . . . . . . . . . . : 192.168.1.102
        Subnet Mask . . . . . . . . . . . : 255.255.255.0
        Default Gateway . . . . . . . . . : 192.168.1.1
        DHCP Server . . . . . . . . . . . : 192.168.1.1
        DNS Servers . . . . . . . . . . . : 65.24.7.3
                                            65.24.7.6
        Lease Obtained. . . . . . . . . . : Thursday, March 29, 2007 6:32:59 AM
        Lease Expires . . . . . . . . . . : Friday, March 30, 2007 6:32:59 AM
! Next, the ARP and name cache are flushed.
C:\> arp -d
C:\> ipconfig /flushdns
Windows IP Configuration


Successfully flushed the DNS Resolver Cache.


! The ping command lists the IP address (198.133.219.25), meaning that the DNS
! request worked.
! However, the ping does not complete, probably due to ACLs filtering ICMP traffic.
C:\> ping www.cisco.com


Pinging www.cisco.com [198.133.219.25] with 32 bytes of data:
Request timed out.
Request timed out.
Request timed out.
Request timed out.


Ping statistics for 192.133.219.25:
    Packets: Sent = 4, Received = 0, Lost = 4 (100% loss),


! Next, the ARP cache lists an entry for the default gateway.
C:\> arp -a


Interface: 192.168.1.102 --- 0x2
  Internet Address      Physical Address      Type
  192.168.1.1           00-13-10-d4-de-08     dynamic
! Next, the local name cache lists the name used in the ping command and the IP
! address
```

```
! learned from the DNS server.
C:\> ipconfig /displaydns

Windows IP Configuration

        www.cisco.com
        _ _ _ _ _ _ _ _ _ _ _ _ _ _ _ _ _ _ _
        Record Name . . . . . : www.cisco.com
        Record Type . . . . . : 1
        Time To Live  . . . . : 26190
        Data Length . . . . . : 4
        Section . . . . . . . : Answer
        A (Host) Record . . . : 198.133.219.25
! Lines omitted for brevity
```

Example 15-1 shows an example of the **ping www.cisco.com** command on a host running Windows XP, just after the ARP cache and hostname cache have been deleted (flushed). The example first shows the DHCP-learned addressing and DNS details, and then shows the flushing of the two caches. At that point, the example shows the **ping www.cisco.com** command, which forces the host to use DNS to learn the IP address of the Cisco web server, and then ARP to learn the MAC address of the default gateway, before sending an ICMP echo request to the Cisco web server.

Note: The ping fails in this example, probably due to ACLs on routers or firewalls in the Internet. However, the **ping** command still drives the DNS and ARP processes as shown in the example. Also, the text is from a DOS window in Windows XP.

In addition to these commands, Figure 15-2 shows an example of the windows used to statically configure a host's IP address, mask, default gateway, and DNS server IP addresses. These details can be configured with commands as well, but most people prefer the easier graphical interface.

Troubleshooting Host Routing Problems

Troubleshooting host routing problems should begin with the same two-step routing logic used by a host. The first question to ask is whether the host can ping other hosts inside the same subnet. If a ping of a same-subnet host fails, the root cause typically falls into one of two categories:

■   The two hosts have incorrect IP address and mask configurations, typically so that at least one of the two hosts thinks it is in a different subnet.

■   The two hosts have correct IP address and mask configurations, but the underlying Ethernet has a problem.

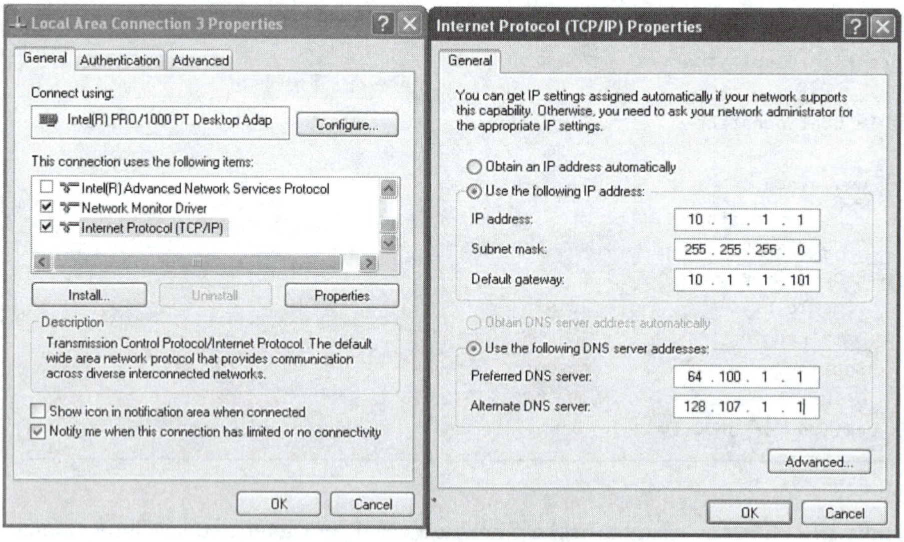

Figure 15-2 *Configuring Static IP Addresses on Windows XP*

Start by looking at the host's addresses and masks, and determine the subnet number and range of addresses for each. If the subnets are the same, then move on to Layer 1 and 2 Ethernet troubleshooting.

If the host can ping other hosts in the same subnet, the next step is to confirm if the host can ping IP addresses in other subnets, thereby testing the second branch of a host's routing logic. Two different pings can be helpful at this step:

- Ping the default gateway IP address to confirm that the host can send packets over the LAN to and from the default gateway.

- Ping a different IP address on the default gateway/router, but not the IP address on the same LAN.

For example, in Figure 15-1 earlier in this chapter, PC1 could first issue the **ping 172.16.1.253** command to confirm whether PC1 can send packets to and from its presumed default gateway. If the ping was successful, PC1 could use a **ping 172.16.2.253** command, which forces PC1 to use its default gateway setting, because PC1 thinks that 172.16.2.253 is in a different subnet.

So, when a host can ping other hosts in the same subnet, but not hosts in other subnets, the root cause typically ends up being one of a few items, as follows:

- There is some mismatch between the host's default gateway configuration and the router acting as default gateway. The problems include mismatched masks between the host and the router, which impacts the perceived range of addresses in the subnet, or the host simply referring to the wrong router IP address.

- If the default gateway settings are all correct, but the ping of the default gateway IP address fails, there is probably some Layer 1 or 2 problem on the LAN.

- If the default gateway settings are all correct and the ping of the default gateway works, but the ping of one of the other router interface IP addresses fails (like the **ping 172.16.2.253** command based on Figure 15-1), then the router's other interface might have failed.

Although all the details in this section can be helpful when troubleshooting problems on hosts, keep in mind that many of the problems stem from incorrect IP address and mask combinations. Mastery of IP addressing and subnetting, both the concepts and the math, can help you find and solve networking problems much more quickly.

Finding the Matching Route on a Router

Chapter 5 summarized the process by which a router forwards a packet. A key part of that process is how a router compares the destination IP address of each packet with the existing contents of that router's IP routing table. The route that matches the packet's destination tells the router out which interface to forward the packet and, in some cases, the IP address of the next-hop router.

In some cases, a particular router's routing table might have more than one route that matches an individual destination IP address. Some legitimate and normal reasons for the overlapping routes in a routing table include auto-summary, route summarization, and the configuration of static routes.

The exams can test your understanding of IP routing by asking questions about which route would be matched for a packet sent to particular IP addresses. To answer such questions, you should keep the following important facts in mind:

- When a particular destination IP address matches more than one route in a router's routing table, the router uses the most specific route—in other words, the route with the longest prefix length.

- Although the router uses binary math to compare the destination IP address to the routing table entries, you can simply compare the destination IP address to each subnet in the routing table. If a subnet's implied address range includes the packet's destination address, the route matches the packet's destination.

- If the question includes a simulator, you can easily find the matched route by using the **show ip route** *address* command, which lists the route matched for the IP address listed in the command.

Example 15-2 shows a sample IP routing table for a router, with many overlapping routes. Read the example, and before reading the explanations after the example, predict which route this router would match for packets destined to the following IP addresses: 172.16.1.1, 172.16.1.2, 172.16.2.2, and 172.16.4.3.

Example 15-2   show ip route *Command with Overlapping Routes*

```
R1# show ip route rip
Codes: C - connected, S - static, R - RIP, M - mobile, B - BGP
       D - EIGRP, EX - EIGRP external, O - OSPF, IA - OSPF inter area
       N1 - OSPF NSSA external type 1, N2 - OSPF NSSA external type 2
```

```
            E1 - OSPF external type 1, E2 - OSPF external type 2
            i - IS-IS, su - IS-IS summary, L1 - IS-IS level-1, L2 - IS-IS level-2
            ia - IS-IS inter area, * - candidate default, U - per-user static route
            o - ODR, P - periodic downloaded static route

Gateway of last resort is not set


     172.16.0.0/16 is variably subnetted, 5 subnets, 4 masks
R        172.16.1.1/32 [120/1] via 172.16.25.2, 00:00:04, Serial0/1/1
R        172.16.1.0/24 [120/2] via 172.16.25.129, 00:00:09, Serial0/1/0
R        172.16.0.0/22 [120/1] via 172.16.25.2, 00:00:04, Serial0/1/1
R        172.16.0.0/16 [120/2] via 172.16.25.129, 00:00:09, Serial0/1/0
R        0.0.0.0/0 [120/3] via 172.16.25.129, 00:00:09, Serial0/1/0
R1# show ip route 172.16.4.3
Routing entry for 172.16.0.0/16
  Known via "rip", distance 120, metric 2
  Redistributing via rip
  Last update from 172.16.25.129 on Serial0/1/0, 00:00:19 ago
  Routing Descriptor Blocks:
  * 172.16.25.129, from 172.16.25.129, 00:00:19 ago, via Serial0/1/0
      Route metric is 2, traffic share count is 1
```

To find the matching route, all you need to know is the destination IP address of the packet and the router's IP routing table. By examining each subnet and mask in the routing table, you can determine the range of IP addresses in each subnet. Then, you can compare the packet's destination to the ranges of addresses, and find all matching routes. In cases where a particular destination IP address falls within the IP address range for multiple routes, then you pick the route with the longest prefix length. In this case:

- Destination address 172.16.1.1 matches all five routes, but the host route for specific IP address 172.16.1.1, prefix length /32, has the longest prefix length.

- Destination address 172.16.1.2 matches four of the routes (all except the host route for 172.16.1.1), but the route to 172.16.1.0/24 has the longest prefix.

- Destination address 172.16.2.2 matches the last three routes listed in R1's routing table in the example, with the route for 172.16.0.0/22 having the longest prefix length.

- Destination address 172.16.4.3 matches the last two routes listed in R1's routing table in the example, with the route for 172.16.0.0/16 having the longest prefix length.

Finally, note the output of the **show ip route 172.16.4.3** command at the end of Example 15-2. This command shows which route the router would match to reach IP address 172.16.4.3—a very handy command for both real life and for Sim questions on the exams. In this case, a packet sent to IP address 172.16.4.3 would match the route for the entire Class B network 172.16.0.0/16, as highlighted near the end of the example.

Troubleshooting Commands

The most popular troubleshooting command on a router or switch is the **ping** command. Chapter 14, "Routing Protocol Concepts and RIP-2 Configuration," already introduced this command, in both its standard form and the extended form. Basically, the **ping** command sends a packet to another host, and the receiving host sends back a packet to the original host, testing to see if packets can be routed between the two hosts.

This section introduces three additional Cisco IOS commands that can be useful when troubleshooting routing problems, namely the **show ip arp**, **traceroute**, and **telnet** commands.

The show ip arp Command

The **show ip arp** command lists the contents of a router's ARP cache. Example 15-3 lists sample output from this command, taken from router R1 in Figure 15-1, after the router and hosts were changed to all use a /24 mask.

Example 15-3 *Sample* **show ip arp** *Command Output*

```
R1# show ip arp
Protocol  Address          Age (min)  Hardware Addr   Type   Interface
Internet  172.16.1.1               8  0013.197b.2f58  ARPA   FastEthernet0/0
Internet  172.16.1.253             -  0013.197b.5004  ARPA   FastEthernet0/0
Internet  172.16.2.253             -  0013.197b.5005  ARPA   FastEthernet0/1
```

The most important parts of each entry are the IP address, MAC address, and interface. When a router needs to send a packet out a particular interface, the router will only use entries associated with that interface. For example, for R1 to send a packet to host PC1 in Figure 15-1 (address 172.16.1.1), R1 needs to forward the packet out its Fa0/0 interface, so R1 will only use ARP cache entries associated with Fa0/0.

Additionally, the Age heading includes a few interesting facts. If it lists a number, the Age value represents the number of minutes since the router last received a packet from the host. For example, it had been 8 minutes since R1 had received a packet from host PC1, source IP address 172.16.1.1, source MAC address 0013.197b.2f58. The Age does not mean how long it has been since the ARP request/reply; the timer is reset to 0 each time a matching packet is received. If the Age is listed as a dash, the ARP entry actually represents an IP address assigned to the router—for example, R1's Fa0/0 interface in Figure 15-1 is shown as 172.16.1.253, which is the second entry in Example 15-3.

The traceroute Command

The Cisco IOS **traceroute** command, like the Cisco IOS **ping** command, tests the route between a router and another host or router. However, the **traceroute** command also identifies the IP addresses of the routers in the route. For example, consider Figure 15-3 and Example 15-4. The figure shows an internetwork with three routers, with the **traceroute 172.16.2.7** command being used on router R1. The arrowed lines show the three IP addresses identified by the command output, which is shown in Example 15-4.

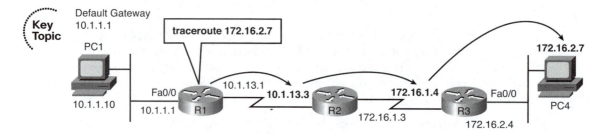

Figure 15-3   *Internetwork Used in* **traceroute** *Example*

Example 15-4   *Sample* **traceroute** *Command Output*

```
R1# traceroute 172.16.2.7


Type escape sequence to abort.
Tracing the route to 172.16.2.7

  1 10.1.13.3    8 msec 4 msec 4 msec
  2 172.16.1.4   24 msec 25 msec 26 msec
  3 172.16.2.7   26 msec 26 msec 28 msec
```

The example shows a working **traceroute** command. However, if a routing problem exists, the command will not complete. For example, imagine that R1 had a route that matched 172.16.2.7, so R1 could forward packets to R2. However, R2 does not have a route that matches destination 172.16.2.7. In that case, the **traceroute** command would list the first line that refers to a router (highlighted in Example 15-4). However, no other routers would be listed, and the user would have to stop the command, typically by pressing the Ctrl-Shift-6 key sequence a few times. 10.1.13.3 is an IP address on the router that has a routing problem (R2), so the next step would be to telnet to R2 and find out why it does not have a route matching destination 172.16.2.7. (Note that Ctl-Shift-6 sends a break character; some international keyboards can map a different key sequence to send a break character.)

It is important to note that the **traceroute** command lists the IP addresses considered to be the next-hop device. For example, in Example 15-4, the first IP address (R2, 10.1.13.3) is the next-hop IP address in the route R1 uses to route the packet. Similarly, the next IP address (R3, 172.16.1.4) is the next-hop router in the route used by R2. (Chapter 20, "Troubleshooting IP Routing II," explains how the **traceroute** command finds these IP addresses.)

Note: Many operating systems have a similar command, including the Microsoft OS **tracert** command, which achieves the same goal.

Telnet and Suspend

Many engineers troubleshoot network problems sitting at their desks. To get access to a router or switch, the engineer just needs to use Telnet or SSH on their desktop PC to connect to each router or switch, often opening multiple Telnet or SSH windows to connect to multiple devices. As an alternative, the engineer could connect to one router or switch using a Telnet or SSH client on their desktop computer, and then use the **telnet** or **ssh** Cisco IOS EXEC commands to connect to other routers and switches. These commands acts as a Telnet or SSH client, respectively, so that you can easily connect to other devices when troubleshooting. When finished, the user could just use the **exit** command to disconnect the Telnet or SSH session.

Frankly, many people who rarely troubleshoot just use multiple windows on their desktop and ignore the Cisco IOS **telnet** and **ssh** commands. However, those who do a lot more troubleshooting tend to use these commands because, with practice, they enable you to move between routers and switches more quickly.

One of the most important advantages of using the Cisco IOS **telnet** and **ssh** commands is the suspend feature. The suspend feature allows a Telnet or SSH connection to remain active while creating another Telnet or SSH connection, so that you can make many concurrent connections, and then easily switch between the connections. Figure 15-4 shows a sample internetwork with which the text will demonstrate the suspend feature and its power.

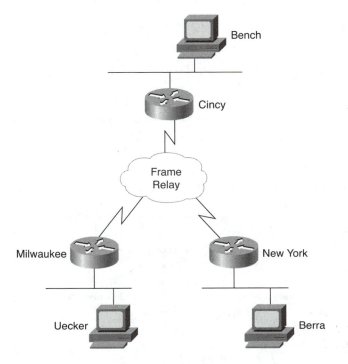

Figure 15-4 *Telnet Suspension*

The router administrator is using the PC named Bench to telnet into the Cincy router. When connected to the Cincy CLI, the user telnets to router Milwaukee. When in Milwaukee, the user suspends the Telnet session by pressing Ctrl-Shift-6, followed by pressing the letter x. The user then telnets to New York and again suspends the connection. At the end of the example, the user is concurrently telnetted into all three routers, with the ability to switch between the connections with just a few keystrokes. Example 15-5 shows example output, with annotations to the side.

Example 15-5   *Telnet Suspensions*

```
Cincy# telnet milwaukee                  (User issues command to Telnet to Milwaukee)
Trying Milwaukee (10.1.4.252)... Open


User Access Verification

Password:                      (User plugs in password, can type commands at Milwaukee)
Milwaukee>
Milwaukee>
Milwaukee>
                          (Note: User pressed Ctrl-Shift-6 and then x)
Cincy# telnet NewYork          (User back at Cincy because Telnet was suspended)
Trying NewYork (10.1.6.253)... Open
                (User is getting into New York now, based on telnet NewYork command)


User Access Verification

Password:
NewYork>                           (User can now type commands on New York)
NewYork>
NewYork>
NewYork>
                      (Note: User pressed Ctrl-Shift-6 and then x)

Cincy# show sessions              (This command lists suspended Telnet sessions)
Conn Host           Address           Byte  Idle Conn Name
   1 Milwaukee      10.1.4.252           0     0 Milwaukee
*  2 NewYork        10.1.6.253           0     0 NewYork

Cincy# where                      (where does the same thing as show sessions)
Conn Host           Address           Byte  Idle Conn Name
   1 Milwaukee      10.1.4.252           0     0 Milwaukee
*  2 NewYork        10.1.6.253           0     0 NewYork
```

```
Cincy# resume 1          (Resume connection 1 (see show session) to Milwaukee)
[Resuming connection 1 to milwaukee ... ]


Milwaukee>                         (User can type commands on Milwaukee)
Milwaukee>
Milwaukee>
! (Note: User pressed Ctrl-Shift-6 and then x, because the user wants to
!  go back to Cincy)
Cincy#         (WOW! User just pressed Enter and resumes the last Telnet)
 [Resuming connection 1 to milwaukee ... ]


Milwaukee>
Milwaukee>
Milwaukee>
               (Note: User pressed Ctrl-Shift-6 and then x)
Cincy# disconnect 1          (No more need to use Milwaukee  Telnet terminated!)
Closing connection to milwaukee [confirm]       (User presses Enter to confirm)
Cincy#
 [Resuming connection 2 to NewYork ... ]
            (Pressing Enter resumes most recently suspended active Telnet)


NewYork>
NewYork>
NewYork>
               (Note: User pressed Ctrl-Shift-6 and then x)
Cincy# disconnect 2                  (Done with New York, terminate Telnet)
Closing connection to NewYork [confirm]       (Just press Enter to confirm)
Cincy#
```

The play-by-play notes in the example explain most of the details. Example 15-5 begins with the Cincy command prompt that would be seen in the Telnet window from host Bench. After telnetting to Milwaukee, the Telnet connection was suspended because the user pressed Ctrl-Shift-6, let go, and then pressed x and let go. Then, after establishing a Telnet connection to New York, that connection was suspended with the same key sequence.

The two connections can be suspended or resumed easily. The **resume** command can be used to resume any suspended connection. To reconnect to a particular session, the **resume** command can list a connection ID, which is shown in the **show sessions** command. (The **where** command provides the same output.) If the **resume** command is used without a connection ID, the command reconnects the user to the most recently suspended connection. Also, instead of using the **resume** command, you can just use the session number as a command. For instance, just typing the command **2** does the same thing as typing the command **resume 2**.

The interesting and potentially dangerous nuance here is that if a Telnet session is suspended and you simply press Enter, Cisco IOS Software resumes the connection to the most recently suspended Telnet connection. That is fine, until you realize that you tend to press the Enter key occasionally to clear some of the clutter from the screen. With a suspended Telnet connection, pressing Enter a few times to unclutter the screen might reconnect to another router. This is particularly dangerous when you are changing the configuration or using potentially damaging EXEC commands, so be careful about what router you are actually using when you have suspended Telnet connections.

If you want to know which session has been suspended most recently, look for the session listed in the **show sessions** command that has an asterisk (*) to the left of the entry. The asterisk marks the most recently suspended session.

In addition to the commands in Example 15-5 that show how to suspend and resume Telnet and SSH connections, two other commands can list useful information about sessions for users logged into a router. The **show users** command lists all users logged into the router on which the command is used. This command lists all sessions, including users at the console, and those connecting using both Telnet and SSH. The **show ssh** command lists the same kind of information, but only for users that connected using SSH. Note that these commands differ from the **show sessions** command, which lists suspended Telnet/SSH sessions from the local router to other devices.

This concludes the first half of the chapter. The remainder of the chapter focuses on how to apply many of the troubleshooting tips covered earlier in this chapter by analyzing an internetwork that has a few problems.

A Routing Troubleshooting Scenario

This section describes a three-part scenario. Each part (A, B, and C) uses figures, examples, and text to explain part of what is happening in an internetwork and asks you to complete some tasks and answer some questions. For each part, the text shows sample answers for the tasks and questions.

The goal of this scenario is to demonstrate how to use some of the troubleshooting tips covered earlier in this chapter. The scenario is just one more tool to help you learn how to apply your knowledge to new unique scenarios.

Scenario Part A: Tasks and Questions

The scenario begins with an internetwork that has just been installed, but the documentation is incomplete. Your job is to examine the existing documentation (in the form of an internetwork diagram), along with the output of several **show** commands. From that information, you should

■   Determine the IP address and subnet mask/prefix length of each router interface.

■   Calculate the subnet number for each subnet in the diagram.

- Complete the internetwork diagram, listing router IP addresses and prefix lengths, as well as the subnet numbers.

- Identify any existing problems with the IP addresses or subnets shown in the existing figure.

- Suggest solutions to any problems you find.

Examples 15-6 through 15-8 list command output from routers R1, R2, and R3 in Figure 15-5. Example 15-9 lists commands as typed into a text editor, which were later pasted into R4's configuration mode.

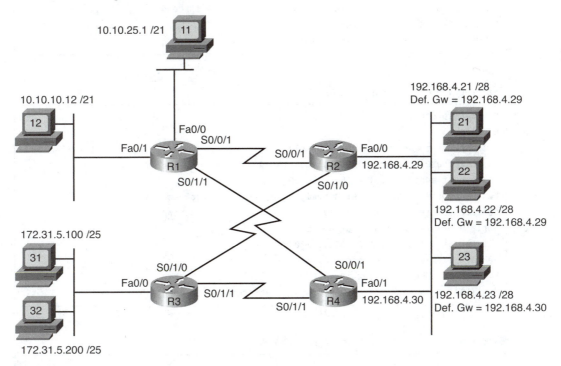

Figure 15-5   *Scenario 3: Incomplete Network Diagram*

Example 15-6   *Scenario Output: Router R1*

```
R1# show ip interface brief
Interface              IP-Address      OK? Method Status                Protocol
FastEthernet0/0        10.10.24.1      YES NVRAM  up                    up
FastEthernet0/1        10.10.15.1      YES NVRAM  up                    up
Serial0/0/0            unassigned      YES NVRAM  administratively down  down
Serial0/0/1            192.168.1.1     YES NVRAM  up                    up
Serial0/1/0            unassigned      YES NVRAM  administratively down  down
Serial0/1/1            192.168.1.13    YES NVRAM  up                    up
R1# show protocols
```

```
Global values:
  Internet Protocol routing is enabled
FastEthernet0/0 is up, line protocol is up
  Internet address is 10.10.24.1/21
FastEthernet0/1 is up, line protocol is up
  Internet address is 10.10.15.1/21
Serial0/0/0 is administratively down, line protocol is down
Serial0/0/1 is up, line protocol is up
  Internet address is 192.168.1.1/30
Serial0/1/0 is administratively down, line protocol is down
Serial0/1/1 is up, line protocol is up
  Internet address is 192.168.1.13/30
```

Example 15-7 *Scenario Output: Router R2*

```
R2# show protocols
Global values:
  Internet Protocol routing is enabled
FastEthernet0/0 is up, line protocol is up
  Internet address is 192.168.4.29/28
FastEthernet0/1 is administratively down, line protocol is down
Serial0/0/0 is administratively down, line protocol is down
Serial0/0/1 is up, line protocol is up
  Internet address is 192.168.1.2/30
Serial0/1/0 is up, line protocol is up
  Internet address is 192.168.1.6/30
Serial0/1/1 is administratively down, line protocol is down
```

Example 15-8 *Scenario Output: Router R3*

```
R3# show ip interface brief
Interface              IP-Address      OK? Method Status                Protocol
FastEthernet0/0        172.31.5.1      YES NVRAM  up                    up
FastEthernet0/1        unassigned      YES NVRAM  administratively down down
Serial0/0/0            unassigned      YES NVRAM  administratively down down
Serial0/0/1            unassigned      YES NVRAM  administratively down down
Serial0/1/0            192.168.1.5     YES NVRAM  up                    up
Serial0/1/1            192.168.1.18    YES NVRAM  up                    up
R3# show ip route connected
     172.31.0.0/25 is subnetted, 1 subnets
C       172.31.5.0 is directly connected, FastEthernet0/0
     192.168.1.0/24 is variably subnetted, 5 subnets, 2 masks
C       192.168.1.4/30 is directly connected, Serial0/1/0
C       192.168.1.16/30 is directly connected, Serial0/1/1
```

Example 15-9 *Scenario Output: Router R4*

```
! The following commands are in a text editor, and will be pasted into
! configuration mode on R4.
interface fa0/1
 ip address 192.168.4.30 255.255.255.240
!
interface serial 0/0/1
 ip address 192.168.1.14 255.255.255.252
!
interface serial 0/1/1
 ip address 192.168.1.19 255.255.255.252
!
! The following three lines correctly configure RIP Version 2
router rip
 version 2
 network 192.168.1.0
 network 192.168.4.0
```

Scenario Part A: Answers

Examples 15-6, 15-7, and 15-8 list the IP addresses of each interface on routers R1, R2, and R3, respectively. However, some of the commands used in the examples do not provide mask information. In particular, the **show ip interface brief** command—a great command for getting a quick look at interfaces, their IP addresses, and the status—does not list the mask. The **show protocols** command lists that same information, as well as the subnet mask.

Example 15-8 (R3) does list the mask information directly, but it can take a little work to find it. You can see the interfaces and their configured IP addresses in the **show ip interfaces brief** command output, and then compare that information to the output of the **show ip route connected** command. This command does list the mask information, and the subnet number connected to an interface. A router determines the subnet number and mask for each connected route based on the configured **ip address** interface subcommand on each interface. From these facts, you can determine the mask used on each of R3's interfaces.

Finally, Example 15-9 lists configuration commands that will be pasted into router R4. These commands explicitly list the IP addresses and subnet masks in the various **ip address** configuration commands.

Figure 15-6 shows the answers to the first three tasks in Part A, listing the IP addresses and masks of each interface, as well as the subnet numbers.

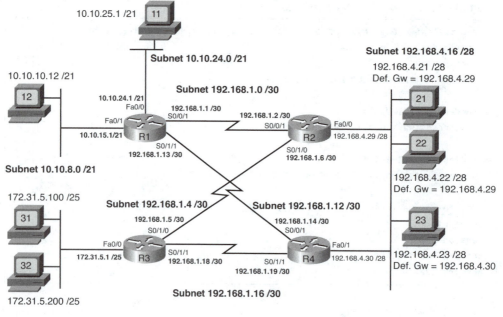

Figure 15-6 *Scenario Part A: Subnet Numbers*

With all the information listed in one internetwork diagram, you can use the suggestions and tips from earlier in this chapter to analyze the IP addresses and subnets. In this case, you should have found two different addressing problems. The first of the two IP addressing problems is the disagreement between PC31 and PC32 regarding the subnet numbers and range of addresses on the lower-left LAN in Figure 15-6. In this case, PC32, with IP address 172.31.5.200 and a prefix length of /25, thinks it is in subnet 172.31.5.128/25, with a range of addresses from 172.31.5.129 to 172.31.5.254. PC31 and R3, attached to the same LAN, think they are attached to subnet 172.31.5.0/25, with the range of addresses being 172.31.5.1–172.31.5.126.

This particular problem results in R3 not being able to forward packets to PC32, because R3's connected route for that interface will refer to subnet 172.31.5.0/25. As a result, packets sent to PC32's IP address would not match that connected route. Additionally, PC32's setting for its default gateway IP address (172.31.5.1) is invalid, because the default gateway IP address should be in the same subnet as the host.

The second addressing problem in this scenario is that on the serial link between routers R3 and R4, R4's IP address and mask (192.168.1.19/30) is actually a broadcast address in subnet 192.168.1.16/30. Subnet 192.168.1.16/30 has an address range of 192.168.1.17–192.168.1.18, with a subnet broadcast address of 192.168.1.19. Note that the scenario suggested that the commands in Example 15-9 would be pasted into R4's configuration mode; R4 would actually reject the **ip address 192.168.1.19 255.255.255.252** command because it is a subnet broadcast address.

Several possible working solutions exist for both problems, but the simple solution in each case is to assign a valid but unused IP address from the correct subnets. In PC32's case, any IP address between 172.31.5.1 and 172.31.5.126, not already used by PC31 or R3, would work fine. For R4, IP address 192.168.1.17 would be the only available IP address, because R3 has already been assigned 192.168.1.18.

Scenario Part B: Analyze Packet/Frame Flow

Part B of this scenario continues with the network shown in Figure 15-6—including the IP addressing errors from Part A. However, no other problems exist. In this case, all physical connections and links are working, and RIP-2 has been correctly configured, and is functional.

With those assumptions in mind, answer the following questions. Note that to answer some questions, you need to refer to MAC addresses that are not otherwise specified. In these cases, a pseudo MAC address is listed—for example, R1-Fa0/1-MAC for R1's Fa0/1 interface's MAC address.

1. PC12 successfully pings PC21, with the packet flowing over the R1-R2 link. What ARP table entries are created to support the forwarding of the ICMP Echo Request packet?

2. Assume when PC12 pings PC23 that the ICMP echo request goes over the R1-R4 path. What ARP table entries are required on PC12? R1? R4?

3. Assume when PC12 pings PC23 that the ICMP echo request goes over the R1-R2 path. What ARP table entries are required in support of the ICMP echo reply from PC23, on PC23? R2? R4? R1?

4. PC31 sends a packet to PC22. When the packet passes over the Ethernet on the right side of the figure, what is the source MAC address? Destination MAC address? Source IP address? Destination IP address?

5. PC31 sends a packet to PC22. When the packet passes over the serial link between R3 and R2, what is the source MAC address? Destination MAC address? Source IP address? Destination IP address?

6. PC21 sends a packet to PC12, with the packet passing over the R2-R1 path. When the packet passes over the Ethernet on the right side of the figure, what is the source MAC address? Destination MAC address? Source IP address? Destination IP address?

7. PC21 sends a packet to PC12, with the packet passing over the R2-R1 path. When the packet passes over the Ethernet on the left side of the figure, what is the source MAC address? Destination MAC address? Source IP address? Destination IP address?

Scenario Part B: Answers

Scenario Part B requires that you think about the theory behind the IP forwarding process. That process includes many details covered in Chapter 5. In particular, to answer the questions in Part B correctly, you need to remember the following key facts:

■ The IP packet flows from the sending host to the receiving host.

■ The data link header and trailer, which encapsulate the packet, do not flow over the complete end-to-end route—instead, each individual data link helps move the packet from a host to a router, between two routers, or from a router to the destination host.

Key
Topic

- For the process to work, the data link frame's destination address lists the next device's data link address.

- The IP header lists the IP address of the sending host and receiving host.

- Routers discard the data link header and trailer for received frames and build a new data link header and trailer—appropriate for the outgoing interface—before forwarding the frame.

- On LANs, hosts and routers use ARP to discover the Ethernet MAC address used by other devices on the same LAN.

- On point-to-point WAN links, ARP is not needed, and the data link addressing is uninteresting and can be ignored.

If your reading of this list caused you to doubt some of your answers, feel free to go back and reevaluate your answers before looking at the actual answers.

Scenario Part B: Question 1

This question focuses on the packet flow from PC12 to PC21, assuming the packet passes over the R1-R2 link. The fact that the packet is created due to a **ping** command, and contains an ICMP echo request, does not impact the answer at all. The question specifically asks about which ARP table entries must be used by each device.

To answer the question, you need to remember how a host or router will choose to which device it sends the frame. PC12 sends the frame to R1 because the destination IP address is in a different subnet than PC12. R1 then sends a new frame to R2. Finally, R2 sends yet another new frame (with new data link header and trailer) to PC21. Figure 15-7 shows the frames, with just the destination MAC address and destination IP address shown.

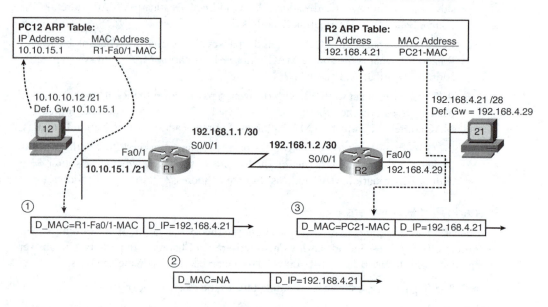

Figure 15-7 *Scenario Part B: Answer to Question 1*

To analyze the frame sent by PC12, remember that PC12's logic is basically "the destination IP address is on another subnet, so send this packet to my default gateway." To do so, PC12 needs to encapsulate the IP packet in an Ethernet frame so that the frame arrives at R1, PC12's default gateway. So, PC12 must find the MAC address of its default gateway (10.10.15.1) in PC12's ARP table. If the ARP table entry exists, PC12 can immediately build the frame shown in Figure 15-7 at step 1. If not, PC12 must first send an ARP broadcast, and receive a reply, to build the correct entry in its ARP table.

Also, note that PC12 does not need to know PC21's MAC address, because PC12 is not trying to send the packet directly to PC21. Instead, PC12 is trying to send the packet to its default gateway, so PC12 needs to know its default gateway's MAC address.

Step 2, as marked in Figure 15-7, shows the frame after R1 has stripped off the incoming frame's Ethernet header and trailer, R1 has decided to forward the packet out R1's S0/0/1 interface to R2 next, and R1 has added a (default) HDLC header and trailer to encapsulate the IP packet. The packet's destination IP address (192.168.4.21) is unchanged. HDLC, used only on point-to-point links, does not use MAC addresses, so it does not need ARP at all. So, no ARP table entries are needed on R1 for forwarding this packet.

Finally, step 3 again shows the frame after the router (R2) has stripped off the incoming HDLC frame's header and trailer and built the new Ethernet header and trailer. R2 needs to forward the packet out R2's Fa0/0 interface, directly to PC21, so R2 builds a header with PC21's MAC address as the destination. To make that happen, R2 needs an ARP table entry listing PC21's IP address (192.168.4.21) and its corresponding MAC address. Again, if R2 does not have an ARP table entry for IP address 192.168.4.21, R2 will send an ARP request (broadcast), and wait for a reply, before R2 would forward the packet.

Scenario Part B: Question 2

The answer to question 2 uses the same logic and reasoning as the answer to question 1. In this case, PC12, R1, and R4 will forward the packet in three successive steps, as follows:

1. PC12 decides to send the packet to its default gateway, because the destination (192.16.4.23) is on a different subnet than PC12. So, PC12 needs an ARP table entry listing the MAC address of its default gateway (10.10.15.1, or R1).

2. R1 receives the frame, strips off the data link header and trailer, and decides to forward the packet over the serial link to R4. The link uses HDLC, so R1 does not need ARP at all.

3. R4 receives the frame and strips off the incoming frame's HDLC header and trailer. R4 then decides to forward the packet directly to PC23, out R4's Fa0/1 interface, so R4 needs an ARP table entry listing the MAC address of host 192.168.4.23 (PC23).

Figure 15-8 shows the ARP table entries required for the flow of a packet from PC12 to PC23. Note that the figure also shows the correlation between the next-hop IP address and the MAC address, with the MAC address then being added to a new Ethernet data link header.

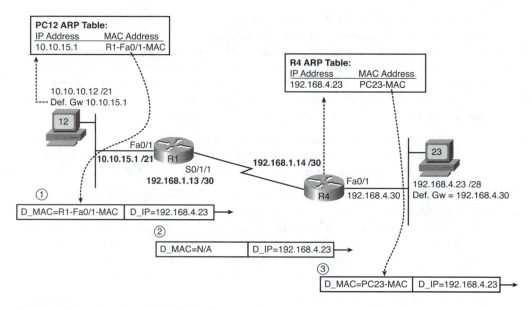

Figure 15-8   *Required ARP Table Entries: Question 2*

Scenario Part B: Question 3

The tricky part of this particular question relates to the fact that two routers connect to the subnet on the right of Figure 15-6, so PC23 appears to have two possible routers to use as its default gateway. The question suggests that an ICMP echo request packet goes from PC12, through R1, then R2, and over the LAN to PC23. PC23 then needs to send the ICMP echo reply to PC12, so to answer the question fully, you need to understand where the packet flows, and then determine the required ARP table entries on each device.

PC23 still uses the same familiar host logic when sending a packet—if the destination is on a different subnet, PC23 will send the packet to its default gateway. In this case, PC23 needs to send the ICMP echo reply to PC12, which is in another subnet, so PC23 will send the packet to 192.168.4.30 (R4)—PC23's configured default gateway. Presumably, R4 would then forward the packet to R1, and then R1 would forward the packet directly to PC12.

The ARP entries required for sending packets from PC23, to R4, to R1, and then to PC12 are as follows:

1. PC23 decides to send the packet to its default gateway, R4. So, PC23 needs an ARP table entry listing the MAC address of its default gateway (192.168.4.30).

2. R4 receives the frame, strips off the data link header and trailer, and decides to forward the packet over the serial link to R1. This links uses HDLC, so R4 does not need ARP at all.

3. R1 receives the frame from R4 and strips off the incoming frame's HDLC header and trailer. R1 then decides to forward the packet directly to PC12, out R1's Fa0/1 interface, so R1 needs an ARP table entry listing the MAC address of host 10.10.10.12 (PC12).

Figure 15-9 shows the ARP table entries required for the flow of a packet from PC23 to PC12. Note that the figure also shows the correlation between the next-hop IP address and the MAC address, with the MAC address then being added to a new Ethernet data link header.

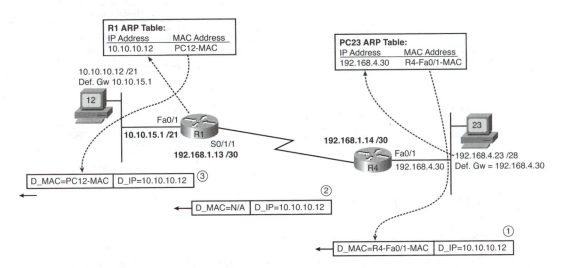

Figure 15-9   *Required ARP Table Entries: Question 3*

Scenario Part B: Question 4

This question uses a packet sent from PC31 to PC22, but with the question focusing on the packet as it crosses the LAN on the right side of Figure 15-6. To answer this question fully, you need to recall that while the source and destination IP addresses of the packet remain unchanged from sending host to receiving host, the data link source and destination addresses change each time a router builds a new data link header when forwarding a packet. Additionally, you need to realize that the R3fiR4 serial link has been misconfigured (R4's proposed IP address of 192.168.1.19 was invalid), so no IP packets can be forwarded over the link between R3 and R4. As a result, the packet will go over this path: PC31fiR3fiR2fiPC22.

The packet in question here (from PC31 to PC22) passes over the LAN on the right side of the figure when R2 forwards the packet over the LAN to PC22. In this case, R2 will build a new Ethernet header, with a source MAC address of R2's Fa0/0 interface MAC address. The destination MAC address will be PC22's MAC address. The source and destination IP addresses of 172.31.5.100 (PC31) and 192.168.4.22 (PC22), respectively, remain unchanged.

Figure 15-10 shows both data link addresses and both network layer addresses in each frame sent from PC31 to PC22. Note that the figure shows the addresses in the data link and network layer headers for each stage of its passage from PC31 to PC22.

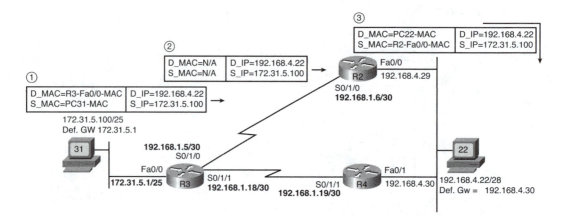

Figure 15-10   *Required ARP Table Entries: Question 4*

Scenario Part B: Question 5

This question uses the same packet flow as question 4, but it focuses on the frame that passes the serial link between R3 and R2. The question can be easily answered as long as you remember that the router discards the data link headers of received frames, and then encapsulates the packet in a new data link header and trailer before forwarding the packet. This new data link header and trailer must be appropriate for the outgoing interface.

In this case, the routers use HDLC, which is the default point-to-point serial data link protocol on Cisco routers. HDLC headers do not include MAC addresses at all—in fact, HDLC addressing is completely uninteresting, because any frame sent by R3 on that link must be destined for R2, because R2 is the only other device on the other end of the link. As a result, there are no MAC addresses, but the source and destination IP addresses of 172.31.5.100 (PC31) and 192.168.4.22 (PC22), respectively, remain unchanged. Figure 15-9, found in the previous answer, shows a representation of the HDLC frame, mainly pointing out that it does not contain MAC addresses.

Scenario Part B: Question 6

This question focuses on a packet sent from PC21 to PC12, as the packet crosses the LAN on the right side of Figure 15-6. Also, the question tells you that the packet goes from PC21 to R2, then to R1, then to PC12.

In this case, PC21 forwards the packet, encapsulated in an Ethernet frame, to R2. To do so, the Ethernet header lists PC21 as the source MAC address, and R2's Fa0/0 interface MAC address as the destination MAC address. The IP addresses—a source of 192.168.4.21 (PC21) and a destination of 10.10.10.12 (PC12)—remain the same for the entire journey from PC21 to PC12. Figure 15-11 summarizes the frame contents for both this question and the next.

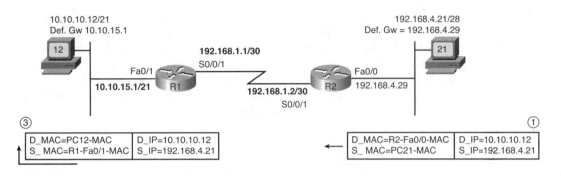

Figure 15-11   *Required ARP Table Entries: Questions 6 and 7*

Scenario Part B: Question 7

Question 7 continues question 6 by examining the same packet, sent from PC21 to PC12, as the packet crosses the LAN on the upper-left part of Figure 15-6. The route taken by this packet is from PC21 to R2, then to R1, then to PC12.

To begin, PC21 sends the IP packet, with a source of 192.168.4.21 (PC21) and a destination of 10.10.10.12 (PC12). To send this packet, PC21 encapsulates the packet in an Ethernet frame to deliver the packet to its default gateway (R2). R2 strips off the Ethernet header of the received frame, and before forwarding the packet to R1, R2 encapsulates the packet in an HDLC frame. When R1 receives the HDLC frame, R1 removes the HDLC header and trailer, deciding to forward the packet out R1's Fa0/1 interface to PC12. As usual, the packet's source and destination address do not change at all during this process.

Before R1 forwards the packet out its Fa0/1 interface, R1 adds an Ethernet header and trailer. The source MAC address is R1's Fa0/1 interface MAC address, and the destination, found in R1's ARP table, is PC12's MAC address. Note that Figure 15-11, shown in the previous section, shows this frame on the left side of the figure.

Scenario Part C: Analyze Connected Routes

For Part C of this scenario, predict the output that would be displayed of the **show ip route connected** command on R4 and R1. You can continue to assume that any IP addressing problems found in Part A still have *not* been corrected. You can refer back to Example 15-5 through Example 15-9, as well as the completed IP address reference of Figure 15-6, for reference.

Scenario Part C: Answers

Routers add connected IP routes to their IP routing tables, referencing the subnet that is connected to an interface, assuming the following are true:

■   The interface's two status codes are "up" and "up."

■   The interface has an IP address correctly configured.

For each interface meeting these two requirements, the router calculates the subnet number based on the IP address and subnet mask listed in the **ip address** interface subcommand. Based on details included in Parts A and B of this scenario, all router interfaces shown in Figure 15-5 have an IP address and are up/up, with the exception of R4's S0/1/1 interface. This one serial interface was to be assigned an IP address that was really a subnet broadcast address, so the router would have rejected the **ip address** command. Table 15-4 lists the location and connected routes added to R1 and R4.

Table 15-4   *Connected Routes Added to R1 and R4*

Location	IP Address	Subnet	Outgoing Interface
R1 Fa0/0	10.10.24.1/21	10.10.24.0/21	Fa0/0
R1 Fa0/1	10.10.15.1/21	10.10.8.0/21	Fa0/1
R1 S0/0/1	192.168.1.1/30	192.168.1.0/30	S0/0/1
R1 S0/1/1	192.168.1.13/30	192.168.1.12/30	S0/1/1
R4 S0/0/1	192.168.1.14/30	192.168.1.12/30	S0/0/1
R4 Fa0/1	192.168.4.30/28	192.168.4.16/28	Fa0/1

To see the connected routes in a concise command, you can use the **show ip route connected** EXEC command. This command simply lists a subset of the routes in the routing table—those that are connected routes. Example 15-10 and Example 15-11 show the contents of the **show ip route connected** command on both R1 and R4, respectively.

Example 15-10   show ip route connected *Command Output for R1*

```
R1# show ip route connected
     10.0.0.0/21 is subnetted, 2 subnets
C       10.10.8.0 is directly connected, FastEthernet0/1
C       10.10.24.0 is directly connected, FastEthernet0/0
     192.168.1.0/24 is variably subnetted, 5 subnets, 2 masks
C       192.168.1.12/30 is directly connected, Serial0/1/1
C       192.168.1.0/30 is directly connected, Serial0/0/1
```

Example 15-11   show ip route connected *Command on R4*

```
R4# show ip route connected
     192.168.4.0/28 is subnetted, 1 subnets
C       192.168.4.16 is directly connected, FastEthernet0/1
     192.168.1.0/24 is variably subnetted, 5 subnets, 2 masks
C       192.168.1.12/30 is directly connected, Serial0/0/1
```

If you compare the highlighted portions of Example 15-11 with Example 15-9's **ip address 192.168.4.30 255.255.255.240** command, a subcommand under R4's Fa0/1 interface, you can correlate the information. The mask from the **ip address** command can be used to determine the prefix notation version of the same mask—/28. The address and mask together can be used to determine the subnet number of 192.168.4.16. These same pieces of information are highlighted in the output of the **show ip route connected** command in Example 15-11.

Chapter Review

Review Key Topics

Review the most important topics from inside the chapter, noted with the Key Topic icon in the outer margin of the page. Table 15-5 lists a reference of these key topics and the page numbers on which each is found.

Key Topic

Table 15-5 *Key Topics for Chapter 15*

Key Topic Element	Description	Page Number
List	First octet values of addresses that are always reserved and cannot be assigned to hosts	358
Table 15-1	Summary of reasons why an engineer should or should not allow the use of the zero and broadcast subnets	359
List	Summary of four tips when approaching IP addressing related questions on the exams	360
List	Summary of how a host thinks about routing, address assignment, name resolution, and ARP	360
List	Two typical reasons why a host cannot ping other hosts in the same subnet	363
List	Three typical reasons why a host can ping other hosts in the same subnet, but not hosts in other subnets	364
List	Tips regarding how a router matches a packet's destination IP address as part of the routing process	365
Figure 15-3	Shows the IP addresses discovered by the Cisco IOS traceroute command	368
List	Reminders that are helpful when thinking about the source and destination MAC and IP addresses used at various points in an internetwork	377
List	Two key requirements for a router to add a connected route	384

Review Command Reference to Check Your Memory

Table 15-6 lists the EXEC commands used in this chapter and a brief description of their use. Additionally, you might want to review the host commands listed earlier in the chapter in Table 15-3. (This chapter did not introduce any new configuration commands.)

Table 15-6 *Chapter 15* show *and* debug *Command Reference*

Command	Purpose
show sessions	Lists the suspended Telnet and SSH session on the router from which the Telnet and SSH sessions were created
where	Does the same thing as the show sessions command
telnet {*hostname* | *ip_address*}	Connects the CLI to another host using Telnet
ssh –l username {*hostname* | *ip_address*}	Connects the CLI to another host using SSH
disconnect [*connection_number*]	Disconnects a currently suspended Telnet or SSH connection, based on the connection number as seen with the **show sessions** command
resume [*connection_number*]	Connects the CLI to a currently suspended Telnet or SSH connection, based on the connection number as seen with the show sessions command
traceroute {*hostname* | *ip_address*}	Discovers whether a path from the router to a destination IP address is working, listing each next-hop router in the route
Ctrl-Shift-6, x	The key sequence required to suspend a Telnet or SSH connection
show ip arp	Lists the contents of the router's ARP cache
show arp	Lists the contents of the router's ARP cache
show ssh	Lists information about the users logged in to the router using SSH
show users	Lists information about users logged in to the router, including Telnet, SSH, and console users

Answer Review Questions

Answer the following review questions:

1. An internetwork diagram shows a router, R1, with the **ip subnet-zero** command configured. The engineer has typed several configuration commands into a word processor for later pasting into the router's configuration. Which of the following IP addresses could not be assigned to the router's Fa0/0 interface?

   a.   172.16.0.200 255.255.255.128

   b.   172.16.0.200 255.255.255.0

   c.   225.1.1.1 255.255.255.0

   d.   10.43.53.63 255.255.255.192

2. Which of the following is a useful command on some Microsoft OSs for discovering a host's current IP address and mask?

   a.   tracert

   b.   ipconfig /all

   c.   arp -a

   d.   ipconfig /displaydns

3. Examine the following command output. If the user typed the **resume** command, what would happen?

   ```
   R1# show sessions
   Conn Host                    Address            Byte  Idle Conn Name
      1 Fred                    10.1.1.1           0     0    Fred
   *  2 Barney                  10.1.2.1           0     0    Barney
   ```

   a.   The command would be rejected, and the R1 CLI command prompt would be displayed again.

   b.   The CLI user would be connected to a suspended Telnet connection to the router with IP address 10.1.1.1.

   c.   The CLI user would be connected to a suspended Telnet connection to the router with IP address 10.1.2.1.

   d.   The result cannot be accurately predicted from the information shown.

Refer to Figure 15-12 for questions 4–9.

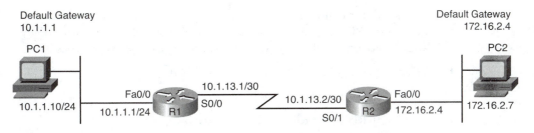

Figure 15-12

4. If PC3 were added to the LAN on the left, with IP address 10.1.1.130/25, default gateway 10.1.1.1, which of the following would be true?

   a. If PC1 issued a **ping 10.1.1.130** command, PC1 would use ARP to learn PC3's MAC address.

   b. If PC3 issued a **ping 10.1.1.10** command, PC3 would ARP trying to learn PC1's MAC address.

   c. If PC1 issued a **ping 10.1.13.1** command, PC1 would ARP trying to learn the MAC address of 10.1.13.1.

   d. If R1 issued a **ping 10.1.1.130** command, R1 would ARP trying to learn the MAC address of 10.1.1.130.

5. A new network engineer is trying to troubleshoot a problem for the user of PC1. Which of the following tasks and results would most likely point to a Layer 1 or 2 Ethernet problem on the LAN on the left side of the figure?

   a. A **ping 10.1.1.1** command on PC1 did not succeed.

   b. A **ping 10.1.13.2** command from PC1 succeeded, but a **ping 172.16.2.4** did not.

   c. A **ping 10.1.1.1** command from PC1 succeeded, but a **ping 10.1.13.1** did not.

   d. A **ping 10.1.1.10** command from PC1 succeeded.

6. The PC2 user issues the **tracert 10.1.1.10** command. Which of the following IP addresses could be shown in the command output?

   a. 10.1.1.10

   b. 10.1.1.1

   c. 10.1.13.1

   d. 10.1.13.2

   e. 172.16.2.4

7. All the devices in the figure just booted, and none of the devices has yet sent any data frames. Both PCs use statically configured IP addresses. Then PC1 successfully pings PC2. Which of the following ARP table entries would you expect to see?

    a. An entry on PC1's ARP cache for IP address 172.16.2.7

    b. An entry on PC1's ARP cache for IP address 10.1.1.1

    c. An entry on R1's ARP cache for IP address 10.1.1.10

    d. An entry on R1's ARP cache for IP address 172.16.2.7

8. All the devices in the figure just booted, and none of the devices has yet sent any data frames. Both PCs use statically configured IP addresses. Then PC1 successfully pings PC2. Which of the following ARP requests would you expect to occur?

    a. PC1 would send an ARP broadcast looking for R1's MAC address of the interface with IP address 10.1.1.1.

    b. PC2 would send an ARP broadcast looking for R2's MAC address of the interface with IP address 172.16.2.4.

    c. R1 would send an ARP broadcast looking for PC1's MAC address.

    d. R2 would send an ARP broadcast looking for PC2's MAC address.

    e. PC1 would send an ARP broadcast looking for PC2's MAC address.

9. PC1 is successfully pinging PC2 in the figure. Which of the following is true about the packets?

    a. The frame going left-to-right, as it crosses the left-side LAN, has a destination MAC address of R1's MAC address.

    b. The frame going left-to-right, as it crosses the right-side LAN, has a destination MAC address of R2's MAC address.

    c. The frame going left-to-right, as it crosses the serial link, has a destination IP address of PC2's IP address.

    d. The frame going right-to-left, as it crosses the left-side LAN, has a source MAC address of PC2's MAC address.

    e. The frame going right-to-left, as it crosses the right-side LAN, has a source MAC address of PC2's MAC address.

    f. The frame going right-to-left, as it crosses the serial link, has a source MAC address of R2's MAC address.

This chapter covers the following subjects:

- **EIGRP Concepts and Operation:** This section explains the concepts behind EIGRP neighbors, exchanging topology information, and calculating routes.

- **EIGRP Configuration and Verification:** This section shows how to configure EIGRP, including authentication and tuning the metric, as well as how to determine the successor and feasible successor routes in the output of **show** commands.

CHAPTER 16

EIGRP Concepts and Configuration

Enhanced Interior Gateway Routing Protocol (EIGRP) provides an impressive set of features and attributes for its main purpose of learning IP routes. EIGRP converges very quickly, on par with or even faster than Open Shortest Path First (OSPF), but without some of the negatives of OSPF. In particular, EIGRP requires much less processing time, much less memory, and much less design effort than OSPF. The only significant negative is that EIGRP is Cisco-proprietary, so if an internetwork uses some non-Cisco routers, EIGRP cannot be used on those routers.

EIGRP does not fit neatly into the general categories of distance vector and link state routing protocols. Sometimes Cisco refers to EIGRP as simply an advanced distance vector protocol, but in other cases, Cisco refers to EIGRP as a new type: a balanced hybrid routing protocol. Regardless of the category, the underlying concepts and processes used by EIGRP might have some similarities with other routing protocols, but EIGRP has far more differences, making EIGRP a unique routing protocol unto itself.

This chapter begins by examining some of the key concepts behind how EIGRP does its work. The second half of this chapter explains EIGRP configuration and verification.

EIGRP Concepts and Operation

Like OSPF, EIGRP follows three general steps to be able to add routes to the IP routing table:

1. **Neighbor discovery:** EIGRP routers send Hello messages to discover potential neighboring EIGRP routers and perform basic parameter checks to determine which routers should become neighbors.
2. **Topology exchange:** Neighbors exchange full topology updates when the neighbor relationship comes up, and then only partial updates as needed based on changes to the network topology.
3. **Choosing routes:** Each router analyzes its respective EIGRP topology tables, choosing the lowest-metric route to reach each subnet.

As a result of these three steps, IOS maintains three important EIGRP tables. The EIGRP neighbor table lists the neighboring routers and is viewed with the **show ip eigrp neighbor** command. The EIGRP topology table holds all the topology information learned from EIGRP neighbors and is displayed with the **show ip eigrp topology** command. Finally, the IP routing table holds all the best routes and is displayed with the **show ip route** command.

The next few sections describe some details about how EIGRP forms neighbor relationships, exchanges routes, and adds entries to the IP routing table. In addition to these three steps, this section explains some unique logic EIGRP uses when converging and reacting to changes in an internetwork—logic that is not seen with the other types of routing protocols.

EIGRP Neighbors

An EIGRP neighbor is another EIGRP-speaking router, connected to a common subnet, with which the router is willing to exchange EIGRP topology information. EIGRP uses EIGRP Hello messages, sent to multicast IP address 224.0.0.10, to dynamically discover potential neighbors. A router learns of potential neighbors by receiving a Hello.

Routers perform some basic checking of each potential neighbor before that router becomes an EIGRP neighbor. A potential neighbor is a router from which an EIGRP Hello has been received. Then the router checks the following settings to determine whether the router should be allowed to be a neighbor:

- It must pass the authentication process.

- It must use the same configured AS number.

- The source IP address used by the neighbors Hello must be in the same subnet.

Note: The router's EIGRP K values must also match, but this topic is outside the scope of this book.

The verification checks are relatively straightforward. If authentication is configured, the two routers must be using the same type of authentication and the same authentication key. EIGRP configuration includes a parameter called an autonomous system number (ASN), which must be the same on two neighboring routers. Finally, the IP addresses used to send the EIGRP Hello messages—the routers' respective interface IP addresses—must be in the range of addresses on the other routers' respective connected subnet.

The EIGRP neighbor relationship is much simpler than OSPF. EIGRP does not have an additional concept of being fully adjacent like OSPF, and there are no neighbor states like OSPF. As soon as an EIGRP neighbor is discovered and passes the basic verification checks, the router becomes a neighbor. At that point, the two routers can begin exchanging topology information. The neighbors send Hellos every EIGRP Hello interval. A router considers its EIGRP neighbor to no longer be reachable after the neighbor's Hellos cease to occur for the number of seconds defined by the EIGRP Hold Timer—the rough equivalent of the OSPF Dead Interval.

Exchanging EIGRP Topology Information

EIGRP uses EIGRP *update messages* to send topology information to neighbors. These Update messages can be sent to multicast IP address 224.0.0.10 if the sending router needs to update multiple routers on the same subnet; otherwise, the updates are sent to the unicast IP address of the particular neighbor. (Hello messages are always sent to the 224.0.0.10 multicast address.) Unlike OSPF, there is no concept of a Designated Router

(DR) or Backup Designated Router (BDR), but the use of multicast packets on LANs allows EIGRP to exchange routing information with all neighbors on the LAN efficiently.

The update messages are sent using *Reliable Transport Protocol (RTP)*. The significance of RTP is that, like OSPF, EIGRP resends routing updates that are lost in transit. By using RTP, EIGRP can better avoid loops.

Note: The acronym RTP also refers to a different protocol, Real-time Transport Protocol (RTP), which is used to transmit voice and video IP packets.

Neighbors use both full routing updates and partial updates, as shown in Figure 16-1. A full update means that a router sends information about all known routes, whereas a partial update includes only information about recently changed routes. Full updates occur when neighbors first come up. After that, the neighbors send only partial updates in reaction to changes to a route. From top to bottom, Figure 16-1 shows neighbor discovery with Hellos, the sending of full updates, the maintenance of the neighbor relationship with ongoing Hellos, and partial updates.

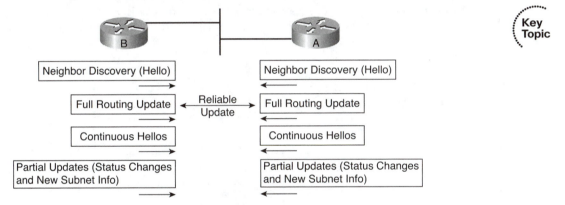

Key Topic

Figure 16-1   *Full and Partial EIGRP Updates*

Calculating the Best Routes for the Routing Table

Metric calculation is one of the more interesting features of EIGRP. EIGRP uses a composite metric, calculated as a function of bandwidth and delay by default. The calculation can also include interface load and interface reliability, although Cisco recommends against using either. EIGRP calculates the metric for each possible route by inserting the values of the composite metric into a formula.

EIGRP's metric calculation formula actually helps describe some of the key points about the metric. The formula, assuming that the default settings use just bandwidth and delay, is as follows:

$$\text{Metric} = \left(\left(\frac{10^7}{\text{least-bandwidth}} \right) + \text{cumulative-delay} \right) * 256$$

In this formula, the term *least-bandwidth* represents the lowest-bandwidth link in the route, using a unit of kilobits per second. For instance, if the slowest link in a route is a 10-Mbps Ethernet link, the first part of the formula is 10^7 / 10^4, which equals 1000. You use 10^4 in the formula because 10 Mbps is equal to 10,000 kbps (10^4 kbps). The cumulative-delay value used in the formula is the sum of all the delay values for all links in the route, with a unit of "tens of microseconds." You can set both bandwidth and delay for each link, using the cleverly named **bandwidth** and **delay** interface subcommands.

Note: Most **show** commands, including **show ip eigrp topology** and **show interfaces,** list delay settings as the number of microseconds of delay. The metric formula uses a unit of tens of microseconds.

EIGRP updates list the subnet number and mask, along with the cumulative delay, minimum bandwidth, along with the other typically unused portions of the composite metric. The router then considers the bandwidth and delay settings on the interface on which the update was received and calculates a new metric. For example, Figure 16-2 shows Albuquerque learning about subnet 10.1.3.0/24 from Seville. The update lists a minimum bandwidth of 100,000 kbps, and a cumulative delay of 100 microseconds. R1 has an interface bandwidth set to 1544 kbps—the default bandwidth on a serial link—and a delay of 20,000 microseconds.

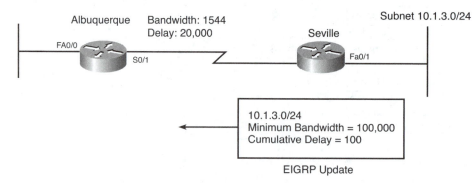

Figure 16-2   *How Albuquerque Calculates Its EIGRP Metric for 10.1.3.0/24*

In this case, Albuquerque discovers that its S0/1 interface bandwidth (1544) is less than the advertised minimum bandwidth of 100,000, so Albuquerque uses this new, slower bandwidth in the metric calculation. (If Albuquerque's S0/1 interface had a bandwidth of 100,000 or more in this case, Albuquerque would instead use the minimum bandwidth listed in the EIGRP Update from Seville.) Albuquerque also adds the interface S0/1 delay (20,000 microseconds, converted to 2000 tens-of-microseconds for the formula) to the cumulative delay received from Seville in the update (100 microseconds, converted to 10 tens-of-microseconds). This results in the following metric calculation:

$$\text{Metric} = \left(\left(\frac{10^7}{1544} \right) + (10 + 2000) \right) * 256 = 2{,}172{,}416$$

Note: IOS rounds down the division in this formula to the nearest integer before performing the rest of the formula. In this case, 10^7 / 1544 is rounded down to 6476.

If multiple possible routes to subnet 10.1.3.0/24 existed, Albuquerque would also calculate the metric for those routes and would choose the route with the best (lowest) metric to be added to the routing table. If the metric is a tie, by default a router would place up to four equal-metric routes into the routing table, sending some traffic over each route. The later section "EIGRP Maximum Paths and Variance" explains a few more details about how EIGRP can add multiple equal-metric routes, and multiple unequal-metric routes, to the routing table.

Feasible Distance and Reported Distance

The example described for Figure 16-2 provides a convenient backdrop to define a couple of EIGRP terms:

- **Feasible Distance (FD):** The metric of the best route to reach a subnet, as calculated on a router

- **Reported Distance (RD):** The metric as calculated on a neighboring router and then reported and learned in an EIGRP Update

Key Topic

For example, in Figure 16-2, Albuquerque calculates an FD of 2,195,631 to reach subnet 10.1.3.0/24 through Seville. Seville also calculates its own metric to reach subnet 10.1.3.0/24. Seville also lists that metric in its EIGRP update sent to Albuquerque. In fact, based on the information in Figure 16-2, Seville's FD to reach subnet 10.1.3.0/24, which is then known by Albuquerque as Seville's RD to reach 10.1.3.0/24, could be easily calculated:

$$\left(\left(\frac{10^7}{100,000}\right) + (10)\right) * 256 = 28,160$$

FD and RD are mentioned in an upcoming discussion of how EIGRP reacts and converges when a change occurs in an internetwork.

Caveats with Bandwidth on Serial Links

EIGRP's robust metric gives it the ability to choose routes that include more router hops but with faster links. However, to ensure that the right routes are chosen, engineers must take care to configure meaningful bandwidth and delay settings. In particular, serial links default to a bandwidth of 1544 and a delay of 20,000 microseconds, as used in the example shown in Figure 16-2. However, IOS cannot automatically change the bandwidth and delay settings based on the Layer 1 speed of a serial link. So, using default bandwidth settings on serial links can lead to problems.

Figure 16-3 shows the problem with using default bandwidth settings and how EIGRP uses the better (faster) route when the bandwidth is set correctly. The figure focuses on router B's route to subnet 10.1.1.0/24 in each case. In the top part of the figure, all serial interfaces use defaults, even though the top serial link is a slow 64 kbps. The bottom figure shows the results when the slow serial link's **bandwidth** command is changed to reflect the correct (slow) speed.

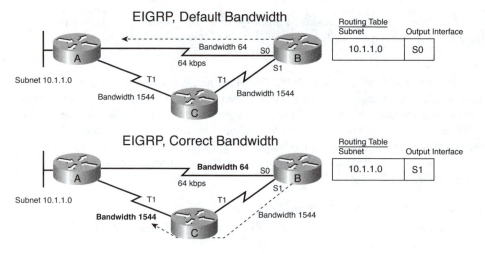

Figure 16-3   *Impact of the Bandwidth on EIGRP's Metric Calculation*

EIGRP Convergence

Loop avoidance poses one of the most difficult problems with any dynamic routing protocol. Distance vector protocols overcome this problem with a variety of tools, some of which create a large portion of the minutes-long convergence time after a link failure. Link-state protocols overcome this problem by having each router keep a full topology of the network, so by running a rather involved mathematical model, a router can avoid any loops.

EIGRP avoids loops by keeping some basic topological information, but it avoids spending too much CPU and memory by keeping the information brief. When a router learns multiple routes to the same subnet, it puts the best route in the IP routing table. EIGRP keeps some topological information for the same reason as OSPF—so that it can very quickly converge and use a new route without causing a loop. Essentially, EIGRP keeps a record of each possible next-hop router, and some details related to those routes, but no information about the topology beyond the next-hop routers. This sparser topology information does not require the sophisticated SPF algorithm, resulting in quick convergence and less overhead, with no loops.

The EIGRP convergence process uses one of two branches in its logic, based on whether the failed route does or does not have a *feasible successor* route. If a feasible successor route exists, the router can immediately use that route. If not, the router must use a *query and response* process to find a loop-free alternative route. Both processes result in fast convergence, typically quicker than 10 seconds, but the query and response process takes slightly longer.

EIGRP Successors and Feasible Successors

EIGRP calculates the metric for each route to reach each subnet. For a particular subnet, the route with the best metric is called the successor, with the router filling the IP routing table with this route. (This route's metric is called the feasible distance, as introduced earlier.)

Of the other routes to reach that same subnet—routes whose metrics were larger than the FD for the route—EIGRP needs to determine which can be used immediately if the currently best route fails, without causing a routing loop. EIGRP runs a simple algorithm to identify which routes could be used, keeping these loop-free backup routes in its topology table and using them if the currently best route fails. These alternative, immediately usable routes are called *feasible successor* routes, because they can feasibly be used when the successor route fails. A router determines if a route is a feasible successor based on the feasibility condition:

If a nonsuccessor route's RD is less than the FD, the route is a feasible successor route.

Although it is technically correct, this definition is much more understandable with the example shown in Figure 16-4. The figure illustrates how EIGRP figures out which routes are feasible successors for subnet 1. In the figure, Router E learns three routes to Subnet 1, from Routers B, C, and D. After calculating each route's metric, based on bandwidth and delay information received in the routing update and on E's corresponding outgoing interfaces, Router E finds that the route through Router D has the lowest metric, so Router E adds that route to its routing table, as shown. The FD is the metric calculated for this route, which is a value of 14,000 in this case.

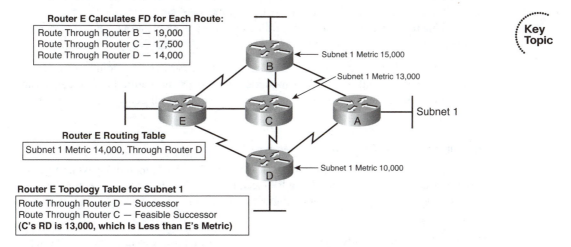

Key
Topic

Figure 16-4 *Successors and Feasible Successors with EIGRP*

EIGRP decides whether a route can be a feasible successor if the reported distance for that route (the metric as calculated on that neighbor) is less than its own best computed metric (the FD). When that neighbor has a lower metric for its route to the subnet in question, that route is said to have met the *feasibility condition*. For example, Router E computes a metric (FD) of 14,000 on its best route (through Router D). Router C's computed metric—its reported distance for this route—is lower than 14,000 (it's 13,000). As a result, E knows that C's best route for this subnet could not possibly point toward router E, so Router E believes that it could start using the route through Router C and not cause a loop. As a result, Router E adds a route through Router C to the topology table as a feasible successor route. Conversely, Router B's reported distance is 15,000, which is larger than Router E's FD of 14,000, so Router E does not consider the route through Router B a feasible successor.

If the route to Subnet 1 through Router D fails, Router E can immediately put the route through Router C into the routing table without fear of creating a loop. Convergence occurs almost instantly in this case.

The Query and Reply Process

When a route fails and has no feasible successor, EIGRP uses a distributed algorithm called *Diffusing Update Algorithm (DUAL)*. DUAL sends queries looking for a loop-free route to the subnet in question. When the new route is found, DUAL adds it to the routing table.

The EIGRP DUAL process simply uses messages to confirm that a route exists, and would not create a loop, before deciding to replace a failed route with an alternative route. For instance, in Figure 16-4, imagine that both Routers C and D fail. Router E does not have a feasible successor route for subnet 1, but there is an obvious physically available path through Router B. To use the route, Router E sends EIGRP *query* messages to its working neighbors (in this case, Router B). Router B's route to subnet 1 is still working fine, so Router B replies to Router E with an EIGRP *reply* message, simply stating the details of the working route to subnet 1 and confirming that it is still viable. Router E can then add a new route to subnet 1 to its routing table, without fear of a loop.

Replacing a failed route with a feasible successor takes a very short amount of time, typically less than a second or two. When queries and replies are required, convergence can take slightly longer, but in most networks, convergence can still occur in less than 10 seconds.

EIGRP Summary and Comparisons with OSPF

EIGRP is a popular IGP for many reasons. It works well, converging quickly while avoiding loops as a side effect of its underlying balanced hybrid/advanced distance vector algorithms. It does not require a lot of configuration or a lot of planning, even when scaling to support larger internetworks.

EIGRP also has another advantage that is not as important today as in years past: the support of Novell's IPX and Apple's AppleTalk Layer 3 protocols. Routers can run EIGRP to learn IP routes, IPX routes, and AppleTalk routes, with the same wonderful performance features. However, like many other Layer 3 protocols, IP has mostly usurped IPX and AppleTalk, making support for these Layer 3 protocols a minor advantage.

Table 16-1 summarizes several important features of EIGRP as compared to OSPF.

Table 16-1   *EIGRP Features Compared to OSPF*

Feature	EIGRP	OSPF
Converges quickly	Yes	Yes
Built-in loop prevention	Yes	Yes

Table 16-1 *EIGRP Features Compared to OSPF*

Feature	EIGRP	OSPF
Sends partial routing updates, advertising only new or changed information	Yes	Yes
Classless; therefore, supports manual summarization and VLSM	Yes	Yes
Allows manual summarization at any router	Yes	No
Sends routing information using IP multicast on LANs	Yes	Yes
Uses the concept of a designated router on a LAN	No	Yes
Flexible network design with no need to create areas	Yes	No
Supports both equal-metric and unequal-metric load balancing	Yes	No
Robust metric based on bandwidth and delay	Yes	No
Can advertise IP, IPX, and AppleTalk routes	Yes	No
Public standard	No	Yes

EIGRP Configuration and Verification

Basic EIGRP configuration closely resembles RIP and OSPF configuration. The **router eigrp** command enables EIGRP and puts the user in EIGRP configuration mode, in which one or more **network** commands are configured. For each interface matched by a **network** command, EIGRP tries to discover neighbors on that interface, and EIGRP advertises the subnet connected to the interface.

This section examines EIGRP configuration, including several optional features. It also explains the meaning of the output of many **show** commands to help connect the theory covered in the first part of this chapter with the reality of the EIGRP implementation in IOS. The following configuration checklist outlines the main configuration tasks covered in this chapter:

Step 1. Enter EIGRP configuration mode, and define the EIGRP ASN by using the **router eigrp** *as-number* global command.

Step 2. Configure one or more **network** *ip-address* [*wildcard-mask*] router subcommands. This enables EIGRP on any matched interface and causes EIGRP to advertise the connected subnet.

Step 3. (Optional) Change the interface Hello and hold timers using the **ip hello-interval eigrp** *asn time* and **ip hold-time eigrp** *asn time* interface subcommands.

Step 4. (Optional) Impact metric calculations by tuning bandwidth and delay using the **bandwidth** *value* and **delay** *value* interface subcommands.

Step 5. (Optional) Configure EIGRP authentication.

Step 6. (Optional) Configure support for multiple equal-cost routes using the **maximum-paths** *number* and **variance** *multiplier* router subcommands.

Basic EIGRP Configuration

Example 16-1 shows a sample EIGRP configuration, along with **show** commands, on Albuquerque in Figure 16-5. The EIGRP configuration required on Yosemite and Seville matches exactly the two lines of EIGRP configuration on Albuquerque.

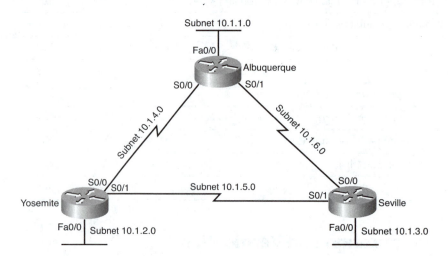

Figure 16-5   *Sample Internetwork Used in Most of the EIGRP Examples*

Example 16-1   *Sample Router Configuration with EIGRP Enabled*

```
router eigrp 1
network 10.0.0.0
Albuquerque# show ip route
Codes: C - connected, S - static, I - IGRP, R - RIP, M - mobile, B - BGP
       D - EIGRP, EX - EIGRP external, O - OSPF, IA - OSPF inter area
       N1 - OSPF NSSA external type 1, N2 - OSPF NSSA external type 2
       E1 - OSPF external type 1, E2 - OSPF external type 2, E - EGP
       i - IS-IS, L1 - IS-IS level-1, L2 - IS-IS level-2, ia - IS-IS inter area
       * - candidate default, U - per-user static route, o - ODR
       P - periodic downloaded static route

Gateway of last resort is not set

     10.0.0.0/24 is subnetted, 6 subnets
D       10.1.3.0 [90/2172416] via 10.1.6.3, 00:00:43, Serial0/1
D       10.1.2.0 [90/2172416] via 10.1.4.2, 00:00:43, Serial0/0
C       10.1.1.0 is directly connected, FastEthernet0/0
C       10.1.6.0 is directly connected, Serial0/1
D       10.1.5.0 [90/2681856] via 10.1.6.3, 00:00:45, Serial0/1
                 [90/2681856] via 10.1.4.2, 00:00:45, Serial0/0
C       10.1.4.0 is directly connected, Serial0/0
```

```
Albuquerque# show ip route eigrp
     10.0.0.0/24 is subnetted, 6 subnets
D        10.1.3.0 [90/2172416] via 10.1.6.3, 00:00:47, Serial0/1
D        10.1.2.0 [90/2172416] via 10.1.4.2, 00:00:47, Serial0/0
D        10.1.5.0 [90/2681856] via 10.1.6.3, 00:00:49, Serial0/1
                  [90/2681856] via 10.1.4.2, 00:00:49, Serial0/0


Albuquerque# show ip eigrp neighbors
IP-EIGRP neighbors for process 1
H    Address                  Interface    Hold Uptime   SRTT   RTO  Q  Seq Type
                                           (sec)         (ms)       Cnt Num
0    10.1.4.2                 Se0/0        11 00:00:54   32     200  0  4
1    10.1.6.3                 Se0/1        12 00:10:36   20     200  0  24

Albuquerque# show ip eigrp interfaces
IP-EIGRP interfaces for process 1


                     Xmit Queue   Mean   Pacing Time   Multicast    Pending
Interface    Peers   Un/Reliable  SRTT   Un/Reliable   Flow Timer   Routes
Fa0/0        0       0/0          0      0/10          0            0
Se0/0        1       0/0          32     0/15          50           0
Se0/1        1       0/0          20     0/15          95           0
Albuquerque# show ip eigrp topology summary
IP-EIGRP Topology Table for AS(1)/ID(10.1.6.1)
Head serial 1, next serial 9
6 routes, 0 pending replies, 0 dummies
IP-EIGRP(0) enabled on 3 interfaces, 2 neighbors present on 2 interfaces
Quiescent interfaces:  Se0/1/0 Se0/0/1
```

For EIGRP configuration, all three routers must use the same AS number in the **router eigrp** command. For instance, they all use **router eigrp 1** in this example. The actual number used doesn't really matter, as long as it is the same on all three routers. (The range of valid AS numbers is 1 through 65,535, as is the range of valid Process IDs with the **router ospf** command.) The **network 10.0.0.0** command enables EIGRP on all interfaces whose IP addresses are in network 10.0.0.0, which includes all three interfaces on Albuquerque. With the identical two EIGRP configuration statements on the other two routers, EIGRP is enabled on all three interfaces on those routers as well, because those interfaces are also in network 10.0.0.0.

The **show ip route** and **show ip route eigrp** commands both list the EIGRP-learned routes with a "D" beside them. "D" signifies EIGRP. The letter E was already being used for Exterior Gateway Protocol (EGP) when Cisco created EIGRP, so Cisco chose the next-closest unused letter, D, to denote EIGRP-learned routes.

You can see information about EIGRP neighbors with the **show ip eigrp neighbors** command and information about the number of active neighbors (called peers in the command output) with the **show ip eigrp interfaces** command, as shown in the last part of the example. These commands also provide some insight into EIGRP's underlying processes, such as the use of RTP for reliable transmission. For instance, the **show ip eigrp neighbors** command shows a "Q Cnt" (Queue Count) column, listing either the number of packets waiting to be sent to a neighbor or packets that have been sent but for which no acknowledgment has been received. The **show ip eigrp interfaces** command lists similar information in the "Xmit Queue Un/Reliable" column, which separates statistics for EIGRP messages that are sent with RTP (reliable) or without it (unreliable).

Finally, the end of the example displays Albuquerque's RID. EIGRP allocates its RID just like OSPF—based on the configured value, or the highest IP address of an up/up loopback interface, or the highest IP address of a nonloopback interface, in that order of precedence. The only difference compared to OSPF is that the EIGRP RID is configured with the **eigrp router-id** *value* router subcommand.

The EIGRP **network** command can be configured without a wildcard mask, as shown in Example 16-1. Without a wildcard mask, the **network** command must use a classful network as the lone parameter, and all interfaces in the classful network are matched. Example 16-2 shows an alternative configuration that uses a **network** command with an address and wildcard mask. In this case, the command matches an interface IP address that would be matched if the address and mask in the **network** command were part of an ACL. The example shows three **network** commands on Albuquerque, one matching each of the three interfaces.

Example 16-2 *Using Wildcard Masks with EIGRP Configuration*

```
Albuquerque# router eigrp 1
Albuquerque(config-router)# network 10.1.1.0 0.0.0.255
Albuquerque(config-router)# network 10.1.4.0 0.0.0.255
Albuquerque(config-router)# network 10.1.6.0 0.0.0.255
```

EIGRP Metrics, Successors, and Feasible Successors

As defined earlier in this chapter, an EIGRP successor route is a route that has the best metric for reaching a subnet, and a Feasible Successor (FS) route is a route that could be used if the successor route failed. This section examines how to see successor and FS routes with EIGRP, along with the calculated metrics. To that end, Example 16-3 shows Albuquerque's single best route to reach subnet 10.1.3.0/24, both in the routing table and as the successor route in the EIGRP topology table. It also lists the two equal-metric successor routes for subnet 10.1.5.0/24, with both of these successor routes being highlighted in the EIGRP topology table. Some of the explanations are listed in the example, and the longer explanations follow the example.

Example 16-3 *Using Wildcard Masks with EIGRP Configuration, and Feasible Successor Examination*

```
! Below, note the single route to subnet 10.1.3.0, and the two
! equal-metric routes to 10.1.5.0.
Albuquerque# show ip route
```

```
Codes: C - connected, S - static, R - RIP, M - mobile, B - BGP
       D - EIGRP, EX - EIGRP external, O - OSPF, IA - OSPF inter area
       N1 - OSPF NSSA external type 1, N2 - OSPF NSSA external type 2
       E1 - OSPF external type 1, E2 - OSPF external type 2
       i - IS-IS, L1 - IS-IS level-1, L2 - IS-IS level-2, ia - IS-IS inter area
       * - candidate default, U - per-user static route, o - ODR
       P - periodic downloaded static route

Gateway of last resort is not set

     10.0.0.0/24 is subnetted, 6 subnets
D       10.1.3.0 [90/2172416] via 10.1.6.3, 00:00:57, Serial0/1
D       10.1.2.0 [90/2172416] via 10.1.4.2, 00:00:57, Serial0/0
C       10.1.1.0 is directly connected, Ethernet0/0
C       10.1.6.0 is directly connected, Serial0/1
D       10.1.5.0 [90/2681856] via 10.1.4.2, 00:00:57, Serial0/0
                 [90/2681856] via 10.1.6.3, 00:00:57, Serial0/1
C       10.1.4.0 is directly connected, Serial0/0
! Next, the EIGRP topology table shows one successor for the route to 10.1.3.0,
! and two successors for 10.1.5.0, reconfirming that EIGRP installs successor
! routes (not feasible successor routes) into the IP routing table.
Albuquerque# show ip eigrp topology
IP-EIGRP Topology Table for AS(1)/ID(10.1.6.1)

Codes: P - Passive, A - Active, U - Update, Q - Query, R - Reply,
       r - reply Status, s - sia Status

P 10.1.3.0/24, 1 successors, FD is 2172416
        via 10.1.6.3 (2172416/28160), Serial0/1
P 10.1.2.0/24, 1 successors, FD is 2172416
        via 10.1.4.2 (2172416/28160), Serial0/0
P 10.1.1.0/24, 1 successors, FD is 281600
        via Connected, Ethernet0/0
P 10.1.6.0/24, 1 successors, FD is 2169856
        via Connected, Serial0/1
P 10.1.5.0/24, 2 successors, FD is 2681856
        via 10.1.4.2 (2681856/2169856), Serial0/0
        via 10.1.6.3 (2681856/2169856), Serial0/1
P 10.1.4.0/24, 1 successors, FD is 2169856
        via Connected, Serial0/0
```

The comments in the example explain the main key points, most of which are relatively straightforward. However, a closer look at the **show ip eigrp topology** command can provide a few insights. First, focus on the EIGRP topology table's listing of the number of successor routes. The entry for 10.1.3.0/24 states that there is one successor, so the IP routing table lists one EIGRP-learned route for subnet 10.1.3.0/24. In comparison, the

EIGRP topology table entry for subnet 10.1.5.0/24 states that two successors exist, so the IP routing table shows two EIGRP-learned routes for that subnet.

Next, focus on the numbers in brackets for the EIGRP topology table entry for 10.1.3.0/24. The first number is the metric calculated by Albuquerque for each route. The second number is the RD—the metric as calculated on neighboring router 10.1.6.3 (Seville) and as reported to Albuquerque. Because these routers have defaulted all bandwidth and delay settings, the metric values match the sample metric calculations shown in the earlier section "Calculating the Best Routes for the Routing Table."

Creating and Viewing a Feasible Successor Route

With all default settings in this internetwork, none of Albuquerque's routes meet the feasibility condition, in which an alternative route's RD is less than or equal to the FD (the metric of the best route). Example 16-4 changes the bandwidth on one of Yosemite's interfaces, lowering Yosemite's FD to reach subnet 10.1.3.0/24. In turn, Yosemite's RD for this same route, as reported to Albuquerque, will now be lower, meeting the feasibility condition, so Albuquerque will now have an FS route.

Example 16-4   *Creating a Feasible Successor Route on Albuquerque*

```
! Below, the bandwidth of Yosemite's link to Seville (Yosemite's S0/1 interface)
! is changed from 1544 to 2000, which lowers Yosemite's metric for
! subnet 10.1.3.0.
Yosemite(config)# interface S0/1
Yosemite(config-if)# bandwidth 2000
! Moving back to Albuquerque
! Below, the EIGRP topology table shows a single successor route for 10.1.3.0,
! but two entries listed - the new entry is a feasible successor route. The new
! entry shows a route to 10.1.3.0 through 10.1.4.2 (which is Yosemite).
Albuquerque# show ip eigrp topology
IP-EIGRP Topology Table for AS(1)/ID(10.1.6.1)

Codes: P - Passive, A - Active, U - Update, Q - Query, R - Reply,
       r - reply Status, s - sia Status


P 10.1.3.0/24, 1 successors, FD is 2172416
        via 10.1.6.3 (2172416/28160), Serial0/1
        via 10.1.4.2 (2684416/1794560), Serial0/0
! the rest of the lines omitted for brevity
! Moving back to Yosemite here
Yosemite# show ip route eigrp
     10.0.0.0/24 is subnetted, 5 subnets
D       10.1.3.0 [90/1794560] via 10.1.5.3, 00:40:14, Serial0/1
D       10.1.1.0 [90/2195456] via 10.1.4.1, 00:42:19, Serial0/0
```

To see the feasible successor route, and why it is a feasible successor, look at the two numbers in parentheses in the second highlighted line from the **show ip eigrp topology** command on Albuquerque. The first of these is Albuquerque's router's calculated metric for the route, and the second number is the neighbor's RD. Of the two possible routes—one through 10.1.6.3 (Seville) and one through 10.1.4.2 (Yosemite)—the route through Seville has the lowest metric (2,172,416), making it the successor route, and making the FD also be 2,172,416. Albuquerque puts this route into the IP routing table. However, note the RD on the second of the two routes (the route through Yosemite), with an RD value of 1,794,560. The feasibility condition is that the route's RD must be smaller than that router's best calculated metric—its FD—for that same destination subnet. So, the route through Yosemite meets this condition, making it a feasible successor route. The following points summarize the key information about the successor and feasible successor routes in this example:

■ The route to 10.1.3.0 through 10.1.6.3 (Seville) is the successor route, because the calculated metric (2,172,416), shown as the first of the two numbers in parentheses, is the best calculated metric.

■ The route to 10.1.3.0 through 10.1.4.2 (Yosemite) is a feasible successor route, because the neighbor's Reported Distance (1,794,560, shown as the second number in parentheses) is lower than Albuquerque's FD.

■ Although both the successor and feasible successor routes are in the EIGRP topology table, only the successor route is added to the IP routing table.

Note: The **show ip eigrp topology** command lists only successor and feasible successor routes. To see other routes, use the **show ip eigrp topology all-links** command.

Convergence Using the Feasible Successor Route

One of the advantages of EIGRP is that it converges very quickly. Example 16-5 shows one such example, using **debug** messages to show the process. Some of the **debug** messages might not make a lot of sense, but the example does highlight a few interesting and understandable **debug** messages.

For this example, the link between Albuquerque and Seville is shut down, but this is not shown in the example. The **debug** messages on Albuquerque show commentary about EIGRP's logic in changing from the original route for 10.1.3.0/24 to the new route through Yosemite. Pay particular attention to the time stamps, which show that the convergence process takes less than 1 second.

Example 16-5 *Debug Messages During Convergence to the Feasible Successor Route for Subnet 10.1.3.0/24*

```
!!!!!!!!!!!!!!!!!!!!!!!!!!!!!!!!!!!!!!!!!!!!!!!!!!!!!!!!!!!!!!!!!!!!!!!!!!!!!!!!!!!!!!
! Below, debug eigrp fsm is enabled, and then Seville's link to Albuquerque
! (Seville's S0/0 interface) will be disabled, but not shown in the example text.
! SOME DEBUG MESSAGES are omitted to improve readability.
Albuquerque# debug eigrp fsm
EIGRP FSM Events/Actions debugging is on
Albuquerque#
```

```
*Mar  1 02:35:31.836: %LINK-3-UPDOWN: Interface Serial0/1, changed state to down
*Mar  1 02:35:31.848: DUAL: rcvupdate: 10.1.6.0/24 via Connected metric 42949672
  95/4294967295
*Mar  1 02:35:31.848: DUAL: Find FS for dest 10.1.6.0/24. FD is 2169856, RD is 2
  169856
*Mar  1 02:35:31.848: DUAL: 0.0.0.0 metric 4294967295/4294967295 not found D
  min is 4294967295
*Mar  1 02:35:31.848: DUAL: Peer total/stub 2/0 template/full-stub 2/0
*Mar  1 02:35:31.848: DUAL: Dest 10.1.6.0/24 entering active state.
*Mar  1 02:35:31.852: DUAL: Set reply-status table. Count is 2.
*Mar  1 02:35:31.852: DUAL: Not doing split horizon
!
! Next, Albuquerque realizes that neighbor 10.1.6.3 (Seville) is down, so
! Albuquerque can react.
!
*Mar  1 02:35:31.852: %DUAL-5-NBRCHANGE: IP-EIGRP(0) 1: Neighbor 10.1.6.3
  (Serial0/1) is down: interface down
!
! The next two highlighted messages imply that the old route to 10.1.3.0 is
! removed, and the new successor route (previously the feasible successor route)
! is added to the "RT" (routing table).
!
*Mar  1 02:35:31.852: DUAL: Destination 10.1.3.0/24
*Mar  1 02:35:31.852: DUAL: Find FS for dest 10.1.3.0/24. FD is 2172416,
  RD is 2172416
*Mar  1 02:35:31.856: DUAL: 10.1.6.3 metric 4294967295/4294967295
*Mar  1 02:35:31.856: DUAL: 10.1.4.2 metric 2684416/1794560 found Dmin is 2684416
!
! The next two highlighted messages state that the old route is removed, and the
! new route through Yosemite is added to the "RT" (routing table).
!
*Mar  1 02:35:31.856: DUAL: Removing dest 10.1.3.0/24, nexthop 10.1.6.3
*Mar  1 02:35:31.856: DUAL: RT installed 10.1.3.0/24 via 10.1.4.2
*Mar  1 02:35:31.856: DUAL: Send update about 10.1.3.0/24.  Reason: metric chg
*Mar  1 02:35:31.860: DUAL: Send update about 10.1.3.0/24.  Reason: new if
```

EIGRP Authentication

EIGRP supports one type of authentication: MD5. Configuring MD5 authentication requires several steps:

Key Topic

Step 1.   Create an (authentication) key chain:

  a.   Create the chain and give it a name with the **key chain** *name* global command (this also puts the user into key chain config mode).

  b.   Create one or more key numbers using the **key** *number* command in key chain configuration mode.

  c. Define the authentication key's value using the **key-string** *value* command in key configuration mode.

  d. (Optional) Define the lifetime (time period) for both sending and accepting this particular key.

Step 2. Enable EIGRP MD5 authentication on an interface, for a particular EIGRP ASN, using the **ip authentication mode eigrp** *asn* **md5** interface subcommand.

Step 3. Refer to the correct key chain to be used on an interface using the **ip authentication key-chain eigrp** *asn name-of-chain* interface subcommand.

The configuration in Step 1 is fairly detailed, but Steps 2 and 3 are relatively simple. Essentially, IOS configures the key values separately, then requires an interface subcommand to refer to the key values. To support the ability to have multiple keys, and even multiple sets of keys, the configuration includes the concept of a key chain and multiple keys on each key chain.

The IOS key chain concept resembles key chains and keys used in everyday life. Most people have at least one key chain, with the keys they typically use every day. If you have a lot of keys for work and home, you might have two key chains to make it a little easier to find the right key. You might even have a key chain with seldom-used keys that you keep on a shelf somewhere. Similarly, IOS allows lets you configure multiple key chains so that different key chains can be used on different interfaces. Each key chain can include multiple keys. Having multiple keys in one key chain allows neighbors to still be up and working while the keys are being changed. (As with all passwords and authentication keys, changing the keys occasionally enhances security.) To configure these main details, follow Steps 1a, 1b, and 1c to create the key chain, create one or more keys, and assign the text key (password).

The last and optional item that can be configured for EIGRP authentication is the useful lifetime of each key. If this isn't configured, the key is valid forever. However, if it is configured, the router uses the key only during the listed times. This feature allows the key chain to include several keys, each with different successive lifetimes. For example, 12 keys could be defined, one for each month of the year. The routers then automatically use the lowest-numbered key whose time range is valid, changing keys automatically every month in this example. This feature allows an engineer to configure the keys once and have the routers use new keys occasionally, improving security.

To support the useful lifetime concept, a router must know the time and date. Routers can set the time and date with the **clock set** EXEC command. Routers can also use Network Time Protocol (NTP), a protocol that allows routers to synchronize their time-of-day clocks.

The best way to appreciate the configuration is to see an example. Example 16-6 shows a sample configuration that uses two key chains. Key chain "fred" has two keys, each with different lifetimes, so that the router will use new keys automatically over time. It also shows the two key chains being referenced on two different interfaces.

Example 16-6   *EIGRP Authentication*

```
! Chain "carkeys" will be used on R1's Fa0/0 interface. R1 will use key "fred"
! for about a month and then start using "wilma."
!
key chain carkeys
  key 1
  key-string fred
  accept-lifetime 08:00:00 Jan 11 2005 08:00:00 Feb 11 2005
  send-lifetime 08:00:00 Jan 11 2005 08:00:00 Feb 11 2005
 key 2
  key-string wilma
  accept-lifetime 08:00:00 Feb 10 2005 08:00:00 Mar 11 2005
  send-lifetime 08:00:00 Feb 10 2005 08:00:00 Mar 11 2005
! Next, key chain "anothersetofkeys" defines the key to be used on
! interface Fa0/1.
key chain anothersetofkeys
 key 1
 key-string barney
!
! Next, R1's interface subcommands are shown. First, the key chain is referenced
! using the ip authentication key-chain command, and the ip authentication mode
  eigrp
! command causes the router to use an MD5 digest of the key string.
interface FastEthernet0/0
ip address 172.31.11.1 255.255.255.0
ip authentication mode eigrp 1 md5
ip authentication key-chain eigrp 1 carkeys
!
! Below, R1 enables EIGRP authentication on interface Fa0/1,
! using the other key chain.
interface FastEthernet0/1
 ip address 172.31.12.1 255.255.255.0
ip authentication eigrp 1 md5
ip authentication key-chain eigrp 1 anothersetofkeys
```

For authentication to work, neighboring routers must both have EIGRP MD5 authentication enabled, and the key strings they currently use must match. Note that the key chain name does not need to match. The most common problems relate to when the useful lifetime settings do not match, or one of the router's clocks has the wrong time. For real-life implementations, NTP should be enabled and used before restricting keys to a particular time frame.

To verify that the authentication worked, use the **show ip eigrp neighbors** command. If the authentication fails, the neighbor relationship will not form. Also, if you see routes learned from a neighbor on that interface, it also proves that authentication worked. You can see more details about the authentication process using the **debug eigrp packets** command, particularly if the authentication fails.

EIGRP Maximum Paths and Variance

Like OSPF, EIGRP supports the ability to put multiple equal-metric routes in the routing table. Like OSPF, EIGRP defaults to support four such routes for each subnet, and it can be configured to support up to 16 using the **maximum-paths** *number* EIGRP subcommand. However, EIGRP's metric calculation often prevents competing routes from having the exact same metric. The formula can result in similar metrics, but given that the metric values can easily be in the millions, calculating the exact same metric is statistically unlikely.

IOS includes the concept of EIGRP variance to overcome this problem. Variance allows routes whose metrics are relatively close in value to be considered equal, allowing multiple unequal-metric routes to the same subnet to be added to the routing table.

The **variance** *multiplier* EIGRP router subcommand defines an integer between 1 and 128. The router then multiplies the variance times a route's FD—the best metric with which to reach that subnet. Any FS routes whose metric is less than the product of the variance times the FD are considered to be equal routes and can be placed in the routing table, depending on the setting of the **maximum-paths** command.

An example of variance can make this concept clear. To keep the numbers more obvious, Table 16-2 lists an example with small metric values. The table lists the metric for three routes to the same subnet, as calculated on router R4. The table also lists the neighboring routers' RD, and the decision to add routes to the routing table based on various variance settings.

Table 16-2   *Example of Routes Chosen as Equal Because of Variance*

Next Hop	Metric	RD	Added to RT at Variance 1?	Added to RT at Variance 2?	Added to RT at Variance 3?
R1	50	30	Yes	Yes	Yes
R2	90	40	No	Yes	Yes
R3	120	60	No	No	No

Before considering the variance, note that in this case, the route through R1 is the successor route because it has the lowest metric. This also means that the metric for the route through R1, 50, is the FD. The route through R2 is an FS route because its RD of 40 is less than the FD of 50. The route through R3 is not an FS route, because R3's RD of 60 is more than the FD of 50.

At a default variance setting of 1, the metrics must be exactly equal to be considered equal, so only the successor route is added to the routing table. With variance 2, the FD (50) is multiplied by the variance (2) for a product of 100. The route through R2, with FD 90, is less than 100, so R4 adds the route through R2 to the routing table as well. The router can then load-balance traffic across these two routes.

In the third case, with variance 3, the product of the FD (50) times 3 results in a product of 150, and all three routes' calculated metrics are less than 150. However, the route through R3 is not an FS route, so it cannot be added to the routing table for fear of causing a routing loop.

The following list summarizes the key points about variance:

Key Topic

- The variance is multiplied by the current FD (the metric of the best route to reach the subnet).

- Any FS routes whose calculated metric is less than or equal to the product of variance times the FD are added to the IP routing table, assuming that the **maximum-paths** setting allows more routes.

- Routes that are neither successor nor feasible successor can never be added to the IP routing table, regardless of the variance setting.

As soon as the routes have been added to the routing table, the router supports a variety of options for how to load-balance traffic across the routes. The router can balance the traffic proportionally with the metrics, meaning that lower metric routes send more packets. The router can send all traffic over the lowest-metric route, with the other routes just being in the routing table for faster convergence in case the best route fails. However, the details of the load-balancing process require a much deeper discussion of the internals of the forwarding process in IOS, and this topic is outside the scope of this book.

Tuning the EIGRP Metric Calculation

By default, EIGRP calculates an integer metric based on the composite metric of bandwidth and delay. Both settings can be changed on any interface using the **bandwidth** *value* and the **delay** *value* interface subcommands.

Cisco recommends setting each interface's bandwidth to an accurate value, rather than setting the bandwidth to change EIGRP's metric calculation. Although LAN interfaces default to accurate bandwidth settings, router serial links should be configured with the **bandwidth** *speed* command, with a speed value in kbps, matching the interface's actual speed.

Because fewer features rely on the interface delay setting, Cisco recommends that if you want to tune EIGRP metric, change the interface delay settings. To change an interface's delay setting, use the **delay** *value* command, where the value is the delay setting with an unusual unit: tens-of-microseconds. Interestingly, the EIGRP metric formula also uses the unit of tens-of-microseconds; however, **show** commands list the delay with a unit of microseconds. Example 16-7 shows an example, with the following details:

1. The router's Fa0/0 has a default delay setting of 100 microseconds (usec).
2. The **delay 123** command is configured on the interface, meaning 123 tens-of-microseconds.
3. The **show interfaces fa0/0** command now lists a delay of 1230 microseconds.

Example 16-7   *Configuring Interface Delay*

```
Yosemite# show interfaces fa0/0
FastEthernet0/0 is up, line protocol is up
  Hardware is Gt96k FE, address is 0013.197b.5026 (bia 0013.197b.5026)
  Internet address is 10.1.2.252/24
  MTU 1500 bytes, BW 100000 Kbit, DLY 100 usec,
! lines omitted for brevity


Yosemite# configure terminal
Enter configuration commands, one per line.  End with CNTL/Z.
Yosemite(config)# interface fa0/0
Yosemite(config-if)# delay 123
Yosemite(config-if)# ^Z


Yosemite# show interfaces fa0/0
FastEthernet0/0 is up, line protocol is up
  Hardware is Gt96k FE, address is 0013.197b.5026 (bia 0013.197b.5026)
  Internet address is 10.1.2.252/24
  MTU 1500 bytes, BW 100000 Kbit, DLY 1230 usec,
! lines omitted for brevity
```

Chapter Review

Review Key Topics

Review the most important topics from this chapter, noted with the Key Topic icons. Table 16-3 lists these key topics and where each is discussed.

Table 16-3   *Key Topics for Chapter 16*

Key Topic Element	Description	Page Number
List	Reasons why EIGRP routers are prevented from becoming neighbors	394
Figure 16-1	Depicts the normal progression through neighbor discovery, full routing updates, ongoing Hellos, and partial updates	395
List	Definitions of Feasible Distance and Reported Distance	397
Figure 16-4	Example of how routers determine which routes are feasible successors	399
Table 16-1	Comparisons of EIGRP and OSPF features	400
List	EIGRP configuration checklist	401
List	Key points about how to determine a feasible successor route from **show** command output	407
List	EIGRP MD5 authentication configuration checklist	408
List	Key points about EIGRP variance	412

Define Key Terms

Define the following key terms from this chapter, and check your answers in the glossary:

feasibility condition, feasible distance, feasible successor, full update, partial update, reported distance, successor

Review Command Reference to Check Your Memory

Although you should not necessarily memorize the information in the tables in this section, this section does include a reference for the configuration and EXEC commands covered in this chapter. Practically speaking, you should memorize the commands as a side effect of reading the chapter and doing all the activities in this "Chapter Review" section. To see how well you have memorized the commands as a side effect of your other studies, cover the left side of the table, read the descriptions on the right side, and see if you remember the command.

Table 16-4 *Chapter 16 Configuration Command Reference*

Command	Description
router eigrp *autonomous-system*	Global command to move the user into EIGRP configuration mode for the listed ASN.
network *network-number* [*wildcard-mask*]	EIGRP router subcommand that matches either all interfaces in a classful network, or a subset of interfaces based on the ACL-style wildcard mask, enabling EIGRP on those interfaces.
maximum-paths *number-paths*	Router subcommand that defines the maximum number of equal-cost routes that can be added to the routing table.
variance *multiplier*	Router subcommand that defines an EIGRP multiplier used to determine if a feasible successor route's metric is close enough to the successor's metric to be considered equal.
bandwidth *bandwidth*	Interface subcommand directly sets the interface bandwidth (kbps).
delay *delay-value*	Interface subcommand to set the interface delay value, with a unit of tens-of-microseconds.
ip hello-interval eigrp *as-number timer-value*	Interface subcommand that sets the EIGRP Hello interval for that EIGRP process.
ip hold-time eigrp *as-number timer-value*	Interface subcommand that sets the EIGRP hold time for the interface.
maximum-paths *number-of-paths*	Router subcommand that defines the maximum number of equal-cost routes that can be added to the routing table.
ip authentication key-chain eigrp *asn chain-name*	Interface subcommand that references the key chain used for MD5 authentication with EIGRP.
ip authentication mode eigrp *asn* **md5**	Interface subcommand that enables EIGRP MD5 authentication for all neighbors reached on the interface.
key chain *name*	Global command to create and name an authentication key chain.
key *integer-number*	Key chain mode command to create a new key number.

Table 16-4   *Chapter 16 Configuration Command Reference*

Command	Description
key-string *text*	Key chain mode command to create the authentication key's value.
accept-lifetime *start-time* {**infinite** | *end-time* | **duration** *seconds*}	Key chain mode command to set the time frame during which a router will accept the use of a particular key.
send-lifetime *start-time* {**infinite** | *end-time* | **duration** *seconds*}	Key chain mode command to set the time frame during which a router will send EIGRP messages using a particular key.

Table 16-5   *Chapter 16 EXEC Command Reference*

Command	Description
show ip route eigrp	Lists routes in the routing table learned by EIGRP.
show ip route *ip-address* [*mask*]	Shows the entire routing table, or a subset if parameters are entered.
show ip protocols	Shows routing protocol parameters and current timer values.
show ip eigrp neighbors	Lists EIGRP neighbors and status.
show ip eigrp topology	Lists the contents of the EIGRP topology table, including successors and feasible successors.
show ip eigrp traffic	Lists statistics on the number of EIGRP messages sent and received by a router.
debug eigrp packets	Displays the contents of EIGRP packets.
debug eigrp fsm	Displays changes to the EIGRP successor and feasible successor routes.
debug ip eigrp	Displays similar output to the **debug eigrp packets** command, but specifically for IP.

Answer Review Questions

Answer the following review questions:

1. Which of the following affect the calculation of EIGRP metrics when all possible default values are used?

   a. Bandwidth

   b. Delay

   c. Load

   d. Reliability

   e. MTU

   f. Hop count

2. How does EIGRP notice when a neighboring router fails?

   a. The failing neighbor sends a message before failing.

   b. The failing neighbor sends a "dying gasp" message.

   c. The router notices a lack of routing updates for a period of time.

   d. The router notices a lack of Hello messages for a period of time.

3. Which of the following is true about the concept of EIGRP feasible distance?

   a. A route's feasible distance is the calculated metric of a feasible successor route.

   b. A route's feasible distance is the calculated metric of the successor route.

   c. The feasible distance is the metric of a route from a neighboring router's perspective.

   d. The feasible distance is the EIGRP metric associated with each possible route to reach a subnet.

4. Which of the following is true about the concept of EIGRP reported distance?

   a. A route's reported distance is the calculated metric of a feasible successor route.

   b. A route's reported distance is the calculated metric of the successor route.

   c. A route's reported distance is the metric of a route from a neighboring router's perspective.

   d. The reported distance is the EIGRP metric associated with each possible route to reach a subnet.

5. Which of the following **network** commands, following the command **router eigrp 1**, tells this router to start using EIGRP on interfaces whose IP addresses are 10.1.1.1, 10.1.100.1, and 10.1.120.1?

   a.   network 10.0.0.0

   b.   network 10.1.1x.0

   c.   network 10.0.0.0 0.255.255.255

   d.   network 10.0.0.0 255.255.255.0

6. Routers R1 and R2 attach to the same VLAN with IP addresses 10.0.0.1 and 10.0.0.2, respectively. R1 is configured with the commands **router eigrp 99** and **network 10.0.0.0**. Which of the following commands might be part of a working EIGRP configuration on R2 that ensures that the two routers become neighbors and exchange routes?

   a.   network 10

   b.   router eigrp 98

   c.   network 10.0.0.2 0.0.0.0

   d.   network 10.0.0.0

7. Examine the following excerpt from a router's CLI:

```
P 10.1.1.0/24, 1 successors, FD is 2172416
        via 10.1.6.3 (2172416/28160), Serial0/1
        via 10.1.4.2 (2684416/2284156), Serial0/0
        via 10.1.5.4 (2684416/2165432), Serial1/0
```

Which of the following identifies a next-hop IP address on a feasible successor route?

   a.   10.1.6.3

   b.   10.1.4.2

   c.   10.1.5.4

   d.   It cannot be determined from this command output.

8. Which of the following must occur to configure MD5 authentication for EIGRP?

   a.   Setting the MD5 authentication key via some interface subcommand

   b.   Configuring at least one key chain

   c.   Defining a valid lifetime for the key

   d.   Enabling EIGRP MD5 authentication on an interface

9. In the **show ip route** command, what code designation implies that a route was learned with EIGRP?

    a.   E

    b.   I

    c.   G

    d.   R

    e.   P

    f.   D

This chapter covers the following subjects:

- **Choosing the Mask(s) to Meet Requirements:** This section discusses the ideas behind choosing a subnet mask—in particular, making sure that the mask meets requirements.

- **Practice Choosing Subnet Masks:** This section supplies suggestions for how to practice the math related to this chapter.

CHAPTER 17

Subnet Mask Design

Earlier, Chapter 8, "IP Subnetting," provided an overall view of the subnet design and implementation process. To begin, the engineer analyzes the needs to decide the required number of subnets and hosts/subnet. During the second major step, the engineer chooses a particular classful network and then picks a single subnet mask to use: a mask that meets the requirements identified at the first step. Figure 17-1 shows the main steps, just as a reminder.

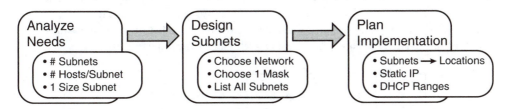

Figure 17-1 *Subnet Design and Implementation Process from Chapter 8*

This chapter examines the choice of subnet mask in more depth. In particular, the text reviews how to determine the minimum number of required subnet and host bits to meet the requirements. The text first examines cases in which no mask meets the requirements. It then examines cases for which only one mask meets the requirements and other cases for which multiple subnet masks meet the requirements. Finally, the chapter examines the trade-offs to consider when choosing masks when multiple options exist.

Choosing the Mask(s) to Meet Requirements

This chapter examines how to find all masks that meet the stated requirements for the number of subnets and the number of hosts per subnet. To that end, this chapter then assumes that the designer has already determined these requirements and has chosen the network number to be subnetted. The designer has also made the choice to use a single subnet mask value throughout the classful network.

Armed with the information in this chapter, you can answer questions like the following:

You are using class B network 172.16.0.0. You need 200 subnets and 200 hosts/subnet. Which of the following subnet mask(s) meet the requirements? (This question is then followed by several answers that list different subnet masks.)

To begin, the following sections review the concepts in Chapter 10's section "Choose the Mask." That section introduced the main concepts about how an engineer, when designing the subnet conventions, must choose the mask based on the requirements.

After reviewing the related concepts from Chapter 10, "Analyzing Existing Subnet Masks," this chapter moves on to examine this topic in more depth. In particular, this chapter looks at three general cases:

- No masks meet the requirements.

- One and only one mask meets the requirements.

- Multiple masks meet the requirements.

For this last case, these sections then discuss how to determine all masks that meet the requirements, and the trade-offs related to choosing which one mask to use.

Review: Choosing the Minimum Number of Subnet and Host Bits

The network designer must examine the requirements for the number of subnets and number of hosts/subnet, and then choose a mask. As discussed in some detail in Chapter 10, a classful view of IP addresses defines the three-part structure of an IP address: network, subnet, and host. The network designer must choose the mask so that the number of subnet and host bits (S and H in Figure 17-2, respectively) meets the requirements.

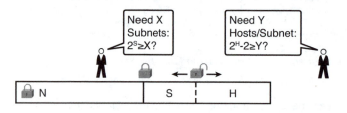

Figure 17-2   *Choosing the Number of Subnet and Host Bits*

Basically, the designer must choose S subnet bits so that the number of subnets that can be uniquely numbered with S bits (2^S) is at least as large as the required number of subnets. The designer applies similar logic to the number of host bits H, while noting that the formula is $2^H - 2$ because of the two reserved numbers in each subnet. So, keeping the powers of 2 handy, as shown in Table 17-1, will be of use when working through these problems.

Table 17-1   *Powers of 2 Reference for Designing Masks*

Number of Bits	2^x
1	2
2	4
3	8
4	16

Table 17-1   *Powers of 2 Reference for Designing Masks*

Number of Bits	2^x
5	32
6	64
7	128
8	256
9	512
10	1,024
11	2,048
12	4,096
13	8,192
14	16,384
15	32,768
16	65,536

More formally, the process to find a subnet mask that meets the requirements must determine the minimum values for S and H that meet the requirements for the numbers of subnets and hosts per subnet. The following list summarizes the initial steps to choose the mask:

Step 1.   Determine the number of network bits (N) based on the class.

Step 2.   Determine the smallest value of S so that 2^s => X, where X represents the required number of subnets.

Step 3.   Determine the smallest value of H so that $2^H - 2$ => Y, where Y represents the required number of hosts/subnet.

The next three sections examine how to use these initial steps to choose a subnet mask.

No Masks Meet Requirements

Keeping these steps in mind, consider the fact that after you determine the required number of subnet and host bits, those bits might not fit into a 32-bit IPv4 subnet mask. Remember, the mask always has a total of 32 bits, with binary 1s in the network and subnet parts and binary 0s in the host part. For the exam, a question might provide a set of requirements that simply cannot be met with 32 total bits.

For example, consider the following sample question:

A network engineer is planning a subnet design. The engineer plans to use class B network 172.16.0.0. The network has a need for 300 subnets and 280 hosts per subnet. Which of the following masks could the engineer choose?

The three-step process shown in the previous section shows that these requirements mean that a total of 34 bits will be needed, so no mask meets the requirements. First, as a class B network, 16 network bits exist, with 16 host bits from which to create the subnet part and to leave enough host bits to number the hosts in each subnet. For the number of subnet bits, S = 8 does not work, because 2^8 = 256 < 300. However, S = 9 works, because 2^9 = 512 => 300. Similarly, because $2^8 - 2$ = 254 < 280, 8 host bits are not enough, but 9 host bits ($2^9 - 2$ = 510 => 280) are enough.

Figure 17-3 shows the resulting format for the IP addresses in this subnet, after the engineer has allocated 9 subnet bits on paper. Only 7 host bits remain, but the engineer needs 9 host bits.

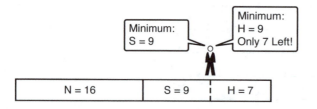

Figure 17-3   *Too Few Bits for the Host Part, Given the Requirements*

One Mask Meets Requirements

The process discussed in this chapter in part focuses on finding the smallest number of subnet bits and the smallest number of host bits to meet the requirements. If the engineer tries to use these minimum values, and the combined network, subnet, and host parts add up to exactly 32 bits, exactly one mask meets the requirements.

For example, consider a revised version of the example in the previous section, with smaller numbers of subnets and hosts, as follows:

> A network engineer is planning a subnet design. The engineer plans to use class B network 172.16.0.0. The network has a need for 200 subnets and 180 hosts per subnet. Which of the following masks could the engineer choose?

The three-step process to determine the numbers of network, minimum subnet, and minimum host bits results in a need for 16, 8, and 8 bits, respectively. As before, with a class B network, 16 network bits exist. With a need for only 200 hosts, S = 8 does work, because 2^8 = 256 => 200; 7 subnet bits would not supply enough subnets (2^7 = 128). Similarly, because $2^8 - 2$ = 254 => 180, 8 host bits meet the requirements; 7 host bits (for 126 total hosts/subnet) would not be enough.

Figure 17-4 shows the resulting format for the IP addresses in this subnet.

The figure shows the mask conceptually. To find the actual mask value, simply record the mask in prefix format (/P), where P = N + S, or in this case, /24.

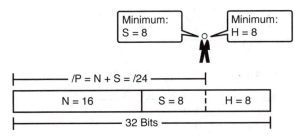

Figure 17-4 *One Mask That Meets Requirements*

Multiple Masks Meet Requirements

Depending on the requirements and choice of network, there can be several masks that meet the requirements for the numbers of subnets and hosts/subnet. In these cases, you need to find all the masks that could be used. Then you have a choice—but what should you consider when choosing one mask among all those that meet your requirements? The following sections examine the concepts related to identifying all the masks that meet the requirements in this case, the math, and the ideas to consider when choosing one mask from the list.

Finding All the Masks: Concepts

To help you better understand how to find all the subnet masks in binary, this section uses two major steps. In the first major step, you build the 32-bit binary subnet mask on paper. You write down binary 1s for the network bits, binary 1s for the subnet bits, and binary 0s for the host bits, just as always. However, you will use the minimum values for S and H. And when you write down these bits, you will not have 32 bits yet!

For example, consider the following problem, similar to the earlier examples in this chapter, but with some changes in the requirements:

> A network engineer is planning a subnet design. The engineer plans to use class B network 172.16.0.0. The network has a need for 50 subnets and 180 hosts per subnet. Which of the following masks could the engineer choose?

This example is similar to an earlier example, except that only 50 subnets are needed in this case. Again, the engineer is using private IP network 172.16.0.0, meaning 16 network bits. The design requires only 6 subnet bits in this case, because $2^6 = 64 => 50$, and with only 5 subnet bits, $2^5 = 32 < 50$. The design then requires a minimum of 8 host bits.

One way to discuss the concepts, and to find all the masks that meet these requirements, is to write down the bits in the subnet mask: binary 1s for the network and subnet parts and binary 0s for the host part. However, think of the 32-bit mask as 32 bit positions, and when writing the binary 0s, *write them on the far right*. Figure 17-5 shows the general idea.

The figure shows 30 bits of the mask, but the mask must have 32 bits. The two remaining bits might become subnet bits, being set to binary 1. Alternately, these 2 bits could be made host bits, being set to binary 0. The engineer simply needs to choose based on whether he would like more subnet bits, to number more subnets, or more host bits, to number more hosts/subnet.

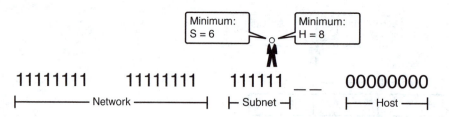

Figure 17-5   *Incomplete Mask with N=16, S=6, and H=8*

However, the engineer cannot just choose any value for these 2 bits. The mask must still follow this rule:

A subnet mask begins with all binary 1s, followed by all binary 0s, with no interleaving of 1s and 0s.

With the example in Figure 17-5, with 2 open bits, one value (binary 01) breaks this rule. However, the other three combinations of 2 bits (00, 10, and 11) do not break the rule. As a result, three masks meet the requirements in this example, as shown in Figure 17-6.

S = 6	H = 8		
11111111 11111111 111111 __ 00000000			
/22 11111111 11111111 1111110̲0̲_ 00000000	S=6	H=10	
/23 11111111 11111111 1111111̲0̲_ 00000000	S=7	H=9	
/24 11111111 11111111 1111111̲1̲_ 00000000	S=8	H=8	

Legend: [minimum value]

Figure 17-6   *Three Masks That Meet the Requirements*

Note that in the three masks, the first has the least number of subnet bits among the three masks but therefore has the most number of host bits. So, the first mask maximizes the number of hosts/subnet. The last mask uses the minimum value for the number of host bits, therefore using the most number of subnet bits allowed while still meeting the requirements. As a result, the last mask maximizes the number of subnets allowed.

Finding All the Masks: Math

Although the concepts related to the example shown in Figures 17-5 and 17-6 are important, you can find the range of masks that meets requirements more easily just using some simple math. The process to find the masks just requires a few steps, after you know N and the minimum values of S and H. The process finds the value of /P when using the least number of subnet bits and when using the least number of host bits, as follows:

Step 1.   Calculate the shortest prefix mask (/P) based on the *minimum value of S*, where P = N + S.

Step 2.   Calculate the longest prefix mask (/P) based on the *minimum value of H*, where P = 32 − H.

Step 3.   The range of valid masks includes all /P values between the two values calculated in the previous steps.

For example, in the example shown in Figure 17-6, N = 16, the minimum S = 6, and the minimum H = 8. The first step identifies the shortest prefix mask (the /P with the smallest value of P) of /22 by adding N and S (16 + 6). The second step identifies the longest prefix mask that meets requirements by subtracting the smallest possible value for H (8 in this case) from 32, for a mask of /24. The third step reminds us that the range is from /22 to /24, meaning that /23 is also an option.

Choosing the Best Mask

When multiple possible masks meet the stated requirements, the engineer has a choice of masks. That, of course, begs some questions. Which mask should you choose? Why would one mask be better than the other? The reasons can be summarized into three main options:

■ **To maximize the number of hosts/subnet:** To make this choice, use the shortest prefix mask (that is, the mask with the smallest /P value), because this mask has the largest host part.

■ **To maximize the number of subnets:** To make this choice, use the longest prefix mask (that is, the mask with the largest /P value), because this mask has the largest subnet part.

■ **To increase both the numbers of supported subnets and hosts:** To make this choice, choose a mask in the middle of the range, which gives you both more subnet bits and more host bits.

For example, in Figure 17-6, the range of masks that meets the requirements is /22 − /24. The shortest mask, /22, has the least subnet bits but the largest number of host bits (10) of the three answers, maximizing the number of hosts/subnet. The longest mask, /24, maximizes the number of subnet bits (8), maximizing the number of subnets, at least among the options that meet the original requirements. The mask in the middle, /23, provides some growth in both subnets and hosts/subnet.

The Formal Process

Although this chapter has explained various steps in finding a subnet mask to meet the design requirements, it has not yet collected these concepts into a list for the entire process. The following list collects all these steps into one place for reference. Note that the following list does not introduce any new concepts compared to the rest of this chapter—it just puts all the ideas in one place:

Step 1.   Find the number of network bits (N) per class rules.

Step 2.   Calculate the minimum number of subnet bits (S) so that 2^S => the number of required subnets.

Step 3. Calculate the minimum number of host bits (H) so that $2^H - 2 =>$ the number of required hosts/subnet.

Step 4. If $N + S + H > 32$, no mask meets the need.

Step 5. If $N + S + H = 32$, one mask meets the need. Calculate the mask as /P, where $P = N + S$.

Step 6. If $N + S + H < 32$, multiple masks meet the need:

> **Step A.** Calculate mask /P, based on the minimum value of S, where $P = N + S$. This mask maximizes the number of hosts/subnet.

> **Step B.** Calculate mask /P, based on the minimum value of H, where $P = 32 - H$. This mask maximizes the number of possible subnets.

> **Step C.** Note the complete range of masks that meets the requirements includes the two masks calculated in Steps 6A and 6B and all masks between these two masks.

Practice Choosing Subnet Masks

To be a well-prepared network engineer, you should master any and all IP addressing processes and calculations by the time you finish this course. Most technical interviews for a job working with IP networking will include some assessment of how well you understand the concepts and how quickly you can calculate various facts about addresses and subnets.

However, you do not need to completely master everything in this chapter right now. Practice now to make sure that you understand the processes, using your notes, the book, and whatever helps. Then you can move on to the next chapter. However, before the midterm and final exams, practice until you master the topics in this chapter. Table 17-2 summarizes the key concepts and suggestions for this two-phase approach.

Table 17-2 *Practice Goals for This Chapter's Topics*

Time Frame	Before Moving to the Next Chapter	Before Taking the Exam
Focus on...	Learning how	Being correct and fast
Tools Allowed	All	Your brain and a notepad
Goal: Accuracy	90% correct	100% correct

Practice Problems for This Chapter

The following list shows three separate problems, each with a classful network number and a required number of subnets and hosts/subnet. For each problem, determine the minimum number of subnet and host bits that meets the requirements. If more than one mask exists, note which mask maximizes the number of hosts/subnet and which maximizes the number of subnets. If only one mask meets the requirements, simply list that mask. List the masks in prefix format.

1. Network 10.0.0.0: Needs 1500 subnets and 300 hosts/subnet.
2. Network 172.25.0.0: Needs 130 subnets and 127 hosts/subnet.
3. Network 192.168.83.0: Needs 8 subnets and 8 hosts/subnet.

Table 17-4, found later in the "Chapter Review" section of the chapter, lists the answers.

Additional Practice

For additional practice, create your own problems. Many subnet calculators let you type the class A, B, or C network and choose the mask, and the calculator then lists the number of subnets and hosts/subnet created by that network/mask. Make up a network number and required numbers of subnets and hosts, derive the answers, and check the math with the calculator. This might take a little more work with a calculator as compared with some of the other subnetting chapters in this book.

Chapter Review

Review Key Topics

Review the key topics as part of your study, but know that you will likely come to know all the information in these key topics through practice and repetition.

Table 17-3 *Key Topics for Chapter 17*

Key Topic Element	Description	Page Number
Definition	Facts about binary values in subnet masks	426
List	The shorter three-step process to find all prefix masks that meet certain requirements	426
List	Reasons to choose one subnet mask versus another	427
List	The complete process for finding and choosing masks to meet certain requirements	427

Define Key Terms

This chapter does not introduce any new terms.

Practice

If you have not done so already, practice finding all subnet masks, based on requirements, as discussed in this chapter. Refer to the earlier section "Practice Choosing Subnet Masks" for suggestions.

Review Answers to Earlier Practice Problems

The earlier section "Practice Problems for This Chapter" listed three practice problems. The answers are listed here so that the answers are nearby but not visible from the list of problems. Table 17-4 lists the answers, with notes related to each problem following the table.

Table 17-4 *Practice Problems: Find the Masks That Meet Requirements*

Problem	Class	Minimum Subnet Bits	Minimum Host Bits	Prefix Range	Prefix to Maximize Subnets	Prefix to Maximize Hosts
1	A	11	9	/19–/23	/23	/19
2	B	8	8	/16	—	—
3	C	3	4	/27–/28	/28	/27

1. N = 8 because the problem lists class A network 10.0.0.0. With a need for 1500 sub-nets, 10 subnet bits supply only 1024 subnets (per Table 17-1), but 11 subnet bits (S) would provide 2048 subnets—more than the required 1500. Similarly, the smallest number of host bits would be 9, because $2^8 - 2 = 254$, and the design requires 300 hosts/subnet. The shortest prefix mask would then be /19, found by adding N (8) and the smallest usable number of subnet bits S (11). Similarly, with a minimum H value of 9, the longest prefix mask, maximizing the number of subnets, is $32 - H = $ /23.

2. N = 16 because the problem lists class B network 172.25.0.0. With a need for 130 sub-nets, 7 subnet bits supply only 128 subnets (per Table 17-1), but 8 subnet bits (S) would provide 256 subnets—more than the required 130. Similarly, the smallest num-ber of host bits would be 8, because $2^7 - 2 = 126$—close to the required 127 but not quite enough, making H = 8 the smallest number of host bits that meets requirements. Note that the network, minimum subnet bits, and minimum host bits add up to 32, so only one mask meets the requirements—namely, /24, found by adding the number of network bits (16) to the minimum number of subnet bits (8).

3. For the last problem, N = 24 because the problem lists class C network 192.168.83.0. With a need for 8 subnets, 3 subnet bits supply enough, but just barely. The smallest number of host bits would be 4, because $2^3 - 2 = 6$, and the design requires 8 hosts/subnet. The shortest prefix mask would then be /27, found by adding N (24) and the smallest usable number of subnet bits S (3). Similarly, with a minimum H value of 4, the longest prefix mask, maximizing the number of subnets, is $32 - H = $ /28.

Answer Review Questions

Answer the following review questions:

1. An IP subnetting design effort is under way at a company. So far, the senior engineer has decided to use class B network 172.23.0.0. The design calls for 100 subnets, with the largest subnet needing 500 hosts. Management requires that the design accom-modate 50 percent growth in the number of subnets and the size of the largest sub-net. The requirements also state that a single mask must be used throughout the class B network. How many masks meet the requirements?

   a. 0

   b. 1

   c. 2

   d. 3+

2. An IP subnetting design effort is under way at a company. So far, the senior engineer has decided to use class C network 192.168.8.0. The design calls for 12 subnets, with the largest subnet needing 8 hosts. The requirements also state that a single mask must be used throughout the class C network. How many masks meet the requirements?

    a.   0

    b.   1

    c.   2

    d.   3+

3. An IP subnetting design requires 200 subnets and 120 hosts/subnet for the largest subnets, and requires that a single mask be used throughout the one private IP network that will be used. The design also requires planning for 20 percent growth in the number of subnets and number of hosts/subnet in the largest subnet. Which of the following answers lists a private IP network and mask that, if chosen, would meet the requirements?

    a.   10.0.0.0/25

    b.   10.0.0.0/22

    c.   172.16.0.0/23

    d.   192.168.7.0/24

4. A subnet design uses class A network 10.0.0.0, and the engineer must choose a single mask to use throughout the network. The design requires 1200 subnets, with the largest subnet needing 300 hosts. Which of the following masks meets the requirements and also maximizes the number of hosts per subnet?

    a.   /16

    b.   /19

    c.   /21

    d.   /23

5. An engineer has planned to use class B network 172.19.0.0 and to use a single subnet mask throughout the network. The answers list the masks considered by the engineer. Choose the mask that supplies the largest number of hosts per subnet while also supplying enough subnet bits to support 1000 subnets.

    a.   255.255.255.0

    b.   /26

    c.   255.255.252.0

    d.   /28

6. An engineer has planned to use class C network 192.168.2.0 and to use a single subnet mask throughout the network. The answers list all the masks considered by the engineer. Choose the mask that supplies the largest number of hosts per subnet while supplying enough subnet bits to support 10 subnets.

   a. 255.255.255.0

   b. /25

   c. 255.255.255.192

   d. /27

   e. 255.255.255.248

7. A subnet design uses class A network 10.0.0.0, and the engineer must choose a single mask to use throughout the network. The design requires 1000 subnets, with the largest subnet needing 200 hosts. Which of the following masks meets the requirements and also maximizes the number of subnets?

   a. /18

   b. /20

   c. /22

   d. /24

This chapter covers the following subjects:

■ **Finding All Subnet IDs:** This section explains the process of making a list of all subnet IDs in a network, based on a classful IP network and the one mask to use throughout the network.

■ **Practice Finding All Subnet IDs:** This section provides tips on how to practice the process to find all subnets of a network.

CHAPTER 18

Finding All Subnet IDs

As described in Chapter 8, "IP Subnetting," the IP subnetting design process requires several choices. The designer must choose a specific private IP network or obtain a registered public IP network. The designer can choose to use either a single mask or multiple masks when subnetting the network. (This book assumes a choice to use a single mask.) Finally, the designer must choose which single mask to use.

This chapter takes the result of these choices—a network ID and one subnet mask—and shows how to then calculate all the subnet IDs for all the subnets that exist in that network when using that one mask.

Finding All Subnet IDs

This chapter focuses on a single question:

> Given a single class A, B, or C network, and the single subnet mask to use for all subnets, what are all the subnet IDs?

When learning how to answer this question, you can think about the problem in either binary or in decimal. This chapter approaches the problem using decimal. And while the process itself requires simple math only, the process does require practice before most people can confidently answer this question.

The decimal process begins by identifying the first, or numerically lowest, subnet ID. After that, the process identifies a pattern in all subnet IDs for a given subnet mask so that you can find each successive subnet ID through simple addition. The following sections examine the key ideas behind this process first, before giving you a formal definition of the process.

The First Subnet ID: The Zero Subnet

The first step in finding all subnet IDs of one network is incredibly simple: Copy the network ID. That is, take the class A, B, or C network ID—in other words, the classful network ID—and write it down as the first subnet ID. No matter what class A, B, or C network you use, and no matter what subnet mask you use, the first (numerically lowest) subnet ID is equal to the network ID.

For example, if you begin with classful network 172.20.0.0, no matter what the mask is, the first subnet ID is 172.20.0.0.

This first subnet ID in each network goes by two special names: either *subnet zero* or the *zero subnet*. The origin of these names is related to the fact that a network's zero subnet, when viewed in binary, has a subnet part of all binary 0s. In decimal, the zero subnet can be easily identified, because the zero subnet always has the same numeric value as the network ID itself.

Note: In years past, IP subnet designs typically avoided the use of the zero subnet because of the confusion that might arise with a network ID and subnet ID that were the same numbers.

Finding the Pattern Using the Magic Number

Subnet IDs follow a predictable pattern, at least when using our assumption of a single subnet mask for all subnets of a network. The pattern is equal to the *magic number*, as discussed earlier in Chapter 13, "Analyzing Existing Subnets." To review, the magic number is 256, minus the mask's decimal value, in a particular octet that the book refers to as the *interesting octet*.

Figure 18-1 shows four number lines, one each for masks /17–/20. The number lines show the pattern of values in the third octet of the subnet IDs when using these masks. The left side of the figure shows the dotted decimal notation (DDN) mask and the calculated magic number. The right side of the figure shows the numeric values in the third octet for each of the subnets of any class B network that used these masks, respectively.

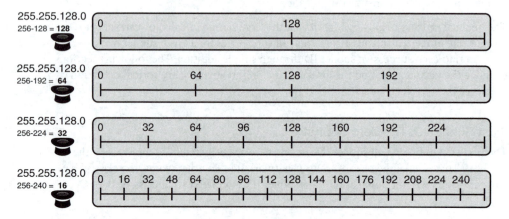

Figure 18-1   *Patterns with Magic Numbers for Masks /17–/20*

For example, if subnetting class B network 172.16.0.0, with the top mask in the figure (/17, or 255.255.128.0), the subnet IDs would be 172.16.0.0 and 172.16.128.0. In particular, note that the third octets of each subnet ID are multiples of the magic number (128), calculated as 256 − 128 = 128. The second row in the figure shows another mask, 255.255.192.0, with magic number 64 (256 − 192 = 64). If used with network 172.16.0.0, the subnet IDs would be 172.16.0.0, 172.16.64.0, 172.16.128.0, and 172.16.192.0, with the pattern in the third octet showing multiples of 64. The same holds true with the other two examples in the figure, with the subnet IDs being either 32 apart (mask /19, 255.255.255.224) or 16 apart (mask /20, 255.255.240.0).

A Formal Process, with Less Than 8 Subnet Bits

While it might be easy to see the patterns in Figure 18-1, it might not be as obvious as to exactly how to apply those concepts to find all the subnet IDs, in every case. This section outlines a specific process to find all the subnet IDs.

To simplify the explanations in this section, the process detailed in this section assumes that less than 8 subnet bits exist. Later, the section "Finding All Subnets with More Than 8 Subnet Bits" describes the full process that can be used in all cases.

First, to organize your thoughts, you might want to organize the data into a table like Table 18-1. The book refers to this chart as the list-all-subnets chart.

Table 18-1   *Generic List-All-Subnets Chart*

Octet	1	2	3	4
Mask				
Magic Number				
Network Number/Zero Subnet				
Next Subnet				
Next Subnet				
Last Subnet				
Broadcast Subnet				
Out of Range (Used by Process)				

A formal process to find all subnet IDs, given a network and a single subnet mask, is as follows:

Step 1.   Write down the subnet mask, in decimal, in the first empty row of the table.

Step 2.   Identify the interesting octet, which is the one octet of the mask with a value other than 255 or 0. Draw a rectangle around the column of the interesting octet.

Step 3.   Calculate and write down the magic number by subtracting the *subnet mask's interesting octet* from 256.

Key Topic

Step 4. Write down the classful network number, which is the same number as the zero subnet, in the next empty row of the list-all-subnets chart.

Step 5. To find each successive subnet number:

    a. For the three uninteresting octets, copy the previous subnet number's values.

    b. For the interesting octet, add the magic number to the previous subnet number's interesting octet.

Step 6. When the sum calculated in Step 5b reaches 256, stop the process. The number with the 256 in it is out of range, and the previous subnet number is the broadcast subnet.

Although the written process is long, with practice, most people can find the answers much more quickly with this decimal-based process than by using binary math. As usual, most people learn this process best by seeing it in action, exercising it, and then practicing it. To that end, review the two examples that follow. You can also use the Subnet Prep application "Find All Subnets" for more practice (http://www.subnetprep.com).

Example 1: Network 172.16.0.0, Mask 255.255.240.0

To begin this example, focus on the first four of the six steps, when subnetting network 172.16.0.0 using mask 255.255.240.0. Figure 18-2 that follows shows the results of these first four steps:

Step 1. Record mask 255.255.240.0, which was given as part of the problem statement. (Figure 18-2 also shows the network ID, 172.16.0.0, for easy reference.)

Step 2. The mask's third octet is neither 0 nor 255, making the third octet interesting.

Step 3. Because the mask's value in the third octet is 240, the magic number = 256 − 240 = 16.

Step 4. Because the network ID is 172.16.0.0, the first subnet ID, the zero subnet, is also 172.16.0.0.

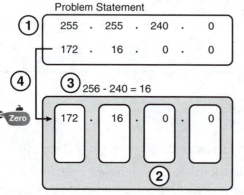

Figure 18-2 *Results of the First Four Steps: 172.16.0.0, 255.255.240.0*

These first four steps discover the first subnet (the zero subnet) and get you ready to do the remaining steps by identifying the interesting octet and the magic number.

Step 5 in the process tells you to copy the three boring octets and to add the magic number (16 in this case) in the interesting octet (octet 3 in this case). You keep repeating this step until the interesting octet value equals 256 (per Step 6). When the total is 256, you have listed all the subnet IDs, and the line with 256 on it is not a correct subnet ID. Figure 18-3 shows the results of these steps.

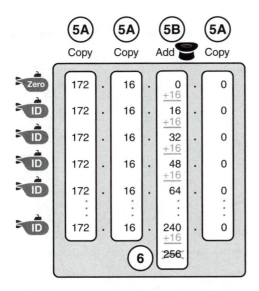

Key Topic

Figure 18-3 *List of Subnet IDs: 172.16.0.0, 255.255.240.0*

Note: In any list of all the subnet IDs of a network, the numerically highest subnet ID is called the *broadcast subnet*. Decades ago, engineers avoided using the broadcast subnet. However, using the broadcast subnet causes no problems. The term *broadcast subnet* has its origins in the fact that if you determine the subnet broadcast address inside the broadcast subnet, it has the same numeric value as the network-wide broadcast address.

Note: People sometimes confuse the terms *broadcast subnet* and *subnet broadcast address*, particularly because people often shorten *subnet broadcast address* to simply *subnet broadcast*. The *broadcast subnet* is one subnet, namely the numerically highest subnet; only one such subnet exists per network. The term *subnet broadcast address* refers to the one number in each subnet that is the numerically highest number in that sub-

Example 2: Network 192.168.1.0, Mask 255.255.255.224

With a class C network and a mask of 255.255.255.224, this next example makes the fourth octet be the interesting octet. However, the process works the same way, with the same logic, just with the interesting logic applied in a different octet. As with the previous

example, the following list outlines the first four steps, with Figure 18-4 that follows showing the results of the first four steps:

Step 1.   Record mask 255.255.255.224, which was given as part of the problem statement, and optionally record the network number (192.168.1.0).

Step 2.   The mask's fourth octet is neither 0 nor 255, making the fourth octet interesting.

Step 3.   Because the mask's value in the fourth octet is 224, the magic number = 256 – 224 = 32.

Step 4.   Because the network ID is 192.168.1.0, the first subnet ID, the zero subnet, is also 192.168.1.0.

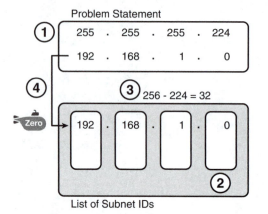

Figure 18-4   *Results of the First Four Steps: 192.168.1.0, 255.255.255.224*

From this point, Step 5 in the process tells you to copy the values in the first three octets, and to then add the magic number (32 in this case) in the interesting octet (octet 4 in this case). You keep doing so until the interesting octet value equals 256 (per Step 6). When the total is 256, you have listed all the subnet IDs, and the line with 256 on it is not a correct subnet ID. Figure 18-5 shows the results of these steps.

Finding All Subnets with Exactly 8 Subnet Bits

The formal process in the earlier section "A Formal Process, with Less Than 8 Subnet Bits" identified the interesting octet as the octet whose mask value is neither a 255 nor a 0. If the mask defines exactly 8 subnet bits, you have to use a little different logic to identify the interesting octet; otherwise, the same process can be used. In fact, the actual subnet IDs can be a little more intuitive.

Only two cases exist with exactly 8 subnet bits:

A class A network with mask 255.255.0.0; the entire second octet contains subnet bits

A class B network with mask 255.255.255.0; the entire third octet contains subnet bits

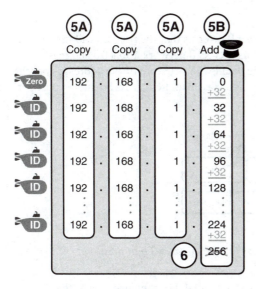

Figure 18-5 *List of Subnet IDs: 192.168.1.0, 255.255.255.224*

In each of these cases, use the same process as with less than 8 subnet bits, but identify the interesting octet as the one octet that contains subnet bits. Also, because the mask's value is 255, the magic number will be 256 − 255 = 1, so the subnet IDs are each 1 larger than the previous subnet ID.

For example, for 172.16.0.0, mask 255.255.255.0, the third octet is the interesting octet and the magic number is 256 − 255 = 1. You start with the zero subnet, equal in value to network number 172.16.0.0, and then add 1 in the third octet. For example, the first four subnets are

172.16.0.0 (zero subnet)

172.16.1.0

172.16.2.0

172.16.3.0

Finding All Subnets with More Than 8 Subnet Bits

Earlier, in the section "A Formal Process, with Less Than 8 Subnet Bits," the text explains that this earlier process assumed less than 8 subnet bits for the purpose of simplifying the discussions while you learn. In real life, you need to be able to find all subnet IDs with any valid mask, so you cannot assume less than 8 subnet bits.

The examples that have at least 9 subnet bits have a minimum of 512 subnet IDs, so writing down such a list would take a lot of time. To conserve space and time, the examples will use shorthand rather than list hundreds or thousands of subnet IDs.

The process with less than eight subnet IDs essentially told you how to count in the one octet where subnet bits existed. With more than 8 subnet bits, the new expanded process must tell you how to count in multiple octets. So, the following sections break down two general cases: when 9–16 subnet bits exist, meaning that the subnet field exists in only two octets, and cases with 17 or more subnet bits, which means that the subnet field exists in three octets.

Process with 9–16 Subnet Bits

To understand the process, you need to know a few terms that the process will use. Figure 18-6 shows the details, with an example that uses class B network 130.4.0.0 and mask 255.255.255.192. The lower part of the figure details the structure of the addresses per the mask: a network part of two octets because it is a class B address, a 10-bit subnet part per the mask (/26), and 6 host bits.

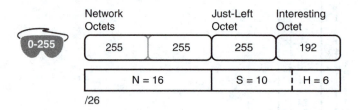

Figure 18-6 *Fundamental Concepts and Terms for the Greater Than 8 Subnet Bit Process*

In this case, subnet bits exist in two octets: octets 3 and 4. For the purposes of the process, the rightmost of these octets is the interesting octet, and the octet just to the left is the cleverly named *just-left* octet.

The updated process tells you to count in increments of the magic number in the interesting octet, but count by 1s in the just-left octet. Formally, follow these steps:

Step 1. Calculate the subnet IDs using the 8-subnet-bits-or-less process. However, when the total adds up to 256, move to the next step; consider the subnet IDs listed so far as a subnet block.

Step 2. Copy the previous subnet block, but add 1 to the just-left octet in all subnet IDs in the new block.

Step 3. Repeat Step 2 until you create the block with a just-left octet of 255, but go no further.

To be honest, the formal concept can cause you problems until you work through some examples, so even if the process remains a bit unclear in your mind, rather than rereading the formal process, work through the following examples instead.

First, consider an example based on Figure 18-6, with network 130.4.0.0 and mask 255.255.255.192. Figure 18-6 already showed the structure, and Figure 18-7 next shows the subnet ID block created at Step 1.

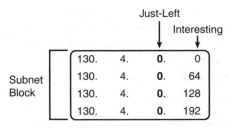

Figure 18-7 *Step 1: Listing the First Subnet ID Block*

The logic at Step 1, to create this subnet ID block of four subnet IDs, follows the same magic number process seen before. The first subnet ID, 130.4.0.0, is the zero subnet. The next three subnet IDs are each 64 bigger, because the magic number in this case is 256 – 192 = 64.

Steps 2 and 3 from the formal process tell you how to create 256 subnet ID blocks, and by doing so, you will list all 1024 subnet IDs. To do so, create 256 total subnet ID blocks: one with a 0 in the just-left octet, one with a 1 in the just-left octet, another with a 2 in the just-left octet, up through 255. The process continues through the step at which you create the subnet block with 255 in the just-left octet (the third octet in this case). Figure 18-8 shows the idea, with the addition of the first few subnet ID blocks.

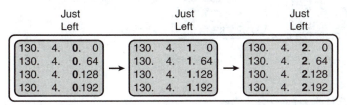

Figure 18-8 *Step 2: Replicating the Subnet Block with +1 in the Just-Left Octet*

This example, with 10 total subnet bits, creates 256 blocks of four subnets each, for a total of 1024 subnets. This math matches the usual method of counting subnets, because $2^{10} = 1024$.

Process with 17 or More Subnet Bits

To create a subnet design that allows 17 or more subnet bits to exist, the design must use a class A network. Additionally, the subnet part will consist of the entire second and third octets, plus part of the fourth octet. That means a lot of subnet IDs: at least 2^{17}, or 131,072, subnets. Figure 18-9 shows an example of just such a structure, with a class A network and a /26 mask.

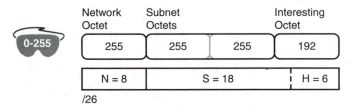

Figure 18-9 *Address Structure with 18 Subnet Bits*

To find all the subnet IDs in this example, you use the same general process as with 9–16 subnet bits, but with many more subnet blocks to create. In effect, you have to create a subnet block for all combinations of values (0–255, inclusive) in both the second and third octet. Figure 18-10 shows the general idea. Note that with only 2 subnet bits in the fourth octet in this example, the subnet blocks will have four subnets each.

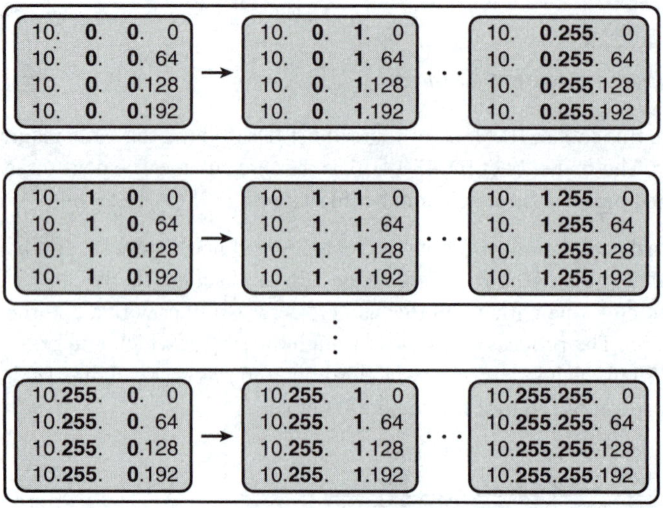

Figure 18-10 *256 Times 256 Subnet Blocks of Four Subnets*

Practice Finding All Subnet IDs

To be a well-prepared network engineer, you should master any and all IP addressing processes and calculations by the time you finish this course. Most technical interviews for a job working with IP networking will include some assessment of how well you understand the concepts and how quickly you can calculate various facts about addresses and subnets.

However, you do not need to completely master everything in this chapter right now. Practice now to make sure that you understand the processes, using your notes, the book, and whatever helps. Then you can move on to the next chapter. However, before the midterm and final exams, practice until you master the topics in this chapter. Table 18-2 summarizes the key concepts and suggestions for this two-phase approach.

Table 18-2 *Practice Goals for This Chapter's Topics*

Time Frame	Before Moving to the Next Chapter	Before Taking the Exam
Focus on...	Learning how	Being correct and fast
Tools Allowed	All	Your brain and a notepad
Goal: Accuracy	90% correct	100% correct

Practice Problems for This Chapter

The following list shows three separate problems, each with a classful network number and prefix-style mask. Find all subnet IDs for each problem:

1. 192.168.9.0/27

2. 172.30.0.0/20

3. 10.0.0.0/17

The section "Review Answers to Earlier Practice Problems," later in this chapter, lists the answers.

Additional Practice

This section lists several options for additional practice:

1. Create your own problems. Some subnet calculators let you type an IP network and mask, and the calculator lists all the subnet IDs. Simply make up a network ID and mask, find the answer on paper, and then plug the values into the calculator to check your work.

2. The Subnet Prep app "Find All Subnets" (http://www.subnetprep.com) provides review videos, but more importantly, practice problem after practice problem. As usual, they guide you to learn the process as described here but give you space to practice without being boxed in to any particular process.

Chapter Review

Review Key Topics

Review the key topics as part of your study, but know that you will likely come to know all the information in these key topics through practice and repetition.

Table 18-3 *Key Topics for Chapter 18*

Key Topic Element	Description	Page Number
Step list	Formal steps to find all subnet IDs when less than 8 subnet bits exist	437
Figure 18-3	An example of adding the magic number in the interesting octet to find all subnet IDs	439
Step list	Formal steps to find all subnet IDs when more than 8 subnet bits exist	442

Define Key Terms

Define the following key terms from this chapter, and check your answers in the glossary:

zero subnet, subnet zero, broadcast subnet

Review Answers to Earlier Practice Problems

The earlier section "Practice Problems for This Chapter" listed three practice problems. The answers are listed here so that the answers are not visible from the same page as the list of problems.

Answer, Practice Problem 1

This problem lists network 192.168.9.0, mask /27. The mask converts to DDN mask 255.255.255.224. When used with a class C network, which has 24 network bits, only 3 subnet bits exist, and they all sit in the fourth octet. So, this problem is a case of less than 8 subnet bits, with the fourth octet as the interesting octet.

To get started listing subnets, first write down the zero subnet and then start adding the magic number in the interesting octet. The zero subnet equals the network ID, or 192.168.9.0 in this case. The magic number, calculated as 256 − 224 = 32, should be added to the previous subnet ID's interesting octet. Table 18-4 lists the results.

Table 18-4   *List-All-Subnets Chart: 192.168.9.0/27*

Octet	1	2	3	4
Mask	255	255	255	224
Magic Number	—	—	—	32
Classful Network/Subnet Zero	192	168	9	0
First Nonzero Subnet	192	168	9	32
Next Subnet	192	168	9	64
Next Subnet	192	168	9	96
Next Subnet	192	168	9	128
Next Subnet	192	168	9	160
Next Subnet	192	168	9	192
Broadcast Subnet	192	168	9	224
Invalid—Used by Process	192	168	9	256

Answer, Practice Problem 2

This problem lists network 172.30.0.0, mask /20. The mask converts to DDN mask 255.255.240.0. When used with a class B network, which has 16 network bits, only 4 subnet bits exist, and they all sit in the third octet. So, this problem is a case of less than 8 subnet bits, with the third octet as the interesting octet.

To get started listing subnets, first write down the zero subnet and then start adding the magic number in the interesting octet. The zero subnet equals the network ID, or 172.30.0.0 in this case. The magic number, calculated as 256 − 240 = 16, should be added to the previous subnet ID's interesting octet. Table 18-5 lists the results.

Table 18-5   *List-All-Subnets Chart: 172.30.0.0/20*

Octet	1	2	3	4
Mask	255	255	240	0
Magic Number	—	—	16	—
Classful Network/Subnet Zero	172	30	0	0
First Nonzero Subnet	172	30	16	0
Next Subnet	172	30	32	0
Next Subnet	172	30	48	0
Next Subnet	172	30	64	0

Table 18-5   *List-All-Subnets Chart: 172.30.0.0/20*

Next Subnet	172	30	Skipping...	0
Next Subnet	172	30	224	0
Broadcast Subnet	172	30	240	0
Invalid—Used by Process	172	30	256	0

Answer, Practice Problem 3

This problem lists network 10.0.0.0, mask /17. The mask converts to DDN mask 255.255.128.0. When used with a class A network, which has 8 network bits, 9 subnet bits exist. Using the terms unique to this chapter, that means octet 3 is the interesting octet, with only 1 subnet bit in that octet, and octet 2 is the just-left octet, with 8 subnet bits.

In this case, begin by finding the first subnet ID block. The magic number is 256 − 128 = 128. The first subnet (zero subnet) equals the network ID. So, the first subnet ID block includes

10.0.0.0
10.0.128.0

Then, you create a subnet ID block for all 256 possible values in the just-left octet, or octet 2 in this case. The following list shows the first three subnet ID blocks and the last, rather than listing page upon page of subnet IDs:

10.0.0.0 (zero subnet)
10.0.128.0
10.1.0.0
10.1.128.0
10.2.0.0
10.2.128.0
...
10.255.0.0
10.255.128.0 (broadcast subnet)

Answer Review Questions

Answer the following review questions:

1. Which of the following are valid subnet IDs for network 10.0.0.0, assuming that mask 255.240.0.0 is used throughout network 10.0.0.0? (Choose two.)

   a.   10.1.16.0

   b.   10.0.0.0

   c.   10.240.0.0

   d.   10.0.0.32

2. An engineer has calculated the list of subnet IDs, in consecutive order, for network 172.30.0.0/22, assuming that the /22 mask is used throughout the network. Which of the following is true? (Choose two.)

   a.   Any two consecutive subnet IDs differ by a value of 22 in the third octet.

   b.   Any two consecutive subnet IDs differ by a value of 16 in the fourth octet.

   c.   The list contains 64 subnet IDs.

   d.   The last subnet ID is 172.30.252.0.

3. Which of the following is a valid subnet ID for network 192.168.9.0, using mask /29, assuming that mask /29 is used throughout the network?

   a.   192.168.9.144

   b.   192.168.9.58

   c.   192.168.9.242

   d.   192.168.9.9

4. An engineer, using class B network 172.20.0.0, correctly claims that the following are valid subnet IDs: 172.20.128.0, 172.20.192.0, and 172.20.80.0. That engineer also confirms that they use a single mask throughout network 172.20.0.0. Which of the following masks could this company be using?

   a.   255.255.252.0

   b.   255.255.192.0

   c.   255.255.224.0

   d.   255.255.0.0

5. Which of the following are not valid subnet IDs for network 172.19.0.0, using mask /24, assuming that mask /24 is used throughout the network?

   a. 172.19.0.0

   b. 172.19.1.0

   c. 172.19.255.0

   d. 172.19.0.16

6. Which of the following is not a valid subnet ID for network 172.19.0.0, using mask /27, assuming that mask /27 is used throughout the network?

   a. 172.19.0.0

   b. 172.19.160.16

   c. 172.19.255.64

   d. 172.19.192.192

7. Which of the following is not a valid subnet ID for network 10.0.0.0, using mask /25, assuming that this mask is used throughout the network?

   a. 10.0.0.0

   b. 10.255.255.0

   c. 10.255.127.128

   d. 10.1.1.192

This chapter covers the following subjects:

- **VLSM:** This section explains the issues and solutions when designing an internetwork that uses VLSM.

- **Manual Route Summarization:** This section explains the concept of manual route summarization and describes how to design internetworks to allow easier summarization.

- **Autosummarization and Discontiguous Classful Networks:** This section examines the autosummarization feature and explains how it must be considered in internetwork designs that use discontiguous networks.

CHAPTER 19

VLSM and Route Summarization

This chapter discusses three related topics: Variable-length subnet masks (VLSM), manual route summarization, and automatic route summarization. These topics mainly relate to each other because of the underlying math, which requires that the engineer be able to look at a subnet number and mask to quickly determine the implied range of addresses. This chapter begins with VLSM, moving on to manual route summarization, and finally autosummarization.

VLSM

VLSM occurs when an internetwork uses more than one mask in different subnets of a single Class A, B, or C network. VLSM allows engineers to reduce the number of wasted IP addresses in each subnet, allowing more subnets and avoiding having to obtain another registered IP network number from regional IP address assignment authorities. Also, even when using private IP networks (as defined in RFC 1918), large corporations might still need to conserve the address space, again creating a need to use VLSM.

Figure 19-1 shows an example of VLSM used in class A network 10.0.0.0.

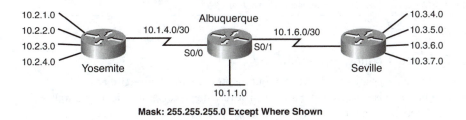

Mask: 255.255.255.0 Except Where Shown

Figure 19-1   *VLSM in Network 10.0.0.0: Masks 255.255.255.0 and 255.255.255.252*

Figure 19-1 shows a typical choice of using a /30 prefix (mask 255.255.255.252) on point-to-point serial links, with some other mask (255.255.255.0, in this example) on the LAN subnets. All subnets are of class A network 10.0.0.0, with two masks being used, therefore meeting the definition of VLSM.

Oddly enough, a common mistake occurs when people think that VLSM means "using more than one mask," rather than "using more than one mask in a single classful network." For example, if in one internetwork diagram, all subnets of network 10.0.0.0 use a

255.255.240.0 mask and all subnets of network 11.0.0.0 use a 255.255.255.0 mask, two different masks are used. However, only one mask is inside each respective classful network, so this particular design would not be using VLSM.

Example 19-1 lists the routing table on Albuquerque from Figure 19-1. Albuquerque uses two masks inside network 10.0.0.0, as noted in the highlighted line in the example.

Example 19-1   *Albuquerque Routing Table with VLSM*

```
Albuquerque# show ip route
Codes: C - connected, S - static, I - IGRP, R - RIP, M - mobile, B - BGP
       D - EIGRP, EX - EIGRP external, O - OSPF, IA - OSPF inter area
       N1 - OSPF NSSA external type 1, N2 - OSPF NSSA external type 2
       E1 - OSPF external type 1, E2 - OSPF external type 2, E - EGP
       i - IS-IS, L1 - IS-IS level-1, L2 - IS-IS level-2, ia - IS-IS inter area
       * - candidate default, U - per-user static route, o - ODR
       P - periodic downloaded static route
Gateway of last resort is not set
     10.0.0.0/8 is variably subnetted, 11 subnets, 2 masks
D       10.2.1.0/24 [90/2172416] via 10.1.4.2, 00:00:34, Serial0/0
D       10.2.2.0/24 [90/2172416] via 10.1.4.2, 00:00:34, Serial0/0
D       10.2.3.0/24 [90/2172416] via 10.1.4.2, 00:00:34, Serial0/0
D       10.2.4.0/24 [90/2172416] via 10.1.4.2, 00:00:34, Serial0/0
D       10.3.4.0/24 [90/2172416] via 10.1.6.2, 00:00:56, Serial0/1
D       10.3.5.0/24 [90/2172416] via 10.1.6.2, 00:00:56, Serial0/1
D       10.3.6.0/24 [90/2172416] via 10.1.6.2, 00:00:56, Serial0/1
D       10.3.7.0/24 [90/2172416] via 10.1.6.2, 00:00:56, Serial0/1
C       10.1.1.0/24 is directly connected, Ethernet0/0
C       10.1.6.0/30 is directly connected, Serial0/1
C       10.1.4.0/30 is directly connected, Serial0/0
```

Classless and Classful Routing Protocols

For a routing protocol to support VLSM, the routing protocol must advertise not only the subnet number but also the subnet mask when advertising routes. Additionally, a routing protocol must include subnet masks in its routing updates to support manual route summarization.

Each IP routing protocol is considered to be either classless or classful, based on whether the routing protocol does (classless) or does not (classful) send the mask in routing updates. Each routing protocol is either classless or classful by its very nature; no commands exist to enable or disable whether a particular routing protocol is a classless or classful routing protocol. Table 19-1 lists the routing protocols, shows whether each is classless or classful, and offers reminders of the two features (VLSM and route summarization) enabled by the inclusion of masks in the routing updates.

Table 19-1 *Classless and Classful Interior IP Routing Protocols*

Routing Protocol	Is It Classless?	Sends Mask in Updates	Supports VLSM	Supports Manual Route Summarization
RIP-1	No	No	No	No
IGRP	No	No	No	No
RIP-2	Yes	Yes	Yes	Yes
EIGRP	Yes	Yes	Yes	Yes
OSPF	Yes	Yes	Yes	Yes

Overlapping VLSM Subnets

The subnets chosen to be used in any IP internetwork design must not overlap their address ranges. With a single subnet mask in a network, the overlaps are somewhat obvious; however, with VLSM, the overlapping subnets might not be as obvious. When multiple subnets overlap, a router's routing table entries overlap. As a result, routing becomes unpredictable, and some hosts can be reached from only particular parts of the internetwork. In short, a design that uses overlapping subnets is considered to be an incorrect design, and should not be used.

Two general types of problems exist that relate to overlapping VLSM subnets: analyzing an existing design to find overlaps, and expanding a design to add VLSM subnets that do not create an overlapped subnet. For example, consider Figure 19-2, which shows a single Class B network (172.16.0.0), using a VLSM design that includes three different masks: /23, /24, and /30.

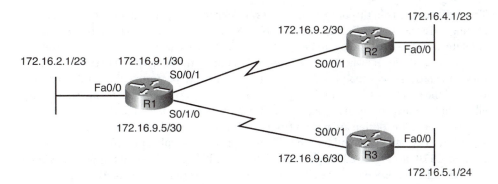

Figure 19-2 *VLSM Design with Possible Overlap*

Now imagine that at a job interview, the interviewer shows you a figure, and asks whether overlapping subnets exist. To answer such a question, you could follow this simple but possibly laborious task:

Step 1. Calculate the subnet number and subnet broadcast address of each subnet; this gives you the range of addresses in that subnet.

Step 2.   Compare the ranges of addresses in each subnet and look for cases in which the address ranges overlap.

For example, in Figure 19-2, you would look at the five subnets, and using Step 1, calculate the subnet numbers, broadcast addresses, and range of addresses, with the answers listed in Table 19-2.

Table 19-2   *Subnets and Address Ranges in Figure 19-2*

Subnet Location	Subnet Number	First Address	Last Address	Broadcast Address
R1 LAN	172.16.2.0	172.16.2.1	172.16.3.254	172.16.3.255
R2 LAN	172.16.4.0	172.16.4.1	172.16.5.254	172.16.5.255
R3 LAN	172.16.5.0	172.16.5.1	172.16.5.254	172.16.5.255
R1-R2 serial	172.16.9.0	172.16.9.1	172.16.9.2	172.16.9.3
R1-R3 serial	172.16.9.4	172.16.9.5	172.16.9.6	172.16.9.7

Step 2 states the somewhat obvious step of comparing the address ranges to see whether any overlaps occur. Note that none of the subnet numbers are identical; however, a closer look at the R2 LAN and R3 LAN subnets shows that these two subnets overlap. In this case, the design is invalid because of the overlap, and one of the two subnets would need to be changed.

Designing a Subnetting Scheme Using VLSM

The earlier chapters in this book that discuss IP subnetting—particularly Chapter 13, "Analyzing Existing Subnets," Chapter 17, "Subnet Mask Design," and Chapter 18, "Finding All Subnet IDs"—explain how to design the IP addressing scheme for a new internetwork by choosing IP subnets when using a single subnet mask throughout a classful network. To do so, the process first analyzes the design requirements to determine the number of subnets and the number of hosts in the largest subnet. Then, a subnet mask is chosen. Finally, all possible subnets of the network, using that mask, are identified, and then the actual subnets used in the design are picked from that list. For example, in Class B network 172.16.0.0, a design might call for ten subnets, with a largest subnet of 200 hosts. Mask 255.255.255.0 meets the requirements, with 8 subnet bits and 8 host bits, supporting 256 subnets and 254 hosts per subnet. The subnet numbers would be 172.16.0.0, 172.16.1.0, 172.16.2.0, and so on.

When using VLSM in a design, the design process starts by deciding how many subnets of each size are required. For example, most installations use subnets with a /30 prefix for serial links because these subnets support exactly two IP addresses, which are all the addresses needed on a point-to-point link. The LAN-based subnets often have different requirements, with shorter prefix lengths (meaning more host bits) for larger numbers of hosts/subnet, and longer prefix lengths (meaning fewer host bits) for smaller numbers of hosts/subnet.

After the number of subnets with each mask has been determined, the next step is to find subnet numbers that match those requirements. This task is not particularly difficult if you already understand how to find subnet numbers when using static-length masks. However, a more formal process can help, which is outlined as follows:

Step 1.   Determine the number of subnets needed for each mask/prefix based on the design requirements.

Step 2.   Using the shortest prefix length (largest number of host bits), identify the subnets of the classful network when using that mask, until the required number of such subnets has been identified.

Step 3.   Identify the next numeric subnet number using the same mask as in the previous step.

Step 4.   Starting with the subnet number identified at the previous step, identify smaller subnets based on the next-longest prefix length required for the design, until the required number of subnets of that size have been identified.

Step 5.   Repeat Steps 3 and 4 until all subnets of all sizes have been found.

Frankly, using the preceding process, as written, can be a little difficult, but an example can certainly help make sense of the process. So, imagine a network design for which the following design requirements were determined, per Step 1 of the previous process. The design calls for the use of Class B network 172.16.0.0:

■   Three subnets with mask /24 (255.255.255.0)

■   Three subnets with mask /26 (255.255.255.192)

■   Four subnets with mask /30 (255.255.255.252)

Step 2 in this case means that the first three subnets of network 172.16.0.0 should be identified, with mask /24, because /24 is the shortest prefix length of the three prefix lengths listed in the design requirements. Using the same math covered in detail in Chapter 18, "Finding All Subnet IDs," the first three subnets would be 172.16.0.0/24, 172.16.1.0/24, and 172.16.2.0/24:

■   172.16.0.0/24: Range 172.16.0.1–172.16.0.254

■   172.16.1.0/24: Range 172.16.1.1–172.16.1.254

■   172.16.2.0/24: Range 172.16.2.1–172.16.2.254

Step 3 in this case says to identify one more subnet using the /24 mask, so the next numeric subnet would be 172.16.3.0/24.

Before moving on to Step 4, take a few minutes to review Figure 19-3. The figure shows the results of Step 2 on the top part of the figure, listing the three subnets identified at this step as "allocated" because they will be used for subnets in this design. It also lists the

next subnet, as found at Step 3, listing it as unallocated, because it has not yet been chosen to be used for a particular part of the design.

Step 2: Find subnets with /24 prefix

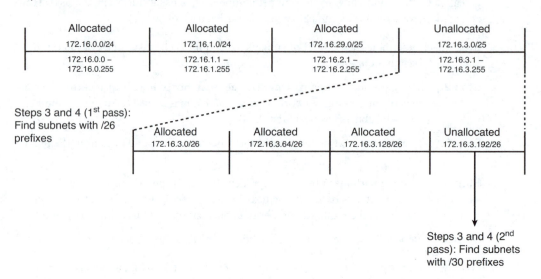

Steps 3 and 4 (1st pass):
Find subnets with /26
prefixes

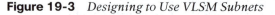

Steps 3 and 4 (2nd
pass): Find subnets
with /30 prefixes

Figure 19-3 *Designing to Use VLSM Subnets*

To find the subnets at Step 4, start with the unallocated subnet number found at Step 3
(172.16.3.0), but with Step 4 applying the next longer prefix length, or /26 in this example.
The process always results in the first subnet number being the subnet number found at
the previous step, or 172.16.3.0 in this case. The three subnets are as follows:

■   172.16.3.0/26: Range 172.16.3.1–172.16.3.62

■   172.16.3.64/26: Range 172.16.3.65–172.16.3.126

■   172.16.3.128/26: Range 172.16.3.129–172.16.3.190

Finally, Step 5 says to repeat Steps 3 and 4 until all subnets have been found. In this case,
repeating Step 3, the next subnet is found, using the /26 prefix length—namely subnet
172.16.3.192/26. This subnet is considered unallocated for the time being. To repeat Step 4
for the next longest prefix length, Step 4 uses the /30 prefix, starting with subnet number
172.16.3.192. The first subnet will be 172.16.3.192, with mask /30, plus the next three subnets with that same mask, as follows:

■   172.16.3.192/30: Range 172.16.3.193–172.16.3.194

■   172.16.3.196/30: Range 172.16.3.197–172.16.3.198

■   172.16.3.200/30: Range 172.16.3.201–172.16.3.202

■   172.16.3.204/30: Range 172.16.3.205–172.16.3.206

The wording in the formalized process might seem to be a bit laborious, but it does result in a set of VLSM subnets that do not overlap. By using a structured approach of essentially allocating the larger subnets first, then the smaller subnets, you can generally choose subnets so that the address ranges do not overlap.

Adding a New Subnet to an Existing Design

Another task required when working with VLSM-based internetworks is to choose a new subnet number for an existing internetwork. In particular, extra care must be taken when choosing new subnet numbers to avoid causing an overlap between the new subnet and any existing subnets. For example, consider the internetwork in Figure 19-2, with classful network 172.16.0.0. You might be given a work request to add a new subnet, with a /23 prefix length, to the design. The work request might also say "Pick the smallest subnet number that can be used for the new subnet." So, the subnets must be identified, and a nonoverlapping subnet must be chosen.

To attack such a problem, you would essentially need to find all the subnet numbers that could be created in that classful network, using the stated or implied mask. Then, you would have to ensure that the new subnet did not overlap with any existing subnets. Specifically, you could use the following steps:

Step 1. If not already listed as part of the question, pick the subnet mask (prefix length) based on the design requirements, typically based on the number of hosts needed in the subnet.

Step 2. Calculate all possible subnet numbers of the classful network, using the mask determined at Step 1. (If you need to use either the numerically largest or smallest subnet number, you might choose to only do this math for the first few or last few subnets.)

Step 3. For the subnets found at Step 2, calculate the subnet broadcast address and range of addresses for each assumed subnet.

Step 4. Compare the lists of potential subnets and address ranges to the existing subnets and address ranges. Rule out any of the potential subnets that overlap with an existing subnet.

Step 5. Pick a subnet number from the list found at Step 2 that does not overlap with any existing subnets, noting whether the question asks for the smallest or largest subnet number.

Using this five-step process with the example started just before the step list with Figure 19-2, the question supplied the prefix length of /23 (Step 1). Table 19-3 lists the results for Steps 2 and 3, listing the subnet numbers, broadcast addresses, and range of addresses for the first five of the possible /23 subnets.

Table 19-3   *First Five Possible /23 Subnets*

Subnet	Subnet Number	First Address	Last Address	Broadcast Address
First (zero)	172.16.0.0	172.16.0.1	172.16.1.254	172.16.1.255
Second	172.16.2.0	172.16.2.1	172.16.3.254	172.16.3.255
Third	172.16.4.0	172.16.4.1	172.16.5.254	172.16.5.255
Fourth	172.16.6.0	172.16.6.1	172.16.7.254	172.16.7.255
Fifth	172.16.8.0	172.16.8.1	172.16.9.254	172.16.9.255

Step 4 compares the information in the table with the existing subnets. In this case, the second, third, and fourth subnets in Table 19-3 overlap with existing subnets in Figure 19-2.

Step 5 has more to do with the types of questions you might see on exams rather than with real networks. Multiple-choice questions sometimes need to force the question to have only a single answer, so asking for the numerically smallest or largest subnet solves the problem. This particular example problem asks for the smallest subnet number, and the zero subnet is still available (172.16.0.0/23, with broadcast address 172.16.1.255). If the question allowed the use of the zero subnet, the zero subnet (172.16.0.0/23) would be the correct answer. However, if the zero subnet was prohibited from use, the first three subnets listed in Table 19-3 would not be available, making the fourth subnet (172.16.8.0/23) the correct answer.

Note: The zero subnet should be avoided if (a) the question implies the use of classful routing protocols or (b) the routers are configured with the **no ip subnet-zero** global configuration command. Otherwise, assume that the zero subnet can be used.

VLSM Configuration

Routers do not enable or disable VLSM as a configuration feature. From a configuration perspective, VLSM is simply a side effect of the **ip address** interface subcommand. Routers configure VLSM by virtue of having at least two router interfaces, on the same router or among all routers in the internetwork, with IP addresses in the same classful network but with different masks. Example 19-2 shows a simple example on Router R3 from Figure 19-2, with interface Fa0/0 being assigned IP address 172.16.5.1/24, and interface S0/0/1 being assigned IP address 172.16.9.6/30, thereby using at least two different masks in network 172.16.0.0.

Example 19-2   *Configuring VLSM*

```
R3# configure terminal
R3(config)# interface Fa0/0
R3(config-if)# ip address 172.16.5.1 255.255.255.0
R3(config-if)# interface S0/0/1
R3(config-if)# ip address 172.16.9.6 255.255.255.252
```

Classless routing protocols, which support VLSM, do not have to be configured to enable VLSM. Support for VLSM is simply a feature inherent to those routing protocols.

Next, the text moves on to the second major section of this chapter, the topic of manual route summarization.

Manual Route Summarization

Small networks might have only a few dozen routes in their routers' routing tables. The larger the network, the larger the number of routes. In fact, Internet routers have more than 100,000 routes in some cases.

The routing table might become too large in large IP networks. As routing tables grow, they consume more memory in a router. Also, each router can take more time to route a packet, because the router has to match a route in the routing table, and searching a larger table generally takes more time. And with a large routing table, it takes more time to troubleshoot problems, because the engineers working on the network need to sift through more information.

Route summarization reduces the size of routing tables while maintaining routes to all the destinations in the network. As a result, routing performance can be improved and memory can be saved inside each router. Summarization also improves convergence time, because the router that summarizes the route no longer has to announce any changes to the status of the individual subnets. By advertising only that the entire summary route is either up or down, the routers that have the summary route do not have to reconverge every time one of the component subnets goes up or down.

This chapter refers to route summarization as manual route summarization, in contrast to the last major topic in this chapter, autosummarization. The term *manual* refers to the fact that manual route summarization only occurs when an engineer configures one or more commands. Autosummarization occurs automatically without a specific configuration command.

The following sections first examine the concepts behind route summarization, followed by some suggestions of how to determine good summary routes. Note that while the concepts are covered, the configuration of manually summarized routes is not covered as an end to itself in this book.

Route Summarization Concepts

Engineers use route summarization to reduce the size of the routing tables in the network. Route summarization causes some number of more-specific routes to be replaced with a single route that includes all the IP addresses covered by the subnets in the original routes.

Summary routes, which replace multiple routes, must be configured by a network engineer. Although the configuration command does not look exactly like a static **ip route** command, the same basic information is configured. Now the routing protocol advertises just the summary route, as opposed to the original routes.

Route summarization works much better when the network was designed with route summarization in mind. For example, Figure 19-1, earlier in this chapter, shows the results of good planning for summarization. In this network, the engineer planned his choices of subnet numbers relative to his goal of using route summarization. All subnets off the main site (Albuquerque), including WAN links, start with 10.1. All LAN subnets off Yosemite start with 10.2, and likewise, all LAN subnets off Seville start with 10.3.

Earlier, Example 19-1 showed a copy of Albuquerque's routing table without summarization. That example shows Albuquerque's four routes to subnets that begin with 10.2, all pointing out its serial 0/0 interface to Yosemite. Similarly, Albuquerque shows four routes to subnets that begin with 10.3, all pointing out its serial 0/1 interface to Seville. This design allows the Yosemite and Seville routers to advertise a single summary route instead of the four routes they currently advertise to Albuquerque, respectively.

Example 19-3 shows the results of the configuration of manual route summarization on both Yosemite and Seville. In this case, Yosemite is advertising a summary route for 10.2.0.0/16, which represents address range 10.2.0.0–10.2.255.255 (all addresses that begin with 10.2). Seville advertises a summary route for 10.3.0.0/16, which represents the address range 10.3.0.0–10.3.255.255 (all addresses that begin 10.3).

Example 19-3   *Albuquerque Routing Table After Route Summarization*

```
Albuquerque# show ip route
Codes: C - connected, S - static, I - IGRP, R - RIP, M - mobile, B - BGP
       D - EIGRP, EX - EIGRP external, O - OSPF, IA - OSPF inter area
       N1 - OSPF NSSA external type 1, N2 - OSPF NSSA external type 2
       E1 - OSPF external type 1, E2 - OSPF external type 2, E - EGP
       i - IS-IS, L1 - IS-IS level-1, L2 - IS-IS level-2, ia - IS-IS inter area
       * - candidate default, U - per-user static route, o - ODR
       P - periodic downloaded static route
Gateway of last resort is not set
     10.0.0.0/8 is variably subnetted, 5 subnets, 3 masks
D       10.2.0.0/16 [90/2172416] via 10.1.4.2, 00:05:59, Serial0/0
D       10.3.0.0/16 [90/2172416] via 10.1.6.3, 00:05:40, Serial0/1
C       10.1.1.0/24 is directly connected, Ethernet0/0
C       10.1.6.0/30 is directly connected, Serial0/1
C       10.1.4.0/30 is directly connected, Serial0/0
```

The resulting routing table on Albuquerque still routes packets correctly, but with more efficiency and less memory. Frankly, improving from 11 routes to 5 routes does not help much, but the same concept, applied to larger networks, does help.

The effects of route summarization can also be seen on the other two routers in the figure. Example 19-4 shows Yosemite, including both the route summarization configuration and Yosemite's routing table. Example 19-5 shows the same kind of information on Seville.

Example 19-4   *Yosemite Configuration and Routing Table After Route Summarization*

```
Yosemite# configure terminal
Enter configuration commands, one per line.  End with CNTL/Z.
Yosemite(config)# interface serial 0/0
```

```
Yosemite(config-if)# ip summary-address eigrp 1 10.2.0.0 255.255.0.0
Yosemite(config-if)# ^Z

Yosemite# show ip route
Codes: C - connected, S - static, I - IGRP, R - RIP, M - mobile, B - BGP
       D - EIGRP, EX - EIGRP external, O - OSPF, IA - OSPF inter area
       N1 - OSPF NSSA external type 1, N2 - OSPF NSSA external type 2
       E1 - OSPF external type 1, E2 - OSPF external type 2, E - EGP
       i - IS-IS, L1 - IS-IS level-1, L2 - IS-IS level-2, ia - IS-IS inter area
       * - candidate default, U - per-user static route, o - ODR
       P - periodic downloaded static route

Gateway of last resort is not set

     10.0.0.0/8 is variably subnetted, 9 subnets, 3 masks
D        10.2.0.0/16 is a summary, 00:04:57, Null0
D        10.3.0.0/16 [90/2684416] via 10.1.4.1, 00:04:30, Serial0/0
C        10.2.1.0/24 is directly connected, FastEthernet0/0
D        10.1.1.0/24 [90/2195456] via 10.1.4.1, 00:04:52, Serial0/0
C        10.2.2.0/24 is directly connected, Loopback2
C        10.2.3.0/24 is directly connected, Loopback3
C        10.2.4.0/24 is directly connected, Loopback4
D        10.1.6.0/30 [90/2681856] via 10.1.4.1, 00:04:53, Serial0/0
C        10.1.4.0/30 is directly connected, Serial0/0
```

Example 19-5 *Seville Configuration and Routing Table After Route Summarization*

```
Seville# configure terminal
Enter configuration commands, one per line.  End with CNTL/Z.
Seville(config)# interface serial 0/0
Seville(config-if)# ip summary-address eigrp 1 10.3.0.0 255.255.0.0
Seville(config-if)# ^Z
Seville# show ip route
Codes: C - connected, S - static, I - IGRP, R - RIP, M - mobile, B - BGP
       D - EIGRP, EX - EIGRP external, O - OSPF, IA - OSPF inter area
       N1 - OSPF NSSA external type 1, N2 - OSPF NSSA external type 2
       E1 - OSPF external type 1, E2 - OSPF external type 2, E - EGP
       i - IS-IS, L1 - IS-IS level-1, L2 - IS-IS level-2, ia - IS-IS inter area
       * - candidate default, U - per-user static route, o - ODR
       P - periodic downloaded static route

Gateway of last resort is not set

     10.0.0.0/8 is variably subnetted, 9 subnets, 3 masks
D        10.2.0.0/16 [90/2684416] via 10.1.6.1, 00:00:36, Serial0/0
```

```
D          10.3.0.0/16 is a summary, 00:00:38, Null0
D          10.1.1.0/24 [90/2195456] via 10.1.6.1, 00:00:36, Serial0/0
C          10.3.5.0/24 is directly connected, Loopback5
C          10.3.4.0/24 is directly connected, FastEthernet0/0
C          10.1.6.0/30 is directly connected, Serial0/0
C          10.3.7.0/24 is directly connected, Loopback7
D          10.1.4.0/30 [90/2681856] via 10.1.6.1, 00:00:36, Serial0/0
C          10.3.6.0/24 is directly connected, Loopback6
```

Route summarization configuration differs with different routing protocols; Enhanced IGRP (EIGRP) is used in this example. The summary routes for EIGRP are created by the **ip summary-address** interface subcommands on Yosemite and Seville in this case. Each command defines a new summarized route and tells EIGRP to only advertise the summary out this interface and not to advertise any routes contained in the larger summary. For example, Yosemite defines a summary route to 10.2.0.0, mask 255.255.0.0, which defines a route to all hosts whose IP addresses begin with 10.2. In effect, this command causes Yosemite and Seville to advertise routes 10.2.0.0 255.255.0.0 and 10.3.0.0 255.255.0.0, respectively, and not to advertise their original four LAN subnets.

Note that back in Example 19-3, Albuquerque's routing table now contains a route to 10.2.0.0 255.255.0.0 (the mask is listed in prefix notation as /16), but none of the original four subnets that begin with 10.2. The same thing occurs for route 10.3.0.0/16.

The routing tables on Yosemite and Seville look a little different from Albuquerque. Focusing on Yosemite (Example 19-4), notice that the four routes to subnets that begin with 10.2 show up because they are directly connected subnets. Yosemite does not see the four 10.3 routes. Instead, it sees a summary route, because Albuquerque now advertises the 10.3.0.0/16 summarized route only. The opposite is true on Seville (Example 19-5), which lists all four connected routes that begin with 10.3 and a summary route for 10.2.0.0/16.

The most interesting part of Yosemite's routing tables is the route to 10.2.0.0/16, with the outgoing interface set to **null0**. Routes referring to an outgoing interface of the null0 interface mean that packets matching this route are discarded. EIGRP added this route, with interface null0, as a result of the **ip summary-address** command. The logic works like this:

Yosemite needs this odd-looking route because now it might receive packets destined for other 10.2 addresses besides the four existing 10.2 subnets. If a packet destined for one of the four existing 10.2.x subnets arrives, Yosemite has a correct, more specific route to match the packet. If a packet whose destination starts with 10.2 arrives, but it is not in one of those four subnets, the null route matches the packet, causing Yosemite to discard the packet—as it should.

The routing table on Seville is similar to Yosemite's in terms of the table entries and why they are in the table.

Route Summarization Strategies

As mentioned earlier, manual route summarization works best when the network engineer plans his choice of subnet numbers anticipating route summarization. For example, the earlier examples assumed a well-thought-out plan, with the engineers only using subnets beginning with 10.2 for subnets off the Yosemite router. That convention allowed the creation of a summary route for all addresses beginning with 10.2 by having Yosemite advertise a route describing subnet 10.2.0.0, mask 255.255.0.0.

Some summarized routes combine many routes into one route, but that might not be the "best" summarization. The word *best*, when applied to choosing what summary route to configure, means that the summary should include all the subnets specified in the question but as few other addresses as is possible. For example, in the earlier summarization example, Yosemite summarized four subnets (10.2.1.0, 10.2.2.0, 10.2.3.0, and 10.2.4.0, all with mask 255.255.255.0) into the 10.2.0.0/16 summary route. However, this summary includes a lot of IP addresses that are not in those four subnets. Does the summary work given that network's design goals? Sure. However, instead of just defining a summary that encompasses lots of additional addresses that do not yet exist in a network, the engineer might instead want to configure the tightest, or most concise, or best summary: the summary that includes all the subnets but as few extra subnets (the ones that have not been assigned yet) as possible. This section describes a strategy for finding those concise best summary routes.

The following list describes a generalized binary process by which you can find a best summary route for a group of subnets:

Step 1. List all to-be-summarized subnet numbers in binary.

Step 2. Find the first N bits of the subnet numbers for which every subnet has the same value, moving from left to right. (For our purposes, consider this first part the "in-common" part.)

Step 3. To find the summary router's subnet number, write down the in-common bits from Step 2 and binary 0s for the remaining bits. Convert back to decimal, 8 bits at a time, when finished.

Step 4. To find the summary route's subnet mask, write down N binary 1s, with N being the number of in-common bits found at Step 2. Complete the subnet mask with all binary 0s. Convert back to decimal, 8 bits at a time, when finished.

Step 5. Check your work by calculating the range of valid IP addresses implied by the new summary route, comparing the range to the summarized subnets. The new summary should encompass all IP addresses in the summarized subnets.

By looking at the subnet numbers in binary, you can more easily discover the bits in common among all the subnet numbers. By using the longest number of bits in common, you can find the best summary. The next two sections show two examples using this process to find the best, most concise, tightest summary routes for the network shown in Figure 19-1.

Key Topic

Sample "Best" Summary on Seville

Seville has subnets 10.3.4.0, 10.3.5.0, 10.3.6.0, and 10.3.7.0, all with mask 255.255.255.0. You start the process by writing down all the subnet numbers in binary:

```
0000 1010 0000 0011 0000 01 | 00 0000 0000 - 10.3.4.0
0000 1010 0000 0011 0000 01 | 01 0000 0000 - 10.3.5.0
0000 1010 0000 0011 0000 01 | 10 0000 0000 - 10.3.6.0
0000 1010 0000 0011 0000 01 | 11 0000 0000 - 10.3.7.0
```

Step 2 requires that you find all in-common bits at the beginning of all the subnets. Even before looking at the numbers in binary, you can guess that the first two octets are identical in all four subnets. So, a quick look at the first 16 bits of all four subnet numbers confirms that all have the same value. This means that the in-common part (Step 2) is at least 16 bits long. Further examination shows that the first 6 bits of the third octet are also identical, but the seventh bit in the third octet has some different values among the different subnets. So, the in-common part of these four subnets is the first 22 bits.

Step 3 says to create a subnet number for the summary by taking the same bits in the in-common part, and write down binary 0s for the rest. In this case:

```
0000 1010 0000 0011 0000 01 | 00 0000 0000 - 10.3.4.0
```

Step 4 creates the mask by using binary 1s for the same bits as the in-common part, which is the first 22 bits in this case, and then binary 0s for the remaining bits, as follows:

```
1111 1111 1111 1111 1111 11 | 00 0000 0000 - 255.255.252.0
```

So, the summary route uses subnet 10.3.4.0, mask 255.255.252.0.

Step 5 suggests a method to check your work. The summary route should include all the IP addresses in the summarized routes. In this case, the range of addresses for the summary route starts with 10.3.4.0. The first valid IP address is 10.3.4.1, the final valid IP address is 10.3.7.254, and the broadcast address is 10.3.7.255. In this case, the summary route includes all the IP addresses in the four routes it summarizes and no extraneous IP addresses.

Sample "Best" Summary on Yosemite

The four subnets on Yosemite cannot be summarized quite as efficiently as those on Seville. On Seville, the summary route itself covers the same set of IP addresses as the four subnets with no extra addresses. As you will see, the best summary route at Yosemite includes twice as many addresses in the summary as exist in the original four subnets.

Yosemite has subnets 10.2.1.0, 10.2.2.0, 10.2.3.0, and 10.2.4.0, all with mask 255.255.255.0. The process starts at Step 1 by writing down all the subnet numbers in binary:

```
0000 1010 0000 0010 0000 0 | 001 0000 0000 - 10.2.1.0
0000 1010 0000 0010 0000 0 | 010 0000 0000 - 10.2.2.0
0000 1010 0000 0010 0000 0 | 011 0000 0000 - 10.2.3.0
0000 1010 0000 0010 0000 0 | 100 0000 0000 - 10.2.4.0
```

At Step 2, it appears that the first two octets are identical in all four subnets, plus the first 5 bits of the third octet. So, the first 21 bits of the four subnet numbers are in common.

Step 3 says to create a subnet number for the summary route by taking the same value for the in-common part and binary 0s for the rest. In this case:

```
0000 1010 0000 0010 0000 0 | 000 0000 0000 - 10.2.0.0
```

Step 4 creates the mask used for the summary route by using binary 1s for the in-common part and binary 0s for the rest. The in-common part in this example is the first 21 bits:

```
1111 1111 1111 1111 1111 1 | 000 0000 0000 - 255.255.248.0
```

So, the best summary is 10.2.0.0, mask 255.255.248.0.

Step 5 suggests a method to check your work. The summary route should define a super-set of the IP addresses in the summarized routes. In this case, the range of addresses starts with 10.2.0.0. The first valid IP address is 10.2.0.1, the final valid IP address is 10.2.7.254, and the broadcast address is 10.2.7.255. In this case, the summary route summarizes a larger set of addresses than just the four subnets, but it does include all addresses in all four subnets.

Autosummarization and Discontiguous Classful Networks

As covered in the previous sections, manual route summarization can improve routing efficiency, reduce memory consumption, and improve convergence by reducing the length of routing tables. The final sections of this chapter examine the automatic summarization of routes at the boundaries of classful networks, using a feature called autosummarization.

Because classful routing protocols do not advertise subnet mask information, the routing updates simply list subnet numbers but no accompanying mask. A router receiving a routing update with a classful routing protocol looks at the subnet number in the update, but the router must make some assumptions about what mask is associated with the subnet.

For example, with Cisco routers, if R1 and R2 have connected networks of the same single Class A, B, or C network, and if R2 receives an update from R1, R2 assumes that the routes described in R1's update use the same mask that R2 uses. In other words, the classful routing protocols require a static-length subnet mask (SLSM) throughout each classful network so that each router can then reasonably assume that the mask configured for its own interfaces is the same mask used throughout that classful network.

When a router has interfaces in more than one Class A, B, or C network, it can advertise a single route for an entire Class A, B, or C network into the other classful network. This feature is called *autosummarization*. It can be characterized as follows:

> When advertised on an interface whose IP address is not in network X, routes related to subnets in network X are summarized and advertised as one route. That route is for the entire Class A, B, or C network X.

In other words, if R3 has interfaces in networks 10.0.0.0 and 11.0.0.0, when R3 advertises routing updates out interfaces with IP addresses that start with 11, the updates advertise a single route for network 10.0.0.0. Similarly, R3 advertises a single route to 11.0.0.0 out its interfaces whose IP addresses start with 10.

An Example of Autosummarization

As usual, an example makes the concept much clearer. Consider Figure 19-4, which shows two networks in use: 10.0.0.0 and 172.16.0.0. Seville has four (connected) routes to subnets of network 10.0.0.0. Example 19-6 shows the output of the **show ip route** command on Albuquerque, as well as RIP-1 **debug ip rip** output.

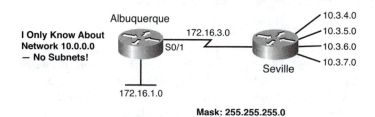

Figure 19-4   *Autosummarization*

Example 19-6   *Albuquerque Routes and RIP Debugs*

```
Albuquerque# show ip route
Codes: C - connected, S - static, I - IGRP, R - RIP, M - mobile, B - BGP
       D - EIGRP, EX - EIGRP external, O - OSPF, IA - OSPF inter area
       N1 - OSPF NSSA external type 1, N2 - OSPF NSSA external type 2
       E1 - OSPF external type 1, E2 - OSPF external type 2, E - EGP
       i - IS-IS, L1 - IS-IS level-1, L2 - IS-IS level-2, ia - IS-IS inter area
       * - candidate default, U - per-user static route, o - ODR
       P - periodic downloaded static route

Gateway of last resort is not set

     172.16.0.0/24 is subnetted, 2 subnets
C       172.16.1.0 is directly connected, Ethernet0/0
C       172.16.3.0 is directly connected, Serial0/1
R    10.0.0.0/8 [120/1] via 172.16.3.3, 00:00:28, Serial0/1


Albuquerque# debug ip rip
RIP protocol debugging is on

00:05:36: RIP: received v1 update from 172.16.3.3 on Serial0/1
00:05:36:      10.0.0.0 in 1 hops
```

As shown in Example 19-6, Albuquerque's received update on Serial0/1 from Seville advertises only the entire Class A network 10.0.0.0 because autosummarization is enabled on

Seville (by default). As a result, the Albuquerque IP routing table lists just one route to network 10.0.0.0.

This example also points out another feature of how classful routing protocols make assumptions. Albuquerque does not have any interfaces in network 10.0.0.0. So, when Albuquerque receives the routing update, it assumes that the mask used with 10.0.0.0 is 255.0.0.0, the default mask for a Class A network. In other words, classful routing protocols expect autosummarization to occur.

Discontiguous Classful Networks

Autosummarization does not cause any problems as long as the summarized network is contiguous rather than discontiguous. U.S. residents can appreciate the concept of a discontiguous network based on the common term *contiguous 48*, referring to the 48 U.S. states besides Alaska and Hawaii. To drive to Alaska from the contiguous 48, for example, you must drive through another country (Canada, for the geographically impaired!), so Alaska is not contiguous with the 48 states. In other words, it is discontiguous.

To better understand what the terms *contiguous* and *discontiguous* mean in networking, refer to the following two formal definitions when reviewing the example of a discontiguous classful network that follows:

■ **Contiguous network:** A classful network in which packets sent between every pair of subnets can pass only through subnets of that same classful network, without having to pass through subnets of any other classful network.

Key
Topic

■ **Discontiguous network:** A classful network in which packets sent between at least one pair of subnets must pass through subnets of a different classful network.

Figure 19-5 shows an example of a discontiguous network 10.0.0.0. In this case, packets sent from the subnets of network 10.0.0.0 on the left, near Yosemite, to the subnets of network 10.0.0.0 on the right, near Seville, have to pass through subnets of network 172.16.0.0.

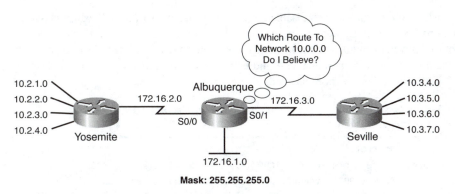

Figure 19-5 *Discontiguous Network 10.0.0.0*

Autosummarization prevents an internetwork with a discontiguous network from working properly. Example 19-7 shows the results of using autosummarization in the internetwork shown in Figure 19-5—in this case, using the classful RIP-1 routing protocol.

Example 19-7   *Albuquerque Routing Table: Autosummarization Causes Routing Problem with Discontiguous Network 10.0.0.0*

```
Albuquerque# show ip route
Codes: C - connected, S - static, I - IGRP, R - RIP, M - mobile, B - BGP
       D - EIGRP, EX - EIGRP external, O - OSPF, IA - OSPF inter area
       N1 - OSPF NSSA external type 1, N2 - OSPF NSSA external type 2
       E1 - OSPF external type 1, E2 - OSPF external type 2, E - EGP
       i - IS-IS, L1 - IS-IS level-1, L2 - IS-IS level-2, ia - IS-IS inter area
       * - candidate default, U - per-user static route, o - ODR
       P - periodic downloaded static route

Gateway of last resort is not set

     172.16.0.0/24 is subnetted, 3 subnets
C       172.16.1.0 is directly connected, Ethernet0/0
C       172.16.2.0 is directly connected, Serial0/0
C       172.16.3.0 is directly connected, Serial0/1
R    10.0.0.0/8 [120/1] via 172.16.3.3, 00:00:13, Serial0/1
                [120/1] via 172.16.2.2, 00:00:04, Serial0/0
```

As shown in Example 19-7, Albuquerque now has two routes to network 10.0.0.0/8: one pointing left toward Yosemite and one pointing right toward Seville. Instead of sending packets destined for Yosemite's subnets out Serial 0/0, Albuquerque sends some packets out S0/1 to Seville! Albuquerque simply balances the packets across the two routes, because as far as Albuquerque can tell, the two routes are simply equal-cost routes to the same destination: the entire network 10.0.0.0. So, applications would cease to function correctly in this network.

The solution to this problem is to disable the use of autosummarization. Because classful routing protocols must use autosummarization, the solution requires migration to a classless routing protocol and disabling the autosummarization feature. Example 19-8 shows the same internetwork from Figure 19-5 and Example 19-7, but this time with (classless) EIGRP, with autosummarization disabled.

Example 19-8   *Classless Routing Protocol with No Autosummarization Allows Discontiguous Network*

```
Albuquerque# show ip route
Codes: C - connected, S - static, I - IGRP, R - RIP, M - mobile, B - BGP
       D - EIGRP, EX - EIGRP external, O - OSPF, IA - OSPF inter area
       N1 - OSPF NSSA external type 1, N2 - OSPF NSSA external type 2
       E1 - OSPF external type 1, E2 - OSPF external type 2, E - EGP
```

```
        i - IS-IS, L1 - IS-IS level-1, L2 - IS-IS level-2, ia - IS-IS inter area
        * - candidate default, U - per-user static route, o - ODR
        P - periodic downloaded static route

Gateway of last resort is not set

      172.16.0.0/24 is subnetted, 3 subnets
C       172.16.1.0 is directly connected, Ethernet0/0
C       172.16.2.0 is directly connected, Serial0/0
C       172.16.3.0 is directly connected, Serial0/1
      10.0.0.0/24 is subnetted, 8 subnets
D       10.2.1.0/24 [90/2172416] via 172.16.2.2, 00:00:01, Serial0/0
D       10.2.2.0/24 [90/2297856] via 172.16.2.2, 00:00:01, Serial0/0
D       10.2.3.0/24 [90/2297856] via 172.16.2.2, 00:00:01, Serial0/0
D       10.2.4.0/24 [90/2297856] via 172.16.2.2, 00:00:01, Serial0/0
D       10.3.5.0/24 [90/2297856] via 172.16.3.3, 00:00:29, Serial0/1
D       10.3.4.0/24 [90/2172416] via 172.16.3.3, 00:00:29, Serial0/1
D       10.3.7.0/24 [90/2297856] via 172.16.3.3, 00:00:29, Serial0/1
D       10.3.6.0/24 [90/2297856] via 172.16.3.3, 00:00:29, Serial0/1
```

With autosummarization disabled on both Yosemite and Seville, neither router advertises an automatic summary of network 10.0.0.0/8 to Albuquerque. Instead, each router advertises the known subnets, so now Albuquerque knows the four LAN subnets off Yosemite as well as the four LAN subnets off Seville.

Autosummarization Support and Configuration

Classful routing protocols must use autosummarization. Some classless routing protocols support autosummarization, defaulting to use it, but with the ability to disable it with the **no auto-summary** router subcommand. Other classless routing protocols, notably Open Shortest Path First (OSPF), simply do not support autosummarization. Table 19-4 summarizes the facts about autosummarization on Cisco routers.

Table 19-4 *Autosummarization Support and Defaults*

Routing Protocol	Classless?	Supports Autosummarization?	Defaults to Use Autosummarization?[1]	Can Disable Autosummarization?
RIP-1	No	Yes	Yes	No
RIP-2	Yes	Yes	Yes	Yes
EIGRP	Yes	Yes	Yes	Yes
OSPF	Yes	No	—	—

[1]As of IOS 12.4 mainline.

Also note that the autosummary feature impacts routers that directly connect to parts of more than one classful network, but it has no impact on routers whose interfaces all connect to the same single classful network. For example, in Figure 19-5, the solution (as shown in Example 19-8) required the **no auto-summary** EIGRP subcommand on both Yosemite and Seville. However, Albuquerque, whose interfaces all sit inside a single network (Class B network 172.16.0.0), would not change its behavior with either the **auto-summary** or **no auto-summary** command configured in this case.

Chapter Review

Review Key Topics

Review the most important topics from this chapter, noted with the Key Topic icon in the outer margin of the page. Table 19-5 lists a reference of these key topics and the page numbers on which each is found.

Table 19-5   *Key Topics for Chapter 19*

Key Topic Element	Description	Page Number
Table 19-1	List of IP routing protocols, with facts about classless/classful, VLSM support, and summarization support	455
List	Two-step strategy for finding overlapping VLSM subnets	455
List	Five-step strategy for choosing a new nonoverlapping VLSM subnet	459
List	Five-step process for finding the best manual summary route	465
Definition	Generalized definition of autosummarization	467
Definitions	Definitions for contiguous network and discontiguous network	469
Table 19-4	List of routing protocols and facts related to autosummarization	471

Define Key Terms

Define the following key terms from this chapter, and check your answers in the glossary:

autosummarization, classful network, classful routing protocol, classless routing protocol, contiguous network, discontiguous network, overlapping subnets, summary route, variable-length subnet masking

Review Command Reference to Check Your Memory

This chapter introduces only one new command that has not already been introduced in this book, namely the [no] **auto-summary** router configuration mode command. This command enables autosummarization (omitting the **no** option) or disables autosummarization (using the **no** option).

This chapter includes this command reference section just as a reminder of the one command to remember from this chapter.

Answer Review Questions

Answer the following review questions:

1. Which of the following routine protocols support VLSM?

   a.   RIP-1

   b.   RIP-2

   c.   EIGRP

   d.   OSPF

2. What does the acronym VLSM stand for?

   a.   Variable-length subnet mask

   b.   Very long subnet mask

   c.   Vociferous longitudinal subnet mask

   d.   Vector-length subnet mask

   e.   Vector loop subnet mask

3. R1 has configured interface Fa0/0 with the **ip address 10.5.48.1 255.255.240.0** command. Which of the following subnets, when configured on another interface on R1, would not be considered to be an overlapping VLSM subnet?

   a.   10.5.0.0 255.255.240.0

   b.   10.4.0.0 255.254.0.0

   c.   10.5.32.0 255.255.224.0

   d.   10.5.0.0 255.255.128.0

4. Which of the following summarized subnets is the smallest (smallest range of addresses) summary route that includes subnets 10.3.95.0, 10.3.96.0, and 10.3.97.0, mask 255.255.255.0?

   a.   10.0.0.0 255.0.0.0

   b.   10.3.0.0 255.255.0.0

   c.   10.3.64.0 255.255.192.0

   d.   10.3.64.0 255.255.224.0

5. Which of the following summarized subnets is not a valid summary that includes subnets 10.1.55.0, 10.1.56.0, and 10.1.57.0, mask 255.255.255.0?

   a.   10.0.0.0 255.0.0.0

   b.   10.1.0.0 255.255.0.0

   c.   10.1.55.0 255.255.255.0

   d.   10.1.48.0 255.255.248.0

   e.   10.1.32.0 255.255.224.0

6. Which of the following routing protocols support manual route summarization?

   a.   RIP-1

   b.   RIP-2

   c.   EIGRP

   d.   OSPF

7. Which routing protocol(s) perform(s) autosummarization by default?

   a.   RIP-1

   b.   RIP-2

   c.   EIGRP

   d.   OSPF

8. An internetwork has a discontiguous network 10.0.0.0, and it is having problems. All routers use RIP-1 with all default configurations. Which of the following answers lists an action that, by itself, would solve the problem and allow the discontiguous network?

   a.   Migrate all routers to use OSPF, using as many defaults as is possible.

   b.   Disable autosummarization with the **no auto-summary** RIP configuration command.

   c.   Migrate to EIGRP, using as many defaults as is possible.

   d.   The problem cannot be solved without first making network 10.0.0.0 contiguous.

This chapter covers the following subjects:

■ **The ping and traceroute Commands:** This section explains how the ping and traceroute commands work, along with the nuances of how they can be used to better troubleshoot routing problems.

■ **Troubleshooting the Packet Forwarding Process:** This section examines the packet forwarding process, focusing on host routing and how routers route packets. It also covers issues related to forwarding packets in both directions between two hosts.

■ **Troubleshooting Tools and Tips:** This section covers a wide variety of topics that have some effect on the packet forwarding process. It includes many tips about various commands and concepts that can aid the troubleshooting process.

CHAPTER 20

Troubleshooting IP Routing II

This troubleshooting chapter has several goals. First, it explains several tools and functions not covered previously in this book—specifically, tools that can be very helpful when you're analyzing problems. This chapter also reviews concepts by showing a suggested process for troubleshooting routing problems, as well as examples of how to use the process. The last major section of this chapter focuses on a series of troubleshooting tips for a variety of features, including VLSM and route summarization.

The ping and traceroute Commands

This section examines a suggested process of troubleshooting IP routing—in other words, troubleshooting the data plane process of how hosts and routers forward IP packets. To that end, this section first examines a set of useful tools and protocols, including ICMP, **ping**, and **traceroute**. Following that, the text suggests a good general troubleshooting process for IP problems, with a few examples to show how to use the processes.

Internet Control Message Protocol (ICMP)

TCP/IP includes ICMP, a protocol designed to help manage and control the operation of a TCP/IP network. The ICMP protocol provides a wide variety of information about a network's health and operational status. *Control Message* is the most descriptive part of the name. ICMP helps control and manage IP's work by defining a set of messages and procedures about the operation of IP. Therefore, ICMP is considered part of TCP/IP's network layer. Because ICMP helps control IP, it can provide useful troubleshooting information. In fact, the ICMP messages sit inside an IP packet, with no transport layer header, so ICMP is truly an extension of the TCP/IP network layer.

RFC 792 defines ICMP. The following excerpt from RFC 792 describes the protocol well:

> Occasionally a gateway (router) or destination host will communicate with a source host, for example, to report an error in datagram processing. For such purposes, this protocol, the Internet Control Message Protocol (ICMP), is used. ICMP uses the basic support of IP as if it were a higher level protocol; however, ICMP is actually an integral part of IP and must be implemented by every IP module.

ICMP defines several different types of messages to accomplish its varied tasks, as summarized in Table 20-1.

Key Topic

Table 20-1 *ICMP Message Types*

Message	Description
Destination Unreachable	Tells the source host that there is a problem delivering a packet.
Time Exceeded	The time that it takes a packet to be delivered has expired, so the packet has been discarded.
Redirect	The router sending this message has received a packet for which another router has a better route. The message tells the sender to use the better route.
Echo Request, Echo Reply	Used by the **ping** command to verify connectivity.

The ping Command and the ICMP Echo Request and Echo Reply

The **ping** command uses the ICMP Echo Request and Echo Reply messages. In fact, when people say they sent a ping packet, they really mean that they sent an ICMP Echo Request. These two messages are somewhat self-explanatory. The Echo Request simply means that the host to which it is addressed should reply to the packet. The Echo Reply is the ICMP message type that should be used in the reply. The Echo Request includes some data that can be specified by the **ping** command; whatever data is sent in the Echo Request is sent back in the Echo Reply.

The **ping** command itself supplies many creative ways to use Echo Requests and Replies. For instance, the **ping** command lets you specify the length as well as the source and destination addresses, and it also lets you set other fields in the IP header. Chapter 12, "IP Routing: Static and Connected Routes," shows an example of the extended **ping** command that lists the various options.

The Destination Unreachable ICMP Message

This book focuses on IP. But if you take a broader view, the role of the entire set of TCP/IP protocols is to deliver data from the sending application to the receiving application. Hosts and routers send ICMP Destination Unreachable messages back to the sending host when that host or router cannot deliver the data completely to the application at the destination host.

To aid in troubleshooting, the ICMP Unreachable message includes five separate unreachable functions (codes) that further identify the reason why the packet cannot be delivered. All five code types pertain directly to an IP, TCP, or UDP feature.

For example, the internetwork shown in Figure 20-1 can be used to better understand some of the Unreachable codes. Assume that Fred is trying to connect to the web server, called Web. (Web uses HTTP, which in turn uses TCP as the transport layer protocol.) Three of the ICMP unreachable codes can possibly be used by Routers A and B. The other two codes are used by the web server. These ICMP codes are sent to Fred as a result of the packet originally sent by Fred.

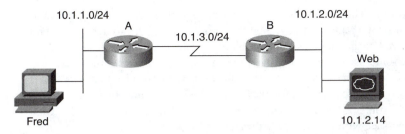

Figure 20-1 *Sample Network for Discussing ICMP Unreachable Codes*

Table 20-2 summarizes the more common ICMP unreachable codes. After the table, the text explains how each ICMP code might be needed for the network shown in Figure 20-1.

Table 20-2 *ICMP Unreachable Codes*

Unreachable Code	When It Is Used	What Typically Sends It
Network unreachable	There is no match in a routing table for the packet's destination.	Router
Host unreachable	The packet can be routed to a router connected to the destination subnet, but the host is not responding.	Router
Can't fragment	The packet has the Don't Fragment bit set, and a router must fragment to forward the packet.	Router
Protocol unreachable	The packet is delivered to the destination host, but the transport layer protocol.	Host
Port unreachable	The packet is delivered to the destination host, but the destination port has not been opened by an application.	Host

The following list explains each code in Table 20-2 in greater detail using the network in Figure 20-1 as an example:

■ **Network unreachable:** Router A uses this code if it does not have a route telling it where to forward the packet. In this case, Router A needs to route the packet to subnet 10.1.2.0/24. If it cannot, Router A sends Fred the ICMP Destination Unreachable message with the code "network unreachable" in response to Fred's packet destined for 10.1.2.14.

■ **Host unreachable:** This code implies that the single destination host is unavailable. If Router A has a route to 10.1.2.0/24, the packet is delivered to Router B. If Router B's LAN interface is working, B also has a connected route to 10.1.2.0/24, so B tries to ARP and learn the web server's MAC address. However, if the web server is down, Router B does not get an ARP reply from the web server. Router B sends Fred the ICMP Destination Unreachable message with the code "host unreachable," meaning that B has a route but cannot forward the packet directly to 10.1.2.14.

- **Can't fragment:** This code is the last of the three ICMP unreachable codes that a router might send. Fragmentation defines the process in which a router needs to forward a packet, but the outgoing interface allows only packets that are smaller than the packet. The router is allowed to fragment the packet into pieces, but the packet header can be set with the "Do Not Fragment" bit in the IP header. In this case, if Router A or B needs to fragment the packet, but the Do Not Fragment bit is set in the IP header, the router discards the packet and sends Fred an ICMP Destination Unreachable message with the code "can't fragment."

- **Protocol unreachable:** If the packet successfully arrives at the web server, two other unreachable codes are possible. One implies that the protocol above IP, typically TCP or UDP, is not running on that host. This is highly unlikely, because most operating systems that use TCP/IP use a single software package that provides IP, TCP, and UDP functions. But if the host receives the IP packet and TCP or UDP is unavailable, the web server host sends Fred the ICMP Destination Unreachable message with the code "protocol unreachable" in response to Fred's packet destined for 10.1.2.14.

- **Port unreachable:** This final code field value is more likely today. If the server—the computer—is up and running, but the web server software is not running, the packet can get to the server but cannot be delivered to the web server software. In effect, the server is not listening on that application protocol's well-known port. So, host 10.1.2.14 sends Fred the ICMP Destination Unreachable message with the code "port unreachable" in response to Fred's packet destined for 10.1.2.14.

Note: Most security policies today filter these various unreachable messages to help bolster the network's security profile.

The **ping** command lists various responses that in some cases imply that an unreachable message was received. Table 20-3 lists the various unreachable codes that can be displayed by the Cisco IOS Software **ping** command.

Table 20-3   *Codes That the* **ping** *Command Receives in Response to Its ICMP Echo Request*

ping Command Code	Description
!	ICMP Echo Reply received
.	Nothing was received before the **ping** command timed out
U	ICMP unreachable (destination) received
N	ICMP unreachable (network/subnet) received
M	ICMP Can't Fragment message received
?	Unknown packet received

The Redirect ICMP Message

The ICMP Redirect message provides a means by which routers can tell hosts to use another router as default gateway for certain destination addresses. Most hosts use the concept of a default router IP address, sending packets destined for subnets to their default router. However, if multiple routers connect to the same subnet, a host's default gateway might not be the best router on that subnet to which to forward packets sent to some destinations. The default gateway can recognize that a different router is a better option. Then it can send ICMP redirect messages to the host to tell it to send the packets for that destination address to this different router.

For example, in Figure 20-2, the PC uses Router B as its default router. However, Router A's route to subnet 10.1.4.0 is a better route. (Assume the use of mask 255.255.255.0 in each subnet in Figure 20-2.) The PC sends a packet to Router B (Step 1 in Figure 20-2). Router B then forwards the packet based on its own routing table (Step 2); that route points through Router A, which has a better route. Finally, Router B sends the ICMP redirect message to the PC (Step 3), telling it to forward future packets destined for 10.1.4.0 to Router A instead. Ironically, the host can ignore the redirect and keep sending the packets to Router B, but in this example, the PC believes the redirect message, sending its next packet (Step 4) directly to Router A.

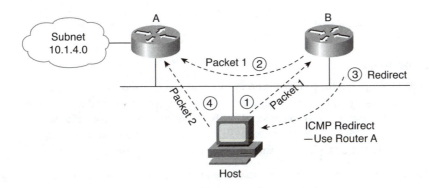

Figure 20-2 *ICMP Redirect*

The ICMP Time Exceeded Message

The ICMP Time Exceeded message notifies a host when a packet it sent has been discarded because it was "out of time." Packets are not actually timed, but to prevent them from being forwarded forever when there is a routing loop, each IP header uses a Time to Live (TTL) field. Routers decrement the TTL by 1 every time they forward a packet; if a router decrements the TTL to 0, it throws away the packet. This prevents packets from rotating forever. Figure 20-3 shows the basic process.

As you can see in the figure, the router that discards the packet also sends an ICMP Time Exceeded message, with a Code field of "time exceeded" to the host that sent the packet. That way, the sender knows that the packet was not delivered. Getting a Time Exceeded message can also help you when you troubleshoot a network. Hopefully, you do not get too many of these; otherwise, you have routing problems.

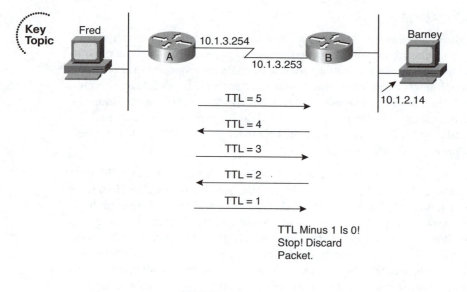

Figure 20-3   *TTL Decremented to 0*

The traceroute Command

The **ping** command is a powerful troubleshooting tool that can be used to answer the question "Does the route from here to there work?" The **traceroute** command provides an arguably better troubleshooting tool because not only can it determine if the route works, but it can supply the IP address of each router in the route. If the route is not working, **traceroute** can identify the best places to start troubleshooting the problem.

The IOS **traceroute** command uses the Time Exceeded message and the IP TTL field to identify each successive router in a route. The **traceroute** command sends a set of messages with increasing TTL values, starting with 1. The **traceroute** command expects these messages to be discarded when routers decrement the TTL to 0, returning Time Exceeded messages to the **traceroute** command. The source IP addresses of the Time Exceeded messages identify the routers that discarded the messages, which can then be displayed by the **traceroute** command.

To see how this command works, consider the first set of packets (three packets by default) sent by the **traceroute** command. The packets are IP packets, with a UDP transport layer, and with the TTL set to 1. When the packets arrive at the next router, the router decrements the TTL to 0 in each packet, discards the packet, and sends a Time Exceeded message back to the host that sent the discarded packet. The **traceroute** command looks at the first router's source IP address in the received Time Exceeded packet.

Next, the **traceroute** command sends another set of three IP packets, this time with TTL = 2. The first router decrements TTL to 1 and forwards the packets, and the second router decrements the TTL to 0 and discards the packets. This second router sends Time

Exceeded messages back to the router where the **traceroute** command was used, and the **traceroute** command now knows the second router in the route.

The **traceroute** command knows when the test packets arrive at the destination host because the host sends back an ICMP Port Unreachable message. The original packets sent by the IOS **traceroute** command use a destination UDP port number that is very unlikely to be used on the destination host, so as soon as the TTL is large enough to allow the packet to arrive at the destination host, the host notices that it does not have an application listening at that particular UDP port. So, the destination host returns a Port Unreachable message, which tells the **traceroute** command that the complete route has been found, and the command can stop.

Figure 20-4 shows an example, but with only one of the three messages at each TTL setting (to reduce clutter). Router A uses the **traceroute** command to try to find the route to Barney. Example 20-1 shows this **traceroute** command on Router A, with debug messages from Router B, showing the three resulting Time Exceeded messages.

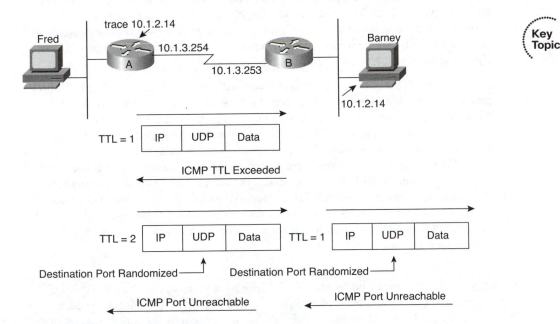

Figure 20-4 *Cisco IOS Software* **traceroute** *Command: Messages Generated*

Example 20-1 *ICMP* **debug** *on Router B When Running the* **traceroute** *Command on Router A*

```
RouterA# traceroute 10.1.2.14

Type escape sequence to abort.
```

```
Tracing the route to 10.1.2.14


  1 10.1.3.253 8 msec 4 msec 4 msec
  2 10.1.2.14 12 msec 8 msec 4 msec
RouterA#
! Moving to Router B now
! The following output occurs in reaction to the traceroute command on A
RouterB# debug ip icmp
RouterB#
ICMP: time exceeded (time to live) sent to 10.1.3.254 (dest was 10.1.2.14)
ICMP: time exceeded (time to live) sent to 10.1.3.254 (dest was 10.1.2.14)
ICMP: time exceeded (time to live) sent to 10.1.3.254 (dest was 10.1.2.14)
```

The **traceroute** command lists the IP address of Router B in the first line and the IP address of the destination host in the second line. Note that it lists Router B's left-side IP address. B replies with the Time Exceeded message, using B's outgoing interface IP address as the source address in that packet. As a result, the **traceroute** command lists that IP address. If the address is known to a DNS server, or if it's in Router A's hostname table, the command can list the hostname instead of the IP address.

Similar to the extended **ping** command as described in the section titled, "The Extended **ping** Command" in Chapter 12, the extended version of the **traceroute** command does a much better job of simulating packets sent by end-user hosts, especially for testing reverse routes. For example, in Example 20-1, A's **traceroute** command uses A's 10.1.3.254 IP address as the source address of sent packets, because A uses the interface with address 10.1.3.254 to send the packets generated by the **traceroute** command. So, the **traceroute** command in Example 20-1 tests the forward route toward 10.1.2.14 and the reverse route to 10.1.3.254. By using the extended **traceroute** command, the command can be used to test a more appropriate reverse route, such as the route to the LAN subnet on the left side of Router A. Example 20-2, later in this chapter, shows an example of the extended **traceroute** command.

Note: The **tracert** command on Microsoft operating systems works much like the IOS **traceroute** command. However, it is important to note that the Microsoft **tracert** command sends ICMP Echo Requests and does not use UDP. So, IP ACLs could cause the IOS **traceroute** to fail while the Microsoft **tracert** worked, and vice versa.

Troubleshooting the Packet Forwarding Process

Troubleshooting the IP routing process is one of the more complex tasks faced by network engineers. As usual, using a structured approach can help. Many of the earlier chapters in this book focus on the first major troubleshooting step, namely, to understand what happens in a network when it is working properly. This section focuses on the second major step: problem isolation. Problem isolation focuses on finding the specific items that fail to occur as they should, to eventually find the specific root cause of the problem.

Note: This chapter defers any detailed troubleshooting of routing protocols until Chapter 22, "Troubleshooting EIGRP and OSPF."

Isolating IP Routing Problems Related to Hosts

The troubleshooting process outlined in this chapter separates the troubleshooting steps—one part for the hosts, and one part for the routers. Essentially, for any problem in which two hosts cannot communicate, the first part of this troubleshooting process examines the issues that might impact each host's ability to send packets to and from its respective default gateway. The second part isolates problems related to how routers forward packets.

The following list outlines the troubleshooting steps focused on testing the host's connectivity to the first router:

Step 1.   Check the host's ability to send packets inside its own subnet. Either ping the host's default gateway IP address from the host, or ping the host's IP address from the default gateway. If the ping fails, do the following:

   a.   Ensure that the router's interface used at the default gateway is in an "up and up" state.

   b.   Check the source host's IP address and mask setting as compared to the router's interface used as the default gateway. Ensure that both agree as to the subnet number and mask, and therefore agree to the range of valid addresses in the subnet.

   c.   If the router uses VLAN trunking, solve any trunk configuration issues, ensuring that the router is configured to support the same VLAN in which the host resides.

   d.   If the other steps do not lead to a solution, investigate Layer 1/2 problems with the LAN, as discussed in more detail in Unit 9.

Step 2.   Verify the default gateway setting on the host by pinging one of the default router's other interface IP addresses. Or, from the default router, use an extended ping of the host's IP address with a source address from another of the router's interfaces.

For example, in Figure 20-5, the problem symptoms might be that PC1 cannot browse the web server at PC4. To test PC1's ability to send packets over its local subnet, PC1 could use the **ping 10.1.1.1** command to test connectivity to the default router in its same subnet. Or the engineer could simply **ping 10.1.1.10** from R1 (Step 1). Either location for the ping works fine, because both ping locations require that a packet be sent in each direction. If the ping fails, further problem isolation should uncover the two specific problem areas listed in Steps 1a, 1b, and 1c. If not, the problem is likely to be some Layer 1 or 2 problem.

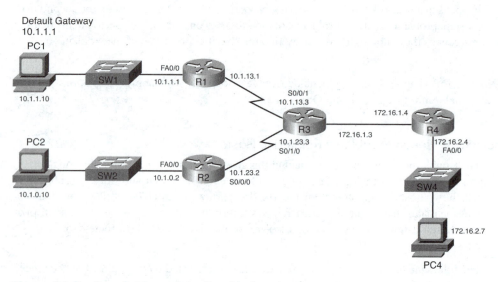

Figure 20-5   *Sample Network for Troubleshooting Scenarios*

Step 2 stresses an often-overlooked troubleshooting concept to verify that the default gateway setting is working. Neither ping option listed in Step 1 requires the host to use its default gateway setting, because the source and destination address in each packet are in the same subnet. Step 2 forces the host to send a packet to an IP address in another subnet, thereby testing the host's default gateway setting. Also, by pinging an IP address on the default gateway (router), instead of some faraway host IP address, this step removes much of the IP routing complexity from the test. Instead, the focus is on whether the host's default gateway setting works. For example, in Figure 20-5, a **ping 10.1.13.1** command on PC1 forces PC1 to use its default gateway setting because 10.1.13.1 is not in PC1's subnet (10.1.1.0/24). But the IP address is on router R1, which removes most of the rest of the network as being a possible cause if the ping fails.

Isolating IP Routing Problems Related to Routers

When the host problem isolation process is complete, and the pings all work, on both the sending and receiving hosts, any remaining IP routing issues should be between the first and last router in both the forward and reverse route between the two hosts. The following list picks up the troubleshooting process with the source host's default gateway/router, relying on the **traceroute** command on the router. (Note that the host's equivalent command, such as **tracert** on Microsoft operating systems, can also be used.)

Note: Although the following list can be useful for reference, it is rather long. Rather than trying to fully digest the meaning of this list by rereading, instead move on to the examples that follow and refer back to the list.

Note: This list includes references to IP access control lists (ACL). ACLs can be configured and enabled on a router for the purpose of filtering (discarding) some IP packets, based on the contents of the packet headers. ACLs exist as an optional topic in this text (see Appendix B, "IP Access Control Lists"), so feel free to ignore the steps that refer to ACLs unless directed otherwise by your instructor.

Step 3. Test connectivity to the destination host by using the extended **traceroute** command on the host's default gateway, using the router's interface attached to the source host for the source IP address of the packets. If the command successfully completes:

> **Key Topic**

   a. No routing problems exist in the forward route or reverse route directions.

   b. If the end-user traffic still does not work (even though the **traceroute** worked), troubleshoot any ACLs on each interface on each router in the route, in both directions.

Step 4. If the **traceroute** command in Step 3 does not complete, test the *forward route* as follows:

   a. Telnet to the last traced router (the last router listed in the **traceroute** command).

   b. Find that router's route that matches the destination IP address that was used in the original **traceroute** command (**show ip route, show ip route** *ip-address*).

   c. If no matching route is found, investigate why the expected route is missing. Typically it's either a routing protocol issue or a static route misconfiguration. It could also be related to a missing connected route.

   d. If a matching route is found, and the route is a default route, confirm that it will be used based on the setting for the **ip classless/no ip classless** commands.

   e. If a matching route is found, ping the next-hop IP address listed in the route. Or, if the route is a connected route, ping the true destination IP address.

   - If the ping fails, investigate Layer 2 problems between this router and the IP address that was pinged, and investigate possible ACL problems.

   - If the ping works, investigate ACL issues.

   f. If a matching route is found, and no other problems are found, confirm that the route is not errantly pointing in the wrong direction.

Step 5. If Step 4 does not identify a problem in the forward route, test the *reverse route*:

   a. If the forward route on the last traced router refers to another router as the next-hop router, repeat the substeps of Step 3 from that next-hop router. Analyze the reverse route—the route to reach the source IP address used by the failed **traceroute** command.

b. If the forward route on the last traced router refers to a connected subnet, check the destination host's IP settings. In particular, confirm the
settings for the IP address, mask, and default gateway.

For example, if PC1 cannot communicate with PC4 in Figure 20-5, and the hosts can both
communicate through their respective default gateways, Step 3 of the router-oriented
problem isolation process could start with a **traceroute 172.16.2.7**, using R1's Fa0/0 IP address (10.1.1.1) as the source IP address. If that **traceroute** command lists 10.1.13.3 as the
last IP address in the command output, rather than completing, you would then start Step
4, which examines R3's forward route toward 172.16.2.7. If the analysis at Step 4 does not
uncover the problem, Step 5 would then move on to the next-hop router, R4 in this case,
and examine R4's reverse route—its route back to the original source address of 10.1.1.1.

Next, two separate scenarios show how to use these troubleshooting steps to isolate some
sample problems.

Troubleshooting Scenario 1: Forward Route Problem

This first example of the router troubleshooting process uses the same internetwork
shown in Figure 20-5. In this case, PC1 cannot use a web browser to connect to the web
service running on PC4. After further investigation, PC1 cannot ping 172.16.2.7 (PC4).
Example 20-2 shows the commands used on R1 and R4 for the host-oriented Steps 1 and
2, as well as a beginning of the router-oriented Step 3.

Example 20-2 *Troubleshooting Scenario 1: Steps 1 and 2 and Part of Step 3*

```
R1# ping 10.1.1.10

Type escape sequence to abort.
Sending 5, 100-byte ICMP Echos to 10.1.1.10, timeout is 2 seconds:
!!!!!
Success rate is 100 percent (5/5), round-trip min/avg/max = 1/2/4 ms
R1# ping
Protocol [ip]:
Target IP address: 10.1.1.10
Repeat count [5]:
Datagram size [100]:
Timeout in seconds [2]:
Extended commands [n]: y
Source address or interface: 10.1.13.1
Type of service [0]:
Set DF bit in IP header? [no]:
Validate reply data? [no]:
Data pattern [0xABCD]:
Loose, Strict, Record, Timestamp, Verbose[none]:
Sweep range of sizes [n]:
Type escape sequence to abort.
```

```
Sending 5, 100-byte ICMP Echos to 10.1.1.10, timeout is 2 seconds:
Packet sent with a source address of 10.1.13.1
!!!!!
Success rate is 100 percent (5/5), round-trip min/avg/max = 1/2/4 ms
R1#
! Now moving to R4 to repeat the test
R4# ping 172.16.2.7

Type escape sequence to abort.
Sending 5, 100-byte ICMP Echos to 172.16.2.7, timeout is 2 seconds:
.....
Success rate is 0 percent (0/5)
R4# show ip interface brief
Interface            IP-Address      OK? Method Status                  Protocol
FastEthernet0/0      172.16.2.4      YES manual administratively down   down
FastEthernet0/1      172.16.1.4      YES manual up                      up
Serial0/0/0          unassigned      YES unset  administratively down   down
Serial0/0/1          unassigned      YES unset  administratively down   down
Serial0/1/0          unassigned      YES unset  administratively down   down
```

The standard and extended pings on R1 at the beginning of the example essentially perform Steps 1 and 2, the host-oriented steps, to confirm that PC1 seems to be working well. However, the example next shows that R4 cannot reach PC4 because R4's LAN interface has been shut down, as shown at the end of the example. Although this scenario might seem a bit simple, it provides a good starting point for troubleshooting a problem.

To get a fuller view of the troubleshooting process, next consider this same scenario, with the same root problem, but now you do not have access to router R4. So, you can only perform Steps 1 and 2 for PC1, which work, but you cannot do those same steps for PC4 from R4. So, Example 20-3 moves on to Steps 3 and 4. The beginning of the example shows Step 3, where R1 uses **traceroute 172.16.2.7**, with a source IP address of 10.1.1.1. This command does not complete, referencing 10.1.13.3 (R3) as the last router. Step 4 proceeds by looking at how R3 then routes packets destined for 172.16.2.7.

Example 20-3 *Troubleshooting Scenario 1: Step 4*

```
R1# traceroute
Protocol [ip]:
Target IP address: 172.16.2.7
Source address: 10.1.1.1
```

```
Numeric display [n]:
Timeout in seconds [3]:
Probe count [3]:
Minimum Time to Live [1]:
Maximum Time to Live [30]:
Port Number [33434]:
Loose, Strict, Record, Timestamp, Verbose[none]:
Type escape sequence to abort.
Tracing the route to 172.16.2.7


  1 10.1.13.3 0 msec 4 msec 0 msec
  2 10.1.13.3 !H  *  !H
! Note above that the command did stop by itself, but it does not list the
! destination host 172.16.2.7
R3# show ip route 172.16.2.7
% Subnet not in table
R3#show ip route
Codes: C - connected, S - static, R - RIP, M - mobile, B - BGP
       D - EIGRP, EX - EIGRP external, O - OSPF, IA - OSPF inter area
       N1 - OSPF NSSA external type 1, N2 - OSPF NSSA external type 2
       E1 - OSPF external type 1, E2 - OSPF external type 2
       i - IS-IS, su - IS-IS summary, L1 - IS-IS level-1, L2 - IS-IS level-2
       ia - IS-IS inter area, * - candidate default, U - per-user static route
       o - ODR, P - periodic downloaded static route


Gateway of last resort is not set


     172.16.0.0/24 is subnetted, 1 subnets
C       172.16.1.0 is directly connected, FastEthernet0/0
     10.0.0.0/24 is subnetted, 4 subnets
C       10.1.13.0 is directly connected, Serial0/0/1
R       10.1.1.0 [120/1] via 10.1.13.1, 00:00:04, Serial0/0/1
R       10.1.0.0 [120/1] via 10.1.23.2, 00:00:01, Serial0/1/0
C       10.1.23.0 is directly connected, Serial0/1/0
```

The extended **traceroute** command at the beginning of the example shows output identifying R3 (10.1.13.3) as the last listed device in the command output (Step 3). Step 4 then proceeds with an examination of the forward route on R3 toward IP address 172.16.2.7. The **show ip route 172.16.2.7** command gets right to the point. The message "subnet not in table" means that R3 does not have a route matching destination address 172.16.2.7. If the question does not supply access to a simulator, only the output of the **show ip route** command, you would need to examine the routes to determine that none of them refer to a range of addresses that includes 172.16.2.7.

Any time the problem isolation process points to a missing route, the next step is to determine how the router should have learned about the route. In this case, R3 should have used RIP-2 to learn the route. So, the next steps would be to troubleshoot any problems with the dynamic routing protocol.

The root cause of this problem has not changed—R4 has shut down its Fa0/0 interface— but the symptoms are somewhat interesting. Because the interface is shut down, R4 does not advertise a route for subnet 172.16.2.0/24 to R3. However, R3 advertises an autosummarized route to network 172.16.0.0/16 to both R1 and R2, so both R1 and R2, because of RIP-2's default autosummary setting, can forward packets destined for 172.16.2.7 to R3. As a result, the **traceroute** command on R1 can forward packets to R3.

Troubleshooting Scenario 2: Reverse Route Problem

This next example uses the same network diagram as shown in Figure 20-5, with all the information shown in the figure still being true. However, the details mentioned in the previous section might have changed—particularly the problem that exists to make the example more interesting. So, approach this second problem only relying on the figure as being true.

In this scenario, PC1 again cannot ping 172.16.2.7 (PC4). The host default gateway checks suggested in Steps 1 and 2 again work for PC1, but the tests cannot be performed for the reverse direction, because the engineer cannot access PC4 or router R4. So, Example 20-4 picks up the suggested troubleshooting process at Step 3, showing the result of the extended **traceroute** command on R1. Note that the command does not even list R3's 10.1.13.3 IP address in this case. So, the rest of Example 20-4 shows the investigations into the specific substeps of Step 4.

Example 20-4   *Troubleshooting Scenario 2: Steps 3 and 4*

```
R1# traceroute ip 172.16.2.7 source fa0/0


Type escape sequence to abort.
Tracing the route to 172.16.2.7

  1  *  *  *
  2  *  *  *
  3  *
R1# show ip route 172.16.2.7
Routing entry for 172.16.0.0/16
  Known via "rip", distance 120, metric 1
  Redistributing via rip
  Last update from 10.1.13.3 on Serial0/1/0, 00:00:05 ago
  Routing Descriptor Blocks:
  * 10.1.13.3, from 10.1.13.3, 00:00:05 ago, via Serial0/1/0
      Route metric is 1, traffic share count is 1

R1# ping 10.1.13.3


Type escape sequence to abort.
```

```
Sending 5, 100-byte ICMP Echos to 10.1.13.3, timeout is 2 seconds:
!!!!!
Success rate is 100 percent (5/5), round-trip min/avg/max = 1/2/4 ms
R1# show ip access-lists

! Switching to router R3 next
R3# show ip access-lists

R3#
```

The example starts by showing the Step 3 part of the process, with the **traceroute** command only listing lines of asterisks. This means that the command did not successfully identify even the very next router in the route.

Next, moving on to Step 4, the following list outlines the substeps of Step 4 as applied to this example:

Step 4a. The example had already begun with a Telnet into R1, so no extra work is required.

Step 4b. The next command, **show ip route 172.16.2.7**, shows that R1 has a nondefault route for network 172.16.0.0, pointing to R3 (10.1.13.3) as the next hop.

Step 4c. This step does not apply in this case, because a matching route was found in Step 4B.

Step 4d. This step does not apply in this case, because the matching route is not a route to 0.0.0.0/0 (the default route).

Step 4e. The next listed command, **ping 10.1.13.3**, tests R1's ability to send packets over the link to the next-hop router identified in Step 4B. The ping works.

Step 4f. On both R1 and the next-hop router (R3), the **show ip access-lists** command confirms that neither router has any IP ACLs configured.

Because all the steps to examine the forward route passed, the process then moves on to Step 5. The original **traceroute** command in Example 20-4 used R1's Fa0/0 interface IP address, 10.1.1.1, as the source IP address. For Step 5, the process begins at R3 with an analysis of R3's reverse route to reach 10.1.1.1. Examine the output in Example 20-5, and look for any problems before reading the explanations following the example.

Example 20-5 *Troubleshooting Scenario 2: Step 5*

```
! The next command shows the matched route, for subnet 10.1.1.0/26,
! with next-hop 10.1.23.2.
R3# show ip route 10.1.1.1
Routing entry for 10.1.1.0/26
  Known via "static", distance 1, metric 0
  Routing Descriptor Blocks:
  * 10.1.23.2
```

```
      Route metric is 0, traffic share count is 1

! The next command shows the overlapping subnets - 10.1.1.0/26 and 10.1.1.0/24.
R3# show ip route
Codes: C - connected, S - static, R - RIP, M - mobile, B - BGP
       D - EIGRP, EX - EIGRP external, O - OSPF, IA - OSPF inter area
       N1 - OSPF NSSA external type 1, N2 - OSPF NSSA external type 2
       E1 - OSPF external type 1, E2 - OSPF external type 2
       i - IS-IS, su - IS-IS summary, L1 - IS-IS level-1, L2 - IS-IS level-2
       ia - IS-IS inter area, * - candidate default, U - per-user static route
       o - ODR, P - periodic downloaded static route

Gateway of last resort is not set

     172.16.0.0/24 is subnetted, 2 subnets
C       172.16.1.0 is directly connected, FastEthernet0/0
R       172.16.2.0 [120/1] via 172.16.1.4, 00:00:18, FastEthernet0/0
     10.0.0.0/8 is variably subnetted, 5 subnets, 2 masks
C       10.1.13.0/24 is directly connected, Serial0/0/1
S       10.1.1.0/26 [1/0] via 10.1.23.2
R       10.1.1.0/24 [120/1] via 10.1.13.1, 00:00:10, Serial0/0/1
R       10.1.0.0/24 [120/1] via 10.1.23.2, 00:00:11, Serial0/1/0
C       10.1.23.0/24 is directly connected, Serial0/1/0
```

R3 has an incorrectly configured static route for subnet 10.1.1.0/26. This subnet includes the address range 10.1.1.0–10.1.1.63, which includes IP address 10.1.1.1. When R3 attempts to send a packet back to 10.1.1.1, R3 has two routes that match the destination address. But R3 picks the more specific (longer prefix) route for subnet 10.1.1.0/26. This route causes R3 to forward packets intended for 10.1.1.1 out R3's link to R2, instead of to R1.

Although you cannot necessarily determine the true intent of this static route, this process has identified the root cause—the static route to 10.1.1.0/26 on R3. If the LAN off R1 should include all addresses between 10.1.1.0 and 10.1.1.255, the static route should just be deleted.

An Alternative Problem Isolation Process for Steps 3, 4, and 5

The router-oriented steps of the IP routing problem isolation process depend on the **traceroute** command, relying on this command's ability to identify on which router the router-oriented troubleshooting should begin. As an alternative, the **ping** and **telnet** commands can be used. However, because these commands cannot quickly identify the most likely routers on which the problem exists, using **ping** and **telnet** requires that you perform a set of tasks on the first router (the host's default gateway/router) in a route, and then the next router, and the next, and so on, until the problem is identified.

So, just to be complete, note that you can do the same specific subtasks as already explained in Steps 4 and 5, but when using **ping**, just repeat the steps at each successive router. For example, to apply this revised process to the first of the two just-completed scenarios, the process would begin with router R1, PC1's default router. In the first scenario, R1 did not have any forward route issues for forwarding packets to 172.16.2.7 (PC4), and R1 had no reverse route issues and no ACLs. This new alternative process would then suggest moving on to the next router (R3). In this example, R3's forward route problem—not having a route that matches destination address 172.16.2.7—would be found.

Troubleshooting Tools and Tips

The second half of this chapter covers a wide variety of troubleshooting tools and tips that can be helpful when you're troubleshooting real networks. As usual, with any discussion of troubleshooting the IP packet forwarding process, this section mentions information about the role of the IP host as well as the role of the router. The majority of this section focuses on troubleshooting the features discussed in Chapter 19, "VLSM and Route Summarization."

Host Routing Tools and Perspectives

When you're trying to isolate the cause of networking problems, the tips in Table 20-4 can help you more quickly find problems related to hosts. The tips are organized by typical symptoms, along with common root causes. Note that the table does not list all possible causes, just the more common ones.

Table 20-4 *Common Host Problem Symptoms and Typical Reasons*

Symptom	Common Root Cause
The host can send packets to hosts in the same subnet, but not to other subnets.	The host does not have a default gateway configured, or the default gateway IP address is incorrect.
The host can send packets to hosts in the same subnet, but not to other subnets.	The host's default gateway is in a different subnet than the host's IP address (according to the host's perception of the subnet).
Some hosts in a subnet can communicate with hosts in other subnets, but others cannot.	This can be caused by the default gateway (router) using a different mask than the hosts. This can result in the router's connected route not including some of the hosts on the LAN.
Some hosts on the same VLAN can send packets to each other, but others cannot.	The hosts might not be using the same mask.

When troubleshooting networking problems in real life, it's helpful to get used to thinking about the symptoms, because that's where the problem isolation process typically begins. However, most host communication problems are caused by just a handful of issues:

Key Topic

Step 1.   Check all hosts and routers that should be in the same subnet to ensure that they all use the same mask and that their addresses are indeed all in the same subnet.

Step 2. Compare each host's default gateway setting with the router's configuration to ensure that it is the right IP address.

Step 3. If the first two items are correct, next look at Layer 1/2 issues.

show ip route Reference

The **show ip route** command plays a huge role in troubleshooting IP routing and IP routing protocol problems. Many chapters in this book mention various facts about this command. This section pulls the concepts together in one place for easier reference and study.

Figure 20-6 shows the output of the **show ip route** command from back in Example 20-3. The figure numbers various parts of the command output for easier reference, with Table 20-5 describing the output noted by each number.

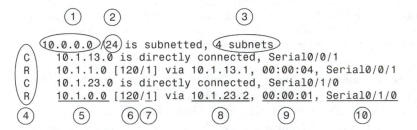

Figure 20-6   show ip route *Command Output Reference*

Table 20-5   *Descriptions of the* show ip route *Command Output*

Item Number	Item	Value in the Figure	Description
1	Classful network	10.0.0.0	The routing table is organized by classful network. This line is the heading line for classful network 10.0.0.0.
2	Prefix length	/24	When this router knows only one subnet mask for all subnets of the network, this location lists that one mask, by default in prefix notation.
3	Number of subnets	4 subnets	Lists the number of routes for subnets of the classful network known to this router.
4	Legend code	R, C	A short code that identifies the source of the routing information. R is for RIP, and C is for connected. The figure omits the legend text at the top of the **show ip route** command output, but it can be seen in Example 20-3.
5	Subnet number	10.1.0.0	The subnet number of this particular route.

Table 20-5   *Descriptions of the* show ip route *Command Output*

Item Number	Item	Value in the Figure	Description
6	Administrative distance	120	If a router learns routes for the listed subnet from more than one source of routing information, the router uses the source with the lowest AD.
7	Metric	1	The metric for this route.
8	Next-hop router	10.1.23.2	For packets matching this route, the IP address of the next router to which the packet should be forwarded.
9	Timer	00:00:01	Time since this route was learned in a routing update.
10	Outgoing interface	Serial0/1/0	For packets matching this route, the interface out which the packet should be forwarded.

The output of the command differs slightly when variable-length subnet masks (VLSM) are used. The figure shows an example in which VLSM is not used in network 10.0.0.0, with mask /24 used for all subnets of that network. So, IOS lists the mask once, in the heading line (/24 in this case). If VLSM were in use, the heading line would simply note that the network is variably subnetted, and each route would list the mask. For an example, see Example 19-1 in Chapter 19.

Interface Status

One of the steps in the IP routing troubleshooting process described earlier, in the "Troubleshooting the Packet Forwarding Process" section, says to check the interface status, ensuring that the required interface is working. For a router interface to be working, the two interface status codes must both be listed as "up," with engineers usually saying the interface is "up and up."

This chapter does not explain the troubleshooting steps for router interfaces, simply assuming that each interface is indeed in an up/up state. Chapter 27's section titled "Troubleshooting Serial Links" covers many of the details for troubleshooting router interfaces. For router LAN interfaces connected to a LAN switch, the main items to check on routers are that the router and switch match each other's duplex and speed settings, and that if trunking is configured, both the router and switch have been manually configured for trunking, because routers do not dynamically negotiate LAN trunking.

VLSM Issues

This section examines several issues when using VLSM:

- Recognizing whether VLSM is used and, if so, which routing protocols can be used

- Understanding the conditions in which routers can allow the misconfiguration of overlapping VLSM subnets

■ Understanding the outward symptoms that can occur when overlapping VLSM subnets exist

Recognizing When VLSM Is Used

One common oversight when troubleshooting a problem in an unfamiliar internetwork is failing to recognize whether VLSM is used. As defined in Chapter 19, an internetwork uses VLSM when multiple subnet masks are used for different subnets of *a single classful network*. For example, if in one internetwork all subnets of network 10.0.0.0 use a 255.255.240.0 mask, and all subnets of network 172.16.0.0 use a 255.255.255.0 mask, the design does not use VLSM. If multiple masks were used for subnets of network 10.0.0.0, VLSM would be in use.

The follow-on concept is that only classless routing protocols (RIP-2, EIGRP, OSPF) can support VLSM; classful routing protocols (RIP-1, IGRP) cannot. So, a quick determination of whether VLSM is actually used can then tell you whether a classless routing protocol is required. Note that the routing protocol does not require any special configuration to support VLSM. It is just a feature of the routing protocol.

Configuring Overlapping VLSM Subnets

IP subnetting rules require that the address ranges in the subnets used in an internetwork should not overlap. IOS can recognize when a new **ip address** command creates an overlapping subnet, but only in some cases. This section examines the conditions under which overlapping subnets can be configured, beginning with the following general statements about when the overlaps cannot and can be configured:

■ **Preventing the overlap:** IOS detects the overlap when the **ip address** command implies an overlap with another **ip address** command *on the same router*. If the interface being configured is up/up, IOS rejects the **ip address** command. If not, IOS accepts the **ip address** command, but IOS will never bring up the interface.

Key Topic

■ **Allowing the overlap:** IOS cannot detect an overlap when an **ip address** command overlaps with an **ip address** command on another router.

The router shown in Example 20-6 prevents the configuration of an overlapping VLSM subnet. The example shows router R3 configuring Fa0/0 with IP address 172.16.5.1/24, and Fa0/1 with 172.16.5.193/26. The ranges of addresses in each subnet are

Subnet 172.16.5.0/24: 172.16.5.1–172.16.5.254

Subnet 172.16.5.192/26: 172.16.5.193–172.16.5.254

Example 20-6 *Single Router Rejects Overlapped Subnets*

```
R3# configure terminal
R3(config)# interface Fa0/0
R3(config-if)# ip address 172.16.5.1 255.255.255.0
R3(config-if)# interface Fa0/1
```

```
R3(config-if)# ip address 172.16.5.193 255.255.255.192
% 172.16.5.192 overlaps with FastEthernet0/0
R3(config-if)#
```

IOS knows that it is illegal to overlap the ranges of addresses implied by a subnet. In this
case, because both subnets would be connected subnets, this single router knows that
these two subnets should not coexist, because that would break subnetting rules, so IOS
rejects the second command.

However, it is possible to configure overlapping subnets if they are connected to different
routers. Figure 20-7 shows a figure very similar to Figure 19-2 in Chapter 19—used in that
chapter to explain the problem of overlapping subnets. Example 20-7 shows the configuration of the two overlapping subnets on R2 and R3, with the resulting routing table on R2.

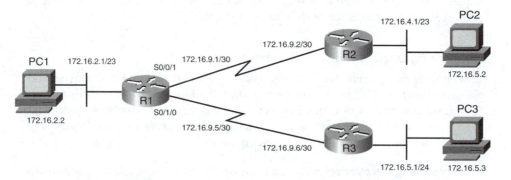

Figure 20-7   *Internetwork That Allows the Configuration of Overlapped Subnets*

Example 20-7   *Two Routers Accept Overlapped Subnets*

```
R2# configure terminal
R2(config)# interface Fa0/0
R2(config-if)# ip address 172.16.4.1 255.255.254.0
R3# configure terminal
R3(config)# interface Fa0/0
R3(config-if)# ip address 172.16.5.1 255.255.255.0
```

Keep in mind that overlapped subnets can be configured if the subnets do not connect to
the same router. So, if a question asks you to pick a new subnet number and configure an
interface to be in that subnet, the router's acceptance of your **ip address** command does
not necessarily tell you that you did the math correctly.

The next topic explains some of the problem symptoms you might see if such an overlap exists.

Symptoms with Overlapping Subnets

The outward problem symptoms differ depending on whether the address in question is in the overlapped portion of the subnets and if multiple hosts are attempting to use the exact same IP address. The addresses in the nonoverlapped parts of the subnet typically work fine, whereas those in the overlapped area might or might not work at all. For example, continuing with the overlapped subnets shown in Figure 20-6, subnets 172.16.4.0/23 and 172.16.5.0/24 overlap—specifically, addresses 172.16.5.0–172.16.5.255. Hosts in the nonoverlapped range of 172.16.4.0–172.16.4.255 probably work fine.

For the addresses in the overlapped address range, in many cases, hosts in the smaller of the two overlapped subnets work fine, but hosts in the larger of the two subnets do not. To see why, consider the case in which PC1 in Figure 20-7 tries to ping both 172.16.5.2 (PC2, off R2) and 172.16.5.3 (PC3, off R3). (For the sake of this example, assume that PC2's and PC3's IP addresses are not duplicated in the opposite overlapped subnet.) As you can see from the routing tables on R1 and R3 and the **traceroute 172.16.5.2** command in Example 20-8, the packet sent by PC1 to PC2 would actually be delivered from R1 to R3, and then onto R3's LAN.

Example 20-8   *Two Routers Accept Overlapped Subnets*

```
! R1's route to reach 172.16.5.2, off R2, points to R3
R1# show ip route 172.16.5.2
Routing entry for 172.16.5.0/24
  Known via "rip", distance 120, metric 1
  Redistributing via rip
  Last update from 172.16.9.6 on Serial0/1/0, 00:00:25 ago
  Routing Descriptor Blocks:
  * 172.16.9.6, from 172.16.9.6, 00:00:25 ago, via Serial0/1/0
      Route metric is 1, traffic share count is 1
! R1's route to reach 172.16.5.3, off R3, points to R3
R1# show ip route 172.16.5.3
Routing entry for 172.16.5.0/24
  Known via "rip", distance 120, metric 1
  Redistributing via rip
  Last update from 172.16.9.6 on Serial0/1/0, 00:00:01 ago
  Routing Descriptor Blocks:
  * 172.16.9.6, from 172.16.9.6, 00:00:01 ago, via Serial0/1/0
      Route metric is 1, traffic share count is 1

! The traceroute to PC2 shows R3, not R2, as the first router, so the packet never
! reaches PC2, and the command never completes until stopped by the user.
R1# traceroute 172.16.5.2

Type escape sequence to abort.
Tracing the route to 172.16.5.2

  1 172.16.9.6 4 msec 0 msec 4 msec
```

```
    2  *  *  *
    3  *  *  *
    4
R1# traceroute 172.16.5.3

Type escape sequence to abort.
Tracing the route to 172.16.5.3

    1 172.16.9.6 0 msec 4 msec 0 msec
    2 172.16.5.3 4 msec *  0 msec
```

The example shows that R1 forwards packets to hosts 172.16.5.2 (PC2) and 172.16.5.3 (PC3) by sending them to R3 next. R3 then tries to send them onto R3's LAN subnet, which works well for PC3 but not so well for PC2. So, PC3, in the smaller of the two overlapped subnets, works fine, whereas PC2, in the larger of the two overlapped subnets, does not.

The symptoms can get even worse when addresses are duplicated. For example, imagine that PC22 has been added to R2's LAN subnet, with IP address 172.16.5.3 duplicating PC3's IP address. Now when the PC22 user calls to say that his PC cannot communicate with other devices, the network support person uses a **ping 172.16.5.3** command to test the problem—and the ping works! The ping works to the wrong instance of 172.16.5.3, but it works. So, the symptoms might be particularly difficult to track down.

Another difficulty with overlapped VLSM subnets is that the problem might not show up for a while. In this same example, imagine that all addresses in both subnets were to be assigned by a DHCP server, beginning with the smallest IP addresses. For the first six months, the server assigned only IP addresses that began with 172.16.4.x on the R2 LAN subnet. Finally, enough hosts were installed on the R2 LAN to require the use of addresses that begin with 172.16.5, like PC2's address of 172.16.5.2 used in the preceding example. Unfortunately, no one can send packets to those hosts. At first glance, the fact that the problem showed up long after the installation and configuration were complete can actually cloud the issue.

VLSM Troubleshooting Summary

The following list summarizes the key troubleshooting points to consider when you're troubleshooting potential VLSM problems:

Key Topic

- Pay close attention to whether the design really uses VLSM. If it does, note whether a classless routing protocol is used.

- Be aware that overlapping subnets can indeed be configured.

- The outward problem symptoms might be that some hosts in a subnet work well, but others cannot send packets outside the local subnet.

- Use the **traceroute** command to look for routes that direct packets to the wrong part of the network. This could be a result of the overlapped subnets.

■   On the exams, you might see a question you think is related to VLSM and IP ad-
    dresses. In that case, the best plan of attack might well be to analyze the math for
    each subnet and ensure that no overlaps exist, rather than troubleshooting using **ping**
    and **traceroute**.

Discontiguous Networks and Autosummary

Chapter 19 also explained the concept of discontiguous networks, along with the solution: using a classless routing protocol with autosummarization disabled. This section examines one particular case in which a discontiguous network exists only part of the time.
Figure 20-8 shows an internetwork with two classful networks: 10.0.0.0 and 172.16.0.0. The
design shows two contiguous networks because a route consisting of only subnets of
each network exists between all subnets of that network.

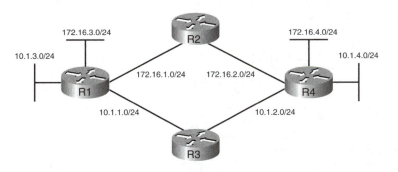

Figure 20-8   *Internetwork with (Currently) Contiguous Networks*

In this figure, with all links up and working, using a routing protocol with autosummary enabled by default, all hosts can ping all other hosts. In this design, packets for network
172.16.0.0 flow over the high route, and packets for network 10.0.0.0 flow over the low route.

Unfortunately, a problem can occur later when one of the four links between routers fails.
If any link between the routers fails, one of the two classful networks becomes discontiguous. For example, if the link between R3 and R4 fails, the route from R1 to R4 passes
through subnets of network 172.16.0.0, so network 10.0.0.0 is discontiguous. Even with a
classless routing protocol, but with autosummarization enabled, both R1 and R4 advertise
a route for 10.0.0.0/8 to R2, and R2 sees two routes to all of network 10.0.0.0—one
through R1, and another through R4. The solution, as always, is to use a classless routing
protocol with autosummary disabled.

Although the design in Figure 20-8 might seem a bit contrived, it happens more often
than you might think. When looking for problems, be sure to think about discontiguous
IP networks, both in cases where all links are working and with different combinations of
failures.

Chapter Review

Review Key Topics

Review the most important topics from this chapter, noted with the Key Topic icon. Table 20-6 lists these key topics and where each is discussed.

Table 20-6   *Key Topics for Chapter 20*

Key Topic Element	Description	Page Number
Table 20-1	Popular ICMP messages and their purpose	478
Figure 20-3	Diagram of how the TTL IP header field and the ICMP Time Exceeded message work	482
Figure 20-4	Demonstration of how the **traceroute** command uses the TTL field and Time Exceeded message	483
List	Two major steps and several substeps in a suggested host-routing problem isolation process	485
List	Three major steps for problem isolation with IP routing in routers, with the list numbered as a continuation of the host-routing problem isolation list	487
List	Three tips for general items to check when troubleshooting host connectivity problems	494
List	Conditions under which overlapping subnets can be configured, and when IOS can prevent this error	497
List	Summary of troubleshooting tips for questions in which VLSM might be causing a problem	500

Define Key Terms

Define the following key terms from this chapter, and check your answers in the glossary:

forward route, reverse route

This chapter covers the following subjects:

- **Link-State Routing Protocol Features:** This section introduces the generic concepts used by any link-state routing protocol.

- **OSPF Protocols and Operation:** This section explains how OSPF implements the same basic link-state concepts discussed in the first section.

- **OSPF Configuration:** This section examines how to configure OSPF in a single area and in multiple areas, describes OSPF authentication, and discusses a few other small features.

CHAPTER 21

OSPF Concepts and Configuration

Link-state routing protocols were originally developed in the early to mid-1990s. The protocol designers assumed that link speeds, router CPUs, and router memory would continue to improve over time, so the protocols were designed to provide much more powerful features by taking advantage of these improvements. By sending more information, and requiring the routers to perform more processing, link-state protocols gain some important advantages over distance vector protocols—in particular, much faster convergence. The goal remains the same—adding the currently best routes to the routing table—but these protocols use different methods to find and add those routes.

This chapter explains the most commonly used IP link-state routing protocol—Open Shortest Path First (OSPF). In particular, the first section examines the concepts that apply to any link-state protocol. The next section explains how OSPF implements some of the same concepts. The last section examines how to configure OSPF on Cisco routers.

Link-State Routing Protocol Features

Like distance vector protocols, link-state protocols send routing updates to neighboring routers, which in turn send updates to their neighboring routers, and so on. At the end of the process, like distance vector protocols, routers that use link-state protocols add the best routes to their routing tables, based on metrics. However, beyond this level of explanation, these two types of routing protocol algorithms have little in common.

This section covers the most basic mechanics of how link-state protocols work, with the examples using Open Shortest Path First (OSPF), the first link-state IP routing protocol, in the examples. The section begins by showing how link-state routing protocols flood routing information throughout the internetwork. Then it describes how link-state protocols process the routing information to choose the best routes.

Building the Same LSDB on Every Router

Routers using link-state routing protocols need to collectively advertise practically every detail about the internetwork to all the other routers. At the end of the process, called flooding, every router in the internetwork has the exact same information about the internetwork. Routers use this information, stored in RAM inside a data structure called the link-state database (LSDB), to perform the other major link-state process to calculate the currently best routes to each subnet. Flooding a lot of detailed information to every router sounds like a lot of work, and relative to distance vector routing protocols, it is.

Open Shortest Path First (OSPF), the most popular link-state IP routing protocol, advertises information in routing update messages of various types, with the updates containing information called link-state advertisements (LSA). LSAs come in many forms, including the following two main types:

- **Router LSA:** Includes a number to identify the router (router ID), the router's interface IP addresses and masks, the state (up or down) of each interface, and the cost (metric) associated with the interface.

- **Link LSA:** Identifies each link (subnet) and the routers that are attached to that link. It also identifies the link's state (up or down).

Some routers must first create the router and link LSAs, and then flood the LSAs to all other routers. Each router creates a router LSA for itself and then floods that LSA to other routers in routing update messages. To flood an LSA, a router sends the LSA to its neighbors. Those neighbors in turn forward the LSA to their neighbors, and so on, until all the routers have learned about the LSA. For the link LSAs, one router attached to a subnet also creates and floods a link LSA for each subnet. (Note that in some cases, a link LSA is not required, typically when only one router connects to the subnet.) At the end of the process, every router has every other router's router LSA and a copy of all the link LSAs as well.

Figure 21-1 shows the general idea of the flooding process, with R8 creating and flooding its router LSA. Note that Figure 21-1 actually shows only a subset of the information in R8's router LSA.

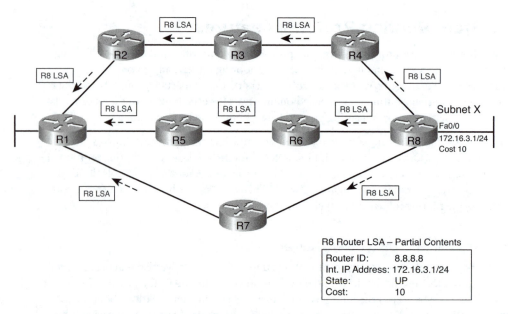

Figure 21-1 *Flooding LSAs Using a Link-State Routing Protocol*

Figure 21-1 shows the rather basic flooding process, with R8 sending the original LSA for itself, and the other routers flooding the LSA by forwarding it until every router has a copy. To prevent looping LSA advertisements, a router that knows about the LSA first asks its neighbor if that neighbor already knows about this LSA. For example, R8 would begin by separately asking R4, R6, and R7 if they know about the router LSA for R8. Those three routers would reply, stating that they do not know about the R8 router LSA. Only at that point does R8 send the LSA to each of those neighboring routers. The process repeats with every neighbor. If a router has already learned the LSA—no matter over what path—it could politely say that it already has the LSA, thereby preventing the LSA from being advertised in loops around the network.

The origins of the term *link state* can be explained by considering the (partial) contents of the router LSA shown in Figure 21-1. The figure shows one of the four interface IP addresses that would be listed in R8's router LSA, along with the interface's state. Link-state protocols get their name from the fact that the LSAs advertise each interface (link) and whether the interface is up or down (state). So, the LSDB contains information about not only the up and working routers and interfaces and links (subnets), but all routers and interfaces and links (subnets), even if the interfaces are down.

After the LSA has been flooded, even if the LSAs do not change, link-state protocols do require periodic reflooding of the LSAs, similar to the periodic updates sent by distance vector protocols. However, distance vector protocols typically use a short timer; for example, RIP sends periodic updates every 30 seconds, and RIP sends a full update listing all normally advertised routes. OSPF refloods each LSA based on each LSA's separate aging timer (default 30 minutes). As a result, in a stable internetwork, link-state protocols actually use less network bandwidth to send routing information than do distance vector protocols. If an LSA changes, the router immediately floods the changed LSA. For example, if Figure 21-1's Router R8's LAN interface failed, R8 would need to reflood the R8 LSA, stating that the interface is now down.

Applying Dijkstra SPF Math to Find the Best Routes

The link-state flooding process results in every router having an identical copy of the LSDB in memory, but the flooding process alone does not cause a router to learn what routes to add to the IP routing table. Although incredibly detailed and useful, the information in the LSDB does not explicitly state each router's best route to reach a destination. Link-state protocols must use another major part of the link-state algorithm to find and add routes to the IP routing table—routes that list a subnet number and mask, an outgoing interface, and a next-hop router IP address. This process uses something called the Dijkstra Shortest Path First (SPF) algorithm.

The SPF algorithm can be compared to how humans think when taking a trip using a road map. Anyone can buy the same road map, so anyone can know all the information about the roads. However, when you look at the map, you first find your starting and ending locations, and then you analyze the map to find the possible routes. If several routes look similar in length, you might decide to take a longer route if the roads are highways rather than country roads. Someone else might own the same map, but they might be starting from a different location, and going to a different location, so they might choose a totally different route.

In the analogy, the LSDB works like the map, and the SPF algorithm works like the person reading the map. The LSDB holds all the information about all the possible routers and links. The SPF algorithm defines how a router should process the LSDB, with each router considering itself to be the starting point for the route. Each router uses itself as the starting point because each router needs to put routes in its own routing table. The SPF algorithm calculates all the possible routes to reach a subnet, and the cumulative metric for each entire route, for each possible destination subnet. In short, each router must view itself as the starting point, and each subnet as the destination, and use the SPF algorithm to look at the LSDB road map to find and pick the best route to each subnet.

Figure 21-2 shows a graphical view of the results of the SPF algorithm run by router R1 when trying to find the best route to reach subnet 172.16.3.0/24 (based on Figure 21-1). Figure 21-2 shows R1 at the top of the figure rather than on the left because SPF creates a mathematical tree. These trees are typically drawn with the base or root of the tree at the top of the figure, and the leaves (subnets) at the bottom.

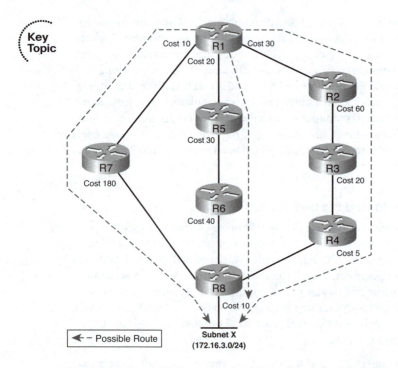

Key Topic

Figure 21-2   *SPF Tree to Find R1's Route to 172.16.3.0/24*

Figure 21-2 does not show the SPF algorithm's math (frankly, almost no one bothers looking at the math), but it does show a drawing of the kind of analysis done by the SPF algorithm on R1. Generally, each router runs the SPF process to find all routes to each subnet, and then the SPF algorithm can pick the best route. To pick the best route, a router's SPF algorithm adds the cost associated with each link between itself and the destination subnet, over each possible route. Figure 21-2 shows the costs associated with each route beside the links, with the dashed lines showing the three routes R1 finds between itself and subnet X (172.16.3.0/24).

Table 21-1 lists the three routes shown in Figure 21-2, with their cumulative costs, showing that R1's best route to 172.16.3.0/24 starts by going through R5.

Table 21-1 *Comparing R1's Three Alternatives for the Route to 172.16.3.0/24*

Route	Location in Figure 21-2	Cumulative Cost
R1–R7–R8	Left	10 + 180 + 10 = 200
R1–R5–R6–R8	Middle	20 + 30 + 40 + 10 = 100
R1–R2–R3–R4–R8	Right	30 + 60 + 20 + 5 + 10 = 125

As a result of the SPF algorithm's analysis of the LSDB, R1 adds a route to subnet 172.16.3.0/24 to its routing table, with the next-hop router of R5.

Convergence with Link-State Protocols

As soon as the internetwork is stable, link-state protocols reflood each LSA on a regular basis. (OSPF defaults to 30 minutes.) However, when an LSA changes, link-state protocols react swiftly, converging the network and using the currently best routes as quickly as possible. For example, imagine that the link between R5 and R6 fails in the internetwork of Figures 21-15 and 21-16. The following list explains the process R1 uses to switch to a different route (similar steps would occur for changes to other routers and routes):

1. R5 and R6 flood LSAs that state that their interfaces are now in a "down" state. (In a network of this size, the flooding typically takes maybe a second or two.)

2. All routers run the SPF algorithm again to see if any routes have changed. (This process can take another second in a network this size.)

3. All routers replace routes, as needed, based on the results of SPF. (This takes practically no additional time after SPF has completed.) For example, R1 changes its route for subnet X (172.16.3.0/24) to use R2 as the next-hop router.

These steps allow the link-state routing protocol to converge quickly—much more quickly than distance vector routing protocols.

Summary and Comparisons to Distance Vector Protocols

Link-state routing protocols provide fast convergence, which is probably the most important feature of a routing protocol, with built-in loop avoidance. Link-state routing protocols do not need to use the large variety of loop-avoidance features used by distance vector protocols, which in itself greatly reduces the convergence time. The main features of a link-state routing protocol are as follows:

■ All routers learn the same detailed information about all routers and subnets in the internetwork.

Key
Topic

■ The individual pieces of topology information are called LSAs. All LSAs are stored in RAM in a data structure called the link-state database (LSDB).

■ Routers flood LSAs when 1) they are created, 2) on a regular (but long) time interval if the LSAs do not change over time, and 3) immediately when an LSA changes.

■ The LSDB does not contain routes, but it does contain information that can be processed by the Dijkstra SPF algorithm to find a router's best route to reach each subnet.

■ Each router runs the SPF algorithm, with the LSDB as input, resulting in the best (lowest-cost/lowest-metric) routes being added to the IP routing table.

■ Link-state protocols converge quickly by immediately reflooding changed LSAs and rerunning the SPF algorithm on each router.

One of the most important comparison points between different routing protocols is how fast the routing protocol converges. Certainly, link-state protocols converge much more quickly than distance vector protocols. The following list summarizes some of the key comparison points for different routing protocols, comparing the strengths of the underlying algorithms:

■ **Convergence:** Link-state protocols converge much more quickly.

■ **CPU and RAM:** Link-state protocols consume much more CPU and memory than distance vector protocols, although with proper design, this disadvantage can be reduced.

■ **Avoiding routing loops:** Link-state protocols inherently avoid loops, whereas distance vector protocols require many additional features (for example, split horizon).

■ **Design effort:** Distance vector protocols do not require much planning, whereas link-state protocols require much more planning and design effort, particularly in larger networks.

■ **Configuration:** Distance vector protocols typically require less configuration, particularly when the link-state protocol requires the use of more-advanced features.

OSPF Protocols and Operation

The OSPF protocol has a wide variety of sometimes-complex features. To aid the learning process, OSPF features can be broken into three major categories: neighbors, database exchange, and route calculation. OSPF routers first form a neighbor relationship that provides a foundation for all continuing OSPF communications. After routers become neighbors, they exchange the contents of their respective LSDBs, through a process called database exchange. Finally, as soon as a router has topology information in its link-state database (LSDB), it uses the Dijkstra Shortest Path First (SPF) algorithm to calculate the now-best routes and add those to the IP routing table.

Interestingly, the IOS **show** commands also support this same structure. IOS has an OSPF neighbor table (**show ip ospf neighbor**), an OSPF LSDB (**show ip ospf database**), and of course an IP routing table (**show ip route**). The processes explained in this section can then be seen in action on routers by displaying the contents of these three tables.

OSPF Neighbors

Although some variations exist, a general definition of an OSPF neighbor is, from one router's perspective, another router that connects to the same data link with which the first router can and should exchange routing information using OSPF. Although this definition is correct, you can better understand the true meaning of the OSPF neighbor concept by thinking about the purpose of OSPF neighbor relationships. First, neighbors check and verify basic OSPF settings before exchanging routing information—settings that must match for OSPF to work correctly. Second, the ongoing process of one router knowing when the neighbor is healthy, and when the connection to a neighbor has been lost, tells the router when it must recalculate the entries in the routing table to reconverge to a new set of routes. Additionally, the OSPF Hello process defines how neighbors can be dynamically discovered, which means that new routers can be added to a network without requiring every router to be reconfigured.

The OSPF Hello process by which new neighbor relationships are formed works somewhat like when you move to a new house and meet your various neighbors. When you see each other outside, you might walk over, say hello, and learn each others' names. After talking a bit, you form a first impression, particularly as to whether you think you'll enjoy chatting with this neighbor occasionally, or whether you might just wave and not take the time to talk the next time you see him outside. Similarly, with OSPF, the process starts with messages called OSPF Hello messages. The Hellos in turn list each router's Router ID (RID), which serves as each router's unique name or identifier for OSPF. Finally, OSPF does several checks of the information in the Hello messages to ensure that the two routers should become neighbors.

Identifying OSPF Routers with a Router ID

OSPF needs to uniquely identify each router for many reasons. First, neighbors need a way to know which router sent a particular OSPF message. Additionally, the OSPF LSDB lists a set of Link State Advertisements (LSA), some of which describe each router in the internetwork, so the LSDB needs a unique identifier for each router. To that end, OSPF uses a concept called the *OSPF router ID (RID)*.

OSPF RIDs are 32-bit numbers written in dotted decimal, so using an IP address is a convenient way to find a default RID. Alternatively, the OSPF RID can be directly configured, as covered in the later section, "Configuring the OSPF Router ID."

Meeting Neighbors by Saying Hello

As soon as a router has chosen its OSPF RID, and some interfaces come up, the router is ready to meet its OSPF neighbors. OSPF routers can become neighbors if they are connected to the same subnet (and in some other special cases not discussed in this book). To discover other OSPF-speaking routers, a router sends multicast OSPF Hello packets to each interface and hopes to receive OSPF Hello packets from other routers connected to those interfaces. Figure 21-3 outlines the basic concept.

Routers A and B both send Hello messages onto the LAN. They continue to send Hellos based on their Hello Timer settings. Soon afterward, the two routers can begin exchanging topology information with each other. Then they run the Dijkstra algorithm to fill the routing table with the best routes. The Hello messages themselves have the following features:

■ The Hello message follows the IP packet header, with IP packet protocol type 89.

■ Hello packets are sent to multicast IP address 224.0.0.5, a multicast IP address intended for all OSPF-speaking routers.

■ OSPF routers listen for packets sent to IP multicast address 224.0.0.5, in part hoping to receive Hello packets and learn about new neighbors.

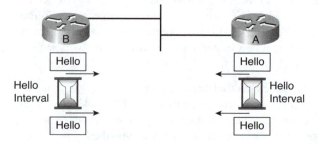

Figure 21-3 *Link-State Hello Packets*

Routers learn several important pieces of information from looking at the received Hello packets. The Hello message includes the sending router's RID, Area ID, Hello interval, dead interval, router priority, the RID of the designated router, the RID of the backup designated router, and a list of neighbors that the sending router already knows about on the subnet. (There's more to come on most of these items.)

The list of neighbors is particularly important to the Hello process. For example, when Router A receives a Hello from Router B, Router A needs to somehow tell Router B that Router A got the Hello. To do so, Router A adds Router B's RID to the list of OSPF neighbors inside the next (and future) Hello that Router A multicasts onto the network. Likewise, when Router B receives Router A's Hello, Router B's next (and ongoing) Hellos include Router A's RID in the list of neighbors.

As soon as a router sees its own RID in a received Hello, the router believes that *two-way* communication has been established with that neighbor. The two-way state for a neighbor is important, because at that point, more detailed information, such as LSAs, can be exchanged. Also, in some cases on LANs, neighbors might reach the two-way state and stop there. You'll read more about that in the later section "Choosing a Designated Router."

Potential Problems in Becoming a Neighbor

Interestingly, receiving a Hello from a router on the same subnet does not always result in two routers becoming neighbors. It's like meeting a new neighbor in real life. If you disagree about a lot of things, and you don't get along, you might not talk all that much. Similarly, with OSPF, routers on the same subnet must agree about several of the parameters exchanged in the Hello; otherwise, the routers simply do not become neighbors. Specifically, the following must match before a pair of routers becomes neighbors:

- Subnet mask used on the subnet

- Subnet number (as derived using the subnet mask and each router's interface IP address)

- Hello interval

- Dead interval

- OSPF area ID

- Must pass authentication checks (if used)

- Value of the stub area flag

If any one of these parameters differs, the routers do not become neighbors. In short, if you're troubleshooting OSPF when routers should be neighbors, and they are not, check this list!

Note: This chapter does not discuss the concepts related to stub areas, including the stub area flag included in this list. However, the text lists this item just so the list will be complete.

A couple of the items in the list need further explanation. First, a potential neighbor confirms that it is in the same subnet by comparing the neighboring router's IP address and subnet mask, as listed in the Hello message, with its own address and mask. If they are in the exact same subnet, with the same range of addresses, this check passes.

Next, two timer settings, the Hello Interval and Dead Interval, must match. OSPF routers send Hello messages every Hello Interval. When a router no longer hears a Hello from a neighbor for the time defined by the Dead Interval, the router believes the neighbor is no longer reachable, and the router reacts and reconverges the network. For instance, on Ethernet interfaces, Cisco routers default to a Hello interval of 10 seconds and a dead interval of 4 times the Hello interval, or 40 seconds. If a router does not hear any Hello messages from that neighbor for 40 seconds, it marks the now-silent router as "down" in its neighbor table. At that point, the routers can react and converge to use the now-currently best routes.

Neighbor States

OSPF defines a large set of potential actions that two neighbors use to communicate with each other. To keep track of the process, OSPF routers set each neighbor to one of many OSPF neighbor states. An OSPF neighbor state is the router's perception of how much work has been completed in the normal processes done by two neighboring routers. For example, if Routers R1 and R2 connect to the same LAN and become neighbors, R1 lists a neighbor state for R2, which is R1's perception of what has happened between the two routers so far. Likewise, R2 lists a neighbor state for R1, representing R2's view of what has happened between R2 and R1 so far. (The most common command to list the neighbors and states is **show ip ospf neighbor.**)

Because the neighbor states reflect various points in the normal OSPF processes used between two routers, it is useful to discuss neighbor states along with these processes and OSPF messages. Also, by understanding the OSPF neighbor states and their meanings, an engineer can more easily determine if an OSPF neighbor is working normally, or if a problem exists.

Figure 21-4 shows several of the neighbor states used by the early formation of a neighbor relationship. The figure shows the Hello messages and the resulting neighbor states.

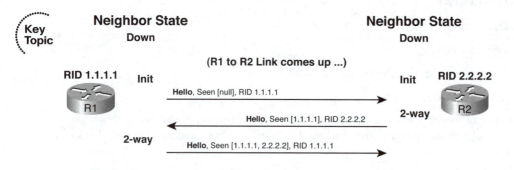

Figure 21-4 *Early Neighbor States*

The first two states, the Down state and the Init state, are relatively simple. In cases when a router previously knew about a neighbor, but the interface failed, the neighbor is listed as a Down state. As soon as the interface comes up, the two routers can send Hellos, transitioning that neighbor to an Init state. Init means that the neighbor relationship is being initialized.

A router changes from Init to a two-way state when two major facts are true: a received Hello lists that router's RID as having been seen, and that router has checked all parameters for the neighbor and they look good. These two facts mean that the router is willing to communicate with this neighbor. To make the process work, when each router receives a Hello from a new neighbor, the router checks the neighbor's configuration details, as described earlier. If all looks good, the router's next Hello lists the neighbor's RID in the list of "seen" routers. After both routers have checked the parameters and sent a Hello listing the other router's RID as "seen," both routers should have reached the two-way state.

For example, in Figure 21-4, R2 receives the first Hello, which lists "Seen [null]." This notation means that R1 has not yet seen any approved potential neighbors. When R2 sends its Hello, R2 lists R1's RID, implying that R2 has seen R1's Hello and has verified that all parameters look good. R1 returns the favor in the third Hello, sent one Hello-interval later than R1's first Hello.

After they are in a two-way state, the two routers are ready to exchange topology information, as covered in the next section.

OSPF Topology Database Exchange

OSPF routers exchange the contents of their LSDBs so that both neighbors have an exact copy of the same LSDB at the end of the database exchange process—a fundamental principle of how link-state routing protocols work. The process has many steps, with much more detail than is described here. This section begins by explaining an overview of the entire process, followed by a deeper look at each of the steps.

Overview of the OSPF Database Exchange Process

Interestingly, after two OSPF routers become neighbors and reach a two-way state, the next step might not be to exchange topology information. First, based on several factors, the routers must first decide if they should directly exchange topology information, or if the two neighbors should learn each other's topology information, in the form of LSAs, indirectly. As soon as a pair of OSPF neighbors knows that they should share topology information directly, they exchange the topology data (LSAs). After this is completed, the process moves to a relatively quiet maintenance state in which the routers occasionally reflood the LSAs and watch for changes to the network.

The overall process flows as follows, with each step explained in the following pages:

Step 1.   Based on the OSPF interface type, the routers might or might not collectively elect a Designated Router (DR) and Backup Designated Router (BDR).

Step 2.   For each pair of routers that need to become fully adjacent, mutually exchange the contents of their respective LSDBs.

Step 3.   When completed, the neighbors monitor for changes and periodically reflood LSAs while in the Full (fully adjacent) neighbor state.

Choosing a Designated Router

OSPF dictates that a subnet either should or should not use a Designated Router (DR) and Backup Designated Router (BDR) based on the OSPF interface type (also sometimes called the OSPF network type). Several OSPF interface types exist, but this books focuses on the two main types: point-to-point and broadcast. (These types can be configured with the **ip ospf network** *type* command.) These OSPF interface types make a general reference to the type of data-link protocol used. As you might guess from the names, the point-to-point type is intended for use on point-to-point links, and the broadcast type is for use on data links that support broadcast frames, such as LANs.

Figure 21-5 shows a classic example of two sets of neighbors—one using the default OSPF interface type of point-to-point on a serial link, and the other using the default OSPF interface type of broadcast on a LAN. The end result of the DR election is that topology information is exchanged only between neighbors shown with arrowed lines in the figure. Focus on the lower-right part of the figure.

When a DR is not required, neighboring routers can go ahead and start the topology exchange process, as shown on the left side of the figure. In OSPF terminology, the two routers on the left should continue working to exchange topology information and become fully adjacent. On the right side of the figure, the top part shows a LAN topology where a DR election has been held, with Router A winning the election. With a DR, the topology exchange process happens between the DR and every other router, but not between every pair of routers. As a result, all routing updates flow to and from Router A, with Router A essentially distributing the topology information to the other routers. All routers learn all topology information from all other routers, but the process only causes a direct exchange of routing information between the DR and each of the non-DR routers.

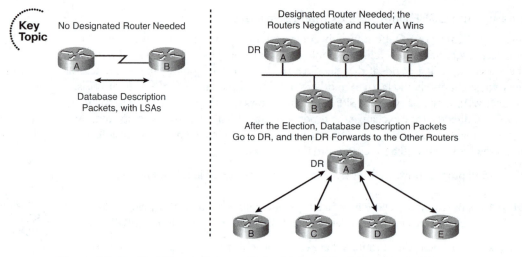

Figure 21-5 *No DR on a Point-to-Point Link, with a DR on the LAN*

The DR concept prevents overloading a subnet with too much OSPF traffic when many routers are on a subnet. Of course, lots of routers could be attached to one LAN, which is why a DR is required for routers attached to a LAN. For instance, if ten routers were attached to the same LAN subnet, and they were allowed to forward OSPF updates to each of the other nine routers, topology updates would flow between 45 different pairs of neighbors—with almost all the information being redundant. With the DR concept, as shown on the right side of Figure 21-5, that same LAN would require routing updates only between the DR and the nine other routers, significantly reducing the flooding of OSPF information across the LAN.

Because the DR is so important to the exchange of routing information, the loss of the elected DR could cause delays in convergence. OSPF includes the concept of a *Backup DR (BDR)* on each subnet, so when the DR fails or loses connectivity to the subnet, the BDR can take over as the DR. (All routers except the DR and BDR are typically called "DROther" in IOS **show** command output.)

Note: All non-DR and non-BDR routers attempt to become fully adjacent with both the DR and BDR, but Figure 21-5 shows only the relationships with the DR to reduce clutter.

When a DR is required, the neighboring routers hold an election. To elect a DR, the neighboring routers look at two fields inside the Hello packets they receive and choose the DR based on the following criteria:

- The router sending the Hello with the *highest OSPF priority* setting becomes the DR.

- If two or more routers tie with the highest priority setting, the router sending the Hello with the *highest RID* wins.

- It's not always the case, but typically the router with the second-highest priority becomes the BDR.

- A priority setting of 0 means that the router does not participate in the election and can never become the DR or BDR.

- The range of priority values that allow a router to be a candidate are 1 through 255.

- If a new, better candidate comes along after the DR and BDR have been elected, the new candidate does not preempt the existing DR and BDR.

Database Exchange

The database exchange process can be quite involved with several OSPF messages. The details of the process can be ignored for the purposes of this book, but a brief overview can help give some perspective on the overall process.

After two routers decide to exchange databases, they do not simply send the contents of the entire database. First, they tell each other a list of LSAs in their respective databases—not all the details of the LSAs, just a list. Each router then compares the other router's list to its own LSDB. For any LSAs that a router does not have a copy of, the router asks the neighbor for a copy of the LSA, and the neighbor sends the full LSA.

When two neighbors complete this process, they are considered to have *fully completed* the database exchange process. So OSPF uses the *Full* neighbor state to mean that the database exchange process has been completed.

Maintaining the LSDB While Being Fully Adjacent

Neighbors in a Full state still do some maintenance work. They keep sending Hellos every Hello interval. The absence of Hellos for a time equal to the Dead Interval means that the connection to the neighbor has failed. Also, if any topology changes occur, the neighbors send new copies of the changed LSAs to each neighbor so that the neighbor can change its LSDBs. For example, if a subnet fails, a router updates the LSA for that subnet to reflect its state as being down. That router then sends the LSA to its neighbors, and they in turn send it to their neighbors, until all routers again have an identical copy of the LSDB. Each router can then also use SPF to recalculate any routes affected by the failed subnet.

The router that creates each LSA also has the responsibility to reflood the LSA every 30 minutes (the default), even if no changes occur. This process is quite different than the distance vector concept of periodic updates. Distance vector protocols send full updates over a short time interval, listing all routes (except those omitted due to loop-avoidance tools such as split horizon). OSPF does not send all routes every 30 minutes. Instead, each LSA has a separate timer, based on when the LSA was created. So, there is no single moment when OSPF sends a lot of messages to reflood all LSAs. Instead, each LSA is reflooded by the router that created the LSA, every 30 minutes.

As a reminder, some routers do not attempt to become fully adjacent. In particular, on interfaces on which a DR is elected, routers that are neither DR nor BDR become neighbors, but they do not become fully adjacent. These non-fully adjacent routers do not directly exchange LSAs. Also, the **show ip ospf neighbor** command on such a router lists these neighbors in a two-way state as the normal stable neighbor state, and Full as the normal stable state for the DR and BDR.

Summary of Neighbor States

For easier reference and study, Table 21-2 lists and briefly describes the neighbor states mentioned in this chapter.

Key Topic

Table 21-2   *OSPF Neighbor and Their Meanings*

Neighbor State	Meaning
Down	A known neighbor is no longer reachable, often because of an underlying interface failure.
Init	An interim state in which a Hello has been heard from the neighbor, but that Hello does not list the router's RID as having been seen yet.
Two-way	The neighbor has sent a Hello that lists the local router's RID in the list of seen routers, also implying that neighbor verification checks all passed.
Full	Both routers know the exact same LSDB details and are fully adjacent.

Building the IP Routing Table

OSPF routers send messages to learn about neighbors, listing those neighbors in the OSPF neighbor table. OSPF routers then send messages to exchange topology data with these same neighbors, storing the information in the OSPF topology table, more commonly called the LSDB or the OSPF database. To fill the third major table used by OSPF, the IP routing table, OSPF does not send any messages. Each router runs the Dijkstra SPF algorithm against the OSPF topology database, choosing the best routes based on that process.

The OSPF topology database consists of lists of subnet numbers (called *links*, hence the name *link-state database*). It also contains lists of routers, along with the links (subnets) to which each router is connected. Armed with the knowledge of links and routers, a router can run the SPF algorithm to compute the best routes to all the subnets. The concept is very much like putting together a jigsaw puzzle. The color and shape of each piece help you identify what pieces might fit next to it. Similarly, the detailed information in each LSA—things such as a *link LSA* listing the routers attached to the subnet, and a *router LSA* listing its IP addresses and masks—gives the SPF algorithm enough information to figure out which routers connect to each subnet and create the mathematical equivalent of a network diagram.

Each router independently uses the Dijkstra SPF algorithm, as applied to the OSPF LSDB, to find the best route from that router to each subnet. The algorithm finds the shortest path from that router to each subnet in the LSDB. Then the router places the best route to each subnet in the IP routing table. It sounds simple, and it is with a drawing of an internetwork that lists all the information. Fortunately, although the underlying math of the SPF algorithm can be a bit daunting, you do not need to know SPF math. However, you do need to be able to predict the routes SPF will choose using network diagrams and documentation.

OSPF chooses the least-cost route between the router and a subnet by adding up the outgoing interfaces' OSPF costs. Each interface has an OSPF cost associated with it. The router looks at each possible route, adds up the costs on the interfaces out which packets would be forwarded on that route, and then picks the least-cost route. For example, Figure 21-6 shows a simple internetwork with the OSPF cost values listed beside each interface. In this figure, router R4 has two possible paths with which to reach subnet 10.1.5.0/24. The two routes are as follows, listing each router and its outgoing interface:

R4 Fa0/0—R1 S0/1—R5 Fa0/0

R4 Fa0/0—R2 S0/1—R5 Fa0/0

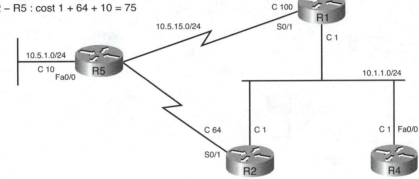

Route R4 – R1 – R5 : cost 1 + 100 + 10 = 111
Route R4 – R2 – R5 : cost 1 + 64 + 10 = 75

Figure 21-6   *Sample OSPF Network with Costs Shown*

If you add up the cost associated with each interface, the first of the two routes totals a cost of 111, and the second totals 75. So, R4 adds the route through R2 as the best route and lists R2's IP address as the next-hop IP address.

Now that you have seen how OSPF routers perform the most fundamental functions of OSPF, the next section takes a broader look at OSPF, particularly some important design points.

Scaling OSPF Through Hierarchical Design

OSPF can be used in some networks with very little thought about design issues. You just turn on OSPF in all the routers, and it works! However, in large networks, engineers need to think about and plan how to use several OSPF features that allow it to scale well in larger networks. To appreciate the issues behind OSPF scalability, and the need for good design to allow scalability, examine Figure 21-7.

In the network shown in Figure 21-7, the topology database on all nine routers is the same full topology that matches the figure. With a network that size, you can just enable OSPF, and it works fine. But imagine a network with 900 routers instead of only nine, and several thousand subnets. In that size of network, the sheer amount of processing required to run the complex SPF algorithm might cause convergence time to be slow, and the routers might experience memory shortages. The problems can be summarized as follows:

Key Topic

■ A larger topology database requires more memory on each router.

■ Processing the larger-topology database with the SPF algorithm requires processing power that grows exponentially with the size of the topology database.

■ A single interface status change (up to down or down to up) forces every router to run SPF again!

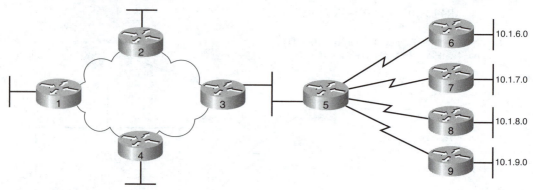

Figure 21-7   *Single-Area OSPF*

Although there is no exact definition of "large" in this context, in networks with at least 50 routers and at least a few hundred subnets, engineers should use OSPF scalability features to reduce the problems just described. These numbers are gross generalizations. They depend largely on the network design, the power of the router CPU, the amount of RAM, and so on.

OSPF Areas

Using OSPF areas solves many, but not all, of the most common problems with running OSPF in larger networks. OSPF areas break up the network so that routers in one area know less topology information about the subnets in the other area—and they do not know about the routers in the other area at all. With smaller-topology databases, routers consume less memory and take less processing time to run SPF. Figure 21-8 shows the same network as Figure 21-7, but with two OSPF areas, labeled Area 1 and Area 0.

The same topology is shown in the upper part of the figure, but the lower part of the figure shows the topology database on Routers 1, 2, and 4. By placing part of the network in another area, the routers inside Area 1 are shielded from some of the details. Router 3 is known as an OSPF Area Border Router (ABR), because it is on the border between two different areas. Router 3 does not advertise full topology information about the part of the network in Area 0 to Routers 1, 2, and 4. Instead, Router 3 advertises summary information about the subnets in Area 0, effectively making Routers 1, 2, and 4 think the topology looks like the lower part of Figure 21-8. Therefore, Routers 1, 2, and 4 view the world as if it has fewer routers. As a result, the SPF algorithm takes less time, and the topology database takes less memory.

OSPF design introduces a few new important terms, as defined in Table 21-3.

Table 21-3   *OSPF Design Terminology*

Term	Description
Area Border Router (ABR)	An OSPF router with interfaces connected to the backbone area and to at least one other area.
Autonomous System Border Router (ASBR)	An OSPF router that connects to routers that do not use OSPF for the purpose of exchanging external routes into and out of the OSPF domain.
Backbone router	A router in one area, the backbone area.
Internal router	A router in a single nonbackbone area.
Area	A set of routers and links that share the same detailed LSDB information, but not with routers in other areas, for better efficiency.
Backbone area	A special OSPF area to which all other areas must connect: Area 0.
External route	A route learned from outside the OSPF domain and then advertised into the OSPF domain.
Intra-area route	A route to a subnet inside the same area as the router.
Interarea route	A route to a subnet in an area of which the router is not a part.
Autonomous system	In OSPF, a reference to a set of routers that use OSPF.

It is very important to note the difference between the summarized information shown in Figure 21-8 versus summarized routes as covered in Chapter 19, "VLSM and Route Summarization." In this case, the term *summary* just means that a router inside one area receives briefer information in the LSA for a subnet, thereby decreasing the amount of memory needed to store the information. For example, in Figure 21-8, router R1 (in Area 1) learns only a very brief LSA about subnets in Area 0. This process reduces the size and complexity of the SPF algorithm. In addition, the term *summary* can refer to a summary route configured in OSPF, with the general concepts covered in Chapter 19. OSPF manual route summarization reduces the number of subnets, which in turn also reduces the size and effort of the SPF calculation.

Note: Although the perspectives of the routers in Area 1 are shown in Figure 21-8, the same thing happens in reverse—routers in Area 0 do not know the details of Area 1's topology.

Notice that the dividing line between areas is not a link, but a router. In Figure 21-8, Router 3 is in both Area 1 and Area 0. OSPF uses the term Area Border Router (ABR) to describe a router that sits in both areas. An ABR has the topology database for both areas and runs SPF when links change status in either area. So, although using areas helps scale OSPF by reducing the size of the LSDB and the time to compute a routing table, the amount of RAM and CPU consumed on ABRs can actually increase. As a result, the routers acting as ABRs should be faster routers with relatively more memory.

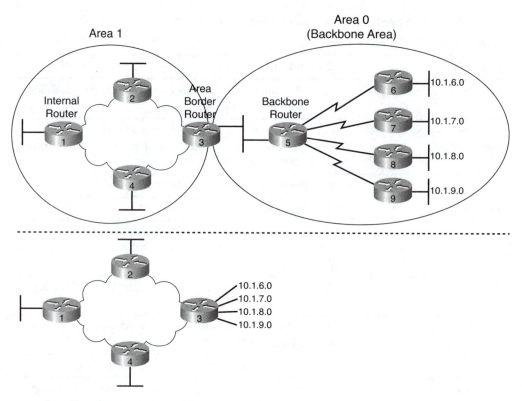

Figure 21-8 *Two-Area OSPF*

OSPF Area Design Advantages

Using areas improves OSPF operations in many ways, particularly in larger internetworks:

- The smaller per-area LSDB requires less memory.

- The router requires fewer CPU cycles to process the smaller per-area LSDB with the SPF algorithm, reducing CPU overhead and improving convergence time.

- The SPF algorithm has to be run on internal routers only when an LSA inside the area changes, so routers have to run SPF less often.

- Less information must be advertised between areas, reducing the bandwidth required to send LSAs.

- Manual summarization can only be configured on ABRs and ASBRs, so areas allow for smaller IP routing tables by allowing for the configuration of manual route summarization.

OSPF Configuration

OSPF configuration includes only a few required steps, but it has many optional steps. After an OSPF design has been chosen—a task that can be complex in larger IP internetworks—the configuration can be as simple as enabling OSPF on each router interface and placing that interface in the correct OSPF area.

This section shows several configuration examples, starting with a single-area OSPF internetwork and then a multiarea OSPF internetwork. Following those examples, the text goes on to cover several of the additional optional configuration settings. For reference, the following list outlines the configuration steps covered in this chapter, as well as a brief reference to the required commands:

Step 1. Enter OSPF configuration mode for a particular OSPF process using the **router ospf** *process-id* global command.

Step 2. (Optional) Configure the OSPF router ID by:

    a. Configuring the **router-id** *id-value* router subcommand.

    b. Configuring an IP address on a loopback interface.

Step 3. Configure one or more **network** *ip-address wildcard-mask* **area** *area-id* router subcommands, with any matched interfaces being added to the listed area.

Step 4. (Optional) Change the interface Hello and Dead intervals using the **ip ospf hello-interval** *time* and **ip ospf dead-interval** *time* interface subcommands.

Step 5. (Optional) Impact routing choices by tuning interface costs as follows:

    a. Configure costs directly using the **ip ospf cost** *value* interface subcommand.

    c. Change interface bandwidths using the **bandwidth** *value* interface subcommand.

    d. Change the numerator in the formula to calculate the cost based on the interface bandwidth, using the **auto-cost reference-bandwidth** *value* router subcommand.

Step 6. (Optional) Configure OSPF authentication:

    a. On a per-interface basis using the **ip ospf authentication** interface subcommand.

    b. For all interfaces in an area using the **area authentication** router subcommand.

Step 7. (Optional) Configure support for multiple equal-cost routes using the **maximum-paths** *number* router subcommand.

OSPF Single-Area Configuration

OSPF configuration differs only slightly from RIP configuration when a single OSPF area is used. The best way to describe the configuration, and the differences with the configuration of the other routing protocols, is to use an example. Figure 21-9 shows a sample network, and Example 21-1 shows the configuration on Albuquerque.

Example 21-1 *OSPF Single-Area Configuration on Albuquerque*

```
interface ethernet 0/0
 ip address 10.1.1.1 255.255.255.0
interface serial 0/0
```

```
  ip address 10.1.4.1 255.255.255.0
 interface serial 0/1
  ip address 10.1.6.1 255.255.255.0
 !
 router ospf 1
 network 10.0.0.0 0.255.255.255 area 0
```

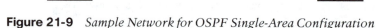

Subnet 10.1.1.0

E0/0

Albuquerque

S0/0   S0/1

Subnet 10.1.4.0

Subnet 10.1.6.0

S0/0
S0/1   Subnet 10.1.5.0   S0/0
S0/1

Yosemite   Seville

E0/0   Subnet 10.1.2.0   E0/0   Subnet 10.1.3.0

Figure 21-9   *Sample Network for OSPF Single-Area Configuration*

The configuration correctly enables OSPF on all three interfaces on Albuquerque. First, the **router ospf 1** global command puts the user in OSPF configuration mode. The **router ospf** command has a parameter called the OSPF *process-id*. In some instances, you might want to run multiple OSPF processes in a single router, so the **router** command uses the *process-id* to distinguish between the processes. The *process-id* does not have to match on each router, and it can be any integer between 1 and 65,535.

The **network** command tells a router to enable OSPF on each matched interface, discover neighbors on that interface, assign the interface to that area, and advertise the subnet connected to each interface. In this case, the **network 10.0.0.0 0.255.255.255 area 0** command matches all three of Albuquerque's interfaces because the OSPF **network** command matches interfaces using an address and a wildcard-style mask like those used with IP ACLs. The wildcard mask shown in Example 21-1 is 0.255.255.255, with address 10.0.0.0. This combination matches all addresses that begin with 10 in the first octet. So, this one **network** command matches all three of Albuquerque's interfaces, puts them in Area 0, and causes Albuquerque to try to discover neighbors on those interfaces. It also causes Albuquerque to advertise the three connected subnets.

The wildcard mask in the OSPF **network** command works like an ACL wildcard mask, but there is one restriction on the values used. The OSPF wildcard mask must have only one string of consecutive binary 1s and one string of consecutive binary 0s. For example, a mask of 0.0.255.255 represents 16 binary 0s and 16 binary 1s and would be allowed. Likewise, a mask of 255.255.255.0 would be allowed, because it has a string of 24 binary 1s followed by eight binary 0s. However, a value of 0.255.255.0 would not be allowed, because it has two sets of eight binary 0s, separated by a string of 16 binary 1s.

Example 21-2 shows an alternative configuration for Albuquerque that also enables OSPF on every interface. In this case, the IP address for each interface is matched with a different **network** command. The wildcard mask of 0.0.0.0 means that all 32 bits must be compared, and they must match—so the **network** commands include the specific IP address of each interface, respectively. Many people prefer this style of configuration in production networks, because it removes any ambiguity about the interfaces on which OSPF is running.

Example 21-2   *OSPF Single-Area Configuration on Albuquerque Using Three* **network** *Commands*

```
interface ethernet 0/0
 ip address 10.1.1.1 255.255.255.0
interface serial 0/0
 ip address 10.1.4.1 255.255.255.0
interface serial 0/1
 ip address 10.1.6.1 255.255.255.0
!
router ospf 1
 network 10.1.1.1 0.0.0.0 area 0
 network 10.1.4.1 0.0.0.0 area 0
 network 10.1.6.1 0.0.0.0 area 0
```

OSPF Configuration with Multiple Areas

Configuring OSPF with multiple areas is simple when you understand OSPF configuration in a single area. Designing the OSPF network by making good choices about which subnets should be placed in which areas is the hard part! After the area design is complete, the configuration is easy. For instance, consider Figure 21-10, which shows some subnets in Area 0 and some in Area 1.

Multiple areas are not needed in such a small network, but two areas are used in this example to show the configuration. Note that Albuquerque and Seville are both ABRs, but Yosemite is totally inside Area 1, so it is not an ABR. Examples 21-3 and 21-4 show the configuration on Albuquerque and Yosemite, along with several **show** commands.

Example 21-3   *OSPF Multiarea Configuration and* **show** *Commands on Albuquerque*

```
! Only the OSPF configuration is shown to conserve space
!
router ospf 1
 network 10.1.1.1 0.0.0.0 area 0
 network 10.1.4.1 0.0.0.0 area 1
 network 10.1.6.1 0.0.0.0 area 0
Albuquerque# show ip route
Codes: C - connected, S - static, I - IGRP, R - RIP, M - mobile, B - BGP
```

```
          D - EIGRP, EX - EIGRP external, O - OSPF, IA - OSPF inter area
          N1 - OSPF NSSA external type 1, N2 - OSPF NSSA external type 2
          E1 - OSPF external type 1, E2 - OSPF external type 2, E - EGP
          i - IS-IS, L1 - IS-IS level-1, L2 - IS-IS level-2, ia - IS-IS inter area
          * - candidate default, U - per-user static route, o - ODR
          P - periodic downloaded static route

Gateway of last resort is not set


     10.0.0.0/24 is subnetted, 6 subnets
O        10.1.3.0 [110/65] via 10.1.6.3, 00:01:04, Serial0/1
O        10.1.2.0 [110/65] via 10.1.4.2, 00:00:39, Serial0/0
C        10.1.1.0 is directly connected, Ethernet0/0
C        10.1.6.0 is directly connected, Serial0/1
O        10.1.5.0 [110/128] via 10.1.4.2, 00:00:39, Serial0/0
C        10.1.4.0 is directly connected, Serial0/0

Albuquerque# show ip route ospf
     10.0.0.0/24 is subnetted, 6 subnets
O        10.1.3.0 [110/65] via 10.1.6.3, 00:01:08, Serial0/1
O        10.1.2.0 [110/65] via 10.1.4.2, 00:00:43, Serial0/0
O        10.1.5.0 [110/128] via 10.1.4.2, 00:00:43, Serial0/0
```

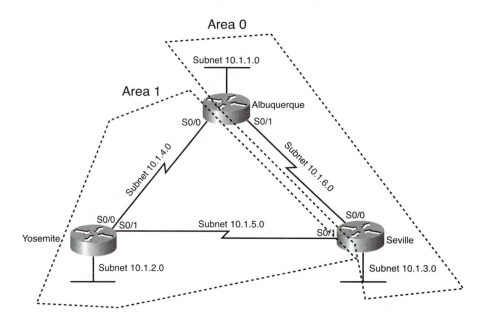

Figure 21-10 *Multiarea OSPF Network*

Example 21-4 *OSPF Multiarea Configuration and* **show** *Commands on Yosemite*

```
! Only the OSPF configuration is shown to conserve space
router ospf 1
 network 10.0.0.0 0.255.255.255 area 1
Yosemite# show ip route
Codes: C - connected, S - static, I - IGRP, R - RIP, M - mobile, B - BGP
       D - EIGRP, EX - EIGRP external, O - OSPF, IA - OSPF inter area
       N1 - OSPF NSSA external type 1, N2 - OSPF NSSA external type 2
       E1 - OSPF external type 1, E2 - OSPF external type 2, E - EGP
       i - IS-IS, L1 - IS-IS level-1, L2 - IS-IS level-2, ia - IS-IS inter area
       * - candidate default, U - per-user static route, o - ODR
       P - periodic downloaded static route

Gateway of last resort is not set

     10.0.0.0/24 is subnetted, 6 subnets
IA      10.1.3.0 [110/65] via 10.1.5.1, 00:00:54, Serial0/1
IA      10.1.1.0 [110/65] via 10.1.4.1, 00:00:49, Serial0/0
C       10.1.2.0 is directly connected, Ethernet0/0
C       10.1.5.0 is directly connected, Serial0/1
IA      10.1.6.0 [110/128] via 10.1.4.1, 00:00:38, Serial0/0
C       10.1.4.0 is directly connected, Serial0/0
```

The configuration needs to set the correct area number on the appropriate interfaces. For instance, the **network 10.1.4.1 0.0.0.0 area 1** command at the beginning of Example 21-3 matches Albuquerque's Serial 0/0 interface IP address, placing that interface in Area 1. The **network 10.1.6.1 0.0.0.0 area 0** and **network 10.1.1.1 0.0.0.0 area 0** commands place Serial 0/1 and Ethernet 0/0, respectively, in Area 0. Unlike Example 21-1, Albuquerque cannot be configured to match all three interfaces with a single **network** command, because one interface (Serial 0/0) is in a different area than the other two interfaces.

Continuing with Example 21-3, the **show ip route ospf** command just lists OSPF-learned routes, as opposed to the entire IP routing table. The **show ip route** command lists all three connected routes, as well as the three OSPF learned routes. Note that Albuquerque's route to 10.1.2.0 has the O designation beside it, meaning *intra-area*, because that subnet resides in Area 1, and Albuquerque is part of Area 1 and Area 0.

In Example 21-4, notice that the OSPF configuration in Yosemite requires only a single **network** command because all interfaces in Yosemite are in Area 1. Also note that the routes learned by Yosemite from the other two routers show up as *interarea (IA) routes*, because those subnets are in Area 0, and Yosemite is in Area 1.

Configuring the OSPF Router ID

OSPF-speaking routers must have a Router ID (RID) for proper operation. To find its RID, a Cisco router uses the following process when the router reloads and brings up the OSPF process. Note that when one of these steps identifies the RID, the process stops.

Key Topic

1. If the **router-id** *rid* OSPF subcommand is configured, this value is used as the RID.

2. If any loopback interfaces have an IP address configured and the interface has a line and protocol status of up/up, the router picks the highest numeric IP address among the up/up loopback interfaces.

3. The router picks the highest numeric IP address from all other working (up/up) interfaces.

The first and third criteria should make some sense right away: the RID is either configured or is taken from a working interface's IP address. However, this book has not yet explained the concept of a *loopback interface*, as mentioned in Step 2. A loopback interface is a virtual interface that can be configured with the **interface loopback** *interface-number* command, where *interface-number* is an integer. Loopback interfaces are always in an "up and up" state unless administratively placed in a shutdown state. For instance, a simple configuration of the command **interface loopback 0**, followed by **ip address 192.168.200.1 255.255.255.0**, would create a loopback interface and assign it an IP address. Because loopback interfaces do not rely on any hardware, these interfaces can be up/up whenever IOS is running, making them good interfaces on which to base an OSPF RID.

Each router chooses its OSPF RID when OSPF is initialized. Initialization happens during the initial load of IOS. So, if OSPF comes up, and later other interfaces come up that happen to have higher IP addresses, the OSPF RID does not change until the OSPF process is restarted. OSPF can be restarted with the **clear ip ospf process** command as well, but depending on circumstances, IOS still might not change its OSPF RID until the next IOS reload.

Many commands list the OSPF RID of various routers. For instance, in Example 21-5, the first neighbor in the output of the **show ip ospf neighbor** command lists Router ID 10.1.5.2, which is Yosemite's RID. Following that, **show ip ospf** lists Albuquerque's own RID.

Example 21-5 *Displaying OSPF-Related Information in Albuquerque*

```
Albuquerque# show ip ospf neighbor



Neighbor ID     Pri   State          Dead Time   Address        Interface
10.1.6.3          1   FULL/  -       00:00:35    10.1.6.3       Serial0/1
10.1.5.2          1   FULL/  -       00:00:37    10.1.4.2       Serial0/0
Albuquerque# show ip ospf neighbor
Routing Process "ospf 1" with ID 10.1.6.1
! lines omitted for brevity
```

OSPF Hello and Dead Timers

The default settings for the OSPF Hello and dead timers typically work just fine. However, it is important to note that a mismatch on either setting causes two potential neighbors to never become neighbors, never reaching the two-way state. Example 21-6 lists the most common way to see the current settings using the **show ip ospf interface** command, as taken from Albuquerque, when configured as shown in the multiarea OSPF example (refer to Examples 21-3 and 21-4).

Example 21-6 *Displaying the Hello and Dead Timers on Albuquerque*

```
Albuquerque# show ip ospf interface
Serial0/1 is up, line protocol is up
  Internet Address 10.1.6.1/24, Area 0
  Process ID 1, Router ID 10.1.6.1, Network Type POINT_TO_POINT, Cost: 64
  Transmit Delay is 1 sec, State POINT_TO_POINT,
  Timer intervals configured, Hello 10, Dead 40, Wait 40, Retransmit 5
    Hello due in 00:00:07
  Index 2/3, flood queue length 0
  Next 0x0(0)/0x0(0)
  Last flood scan length is 2, maximum is 2
  Last flood scan time is 0 msec, maximum is 0 msec
  Neighbor Count is 1, Adjacent neighbor count is 1
    Adjacent with neighbor 10.1.6.3
  Suppress hello for 0 neighbor(s)
Ethernet0/0 is up, line protocol is up
  Internet Address 10.1.1.1/24, Area 0
  Process ID 1, Router ID 10.1.6.1, Network Type BROADCAST, Cost: 10
  Transmit Delay is 1 sec, State DR, Priority 1
  Designated Router (ID) 10.1.6.1, Interface address 10.1.1.1
  No backup designated router on this network
  Timer intervals configured, Hello 10, Dead 40, Wait 40, Retransmit 5
    Hello due in 00:00:08
  Index 1/1, flood queue length 0
  Next 0x0(0)/0x0(0)
  Last flood scan length is 0, maximum is 0
  Last flood scan time is 0 msec, maximum is 0 msec
  Neighbor Count is 0, Adjacent neighbor count is 0
  Suppress hello for 0 neighbor(s)
Serial0/0 is up, line protocol is up
  Internet Address 10.1.4.1/24, Area 1
  Process ID 1, Router ID 10.1.6.1, Network Type POINT_TO_POINT, Cost: 64
  Transmit Delay is 1 sec, State POINT_TO_POINT,
  Timer intervals configured, Hello 10, Dead 40, Wait 40, Retransmit 5
    Hello due in 00:00:01
  Index 1/2, flood queue length 0
  Next 0x0(0)/0x0(0)
  Last flood scan length is 1, maximum is 1
  Last flood scan time is 0 msec, maximum is 0 msec
  Neighbor Count is 1, Adjacent neighbor count is 1
    Adjacent with neighbor 10.1.5.2
  Suppress hello for 0 neighbor(s)
```

Note also that the **show ip ospf interface** command lists more detailed information about OSPF operation on each interface. For instance, this command lists the area number, OSPF cost, and any neighbors known on each interface. The timers used on the interface, including the Hello and dead timer, are also listed.

To configure the Hello and Dead intervals, you can use the **ip ospf hello-interval** *value* and **ip ospf dead-interval** *value* interface subcommands. Interestingly, if the Hello interval is configured, IOS automatically reconfigures the interface's dead interval to be four times the Hello interval.

OSPF Metrics (Cost)

OSPF calculates the metric for each possible route by adding up the outgoing interfaces' OSPF costs. The OSPF cost for an interface can be configured, or a router can calculate the cost based on the interface's bandwidth setting.

As a reminder, the bandwidth setting on an interface can be configured using the **bandwidth** interface subcommand. This command sets the router's perception of interface speed, with a unit of Kbps. Note that the interface's bandwidth setting does not have to match the physical interface speed, but it usually makes sense to set the bandwidth to match the physical interface speed. On Ethernet interfaces, the bandwidth reflects the current negotiated speed—10,000 (meaning 10,000 Kbps or 10 Mbps) for 10 Mbps Ethernet, and 100,000 (meaning 100,000 Kbps or 100 Mbps) for 100 Mbps. For serial interfaces, the bandwidth defaults to 1544 (meaning 1544 Kbps, or T1 speed), but IOS cannot adjust this setting dynamically.

IOS chooses an interface's cost based on the following rules:

1. The cost can be explicitly set using the **ip ospf cost** *x* interface subcommand, to a value between 1 and 65,535, inclusive.

2. IOS can calculate a value based on the generic formula *Ref-BW* / *Int-BW*, where *Ref-BW* is a reference bandwidth that defaults to 100 Mbps, and *Int-BW* is the interface's bandwidth setting.

3. The reference bandwidth can be configured from its default setting of 100 (100 Mbps) using the router OSPF subcommand **auto-cost reference-bandwidth** *ref-bw*, which in turn affects the calculation of the default interface cost.

The simple formula to calculate the default OSPF cost has one potentially confusing part. The calculation requires that the numerator and denominator use the same units, whereas the **bandwidth** and **auto-cost reference-bandwidth** commands use different units. For instance, Cisco IOS software defaults Ethernet interfaces to use a bandwidth of 10,000, meaning 10,000 Kbps, or 10 Mbps. The reference bandwidth defaults to a value of 100, meaning 100 Mbps. So, the default OSPF cost on an Ethernet interface would be 100 Mbps / 10 Mbps, after making both values use a unit of Mbps. Higher-speed serial interfaces default to a bandwidth of 1544, giving a default cost of 10^8 bps / 1,544,000 bps, which is rounded down to a value of 64, as shown for interface S0/1 in Example 21-6. If the reference bandwidth had been changed to 1000, using the router OSPF subcommand **auto-cost reference-bandwidth 1000**, the calculated metric would be 647.

The main motivation for changing the reference bandwidth is so that routers can have different cost values for interfaces running at speeds of 100 Mbps and higher. With the default setting, an interface with a 100 Mbps bandwidth setting (for example, an FE interface) and an interface with a 1000 Mbps bandwidth (for example, a GE interface) would both have a default cost of 1. By changing the reference bandwidth to 1000, meaning 1000 Mbps, the default cost on a 100-Mbps bandwidth interface would be 10, versus a default cost of 1 on an interface with a bandwidth of 1000 Mbps.

Note: Cisco recommends making the OSPF reference bandwidth setting the same on all OSPF routers in a network.

OSPF Authentication

Authentication is arguably the most important of the optional configuration features for OSPF. The lack of authentication opens the network to attacks in which an attacker connects a router to the network, with the legitimate routers believing the OSPF data from the rogue router. As a result, the attacker can easily cause a denial-of-service (DoS) attack by making all routers remove the legitimate routes to all subnets, instead installing routes that forward packets to the attacking router. The attacker can also perform a reconnaissance attack, learning information about the network by listening for and interpreting the OSPF messages.

OSPF supports three types of authentication—one called null authentication (meaning no authentication), one that uses a simple text password and therefore is easy to break, and one that uses MD5. Frankly, if you bother to configure an option in real life, the MD5 option is the only reasonable option. As soon as a router has configured OSPF authentication on an interface, that router must pass the authentication process for every OSPF message, with every neighboring router on that interface. This means that each neighboring router on that interface must also have the same authentication type and the same authentication password configured.

The configuration can use two interface subcommands on each interface—one to enable the particular type of authentication, and one to set the password used for the authentication. Example 21-7 shows a sample configuration in which simple password authentication is configured on interface Fa0/0, and MD5 authentication is configured on Fa0/1.

Example 21-7 *OSPF Authentication Using Only Interface Subcommands*

```
! The following commands enable OSPF simple password authentication and
! set the password to a value of "key-t1".
R1# show running-config
! lines omitted for brevity
interface FastEthernet0/0
 ip ospf authentication
 ip ospf authentication-key key-t1
! Below, the neighbor relationship formed, proving that authentication worked.
R1# show ip ospf neighbor fa 0/0
Neighbor ID    Pri   State          Dead Time   Address      Interface
```

```
2.2.2.2              1   FULL/BDR       00:00:37   10.1.1.2        FastEthernet0/0
! Next, each interface's OSPF authentication type can be seen in the last line
! or two in the output of the show ip ospf interface command.
R1# show ip ospf interface fa 0/0
! Lines omitted for brevity
 Simple password authentication enabled


! Below, R1's Fa0/1 interface is configured to use type 2 authentication.
! Note that the key must be defined with
! the ip ospf message-digest-key interface subcommand.
R1# show running-config
! lines omitted for brevity
interface FastEthernet0/1
  ip ospf authentication message-digest
  ip ospf message-digest-key 1 md5 key-t2
! Below, the command confirms type 2 (MD5) authentication, key number 1.
R1# show ip ospf interface fa 0/1
! Lines omitted for brevity
Message digest authentication enabled
Youngest key id is 1
```

The trickiest part of the configuration is to remember the command syntax used on two interface subcommands. Note the interface subcommands used to configure the authentication keys, with the syntax differing depending on the type of authentication. For reference, Table 21-4 lists the three OSPF authentication types and the corresponding commands.

Key Topic

Table 21-4 *OSPF Authentication Types*

Type	Meaning	Command to Enable Authentication	What the Password Is Configured With
0	None	**ip ospf authentication null**	—
1	Clear text	**ip ospf authentication**	**ip ospf authentication-key** *key-value*
2	MD5	**ip ospf authentication message-digest**	**ip ospf message-digest-key** *key-number* **md5** *key-value*

Note that the passwords, or authentication keys, are kept in clear text in the configuration, unless you add the **service password-encryption** global command to the configuration. (Refer back to Chapter 11, "Cisco Router Configuration," for more information on the **service password-encryption** command.)

The default setting to use type 0 authentication—which really means no authentication—can be overridden on an area-by-area basis by using the **area authentication** router command. For example, Router R1 in Example 21-7 could be configured with the **area 1 authentication message-digest** router subcommand, which makes that router default to use MD5 authentication on all its interfaces in Area 1. Similarly, the **area 1 authentication** router subcommand enables simple password authentication for all interfaces in Area 1, making the **ip ospf authentication** interface subcommand unnecessary. Note that the authentication keys (passwords) must still be configured with the interface subcommands listed in Table 21-4.

OSPF Load Balancing

When OSPF uses SPF to calculate the metric for each of several routes to reach one subnet, one route might have the lowest metric, so OSPF puts that route in the routing table. However, when the metric is a tie, the router can put up to 16 different equal-cost routes in the routing table (the default is four different routes) based on the setting of the **maximum-paths** *number* router subcommand. For example, if an internetwork had six possible paths between some parts of the network, and the engineer wanted all routes to be used, the routers could be configured with the **maximum-paths 6** subcommand under **router ospf**.

The more challenging concept relates to how the routers use those multiple routes. A router could load-balance the packets on a per-packet basis. For example, if the router had three equal-cost OSPF routes for the same subnet in the routing table, the router could send the next packet over the first route, the next packet over the second route, the next packet over the third route, and then start over with the first route for the next packet. Alternatively, the load balancing could be on a per-destination IP address basis.

Chapter Review

Review Key Topics

Review the most important topics from this chapter, noted with the key topics icon. Table 21-5 lists these key topics and where each is discussed.

Table 21-5   *Key Topics for Chapter 21*

Key Topic Element	Description	Page Number
Figure 21-2	Figure that shows SPF shortest-path computation results	508
List	Comparisons between distance vector and link-state protocols	509
List	Items that must match on OSPF neighbors before they will become neighbors and reach the two-way state (at least)	513
Figure 21-4	Neighbor states and messages during OSPF neighbor formation	514
List	Three-step summary of the OSPF topology database exchange process	515
Figure 21-5	Drawing comparing full adjacencies formed with and without a DR	516
List	Rules for electing a designated router	516
Table 21-2	OSPF neighbor states and their meanings	518
List	List of reasons why OSPF needs areas to scale well	520
Table 21-3	OSPF design terms and definitions	521
List	Configuration checklist for OSPF	523
List	Details of how IOS determines an interface's OSPF cost	528
Table 21-4	OSPF authentication types and configuration commands	532

Define Key Terms

Define the following key terms from this chapter, and check your answers in the glossary:

two-way state, Area Border Router (ABR), Autonomous System Border Router (ASBR), Backup Designated Router, database description, dead interval, designated router, Full state, fully adjacent, Hello interval, link-state advertisement, link-state request, link-state update, neighbor, neighbor table, router ID (RID), topology database

Review Command Reference to Check Your Memory

Although you should not necessarily memorize the information in the tables in this section, this section does include a reference for the configuration and EXEC commands covered in this chapter. Practically speaking, you should memorize the commands as a side effect of reading the chapter and doing all the activities in this "Chapter Review" section. To see how well you have memorized the commands as a side effect of your other studies, cover the left side of the table, read the descriptions on the right side, and see if you remember the command.

Table 21-6   *Chapter 21 Configuration Command Reference*

Command	Description
router ospf *process-id*	Enters OSPF configuration mode for the listed process.
network *ip-address wildcard-mask* **area** *area-id*	Router subcommand that enables OSPF on interfaces matching the address/wildcard combination and sets the OSPF area.
ip ospf cost *interface-cost*	Interface subcommand that sets the OSPF cost associated with the interface.
bandwidth *bandwidth*	Interface subcommand that directly sets the interface bandwidth (Kbps).
auto-cost reference-bandwidth *number*	Router subcommand that tells OSPF the numerator in the *Ref-BW/Int-BW* formula used to calculate the OSPF cost based on the interface bandwidth.
ip ospf hello-interval *number*	Interface subcommand that sets the OSPF Hello interval, and also resets the Dead interval to four times this number.
ip ospf dead-interval *number*	Interface subcommand that sets the OSPF dead timer.
ip ospf network *type*	Interface subcommand that defines the OSPF network type.
router-id *id*	OSPF command that statically sets the router ID.
ip ospf hello-interval *seconds*	Interface subcommand that sets the interval for periodic Hellos.
ip ospf priority *number-value*	Interface subcommand that sets the OSPF priority on an interface.
maximum-paths *number-of-paths*	Router subcommand that defines the maximum number of equal-cost routes that can be added to the routing table.

Table 21-6   *Chapter 21 Configuration Command Reference*

Command	Description
ip ospf authentication [null | message-digest]	Interface subcommand that enables type 0 (null), type 1 (no optional parameter listed), or type 2 (message-digest) authentication.
ip ospf message-digest-key *key-number* **md5** *key-value*	Interface subcommand that sets the OSPF authentication key if MD5 authentication is used.
ip ospf authentication *key-value*	Interface subcommand that sets the OSPF authentication key if simple password authentication is used.
area *area* **authentication [message-digest | null]**	Router subcommand that configures the default authentication service for interfaces in the listed area.

Table 21-7   *Chapter 21 EXEC Command Reference*

Command	Description
show ip route ospf	Lists routes in the routing table learned by OSPF.
show ip protocols	Shows routing protocol parameters and current timer values.
show ip ospf interface	Lists the area in which the interface resides, neighbors adjacent on this interface, and Hello and dead timers.
show ip ospf neighbor [*neighbor-RID*]	Lists neighbors and current status with neighbors, per interface, and optionally lists details for the router ID listed in the command.
debug ip ospf events	Issues log messages for each OSPF packet.
debug ip ospf packet	Issues log messages describing the contents of all OSPF packets.
debug ip ospf hello	Issues log messages describing Hellos and Hello failures.

Answer Review Questions

Answer the following review questions:

1. An internetwork is using a link-state routing protocol. The routers have flooded all LSAs, and the network is stable. Which of the following describes what the routers will do to reflood the LSAs?

   a. Each router refloods each LSA using a periodic timer that has a time similar to distance vector update timers.

   b. Each router refloods each LSA using a periodic timer that is much longer than distance vector update timers.

   c. The routers never reflood the LSAs as long as the LSAs do not change.

   d. The routers reflood all LSAs whenever one LSA changes.

2. Which of the following is true about how a router using a link-state routing protocol chooses the best route to reach a subnet?

   a. The router finds the best route in the link-state database.

   b. The router calculates the best route by running the SPF algorithm against the information in the link-state database.

   c. The router compares the metrics listed for that subnet in the updates received from each neighbor and picks the best (lowest) metric route.

3. Which of the following affects the calculation of OSPF routes when all possible default values are used?

   a. Bandwidth

   b. Delay

   c. Load

   d. Reliability

   e. MTU

   f. Hop count

4. OSPF runs an algorithm to calculate the currently best route. Which of the following terms refer to that algorithm?

   a. SPF

   b. DUAL

   c. Feasible successor

   d. Dijkstra

   e. Good old common sense

5. Two OSPF routers connect to the same VLAN using their Fa0/0 interfaces. Which of the following settings on the interfaces of these two potentially neighboring routers would prevent the two routers from becoming OSPF neighbors?

   a. IP addresses of 10.1.1.1/24 and 10.1.1.254/25, respectively

   b. The addition of a secondary IP address on one router's interface, but not the other

   c. Both router interfaces assigned to area 3

   d. One router is configured to use MD5 authentication, and the other is not configured to use authentication

6. Which of the following OSPF neighbor states is expected when the exchange of topology information is complete so that neighboring routers have the same LSDB?

   a. Two-way

   b. Full

   c. Exchange

   d. Loading

7. Which of the following is true about an existing OSPF designated router?

   a. A newly connected router in the same subnet, with a higher OSPF priority, preempts the existing DR to become the new DR.

   b. A newly connected router in the same subnet, with a lower OSPF priority, preempts the existing DR to become the new DR.

   c. The DR can be elected based on the lowest OSPF Router ID.

   d. The DR can be elected based on the highest OSPF Router ID.

   e. The DR attempts to become fully adjacent with every other neighbor on the subnet.

8. Which of the following **network** commands, following the command **router ospf 1**, tells this router to start using OSPF on interfaces whose IP addresses are 10.1.1.1, 10.1.100.1, and 10.1.120.1?

   a. network 10.0.0.0 255.0.0.0 area 0

   b. network 10.0.0.0 0.255.255.255 area 0

   c. network 10.0.0.1 255.0.0.255 area 0

   d. network 10.0.0.1 0.255.255.0 area 0

9. Which of the following **network** commands, following the command **router ospf 1**, tells this router to start using OSPF on interfaces whose IP addresses are 10.1.1.1, 10.1.100.1, and 10.1.120.1?

    a. network 0.0.0.0 255.255.255.255 area 0

    b. network 10.0.0.0 0.255.255.0 area 0

    c. network 10.1.1.0 0.x.1x.0 area 0

    d. network 10.1.1.0 255.0.0.0 area 0

    e. network 10.0.0.0 255.0.0.0 area 0

10. Which of the following commands list the OSPF neighbors off interface serial 0/0?

    a. show ip ospf neighbor

    b. show ip ospf interface

    c. show ip neighbor

    d. show ip interface

    e. show ip ospf neighbor serial 0/0

11. OSPF routers R1, R2, and R3 attach to the same VLAN. R2 has been configured with the **ip ospf authentication message-digest** and the **ip ospf message-digest-key 1 md5 fred** interface subcommand on the LAN interface connected to the common VLAN. The **show ip ospf neighbor** command lists R1 and R3 as neighbors, in an Init and Full state, respectively. Which of the following are true?

    a. R3 must have an **ip ospf authentication message-digest** interface subcommand configured.

    b. R3 must have an **ip ospf message-digest-key** interface subcommand configured.

    c. R1's failure must be because of having configured an incorrect OSPF authentication type.

    d. R1's failure might or might not be related to authentication.

12. An OSPF router learns about six possible routes to reach subnet 10.1.1.0/24. All six routes have a cost of 55, and all six are interarea routes. By default, how many of these routes are placed in the routing table?

    a. 1

    b. 2

    c. 3

    d. 4

    e. 5

    f. 6

This chapter covers the following subjects:

- **Perspectives on Troubleshooting Routing Protocol Problems:** This short introductory section explains the troubleshooting process this book suggests for solving routing protocol problems.

- **Interfaces Enabled with a Routing Protocol:** This section shows how to determine the interfaces on which a router attempts to form neighbor relationships and whose connected subnets to advertise.

- **Neighbor Relationships:** This section examines why routers can fail to become neighbors with routers that they should become neighbors with.

CHAPTER 22

Troubleshooting EIGRP and OSPF

Chapter 15, "Troubleshooting IP Routing," and Chapter 20, "Troubleshooting IP Routing II," the other two chapters of this book that are dedicated to troubleshooting, focus on the process of forwarding data. In particular, Chapter 15 mostly ignores how routes are added to the routing table, focusing entirely on the data plane process of IP packet forwarding and discussing how to troubleshoot that process. That chapter assumes that the control plane processes related to filling the routing table will be covered elsewhere.

This chapter wraps up the coverage of the IPv4 control plane—the process of filling routers' routing tables with good routes—by examining how to troubleshoot problems with Open Shortest Path First (OSPF) and Enhanced Interior Gateway Routing Protocol (EIGRP). The troubleshooting process itself is relatively straightforward. However, as usual, you need to think about many different details while troubleshooting, so the process can help ensure that you verify each component before moving on to the next function.

Perspectives on Troubleshooting Routing Protocol Problems

Because a routing protocol's job is to fill a router's routing table with the currently best routes, it makes sense that troubleshooting potential problems with routing protocols could begin with the IP routing table. Given basic information about an internetwork, including the routers, their IP addresses and masks, and the routing protocol, you could calculate the subnet numbers that should be in the router's routing table and list the likely next-hop router(s) for each route. For example, Figure 22-1 shows an internetwork with six subnets. Router R1's routing table should list all six subnets, with three connected routes, two routes learned from R2 (172.16.4.0/24 and 172.16.5.0/24), and one route learned from R3 (172.16.6.0/24).

So, one possible troubleshooting process would be to analyze the internetwork, look at the routing table, and look for missing routes. If one or more expected routes are missing, the next step would be to determine if that router has learned any routes from the expected next-hop (neighbor) router. The next steps to isolate the problem differ greatly if a router is having problems forming a neighbor relationship with another router, versus having a working neighbor relationship but not being able to learn all routes.

For example, imagine that R1 in Figure 22-1 has learned a route for subnet 172.16.4.0/24 in Figure 22-1 but not for subnet 172.16.5.0/24. In this case, it is clear that R1 has a working neighbor relationship with R2. In these cases, the root cause of this problem can still be related to the routing protocol, or it might be unrelated to the routing protocol. For example, the problem might be that R2's lower LAN interface is down. However, if R1 did not have a route for either 172.16.4.0/24 or 172.16.5.0/24, R1's neighbor relationship with R2 could be the problem.

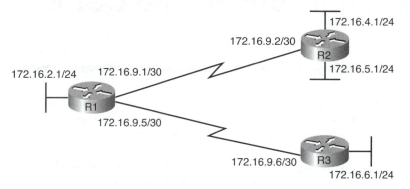

Figure 22-1 *Internetwork with Six Subnets*

Troubleshooting routing protocol problems in real internetworks can be very complex. Defining a generic troubleshooting process with which to attack both simple and complex routing protocol problems would require a lot of space, and be counterproductive. This chapter offers a straightforward process for attacking routing protocol problems.

If you suspect a problem with a routing protocol, you can quickly identify some common configuration errors with the following process—even without the configuration or the ability to use the **show running-config** command. The process has three main branches:

Step 1. Examine the internetwork design to determine on which interfaces the routing protocol should be enabled and which routers are expected to become neighbors.

Step 2. Verify whether the routing protocol is enabled on each interface (as per Step 1). If it isn't, determine the root cause and fix the problem.

Step 3. Verify that each router has formed all expected neighbor relationships. If it hasn't, find the root cause and fix the problem.

At this point, having completed Chapters 16, "EIGRP Concepts and Configuration," and 21, "OSPF Concepts and Configuration," Step 1 should not require any further explanation. The two remaining major sections of this chapter examine Steps 2 and 3.

Interfaces Enabled with a Routing Protocol

This section examines the second major troubleshooting step outlined in the previous section of the chapter: how to verify the interfaces on which the routing protocol has been enabled. Both EIGRP and OSPF configuration enables the routing protocol on an interface by using the **network** router subcommand. For any interfaces matched by the **network** commands, the routing protocol tries the following two actions:

Key Topic

■ Attempt to find potential neighbors on the subnet connected to the interface

■   Advertise the subnet connected to that interface

At the same time, the **passive-interface** router subcommand can be configured so that the router does not attempt to find neighbors on the interface (the first action just listed) but still advertises the connected subnet (the second action).

Three **show** commands are all that is needed to know exactly which interfaces have been enabled with EIGRP and OSPF and which interfaces are passive. In particular, the **show ip eigrp interfaces** command lists all EIGRP-enabled interfaces that are not passive interfaces. The **show ip protocols** command essentially lists the contents of the configured **network** commands for each routing protocol, as well as a separate list of the passive interfaces. Comparing these two commands identifies all EIGRP-enabled interfaces and those that are passive. For OSPF, the command works slightly differently, with the **show ip ospf interface brief** command listing all OSPF-enabled interfaces (including passive interfaces). Table 22-1 summarizes these commands for easier reference.

Table 22-1   *Key Commands to Find Routing Protocol–Enabled Interfaces*

Command	Key Information
show ip eigrp interfaces	Lists the interfaces on which the routing protocol is enabled (based on the **network** commands), except passive interfaces.
show ip ospf interface brief	Lists the interfaces on which the OSPF is enabled (based on the **network** commands), including passive interfaces.
show ip protocols	Lists the contents of the **network** configuration commands for each routing process, and lists enabled but passive interfaces.

Note: All the commands in Table 22-1 list the interfaces regardless of interface status, in effect telling you the results of the **network** and **passive-interface** configuration commands.

So, for the major troubleshooting step covered in this section, the task is to use the commands in Table 22-1 and analyze the output. First, an EIGRP example will be shown, followed by an OSPF example.

EIGRP Interface Troubleshooting Example

This section shows a few examples of the commands in the context of Figure 22-2, which is used in all the examples in this chapter.

This example includes four routers, with the following scenario in this case:

■   R1 and R2 are configured correctly on both LAN interfaces.

■   R3 is mistakenly not enabled with EIGRP on its Fa0/1 interface.

■   R4 meant to use a **passive-interface fa0/1** command, because no other routers are off R4's Fa0/1 LAN, but instead R4 has configured a **passive-interface fa0/0** command.

Example 22-1 begins by showing the pertinent commands, with an example on either R1 or on R2. It also shows the configuration on R1 for the sake of comparison.

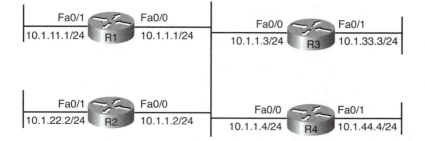

Figure 22-2   *Sample Internetwork for EIGRP/OSPF Troubleshooting Examples*

Example 22-1   *EIGRP Problems with Interfaces*

```
R1# show running-config
! only pertinent lines shown
router eigrp 99
 network 10.0.0.0
!
R1> show ip eigrp interfaces
IP-EIGRP interfaces for process 99

                      Xmit Queue    Mean    Pacing Time    Multicast    Pending
Interface      Peers  Un/Reliable   SRTT    Un/Reliable    Flow Timer   Routes
Fa0/0            2       0/0         620        0/10           50          0
Fa0/1            0       0/0          0         0/10            0          0
R1> show ip protocols
Routing Protocol is "eigrp 99"
  Outgoing update filter list for all interfaces is not set
  Incoming update filter list for all interfaces is not set
  Default networks flagged in outgoing updates
  Default networks accepted from incoming updates
  EIGRP metric weight K1=1, K2=0, K3=1, K4=0, K5=0
  EIGRP maximum hopcount 100
  EIGRP maximum metric variance 1
  Redistributing: eigrp 99
  EIGRP NSF-aware route hold timer is 240s
  Automatic network summarization is in effect
  Maximum path: 4
  Routing for Networks:
    10.0.0.0
  Routing Information Sources:
    Gateway         Distance      Last Update
    10.1.1.2          90          00:13:11
    10.1.1.3          90          00:13:09
  Distance: internal 90 external 170
! The next commands are on router R2
```

```
!
R2> show ip eigrp interfaces
IP-EIGRP interfaces for process 99

                          Xmit Queue    Mean   Pacing Time   Multicast    Pending
Interface        Peers   Un/Reliable    SRTT   Un/Reliable   Flow Timer   Routes
Fa0/0              2        0/0          736      0/1           3684         0
Fa0/1              0        0/0           0       0/1            0           0
R2> show ip protocols
Routing Protocol is "eigrp 99"
  Outgoing update filter list for all interfaces is not set
  Incoming update filter list for all interfaces is not set
  Default networks flagged in outgoing updates
  Default networks accepted from incoming updates
  EIGRP metric weight K1=1, K2=0, K3=1, K4=0, K5=0
  EIGRP maximum hopcount 100
  EIGRP maximum metric variance 1
  Redistributing: eigrp 99
  EIGRP NSF-aware route hold timer is 240s
  Automatic network summarization is in effect
  Maximum path: 4
  Routing for Networks:
    10.0.0.0
  Routing Information Sources:
    Gateway         Distance      Last Update
    10.1.1.3              90      00:13:25
    10.1.1.1              90      00:13:25
  Distance: internal 90 external 170

R2> show ip route eigrp
     10.0.0.0/24 is subnetted, 3 subnets
D       10.1.11.0 [90/30720] via 10.1.1.1, 00:13:38, FastEthernet0/0
```

The **show ip eigrp interfaces** command output on both R1 and R2 shows how both R1 and R2 have configured EIGRP using process ID 99, and that EIGRP has been enabled on both Fa0/0 and Fa0/1 on R1 and R2. This command lists only interfaces on which EIGRP has been enabled, excluding passive interfaces.

The highlighted parts of the **show ip protocols** command output on each router are particularly interesting. These sections show the parameters of the configured **network** commands. For each **network** command, the **show ip protocols** command lists a separate line under the header "Routing for Networks," with each line listing the contents of the various **network** router subcommands. For example, R1 uses the **network 10.0.0.0** configuration command (shown at the beginning of the example), which matches the "10.0.0.0" line in the output of the **show ip protocols** command.

The end of the example gives brief insight into the current problem on R3 from R2's perspective. The end of the **show ip protocols** command on R2 lists two routing information sources: 10.1.1.1 (R1) and 10.1.1.3 (R3). However, R2 has learned only one EIGRP route (10.1.11.0/24), as shown in the **show ip route eigrp** command output. When working properly, R2 should learn three EIGRP routes—one for each of the outer LAN subnets shown in Figure 22-2.

Next, Example 22-2 shows the problems on R3 and R4 that prevent R1 and R2 from learning about subnets 10.1.33.0/24 and 10.1.44.0/24. The example shows the pertinent configuration on each router for perspective, as well as **show** commands that point out the problems.

Example 22-2   *EIGRP Problems on R3 and R4*

```
R3# show running-config
! lines omitted for brevity
router eigrp 99
 network 10.1.1.3 0.0.0.0
 network 10.1.13.3 0.0.0.0
 auto-summary
R3# show ip eigrp interfaces
IP-EIGRP interfaces for process 99

                        Xmit Queue   Mean   Pacing Time   Multicast    Pending
Interface        Peers  Un/Reliable  SRTT   Un/Reliable   Flow Timer   Routes
Fa0/0              2       0/0         1        0/10          50          0
R3# show ip protocols
Routing Protocol is "eigrp 99"
  Outgoing update filter list for all interfaces is not set
  Incoming update filter list for all interfaces is not set
  Default networks flagged in outgoing updates
  Default networks accepted from incoming updates
  EIGRP metric weight K1=1, K2=0, K3=1, K4=0, K5=0
  EIGRP maximum hopcount 100
  EIGRP maximum metric variance 1
  Redistributing: eigrp 99
  EIGRP NSF-aware route hold timer is 240s
  Automatic network summarization is in effect
  Maximum path: 4
  Routing for Networks:
    10.1.1.3/32
    10.1.13.3/32
  Routing Information Sources:
    Gateway         Distance      Last Update
    10.1.1.2            90        00:28:16
    10.1.1.1            90        00:28:14
  Distance: internal 90 external 170
```

```
! R4 output starts here

R4# show running-config
! lines omitted for brevity
router eigrp 99
 passive-interface FastEthernet0/0
 network 10.0.0.0
 auto-summary

R4# show ip eigrp interfaces
IP-EIGRP interfaces for process 99

                        Xmit Queue    Mean   Pacing Time   Multicast    Pending
Interface       Peers   Un/Reliable   SRTT   Un/Reliable   Flow Timer   Routes
Fa0/1             0        0/0          0        0/1           0           0
R4# show ip protocols
Routing Protocol is "eigrp 99"
  Outgoing update filter list for all interfaces is not set
  Incoming update filter list for all interfaces is not set
  Default networks flagged in outgoing updates
  Default networks accepted from incoming updates
  EIGRP metric weight K1=1, K2=0, K3=1, K4=0, K5=0
  EIGRP maximum hopcount 100
  EIGRP maximum metric variance 1
  Redistributing: eigrp 99
  EIGRP NSF-aware route hold timer is 240s
  Automatic network summarization is in effect
  Maximum path: 4
  Routing for Networks:
    10.0.0.0
  Passive Interface(s):
    FastEthernet0/0
  Routing Information Sources:
    Gateway         Distance      Last Update
  Distance: internal 90 external 170
```

The root cause of R3's problem is that R3 has a **network 10.1.13.3 0.0.0.0** configuration command, which does not match R3's 10.1.33.3 Fa0/1 IP address. If the configuration is not available, the **show ip protocols** command could be used to essentially see the same configuration details. In this case, the **show ip protocols** command on R3 lists the text "10.1.13.3/32" as a reference to the contents of the incorrect **network** command's parameters. As a result, R3 does not try to find neighbors on its Fa0/1 interface, which is not a big deal in this case, but R3 also does not advertise subnet 10.1.33.0/24, the connected subnet off its Fa0/1 interface. Also note that R3's **show ip eigrp interfaces** command omits interface Fa0/1, which does not by itself determine the root cause, but it can help you isolate the problem.

On R4, the engineer could have correctly used a **passive-interface fastethernet0/1** router subcommand, because no other routers should exist off R4's Fa0/1 interface. However, the engineer mistakenly referred to R4's Fa0/0 interface instead of Fa0/1. R4's **show ip eigrp interfaces** command purposefully omits the (Fa0/0) passive interface, and the highlighted part of R4's **show ip protocols** command output lists Fa0/0 as a passive interface. Because R4's Fa0/0 is passive, R4 does not even attempt to become neighbors with other routers on the same LAN.

OSPF Interface Troubleshooting Example

OSPF has the same basic requirements as EIGRP for interfaces, with a few exceptions. First, EIGRP routers need to use the same ASN or process ID as their neighboring routers, as configured in the **router** global configuration command. OSPF routers can use any process ID, with no need to match their neighbors. Second, OSPF requires that the interfaces connected to the same subnet be assigned to the same OSPF area, whereas EIGRP has no concept of areas.

Example 22-3 shows a mostly working OSPF internetwork, again based on Figure 22-2. The following problems exist:

R2 has been configured to put both interfaces in area 1. R1, R3, and R4 have been configured to put their common LAN interfaces (Fa0/0 in each case) in area 0, breaking OSPF design rules.

Example 22-3 shows how to isolate the root cause of the problem. It also shows the normal working output, with the **show ip ospf interface brief** and **show ip protocols** commands.

Example 22-3   *OSPF Problems on R2*

```
R1> show ip ospf interface brief
Interface    PID    Area          IP Address/Mask    Cost  State Nbrs F/C
Fa0/1        11     0             10.1.11.1/24       1     DR    0/0
Fa0/0        11     0             10.1.1.1/24        1     DROTH 2/2
R1> show ip protocols
Routing Protocol is "ospf 11"
  Outgoing update filter list for all interfaces is not set
  Incoming update filter list for all interfaces is not set
 Router ID 1.1.1.1
  Number of areas in this router is 1. 1 normal 0 stub 0 nssa
  Maximum path: 4
  Routing for Networks:
    10.0.0.0 0.255.255.255 area 0
  Routing Information Sources:
    Gateway         Distance      Last Update
    3.3.3.3              110      00:01:12
    4.4.4.4              110      00:01:12
    1.1.1.1              110      00:01:12
  Distance: (default is 110)
R1> show ip route ospf
```

```
     10.0.0.0/24 is subnetted, 5 subnets
O        10.1.44.0 [110/2] via 10.1.1.4, 00:01:19, FastEthernet0/0
O        10.1.33.0 [110/2] via 10.1.1.3, 00:01:19, FastEthernet0/0
! Now moving to router R2
R2> show ip ospf interface brief
Interface   PID   Area        IP Address/Mask   Cost  State Nbrs F/C
Fa0/1       22    1           10.1.22.2/24      1     DR    0/0
Fa0/0       22    1           10.1.1.2/24       1     DR    0/0
R2> show ip protocols
Routing Protocol is "ospf 22"
  Outgoing update filter list for all interfaces is not set
  Incoming update filter list for all interfaces is not set
 —More—  _____        _____    Router ID 2.2.2.2
  Number of areas in this router is 1. 1 normal 0 stub 0 nssa
  Maximum path: 4
  Routing for Networks:
    10.0.0.0 0.255.255.255 area 1
  Reference bandwidth unit is 100 mbps
  Routing Information Sources:
    Gateway         Distance      Last Update
  Distance: (default is 110)
R2>
!!!!!!!!!!!!!!!!!!!!!!!!!!!!!!!!!!!!!!!!!!!!!!!!!!!!!!!!!!!!!!!!!!!!!!!!!!!!!!!!!
May 28 18:30:26.659: %OSPF-4-ERRRCV: Received invalid packet: mismatch area ID,
from backbone area must be virtual-link but not found from 10.1.1.4,
FastEthernet0/0
```

For OSPF, the **show ip ospf interface brief** command lists output similar to the **show ip eigrp interface** command, with one line for each enabled interface. (The **show ip ospf interface** command, not shown in the example, lists detailed OSPF information for each interface.) In this example, both R1 and R2 have OSPF enabled on both LAN interfaces, but this command also lists the area number for each interface, with R2 having both LAN interfaces in area 1. As a result, R2's Fa0/0 interface is in a different area than the other three routers' interfaces on the same LAN.

A closer look at R2's **show ip protocols** command output, particularly the highlighted portion, points out the configuration error. The highlighted phrase "10.0.0.0 0.255.255.255 area 1" is actually the exact syntax of the one **network** command on router R2, minus the word "network." Reconfiguring R2 so that its Fa0/0 interface matches the other three routers would solve this particular problem.

The end of the example shows an unsolicited log message generated by router R2, notifying the console user that this router has received a Hello from a router in a different area.

As you check the interfaces, you could also check several other details mentioned in Chapter 15's IP troubleshooting coverage. It makes sense to go ahead and check the interface IP addresses, masks, and interface status, using the **show interfaces** and **show ip**

interface brief commands. In particular, it is helpful to note which interfaces are up/up, because a routing protocol will not attempt to find neighbors or advertise connected subnets for an interface that is not in an up/up state. These verification checks were discussed in detail in Chapter 15, so they are not repeated here.

Neighbor Relationships

As mentioned near the beginning of this chapter, when a routing protocol has been enabled on an interface, and the interface is not configured as a passive interface, the routing protocol attempts to discover neighbors and form a neighbor relationship with each neighbor that shares the common subnet. This section examines the large number of facts that each router must check with each potential neighbor before the two routers become neighbors.

OSPF and EIGRP both use Hello messages to learn about new neighbors and to exchange information used to perform some basic verification checks. For example, as just shown in Example 22-3, an OSPF router should not become neighbors with another router in another area, because all routers on a common subnet should be in the same area by design. (The border between areas is a router, not a link.)

After an EIGRP or OSPF router hears a Hello from a new neighbor, the routing protocol examines the information in the Hello, along with some local settings, to decide if the two neighbors should even attempt to become neighbors. Because there is no formal term for all these items that a routing protocol considers, this book just calls them *neighbor requirements*. Table 22-2 lists the neighbor requirements for both EIGRP and OSPF. Following the table, the next few pages examine some of these settings for both EIGRP and OSPF, again using examples based on Figure 22-2.

Table 22-2   *Neighbor Requirements for EIGRP and OSPF*

Requirement	EIGRP	OSPF
Interfaces must be in an up/up state	Yes	Yes
Interfaces must be in the same subnet	Yes	Yes
Must pass neighbor authentication (if configured)	Yes	Yes
Must use the same ASN/process-ID on the **router** configuration command	Yes	No
Hello and hold/dead timers must match	No	Yes
IP MTU must match	No	Yes
Router IDs must be unique	No[1]	Yes
K-values must match	Yes	N/A
Must be in the same area	N/A	Yes

[1]Having duplicate EIGRP RIDs does not prevent routers from becoming neighbors, but it can cause problems when external EIGRP routes are added to the routing table.

Note: Even though it is important to study and remember the items in this table, it might be best not to study this table right now. Instead, read the rest of the chapter first, because the items in the table will be mentioned and reviewed throughout the rest of this chapter.

Unlike the rest of the neighbor requirements listed in Table 22-2, the first requirement has very little to do with the routing protocols themselves. The two routers must be able to send packets to each other over the physical network to which they are both connected. To do that, the router interfaces must be up/up. In practice, before examining the rest of the details of why two routers do not become neighbors, confirm that the two routers can ping each other on the local subnet. If the ping fails, investigate all the Layer 1, 2, and 3 issues that could prevent the ping from working (such as an interface not being up/up), as covered in various chapters of this book.

Because the details differ slightly between the two routing protocols, this section first examines EIGRP, followed by OSPF.

Note: This section assumes that the routing protocol has actually been enabled on each required interface, as covered earlier in this chapter in the section "Interfaces Enabled with a Routing Protocol."

EIGRP Neighbor Requirements

Any two EIGRP routers that connect to the same data link, and whose interfaces have been enabled for EIGRP and are not passive, will at least consider becoming neighbors. To quickly and definitively know which potential neighbors have passed all the neighbor requirements for EIGRP, just look at the output of the **show ip eigrp neighbors** command. This command lists only neighbors that have passed all the neighbor verification checks. Example 22-4 shows an example, with the four routers from Figure 22-2 again, but with all earlier EIGRP configuration problems having been fixed.

Example 22-4   *R1* **show ip eigrp neighbors** *Command with All Problems Fixed*

```
R1# show ip eigrp neighbors
IP-EIGRP neighbors for process 99
H   Address            Interface       Hold Uptime   SRTT   RTO  Q  Seq
                                       (sec)         (ms)       Cnt Num
2   10.1.1.3           Fa0/0            13 00:00:04   616   3696  0  8
1   10.1.1.4           Fa0/0            12 00:00:54     1    200  0  45
0   10.1.1.2           Fa0/0            14 00:01:19   123    738  0  43
```

If the **show ip eigrp neighbors** command does not list one or more expected neighbors, and the two routers can ping each other's IP address on their common subnet, the problem is probably related to one of the neighbor requirements listed in Tables 22-2 and 22-3. Table 22-3 summarizes the EIGRP neighbor requirements and notes the best commands with which to determine which requirement is the root cause of the problem.

Key Topic

Table 22-3 *EIGRP Neighbor Requirements and the Best* **show/debug** *Commands*

Requirement	Best Command(s) to Isolate the Problem
Must be in the same subnet	show interfaces
Must pass any neighbor authentication	debug eigrp packets
Must use the same ASN on the **router** configuration command	show ip eigrp interfaces, show ip protocols
K-values must match	show ip protocols

All the requirements listed in Table 22-3, except the last one, were explained in Chapter 16, "EIGRP Concepts and Configuration." EIGRP K-values refer to the parameters that can be configured to change what EIGRP uses in its metric calculation. Cisco recommends leaving these values at their default settings, using only bandwidth and delay in the metric calculation. Because Cisco recommends that you not change these values, this particular problem is not very common. However, you can check the K-values on both routers with the **show ip protocols** command.

Example 22-5 shows three problems that can cause two routers that should become EIGRP neighbors to fail to do so. For this example, the following problems have been introduced:

■ R2 has been configured with IP address 10.1.2.2/24, in a different subnet than R1, R3, and R4.

■ R3 has been configured to use ASN 199 with the **router eigrp 199** command, instead of ASN 99, as used on the other three routers.

■ R4 has been configured to use MD5 authentication, like the other routers, but R4 has a key value of "FRED" instead of the value "fred," used by the other three routers.

R1 can actually detect two of the problems without having to use commands on the other routers. R1 generates an unsolicited log message for the mismatched subnet problem, and a **debug** command on R1 can reveal the authentication failure. A quick examination of a few **show** commands on R3 can identify that the wrong ASN has been used in the **router** configuration command. Example 22-5 shows the details.

Example 22-5 *Common Problems Preventing the Formation of EIGRP Neighbors*

```
! First, R1 has no neighbor relationships yet. R1 uses ASN (process) 99.
R1# show ip eigrp neighbors
IP-EIGRP neighbors for process 99

R1#
! Next, R1 generates a log message, which shows up at the console, stating
! that the router with IP address 10.1.2.2 is not on the same subnet as R1.
!
*May 28 20:02:22.355: IP-EIGRP(Default-IP-Routing-Table:99): Neighbor
```

```
      10.1.2.2 not on common subnet for FastEthernet0/0

! Next, R1 enables a debug that shows messages for each packet received from R4,
! which uses the wrong password (authentication key string)
!
R1# debug eigrp packets
EIGRP Packets debugging is on
    (UPDATE, REQUEST, QUERY, REPLY, HELLO, IPXSAP, PROBE, ACK, STUB, SIAQUERY,
    SIAREPLY)
*May 28 20:04:00.931: EIGRP: pkt key id = 1, authentication mismatch
*May 28 20:04:00.931: EIGRP: FastEthernet0/0: ignored packet from 10.1.1.4,
  opcode = 5 (invalid authentication)
! The rest of the output is from R3
! The first line of output from the show ip protocols command lists ASN 199
!
R3# show ip protocols
Routing Protocol is "eigrp 199"
!
! The first line of output from show ip eigrp interfaces lists ASN 199
!
R3# show ip eigrp interfaces
IP-EIGRP interfaces for process 199

                       Xmit Queue   Mean   Pacing Time   Multicast   Pending
Interface      Peers   Un/Reliable  SRTT   Un/Reliable   Flow Timer  Routes
Fa0/0          0       0/0          0      0/10          0           0
Fa0/1          0       0/0          0      0/10          0           0
```

OSPF Neighbor Requirements

Similar to EIGRP, a router's **show ip ospf neighbor** command lists all the neighboring routers that have met all the requirements to become an OSPF neighbor as listed in Table 22-2—with one minor exception (mismatched MTU). (If the MTU is mismatched, the two routers are listed in the **show ip ospf neighbor** command. This particular problem is discussed later, in the section "The MTU Matching Requirement.") So, the first step in troubleshooting OSPF neighbors is to look at the list of neighbors.

Example 22-6 lists the output of a **show ip ospf neighbor** command on router R2, from Figure 22-2, with the configuration correct on each of the four routers in the figure.

Example 22-6 *Normal Working* **show ip ospf neighbors** *Command on Router R2*

```
R2# show ip ospf neighbor

Neighbor ID     Pri   State           Dead Time   Address     Interface
1.1.1.1         1     FULL/BDR        00:00:37    10.1.1.1    FastEthernet0/0
3.3.3.3         1     2WAY/DROTHER    00:00:37    10.1.1.3    FastEthernet0/0
4.4.4.4         1     FULL/DR         00:00:31    10.1.1.4    FastEthernet0/0
```

A brief review of OSPF neighbor states (as explained in Chapter 21, "OSPF Concepts and Configuration") can help you understand a few of the subtleties of the output in the example. A router's listed status for each of its OSPF neighbors—the neighbor's state—should settle into either a *two-way* or *Full* state under normal operation. For neighbors that do not need to directly exchange their databases, typically two non-DR routers on a LAN, the routers should settle into a *two-way* neighbor state. In most cases, two neighboring routers need to directly exchange their complete full LSDBs with each other. As soon as that process has been completed, the two routers settle into a Full neighbor state. In Example 22-6, router R4 is the DR, and R1 is the BDR, so R2 and R3 (as non-DRs) do not need to directly exchange routes. Therefore, R2's neighbor state for R3 (RID 3.3.3.3) in Example 22-6 is listed as two-way.

Note: Notably, OSPF neighbors do not have to use the same process ID on the **router ospf** *process-id* command to become neighbors. In Example 22-6, all four routers use different process IDs.

If the **show ip ospf neighbor** command does not list one or more expected neighbors, before moving on to look at OSPF neighbor requirements, you should confirm that the two routers can ping each other on the local subnet. As soon as the two neighboring routers can ping each other, if the two routers still do not become OSPF neighbors, the next step is to examine each of the OSPF neighbor requirements. Table 22-4 summarizes the requirements, listing the most useful commands with which to find the answers.

Table 22-4   *OSPF Neighbor Requirements and the Best* **show/debug** *Commands*

Requirement	Best Command(s) to Isolate the Problem
Must be in the same subnet	show interfaces, debug ip ospf hello
Must pass any neighbor authentication	debug ip ospf adj
Hello and hold/dead timers must match	show ip ospf interface, debug ip ospf hello
Must be in the same area	debug ip ospf adj, show ip ospf interface brief
Router IDs must be unique	show ip ospf

The rest of this section looks at a couple of examples in which two OSPF routers could become neighbors but do not because of some of the reasons in the table. This is followed by information on the MTU matching requirement.

OSPF Neighbor Example 1

In this first example of OSPF neighbor problems, the usual four-router network from Figure 22-2 is used. This internetwork is designed to use a single area, area 0. In this case, the following problems have been introduced into the design:

- R2 has been configured with both LAN interfaces in area 1, whereas the other three routers' Fa0/0 interfaces are assigned to area 0.

- R3 is using the same RID (1.1.1.1) as R1.

- R4 is using MD5 authentication like the other three routers, but R4 has misconfigured its authentication key value (FRED instead of fred).

Example 22-7 shows the evidence of the problems, with comments following the example.

Example 22-7   *Finding Mismatch Area, Same RID, and Authentication Problems*

```
R1# debug ip ospf adj
OSPF adjacency events debugging is on
R1#
*May 28 23:59:21.031: OSPF: Send with youngest Key 1
*May 28 23:59:24.463: OSPF: Rcv pkt from 10.1.1.2, FastEthernet0/0, area 0.0.0.0
     mismatch area 0.0.0.1 in the header
*May 28 23:59:24.907: OSPF: Rcv pkt from 10.1.1.4, FastEthernet0/0 :
 Mismatch Authentication Key - Message Digest Key 1


R1# undebug all
All possible debugging has been turned off
R1# show ip ospf interface brief
Interface   PID   Area          IP Address/Mask    Cost   State Nbrs F/C
Fa0/1       11    0             10.1.11.1/24       1      DR    0/0
Fa0/0       11    0             10.1.1.1/24        1      DR    0/0
! Now to R2
! R2 shows that Fa0/0 is in area 1
!
R2# show ip ospf interface brief
Interface   PID   Area          IP Address/Mask    Cost   State Nbrs F/C
Fa0/1       22    1             10.1.22.2/24       1      DR    0/0
Fa0/0       22    1             10.1.1.2/24        1      DR    0/0
! Next, on R3
! R3 lists the RID of 1.1.1.1
!
R3# show ip ospf
 Routing Process "ospf 33" with ID 1.1.1.1
 Supports only single TOS(TOS0) routes
! lines omitted for brevity
! Back to R1 again
! Next command confirms that R1 is also trying to use RID 1.1.1.1
```

```
!
R1# show ip ospf
 Routing Process "ospf 11" with ID 1.1.1.1
 Supports only single TOS(TOS0) routes
 ! lines omitted for brevity
*May 29 00:01:25.679: %OSPF-4-DUP_RTRID_NBR: OSPF detected duplicate router-id
1.1.1.1 from 10.1.1.3 on interface FastEthernet0/0
```

As noted in Table 22-4, the **debug ip ospf adj** command helps troubleshoot mismatched OSPF area problems as well as authentication problems. The highlighted messages in the first few lines of the example point out that the router with address 10.1.1.2 (R2) has a mismatched area ID 0.0.0.1, meaning area 1. Indeed, R2 was misconfigured to put its Fa0/0 interface in area 1. Immediately following is a reference to a "mismatched authentication key," meaning that the correct authentication type was used, but the configured keys have different values, specifically for router 10.1.1.4 (R4).

Note: Routers treat debug messages as log messages, which IOS sends to the console by default. To see these messages from a Telnet or SSH connection, use the **terminal monitor** command. To disable the display of these messages, use the **terminal no monitor** command.

The next part of the example shows the **show ip ospf interface brief** command on both R1 and R2, pointing out how each router's Fa0/0 interface is in a different OSPF area.

The end of the example lists the information that shows R1 and R3 both trying to use RID 1.1.1.1. Interestingly, both routers automatically generate a log message for the duplicate OSPF RID problem between R1 and R3. A duplicate RID causes significant problems with OSPF, far beyond just whether two routers can become neighbors. The end of Example 22-7 shows the (highlighted) log message. The **show ip ospf** commands on both R3 and R1 also show how you can easily list the RID on each router, noting that they both use the same value.

OSPF Neighbor Example 2

In this next example, the same network from Figure 22-2 is used again. The problems on R2, R3, and R4 from the previous example have been fixed, but new problems have been introduced on R2 and R4 to show the symptoms. In this case, the following problems have been introduced into the design:

- R2 has been configured with a Hello/Dead timer of 5/20 on its Fa0/0 interface, instead of the 10/40 used (by default) on R1, R3, and R4.

- R3's problems have been solved; no problems related to OSPF neighbors exist.

- R4 is now using the correct key string (fred), but with clear-text authentication instead of the MD5 authentication used by the other three routers.

Example 22-8 shows the evidence of the problems, with comments following the example. As usual, the **debug ip ospf adj** command helps discover authentication problems. Also, the **debug ip ospf hello** command helps uncover mismatches discovered in the Hello message, including mismatched IP addresses/masks and timers.

Example 22-8 *Finding Mismatched Hello/Dead Timers and Wrong Authentication Types*

```
R1# debug ip ospf adj
OSPF adjacency events debugging is on
R1#
*May 29 10:41:30.639: OSPF: Rcv pkt from 10.1.1.4, FastEthernet0/0 :
  Mismatch Authentication type. Input packet specified type 1, we use type 2

R1#
R1# undebug all
All possible debugging has been turned off
R1# debug ip ospf hello
OSPF hello events debugging is on
R1#
*May 29 10:41:42.603: OSPF: Rcv hello from 2.2.2.2 area 0 from
  FastEthernet0/0 10.1.1.2
*May 29 10:41:42.603: OSPF: Mismatched hello parameters from 10.1.1.2
*May 29 10:41:42.603: OSPF: Dead R 20 C 40, Hello R 5 C 10
  Mask R 255.255.255.0 C 255.255.255.0
R1# undebug all
All possible debugging has been turned off
R1# show ip ospf interface fa0/0
FastEthernet0/0 is up, line protocol is up
  Internet Address 10.1.1.1/24, Area 0
  Process ID 11, Router ID 1.1.1.1, Network Type BROADCAST, Cost: 1
  Transmit Delay is 1 sec, State DR, Priority 1
  Designated Router (ID) 1.1.1.1, Interface address 10.1.1.1
  Backup Designated router (ID) 3.3.3.3, Interface address 10.1.1.3
  Timer intervals configured, Hello 10, Dead 40, Wait 40, Retransmit 5
! lines omitted for brevity
! Moving on to R2 next
!
R2# show ip ospf interface fa0/0
FastEthernet0/0 is up, line protocol is up
  Internet Address 10.1.1.2/24, Area 0
  Process ID 22, Router ID 2.2.2.2, Network Type BROADCAST, Cost: 1
  Transmit Delay is 1 sec, State DR, Priority 1
  Designated Router (ID) 2.2.2.2, Interface address 10.1.1.2
  No backup designated router on this network
  Timer intervals configured, Hello 5, Dead 20, Wait 20, Retransmit 5
! lines omitted for brevity
```

The example begins with the debug messages related to the authentication problem between R1, which uses MD5 authentication, and R4, which now uses clear-text authentication. As listed in Chapter 21's Table 21-4, IOS considers OSPF clear-text authentication to be type 1 authentication and MD5 to be type 2. The highlighted debug message confirms that thinking, stating that R1 received a packet from 10.1.1.4 (R4), with type 1 authentication, but with R1 expecting type 2 authentication.

Next, the example shows the messages generated by the **debug ip ospf hello** command—specifically, those related to the Hello/Dead timer mismatch. The highlighted message uses a "C" to mean "configured value"—in other words, the value on the local router, or R1 in this case. The "R" in the message means "Received value," or the value listed in the received Hello. In this case, the phrase "Dead R 20 C 40" means that the router that generated this message, R1, received a Hello with a Dead timer set to 20, but R1's configured value on the interface is 40, so the values don't match. Similarly, the message shows the mismatch in the Hello timers as well. Note that any IP subnet mismatch problems could also be found with this same debug, based on the received and configured subnet masks.

The majority of the space in the example shows the output of the **show ip ospf interface** command on both R1 and R2, which lists the Hello and Dead timers on each interface, confirming the details listed in the debug messages.

The MTU Matching Requirement

Of all the potential problems between two potential OSPF neighbors listed in Table 22-2, only one problem, the mismatched MTU problem, allows the neighbor to be listed in the other router's **show ip ospf neighbor** command output. When two routers connect to the same subnet, with different interface IP MTU settings, the two routers can become neighbors and reach the two-way state. However, when the two routers attempt to exchange LS-DBs, the database exchange process fails because of the MTU mismatch.

When the MTU mismatch occurs, the routers typically move between a few neighbor states while trying to overcome the problem. The most common state is the Exchange state, as shown in Example 22-9. In this case, R1 and R3 have no other problems that prevent them from becoming OSPF neighbors, except that R3 has been configured with an IP MTU of 1200 bytes on its Fa0/0 interface, instead of the default 1500 used by R1.

Example 22-9 *Results of Mismatched MTUs on OSPF Neighbors*

```
R1# show ip ospf neighbor

Neighbor ID     Pri   State        Dead Time   Address      Interface
3.3.3.3          1    EXCHANGE/DR  00:00:36    10.1.1.3     FastEthernet0/0
```

The state typically cycles from Exchange state, back to Init state, and then back to Exchange state.

Chapter Review

Review Key Topics

Review the most important topics from this chapter, noted with the Key Topic icon. Table 22-5 lists these key topics and where each is discussed.

Table 22-5 *Key Topics for Chapter 22*

Key Topic Element	Description	Page Number
List	Two things that happen when EIGRP or OSPF is enabled on a router's interface	542
Table 22-1	List of three commands that are useful when determining on which interfaces EIGRP or OSPF has been enabled	543
Table 22-2	List of neighbor requirements for both EIGRP and OSPF	550
Table 22-3	List of EIGRP neighbor requirements and useful commands to isolate that requirement as the root cause of a neighbor problem	552
Table 22-4	The same information as Table 22-3, but for OSPF	554

Key
Topic

Review Command Reference to Check Your Memory

Although you should not necessarily memorize the information in the tables in this section, this section does include a reference for the configuration and EXEC commands covered in this chapter. Practically speaking, you should memorize the commands as a side effect of reading the chapter and doing all the activities in this "Chapter Review" section. To see how well you have memorized the commands as a side effect of your other studies, cover the left side of the table, read the descriptions on the right side, and see if you remember the command.

Table 22-6 *Chapter 22 Configuration Command Reference*

Command	Description
ip hello-interval eigrp *as-number timer-value*	Interface subcommand that sets the EIGRP Hello interval for that EIGRP process.
ip hold-time eigrp *as-number timer-value*	Interface subcommand that sets the EIGRP hold time for the interface.
ip ospf hello-interval *seconds*	Interface subcommand that sets the interval for periodic Hellos.
ip ospf dead-interval *number*	Interface subcommand that sets the OSPF Dead Timer.

Table 22-7 *Chapter 22 EXEC Command Reference*

Command	Description
show ip protocols	Shows routing protocol parameters and current timer values, including an effective copy of the routing protocols' **network** commands, and a list of passive interfaces.
show ip eigrp interfaces	Lists the interfaces on which EIGRP has been enabled for each EIGRP process, except passive interfaces.
show ip route eigrp	Lists only EIGRP-learned routes from the routing table.
debug eigrp packets	Displays the contents of EIGRP packets, including many useful notices about reasons why neighbor relationships fail to form.
show ip eigrp neighbors	Lists EIGRP neighbors and status.
show ip ospf interface brief	Lists the interfaces which the OSPF protocol is enabled (based on the **network** commands), including passive interfaces.
show ip ospf interface [*type number*]	Lists detailed OSPF settings for all interfaces, or the listed interface, including Hello and Dead timers and OSPF area.
show ip route ospf	Lists routes in the routing table learned by OSPF.
show ip ospf neighbor	Lists neighbors and current status with neighbors, per interface.
debug ip ospf events	Issues log messages for each action taken by OSPF, including the receipt of messages.
debug ip ospf packet	Issues log messages describing the contents of all OSPF packets.
debug ip ospf hello	Issues log messages describing Hellos and Hello failures.

This chapter covers the following subjects:

■ **Global Unicast Addressing, Routing, and Subnetting:** This section introduces the concepts behind unicast IPv6 addresses, IPv6 routing, and subnetting using IPv6, all in comparison to IPv4.

■ **IPv6 Protocols and Addressing:** This section examines the most common protocols used in conjunction with IPv6.

■ **Configuring IPv6 Routing and Routing Protocols:** This section shows how to configure IPv6 routing and routing protocols on Cisco routers.

■ **IPv6 Transition Options:** This section explains some of the options for migrating from IPv4 to IPv6.

CHAPTER 23

IP Version 6

The world has changed tremendously over the last 10–20 years as a result of the growth and maturation of the Internet and networking technologies in general. By the year 2000, almost everyone with a home computer also connected to the Internet.

The eventual migration to IPv6 will likely be driven by the need for more addresses. Practically every mobile phone supports Internet traffic, requiring the use of an IP address. Most new cars have the ability to acquire and use an IP address, along with wireless communications, allowing the car dealer to contact the customer when the car's diagnostics detect a problem with the car. Some manufacturers have embraced the idea that all their appliances need to be IP enabled.

Besides the sheer growth in the need for IPv4 addresses, edicts from governmental agencies could drive demand for IPv6. At one point, the U.S. government had set a date in 2008 by which all government agencies should be running IPv6 in their core IP networks. Although the United States backed off that edict, such initiatives can help drive adoption of IPv6. Also, the last of the IPv4 address space has been allocated to the regional IPv4 numbering authorities, so the day at which some company asks for public IPv4 addresses, and is rejected, might finally tip the balance toward IPv6.

Although the two biggest reasons why networks might migrate to IPv6 are the need for more addresses and mandates from government organizations, at least IPv6 includes some attractive features and migration tools. Some of those advantages are as follows:

■ **Address assignment features:** IPv6 address assignment allows easier renumbering, dynamic allocation, and recovery of addresses, with nice features for mobile devices to move around and keep their IP address (thereby avoiding having to close and reopen an application).

■ **Aggregation:** IPv6's huge address space allows much easier aggregation of blocks of addresses in the Internet.

■ **No need for NAT/PAT:** Using publicly registered unique addresses on all devices removes the need for Network Address Translation/Port Address Translation (NAT/PAT), which also avoids some of the application layer and VPN-tunneling issues caused by NAT.

■ **IPsec:** IPsec works with both IPv4 and IPv6, but it is required on IPv6 hosts, so you can rely on support for IPsec as needed for VPN tunneling.

- ■ **Header improvements:** Although it might seem like a small issue, the IPv6 header improves several things compared to IPv4. In particular, routers do not need to recalculate a header checksum for every packet, reducing per-packet overhead. Additionally, the header includes a flow label that allows easy identification of packets sent over the same single TCP or User Datagram Protocol (UDP) connection.

- ■ **Transition tools:** As is covered in the last major section of this chapter, IPv6 has many tools to help with the transition from IPv4 to IPv6.

The worldwide migration from IPv4 to IPv6 will not be an event, or even a year on the calendar. Rather, it will be a long process, a process that has already begun. Network engineers have a growing need to learn more about IPv6. This chapter covers the basics of IPv6, ending with some discussions about the issues of living in a world in which both IPv4 and IPv6 will likely coexist for quite a long time.

Note: Many articles were posted online around the end of January 2011 regarding the event at which the Internet Assigned Numbers Authority (IANA) assigned the last of the IPv4 address blocks to regional numbering registries. See the author's web page for this book as referenced in the Introduction for some links.

Global Unicast Addressing, Routing, and Subnetting

One of the original design goals for the Internet was that all organizations would register and be assigned one or more public IP networks (Class A, B, or C). By registering to use a particular public network number, the company or organization using that network was assured by the numbering authorities that no other company or organization in the world would be using the addresses in that network. As a result, all hosts in the world would have globally unique IP addresses.

From the perspective of the Internet infrastructure, in particular the goal of keeping Internet routers' routing tables from getting too large, assigning an entire network to each organization helped to some degree. The Internet routers could ignore all subnets, instead having a route for each classful network. For example, if a company registered and was assigned Class B network 128.107.0.0/16, the Internet routers just needed one route for that entire network.

Over time, the Internet grew tremendously. It became clear by the early 1990s that something had to be done, or the growth of the Internet would grind to a halt when all the public IP networks were assigned, and no more existed. Additionally, the IP routing tables in Internet routers were becoming too large for the router technology of that day. So, the Internet community worked together to come up with both some short-term and long-term solutions to two problems: the shortage of public addresses and the size of the routing tables.

The short-term solutions included a much smarter public address assignment policy, where public addresses were not assigned as only Class A, B, and C networks, but as smaller subdivisions (prefixes), reducing waste. Additionally, the growth of the Internet routing tables was reduced by smarter assignment of the address ranges. For example, assigning the Class C networks that begin with 198 to only a particular Internet service provider (ISP) in a particular part of the world allowed other ISPs to use one route for 198.0.0.0/8—in other words, all addresses that begin with 198—rather than a route for each of the 65,536 different Class C networks that begin with 198. Finally, NAT/PAT achieved amazing results by allowing a typical home or small office to consume only one public IPv4 address, greatly reducing the need for public IPv4 addresses.

The ultimate solution to both problems is IPv6. The sheer number of IPv6 addresses takes care of the issue of running out of addresses. The address assignment policies already used with IPv4 have been refined and applied to IPv6, with good results for keeping the size of IPv6 routing tables smaller in Internet routers. The following sections provide a general discussion of both issues, in particular how global unicast addresses, along with good administrative choices for how to assign IPv6 address prefixes, aid in routing in the global Internet. These sections conclude with a discussion of subnetting in IPv6.

Global Route Aggregation for Efficient Routing

By the time IPv6 was being defined in the early 1990s, it was clear that thoughtful choices about how to assign the public IPv4 address space could help with the efficiency of Internet routers by keeping their routing tables much smaller. By following those same well-earned lessons, IPv6 public IP address assignment can make for even more efficient routing as the Internet migrates to IPv6.

The address assignment strategy for IPv6 is elegant, but simple, and can be roughly summarized as follows:

- Public IPv6 addresses are grouped (numerically) by major geographic region.

- Inside each region, the address space is further subdivided by ISP inside that region.

- Inside each ISP in a region, the address space is further subdivided for each customer.

The same organizations handle this address assignment for IPv6 as for IPv4. The Internet Corporation for Assigned Network Numbers (ICANN, http://www.icann.org) owns the process. ICANN assigns one or more IPv6 address ranges to each Regional Internet Registry (RIR), of which five exist at the time of publication, roughly covering North America, Central/South America, Europe, Asia/Pacific, and Africa. These RIRs then subdivide their assigned address space into smaller portions, assigning prefixes to different ISPs and other smaller registries, with the ISPs then assigning even smaller ranges of addresses to their customers.

Note: The Internet Assigned Numbers Authority (IANA) formerly owned the address assignment process, but it was transitioned to ICANN.

The IPv6 global address assignment plan results in more efficient routing, as shown in Figure 23-1. The figure shows a fictitious company (Company1) that has been assigned an IPv6 prefix by a fictitious ISP, NA-ISP1 (standing for North American ISP number 1). The figure lists the American Registry for Internet Numbers (ARIN), which is the RIR for North America.

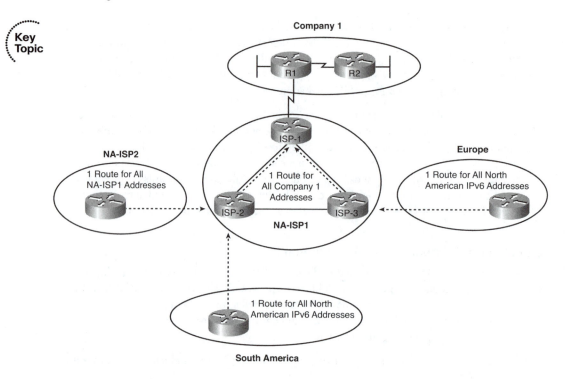

Figure 23-1   *Conceptual View of IPv6 Global Routes*

As shown in the figure, the routers installed by ISPs in other major geographies of the world can have a single route that matches all IPv6 addresses in North America. While hundreds of ISPs might be operating in north America, and hundreds of thousands of enterprise customers of those ISPs, and tens of millions of individual customers of those ISPs, all the public IPv6 addresses can be from one (or a few) very large address blocks—requiring only one (or a few) routes on the Internet routers in other parts of the world. Similarly, routers inside other ISPs in North America (for example, NA-ISP2, indicating North American ISP number 2 in the figure) can have one route that matches all address ranges assigned to NA-ISP2. And the routers inside NA-ISP1 just need to have one route that matches the entire address range assigned to Company1, rather than needing to know about all the subnets inside Company1.

Besides keeping the routers' routing table much smaller, this process also results in fewer changes to Internet routing tables. For example, if NA-ISP1 signed a service contract with another enterprise customer, NA-ISP1 could assign another prefix inside the range of addresses already assigned to NA-ISP1 by ARIN. The routers outside NA-ISP1's network—the majority of the Internet—do not need to know any new routes, because their existing routes already match the address range assigned to the new customer. The NA-ISP2 routers (another ISP) already have a route that matches the entire address range assigned to NA-ISP1, so they do not need any more routes. Likewise, the routers in ISPs in Europe and South America already have a route that works as well.

Although the general concept might not be too difficult, a specific example can help. Before seeing a specific example, however, it helps to know a bit about how IPv6 addresses and prefixes are written.

Conventions for Representing IPv6 Addresses

IPv6 conventions use 32 hexadecimal numbers, organized into 8 quartets of 4 hex digits separated by a colon, to represent a 128-bit IPv6 address. For example:

2340:1111:AAAA:0001:1234:5678:9ABC

Each hex digit represents 4 bits, so if you want to examine the address in binary, the conversion is relatively easy if you memorize the values shown in Table 23-1.

Table 23-1   *Hexadecimal/Binary Conversion Chart*

Hex	Binary	Hex	Binary
0	0000	8	1000
1	0001	9	1001
2	0010	A	1010
3	0011	B	1011
4	0100	C	1100
5	0101	D	1101
6	0110	E	1110
7	0111	F	1111

Writing or typing 32 hexadecimal digits, while more convenient than doing the same with 128 binary digits, can still be a pain. To make things a little easier, two conventions allow you to shorten what must be typed for an IPv6 address:

■   Omit the leading 0s in any given quartet.

■   Represent 1 or more consecutive quartets of all hex 0s with a double colon (::), but only for one such occurrence in a given address.

Key Topic

Note: For IPv6, a quartet is one set of 4 hex digits in an IPv6 address. Eight quartets are in each IPv6 address.

For example, consider the following address. The bold digits represent digits in which the address could be abbreviated.

FE00:**0000**:**0000**:**000**1:**0000**:**0000**:**0000**:**00**56

This address has two different locations in which one or more quartets have 4 hex 0s, so two main options exist for abbreviating this address, using the :: abbreviation in one or the other location. The following two options show the two briefest valid abbreviations:

■   FE00::1:0:0:0:56

■   FE00:0:0:1::56

In particular, note that the :: abbreviation, meaning "one or more quartets of all 0s," cannot be used twice, because that would be ambiguous. So, the abbreviation FE00::1::56 would not be valid.

Conventions for Writing IPv6 Prefixes

IPv6 prefixes represent a range or block of consecutive IPv6 addresses. The number that represents the range of addresses, called a *prefix*, is usually seen in IP routing tables, just like you see IP subnet numbers in IPv4 routing tables.

Before examining IPv6 prefixes in more detail, it is helpful to review a few terms used with IPv4. IPv4 addresses can be analyzed and understood using either *classful addressing* rules or *classless addressing* rules, as discussed earlier in Chapter 10, "Analyzing Existing Subnet Masks." Classful addressing means that the analysis of an IP address or subnet includes the idea of a classful network number, with a separate network part of the address. The top part of Figure 23-2 reviews these concepts.

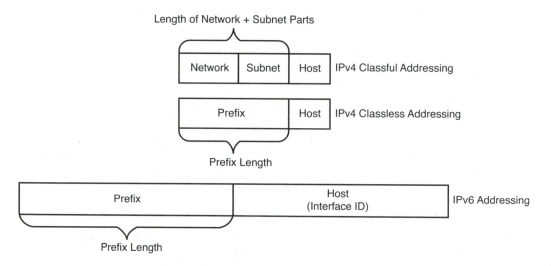

Figure 23-2   *IPv4 Classless and Classful Addressing, and IPv6 Addressing*

Thinking about IPv4 addressing as classful addresses helps to fully understand some issues in networking. With classful addressing, for example, the written value

128.107.3.0/24 means 16 network bits (because the address is in a Class B network) and 8 host bits (because the mask has 8 binary 0s), leaving 8 subnet bits. The same value, interpreted with classless rules, means prefix 128.107.3.0, prefix length 24. Same subnet/prefix, same meaning, same router operation, same configuration—it's just two different ways to think about the meaning of the numbers.

IPv6 uses a classless view of addressing, with no concept of classful addressing. Like IPv4, IPv6 prefixes list some value, a slash, and then a numeric prefix length. Like IPv4 prefixes, the last part of the number, beyond the length of the prefix, is represented by binary 0s. And finally, IPv6 prefix numbers can be abbreviated with the same rules as IPv4 addresses. For example, consider the following IPv6 address that is assigned to a host on a LAN:

2000:1234:5678:9ABC:1234:5678:9ABC:1111/64

This value represents the full 128-bit IP address; in fact, you have no opportunities to abbreviate this address. However, the /64 means that the prefix (subnet) in which this address resides is the subnet that includes all addresses that begin with the same first 64 bits as the address. Conceptually, it is the same logic as an IPv4 address. For example, address 128.107.3.1/24 is in the prefix (subnet) whose first 24 bits are the same values as address 128.107.3.1.

Like with IPv4, when writing or typing a prefix, the bits past the end of the prefix length are all binary 0s. In the IPv6 address shown previously, the prefix in which the address resides would be as follows:

2000:1234:5678:9ABC:**0000:0000:0000:0000**/64

When abbreviated, this would be

2000:1234:5678:9ABC::/64

Next, here's one last fact about the rules for writing prefixes before seeing some examples and moving on. If the prefix length is not a multiple of 16, the boundary between the prefix and the host part of the address is inside a quartet. In such cases, the prefix value should list all the values in the last octet in the prefix part of the value. For example, if the address just shown with a /64 prefix length instead had a /56 prefix length, the prefix would include all the first 3 quartets (a total of 48 bits), plus the first 8 bits of the fourth octet. The last 8 bits (last 2 hex digits) of the fourth octet should now be binary 0s. So, by convention, the rest of the fourth octet should be written, after being set to binary 0s, as follows:

2000:1234:5678:9A00::/56

The following list summarizes some key points about how to write IPv6 prefixes:

- The prefix has the same value as the IP addresses in the group for the first number of bits, as defined by the prefix length.

- Any bits after the prefix-length number of bits are binary 0s.

- The prefix can be abbreviated with the same rules as IPv6 addresses.

- If the prefix length is not on a quartet boundary, write down the value for the entire quartet.

Examples can certainly help a lot in this case. Table 23-2 shows several sample prefixes, their format, and a brief explanation.

Table 23-2   *Example IPv6 Prefixes and Their Meanings*

Prefix	Explanation	Incorrect Alternative
2000::/3	All addresses whose first 3 bits are equal to the first 3 bits of hex number 2000 (bits are 001)	2000/3 (omits ::) 2::/3 (omits the rest of the first quartet)
2340:1140::/26	All addresses whose first 26 bits match the listed hex number	2340:114::/26 (omits the last digit in the second quartet)
2340:1111::/32	All addresses whose first 32 bits match the listed hex number	2340:1111/32 (omits ::)

Almost as important to this convention is to note which options are not allowed. For example, 2::/3 is not allowed instead of 2000::/3, because it omits the rest of the octet, and a device could not tell whether 2::/3 means "hex 0002" or "hex 2000." Only leading 0s in a quartet, and not trailing 0s, can be omitted when abbreviating an IPv6 address or prefix.

Now that you understand a few of the conventions about how to represent IPv6 addresses and prefixes, a specific example can show how ICANN's IPv6 global unicast IP address assignment strategy can allow the easy and efficient routing shown back in Figure 23-1.

Global Unicast Prefix Assignment Example

IPv6 standards reserve the 2000::/3 prefix—which, when interpreted more fully, means all addresses that begin with binary 001 or either a hex 2 or 3—as global unicast addresses. Global unicast addresses are addresses that have been assigned as public and globally unique IPv6 addresses, allowing hosts using those addresses to communicate through the Internet without the need for NAT. In other words, these addresses fit the purest design for how to implement IPv6 for the global Internet.

Figure 23-3 shows an example set of prefixes that could result in a company (Company1) being assigned a prefix of 2340:1111:AAAA::/48.

The process starts with ICANN, which owns the entire IPv6 address space, and assigns the rights to *registry prefix* 2340::/12 to one of the RIRs—ARIN in this case (North America). This means that ARIN has the rights to assign any IPv6 addresses that begin with the first 12 bits of hex 2340 (binary value 0010 0011 0100). For perspective, that's a large group of addresses—2^{116} to be exact.

Next, NA-ISP1 asks ARIN for a prefix assignment. After ARIN ensures that NA-ISP1 meets some requirements, ARIN might assign *ISP prefix* 2340:1111::/32 to NA-ISP1. This too is a large group—2^{96} addresses to be exact. For perspective, this one address block might well be enough public IPv6 addresses for even the largest ISP, without that ISP ever needing another IPv6 prefix.

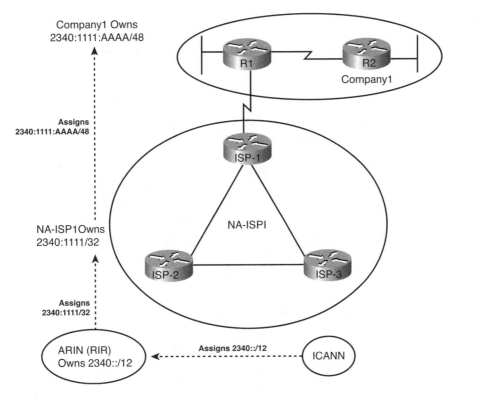

Figure 23-3 *Example IPv6 Prefix Assignment in the Internet*

Finally, Company1 asks its ISP, NA-ISP1, for the assignment of an IPv6 prefix. NA-ISP1 assigns Company1 the site prefix 2340:1111:AAAA::/48, which is again a large range of addresses—2^{80} in this case. In the next paragraph, the text shows what Company1 could do with that prefix, but first, examine Figure 23-4, which presents the same concepts as shown in Figure 23-1, but now with the prefixes shown.

The figure shows the perspectives of routers outside North America, routers from another ISP in North America, and other routers in the same ISP. Routers outside North America can use a route for prefix 2340::/12, knowing that ICANN assigned this prefix to be used only by ARIN. This one route could match all IPv6 addresses assigned in North America. Routers in NA-ISP2, an example alternative ISP in North America, need one route for 2340:1111::/32, the prefix assigned to NA-ISP1. This one route could match all packets destined for all customers of NA-ISP1. Inside NA-ISP1, its routers need to know to which NA-ISP1 router to forward packets for that particular customer (the router named ISP-1 in this case), so the routes inside NA-ISP1's routers lists a prefix of 2340:1111:AAAA::/48.

Subnetting Global Unicast IPv6 Addresses Inside an Enterprise

The original IPv4 Internet design called for each organization to be assigned a classful network number, with the enterprise subdividing the network into smaller address ranges by subnetting the classful network. This same concept of subnetting carries over from

IPv4 to IPv6, with the enterprise subnetting the prefix assigned by its ISP into smaller prefixes. When thinking about the IPv6 subnetting concept, you could make the following general analogies with classful IPv4 subnetting to help understand the process:

- The prefix assigned to the enterprise by the ISP, which must be the same for all IPv6 addresses in one enterprise, is like the IPv4 network part of an address.

- The enterprise engineer extends the length of the prefix, borrowing host bits, to create a subnet part of the address.

- The last/third major part is the host part of the address, called the *interface ID* in IPv6, and is meant to uniquely identify a host inside a subnet.

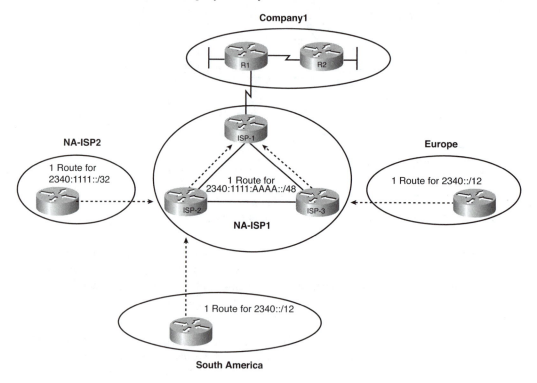

Figure 23-4 *IPv6 Global Routing Concepts*

For example, Figure 23-5 shows a more detailed view of the Company1 enterprise network shown in several of the earlier figures in this chapter. The design concepts behind how many subnets are needed with IPv6 are identical to those for IPv4: A subnet is needed for each VLAN and for each serial link, with the same options for subnets with Frame Relay. In this case, two LANs and two serial links exist, so Company1 needs four subnets.

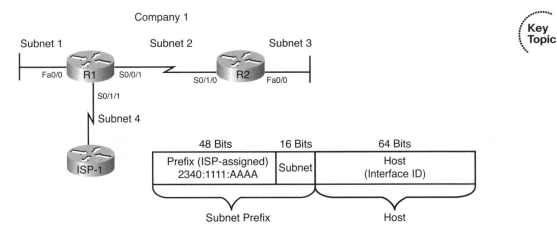

Figure 23-5   *Company1 Needs Four Subnets*

The figure also shows how the enterprise engineer extended the length of the prefix as assigned by the ISP (/48) to /64, thereby creating a 16-bit subnet part of the address structure. The /48 prefix is generally called the *site prefix*, and the longer prefix used on each link is called a *subnet prefix*. To create this extra 16-bit subnet field, the engineer uses the same concept as with IPv4 when choosing a subnet mask by borrowing bits from the host field of an IPv4 address. In this case, think of the host field as having 80 bits (because the prefix assigned by the ISP is 48 bits long, leaving 80 bits), and the design in Figure 23-5 borrows 16 bits for the subnet field, leaving a measly 64 bits for the host field.

A bit of math about the design choices can help provide some perspective on the scale of IPv6. The 16-bit subnet field allows 2^{16}, or 65,536, subnets—overkill for all but the very largest organizations or companies. (There are also no worries about a zero or broadcast subnet in IPv6!) The host field is seemingly even more overkill: 2^{64} hosts per subnet, which is more than 1,000,000,000,000,000,000 addresses per subnet. However, a good reason exists for this large host or interface ID part of the address, because it allows one of the automatic IPv6 address assignment features to work well, as is covered in the section "IPv6 Host Address Assignment," later in this chapter.

Figure 23-6 takes the concept to the final conclusion, assigning the specific four subnets to be used inside Company1. Note that the figure shows the subnet fields and prefix lengths (64 in this case) in bold.

Note: The subnet numbers in the figure could be abbreviated slightly, removing the three leading 0s from the last shown quartets.

Figure 23-6 just shows one option for subnetting the prefix assigned to Company1. However, any number of subnet bits could be chosen, as long as the host field retained enough bits to number all hosts in a subnet. For example, a /112 prefix length could be used, extending the /48 prefix by 64 bits (4 hex quartets). Then, for the design in Figure 23-6, you could choose the following four subnets:

- 2340:1111:AAAA::0001:0000/112

- 2340:1111:AAAA::0002:0000/112

- 2340:1111:AAAA::0003:0000/112

- 2340:1111:AAAA::0004:0000/112

By using global unicast IPv6 addresses, Internet routing can be very efficient, and enterprises can have plenty of IP addresses and plenty of subnets, with no requirement for NAT functions to conserve the address space.

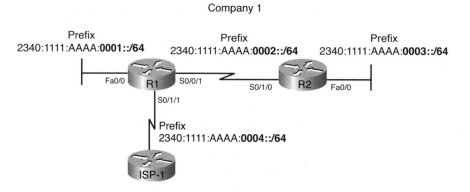

Figure 23-6 *Company1 with Four Subnets Assigned*

Prefix Terminology

Before wrapping up this topic, a few new terms need to be introduced. The process of global unicast IPv6 address assignment examines many different prefixes, with many different prefix lengths. The text scatters a couple of more specific terms, but for easier study, Table 23-3 summarizes the four key terms, with some reminders of what each means.

The next sections of this chapter broaden the discussion of IPv6 to include additional types of IPv6 addresses, along with the protocols that control and manage several common functions for IPv6.

Table 23-3 *Example IPv6 Prefixes and Their Meanings*

Term	Assignment	Example from This Chapter
Registry prefix	By ICANN to an RIR	2340::/12
ISP prefix	By an RIR to an ISP[1]	2340:1111::/32
Site prefix	By an ISP to a customer (site)	2340:1111:AAAA::/48
Subnet prefix	By an enterprise engineer for each individual link	2340:1111:AAAA:0001::/64

[1]Although an RIR can assign a prefix to an ISP, an RIR can also assign a prefix to other Internet registries, which can subdivide and assign additional prefixes, until eventually an ISP and then its customers are assigned some unique prefix.

IPv6 Protocols and Addressing

IPv4 hosts need to know several basic facts before they can succeed in simple tasks like opening a web browser to view a web page. IPv4 hosts typically need to know the IP address of one or more Domain Name System (DNS) servers so that they can use DNS protocol messages to ask a DNS server to resolve that name into an IPv4 address. They need to know an IP address of a router to use as a default gateway (default router), with the host sending packets destined to a host in a different subnet to that default router. The host, of course, needs to know its unicast IPv4 IP address and mask—or, as stated with classless terminology, its IPv4 address and prefix length—from which the host can calculate the prefix (subnet) on that link.

IPv6 hosts need the same information—DNS IP addresses, default router IP address, and their own address/prefix length—for the same reasons. IPv6 hosts still use host names, and they need to have the host name resolved into an IPv6 address. IPv6 hosts still send packets directly to hosts on the same subnet, but they send packets to the default router for off-subnet destinations.

While IPv6 hosts need to know the same information, IPv6 changes the mechanisms for learning some of these facts compared to IPv4. The following sections examine the options and protocols through which a host can learn these key pieces of information. At the same time, these sections introduce several other types of IPv6 addresses that are used by the new IPv6 protocols. The end of these sections summarizes the details and terminology for the various types of IPv6 addresses.

DHCP for IPv6

IPv6 hosts can use Dynamic Host Configuration Protocol (DHCP) to learn and lease an IP address and corresponding prefix length (mask), the IP address of the default router, and the DNS IP address(es). The concept works basically like DHCP for IPv4: The host sends a (multicast) IPv6 packet searching for the DHCP server. When a server replies, the DHCP client sends a message asking for a lease of an IP address, and the server replies, listing an IPv6 address, prefix length, default router, and DNS IP addresses. The names and formats of the actual DHCP messages have changed quite a bit from IPv4 to IPv6, so DHCPv4 and DHCPv6 differ in detail, but the basic process remains the same. (DHCPv4 refers to the version of DHCP used for IPv4, and DHCPv6 refers to the version of DHCP used for IPv6.)

DHCPv4 servers retain information about each client, like the IP address leased to that client and the length of time for which the lease is valid. This type of information is called *state information*, because it tracks the state or status of each client. DHCPv6 servers happen to have two operational modes: stateful, in which the server tracks state information, and stateless, in which the server does not track state information. Stateful DHCPv6 servers fill the same role as the older DHCPv4 servers, whereas stateless DHCPv6 servers fill one role in an IPv6 alternative to stateful DHCP. (Stateless DHCP, and its purpose, is covered in the upcoming section.)

One difference between DHCPv4 and stateful DHCPv6 is that IPv4 hosts send IP broadcasts to find DHCP servers, whereas IPv6 hosts send IPv6 multicasts. IPv6 multicast addresses have a prefix of FF00::/8, meaning that the first 8 bits of an address are binary

11111111, or FF in hex. The multicast address FF02::1:2 (longhand FF02:0000:0000:0000:0000:0000:0001:0002) has been reserved in IPv6 to be used by hosts to send packets to an unknown DHCP server, with the routers working to forward these packets to the appropriate DHCP server.

IPv6 Host Address Assignment

When using IPv4 in enterprise networks, engineers typically configure static IPv4 addresses on each router interface with the **ip address** interface subcommand. At the same time, most end-user hosts use DHCP to dynamically learn their IP address and mask. For Internet access, the router can use DHCP to learn its own public IPv4 address from the ISP.

IPv6 follows the same general model, but with routers using one of two options for static IPv6 address assignment, and with end-user hosts using one of two options for dynamic IPv6 address assignment. The following sections examine all four options. But first, to appreciate the configuration options, you need a little more information about the low-order 64 bits of the IPv6 address format: the interface ID.

The IPv6 Interface ID and EUI-64 Format

Earlier in this chapter, Figure 23-5 shows the format of an IPv6 global unicast address, with the second half of the address called the host or interface ID. The value of the interface ID portion of a global unicast address can be set to any value, as long as no other host in the same subnet attempts to use the same value. (IPv6 includes a dynamic method for hosts to find out whether a duplicate address exists on the subnet before starting to use the address.) However, the size of the interface ID was purposefully chosen to allow easy autoconfiguration of IP addresses by plugging the MAC address of a network card into the interface ID field in an IPv6 address.

MAC addresses are 6 bytes (48 bits) in length, so for a host to automatically decide on a value to use in the 8-byte (64-bit) interface ID field, IPv6 cannot simply copy just the MAC address. To complete the 64-bit interface ID, IPv6 fills in 2 more bytes. Interestingly, to do so, IPv6 separates the MAC address into two 3-byte halves, and inserts hex FFFE in between the halves, to form the interface ID field, as well as inverting 1 special bit. This format, called the EUI-64 format, is shown in Figure 23-7.

Although it might seem a bit convoluted, it works. Also, with a little practice, you can look at an IPv6 address and quickly notice the FFFE late in the address, and then easily find the two halves of the corresponding interface's MAC address.

To be complete, the figure points out one other small detail regarding the EUI-64 interface ID value. Splitting the MAC address into two halves, and injecting FFFE, is easy. However, the EUI-64 format requires inverting the seventh bit in the first byte of the value. In other words, the host will look at the seventh bit, and if it's a 0, change it to a 1, or if it's a 1, change it to a 0.

For example, the following two lines list a host's MAC address and corresponding EUI-64 format interface ID, assuming the use of an address configuration option that uses the EUI-64 format:

■   0034:5678:9ABC

■   0234:56FF:FE78:9ABC

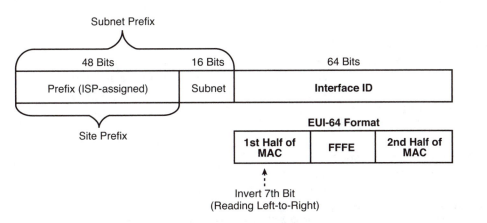

Figure 23-7   *IPv6 Address Format with Interface ID and EUI-64*

Note: To change the seventh bit (reading left-to-right) in the example, convert hex 00 to binary 00000000, change the seventh bit to 1 (00000010), and then convert back to hex, for hex 02 as the first two digits.

Static IPv6 Address Configuration

Two options for static IPv6 address configuration are covered in this book, and both are available on both routers and hosts: static configuration of the entire address, and static configuration of a /64 prefix with the host calculating its EUI-64 interface ID to complete the IP address. This section shows the concept using routers.

To configure an IPv6 address on an interface, the router needs an **ipv6 address** *address/prefix-length* [**eui-64**] interface subcommand on each interface. If the **eui-64** keyword is not included, the address must represent the entire 128-bit address. If the **eui-64** keyword is included, the address should represent the 64-bit prefix, with the router creating the interface ID using the EUI-64 format. The *prefix-length* parameter should be the length of the subnet prefix. For example, Example 23-1 lists the commands on Router R1 from Figure 23-6 earlier in this chapter, which is one of Company1's enterprise routers. It uses the site prefix length of /64. The example shows both versions of the command (with and without the **eui-64** keyword).

Example 23-1   *Configuring Static IPv6 Addresses*

```
! The first interface is in subnet 1, and will use EUI-64 as the Interface ID
!
interface FastEthernet0/0
 ipv6 address 2340:1111:AAAA:1::/64 eui-64
! The next interface spells out the whole 128 bits, abbreviated. The longer
! version is 2340:1111:AAAA:0003:0000:0000:0001/64. It is in subnet 2.
```

```
!
interface Serial0/0/1
 ipv6 address 2340:1111:AAAA:2::1/64
! The third interface is in subnet 4, with EUI-64 format Interface ID again.
!
interface Serial0/1/1
 ipv6 address 2340:1111:AAAA:4::/64 eui-64
!
R1# show ipv6 interface fa0/0
FastEthernet0/0 is up, line protocol is up
  IPv6 is enabled, link-local address is FE80::213:19FF:FE7B:5004
  Global unicast address(es):
    2340:1111:AAAA:1:213:19FF:FE7B:5004, subnet is 2340:1111:AAAA:1::/64 [EUI]
! Lines omitted for brevity
R1# show ipv6 interface S0/0/1
Serial0/0/1 is up, line protocol is up
  IPv6 is enabled, link-local address is FE80::213:19FF:FE7B:5004
  Global unicast address(es):
    2340:1111:AAAA:3::1, subnet is 2340:1111:AAAA:3::/64
! Lines omitted for brevity
R1# show ipv6 interface s0/1/1
Serial0/1/1 is up, line protocol is up
  IPv6 is enabled, link-local address is FE80::213:19FF:FE7B:5004
  Global unicast address(es):
    2340:1111:AAAA:4:213:19FF:FE7B:5004, subnet is 2340:1111:AAAA:4::/64 [EUI]
! Lines omitted for brevity
```

The end of the example lists the full global unicast IPv6 address as part of the **show ipv6 interface** command. When using the EUI-64 option, this command is particularly useful, because the configuration command does not list the entire IPv6 address. Note that if the EUI format is used, the **show ipv6 interface** command notes that fact (see interfaces Fa0/0 and S0/1/1, versus S0/0/1). Also, routers do not have MAC addresses associated with some interfaces, including serial interfaces, so to form the EUI-64–formatted interface ID on those interfaces, routers use the MAC address of a LAN interface. In this case, S0/1/1's interface ID is based on Fa0/0's MAC address.

Stateless Autoconfiguration and Router Advertisements

IPv6 supports two methods of dynamic configuration of IPv6 addresses. One uses a stateful DHCPv6 server, which as mentioned earlier, works the same as DHCP in IPv4 in concept, although many details in the messages differ between DHCPv4 and DHCPv6. IPv6 also supplies an alternative called *stateless autoconfiguration* (not to be confused with stateless DHCP, which is covered in this section). With stateless autoconfiguration, a host dynamically learns the /64 prefix used on the subnet, and then calculates the rest of its address by using an EUI-64 interface ID based on its network interface card (NIC) MAC address.

The stateless autoconfiguration process uses one of many features of the IPv6 Neighbor Discovery Protocol (NDP) to discover the prefix used on the LAN. NDP performs many functions for IPv6, all related to something that occurs between two hosts in the same subnet. For example, one part of NDP replaces the IPv4 ARP protocol. IPv4 ARP allows devices on the same subnet—neighbors—to learn each other's MAC address. Because this and many other activities occur only inside the local subnet between neighbors on the same link, IPv6 collected these basic functions into one protocol suite, called NDP.

Stateless autoconfiguration uses two NDP messages, namely router solicitation (RS) and router advertisement (RA) messages, to discover the IPv6 prefix used on a LAN. The host sends the RS message as an IPv6 multicast message, asking all routers to respond to the questions "What IPv6 prefix(s) is used on this subnet?" and "What is the IPv6 address(s) of any default routers on this subnet?" Figure 23-8 shows the general idea, on subnet 1 from Figure 23-6, with PC1 sending an RS, and router R1 replying with the IPv6 prefix used on the LAN and R1's own IPv6 address as a potential default router.

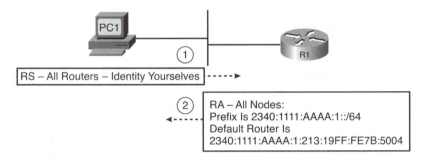

Figure 23-8 *Example NDP RS/RA Process to Find the Default Routers*

IPv6 does not use broadcasts. In fact, there is no such thing as a subnet broadcast address, a network-wide broadcast address, or an equivalent of the all-hosts 255.255.255.255 broadcast IPv4 address. Instead, IPv6 uses multicast addresses. By using a different multicast IPv6 address for different functions, a computer that has no need to participate in a particular function can simply ignore those particular multicasts, reducing the impact to the host. For example, the RS message only needs to be received and processed by routers, so the RS message's destination IP address is FF02::2, which is the address reserved in IPv6 to be used only by IPv6 routers. RA messages are sent to a multicast address intended for use by all IPv6 hosts on the link (FF02::1), so not only will the host that sent the RS learn the information, but all other hosts on the link will also learn the details.

Table 23-4 summarizes some of the key details about the RS/RA messages.

Table 23-4 *Details of the RS/RA Process*

Message	RS	RA
Multicast destination	FF02::2	FF02::1
Meaning of multicast address	All routers on this link	All IPv6 nodes on this link

IPv6 Address Configuration Summary

This chapter covers four methods for assigning IPv6 addresses to hosts or router interfaces. Two variations use static configuration, while two dynamically learn the address. However, with both static and dynamic configuration, two alternatives exist—one that supplies the entire IPv6 address and one that allows the host to calculate the EUI-64 interface ID. Table 23-5 summarizes the configuration methods.

Key Topic

Table 23-5 *IPv6 Address Configuration Options*

Static or Dynamic	Option	Portion Configured or Learned
Static	Do not use EUI-64	Entire 128-bit address
Static	Use EUI-64	Just the /64 prefix
Dynamic	Stateful DHCPv6	Entire 128-bit address
Dynamic	Stateless autoconfiguration	Just the /64 prefix

Discovering the Default Router with NDP

In IPv4, hosts discover their default router (default gateway) either through static configuration on the host or, more typically, with DHCP. IPv6 can use both of these same options as well, plus the NDP RS/RA messages as explained in the previous section. The NDP router discovery process occurs by default on IPv6 hosts and routers, so while the stateful DHCPv6 server can supply the IP address(es) of the possible default routers, it is perfectly reasonable in IPv6 to simply not bother to configure these details in a stateful DHCP server, allowing the built-in NDP RS/RA messages to be used instead.

The default router discovery process is relatively simple. Routers automatically send RA messages on a periodic basis. These messages list not only the sending router's IPv6 address but also all the known routers on that subnet. A host can wait for the next periodic RA message or request that all local routers send an RA immediately by soliciting the routers using the RS message.

Learning the IP Address(es) of DNS Servers

Like IPv4 hosts, IPv6 hosts typically need to know the IP address of one or more DNS servers to resolve names into the corresponding IP address. Oftentimes, the host also needs to learn the DNS domain name to use. And like IPv4 hosts, IPv6 hosts can be told these IP addresses using (stateful) DHCP. When a host (or router for that matter) learns its IPv6 address using stateful DHCP, the host can also learn the DNS server IP addresses and the domain name, taking care of this particular detail.

Stateless DHCP, which is most useful in conjunction with stateless autoconfiguration, is an alternative method for finding the DNS server IP addresses and the domain name. A host that uses stateless autoconfiguration can learn its IPv6 address and prefix automatically, as well as learn its default router IP address, in both cases using NDP RS/RA messages. However, the stateless autoconfiguration process does not help a host learn the DNS IP addresses and domain name. So, stateless DHCP supplies that information using the same messages as stateful DHCP. However, to supply this information, the server does not need to track any state information about each client, so a stateless DHCP server can be used.

Table 23-6 summarizes some of the key features of stateful and stateless DHCPv6.

Table 23-6   *Comparison of Stateless and Stateful DHCPv6 Services*

Feature	Stateful DHCP	Stateless DHCP
Remembers IPv6 address (state information) of clients that make requests	Yes	No
Assigns IPv6 address to client	Yes	No
Supplies useful information, like DNS server IP addresses	Yes	Yes
Is most useful in conjunction with stateless autoconfiguration	No	Yes

IPv6 Addresses

This chapter has already introduced the concepts behind the general format of IPv6 addresses, the ideas behind global unicast IPv6 addresses, and some details about multicast IPv6 addresses. The following sections round out the coverage of addressing, specifically the three categories of IPv6 address:

- **Unicast:** IP addresses assigned to a single interface for the purpose of allowing that one host to send and receive data.

- **Multicast:** IP addresses that represent a dynamic group of hosts for the purpose of sending packets to all current members of the group. Some multicast addresses are used for special purposes, like with NDP messages, while most support end-user applications.

- **Anycast:** A design choice by which servers that support the same function can use the same unicast IP address, with packets sent by clients being forwarded to the nearest server, allowing load balancing across different servers.

Unicast IPv6 Addresses

IPv6 supports three main classes of unicast addresses. One of these classes, global unicast IP addresses, closely matches the purpose of IPv4 public IP addresses. Global unicast addresses are assigned by ICANN and the RIRs for the purpose of allowing globally unique IPv6 addresses for all hosts. These addresses come from inside the 2000::/3 prefix, which includes all addresses that begin with 2 or 3 (hex).

The next class of IPv6 unicast addresses covered here, *unique local* unicast addresses, have the same function as IPv4 RFC 1918 private addresses. In IPv4, most every enterprise, and most every Internet-connected small or home office, uses IPv4 private networks. *Unique local* unicast addresses begin with hex FD (FD00::/8), with the format shown in Figure 23-9.

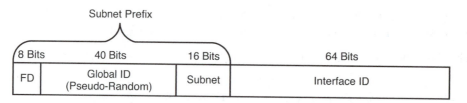

Figure 23-9 *Unique Local Address Format*

> **Note:**   The original IPv6 RFCs defined a private address class called *site local*, meaning local within a site (organization). The original site local address class has been deprecated and replaced with unique local unicast addresses.

To use these addresses, an enterprise engineer would choose a 40-bit global ID in a pseudorandom manner, with the goal that hopefully the addresses will be unique in the universe. In reality, pseudorandom is probably a number made up by the engineer. The 16-bit subnet field and 64-bit interface ID work just like with global unicast addresses, numbering different subnets and hosts and allowing EUI-64 assignment of the interface ID. As usual, the engineer could avoid using EUI-64, using easier-to-remember values like 0000:0000:0000:0001 as the interface ID.

Link local addresses are the third class of unicast IPv6 addresses covered here. IPv4 has no concepts like the link local IP address. IPv6 uses these addresses when sending packets over the local subnet; routers never forward packets destined for link local addresses to other subnets.

Link local addresses can be useful for functions that do not need to leave the subnet, in particular because a host can automatically derive its own link local IP address without sending packets over the subnet. So, before sending the first packets, the host can calculate its own link local address so that the host has an IPv6 address to use when doing its first overhead messages. For example, before a host sends an NDP RS (router solicitation) message, the host will have already calculated its link local address. The host uses its link local address as the source IP address in the RS message.

Link local addresses come from the FE80::/10 range. No specific configuration is required, because a host forms these addresses by using the first 10 bits of hex FE80 (binary 1111111010), 54 more binary 0s, and the last 64 bits being the host's EUI-64 format interface ID. Figure 23-10 shows the format.

Figure 23-10 *Link Local Address Format*

Routers also use link local addresses on each interface enabled to support IPv6. Like hosts, routers automatically calculate their link local IP addresses. In fact, Example 23-1 earlier in this chapter listed the (R1) router's link local IP addresses in the output of the **show ipv6 interface** command output. Interestingly, routers normally use link local addresses as the next-hop IP address in IPv6 routes, rather than the neighboring router's global unicast or unique local unicast address.

Multicast and Other Special IPv6 Addresses

Multicast addresses can be used to communicate to dynamic groupings of hosts, with the sender sending a single packet and with the network replicating that packet as needed so that all hosts listening for packets sent to that multicast address receive a copy of the packet. IPv6 can limit the scope of where routers forward multicasts based on the value in the first quartet of the address. This book only examines multicasts that should stay on a local link; these addresses all begin with FF02::/16, so they are easily recognized.

For reference, Table 23-7 lists some of the more commonly seen IPv6 multicast addresses. Of particular interest are the addresses chosen for use by Routing Information Protocol (RIP), Open Shortest Path First (OSPF), and Enhanced IGRP (EIGRP), which somewhat mirror the multicast addresses each protocol uses for IPv4.

Table 23-7   *Common Link Local Multicast Addresses*

Purpose	IPv6 Address	IPv4 Equivalent
All IP nodes on the link	FF02::1	Subnet broadcast address
All routers on the link	FF02::2	N/A
OSPF messages	FF02::5, FF02::6	224.0.0.5, 224.0.0.6
RIP-2 messages	FF02::9	224.0.0.9
EIGRP messages	FF02::A	224.0.0.10
DHCP relay agents (routers that forward to the DHCP server)	FF02:1:2	N/A

Before completing the discussion of IPv6 addressing, you should know about a couple of special IPv6 addresses. First, IPv6 supports the concept of a loopback IP address, as follows:

::1 (127 binary 0s and a 1)

Just like the IPv4 127.0.0.1 loopback address, this address can be used to test a host's software. A packet sent by a host to this address goes down the protocol stack, and then right back up the stack, with no communication with the underlying network card. This allows testing of the software on a host, particularly when testing new applications.

The other special address is the :: address (all binary 0s). This address represents the unknown address, which a host can use temporarily during the address discovery process, before the host knows its own IPv6 address.

Summary of IP Protocols and Addressing

This chapter has covered a lot of concepts and details about IPv6 addresses, many of which require some work to remember or memorize. This short section pulls several concepts from throughout this major section on IPv6 protocols and addresses together before moving on to some details about routing protocols and router configuration.

When an IPv6 host first boots, it needs to do several tasks before it can send packets through a router to another host. When using one of the two methods of dynamically learning an IPv6 address that can be used to send packets past the local routers to the rest of a network, the first few initialization steps are the same, with some differences in the later steps. The following list summarizes the steps a host takes when first booting, at least for the functions covered in this chapter:

Key Topic

Step 1.   The host calculates its IPv6 link local address (begins with FE80::/10).

Step 2.   The host sends an NDP router solicitation (RS) message, with its link local address as the source address and the all-routers FF02::2 multicast destination address, to ask routers to supply a list of default routers and the prefix/length used on the LAN.

Step 3.   The router(s) replies with an RA message, sourced from the router's link local address, sent to the all-IPv6-hosts-on-the-link multicast address (FF02::1), supplying the default router and prefix information.

Step 4.   If the type of dynamic address assignment is stateless autoconfiguration, the following occur:

    a.   The host builds the unicast IP address it can use to send packets through the router by using the prefix learned in the RA message and calculating an EUI-64 interface ID based on the NIC MAC address.

    b.   The host uses DHCP messages to ask a stateless DHCP server for the DNS server IP addresses and domain name.

Step 5.   If the type of dynamic address assignment is stateful DHCP, the host uses DHCP messages to ask a stateful DHCP server for a lease of an IP address/prefix length, as well as default router addresses, the DNS server IP addresses, and domain name.

Other tasks occur when a host initializes as well, but they are beyond the scope of this book.

IPv6 includes many different types of addresses, including unicast and multicast. By way of summary, Table 23-8 lists the types of IPv6 addresses mentioned by this chapter, with a few details, for easier reference when studying.

Table 23-8 *IPv6 Address Types*

Type of Address	Purpose	Prefix	Easily Seen Hex Prefix(es)
Global unicast	Unicast packets sent through the public Internet	2000::/3	2 or 3
Unique local	Unicast packets inside one organization	FD00::/8	FD
Link Local	Packets sent in the local subnet	FE80::/10	FE8, FE9, FEA, FEB
Multicast (link local scope)	Multicasts that stay on the local subnet	FF02::/16	FF02

Key Topic

Configuring IPv6 Routing and Routing Protocols

To support IPv6, all the IPv4 routing protocols had to go through varying degrees of changes, with the most obvious being that each had to be changed to support longer addresses and prefixes. The following sections first examine a few details about routing protocols and then show how to configure IPv6 routing and routing protocols on Cisco routers.

IPv6 Routing Protocols

As with IPv4, most IPv6 routing protocols are interior gateway protocols (IGP), with Border Gateway Protocol (BGP) still being the only exterior gateway protocol (EGP) of note. All these current IGPs and BGP have been updated to support IPv6. Table 23-9 lists the routing protocols and their new RFCs (as appropriate).

Table 23-9 *Updates to Routing Protocols for IPv6*

Routing Protocol	Full Name	RFC
RIPng	RIP Next Generation	2080
OSPFv3	OSPF version 3	2740
MP-BGP4	Multiprotocol BGP-4	2545/4760
EIGRP for IPv6	EIGRP for IPv6	Proprietary

Each of these routing protocols has to make several changes to support IPv6. The actual messages used to send and receive routing information have changed, using IPv6 headers instead of IPv4 headers and using IPv6 addresses in those headers. For example, RIPng sends routing updates to the IPv6 destination address FF02::9, instead of the old RIP-2 IPv4 224.0.0.9 address. Also, the routing protocols typically advertise their link local IP address as the next hop in a route, as will be shown in the upcoming Example 23-2.

The routing protocols still retain many of the same internal features. For example, RIPng, being based on RIP-2, is still a distance vector protocol, with hop count as the metric and 15 hops as the longest valid route (16 is infinity). OSPFv3, created specifically to support IPv6, is still a link-state protocol, with cost as the metric but with many of the internals, including link-state advertisement (LSA) types, changed. As a result, OSPFv2, as covered in Chapter 21, "OSPF Concepts and Configuration," is not compatible with OSPFv3. However, the core operational concepts remain the same.

IPv6 Configuration

Cisco router IOS enables the routing (forwarding) of IPv4 packets by default, with IPv4 being enabled on an interface when the interface has an IPv4 address configured. For IPv4 routing protocols, the routing protocol must be configured, with the **network** command indirectly enabling the routing protocol on an interface.

IPv6 configuration follows some of these same guidelines, with the largest difference being how to enable a routing protocol on an interface. Cisco router IOS does not enable IPv6 routing by default, so a global command is required to enable IPv6 routing. The unicast IP addresses need to be configured on the interfaces, similar to IPv4. The routing protocol needs to be globally configured, similar to IPv4. Finally, the routing protocol has to be configured on each interface as needed, but with IPv6, the process does not use the **network** router subcommand.

This section shows an example configuration, again showing Router R1 from the Company1 enterprise network shown in earlier figures in this chapter. The example uses RIPng as the routing protocol. The following list outlines the four main steps to configure IPv6:

Step 1.   Enable IPv6 routing with the **ipv6 unicast-routing** global command.

Step 2.   Enable the chosen routing protocol. For example, for RIPng, use the **ipv6 router rip** *name* global configuration command.

Step 3.   Configure an IPv6 unicast address on each interface using the **ipv6 address** *address/prefix-length* [**eui-64**] interface command.

Step 4.   Enable the routing protocol on the interface, for example, with the **ipv6 rip** *name* **enable** interface subcommand (where the name matches the **ipv6 router rip** *name* global configuration command).

Example 23-2 shows the configuration, plus a few **show** commands. Note that the IP address configuration matches the earlier Example 23-1. Because Example 23-1 showed the address configuration, this example shows gray highlights on the new configuration commands only.

Example 23-2 *Configuring IPv6 Routing and Routing Protocols on R1*

```
R1# show running-config
! output is edited to remove lines not pertinent to this example
ipv6 unicast-routing
!
interface FastEthernet0/0
 ipv6 address 2340:1111:AAAA:1::/64 eui-64
 ipv6 rip atag enable
!
interface Serial0/0/1
 ipv6 address 2340:1111:AAAA:2::1/64
 ipv6 rip atag enable
!
interface Serial0/1/1
 ipv6 address 2340:1111:AAAA:4::/64 eui-64
 ipv6 rip atag enable
!
ipv6 router rip atag
!
R1# show ipv6 route
IPv6 Routing Table - 10 entries
Codes: C - Connected, L - Local, S - Static, R - RIP, B - BGP
       U - Per-user Static route
       I1 - ISIS L1, I2 - ISIS L2, IA - ISIS interarea, IS - ISIS summary
       O - OSPF intra, OI - OSPF inter, OE1 - OSPF ext 1, OE2 - OSPF ext 2
       ON1 - OSPF NSSA ext 1, ON2 - OSPF NSSA ext 2
R   ::/0 [120/2]
     via FE80::213:19FF:FE7B:2F58, Serial0/1/1
C   2340:1111:AAAA:1::/64 [0/0]
     via ::, FastEthernet0/0
L   2340:1111:AAAA:1:213:19FF:FE7B:5004/128 [0/0]
     via ::, FastEthernet0/0
C   2340:1111:AAAA:2::/64 [0/0]
     via ::, Serial0/0/1
L   2340:1111:AAAA:2::1/128 [0/0]
     via ::, Serial0/0/1
R   2340:1111:AAAA:3::/64 [120/2]
     via FE80::213:19FF:FE7B:5026, Serial0/0/1
C   2340:1111:AAAA:4::/64 [0/0]
     via ::, Serial0/1/1
```

```
L    2340:1111:AAAA:4:213:19FF:FE7B:5004/128 [0/0]
      via ::, Serial0/1/1
L    FE80::/10 [0/0]
      via ::, Null0
L    FF00::/8 [0/0]
      via ::, Null0
R1# show ipv6 interface brief
FastEthernet0/0              [up/up]
    FE80::213:19FF:FE7B:5004
    2340:1111:AAAA:1:213:19FF:FE7B:5004
FastEthernet0/1              [up/up]
   unassigned
Serial0/0/0                  [administratively down/down]
   unassigned
Serial0/0/1                  [up/up]
   FE80::213:19FF:FE7B:5004
   2340:1111:AAAA:2::1
Serial0/1/0                  [administratively down/down]
   unassigned
Serial0/1/1                  [up/up]
   FE80::213:19FF:FE7B:5004
   2340:1111:AAAA:4:213:19FF:FE7B:5004
```

The configuration itself does not require a lot of work beyond the IPv6 address configuration shown previously in Example 23-1. The **ipv6 router rip** *name* command requires a name (formally called a tag) that is just a text name for the routing process. Example 23-2 shows the configuration, using a RIP tag named "atag." This tag does not have to match between the various routers. Otherwise, the configuration itself is straightforward.

The **show ipv6 route** command lists all the IPv6 routes, listing some important differences as highlighted in the command output. First, note the first few lines of highlighted output in that command, and the new routing code "L." For each interface with a unicast address, the router adds the usual connected route for the prefix connected to that interface. For example, the first highlighted line inside this command lists 2340:1111:AAAA:1::/64, which is the subnet connected to R1's Fa0/0 interface. The output also lists a host route—a /128 prefix length route—as a local route. Each of these local routes, as noted with the code "L," lists the specific address on each interface, respectively.

The next highlighted lines in that same **show ipv6 route** command list some interesting next-hop information in a RIP-learned route. The example highlights the route to subnet 3, listing outgoing interface S0/0/1, but the next-hop address is R2's link local IP address of FE80::213:19FF:FE7B:5026. IPv6 routing protocols typically advertise the link local addresses as next-hop addresses.

Finally, the last part of the example shows the output of the **show ipv6 interface brief** command, which lists the unicast IP addresses on each interface. The highlighted lines first show the link local address (each starts with FE8), and then the global unicast address, on

R1's Fa0/0 interface. Each of the three interfaces used in this example has both the link local address, which is automatically generated, and the global unicast addresses configured, as shown in the first part of Example 23-2.

Configuring host names and DNS servers on routers for IPv4 can be a small convenience, but for IPv6, it might well be a necessity. Because of the length of IPv6 addresses, even a simple **ping** command requires a fair amount of typing and referring to other command output or documentation. So, just as with IPv4, you might want to configure static host names on routers, or refer to a DNS server, with the following two commands. Note that the commands and syntax are the same as the commands for IPv4, just with IPv6 addresses used as parameters.

- **ipv6 host** *name ipv6-address* [*second-address* [*third-address* [*fourth-address*]]]
- **ipv6 name-server** *server-address1* [*server-address2...server-address6*]

The first command configures a host name only known to the local routers, while the second refers to a DNS server. Note that the router attempts to act as a DNS client by default, based on the default **ip domain-lookup** global configuration command. However, if the **no ip domain-lookup** command has been configured, change the command back to **ip domain-lookup** to begin using DNS services.

Although the configuration and **show** commands in Example 23-2 can be useful for learning the basics, much more is required before an internetwork can be ready for an IPv6 deployment. (*IPv6 for Enterprise Networks*, by Shannon McFarland et al., published by Cisco Press, is a great resource if you want to read more.) The next section takes a brief look at one of the larger deployment issues, namely, how to support users during a worldwide migration from IPv4 to IPv6, which might take decades.

IPv6 Transition Options

While IPv6 solves a lot of problems, an overnight migration from IPv4 to IPv6 is ridiculous. The number of devices on Earth that use IPv4 number is well into the billions, and in some cases, even if you wanted to migrate to IPv6, the devices or their software might not even have IPv6 support, or at least well-tested IPv6 support. The migration from IPv4 to IPv6 will at least take years, if not decades.

Thankfully, much time and effort have been spent thinking about the migration process and developing standards for how to approach the migration or transition issue. The following sections introduce the main options and explain the basics. In particular, these sections examine the idea of using dual stacks, tunneling, and translation between the two versions of IP. Note that no one solution is typically enough to solve all problems; in all likelihood, a combination of these tools will need to be used in most every network.

IPv4/IPv6 Dual Stacks

The term *dual stacks* means that the host or router uses both IPv4 and IPv6 at the same time. For hosts, this means that the host has both an IPv4 and IPv6 address associated with each NIC, that the host can send IPv4 packets to other IPv4 hosts, and that the host can send IPv6 packets to other IPv6 hosts. For routers, it means that in addition to the usual IPv4 IP addresses and routing protocols covered in many of the other chapters of this book, the routers would also have IPv6 addresses and routing protocols configured, as shown in this chapter. To support both IPv4 and IPv6 hosts, the router could then receive and forward both IPv4 packets and IPv6 packets.

The dual-stack approach can be a reasonable plan of attack to migrate an enterprise to IPv6 for communications inside the enterprise. The routers could be easily migrated to use dual stacks, and most desktop operating systems (OS) support IPv6 today. In some cases, the upgrade may require new software or hardware, but this approach allows a slower migration, which is not necessarily a bad thing, because the support staff needs time to learn how IPv6 works.

Tunneling

Another tool to support the IPv4-to-IPv6 transition is tunneling. Many types of tunneling exist, but in this case, the tunnel function typically takes an IPv6 packet sent by a host and encapsulates it inside an IPv4 packet. The IPv4 packet can then be forwarded over an existing IPv4 internetwork, with another device removing the IPv4 header, revealing the original IPv6 packet.

Figure 23-11 shows a typical example with a type of tunnel generically called an IPv6-to-IPv4 tunnel, meaning IPv6 inside IPv4. The figure shows a sample enterprise internetwork in which hosts on some of the LANs have migrated to IPv6, but the core of the network still runs IPv4. This might be the case during an initial testing phase inside an enterprise, or it could be commonly done with an IPv4-based ISP that has customers wanting to migrate to IPv6.

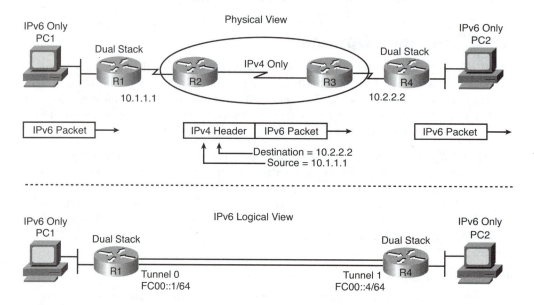

Figure 23-11 *Example IPv6-to-IPv4 Tunnel, Physical and Logical View*

In the figure, the IPv6-based PC1 sends an IPv6 packet. Router R1 then encapsulates or tunnels the IPv6 packet into a new IPv4 header, with a destination IPv4 address of an address on Router R4. Routers R2 and R3 happily forward the packet, because it has a normal IPv4 header, while R4 de-encapsulates the original IPv6 packet, forwarding it to IPv6-based PC2. It's called a tunnel in part because the IPv6 packets inside the tunnel can't be seen while traversing the tunnel; the routers in the middle of the network, R2 and R3 in this case, perceive the packets as IPv4 packets.

Several types of IPv6-to-IPv4 tunnels exist. To perform the tunneling shown by the routers in Figure 23-11, the first three of the following types of tunnels could be used, with the fourth type (Teredo tunnels) being used by hosts:

■ **Manually configured tunnels (MCT):** A simple configuration in which tunnel interfaces, a type of virtual router interface, are created, with the configuration referencing the IPv4 addresses used in the IPv4 header that encapsulates the IPv6 packet.

■ **Dynamic 6to4 tunnels:** This term refers to a specific type of dynamically created tunnel, typically done on the IPv4 Internet, in which the IPv4 addresses of the tunnel endpoints can be dynamically found based on the destination IPv6 address.

■ **Intra-site Automatic Tunnel Addressing Protocol (ISATAP):** Another dynamic tunneling method, typically used inside an enterprise. Unlike 6to4 tunnels, ISATAP tunnels do not work if IPv4 NAT is used between the tunnel endpoints.

■ **Teredo tunneling:** This method allows dual-stack hosts to create a tunnel to another host, with the host itself both creating the IPv6 packet and encapsulating the packet inside an IPv4 header.

Figure 23-12 shows the basic idea behind the Teredo tunnel.

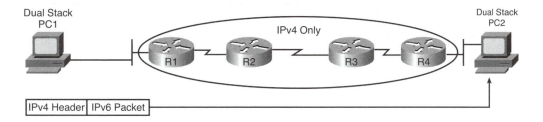

Figure 23-12   *Example Encapsulation for a Teredo Host-Host Tunnel*

Translating Between IPv4 and IPv6 with NAT-PT

Both classes of IPv6 transition features mentioned so far in this chapter, dual stack and tunnels, rely on the end hosts to at least support IPv6, if not both IPv4 and IPv6. However, in some cases, an IPv4-only host needs to communicate with an IPv6-only host. A third class of transition features needs to be used in this case: a tool that translates the headers of an IPv6 packet to look like an IPv4 packet, and vice versa.

In Cisco routers, Network Address Translation–Protocol Translation (NAT-PT), defined in RFC 2766, can be used to perform the translation. To do its work, a router configured with NAT-PT must know what IPv6 address to translate to which IPv4 address and vice versa, the same kind of information held in the traditional NAT translation table. And like traditional NAT, NAT-PT allows static definition, dynamic NAT, and dynamic PAT, which can be used to conserve IPv4 addresses.

Transition Summary

Table 23-10 summarizes the transition options for IPv6 for easier reference and study.

Table 23-10   *Summary of IPv6 Transition Options*

Key Topic

Name	Particular Type	Description
Dual stack	—	Supports both protocols, and sends IPv4 to IPv4 hosts and IPv6 to IPv6 hosts
Tunnel	MCT	Tunnel is manually configured; sends IPv6 through IPv4 network, typically between routers
Tunnel	6to4	Tunnel endpoints are dynamically discovered; sends IPv6 through IPv4 network, typically between routers
Tunnel	ISATAP	Tunnel endpoints are dynamically discovered; sends IPv6 through IPv4 network between routers; does not support IPv4 NAT
Tunnel	Teredo	Typically used by hosts; host creates IPv6 packet and encapsulates in IPv4
NAT-PT	—	Router translates between IPv4 and IPv6; allows IPv4 hosts to communicate with IPv6 hosts

Chapter Review

Review Key Topics

Review the most important topics from this chapter, noted with the Key Topic icons in the outer margin of the page. Table 23-11 lists a reference of these key topics and the page numbers on which each is found.

Table 23-11 *Key Topics for Chapter 23*

Key Topic Element	Description	Page Number
Figure 23-1	Route aggregation concepts in the global IPv6 Internet	566
List	Rules for abbreviating IPv6 addresses	567
List	Rules for writing IPv6 prefixes	569
Figure 23-3	Example prefix assignment process	571
List	Major steps in subdividing a prefix into a subnet prefix in an enterprise	572
Figure 23-5	Example and structure of IPv6 subnets	573
Figure 23-7	Structure of IPv6 addresses and EUI-64 formatted interface ID	577
Table 23-5	List of four main options to IPv6 address configuration	580
Table 23-6	Comparisons of IPv6 stateful and stateless DHCP services	581
List	Different types and purposes of IPv6 addresses	581
Figure 23-10	Format and structure of link local addresses	582
List	Summary of the steps a host takes to learn its address, prefix length, DNS, and default router	584
Table 23-8	Summary of prefixes and purpose of most common types of IPv6 addresses	585
List	Configuration checklist for IPv6 configuration	586
Table 23-10	List of IPv6 transition options	592

Define Key Terms

Define the following key terms from this chapter, and check your answers in the glossary:

global unicast address, ISP prefix, link local address, Neighbor Discovery Protocol (NDP), Regional Internet Registry (RIR), registry prefix, site prefix, stateful DHCP, stateless autoconfiguration, stateless DHCP, subnet prefix, unique local address

Review Command Reference to Check Your Memory

Although you should not necessarily memorize the information in the tables in this section, this section does include a reference for the configuration and EXEC commands covered in this chapter. Practically speaking, you should memorize the commands as a side effect of reading the chapter and doing all the activities in this "Chapter Review" section. To check to see how well you have memorized the commands as a side effect of your other studies, cover the left side of the table with a piece of paper, read the descriptions on the right side, and see whether you remember the command.

Table 23-12   *Chapter 23 Configuration Command Reference*

Command	Description
ipv6 unicast-routing	Global command that enables IPv6 routing on the router
ipv6 router rip *tag*	Global command that enables RIPng
ipv6 rip *name* **enable**	Interface subcommand that enables RIPng on the interface
ipv6 address {*ipv6-address/prefix-length* | *prefix-name sub-bits/prefix-length*} **eui-64**	Interface subcommand that manually configures either the entire interface IP address, or a /64 prefix with the router building the EUI-64 format interface ID automatically
ipv6 host *name ipv6-address1* [*ipv6-address2...ipv6-address4*]	Global command to create a static host name definition
ip name-server *server-address1* [*server-address2...server-address6*]	Global command to point to one or more name servers, to resolve a name into either an IPv4 or IPv6 address
[no] **ip domain-lookup**	Global command that enables the router as a DNS client, or with the **no** option, disables the router as a DNS client

Table 23-13   *Chapter 23 EXEC Command Reference*

Command	Description
show ipv6 route	Lists IPv6 routes
show ipv6 route *ip-address*	Lists the route(s) this router would match for packets sent to the listed address
show ipv6 route [*prefix/prefix-length*]	Lists the route for the specifically listed prefix/length
show ipv6 interface [*type number*]	Lists IPv6 settings on an interface, including link local and other unicast IP addresses
show ipv6 interface brief	Lists interface status and IPv6 addresses for each interface

Answer Review Questions

Answer the following review questions:

1. Which of the following is the most likely organization from which an enterprise could obtain an administrative assignment of a block of IPv6 global unicast IP addresses?

   a. An ISP

   b. ICANN

   c. An RIR

   d. Global unicast addresses are not administratively assigned by an outside organization.

2. Which of the following is the shortest valid abbreviation for FE80:0000:0000:0100:0000:0000:0000:0123?

   a. FE80::100::123

   b. FE8::1::123

   c. FE80::100:0:0:0:123:4567

   d. FE80:0:0:100::123

3. Which of the following answers lists a multicast IPv6 address?

   a. 2000::1:1234:5678:9ABC

   b. FD80::1:1234:5678:9ABC

   c. FE80::1:1234:5678:9ABC

   d. FF80::1:1234:5678:9ABC

4. Which of the following answers lists either a protocol or function that can be used by a host to dynamically learn its own IPv6 address?

   a. Stateful DHCP

   b. Stateless DHCP

   c. Stateless autoconfiguration

   d. Neighbor Discovery Protocol

5. Which of the following help allow an IPv6 host to learn the IP address of a default gateway on its subnet?

   a. Stateful DHCP

   b. Stateless RS

   c. Stateless autoconfiguration

   d. NDP

6. Which of the following are routing protocols that support IPv6?

   a.   RIPng

   b.   RIP-2

   c.   OSPFv2

   d.   OSPFv3

   e.   OSPFv4

7. In the following configuration, this router's Fa0/0 interface has a MAC address of 4444.4444.4444. Which of the following IPv6 addresses will the interface use?

```
ipv6 unicast-routing
ipv6 router rip tag1
interface FastEthernet0/0
ipv6 address 3456::1/64
```

   a.   3456::C444:44FF:FE44:4444

   b.   3456::4444:44FF:FE44:4444

   c.   3456::1

   d.   FE80::1

   e.   FE80::6444:44FF:FE44:4444

   f.   FE80::4444:4444:4444

8. In the configuration text in the previous question, RIP was not working on interface Fa0/0. Which of the following configuration commands would enable RIP on Fa0/0?

   a.   network 3456::/64

   b.   network 3456::/16

   c.   network 3456::1/128

   d.   ipv6 rip enable

   e.   ipv6 rip tag1 enable

9. Which of the following IPv4-to-IPv6 transition methods allows an IPv4-only host to communicate with an IPv6-only host?

   a.   Dual-stack

   b.   6to4 tunneling

   c.   ISATAP tunneling

   d.   NAT-PT

This chapter covers the following subjects:

■ **LAN Switching Concepts:** Explains the basic processes used by LAN switches to forward frames.

■ **LAN Design Considerations:** Describes the reasoning and terminology for how to design a switched LAN that operates well.

CHAPTER 24

Ethernet LAN Switch Concepts

Chapter 2, "LAN Fundamentals," provides enough of the basics about Ethernet LANs so that the discussions of routing make more sense. That chapter explains a wide variety of Ethernet concepts, including the basics of unshielded twisted-pair (UTP) cabling, the basic operation of and concepts behind hubs and switches, comparisons of different kinds of Ethernet standards, and Ethernet data link layer concepts such as addressing and framing.

This chapter begins Unit 9, "LANs," which looks at the most common Ethernet LAN features in more detail. In particular, this chapter contains a more detailed examination of how switches work, as well as the LAN design implications of using hubs, bridges, switches, and routers. Chapter 25, "Ethernet Switch Configuration," then looks specifically at Cisco LAN switches, showing the configuration of switch interfaces, switch IP addresses, and a few other features. Finally, Chapter 26, "Virtual LANs," examines virtual LANs (VLAN) in more depth, including VLAN trunking and VLAN Trunking Protocol (VTP).

LAN Switching Concepts

When thinking about how LAN switches work, it can be helpful to think about how earlier products (hubs and bridges) work. The first part of this section briefly looks at why switches were created. Following that, this section explains the three main functions of a switch, plus a few other details.

Historical Progression: Hubs, Bridges, and Switches

As mentioned in Chapter 2, Ethernet started out with standards that used a physical electrical bus created with coaxial cabling. 10BASE-T Ethernet came next. It offered improved LAN availability, because a problem on a single cable did not affect the rest of the LAN—a common problem with 10BASE2 and 10BASE5 networks. 10BASE-T allowed the use of unshielded twisted-pair (UTP) cabling, which is much cheaper than coaxial cable. Also, many buildings already had UTP cabling installed for phone service, so 10BASE-T quickly became a popular alternative to 10BASE2 and 10BASE5 Ethernet networks. For perspective and review, Figure 24-1 depicts the typical topology for 10BASE2 and for 10BASE-T with a hub.

Although using 10BASE-T with a hub improved Ethernet as compared to the older standards, several drawbacks continued to exist, even with 10BASE-T using hubs:

■ Any device sending a frame could have the frame collide with a frame sent by any other device attached to that LAN segment.

- Only one device could send a frame at a time, so the devices shared the (10-Mbps) bandwidth.

- Broadcasts sent by one device were heard by, and processed by, all other devices on the LAN.

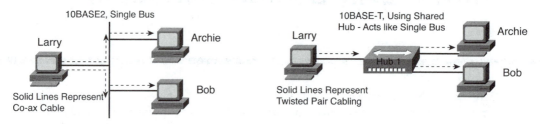

Figure 24-1   *Ethernet Bus Compared to Ethernet Hub*

When these three types of Ethernet were introduced, a shared 10 Mbps of bandwidth was a huge amount! Before the introduction of LANs, people often used dumb terminals, with a 56-kbps WAN link being a really fast connection to the rest of the network—and that 56 kbps was shared among everyone in a remote building. So, in the days when 10BASE-T was first used, getting a connection to a 10BASE-T Ethernet LAN was like getting a Gigabit Ethernet connection for your work PC today. It was more bandwidth than you thought you would ever need.

Over time, the performance of many Ethernet networks started to degrade. People developed applications to take advantage of the LAN bandwidth. More devices were added to each Ethernet. Eventually, an entire network became congested. The devices on the same Ethernet could not send (collectively) more than 10 Mbps of traffic because they all shared the 10 Mbps of bandwidth. In addition, the increase in traffic volumes increased the number of collisions. Long before the overall utilization of an Ethernet approached 10 Mbps, Ethernet began to suffer because of increasing collisions.

Ethernet bridges were created to solve some of the performance issues. Bridges solved the growing Ethernet congestion problem in two ways:

- They reduced the number of collisions that occurred in the network.

- They added bandwidth to the network.

Figure 24-2 shows the basic premise behind an Ethernet transparent bridge. The top part of the figure shows a 10BASE-T network before adding a bridge, and the lower part shows the network after it has been *segmented* using a bridge. The bridge creates two separate *collision domains*. Fred's frames can collide with Barney's, but they cannot collide with Wilma's or Betty's. If one LAN segment is busy, and the bridge needs to forward a frame onto the busy segment, the bridge simply buffers the frame (holds the frame in memory) until the segment is no longer busy. Reducing collisions, and assuming no significant change in the number of devices or the load on the network, greatly improves network performance.

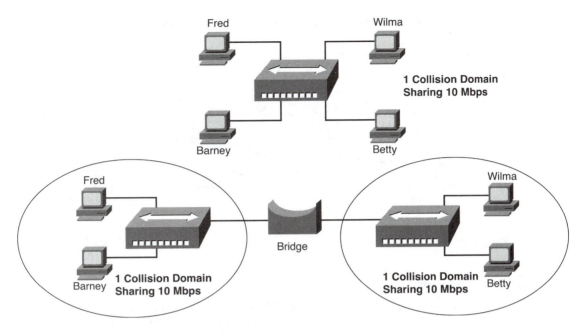

Figure 24-2   *Bridge Creates Two Collision Domains and Two Shared Ethernets*

Adding a bridge between two hubs really creates two separate 10BASE-T networks—one on the left and one on the right. The 10BASE-T network on the left has its own 10 Mbps to share, as does the network on the right. So, in this example, the total network bandwidth is doubled to 20 Mbps, as compared with the 10BASE-T network at the top of the figure.

LAN switches perform the same basic core functions as bridges, but with many enhanced features. Like bridges, switches segment a LAN into separate parts, each part being a separate collision domain. Switches have potentially large numbers of interfaces, with highly optimized hardware, allowing even small Enterprise switches to forward millions of Ethernet frames per second. By creating a separate collision domain for each interface, switches multiply the amount of available bandwidth in the network. And, as mentioned in Chapter 2, if a switch port connects to a single device, that Ethernet segment can use full-duplex logic, essentially doubling the speed on that segment.

Note: A switch's effect of segmenting an Ethernet LAN into one collision domain per interface is sometimes called *microsegmentation*.

Figure 24-3 summarizes some of these key concepts, showing the same hosts as in Figure 24-2, but now connected to a switch. In this case, all switch interfaces are running at 100 Mbps, with four collision domains. Note that each interface also uses full duplex. This is possible because only one device is connected to each port, essentially eliminating collisions for the network shown.

The next section examines how switches forward Ethernet frames.

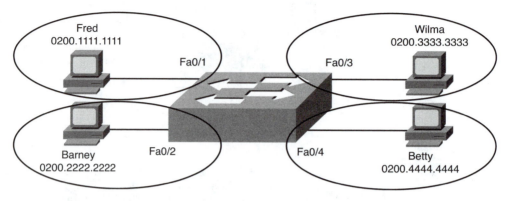

Figure 24-3 *Switch Creates Four Collision Domains and Four Ethernet Segments*

Switching Logic

Ultimately, the role of a LAN switch is to forward Ethernet frames. To achieve that goal, switches use logic—logic based on the source and destination MAC address in each frame's Ethernet header. To help you appreciate how switches work, first a review of Ethernet addresses is in order.

The IEEE defines three general categories of Ethernet MAC addresses:

■ **Unicast addresses:** MAC addresses that identify a single LAN interface card.

■ **Broadcast addresses:** A frame sent with a destination address of the broadcast address (FFFF.FFFF.FFFF) implies that all devices on the LAN should receive and process the frame.

■ **Multicast addresses:** Multicast MAC addresses are used to allow a dynamic subset of devices on a LAN to communicate.

Note: The IP protocol supports the multicasting of IP packets. When IP multicast packets are sent over an Ethernet, the multicast MAC addresses used in the Ethernet frame follow this format: 0100.5e*xx.xxxx*, where a value between 00.0000 and 7f . ffff can be used in the last half of the address. Ethernet multicast MAC addresses are not covered in this book.

The primary job of a LAN switch is to receive Ethernet frames and then make a decision: either forward the frame out some other port(s), or ignore the frame. To accomplish this primary mission, transparent bridges perform three actions:

Key Topic

1. Deciding when to forward a frame or when to filter (not forward) a frame, based on the destination MAC address.

2. Learning MAC addresses by examining the source MAC address of each frame received by the bridge.

3. Creating a (Layer 2) loop-free environment with other bridges by using Spanning Tree Protocol (STP).

The first action is the switch's primary job, whereas the other two items are overhead functions. The next sections examine each of these steps in order.

The Forward Versus Filter Decision

To decide whether to forward a frame, a switch uses a dynamically built table that lists MAC addresses and outgoing interfaces. Switches compare the frame's destination MAC address to this table to decide whether the switch should forward a frame or simply ignore it. For example, consider the simple network shown in Figure 24-4, with Fred sending a frame to Barney.

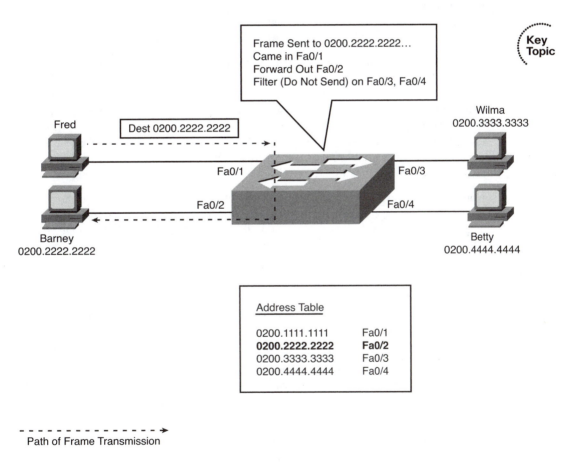

Figure 24-4 *Sample Switch Forwarding and Filtering Decision*

Figure 24-4 shows an example of both the forwarding decision and the filtering decision. Fred sends a frame with destination address 0200.2222.2222 (Barney's MAC address). The switch compares the destination MAC address (0200.2222.2222) to the MAC address table, finding the matching entry. This is the interface out which a frame should be sent to deliver it to that listed MAC address (0200.2222.2222). Because the interface in which the frame arrived (Fa0/1) is different than the listed outgoing interface (Fa0/2), the switch decides to forward the frame out interface Fa0/2, as shown in the figure's table.

> **Note:**   A switch's MAC address table is also called the switching table, or bridging table, or even the Content Addressable Memory (CAM), in reference to the type of physical memory used to store the table.

The key to anticipating where a switch should forward a frame is to examine and understand the address table. The table lists MAC addresses and the interface the switch should use when forwarding packets sent to that MAC address. For example, the table lists 0200.3333.3333 off Fa0/3, which is the interface out which the switch should forward frames sent to Wilma's MAC address (0200.3333.3333).

Figure 24-5 shows a different perspective, with the switch making a filtering decision. In this case, Fred and Barney connect to a hub, which is then connected to the switch. The switch's MAC address table lists both Fred's and Barney's MAC addresses off that single switch interface (Fa0/1), because the switch would forward frames to both Fred and Barney out its FA0/1 interface. So, when the switch receives a frame sent by Fred (source MAC address 0200.1111.1111) to Barney (destination MAC address 0200.2222.2222), the switch thinks like this: "Because the frame entered my Fa0/1 interface, and I would send it out that same Fa0/1 interface, do not send it (filter it), because sending it would be pointless."

Note that the hub simply regenerates the electrical signal out each interface, so the hub forwards the electrical signal sent by Fred to both Barney and the switch. The switch decides to filter (not forward) the frame, noting that the MAC address table's interface for 0200.2222.2222 (Fa0/1) is the same as the incoming interface.

How Switches Learn MAC Addresses

The second main function of a switch is to learn the MAC addresses and interfaces to put into its address table. With a full and accurate MAC address table, the switch can make accurate forwarding and filtering decisions.

Switches build the address table by listening to incoming frames and examining the *source MAC address* in the frame. If a frame enters the switch and the source MAC address is not in the MAC address table, the switch creates an entry in the table. The MAC address is placed in the table, along with the interface from which the frame arrived. Switch learning logic is that simple.

Figure 24-6 depicts the same network as Figure 24-4, but before the switch has built any address table entries. The figure shows the first two frames sent in this network—first a frame from Fred, addressed to Barney, and then Barney's response, addressed to Fred.

As shown in the figure, after Fred sends his first frame (labeled "1") to Barney, the switch adds an entry for 0200.1111.1111, Fred's MAC address, associated with interface Fa0/1. When Barney replies in Step 2, the switch adds a second entry, this one for 0200.2222.2222, Barney's MAC address, along with interface Fa0/2, which is the interface in which the switch received the frame. Learning always occurs by looking at the source MAC address in the frame.

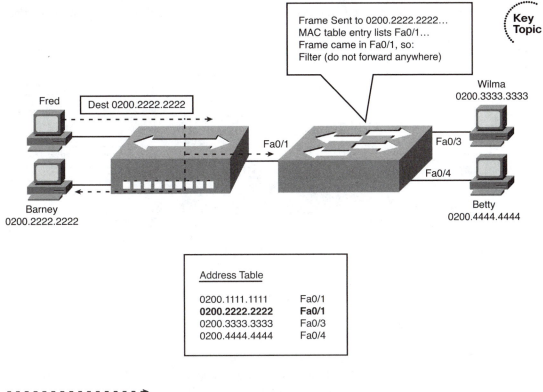

Figure 24-5 *Sample Switch Filtering Decision*

Flooding Frames

Now again turn your attention to the forwarding process, using Figure 24-6. What do you suppose the switch does with Fred's first frame in Figure 24-6, the one that occurred when there were no entries in the MAC address table? As it turns out, when there is no matching entry in the table, switches forward the frame out all interfaces (except the incoming interface). Switches forward these *unknown unicast frames* (frames whose destination MAC addresses are not yet in the bridging table) out all other interfaces, with the hope that the unknown device will be on some other Ethernet segment and will reply, allowing the switch to build a correct entry in the address table.

For example, in Figure 24-6, the switch forwards the first frame out Fa0/2, Fa0/3, and Fa0/4, even though 0200.2222.2222 (Barney) is only off Fa0/2. The switch does not forward the frame back out Fa0/1, because a switch never forwards a frame out the same interface on which it arrived. (As a side note, Figure 24-6 does not show the frame being forwarded out interfaces Fa0/3 and Fa0/4, because this figure is focused on the learning process.) When Barney replies to Fred, the switch correctly adds an entry for 0200.2222.2222 (Fa0/2) to its address table. Any later frames sent to destination address 0200.2222.2222 will no longer need to be sent out Fa0/3 and Fa0/4, only being forwarded out Fa0/2.

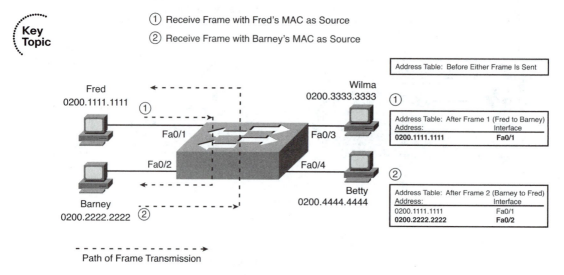

Figure 24-6 *Switch Learning: Empty Table and Adding Two Entries*

The process of sending frames out all other interfaces, except the interface on which the frame arrived, is called *flooding*. Switches flood unknown unicast frames as well as broadcast frames. Switches also flood LAN multicast frames out all ports, unless the switch has been configured to use some multicast optimization tools that are not covered in this book.

Switches keep a timer for each entry in the MAC address table, called an *inactivity timer*. The switch sets the timer to 0 for new entries. Each time the switch receives another frame with that same source MAC address, the timer is reset to 0. The timer counts upward, so the switch can tell which entries have gone the longest time since receiving a frame from that device. If the switch ever runs out of space for entries in the MAC address table, the switch can then remove table entries with the oldest (largest) inactivity timers.

Avoiding Loops Using Spanning Tree Protocol

The third primary feature of LAN switches is loop prevention, as implemented by Spanning Tree Protocol (STP). Without STP, frames would loop for an indefinite period of time in Ethernet networks with physically redundant links. To prevent looping frames, STP blocks some ports from forwarding frames so that only one active path exists between any pair of LAN segments (collision domains). The result of STP is good: frames do not loop infinitely, which makes the LAN usable. However, although the network can use some redundant links in case of a failure, the LAN does not load-balance the traffic.

To avoid Layer 2 loops, all switches need to use STP. STP causes each interface on a switch to settle into either a blocking state or a forwarding state. *Blocking* means that the interface cannot forward or receive data frames. *Forwarding* means that the interface can send and receive data frames. If a correct subset of the interfaces is blocked, a single currently active logical path exists between each pair of LANs.

Note: STP behaves identically for a transparent bridge and a switch. Therefore, the terms *bridge*, *switch*, and *bridging device* all are used interchangeably when discussing STP.

A simple example makes the need for STP more obvious. Remember, switches flood frames sent to both unknown unicast MAC addresses and broadcast addresses. Figure 24-7 shows that a single frame, sent by Larry to Bob, loops forever because the network has redundancy but no STP.

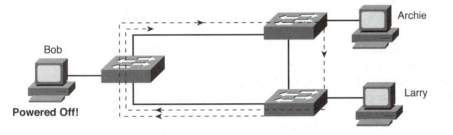

Figure 24-7 *Network with Redundant Links But Without STP: The Frame Loops Forever*

Larry sends a single unicast frame to Bob's MAC address, but Bob is powered off, so none of the switches has learned Bob's MAC address yet. Bob's MAC address would be an unknown unicast address at this point in time. Therefore, frames destined for Bob's MAC address are forwarded by each switch out every port. These frames loop indefinitely. Because the switches never learn Bob's MAC address (remember, he's powered off and can send no frames), they keep forwarding the frame out all ports, and copies of the frame go around and around.

Similarly, switches flood broadcasts as well, so if any of the PCs sent a broadcast, the broadcast would also loop indefinitely.

One way to solve this problem is to design the LAN with no redundant links. However, most network engineers purposefully design LANs to use physical redundancy between the switches. Eventually, a switch or a link will fail, and you want the network to still be available by having some redundancy in the LAN design. The right solution includes switched LANs with physical redundancy, while using STP to dynamically block some interface(s) so that only one active path exists between two endpoints at any instant in time.

Internal Processing on Cisco Switches

This chapter has already explained how switches decide whether to forward or filter a frame. As soon as a Cisco switch decides to forward a frame, the switch can use a couple of different types of internal processing variations. Almost all of the more recently released switches use store-and-forward processing, but all three types of these internal processing methods are supported in at least one type of currently available Cisco switch.

Some switches, and transparent bridges in general, use *store-and-forward processing*. With store-and-forward, the switch must receive the entire frame before forwarding the first bit of the frame. However, Cisco also offers two other internal processing methods for switches: *cut-through* and *fragment-free*. Because the destination MAC address occurs very early in the Ethernet header, a switch can make a forwarding decision long before the switch has received all the bits in the frame. The cut-through and fragment-free processing methods allow the switch to start forwarding the frame before the entire frame has been received, reducing time required to send the frame (the latency, or delay).

With *cut-through* processing, the switch starts sending the frame out the output port as soon as possible. Although this might reduce latency, it also propagates errors. Because the frame check sequence (FCS) is in the Ethernet trailer, the switch cannot determine whether the frame had any errors before starting to forward the frame. So, the switch reduces the frame's latency, but with the price of having forwarded some frames that contain errors.

Fragment-free processing works similarly to cut-through, but it tries to reduce the number of errored frames that it forwards. One interesting fact about Ethernet carrier sense multiple access with collision detection (CSMA/CD) logic is that collisions should be detected within the first 64 bytes of a frame. Fragment-free processing works like cut-through logic, but it waits to receive the first 64 bytes before forwarding a frame. The frames experience less latency than with store-and-forward logic and slightly more latency than with cut-through, but frames that have errors as a result of collisions are not forwarded.

With many links to the desktop running at 100 Mbps, uplinks at 1 Gbps, and faster application-specific integrated circuits (ASIC), today's switches typically use store-and-forward processing, because the improved latency of the other two switching methods is negligible at these speeds.

The internal processing algorithms used by switches vary among models and vendors; regardless, the internal processing can be categorized as one of the methods listed in Table 24-1.

Table 24-1   *Switch Internal Processing*

Switching Method	Description
Store-and-forward	The switch fully receives all bits in the frame (store) before forwarding the frame (forward). This allows the switch to check the FCS before forwarding the frame.
Cut-through	The switch forwards the frame as soon as it can. This reduces latency but does not allow the switch to discard frames that fail the FCS check.

Key Topic

Table 24-1 *Switch Internal Processing*

Switching Method	Description
Fragment-free	The switch forwards the frame after receiving the first 64 bytes of the frame, thereby avoiding forwarding frames that were errored due to a collision.

LAN Switching Summary

Switches provide many additional features not offered by older LAN devices such as hubs and bridges. In particular, LAN switches provide the following benefits:

■ Switch ports connected to a single device microsegment the LAN, providing dedicated bandwidth to that single device.

■ Switches allow multiple simultaneous conversations between devices on different ports.

■ Switch ports connected to a single device support full duplex, in effect doubling the amount of bandwidth available to the device.

■ Switches support rate adaptation, which means that devices that use different Ethernet speeds can communicate through the switch (hubs cannot).

Switches use Layer 2 logic, examining the Ethernet data-link header to choose how to process frames. In particular, switches make decisions to forward and filter frames, learn MAC addresses, and use STP to avoid loops, as follows:

Step 1.   Switches forward frames based on the destination address:

    a.   If the destination address is a broadcast, multicast, or unknown destination unicast (a unicast not listed in the MAC table), the switch floods the frame.

    b.   If the destination address is a known unicast address (a unicast address found in the MAC table):

       i.   If the outgoing interface listed in the MAC address table is different from the interface in which the frame was received, the switch forwards the frame out the outgoing interface.

      ii.   If the outgoing interface is the same as the interface in which the frame was received, the switch filters the frame, meaning that the switch simply ignores the frame and does not forward it.

Step 2.   Switches use the following logic to learn MAC address table entries:

    a.   For each received frame, examine the source MAC address and note the interface from which the frame was received.

    b.   If they are not already in the table, add the address and interface, setting the inactivity timer to 0.

    c.   If it is already in the table, reset the inactivity timer for the entry to 0.

Step 3.   Switches use STP to prevent loops by causing some interfaces to block, meaning that they do not send or receive frames.

LAN Design Considerations

So far, the LAN coverage in this book has mostly focused on individual functions of LANs. For example, you have read about how switches forward frames, the details of UTP cables and cable pinouts, the CSMA/CD algorithm that deals with the issue of collisions, and some of the differences between how hubs and switches operate to create either a single collision domain (hubs) or many collision domains (switches).

This section now takes a broader look at LANs—particularly, how to design medium to larger LANs. When building a small LAN, you might simply buy one switch, plug in cables to connect a few devices, and you're finished. However, when building a medium to large LAN, you have more product choices to make, such as when to use hubs, switches, and routers. Additionally, you must weigh the choice of which LAN switch to choose (switches vary in size, number of ports, performance, features, and price). The types of LAN media differ as well. Engineers must weigh the benefits of UTP cabling, like lower cost and ease of installation, versus fiber optic cabling options, which support longer distances and better physical security.

This section examines a variety of topics that all relate to LAN design in some way. In particular, this section begins by looking at the impact of the choice of using a hub, switch, or router to connect parts of LANs. Following that, some Cisco design terminology is covered. Finishing this section is a short summary of some of the more popular types of Ethernet and cabling types, and cable length guidelines for each.

Collision Domains and Broadcast Domains

When creating any Ethernet LAN, you use some form of networking devices—typically switches today—a few routers, and possibly a few hubs. The different parts of an Ethernet LAN might behave differently, in terms of function and performance, depending on which types of devices are used. These differences then affect a network engineer's decision when choosing how to design a LAN.

The terms *collision domain* and *broadcast domain* define two important effects of the process of segmenting LANs using various devices. This section examines the concepts behind Ethernet LAN design. The goal is to define these terms and to explain how hubs, switches, and routers impact collision domains and broadcast domains.

Collision Domains

As mentioned earlier, a *collision domain* is the set of LAN interfaces whose frames could collide with each other, but not with frames sent by any other devices in the network. To review the core concept, Figure 24-8 illustrates collision domains.

Note: The LAN design in Figure 24-8 is not a typical design today. Instead, it simply provides enough information to help you compare hubs, switches, and routers.

Each separate segment, or collision domain, is shown with a dashed-line circle in the figure. The switch on the right separates the LAN into different collision domains for each port. Likewise, both bridges and routers also separate LANs into different collision domains (although this effect with routers was not covered earlier in this book). Of all the devices in the figure, only the hub near the center of the network does not create multiple collision domains for each interface. It repeats all frames out all ports without any regard for buffering and waiting to send a frame onto a busy segment.

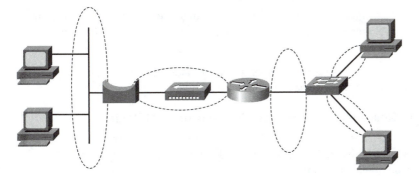

Figure 24-8 *Collision Domains*

Broadcast Domains

The term *broadcast domain* relates to where broadcasts can be forwarded. A *broadcast domain* encompasses a set of devices for which, when one of the devices sends a broadcast, all the other devices receive a copy of the broadcast. For example, switches flood broadcasts and multicasts on all ports. Because broadcast frames are sent out all ports, a switch creates a single broadcast domain.

Conversely, only routers stop the flow of broadcasts. For perspective, Figure 24-9 provides the broadcast domains for the same network depicted in Figure 24-8.

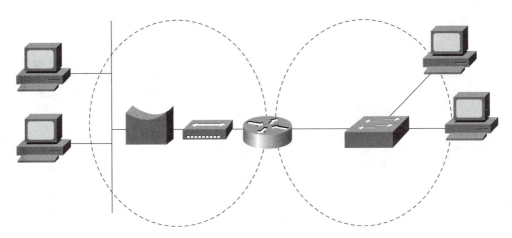

Figure 24-9 *Broadcast Domains*

Broadcasts sent by a device in one broadcast domain are not forwarded to devices in another broadcast domain. In this example, there are two broadcast domains. For instance, the router does not forward a LAN broadcast sent by a PC on the left to the network segment on the right. In the old days, the term *broadcast firewall* described the fact that routers did not forward LAN broadcasts.

General definitions for a collision domain and a broadcast domain are as follows:

- A *collision domain* is a set of network interface cards (NIC) for which a frame sent by one NIC could result in a collision with a frame sent by any other NIC in the same collision domain.

- A *broadcast domain* is a set of NICs for which a broadcast frame sent by one NIC is received by all other NICs in the same broadcast domain.

The Impact of Collision and Broadcast Domains on LAN Design

When designing a LAN, you need to keep in mind the trade-offs when choosing the number of devices in each collision domain and broadcast domain. First, consider the devices in a single collision domain for a moment. For a single collision domain:

- The devices share the available bandwidth.

- The devices might inefficiently use that bandwidth due to the effects of collisions, particularly under higher utilization.

For example, you might have ten PCs with 10/100 Ethernet NICs. If you connect all ten PCs to ten different ports on a single 100-Mbps hub, you have one collision domain, and the PCs in that collision domain share the 100 Mbps of bandwidth. That can work well and meet the needs of those users. However, with heavier traffic loads, the hub's performance would be worse than it would be if you had used a switch. Using a switch instead of a hub, with the same topology, would create ten different collision domains, each with 100 Mbps of bandwidth. Additionally, with only one device on each switch interface, no collisions would occur. This means that you could enable full duplex on each interface, effectively giving each interface 200 Mbps, and a theoretical maximum of 2 Gbps of bandwidth—a considerable improvement!

Using switches instead of hubs seems like an obvious choice given the overwhelming performance benefits. Frankly, most new installations today use switches exclusively. However, vendors still offer hubs, mainly because hubs are still slightly less expensive than switches, so you might still see hubs in networks today.

Now consider the issue of broadcasts. When a host receives a broadcast, the host must process the received frame. This means that the NIC must interrupt the computer's CPU, and the CPU must spend time thinking about the received broadcast frame. All hosts need to send some broadcasts to function properly (for example, IP ARP messages are LAN broadcasts, as mentioned in Chapter 5, "Fundamentals of IP Addressing and Routing"). So, broadcasts happen, which is good, but broadcasts do require all the hosts to spend time processing each broadcast frame.

Next, consider a large LAN, with multiple switches, with 500 PCs total. The switches create a single broadcast domain, so a broadcast sent by any of the 500 hosts should be sent to, and then processed by, all 499 other hosts. Depending on the number of broadcasts, the broadcasts could start to impact performance of the end-user PCs. However, a design that separated the 500 PCs into five groups of 100, separated from each other by a router, would create five broadcast domains. Now, a broadcast by one host would interrupt only 99 other hosts, and not the other 400 hosts, resulting in generally better performance on the PCs.

Note: Using smaller broadcast domains can also improve security, due to limiting broadcasts, and due to robust security features in routers.

The choice about when to use a hub versus a switch was straightforward, but the choice of when to use a router to break up a large broadcast domain is more difficult. A meaningful discussion of the trade-offs and options is beyond the scope of this book. However, you should understand the concepts behind broadcast domains—specifically, that a router breaks LANs into multiple broadcast domains, but switches and hubs do not.

Today, most LANs consist of switches and a few routers, plus the hosts that connect to the LAN. However, as a way to categorize the different behavior of hubs, switches, and routers, imagine a LAN using a bus created with a coaxial cable. If you then think about migrating that old LAN to use either hubs, switches, or routers, what design benefits will you gain? Table 24-2 lists some of the key benefits. The features in the table should be interpreted within the following context: "Which of the following benefits are gained by using a hub/switch/router between Ethernet devices?"

Table 24-2   *Benefits of Segmenting Ethernet Devices Using Hubs, Switches, and Routers*   ⫶Key Topic

Feature	Hub	Switch	Router
Greater cabling distances are allowed	Yes	Yes	Yes
Creates multiple collision domains	No	Yes	Yes
Increases bandwidth	No	Yes	Yes
Creates multiple broadcast domains	No	No	Yes

Virtual LANs (VLAN)

Almost every Enterprise network today uses the concept of virtual LANs (VLAN). Before understanding VLANs, you must have a very specific understanding of the definition of a LAN. Although you can think about and define the term "LAN" from many perspectives, one perspective in particular will help you understand VLANs:

A LAN consists of all devices in the same broadcast domain.

Without VLANs, a switch considers all interfaces on the switch to be in the same broadcast domain. In other words, all connected devices are in the same LAN. (Cisco switches accomplish this by putting all interfaces in VLAN 1 by default.) With VLANs, a switch can put some interfaces into one broadcast domain and some into another based on some simple configuration. Essentially, the switch creates multiple broadcast domains by putting some interfaces into one VLAN and other interfaces into other VLANs. These individual broadcast domains created by the switch are called virtual LANs.

So, instead of all ports on a switch forming a single broadcast domain, the switch separates them into many, based on configuration. It's really that simple.

The next two figures compare two LANs for the purpose of explaining a little more about VLANs. First, before VLANs existed, if a design specified two separate broadcast domains, two switches would be used—one for each broadcast domain, as shown in Figure 24-10.

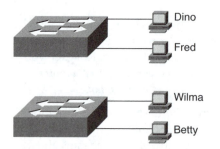

Figure 24-10   *Sample Network with Two Broadcast Domains and No VLANs*

Alternatively, you can create multiple broadcast domains using a single switch. Figure 24-11 shows the same two broadcast domains as in Figure 24-10, now implemented as two different VLANs on a single switch.

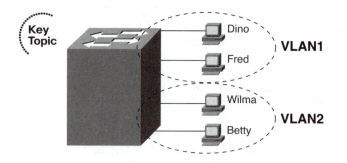

Figure 24-11   *Sample Network with Two VLANs Using One Switch*

In a network as small as the one shown in Figure 24-11, you might not really need to use VLANs. However, there are many motivations for using VLANs, including the following:

■   To create more flexible designs that group users by department, or by groups that work together, instead of by physical location

■   To segment devices into smaller LANs (broadcast domains) to reduce overhead caused to each host in the VLAN

■   To reduce the workload for STP by limiting a VLAN to a single access switch

- To enforce better security by keeping hosts that work with sensitive data on a separate VLAN

- To separate traffic sent by an IP phone from traffic sent by PCs connected to the phones

Chapter 26 explains VLAN configuration along with several related concepts.

Campus LAN Design Terminology

The term *campus LAN* refers to the LAN created to support larger buildings, or multiple buildings in somewhat close proximity to one another. For instance, a company might lease office space in several buildings in the same office park. The network engineers can then build a campus LAN that includes switches in each building, plus Ethernet links between the switches in the buildings, to create a larger campus LAN.

When planning and designing a campus LAN, the engineers must consider the types of Ethernet available and the cabling lengths supported by each type. The engineers also need to choose the speeds required for each Ethernet segment. Additionally, some thought needs to be given to the idea that some switches should be used to connect directly to end-user devices, whereas other switches might need to simply connect to a large number of these end-user switches. Finally, most projects require that the engineer consider the type of equipment that is already installed and whether an increase in speed on some segments is worth the cost of buying new equipment.

For example, the vast majority of PCs that are already installed in networks today have 10/100 NICs, with many new PCs today having 10/100/1000 NICs built into the PC. Assuming that the appropriate cabling has been installed, a 10/100/1000 NIC can use autonegotiation to use either 10BASE-T (10 Mbps), 100BASE-TX (100 Mbps), or 1000BASE-T (1000 Mbps, or 1 Gbps) Ethernet, each using the same UTP cable. However, one trade-off the engineer must make is whether to buy switches that support only 10/100 interfaces or that support 10/100/1000 interfaces. The price difference per port for switches with 10/100 ports versus switches with 10/100/1000 ports, might still be enough to make you think about whether the extra expense is worth the money. However, spending the money on switches that include 10/100/1000 interfaces allows you to connect pretty much any end-user device. You'll also be ready to migrate from 100 Mbps to the desktop device to 1000 Mbps (gigabit) as new PCs are bought.

To sift through all the requirements for a campus LAN, and then have a reasonable conversation about it with peers, most Cisco-oriented LAN designs use some common terminology to refer to the design. For this book's purposes, you should be aware of some of the key campus LAN design terminology. Figure 24-12 shows a typical design of a large campus LAN, with the terminology included in the figure. Explanations of the terminology follow the figure.

Cisco uses three terms to describe the role of each switch in a campus design: *access*, *distribution*, and *core*. The roles differ mainly in two main concepts:

- Whether the switch should connect to end-user devices

- Whether the switch should forward frames between other switches by connecting to multiple different switches

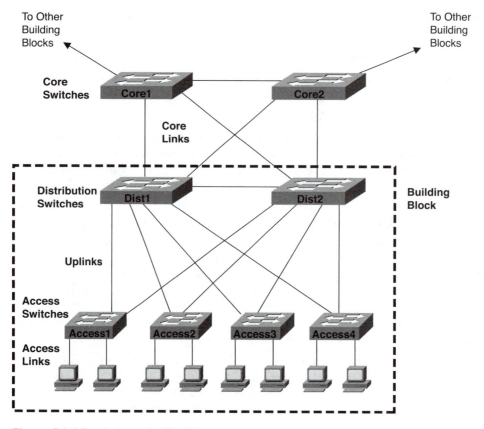

Figure 24-12   *Campus LAN with Design Terminology Listed*

Access switches connect directly to end users, providing access to the LAN. Under normal circumstances, access switches normally send traffic to and from the end-user devices to which they are connected. However, access switches should not, at least by design, be expected to forward traffic between two other switches. For example, in Figure 24-12, switch Access1 normally would not forward traffic going from PCs connected to switch Access3 to a PC off switch Access4. Because access layer switches support only the traffic for the locally attached PCs, access switches tend to be smaller and less expensive, often supporting just enough ports to support a particular floor of a building.

In larger campus LANs, distribution switches provide a path through which the access switches can forward traffic to each other. By design, each of the access switches connects to at least one distribution switch. However, designs use at least two uplinks to two different distribution switches (as shown in Figure 24-12) for redundancy.

Using distribution switches provides some cabling advantages and potential performance advantages. For example, if a network had 30 access layer switches, and the network engineer decided that each access layer switch should be cabled directly to every other access layer switch, the LAN would need 435 cables between switches! Furthermore, that design includes only one segment between each pair of switches. A possibly worse side effect is that if a link fails, the access layer switches might forward traffic to and from other switches, stressing the performance of the access switch, which typically is a less expensive but less powerful switch. Instead, by connecting each of the 30 access switches to two different distribution switches, only 60 cables are required. Well-chosen distribution switches, with faster forwarding rates, can handle the larger amount of traffic between switches. Additionally, the design with two distribution switches, with two uplinks from each access switch to the distribution switches, actually has more redundancy and therefore better availability.

Core switches provide even more aggregation benefits than do the distribution switches. Core switches provide extremely high forwarding rates—these days into the hundreds of millions of frames per second. The reasons for core switches are generally the same as for distribution switches. However, medium to smaller campus LANs often forego the concept of core switches.

The following list summarizes the terms that describe the roles of campus switches:

- **Access:** Provides a connection point (access) for end-user devices. Does not forward frames between two other access switches under normal circumstances.

- **Distribution:** Provides an aggregation point for access switches, forwarding frames between switches, but not connecting directly to end-user devices.

- **Core:** Aggregates distribution switches in very large campus LANs, providing very high forwarding rates.

Ethernet LAN Media and Cable Lengths

When designing a campus LAN, an engineer must consider the length of each cable run and then find the best type of Ethernet and cabling type that supports that length of cable. For example, if a company leases space in five buildings in the same office park, the engineer needs to figure out how long the cables between the buildings need to be and then pick the right type of Ethernet.

The three most common types of Ethernet today (10BASE-T, 100BASE-TX, and 1000BASE-T) have the same 100-meter cable restriction, but they use slightly different cables. The EIA/TIA defines Ethernet cabling standards, including the cable's quality. Each Ethernet standard that uses UTP cabling lists a cabling quality category as the minimum category that the standard supports. For example, 10BASE-T allows for Category 3 (CAT3) cabling or better, whereas 100BASE-TX calls for higher-quality CAT5 cabling, and 1000BASE-TX requires even higher-quality CAT5e or CAT6 cabling. If an engineer plans on using existing cabling, he or she must be aware of the types of UTP cables and the speed restrictions implied by the type of Ethernet the cabling supports.

Several types of Ethernet define the use of fiber-optic cables. UTP cables include copper wires over which electrical currents can flow, whereas optical cables include ultra-thin strands of glass through which light can pass. To send bits, the switches can alternate between sending brighter and dimmer light to encode 0s and 1s on the cable.

Optical cables support a variety of much longer distances than the 100 meters supported by Ethernet on UTP cables. Optical cables experience much less interference from outside sources as compared to copper cables. Additionally, switches can use lasers to generate the light, as well as light-emitting diodes (LED). Lasers allow for even longer cabling distances, up to 100 km today, at higher cost, whereas less-expensive LEDs can support plenty of distance for campus LANs in most office parks.

Finally, the type of optical cabling can also impact the maximum distances per cable. Of the two types, multimode fiber supports shorter distances, but it is generally cheaper cabling, and it works fine with less-expensive LEDs. The other optical cabling type, single-mode fiber, supports the longest distances but is more expensive. Also note that the switch hardware to use LEDs (often with multimode fiber) is much less expensive than the switch hardware to support lasers (often with single-mode fiber).

Table 24-3 lists the more common types of Ethernet and their cable types and length limitations.

Table 24-3   *Ethernet Types, Media, and Segment Lengths (Per IEEE)*

Ethernet Type	Media	Maximum Segment Length
10BASE-T	TIA/EIA CAT3 or better, two pair	100 m (328 feet)
100BASE-TX	TIA/EIA CAT5 UTP or better, two pair	100 m (328 feet)
100BASE-FX	62.5/125-micron multimode fiber	400 m (1312.3 feet)
1000BASE-CX	STP	25 m (82 feet)
1000BASE-T	TIA/EIA CAT5e UTP or better, four pair	100 m (328 feet)
1000BASE-SX	Multimode fiber	275 m (853 feet) for 62.5-micron fiber 550 m (1804.5 feet) for 50-micron fiber
1000BASE-LX	Multimode fiber	550 m (1804.5 feet) for 50- and 62.5-micron fiber
1000BASE-LX	9-micron single-mode fiber	5 km (3.1 miles)

Most engineers simply remember the general distance limitations and then use a reference chart (such as Table 24-3) to remember each specific detail. An engineer must also consider the physical paths that the cables will use to run through a campus or building and the impact on the required cable length. For example, a cable might have to run from one end of the building to the other, and then through a conduit that connects the floors of the building, and then horizontally to a wiring closet on another floor. Often those paths are not the shortest way to get from one place to the other. So the chart's details are important to the LAN planning process and the resulting choice of LAN media.

Chapter Review

Review Key Topics

Review the most important topics from this chapter, noted with the Key Topic icons. Table 24-4 lists these key topics and where each is discussed.

Table 24-4 *Key Topics for Chapter 24*

Key Topic Element	Description	Page Number
List	LAN switch actions	602
Figure 24-4	Example of switch forwarding logic	603
Figure 24-5	Example of switch filtering logic	605
Figure 24-6	Example of how a switch learns MAC addresses	606
Table 24-1	Summary of three switch internal forwarding options	608
List	Some of the benefits of switching	609
List	Summary of logic used to forward and filter frames and to learn MAC addresses	609
List	Definitions of collision domain and broadcast domain	612
Table 24-2	Four LAN design feature comparisons with hubs, switches, and routers	613
Figure 24-11	Illustration of the concept of a VLAN	614

Define Key Terms

Define the following key terms from this chapter, and check your answers in the glossary:

broadcast domain, broadcast frame, collision domain, cut-through switching, flooding, fragment-free switching, microsegmentation, segmentation, Spanning Tree Protocol (STP), store-and-forward switching, unknown unicast frame, virtual LAN

Answer Review Questions

Answer the following review questions:

1. Which of the following statements describes part of the process of how a switch decides to forward a frame destined for a known unicast MAC address?

   a. It compares the unicast destination address to the bridging, or MAC address, table.

   b. It compares the unicast source address to the bridging, or MAC address, table.

   c. It forwards the frame out all interfaces in the same VLAN except for the incoming interface.

   d. It compares the destination IP address to the destination MAC address.

   e. It compares the frame's incoming interface to the source MAC entry in the MAC address table.

2. Which of the following statements describes part of the process of how a LAN switch decides to forward a frame destined for a broadcast MAC address?

   a. It compares the unicast destination address to the bridging, or MAC address, table.

   b. It compares the unicast source address to the bridging, or MAC address, table.

   c. It forwards the frame out all interfaces in the same VLAN except for the incoming interface.

   d. It compares the destination IP address to the destination MAC address.

   e. It compares the frame's incoming interface to the source MAC entry in the MAC address table.

3. Which of the following statements best describes what a switch does with a frame destined for an unknown unicast address?

   a. It forwards out all interfaces in the same VLAN except for the incoming interface.

   b. It forwards the frame out the one interface identified by the matching entry in the MAC address table.

   c. It compares the destination IP address to the destination MAC address.

   d. It compares the frame's incoming interface to the source MAC entry in the MAC address table.

4. Which of the following comparisons does a switch make when deciding whether a new MAC address should be added to its bridging table?

   a. It compares the unicast destination address to the bridging, or MAC address, table.

   b. It compares the unicast source address to the bridging, or MAC address, table.

   c. It compares the VLAN ID to the bridging, or MAC address, table.

   d. It compares the destination IP address's ARP cache entry to the bridging, or MAC address, table.

5. PC1, with MAC address 1111.1111.1111, is connected to Switch SW1's Fa0/1 interface. PC2, with MAC address 2222.2222.2222, is connected to SW1's Fa0/2 interface. PC3, with MAC address 3333.3333.3333, connects to SW1's Fa0/3 interface. The switch begins with no dynamically learned MAC addresses, followed by PC1 sending a frame with a destination address of 2222.2222.2222. If the next frame to reach the switch is a frame sent by PC3, destined for PC2's MAC address of 2222.2222.2222, which of the following are true?

   a.   The switch forwards the frame out interface Fa0/1.

   b.   The switch forwards the frame out interface Fa0/2.

   c.   The switch forwards the frame out interface Fa0/3.

   d.   The switch discards (filters) the frame.

6. Which of the following devices would be in the same collision domain as PC1?

   a.   PC2, which is separated from PC1 by an Ethernet hub

   b.   PC3, which is separated from PC1 by a transparent bridge

   c.   PC4, which is separated from PC1 by an Ethernet switch

   d.   PC5, which is separated from PC1 by a router

7. Which of the following devices would be in the same broadcast domain as PC1?

   a.   PC2, which is separated from PC1 by an Ethernet hub

   b.   PC3, which is separated from PC1 by a transparent bridge

   c.   PC4, which is separated from PC1 by an Ethernet switch

   d.   PC5, which is separated from PC1 by a router

8. Which of the following Ethernet standards support a maximum cable length of longer than 100 meters?

   a.   100BASE-TX

   b.   1000BASE-LX

   c.   1000BASE-T

   d.   100BASE-FX

This chapter covers the following subjects:

- **Comparing Cisco Router and Switch Configuration:** This section briefly reviews the configuration details in common between Cisco routers and switches.

- **LAN Switch Configuration and Operation:** This section explains how to configure a variety of switch features that happen to be unique to switches and are not used on routers, or are configured differently than the configuration on Cisco routers.

CHAPTER 25

Ethernet Switch Configuration

Many Cisco Catalyst switches use the same Cisco IOS Software command-line interface (CLI) as Cisco routers. In addition to having the same look and feel, the switches and routers sometimes support the same configuration and **show** commands. Additionally, some of the same commands and processes shown for Cisco routers work the same way for Cisco switches.

This short chapter explains a small set of configurable items on Cisco switches. The chapter begins with a review of the features in common between Cisco routers and switches, at least from the perspective of configuration. The last part of the chapter examines several configuration topics specific to Cisco switches.

Comparing Cisco Router and Switch Configuration

Cisco switches use the same switch IOS CLI for routers as described in Chapter 7, "Operating Cisco Routers." However, because routers and switches perform different functions, the actual commands differ in some cases. This section begins by listing some of the key features that work exactly the same on both switches and routers, and then lists and describes in detail some of the key features that differ between switches and routers.

The following list details the many items covered in Chapter 7 for which the router CLI behaves the same. If these details are not fresh in your memory, it might be worthwhile to spend a few minutes briefly reviewing Chapter 7. The configuration commands used for the following features are the same on both routers and switches:

- User and Enable (privileged) mode
- Entering and exiting configuration mode, using the **configure terminal**, **end**, and **exit** commands, and the Ctrl-Z key sequence

  Key Topic
- Configuration of console, Telnet, and enable secret passwords
- Configuration of SSH encryption keys and username/password login credentials
- Configuration of the host name and interface description
- Configuration of Ethernet interfaces that can negotiate speed, using the **speed** and **duplex** commands
- Configuring an interface to be administratively disabled (**shutdown**) and administratively enabled (**no shutdown**)

- Navigation through different configuration mode contexts using commands like **line console 0** and **interface**

- CLI help, command editing, and command recall features

- The meaning and use of the startup-config (in NVRAM), running-config (in RAM), and external servers (like TFTP), along with how to use the **copy** command to copy the configuration files and IOS images

- The process of reaching setup mode either by reloading the router with an empty startup-config or by using the **setup** command

At first glance, this list seems to cover most everything covered in Chapter 7—and it does cover most of the details. However, a couple of topics covered in Chapter 7 do work differently with the switch CLI as compared to the switch CLI, namely:

> **Key Topic**

- The configuration of IP addresses differs in some ways.

- Switches do not have an auxiliary (Aux) port, intended to be connected to an external modem and phone line.

Beyond these three items from Chapter 7, the switch CLI does differ from a router CLI just because switches and routers do different things. For instance, a switch forwards Ethernet frames based on the MAC address table; to display this table, switches support the **show mac address-table dynamic** command. Routers do not support this command. However, routers forward IP packets based on their IP routing tables, so routers (but not switches) support the **show ip route** command.

LAN Switch Configuration and Operation

One of the most convenient facts about LAN switch configuration is that Cisco switches work without any configuration. Cisco switches ship from the factory with all interfaces enabled (a default configuration of **no shutdown**) and with autonegotiation enabled for ports that run at multiple speeds and duplex settings (a default configuration of **duplex auto** and **speed auto**). All you have to do is connect the Ethernet cables and plug in the power cord to a power outlet, and the switch is ready to work—learning MAC addresses, making forwarding/filtering decisions, and even using STP by default.

The second half of this chapter continues the coverage of switch configuration, mainly covering features that apply only to switches and not routers. In particular, this section covers the following:

- Switch IP configuration

- Interface configuration (including speed and duplex)

- Port security

- VLAN configuration

- Securing unused switch interfaces

Configuring the Switch IP Address

To allow Telnet or SSH access to the switch, to allow other IP-based management protocols such as Simple Network Management Protocol (SNMP) to function as intended, or to
allow access to the switch using graphical tools such as Cisco Device Manager (CDM), the
switch needs an IP address. Switches do not need an IP address to be able to forward Ethernet frames. The need for an IP address is simply to support overhead management traffic, such as logging into the switch.

A switch's IP configuration essentially works like a host with a single Ethernet interface.
The switch needs one IP address and a matching subnet mask. The switch also needs to
know its default gateway—in other words, the IP address of some nearby router. As with
hosts, you can statically configure a switch with its IP address/mask/gateway, or the
switch can dynamically learn this information using DHCP.

An IOS-based switch configures its IP address and mask on a special virtual interface
called the *VLAN 1 interface*. This interface plays the same role as an Ethernet interface on
a PC. In effect, a switch's VLAN 1 interface gives the switch an interface into the default
VLAN used on all ports of the switch—namely, VLAN 1. The following steps list the
commands used to configure IP on a switch:

Step 1. Enter VLAN 1 configuration mode using the **interface vlan 1** global configuration command (from any config mode).

Step 2. Assign an IP address and mask using the **ip address** *ip-address mask* interface
subcommand.

Step 3. Enable the VLAN 1 interface using the **no shutdown** interface subcommand.

Step 4. Add the **ip default-gateway** *ip-address* global command to configure the default gateway.

> **Key Topic**

Example 25-1 shows a sample configuration.

Example 25-1 *Switch Static IP Address Configuration*

```
Emma# configure terminal
Emma(config)# interface vlan 1
Emma(config-if)# ip address 192.168.1.200 255.255.255.0
Emma(config-if)# no shutdown
00:25:07: %LINK-3-UPDOWN: Interface Vlan1, changed state to up
00:25:08: %LINEPROTO-5-UPDOWN: Line protocol on Interface Vlan1, changed
  state to up
Emma(config-if)# exit
Emma(config)# ip default-gateway 192.168.1.1
```

Of particular note, this example shows how to enable any interface, VLAN interfaces included. To administratively enable an interface on a switch or router, you use the **no shutdown** interface subcommand. To administratively disable an interface, you would use the
shutdown interface subcommand. The messages shown in Example 25-1, immediately

following the **no shutdown** command, are syslog messages generated by the switch stating that the switch did indeed enable the interface.

To verify the configuration, you can again use the **show running-config** command to view the configuration commands and confirm that you entered the right address, mask, and default gateway.

For the switch to act as a DHCP client to discover its IP address, mask, and default gateway, you still need to configure it. You use the same steps as for static configuration, with the following differences in Steps 2 and 4:

Step 2:   Use the **ip address dhcp** command, instead of the **ip address** *ip-address mask* command, on the VLAN 1 interface.

Step 4:   Do not configure the **ip default-gateway** global command.

Example 25-2 shows an example of configuring a switch to use DHCP to acquire an IP address.

Example 25-2   *Switch Dynamic IP Address Configuration with DHCP*

```
Emma# configure terminal
Enter configuration commands, one per line.  End with CNTL/Z.
Emma(config)# interface vlan 1
Emma(config-if)# ip address dhcp
Emma(config-if)# no shutdown
Emma(config-if)# ^Z
Emma#
00:38:20: %LINK-3-UPDOWN: Interface Vlan1, changed state to up
00:38:21: %LINEPROTO-5-UPDOWN: Line protocol on Interface Vlan1, changed state to up
Emma#
Interface Vlan1 assigned DHCP address 192.168.1.101, mask 255.255.255.0
Emma# show dhcp lease
Temp IP addr: 192.168.1.101  for peer on Interface: Vlan1
Temp  sub net mask: 255.255.255.0
   DHCP Lease server: 192.168.1.1, state: 3 Bound
   DHCP transaction id: 1966
   Lease: 86400 secs,  Renewal: 43200 secs,  Rebind: 75600 secs
Temp default-gateway addr: 192.168.1.1
   Next timer fires after: 11:59:45
   Retry count: 0    Client-ID: cisco-0019.e86a.6fc0-Vl1
   Hostname: Emma
Emma# show interface vlan 1
Vlan1 is up, line protocol is up
   Hardware is EtherSVI, address is 0019.e86a.6fc0 (bia 0019.e86a.6fc0)
   Internet address is 192.168.1.101/24
   MTU 1500 bytes, BW 1000000 Kbit, DLY 10 usec,
      reliability 255/255, txload 1/255, rxload 1/255
! lines omitted for brevity
```

When configuring a static interface IP address, you can use the **show running-config** command to see the IP address. However, when using the DHCP client, the IP address is not in the configuration, so you need to use the **show dhcp lease** command to see the (temporarily) leased IP address and other parameters.

Note: Some older models of Cisco IOS switches might not support the DHCP client function on the VLAN 1 interface. Example 25-2 was taken from a 2960 switch running Cisco IOS Software Release 12.2.

Finally, the output of the **show interface vlan 1** command, shown at the end of Example 25-2, lists two very important details related to switch IP addressing. First, this **show** command lists the interface status of the VLAN 1 interface—in this case, "up and up." If the VLAN 1 interface is not up, the switch cannot use its IP address to send and receive traffic. Notably, if you forget to issue the **no shutdown** command, the VLAN 1 interface remains in its default shutdown state and is listed as "administratively down" in the **show** command output. Second, note that the output lists the interface's IP address on the third line of the output. If the switch fails to acquire an IP address with DHCP, the output would instead list the fact that the address will (hopefully) be acquired by DHCP. As soon as an address has been leased using DHCP, the output of the command looks like Example 25-2. However, nothing in the **show interface vlan 1** command output mentions that the address is either statically configured or DHCP-leased.

Configuring Switch Interfaces

IOS uses the term *interface* to refer to physical ports used to forward data to and from other devices. Each interface can be configured with several settings, each of which might differ from interface to interface.

IOS uses interface subcommands to configure these settings. For instance, interfaces can be configured to use the **duplex** and **speed** interface subcommands to configure those settings statically, or an interface can use autonegotiation (the default). Example 25-3 shows how to configure duplex and speed, as well as the **description** command, which is simply a text description of what an interface does.

Example 25-3 *Interface Configuration Basics*

```
Emma# configure terminal
Enter configuration commands, one per line.  End with CNTL/Z.
Emma(config)# interface FastEthernet 0/1
Emma(config-if)# duplex full
Emma(config-if)# speed 100
Emma(config-if)# description Server1 connects here
Emma(config-if)# exit
Emma(config)# interface range FastEthernet 0/11 - 20
Emma(config-if-range)# description end-users connect_here
Emma(config-if-range)# ^Z
Emma#
```

```
Emma# show interfaces status

Port     Name               Status       Vlan   Duplex  Speed  Type
Fa0/1    Server1 connects h notconnect   1      full    100    10/100BaseTX
Fa0/2                       notconnect   1      auto    auto   10/100BaseTX
Fa0/3                       notconnect   1      auto    auto   10/100BaseTX
Fa0/4                       connected    1      a-full  a-100  10/100BaseTX
Fa0/5                       notconnect   1      auto    auto   10/100BaseTX
Fa0/6                       connected    1      a-full  a-100  10/100BaseTX
Fa0/7                       notconnect   1      auto    auto   10/100BaseTX
Fa0/8                       notconnect   1      auto    auto   10/100BaseTX
Fa0/9                       notconnect   1      auto    auto   10/100BaseTX
Fa0/10                      notconnect   1      auto    auto   10/100BaseTX
Fa0/11   end-users connect  notconnect   1      auto    auto   10/100BaseTX
Fa0/12   end-users connect  notconnect   1      auto    auto   10/100BaseTX
Fa0/13   end-users connect  notconnect   1      auto    auto   10/100BaseTX
Fa0/14   end-users connect  notconnect   1      auto    auto   10/100BaseTX
Fa0/15   end-users connect  notconnect   1      auto    auto   10/100BaseTX
Fa0/16   end-users connect  notconnect   1      auto    auto   10/100BaseTX
Fa0/17   end-users connect  notconnect   1      auto    auto   10/100BaseTX
Fa0/18   end-users connect  notconnect   1      auto    auto   10/100BaseTX
Fa0/19   end-users connect  notconnect   1      auto    auto   10/100BaseTX
Fa0/20   end-users connect  notconnect   1      auto    auto   10/100BaseTX
Fa0/21                      notconnect   1      auto    auto   10/100BaseTX
Fa0/22                      notconnect   1      auto    auto   10/100BaseTX
Fa0/23                      notconnect   1      auto    auto   10/100BaseTX
Fa0/24                      notconnect   1      auto    auto   10/100BaseTX
Gi0/1                       notconnect   1      auto    auto   10/100/1000BaseTX
Gi0/2                       notconnect   1      auto    auto   10/100/1000BaseTX
Emma#
```

You can see some of the details of interface configuration with both the **show running-config** command (not shown in the example) and the handy **show interfaces status** command. This command lists a single line for each interface, the first part of the interface description, and the speed and duplex settings. Note that interface FastEthernet 0/1 (abbreviated as Fa0/1 in the command output) lists a speed of 100, and duplex full, as configured earlier in the example. Compare those settings with Fa0/2, which does not have any cable connected yet, so the switch lists this interface with the default setting of auto, meaning autonegotiate. Also, compare these settings to interface Fa0/4, which is physically connected to a device and has completed the autonegotiation process. The command output lists the results of the autonegotiation—in this case, using 100 Mbps and full duplex. The **a-** in **a-full** and **a-100** refers to the fact that these values were autonegotiated.

Also, note that for the sake of efficiency, you can configure a command on a range of interfaces at the same time using the **interface range** command. In the example, the

interface range FastEthernet 0/11 - 20 command tells IOS that the next subcommand(s) apply to interfaces Fa0/11 through Fa0/20.

Port Security

If the network engineer knows what devices should be cabled and connected to particular interfaces on a switch, the engineer can use *port security* to restrict that interface so that only the expected devices can use it. This reduces exposure to some types of attacks in which the attacker connects a laptop to the wall socket that connects to a switch port that has been configured to use port security. When that inappropriate device attempts to send frames to the switch interface, the switch can issue informational messages, discard frames from that device, or even discard frames from all devices by effectively shutting down the interface.

Port security configuration involves several steps. Basically, you need to make the port an access port, which means that the port is not doing any VLAN trunking. You then need to enable port security and then configure the actual MAC addresses of the devices allowed to use that port. The following list outlines the steps, including the configuration commands used:

Step 1. Make the switch interface an access interface using the **switchport mode access** interface subcommand.

Key Topic

Step 2. Enable port security using the **switchport port-security** interface subcommand.

Step 3. (Optional) Specify the maximum number of allowed MAC addresses associated with the interface using the **switchport port-security maximum** *number* interface subcommand. (Defaults to one MAC address.)

Step 4. (Optional) Define the action to take when a frame is received from a MAC address other than the defined addresses using the **switchport port-security violation {protect | restrict | shutdown}** interface subcommand. (The default action is to shut down the port.)

Step 5a. Specify the MAC address(es) allowed to send frames into this interface using the **switchport port-security mac-address** *mac-address* command. Use the command multiple times to define more than one MAC address.

Step 5b. Alternatively, instead of Step 5a, use the "sticky learning" process to dynamically learn and configure the MAC addresses of currently connected hosts by configuring the **switchport port-security mac-address sticky** interface subcommand.

For example, in Figure 25-1, Server 1 and Server 2 are the only devices that should ever be connected to interfaces FastEthernet 0/1 and 0/2, respectively. When you configure port security on those interfaces, the switch examines the source MAC address of all frames received on those ports, allowing only frames sourced from the configured MAC addresses. Example 25-4 shows a sample port security configuration matching Figure 25-1, with interface Fa0/1 being configured with a static MAC address, and with interface Fa0/2 using sticky learning.

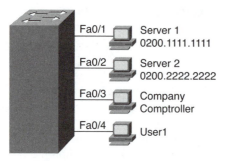

Figure 25-1   *Port Security Configuration Example*

Example 25-4   *Using Port Security to Define Correct MAC Addresses of Particular Interfaces*

```
fred# show running-config
(Lines omitted for brevity)


interface FastEthernet0/1
 switchport mode access
 switchport port-security
 switchport port-security mac-address 0200.1111.1111
!
interface FastEthernet0/2
 switchport mode access
 switchport port-security
 switchport port-security mac-address sticky


fred# show port-security interface fastEthernet 0/1
Port Security               : Enabled
Port Status                 : Secure-shutdown
Violation Mode              : Shutdown
Aging Time                  : 0 mins
Aging Type                  : Absolute
SecureStatic Address Aging  : Disabled
Maximum MAC Addresses       : 1
Total MAC Addresses         : 1
Configured MAC Addresses    : 1
Sticky MAC Addresses        : 0
Last Source Address:Vlan    : 0013.197b.5004:1
Security Violation Count    : 1
fred# show port-security interface fastEthernet 0/2
Port Security               : Enabled
Port Status                 : Secure-up
Violation Mode              : Shutdown
Aging Time                  : 0 mins
```

```
Aging Type                  : Absolute
SecureStatic Address Aging : Disabled
Maximum MAC Addresses       : 1
Total MAC Addresses         : 1
Configured MAC Addresses    : 1
Sticky MAC Addresses        : 1
Last Source Address:Vlan    : 0200.2222.2222:1
Security Violation Count    : 0
fred#show running-config
(Lines omitted for brevity)
interface FastEthernet0/2
 switchport mode access
 switchport port-security
 switchport port-security mac-address sticky
 switchport port-security mac-address sticky 0200.2222.2222
```

For FastEthernet 0/1, Server 1's MAC address is configured with the **switchport port-security mac-address 0200.1111.1111** command. For port security to work, the 2960 must think that the interface is an access interface, so the **switchport mode access** command is required. Furthermore, the **switchport port-security** command is required to enable port security on the interface. Together, these three interface subcommands enable port security, and only MAC address 0200.1111.1111 is allowed to use the interface. This interface uses defaults for the other settings, allowing only one MAC address on the interface, and causing the switch to disable the interface if the switch receives a frame whose source MAC address is not 0200.1111.111.

Interface FastEthernet 0/2 uses a feature called *sticky secure MAC addresses*. The configuration still includes the **switchport mode access** and **switchport port-security** commands for the same reasons as on FastEthernet 0/1. However, the **switchport port-security mac-address sticky** command tells the switch to learn the MAC address from the first frame sent to the switch and then add the MAC address as a secure MAC to the running configuration. In other words, the first MAC address heard "sticks" to the configuration, so the engineer does not have to know the MAC address of the device connected to the interface ahead of time.

The **show running-config** output at the beginning of Example 25-4 shows the configuration for Fa0/2, before any sticky learning occurred. The end of the example shows the configuration after an address was sticky-learned, including the **switchport port-security mac-address sticky 0200.2222.2222** interface subcommand, which the switch added to the configuration. If you wanted to save the configuration so that only 0200.2222.2222 is used on that interface from now on, you would simply need to use the **copy running-config startup-config** command to save the configuration.

As it turns out, a security violation has occurred on FastEthernet 0/1 in Example 25-4, but no violations have occurred on FastEthernet 0/2. The **show port-security interface fastethernet 0/1** command shows that the interface is in a *secure-shutdown* state, which means that the interface has been disabled due to port security. The device connected to interface FastEthernet 0/1 did not use MAC address 0200.1111.1111, so the switch received a frame in Fa0/1 with a different source MAC, causing a violation.

The switch can be configured to use one of three actions when a violation occurs. All three configuration options cause the switch to discard the offending frame, but some of the configuration options include additional actions. The actions include the sending of syslog messages to the console and SNMP trap message to the network management station, as well as whether the switch should shut down (err-disable) the interface. The **shutdown** option actually puts the interface in an error disabled (err-disabled) state, making it unusable. An interface in err-disabled state requires that someone manually shut down the interface and then use the **no shutdown** command to recover the interface. Table 25-1 lists the options on the **switchport port-security violation** command and which actions each option sets.

Table 25-1 *Actions When Port Security Violation Occurs*

Option on the switchport port-security violation Command	Protect	Restrict	Shutdown*
Discards offending traffic	Yes	Yes	Yes
Sends log and SNMP messages	No	Yes	Yes
Disables the interface, discarding all traffic	No	No	Yes

*shutdown is the default setting.

VLAN Configuration

Cisco switch interfaces are considered to be either access interfaces or trunk interfaces. By definition, access interfaces send and receive frames only in a single VLAN, called the access VLAN. Trunking interfaces send and receive traffic in multiple VLANs. This section introduces how to configure access VLANs, whereas Chapter 26, "Virtual LANs," explains several details beyond this basic configuration.

For a Cisco switch to forward frames on access interfaces in a particular VLAN, the switch must be configured to believe that the VLAN exists. Additionally, the switch must have one or more access interfaces assigned to the VLAN. By default, Cisco switches already have VLAN 1 configured, and all interfaces default to be assigned to VLAN 1. However, to add another VLAN, and assign access interfaces to be in that VLAN, you can follow these steps:

Step 1. To configure a new VLAN:

a. From configuration mode, use the **vlan** *vlan-id* global configuration command to create the VLAN and move the user into VLAN configuration mode.

b. (Optional) Use the **name** *name* VLAN subcommand to list a name for the VLAN. If not configured, the VLAN name is VLANZZZZ, where *ZZZZ* is the four-digit decimal VLAN ID.

Step 2. To configure a VLAN for each access interface:

    a. Use the **interface** command to move into interface configuration mode for each desired interface.

    b. Use the **switchport access vlan** *id-number* interface subcommand to specify the VLAN number associated with that interface.

    c. (Optional) To disable trunking so that the switch will not dynamically decide to use trunking on the interface, and it will remain an access interface, use the **switchport mode access** interface subcommand.

Example 25-5 shows the configuration process to add a new VLAN and assign access interfaces to it. Figure 25-2 shows the network used in the example, with one LAN switch (SW1) and two hosts in each of two VLANs (1 and 2). Example 25-5 shows the details of the two-step configuration process for VLAN 2 and the two access interfaces assigned to VLAN 2.

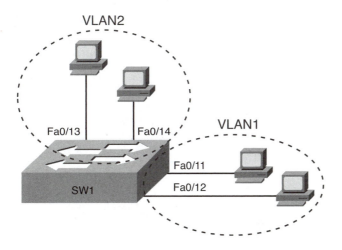

Figure 25-2 *Network with One Switch and Two VLANs*

Example 25-5 *Configuring VLANs and Assigning Them to Interfaces*

```
! to begin, 5 VLANs exist, with all interfaces assigned to VLAN 1 (default setting)
SW1# show vlan brief
VLAN Name                             Status    Ports
---- -------------------------------- --------- -------------------------------
1    default                          active    Fa0/1, Fa0/2, Fa0/3, Fa0/4
                                                Fa0/5, Fa0/6, Fa0/7, Fa0/8
                                                Fa0/9, Fa0/10, Fa0/11, Fa0/12
                                                Fa0/13, Fa0/14, Fa0/15, Fa0/16
                                                Fa0/17, Fa0/18, Fa0/19, Fa0/20
                                                Fa0/21, Fa0/22, Fa0/23, Fa0/24
                                                Gi0/1, Gi0/2
1002 fddi-default                     act/unsup
1003 token-ring-default               act/unsup
1004 fddinet-default                  act/unsup
```

```
1005 trnet-default                   act/unsup
! Above, VLAN 2 did not yet exist. Below, VLAN 2 is added, with name Freds-vlan,
! with two interfaces assigned to VLAN 2.
SW1# configure terminal
Enter configuration commands, one per line.  End with CNTL/Z.
SW1(config)# vlan 2
SW1(config-vlan)# name Freds-vlan
SW1(config-vlan)# exit
SW1(config)# interface range fastethernet 0/13 - 14
SW1(config-if)# switchport access vlan 2
SW1(config-if)# exit
! Below, the show running-config command lists the interface subcommands on
! interfaces Fa0/13 and Fa0/14. The vlan 2 and name Freds-vlan commands do
! not show up in the running-config.
SW1# show running-config
! lines omitted for brevity
interface FastEthernet0/13
 switchport access vlan 2
 switchport mode access
!
interface FastEthernet0/14
 switchport access vlan 2
 switchport mode access
!
SW1# show vlan brief

VLAN Name                             Status    Ports
---- -------------------------- ---------- ----------------------------
1    default                        active    Fa0/1, Fa0/2, Fa0/3, Fa0/4
                                              Fa0/5, Fa0/6, Fa0/7, Fa0/8
                                              Fa0/9, Fa0/10, Fa0/11, Fa0/12
                                              Fa0/15, Fa0/16, Fa0/17, Fa0/18
                                              Fa0/19, Fa0/20, Fa0/21, Fa0/22
                                              Fa0/23, Fa0/24, Gi0/1, Gi0/2
2    Freds-vlan                     active    Fa0/13, Fa0/14
1002 fddi-default                   act/unsup
1003 token-ring-default             act/unsup
1004 fddinet-default                act/unsup
1005 trnet-default                  act/unsup
```

The example begins with the **show vlan brief** command confirming the default settings of five nondeletable VLANs (VLANs 1 and 1002–1005), with all interfaces assigned to VLAN 1. In particular, note that this 2960 switch has 24 Fast Ethernet ports (Fa0/1–Fa0/24) and two Gigabit Ethernet ports (Gi0/1 and Gi0/2), all of which are listed as being assigned to VLAN 1.

Following the first **show vlan brief** command, the example shows the entire configuration process. The configuration shows the creation of VLAN 2, named "Freds-vlan," and the assignment of interfaces Fa0/13 and Fa0/14 to VLAN 2. Note in particular that the example uses the **interface range** command, which causes the **switchport access vlan 2** interface subcommand to be applied to both interfaces in the range, as confirmed in the **show running-config** command output at the end of the example.

After the configuration has been added, to list the new VLAN, the example repeats the **show vlan brief** command. Note that this command lists VLAN 2, named "Freds-vlan," and the interfaces assigned to that VLAN (Fa0/13 and Fa0/14).

Securing Unused Switch Interfaces

Cisco originally chose the default interface configuration settings on Cisco switches so that the interfaces would work without any overt configuration. The interfaces automatically negotiate the speed and duplex, and each interface begins in an enabled (**no shutdown**) state, with all interfaces assigned to VLAN 1. Additionally, every interface defaults to negotiate to use VLAN features called VLAN trunking and VLAN Trunking Protocol (VTP), which are covered in more detail in Chapter 26.

The good intentions of Cisco for "plug and play" operation have an unfortunate side effect in that the defaults expose switches to some security threats. So, for any currently unused switch interfaces, Cisco makes some general recommendations to override the default interface settings to make the unused ports more secure. The recommendations for unused interfaces are as follows:

- Administratively disable the interface using the **shutdown** interface subcommand.

- Prevent VLAN trunking and VTP by making the port a nontrunking interface using the **switchport mode access** interface subcommand.

- Assign the port to an unused VLAN using the **switchport access vlan** *number* interface subcommand.

Key Topic

Frankly, if you just shut down the interface, the security exposure goes away, but the other two tasks prevent any immediate problems if someone else comes around and enables the interface by configuring a **no shutdown** command.

Chapter Review

Review Key Topics

Review the most important topics from this chapter, noted with the Key Topic icons. Table 25-2 describes these key topics and where each is discussed.

Table 25-2 *Key Topics for Chapter 25*

Key Topic Element	Description	Page Number
List	Key configuration similarities between Cisco routers and switches	623
List	Key configuration differences between Cisco routers and switches	624
List	Configuration checklist for a switch's IP address and default gateway configuration	625
List	Port security configuration checklist	629
Table 25-1	Port security actions and the results of each action	632
List	VLAN configuration checklist	632
List	Suggested security actions for unused switch ports	635
Table 25-4	**show** and **debug** command reference (at the end of the chapter). This chapter describes many small but important commands!	638

Note: There is no need to memorize any configuration step list referenced as a key topic; these lists are just study aids.

Define Key Terms

Define the following key terms from this chapter, and check your answers in the glossary:

access interface, trunk interface

Review Command Reference to Check Your Memory

Table 25-3 lists and briefly describes the configuration commands used in this chapter.

Table 25-3   *Chapter 25 Configuration Command Reference*

Command	Mode/Purpose/Description
IP Address Configuration	
The following four commands are related to IP address configuration.	
interface vlan *number*	Changes the context to VLAN interface mode. For VLAN 1, allows the configuration of the switch's IP address.
ip address *ip-address subnet-mask*	VLAN interface mode. Statically configures the switch's IP address and mask.
ip address dhcp	VLAN interface mode. Configures the switch as a DHCP client to discover its IP address, mask, and default gateway.
ip default-gateway *address*	Global command. Configures the switch's default gateway IP address. Not required if the switch uses DHCP.
Interface Configuration	
The following six commands are related to interface configuration.	
interface *type port-number*	Changes context to interface mode. The type is typically FastEthernet or gigabitEthernet. The possible port numbers vary depending on the model of switch—for example, Fa0/1, Fa0/2, and so on.
interface range *type port-range*	Changes the context to interface mode for a range of consecutively numbered interfaces. The subcommands that follow then apply to all interfaces in the range.
shutdown **no shutdown**	Interface mode. Disables or enables the interface, respectively.
speed {**10** | **100** | **1000** | **auto**}	Interface mode. Manually sets the speed to the listed speed or, with the auto setting, automatically negotiates the speed.
duplex {**auto** | **full** | **half**}	Interface mode. Manually sets the duplex to half or full, or to autonegotiate the duplex setting.
description *text*	Interface mode. Lists any information text that the engineer wants to track for the interface, such as the expected device on the other end of the cable.

Table 25-3   *Chapter 25 Configuration Command Reference*

Command	Mode/Purpose/Description
Port Security	
The remaining commands are related to port security.	
switchport port-security mac-address *mac-address*	Interface configuration mode command that statically adds a specific MAC address as an allowed MAC address on the interface.
switchport port-security mac-address sticky	Interface subcommand that tells the switch to learn MAC addresses on the interface and add them to the configuration for the interface as secure MAC addresses.
switchport port-security maximum *value*	Interface subcommand that sets the maximum number of static secure MAC addresses that can be assigned to a single interface.
switchport port-security violation {protect | restrict | shutdown}	Interface subcommand that tells the switch what to do if an inappropriate MAC address tries to access the network through a secure switch port.

Table 25-4 lists and briefly describes the EXEC commands used in this chapter.

Key Topic

Table 25-4   *Chapter 25 EXEC Command Reference*

Command	Purpose
show mac address-table dynamic	Lists the dynamically learned entries in the switch's address (forwarding) table.
show dhcp lease	Lists any information the switch acquires as a DHCP client. This includes IP address, subnet mask, and default gateway information.
show crypto key mypubkey rsa	Lists the public and shared key created for use with SSH using the **crypto key generate rsa** global configuration command.
show interfaces status	Lists one output line per interface, noting the description, operating state, and settings for duplex and speed on each interface.
show interfaces vlan 1	Lists the interface status, the switch's IP address and mask, and much more.
show port-security interface *type number*	Lists an interface's port security configuration settings and security operational status.

Answer Review Questions

Answer the following review questions:

1. Imagine that you have configured the **enable secret** command, followed by the **enable password** command, from the console. You log out of the switch and log back in at the console. Which command defines the password that you had to enter to access privileged mode?

    a.   enable password

    b.   enable secret

    c.   Neither

    d.   The **password** command, if it's configured

2. An engineer had formerly configured a Cisco 2960 switch to allow Telnet access so that the switch expected a password of **mypassword** from the Telnet user. The engineer then changed the configuration to support Secure Shell. Which of the following commands could have been part of the new configuration?

    a.   A **username** *name* **password** *password* command in vty config mode

    b.   A **username** *name* **password** *password* global configuration command

    c.   A **transport input ssh** command in vty config mode

    d.   A **transport input ssh** global configuration command

3. The following command was copied and pasted into configuration mode when a user was telnetted into a Cisco switch:
   banner login this is the login banner

    Which of the following is true about what occurs the next time a user logs in from the console?

    a.   No banner text is displayed.

    b.   The banner text "his is" is displayed.

    c.   The banner text "this is the login banner" is displayed.

    d.   The banner text "Login banner configured, no text defined" is displayed.

4. Which of the following is not required when configuring port security without sticky learning?

   a. Setting the maximum number of allowed MAC addresses on the interface with the **switchport port-security maximum** interface subcommand.

   b. Enabling port security with the **switchport port-security** interface subcommand.

   c. Defining the allowed MAC addresses using the **switchport port-security mac-address** interface subcommand.

   d. All the other answers list required commands.

5. An engineer's desktop PC connects to a switch at the main site. A router at the main site connects to each branch office via a serial link, with one small router and switch at each branch. Which of the following commands must be configured, in the listed configuration mode, to allow the engineer to telnet to the branch office switches?

   a. The **ip address** command in VLAN 1 configuration mode

   b. The **ip address** command in global configuration mode

   c. The **ip default-gateway** command in VLAN 1 configuration mode

   d. The **ip default-gateway** command in global configuration mode

   e. The **password** command in console line configuration mode

   f. The **password** command in vty line configuration mode

6. Which of the following describes a way to disable IEEE standard autonegotiation on a 10/100 port on a Cisco switch?

   a. Configure the **negotiate disable** interface subcommand

   b. Configure the **no negotiate** interface subcommand

   c. Configure the **speed 100** interface subcommand

   d. Configure the **duplex half** interface subcommand

   e. Configure the **duplex full** interface subcommand

   f. Configure the **speed 100** and **duplex full** interface subcommands

7. In which of the following modes of the CLI could you configure the duplex setting for interface fastethernet 0/5?

   a. User mode

   b. Enable mode

   c. Global configuration mode

   d. Setup mode

   e. Interface configuration mode

8. The **show vlan brief** command lists the following output:

```
2    my-vlan                        active    Fa0/13, Fa0/15
```

Which of the following commands could have been used as part of the configuration for this switch?

a. The **vlan 2** global configuration command

b. The **name MY-VLAN** vlan subcommand

c. The **interface range Fa0/13 - 15** global configuration command

d. The **switchport vlan 2** interface subcommand

This chapter covers the following subjects:

- **Virtual LAN Concepts:** This section explains the meaning and purpose for VLANs, VLAN trunking, and the VLAN Trunking Protocol (VTP).

- **VLAN and VLAN Trunking Configuration and Verification:** This section shows how to configure VLANs and trunks on Cisco Catalyst switches.

- **VTP Configuration and Verification:** This final section explains how to configure and troubleshoot VTP installations.

CHAPTER 26

Virtual LANs

This chapter completes Unit 9's look at Ethernet LANs with a more detailed examination of virtual LANs. The first major section of this chapter explains the core concepts, including how to pass VLAN traffic between switches using VLAN trunks, and how the Cisco-proprietary VLAN Trunking Protocol (VTP) aids the process of configuring VLANs in a campus LAN. The second major section of this chapter shows how to configure VLANs and VLAN trunks, how to statically assign interfaces to a VLAN, and how to configure a switch so that a phone and PC on the same interface are in two different VLANs. The final major section covers VTP configuration and troubleshooting.

Virtual LAN Concepts

Before understanding VLANs, you must first have a specific understanding of the definition of a LAN. Although you can think about LANs from many perspectives, one perspective in particular can help you understand VLANs:

A LAN includes all devices in the same broadcast domain.

A broadcast domain includes the set of all LAN-connected devices that when any of the devices sends a broadcast frame, all the other devices get a copy of the frame. So, you can think of a LAN and a broadcast domain as being basically the same thing.

Without VLANs, a switch considers all its interfaces to be in the same broadcast domain; in others words, all connected devices are in the same LAN. With VLANs, a switch can put some interfaces into one broadcast domain and some into another, creating multiple broadcast domains. These individual broadcast domains created by the switch are called virtual LANs. Figure 26-1 shows an example, with two VLANs and two devices in each VLAN.

Putting hosts into different VLANs provides many benefits, although the reasons might not be obvious from Figure 26-1. The key to appreciating these benefits is to realize that a broadcast sent by one host in a VLAN will be received and processed by all the other hosts in the VLAN, but not by hosts in a different VLAN. The more hosts in a single VLAN, the larger the number of broadcasts, and the greater the processing time required by each host in the VLAN. Additionally, anyone can download several free software packages, generically called protocol analyzer software, which can capture all the frames received by a host. (Visit Wireshark, at http://www.wireshark.org, for a good free analyzer package.) As a result, larger VLANs expose larger numbers and types of broadcasts to other hosts, exposing more frames to hosts that could be used by an attacker that uses protocol analyzer software to try and perform a reconnaissance attack. These are just a few reasons for separating hosts into different VLANs. The following summarizes the most common reasons:

■ To create more flexible designs that group users by department, or by groups that work together, instead of by physical location

■ To segment devices into smaller LANs (broadcast domains) to reduce overhead caused to each host in the VLAN

■ To reduce the workload for the Spanning Tree Protocol (STP) by limiting a VLAN to a single access switch

■ To enforce better security by keeping hosts that work with sensitive data on a separate VLAN

■ To separate traffic sent by an IP phone from traffic sent by PCs connected to the phones

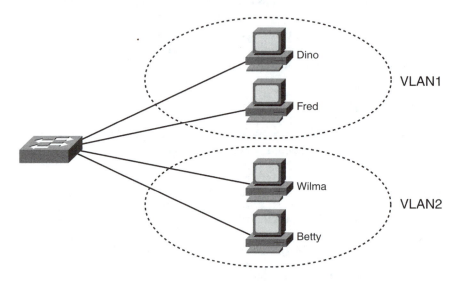

Figure 26-1 *Sample Network with Two VLANs Using One Switch*

This chapter does not examine the reasons for VLANs in any more depth, but it does closely examine the mechanics of how VLANs work across multiple Cisco switches, including the required configuration. To that end, the next section examines VLAN trunking, a feature required when installing a VLAN that exists on more than one LAN switch.

Trunking with ISL and 802.1Q

When using VLANs in networks that have multiple interconnected switches, the switches need to use *VLAN trunking* on the segments between the switches. VLAN trunking causes the switches to use a process called *VLAN tagging*, by which the sending switch adds another header to the frame before sending it over the trunk. This extra VLAN header includes a *VLAN identifier* (VLAN ID) field so that the sending switch can list the VLAN ID and the receiving switch can then know in what VLAN each frame belongs. Figure 26-2 outlines the basic idea.

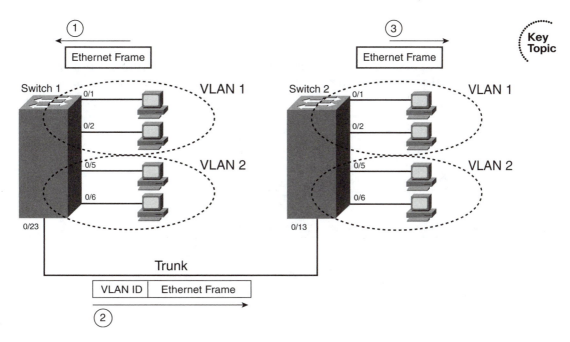

Figure 26-2 *VLAN Trunking Between Two Switches*

The use of trunking allows switches to pass frames from multiple VLANs over a single physical connection. For example, Figure 26-2 shows switch 1 receiving a broadcast frame on interface Fa0/1 at Step 1. To flood the frame, switch 1 needs to forward the broadcast frame to switch 2. However, switch 1 needs to let switch 2 know that the frame is part of VLAN 1. So, as shown at Step 2, before sending the frame, switch 1 adds a VLAN header to the original Ethernet frame, with the VLAN header listing a VLAN ID of 1 in this case. When switch 2 receives the frame, it sees that the frame was from a device in VLAN 1, so switch 2 knows that it should only forward the broadcast out its own interfaces in VLAN 1. Switch 2 removes the VLAN header, forwarding the original frame out its interfaces in VLAN 1 (Step 3).

For another example, consider the case when the device on switch 1's Fa0/5 interface sends a broadcast. Switch 1 sends the broadcast out port Fa0/6 (because that port is in VLAN 2) and out Fa0/23 (because it is a trunk, meaning that it supports multiple different VLANs). Switch 1 adds a trunking header to the frame, listing a VLAN ID of 2. Switch 2 strips off the trunking header after noticing that the frame is part of VLAN 2, so switch 2 knows to forward the frame out only ports Fa0/5 and Fa0/6, and not ports Fa0/1 and Fa0/2.

Cisco switches support two different trunking protocols: Inter-Switch Link (ISL) and IEEE 802.1Q. Trunking protocols provide several features, most importantly that they define headers which identify the VLAN ID, as shown in Figure 26-2. They do have some differences as well, as discussed next.

ISL

Cisco created ISL many years before the IEEE created the 802.1Q standard VLAN trunk-ing protocol. Because ISL is Cisco proprietary, it can be used only between two Cisco switches that support ISL. (Some newer Cisco switches do not even support ISL, instead supporting only the standardized alternative, 802.1Q.) ISL fully encapsulates each original Ethernet frame in an ISL header and trailer. The original Ethernet frame inside the ISL header and trailer remains unchanged. Figure 26-3 shows the framing for ISL.

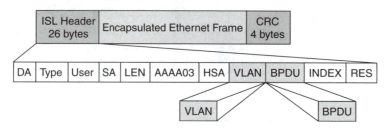

Figure 26-3   *ISL Header*

The ISL header includes several fields, but most importantly, the ISL header VLAN field provides a place to encode the VLAN number. By tagging a frame with the correct VLAN number inside the header, the sending switch can ensure that the receiving switch knows to which VLAN the encapsulated frame belongs. Also, the source and destination ad-dresses in the ISL header use MAC addresses of the sending and receiving switch, as op-posed to the devices that actually sent the original frame. Other than that, the details of the ISL header are not that important.

IEEE 802.1Q

The IEEE standardizes many of the protocols that relate to LANs today, and VLAN trunk-ing is no exception. Years after Cisco created ISL, the IEEE completed work on the 802.1Q standard, which defines a different way to do trunking. Today, 802.1Q has become the more popular trunking protocol, with Cisco not even supporting ISL in some of its newer models of LAN switches, including the 2960 switches used in the examples in this book.

802.1Q uses a different style of header than does ISL to tag frames with a VLAN number. In fact, 802.1Q does not actually encapsulate the original frame in another Ethernet header and trailer. Instead, 802.1Q inserts an extra 4-byte VLAN header into the original frame's Ethernet header. As a result, unlike ISL, the frame still has the same original source and destination MAC addresses. Also, because the original header has been expanded, 802.1Q encapsulation forces a recalculation of the original frame check sequence (FCS) field in the Ethernet trailer, because the FCS is based on the contents of the entire frame. Figure 26-4 shows the 802.1Q header and framing of the revised Ethernet header.

ISL and 802.1Q Compared

So far, the text has described one major similarity between ISL and 802.1Q, with a couple of differences. The similarity is that both ISL and 802.1Q define a VLAN header that has a

VLAN ID field. However, each trunking protocol uses a different overall header, plus one is standardized (802.1Q) and one is proprietary (ISL). This section points out a few other key comparison points between the two.

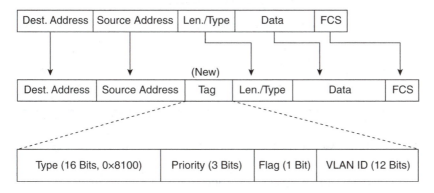

Figure 26-4 *802.1Q Trunking Header*

Both trunking protocols support the same number of VLANs, specifically 4094 VLANs. Both protocols use 12 bits of the VLAN header to number VLANs, supporting 2^{12}, or 4096, VLAN IDs, minus two reserved values (0 and 4095). Of the supported VLANs, note that VLAN IDs 1–1005 are considered to be *normal range* VLANs, whereas values higher than 1005 are called *extended range* VLANs. This distinction matters in regard to the VLAN Trunking Protocol (VTP), which is covered in the next section.

ISL and 802.1Q both support a separate instance of Spanning Tree Protocol (STP) for each VLAN, but with different implementation details. For campus LANs with redundant links, using only one instance of STP means that some links sit idle under normal operations, with those links only being used when another link fails. By supporting multiple instances of STP, engineers can tune the STP parameters so that under normal operations, some VLANs' traffic uses one set of links and other VLANs' traffic uses other links, taking advantage of all the links in the network.

Note: 802.1Q has not always supported multiple instances of STP, so some older references might have accurately stated that, at that time, 802.1Q only supported a single instance of STP.

One final key difference between ISL and 802.1Q covered here relates to a feature called the *native VLAN*. 802.1Q defines one VLAN on each trunk as the native VLAN, whereas ISL does not use the concept. By default, the 802.1Q native VLAN is VLAN 1. By definition, 802.1Q simply does not add an 802.1Q header to frames in the native VLAN. When the switch on the other side of the trunk receives a frame that does not have an 802.1Q header, the receiving switch knows that the frame is part of the native VLAN. Note that because of this behavior, both switches must agree which VLAN is the native VLAN.

The 802.1Q native VLAN provides some interesting functions, mainly to support connections to devices that do not understand trunking. For example, a Cisco switch could be cabled to a switch that does not understand 802.1Q trunking. The Cisco switch could send frames in the native VLAN—meaning that the frame has no trunking header—so the other switch would understand the frame. The native VLAN concept gives switches the capability of at least passing traffic in one VLAN (the native VLAN), which can allow some basic functions, like reachability to telnet into a switch.

Table 26-1 summarizes the key features and points of comparison between ISL and 802.1Q.

Table 26-1   *ISL and 802.1Q Compared*

Function	ISL	802.1Q
Defined by	Cisco	IEEE
Inserts another 4-byte header instead of completely encapsulating the original frame	No	Yes
Supports normal-range (1–1005) and extended-range (1006–4094) VLANs	Yes	Yes
Allows multiple spanning trees	Yes	Yes
Uses a native VLAN	No	Yes

IP Subnets and VLANs

When including VLANs in a design, the devices in a VLAN need to be in the same subnet. Following the same design logic, devices in different VLANs need to be in different subnets.

Because of these design rules, many people think that a VLAN is a subnet and that a subnet is a VLAN. Although not completely true, because a VLAN is a Layer 2 concept and a subnet is a Layer 3 concept, the general idea is reasonable because the same devices in a single VLAN are the same devices in a single subnet.

As with all IP subnets, for a host in one subnet to forward packets to a host in another subnet, at least one router must be involved. For example, consider Figure 26-5, which shows a switch with three VLANs, shown inside the dashed lines, with some of the logic used when a host in VLAN 1 sends an IP packet to a host in VLAN 2.

In this case, when Fred sends a packet to Wilma's IP address, Fred sends the packet to his default router, because Wilma's IP address is in a different subnet. The router receives the frame, with a VLAN header that implies the frame is part of VLAN 1. The router makes a forwarding decision, sending the frame back out the same physical link, but this time with a VLAN trunking header that lists VLAN 2. The switch forwards the frame in VLAN 2 to Wilma.

It might seem a bit inefficient to send the packet from the switch, to the router, and right back to the switch—and it is. A more likely option in real campus LANs today is to use a switch called either a multilayer switch or a Layer 3 switch. These switches can perform both Layer 2 switching and Layer 3 routing, combining the router function shown in Figure 26-5 into the switch.

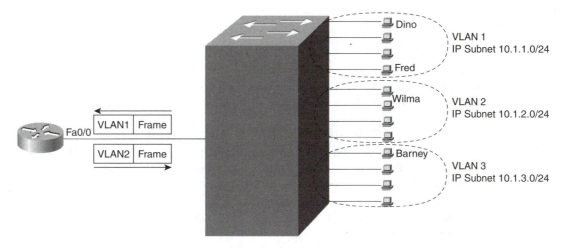

Figure 26-5 *Routing Between VLANs*

VLAN Trunking Protocol (VTP)

The Cisco-proprietary VLAN Trunking Protocol (VTP) provides a means by which Cisco switches can exchange VLAN configuration information. In particular, VTP advertises about the existence of each VLAN based on its VLAN ID and the VLAN name. However, VTP does not advertise the details about which switch interfaces are assigned to each VLAN.

Because this book has not yet shown how to configure VLANs, to better appreciate VTP, consider this example of what VTP can do. Imagine that a network has ten switches connected somehow using VLAN trunks, and each switch has at least one port assigned to a VLAN with VLAN ID 3 and the name Accounting. Without VTP, an engineer would have to log in to all ten switches and enter the same two config commands to create the VLAN and define its name. With VTP, you would create VLAN 3 on one switch, and the other nine switches would learn about VLAN 3 and its name using VTP.

VTP defines a Layer 2 messaging protocol that the switches use to exchange VLAN configuration information. When a switch changes its VLAN configuration—in other words, when a VLAN is added or deleted, or an existing VLAN is changed—VTP causes all the switches to synchronize their VLAN configuration to include the same VLAN IDs and VLAN names. The process is somewhat like a routing protocol, with each switch sending periodic VTP messages. Switches also send VTP messages as soon as their VLAN configuration changes. For example, if you configured a new VLAN 3, with the name Accounting, the switch would immediately send VTP updates out all trunks, causing the distribution of the new VLAN information to the rest of the switches.

Each switch uses one of three VTP modes: server mode, client mode, or transparent mode. To use VTP, an engineer sets some switches to use server mode and the rest to use client mode. Then, VLAN configuration can be added on the servers, with all other servers and clients learning about the changes to the VLAN database. Clients cannot be used to configure VLAN information.

Oddly enough, Cisco switches cannot disable VTP. The closest option is to use transparent mode, which causes a switch to ignore VTP, other than to forward VTP messages so that any other clients or servers can receive a copy.

The next section explains the normal operations when the engineer uses server and client modes to take advantage of VTP's capabilities, followed by an explanation of the rather unusual way to essentially disable VTP by enabling VTP transparent mode.

Normal VTP Operation Using VTP Server and Client Modes

The VTP process begins with VLAN creation on a switch called a VTP server. The VTP server then distributes VLAN configuration changes through VTP messages, sent only over ISL and 802.1Q trunks, throughout the network. Both VTP servers and clients process the received VTP messages, update their VTP configuration database based on those messages, and then independently send VTP updates out their trunks. At the end of the process, all switches learn the new VLAN information.

VTP servers and clients choose whether to react to a received VTP update, and update their VLAN configurations based on whether the *VLAN database configuration revision number* increases. Each time a VTP server modifies its VLAN configuration, the VTP server increments the current configuration revision number by 1. The VTP update messages list the new configuration revision number. When another client or server switch receives a VTP message with a higher configuration revision number than its own, the switch updates its VLAN configuration. Figure 26-6 illustrates how VTP operates in a switched network.

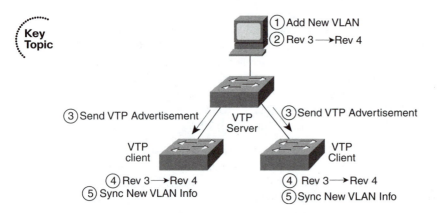

Figure 26-6   *VTP Configuration Revision Numbers and the VTP Update Process*

Figure 26-6 begins with all switches having the same VLAN configuration revision number, meaning that they have the same VLAN configuration database; this means that all switches know about the same VLAN numbers and VLAN names. The process begins with each switch knowing that the current configuration revision number is 3. The steps shown in Figure 26-6 are as follows:

1. Someone configures a new VLAN from the command-line interface (CLI) of a VTP server.

2. The VTP server updates its VLAN database revision number from 3 to 4.

3. The server sends VTP update messages out its trunk interfaces, stating revision number 4.

4. The two VTP client switches notice that the updates list a higher revision number (4) than their current revision numbers (3).

5. The two client switches update their VLAN databases based on the server's VTP updates.

Although this example shows a very small LAN, the process works the same for larger networks. When a VTP server updates the VLAN configuration, the server immediately sends VTP messages out all trunks. The neighboring switches on the other end of the trunks process the received messages and update their VLAN databases, and then they send VTP messages to their neighbors. The process repeats on the neighboring switches, until eventually, all switches have heard of the new VLAN database.

Note: The complete process by which a server changes the VLAN configuration, and all VTP switches learn the new configuration, resulting in all switches knowing the same VLAN IDs and name, is called *synchronization*.

VTP servers and clients also send periodic VTP messages every 5 minutes, in case any newly added switches need to know the VLAN configuration. Additionally, when a new trunk comes up, switches can immediately send a VTP message asking the neighboring switch to send its VLAN database.

So far, this chapter has referred to VTP messages as either VTP updates or VTP messages. In practice, VTP defines three different types of messages: summary advertisements, subset advertisements, and advertisement requests. The summary advertisements list the revision number, domain name, and other information, but no VLAN information. The periodic VTP messages that occur every five minutes are VTP summary advertisements. If something changes, as indicated by a new 1-larger revision number, the summary advertisement message is followed by one or more subset advertisements, each of which advertises some subset of the VLAN database. The third message, the advertisement request message, allows a switch to immediately request VTP messages from a neighboring switch as soon as a trunk comes up. However, the examples shown for the purposes of this book do not make distinctions about the use of the messages.

Three Requirements for VTP to Work Between Two Switches

When a VTP client or server connects to another VTP client or server switch, Cisco IOS requires that the following three facts be true before the two switches can exchange VTP messages:

■ The link between the switches must be operating as a VLAN trunk (ISL or 802.1Q).

■ The two switches' case-sensitive VTP domain name must match.

■ If configured on at least one of the switches, the two switches' case-sensitive VTP password must match.

Key
Topic

The VTP domain name provides a design tool by which engineers can create multiple groups of VTP switches, called domains, whose VLAN configurations are autonomous. To do so, the engineer can configure one set of switches in one VTP domain and another set in another VTP domain, and switches in the different domains will ignore each other's VTP messages. VTP domains allow engineers to break up the switched network into different administrative domains. For example, in a large building with a large IT staff, one division's IT staff might use a VTP domain name of Accounting, while another part of the IT staff might use a domain name of Sales, maintaining control of their configurations but still being able to forward traffic between divisions through the LAN infrastructure.

The VTP password mechanism provides a means by which a switch can prevent malicious attackers from forcing a switch to change its VLAN configuration. The password itself is never transmitted in clear text.

Avoiding VTP by Using VTP Transparent Mode

Interestingly, to avoid using VTP to exchange VLAN information in Cisco switches, switches cannot simply disable VTP. Instead, switches must use the third VTP mode: VTP transparent mode. Transparent mode gives a switch autonomy from the other switches. Like VTP servers, VTP transparent mode switches can configure VLANs. However, unlike servers, transparent mode switches never update their VLAN databases based on incoming VTP messages, and transparent mode switches never try to create VTP messages to tell other switches about their own VLAN configuration.

VTP transparent mode switches essentially behave as if VTP does not exist, other than one small exception: Transparent mode switches forward VTP updates received from other switches, just to help out any neighboring VTP server or client switches.

From a design perspective, because of the dangers associated with VTP (as covered in the next section), some engineers just avoid VTP altogether by using VTP transparent mode on all switches. In other cases, engineers might make a few switches transparent mode switches to give autonomy to the engineers responsible for those switches, while using VTP server and client modes on other switches.

Storing VLAN Configuration

To forward traffic for a VLAN, a switch needs to know the VLAN's VLAN ID and its VLAN name. VTP's job is to advertise these details, with the full set of configuration for all VLANs being called the *VLAN configuration database*, or simply VLAN database.

Interestingly, Cisco IOS stores the information in the VLAN database differently than for most other Cisco IOS configuration commands. When VTP clients and servers store VLAN configuration—specifically, the VLAN ID, VLAN name, and other VTP configuration settings—the configuration is stored in a file called vlan.dat in flash memory. (The filename is short for "VLAN database.") Even more interesting is the fact that Cisco IOS does not put this VLAN configuration in the running-config file or the startup-config file. No command exists to view the VTP and VLAN configuration directly; instead, you need to use several **show** commands to list the information about VLANs and VTP output.

The process of storing the VLAN configuration in flash in the vlan.dat file allows both clients and servers to dynamically learn about VLANs, and have the configuration automatically stored, therefore making both client and server prepared for their next re-load. If the dynamically learned VLAN configuration was only added to the running con-fig file, the campus LAN could be exposed to cases in which all switches lost power around the same time (easily accomplished with a single power source into the building), resulting in loss of all VLAN configuration. By automatically storing the configuration in the vlan.dat file in flash memory, each switch has at least a recent VLAN configuration database, and can then rely on VTP updates from other switches if any VLAN configura-tion has changed recently.

An interesting side effect of this process is that when you use a VTP client or server switch in a lab, and you want to remove all the configuration to start with a clean switch, you must issue more than the **erase startup-config** command. If you only erase the startup-config and reload the switch, the switch remembers all VLAN config and VTP configuration that is instead stored in the vlan.dat file in flash. To remove those configura-tion details before reloading a switch, you would have to delete the vlan.dat file in flash with a command such as **delete flash:vlan.dat**.

Switches in transparent mode store VLAN configuration in both the running-config file as well as the vlan.dat file in flash. The running-config can be saved to the startup-config as well.

Note: In some older switch Cisco IOS versions, VTP servers stored VLAN configuration in both vlan.dat and the running-config file.

VTP Versions

Cisco supports three VTP versions, aptly named versions 1, 2, and 3. Most of the differ-ences between these versions are unimportant to the discussions in this book. However, VTP version 2 made one important improvement over version 1 relative to VTP transpar-ent mode, an improvement that is briefly described in this section.

The section "Avoiding VTP by Using VTP Transparent Mode," earlier in this chapter, de-scribed how a switch using VTP version 2 would work. However, in VTP version 1, a VTP transparent mode switch would first check a received VTP update's domain name and password. If the transparent mode switch did not match both parameters, the transparent mode switch discarded the VTP update, rather than forwarding the update. The problem with VTP version 1 is that in cases where a transparent mode switch existed in a network with multiple VTP domains, the switch wouldn't forward all VTP updates. So, VTP ver-sion 2 changed transparent mode logic, ignoring the domain name and password, allowing a VTP version 2 transparent mode switch to forward all received VTP updates.

Note: Version 3 is available only in higher-end Cisco switches today, and will be ignored for the purposes of this book.

VTP Pruning

By default, Cisco switches flood broadcasts (and unknown destination unicasts) in each active VLAN out all trunks, as long as the current STP topology does not block the trunk. However, in most campus networks, many VLANs exist on only a few switches, but not all switches. Therefore, it is wasteful to forward broadcasts over all trunks, causing the frames to arrive at switches that do not have any ports in that VLAN.

Switches support two methods by which an engineer can limit which VLAN's traffic flows over a trunk. One method requires the manual configuration of the *allowed VLAN list* on each trunk; this manual configuration is covered later in the chapter. The second method, VTP pruning, allows VTP to dynamically determine which switches do not need frames from certain VLANs, and then VTP prunes those VLANs from the appropriate trunks. Pruning simply means that the appropriate switch trunk interfaces do not flood frames in that VLAN. Figure 26-7 shows an example, with the dashed-line rectangles denoting the trunks from which VLAN 10 has been automatically pruned.

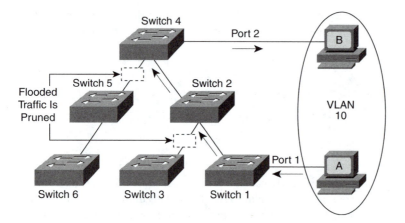

Figure 26-7   *VTP Pruning*

In Figure 26-7, switches 1 and 4 have ports in VLAN 10. With VTP pruning enabled network-wide, switch 2 and switch 4 automatically use VTP to learn that none of the switches in the lower-left part of the figure have any ports assigned to VLAN 10. As a result, switch 2 and switch 4 prune VLAN 10 from the trunks as shown. The pruning causes switch 2 and switch 4 to not send frames in VLAN 10 out these trunks. For example, when station A sends a broadcast, the switches flood the broadcast, as shown by the arrowed lines in Figure 26-7.

VTP pruning increases the available bandwidth by restricting flooded traffic. VTP pruning is one of the two most compelling reasons to use VTP, with the other reason being to make VLAN configuration easier and more consistent.

Summary of VTP Features

Table 26-2 offers a comparative overview of the three VTP modes.

Table 26-2 *VTP Features*

Function	Server	Client	Transparent
Only sends VTP messages out ISL or 802.1Q trunks	Yes	Yes	Yes
Supports CLI configuration of VLANs	Yes	No	Yes
Can use normal-range VLANs (1–1005)	Yes	Yes	Yes
Can use extended-range VLANs (1006–4095)	No	No	Yes
Synchronizes (updates) its own config database when receiving VTP messages with a higher revision number	Yes	Yes	No
Creates and sends periodic VTP updates every 5 minutes	Yes	Yes	No
Does not process received VTP updates, but does forward received VTP updates out other trunks	No	No	Yes
Places the VLAN ID, VLAN name, and VTP configuration into the running-config file	No	No	Yes
Places the VLAN ID, VLAN name, and VTP configuration into the vlan.dat file in flash	Yes	Yes	Yes

VLAN and VLAN Trunking Configuration and Verification

Cisco switches do not require any configuration to work. You can purchase Cisco switches, install devices with the correct cabling, and turn on the switches, and they work. You would never need to configure the switch and it would work fine, even if you interconnected switches, until you needed more than one VLAN. Even the default STP settings would likely work just fine, but if you want to use VLANs—and most every enterprise network does—you need to add some configuration.

This chapter separates the VLAN configuration details into two major sections. The current section focuses on configuration and verification tasks when VTP is ignored, either by using the default VTP settings or if using VTP transparent mode. The final major section of this chapter, "VTP Configuration and Verification," examines VTP specifically.

Creating VLANs and Assigning Access VLANs to an Interface

This section shows how to create a VLAN, give the VLAN a name, and assign interfaces to a VLAN. To focus on these basic details, this section shows examples using a single switch, so VTP and trunking are not needed.

For a Cisco switch to forward frames in a particular VLAN, the switch must be configured to believe that the VLAN exists. Additionally, the switch must have nontrunking interfaces (called *access interfaces*) assigned to the VLAN and/or trunks that support the VLAN. The configuration steps for creating the VLAN, and assigning a VLAN to an access interface, are as follows. (Note that the trunk configuration is covered in the section "VLAN Trunking Configuration," later in this chapter.)

Step 1. To configure a new VLAN, follow these steps:

  a. From configuration mode, use the **vlan** *vlan-id* global configuration command to create the VLAN and to move the user into VLAN configuration mode.

  b. (Optional) Use the **name** *name* VLAN subcommand to list a name for the VLAN. If not configured, the VLAN name is VLAN*ZZZZ*, where *ZZZZ* is the 4-digit decimal VLAN ID.

Step 2. To configure a VLAN for each access interface, follow these steps:

  a. Use the **interface** command to move into interface configuration mode for each desired interface.

  b. Use the **switchport access vlan** *id-number* interface subcommand to specify the VLAN number associated with that interface.

  c. (Optional) To disable trunking on that same interface, ensuring that the interface is an access interface, use the **switchport mode access** interface subcommand.

Note: VLANs can be created and named in configuration mode (as described in Step 1) or by using a configuration tool called VLAN database mode. The VLAN database mode is not covered in this book.

Note: Cisco switches also support a dynamic method of assigning devices to VLANs, based on the device's MAC addresses, using a tool called the VLAN Management Policy Server (VMPS). This tool is seldom, if ever, used.

The previous process can be used on a switch either configured to be a transparent mode switch or a switch with all default VTP settings. For reference, the following list outlines the key Cisco switch defaults related to VLANs and VTP. For now, this chapter assumes either default VTP settings or a setting of VTP transparent mode. Later in this chapter, the section "Caveats When Moving Away from Default VTP Configuration" revisits Cisco switch defaults and the implication of how to go from not using VTP, based on the default settings, to how to use VTP.

- VTP server mode.

- No VTP domain name.

- VLAN 1 and VLANs 1002–1005 are automatically configured (and cannot be deleted).

- All access interfaces are assigned to VLAN 1 (an implied **switchport access vlan 1** command).

VLAN Configuration Example 1: Full VLAN Configuration

Example 26-1 shows the configuration process of adding a new VLAN and assigning access interfaces to that VLAN. Figure 26-8 shows the network used in the example, with one LAN switch (SW1) and two hosts in each of three VLANs (1, 2, and 3). The example shows the details of the two-step process for VLAN 2 and the interfaces in VLAN 2, with the configuration of VLAN 3 deferred until the next example.

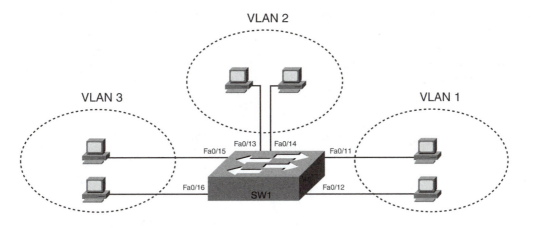

Figure 26-8   *Network with One Switch and Three VLANs*

Example 26-1   *Configuring VLANs and Assigning VLANs to Interfaces*

```
sw1-2960# show vlan brief
VLAN Name                             Status    Ports
---- -------------------------------- --------- -------------------------------
1    default                          active    Fa0/1, Fa0/2, Fa0/3, Fa0/4
                                                Fa0/5, Fa0/6, Fa0/7, Fa0/8
                                                Fa0/9, Fa0/10, Fa0/11, Fa0/12
                                                Fa0/13, Fa0/14, Fa0/15, Fa0/16
                                                Fa0/17, Fa0/18, Fa0/19, Fa0/20
                                                Fa0/21, Fa0/22, Fa0/23, Fa0/24
                                                Gi0/1, Gi0/2
1002 fddi-default                     act/unsup
1003 token-ring-default               act/unsup
1004 fddinet-default                  act/unsup
1005 trnet-default                    act/unsup
! Above, VLAN 2 did not yet exist. Below, VLAN 2 is added, with name Freds-vlan,
! with two interfaces assigned to VLAN 2.
sw1-2960# configure terminal
Enter configuration commands, one per line.  End with CNTL/Z.
sw1-2960(config)# vlan 2
sw1-2960(config-vlan)# name Freds-vlan
sw1-2960(config-vlan)# exit
sw1-2960(config)# interface range fastethernet 0/13 - 14
```

```
sw1-2960(config-if)# switchport access vlan 2
sw1-2960(config-if)# exit
! Below, the show running-config command lists the interface subcommands on
! interfaces Fa0/13 and Fa0/14. The vlan 2 and name Freds-vlan commands do
! not show up in the running-config.
sw1-2960# show running-config
! lines omitted for brevity
interface FastEthernet0/13
 switchport access vlan 2
 switchport mode access
!
interface FastEthernet0/14
 switchport access vlan 2
 switchport mode access
!
SW1# show vlan brief


VLAN Name                             Status     Ports
---- -------------------------------- ---------- -------------------------------
1    default                          active     Fa0/1, Fa0/2, Fa0/3, Fa0/4
                                                 Fa0/5, Fa0/6, Fa0/7, Fa0/8
                                                 Fa0/9, Fa0/10, Fa0/11, Fa0/12
                                                 Fa0/15, Fa0/16, Fa0/17, Fa0/18
                                                 Fa0/19, Fa0/20, Fa0/21, Fa0/22
                                                 Fa0/23, Fa0/24, Gi0/1, Gi0/2
2    Freds-vlan                       active     Fa0/13, Fa0/14
1002 fddi-default                     act/unsup
1003 token-ring-default               act/unsup
1004 fddinet-default                  act/unsup
1005 trnet-default                    act/unsup
```

The example begins with the **show vlan brief** command, confirming the default settings of five nondeletable VLANs, with all interfaces assigned to VLAN 1. In particular, note that this 2960 switch has 24 Fast Ethernet ports (Fa0/1–Fa0/24) and two Gigabit Ethernet ports (Gi0/1 and Gi0/2), all of which are listed as being in VLAN 1.

Next, the example shows the process of creating VLAN 2 and assigning interfaces Fa0/13 and Fa0/14 to VLAN 2. Note in particular that the example uses the **interface range** command, which causes the **switchport access vlan 2** interface subcommand to be applied to both interfaces in the range, as confirmed in the **show running-config** command output at the end of the example.

After the configuration has been added, to list the new VLAN, the example repeats the **show vlan brief** command. Note that this command lists VLAN 2, name Freds-vlan, and the interfaces assigned to that VLAN (Fa0/13 and Fa0/14).

Note: Example 26-1 uses default VTP configuration. However, if the switch had been configured for VTP transparent mode, the **vlan 2** and **name Freds-vlan** configuration commands would have also been seen in the output of the **show running-config** command. Because this switch is in VTP server mode (default), the switch stores these two commands only in the vlan.dat file.

A switch might not use the VLAN assigned by the **switchport access vlan** *vlan-id* command in some cases, depending on the operational mode of an interface. A Cisco switch's operational mode relates to whether the interface is currently using a trunking protocol. An interface that is currently using trunking is called a *trunk interface*, and all other interfaces are called *access interfaces*. So, engineers use phrases like "Fa0/12 is a trunk port" or "Fa0/13 is an access interface," referring to whether the design intends to use a particular interface to trunk (trunk mode) or to connect to just one VLAN (access mode).

The optional interface subcommand **switchport mode access** tells the switch to allow the interface to be only an access interface, which means the interface will not use trunking and will use the assigned access VLAN. If you omit the optional **switchport mode access** interface subcommand, the interface could negotiate to use trunking, becoming a trunk interface and ignoring the configured access VLAN.

VLAN Configuration Example 2: Shorter VLAN Configuration

Example 26-1 shows several of the optional configuration commands, with a side effect of being a bit longer than is required. Example 26-2 shows a much briefer alternative configuration, picking up the story where Example 26-1 ended, showing the addition of VLAN 3 (as seen in Figure 26-8). Note that SW1 does not know about VLAN 3 at the beginning of this example.

Example 26-2 *Shorter VLAN Configuration Example (VLAN 3)*

```
SW1# configure terminal
Enter configuration commands, one per line.  End with CNTL/Z.
SW1(config)# interface range Fastethernet 0/15 - 16
SW1(config-if-range)# switchport access vlan 3
% Access VLAN does not exist. Creating vlan 3
SW1(config-if-range)# ^Z
SW1# show vlan brief


VLAN Name                             Status    Ports
---- -------------------------------- --------- -------------------------------
1    default                          active    Fa0/1, Fa0/2, Fa0/3, Fa0/4
                                                Fa0/5, Fa0/6, Fa0/7, Fa0/8
                                                Fa0/9, Fa0/10, Fa0/11, Fa0/12
                                                Fa0/17, Fa0/18, Fa0/19, Fa0/20
                                                Fa0/21, Fa0/22, Fa0/23, Fa0/24
                                                Gi0/1, Gi0/2
```

```
2      Freds-vlan                       active    Fa0/13, Fa0/14
3      VLAN0003                         active    Fa0/15, Fa0/16
1002   fddi-default                     act/unsup
1003   token-ring-default               act/unsup
1004   fddinet-default                  act/unsup
1005   trnet-default                    act/unsup
SW1#
```

Example 26-2 shows how a switch can dynamically create a VLAN—the equivalent of the **vlan** *vlan-id* global config command—when the **switchport access vlan** interface subcommand refers to a currently unconfigured VLAN. This example begins with SW1 not knowing about VLAN 3. When the **switchport access vlan 3** interface subcommand was used, the switch realized that VLAN 3 did not exist, and as noted in the shaded message in the example, the switch created VLAN 3, using a default name (VLAN0003). No other steps are required to create the VLAN. At the end of the process, VLAN 3 exists in the switch, and interfaces Fa0/15 and Fa0/16 are in VLAN 3, as noted in the shaded part of the **show vlan brief** command output.

As a reminder, note that some of the configuration shown in Examples 26-1 and 26-2 ends up only in the vlan.dat file in flash memory, and some ends up only in the running-config file. In particular, the interface subcommands are in the running-config file, so a **copy running-config startup-config** command would be needed to save the configuration. However, the definitions of new VLANs 2 and 3 have already been automatically saved in the vlan.dat file in flash. Table 26-6, later in this chapter, lists a reference of the various configuration commands, where they are stored, and how to confirm the configuration settings.

VLAN Trunking Configuration

Trunking configuration on Cisco switches involves two important configuration choices, as follows:

- The type of trunking: IEEE 802.1Q, ISL, or negotiate which one to use

- The *administrative mode*: Whether to trunk, not trunk, or negotiate

Cisco switches can either negotiate or configure the type of trunking to use (ISL or 802.1Q). By default, Cisco switches negotiate the type of trunking with the switch on the other end of the trunk, using the Dynamic Trunk Protocol (DTP). When negotiating, if both switches support both ISL and 802.1Q, they choose ISL. If one switch is willing to use either type, and the other switch is only willing to use one type of trunking, the two switches agree to use that one type of trunking supported by both switches. The type of trunking preferred on an interface, for switches that support both types, is configured using the **switchport trunk encapsulation {dot1q | isl | negotiate}** interface subcommand. (Many of the most recently developed Cisco switches, including 2960s, only support the IEEE-standard 802.1Q trunking today, so these switches simply default to a setting of **switchport trunk encapsulation dot1q**.)

The administrative mode refers to the configuration setting for whether trunking should be used on an interface. The term *administrative* refers to what is configured, whereas an interface's *operational* mode refers to what is currently happening on the interface. Cisco switches use an interface's *administrative mode*, as configured with the **switchport mode** interface subcommand, to determine whether to use trunking. Table 26-3 lists the options of the **switchport mode** command.

Table 26-3   *Trunking Administrative Mode Options with the switchport mode Command*

Key Topic

Command Option	Description
access	Prevents the use of trunking, making the port always act as an access (non-trunk) port
trunk	Always uses trunking
dynamic desirable	Initiates negotiation messages and responds to negotiation messages to dynamically choose whether to start using trunking, and defines the trunking encapsulation
dynamic auto	Passively waits to receive trunk negotiation messages, at which point the switch will respond and negotiate whether to use trunking, and if so, the type of trunking

For example, consider the two switches shown in Figure 26-9. This figure shows an expansion of the network of Figure 26-8, with a trunk to a new switch (SW2) and with parts of VLANs 1 and 3 on ports attached to SW2. The two switches use a Gigabit Ethernet link for the trunk. In this case, the trunk does not dynamically form by default, because both (2960) switches default to an administrative mode of *dynamic auto*, meaning that neither switch initiates the trunk negotiation process. By changing one switch to use *dynamic desirable* mode, which does initiate the negotiation, the switches negotiate to use trunking—specifically 802.1Q because the 2960s only support 802.1Q.

Example 26-3 begins by showing the two switches with the default configuration so that the two switches do not trunk. The example then shows the configuration of SW1 so that the two switches negotiate and use 802.1Q trunking.

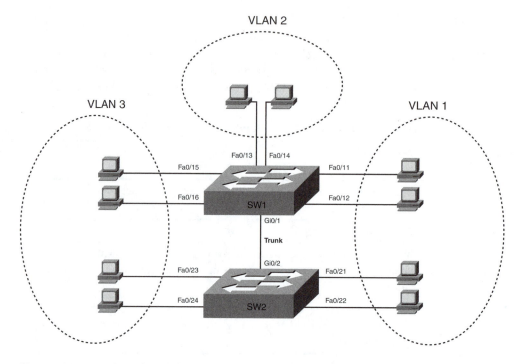

Figure 26-9 *Network with Two Switches and Three VLANs*

Example 26-3 *Trunking Configuration and* show *Commands on 2960 Switches*

```
SW1# show interfaces gigabit 0/1 switchport
Name: Gi0/1
Switchport: Enabled
Administrative Mode: dynamic auto
Operational Mode: static access
Administrative Trunking Encapsulation: dot1q
Operational Trunking Encapsulation: native
Negotiation of Trunking: On
Access Mode VLAN: 1 (default)
Trunking Native Mode VLAN: 1 (default)
Administrative Native VLAN tagging: enabled
Voice VLAN: none
Access Mode VLAN: 1 (default)
Trunking Native Mode VLAN: 1 (default)
Administrative Native VLAN tagging: enabled
Voice VLAN: none
Administrative private-vlan host-association: none
Administrative private-vlan mapping: none
Administrative private-vlan trunk native VLAN: none
Administrative private-vlan trunk Native VLAN tagging: enabled
```

```
Administrative private-vlan trunk encapsulation: dot1q
Administrative private-vlan trunk normal VLANs: none
Administrative private-vlan trunk private VLANs: none
Operational private-vlan: none
Trunking VLANs Enabled: ALL
Pruning VLANs Enabled: 2-1001
Capture Mode Disabled
Capture VLANs Allowed: ALL


Protected: false
Unknown unicast blocked: disabled
Unknown multicast blocked: disabled
Appliance trust: none
! Note that the next command results in a single empty line of output.
SW1# show interfaces trunk


SW1#
! Next, the administrative mode is set to dynamic desirable.
SW1# configure terminal
Enter configuration commands, one per line.  End with CNTL/Z.
SW1(config)# interface gigabit 0/1
SW1(config-if)# switchport mode dynamic desirable
SW1(config-if)# ^Z
SW1#
01:43:46: %LINEPROTO-5-UPDOWN: Line protocol on Interface GigabitEthernet0/1,
changed state to down
SW1#
01:43:49: %LINEPROTO-5-UPDOWN: Line protocol on Interface GigabitEthernet0/1,
changed state to up
SW1# show interfaces gigabit 0/1 switchport
Name: Gi0/1
Switchport: Enabled
Administrative Mode: dynamic desirable
Operational Mode: trunk
Administrative Trunking Encapsulation: dot1q
Operational Trunking Encapsulation: dot1q
Negotiation of Trunking: On
Access Mode VLAN: 1 (default)
Trunking Native Mode VLAN: 1 (default)
! lines omitted for brevity
! The next command formerly listed a single empty line of output; now it lists
! information about the 1 operational trunk.
SW1# show interfaces trunk


Port          Mode         Encapsulation  Status        Native vlan
Gi0/1         desirable    802.1q         trunking      1
```

```
Port          Vlans allowed on trunk
Gi0/1         1-4094


Port          Vlans allowed and active in management domain
Gi0/1         1-3


Port          Vlans in spanning tree forwarding state and not pruned
Gi0/1.        1-3
```

First, focus on important items from the output of the **show interfaces switchport** command at the beginning of Example 26-3. The output lists the default administrative mode setting of dynamic auto. Because SW2 also defaults to dynamic auto, the command lists SW1's operational status as access, meaning that it is not trunking. The third shaded line points out the only supported type of trunking (802.1Q) on this 2960 switch. (On a switch that supports both ISL and 802.1Q, this value would by default list "negotiate," to mean that the type or encapsulation is negotiated.) Finally, the operational trunking type is listed as "native," which is a subtle way to say that the switch does not add any trunking header to forwarded frames on this port, treating frames as if they are in an 802.1Q native VLAN.

To enable trunking, the two switches' administrative modes must be set to a combination of values that result in trunking. By changing SW1 to use dynamic desirable mode, as shown next in Example 26-3, SW1 will now initiate the negotiations, and the two switches will use trunking. Of particular interest is the fact that the switch brings the interface to a down state, and then back up again, as a result of the change to the administrative mode of the interface.

To verify that trunking is working now, the end of Example 26-3 lists the **show interfaces switchport** command. Note that the command still lists the administrative settings, which denote the configured values, along with the operational settings, which list what the switch is currently doing. In this case, SW1 now claims to be in an operational mode of trunk, with an operational trunking encapsulation of dot1Q.

You should be ready to interpret the output of the **show interfaces switchport** command, realize the administrative mode implied by the output, and know whether the link should operationally trunk based on those settings. Table 26-4 lists the combinations of the trunking administrative modes and the expected operational mode (trunk or access) resulting from the configured settings. The table lists the administrative mode used on one end of the link on the left, and the administrative mode on the switch on the other end of the link across the top of the table.

Table 26-4 *Expected Trunking Operational Mode Based on the Configured Administrative Modes*

Administrative Mode	Access	Dynamic Auto	Trunk	Dynamic Desirable
access	Access	Access	Access	Access
dynamic auto	Access	Access	Trunk	Trunk
trunk	Access	Trunk	Trunk	Trunk
dynamic desirable	Access	Trunk	Trunk	Trunk

Controlling Which VLANs Can Be Supported on a Trunk

The *allowed VLAN list* feature provides a mechanism for engineers to administratively disable a VLAN from a trunk. By default, switches include all possible VLANs (1–4094) in each trunk's allowed VLAN list. However, the engineer can then limit the VLANs allowed on the trunk by using the following interface subcommand:

```
switchport trunk allowed vlan {add ¦ all ¦ except ¦ remove} vlan-list
```

This command provides a way to easily add and remove VLANs from the list. For example, the **add** option permits the switch to add VLANs to the existing allowed VLAN list, and the **remove** option permits the switch to remove VLANs from the existing list. The **all** option means all VLANs, so you can use it to reset the switch to its original default setting (permitting VLANs 1–4094 on the trunk). The **except** option is rather tricky: It adds all VLANs to the list that are not part of the command. For example, the **switchport trunk allowed vlan except 100-200** interface subcommand adds VLANs 1 through 99 and 201 through 4094 to the existing allowed VLAN list on that trunk.

In addition to the allowed VLAN list, a switch has three other reasons to prevent a particular VLAN's traffic from crossing a trunk. All four reasons are summarized in the following list:

- A VLAN has been removed from the trunk's *allowed VLAN* list.
- A VLAN does not exist, or is not active, in the switch's VLAN database (as seen with the **show vlan** command).
- A VLAN has been automatically pruned by VTP.
- A VLAN's STP instance has placed the trunk interface into a state other than a Forwarding State.

This section takes a closer look at the second item in the list only. Of the other reasons in the list, the first and third have already been discussed in this chapter. The fourth reason relates to STP, which is only briefly mentioned in this book.

Switches must believe a VLAN exists, and is active, before the switch will try to send frames in that VLAN. First, if a switch does not know that a VLAN exists, as evidenced by the VLAN's absence from the output of the **show vlan** command, the switch will not forward frames in that VLAN over any interface. Additionally, a VLAN can be administratively shut down on any switch by using the **shutdown vlan** *vlan-id* global configuration command, which also causes the switch to no longer forward frames in that VLAN, even over trunks. So, switches do not forward frames in a nonexistent or shutdown VLAN over any of the switch's trunks.

The book lists the four reasons for limiting VLANs on a trunk in the same order in which IOS describes these reasons in the output of the **show interfaces trunk** command. This command includes a progression of three lists of the VLANs supported over a trunk. These three lists are as follows:

- VLANs in the allowed VLAN list on the trunk

- VLANs in the previous group that are also configured and active (not shut down) on the switch

- VLANs in the previous group that are also not pruned and are in an STP Forwarding State

To get an idea of these three lists inside the output of the **show interfaces trunk** command, Example 26-4 shows how VLANs might be disallowed on a trunk for various reasons. The command output is taken from SW1 in Figure 26-9, after the completion of the configuration as shown in Examples 26-1, 26-2, and 26-3. In other words, VLANS 1 through 3 exist, and trunking is operational. Then, during the example, the following items are configured on SW1:

Step 1.   VLAN 4 is added.

Step 2.   VLAN 2 is shut down.

Step 3.   VLAN 3 is removed from the trunk's allowed VLAN list.

Example 26-4   *Allowed VLAN List and the List of Active VLANs*

```
! The three lists of VLANs in the next command list allowed VLANs (1-4094),
! Allowed and active VLANs (1-3), and allowed/active/not pruned/STP forwarding
! VLANs (1-3)
SW1# show interfaces trunk

Port        Mode          Encapsulation  Status        Native vlan
Gi0/1       desirable     802.1q         trunking      1


Port        Vlans allowed on trunk
Gi0/1       1-4094


Port        Vlans allowed and active in management domain
Gi0/1       1-3


Port        Vlans in spanning tree forwarding state and not pruned
Gi0/1       1-3
```

```
! Next, the switch is configured with new VLAN 4; VLAN 2 is shutdown;
! and VLAN 3 is removed from the allowed VLAN list on the trunk.
SW1# configure terminal
Enter configuration commands, one per line.  End with CNTL/Z.
SW1(config)# vlan 4
SW1(config-vlan)# vlan 2
SW1(config-vlan)# shutdown
SW1(config-vlan)# interface gi0/1
SW1(config-if)# switchport trunk allowed vlan remove 3
SW1(config-if)# ^Z
! The three lists of VLANs in the next command list allowed VLANs (1-2, 4-4094),
! allowed and active VLANs (1,4), and allowed/active/not pruned/STP forwarding
! VLANs (1,4)
SW1# show interfaces trunk


Port        Mode        Encapsulation  Status       Native vlan
Gi0/1       desirable   802.1q         trunking     1


! VLAN 3 is omitted next, because it was removed from the allowed VLAN list.
Port        Vlans allowed on trunk
Gi0/1       1-2,4-4094


! VLAN 2 is omitted below because it is shutdown. VLANs 5-4094 are omitted below
! because SW1 does not have them configured.
Port        Vlans allowed and active in management domain
Gi0/1       1,4


Port        Vlans in spanning tree forwarding state and not pruned
Gi0/1       1,4
```

Trunking to Cisco IP Phones

Cisco IP phones use Ethernet to connect to the IP network for the purpose of sending Voice over IP (VoIP) packets. Cisco IP phones can send VoIP packets to other IP phones to support voice calls, as well as send VoIP packets to voice gateways, which in turn connect to the existing traditional telephone network, supporting the ability to call most any phone in the world.

Cisco anticipated that each desk in an enterprise might have both a Cisco IP phone and a PC on it. To reduce cabling clutter, Cisco includes a small LAN switch in the bottom of each Cisco IP phone. The small switch allows one cable to run from the wiring closet to the desk and connect to the IP phone, and then the PC can connect to the switch by connecting a short Ethernet (straight-through) cable from the PC to the bottom of the IP phone. Figure 26-10 shows the cabling as well as a few more details.

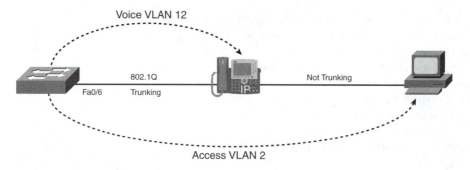

Figure 26-10   *Typical Connection of a Cisco IP Phone and PC to a Cisco Switch*

Cisco IP telephony design guidelines suggest that the link between the phone and switch should use 802.1Q trunking, and that the phone and PC should be in different VLANs (and therefore in different subnets). By placing the phones in one VLAN, and the PCs connected to the phones in a different VLAN, engineers can more easily manage the IP address space, more easily apply quality of service (QoS) mechanisms to the VoIP packets, and provide better security by separating the data and voice traffic.

Cisco calls the VLAN used for the phone's traffic the voice VLAN and the VLAN used for data the data or access VLAN. For the switch to forward traffic correctly, Cisco switches need to know the VLAN ID of both the voice VLAN and the data VLAN. The data (or access) VLAN is configured just as seen in the last few examples, using the **switchport access vlan** *vlan-id* command. The voice vlan is configured with the **switchport voice vlan** *vlan-id* interface subcommand. For example, to match Figure 26-10, interface Fa0/6 would need both the **switchport access vlan 2** interface subcommand and the **switchport voice vlan 12** subcommand.

Table 26-5 summarizes the key points about the voice VLAN.

Key
Topic

Table 26-5   *Voice and Data VLAN Configuration*

Device	Name of the VLAN	Configured with This Command
Phone	Voice or auxiliary VLAN	**switchport voice vlan** *vlan-id*
PC	Data or access VLAN	**switchport access vlan** *vlan-id*

Securing VLANs and Trunking

Switches are exposed to several types of security vulnerabilities over both used ports and unused ports. For example, an attacker could connect a computer to a wall plug cabled to a switch port and cause problems on the VLAN assigned to that port. Additionally, the attacker could negotiate trunking and cause many other types of problems, some related to VTP.

Cisco makes some recommendations for how to protect unused switch ports. Instead of using default settings, Cisco recommends configuring these interfaces as follows:

Key
Topic

■ Administratively disable the unused interface, using the **shutdown** interface subcommand.

■ Prevent trunking from being negotiated when the port is enabled by using the **switchport nonegotiate** interface subcommand to disable negotiation, or the **switchport mode access** interface subcommand to statically configure the interface as an access interface.

■ Assign the port to an unused VLAN, sometimes called a *parking lot VLAN*, using the **switchport access vlan** *number* interface subcommand.

Frankly, if you just shut down the interface, the security exposure goes away, but the other two tasks prevent any immediate problems if some other engineer enables the interface by configuring a **no shutdown** command.

Besides these recommendations on unused ports, Cisco recommends that the negotiation of trunking be disabled on all in-use access interfaces, with all trunks being manually configured to trunk. The exposure is that an attacker could disconnect a legitimate user's computer from the RJ-45 port, connect the attacker's PC, and try to negotiate trunking. By configuring all in-use interfaces that should not be trunking with the **switchport nonegotiate** interface subcommand, these interfaces will not dynamically decide to trunk, reducing the exposure to trunking-related problems. For any interfaces that need to trunk, Cisco recommends manually configuring trunking.

VTP Configuration and Verification

VTP configuration requires only a few simple steps, but VTP has the power to cause significant problems, either by accidental poor configuration choices or by malicious attacks. The following sections first examine the overall configuration, followed by some comments about potential problems created by the VTP process. These sections then end with a discussion of how to troubleshoot problems related to VTP.

Using VTP: Configuring Servers and Clients

Before configuring VTP, several VTP settings must be chosen. In particular, assuming that the engineer wants to make use of VTP, the engineer needs to decide which switches will be in the same VTP domain, meaning that these switches will learn VLAN configuration information from each other. The VTP domain name must be chosen, along with an optional but recommended VTP password. (Both values are case sensitive.) The engineer must also choose which switches will be servers (usually at least two for redundancy), and which will be clients.

After the planning steps are completed, the following steps can be used to configure VTP:

Step 1. Configure the VTP mode using the **vtp mode** {**server** | **client**} global configuration command.

Step 2. Configure the VTP (case-sensitive) domain name using the **vtp domain** *domain-name* global configuration command.

Step 3. (Optional) On both clients and servers, configure the same case-sensitive password using the **vtp password** *password-value* global configuration command.

Step 4. (Optional) Configure VTP pruning on the VTP servers using the **vtp pruning** global configuration command.

Step 5. (Optional) Enable VTP version 2 with the **vtp version 2** global configuration command.

Step 6. Bring up trunks between the switches.

Example 26-5 shows a sample configuration, along with a **show vtp status** command, for the two switches in Figure 26-11. The figure points out the configuration settings on the two switches before Example 26-5 shows VTP configuration being added. In particular, note that both switches use default VTP configuration settings.

```
SW1
  Gi0/1        VLANs:         1, 2, 3,1002-1005
               VTP Mode:      Server
               VTP Domain:    <null>
               VTP Password:  <null>
               VTP Revision:  5
               IP Address:    192.168.1.105
  Trunk

  Gi0/2
SW2            VLANs:         1,1002-1005
               VTP Mode:      Server
               VTP Domain:    <null>
               VTP Password:  <null>
               Revision:      1
               IP Address:    192.168.1.106
```

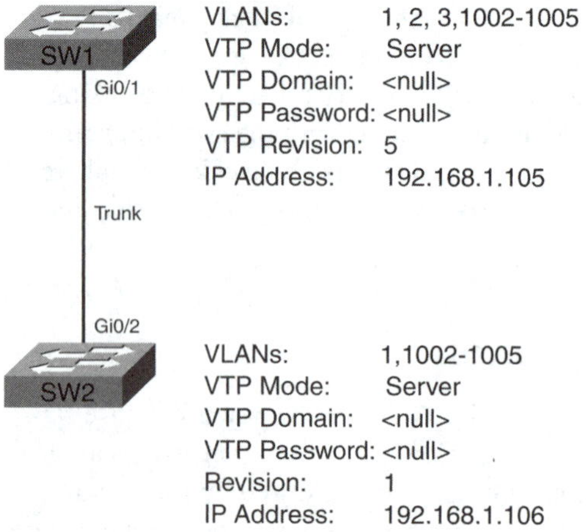

Figure 26-11 *Switch Configuration Before Example 26-5*

Example 26-5 shows the following configuration on both SW1 and SW2, and the results:

■ **SW1:** Configured as a server, with VTP domain name Freds-domain, VTP password Freds-password, and VTP pruning enabled

■ **SW2:** Configured as a client, with VTP domain name Freds-domain and VTP password Freds-password

Example 26-5 *Basic VTP Client and Server Configuration*

```
! IOS generates at least one informational message after each VTP command listed
! below. The comments added by the author begin with an exclamation point.
SW1# configure terminal
Enter configuration commands, one per line.  End with CNTL/Z.
SW1(config)# vtp mode server
Setting device to VTP SERVER mode
SW1(config)# vtp domain Freds-domain
Changing VTP domain name from NULL to Freds-domain
SW1(config)# vtp password Freds-password
Setting device VLAN database password to Freds-password
SW1(config)# vtp pruning
Pruning switched on
SW1(config)# ^Z
! Switching to SW2 now
SW2# configure terminal
Enter configuration commands, one per line.  End with CNTL/Z.
SW2(config)# vtp mode client
Setting device to VTP CLIENT mode.
SW2(config)# vtp domain Freds-domain
Domain name already set to Freds-domain.
SW2(config)# vtp password Freds-password
Setting device VLAN database password to Freds-password
SW2(config)# ^Z
! The output below shows configuration revision number 5, with 7 existing VLANs
! (1 through 3, 1002 through 1005), as learned from SW1
SW2# show vtp status
VTP Version                     : 2
Configuration Revision          : 5
Maximum VLANs supported locally : 255
Number of existing VLANs        : 7
VTP Operating Mode              : Client
VTP Domain Name                 : Freds-domain
VTP Pruning Mode                : Enabled
VTP V2 Mode                     : Disabled
VTP Traps Generation            : Disabled
MD5 digest                      : 0x22 0x07 0xF2 0x3A 0xF1 0x28 0xA0 0x5D
Configuration last modified by 192.168.1.105 at 3-1-93 00:28:35
! The next command lists the known VLANs, including VLANs 2 and 3, learned
! from SW1
SW2# show vlan brief

VLAN Name                        Status    Ports
---- -------------------------- --------- ------------------------------
1    default                     active    Fa0/1, Fa0/2, Fa0/3, Fa0/4
```

```
                                                      Fa0/5, Fa0/6, Fa0/7, Fa0/8
                                                      Fa0/9, Fa0/10, Fa0/11, Fa0/12
                                                      Fa0/13, Fa0/14, Fa0/15, Fa0/16
                                                      Fa0/17, Fa0/18, Fa0/19, Fa0/20
                                                      Fa0/21, Fa0/22, Fa0/23, Fa0/24
                                                      Gi0/1
2    Freds-vlan                        active
3    VLAN0003                          active
1002 fddi-default                      act/unsup
1003 token-ring-default                act/unsup
1004 fddinet-default                   act/unsup
1005 trnet-default                     act/unsup
! Switching to SW1 now
! Back on SW1, the output below confirms the same revision number as SW2, meaning
! that the two switches have synchronized their VLAN databases.
SW1# show vtp status
VTP Version                 : 2
Configuration Revision      : 5
Maximum VLANs supported locally : 255
Number of existing VLANs    : 7
VTP Operating Mode          : Server
VTP Domain Name             : Freds-domain
VTP Pruning Mode            : Enabled
VTP V2 Mode                 : Disabled
VTP Traps Generation        : Disabled
MD5 digest                  : 0x22 0x07 0xF2 0x3A 0xF1 0x28 0xA0 0x5D
Configuration last modified by 192.168.1.105 at 3-1-93 00:28:35
Local updater ID is 192.168.1.105 on interface Vl1 (lowest numbered VLAN
interface found)
SW1# show vtp password
VTP Password: Freds-password
```

The example is relatively long, but the configuration is straightforward. Both switches were configured with the VTP mode (server and client), the same domain name, and the same password, with trunking already having been configured. The configuration resulted in SW2 (client) synchronizing its VLAN database to match SW1 (server).

Cisco IOS switches in VTP server or client mode store the **vtp** configuration commands, and some other configuration commands, in the vlan.dat file in flash, and the switches do not store the configuration commands in the running-config file. Instead, to verify these configuration commands and their settings, the **show vtp status** and **show vlan** commands are used. For reference, Table 26-6, lists the VLAN-related configuration commands, the location in which a VTP server or client stores the commands, and how to view the settings for the commands.

Table 26-6   *Where VTP Clients and Servers Store VLAN-Related Configuration*

Key
Topic

Configuration Commands	Where Stored	How to View
vtp domain	vlan.dat	**show vtp status**
vtp mode	vlan.dat	**show vtp status**
vtp password	vlan.dat	**show vtp password**
vtp pruning	vlan.dat	**show vtp status**
vlan *vlan-id*	vlan.dat	**show vlan [brief]**
name *vlan-name*	vlan.dat	**show vlan [brief]**
switchport access vlan *vlan-id*	running-config	**show running-config, show interfaces switchport**
switchport voice vlan *vlan-id*	running-config	**show running-config, show interfaces switchport**

Any analysis of VTP and VLANs on Cisco switches depends on two important commands: the **show vtp status** and **show vlan** commands. First, note that when the domain is synchronized, the **show vtp status** command on all switches should have the same configuration revision number. Additionally, the **show vlan** command should list the same VLANs and VLAN names. For example, both SW1 and SW2 end Example 26-5 with a revision number of 5, and both know about seven VLANs: 1–3 and 1002–1005. Both instances of the **show vtp status** command in Example 26-5 list the IP address of the last switch to modify the VLAN database—namely SW1, 192.168.1.105—so it is easier to find which switch last changed the VLAN configuration. Only on VTP servers, the **show vtp status** command ends with a line that lists that switch's IP address that identifies itself when advertising VTP updates, making it easier to confirm which switch last changed the VLAN configuration.

Note that the VTP password can only be displayed with the **show vtp password** command. The **show vtp status** command displays an MD5 digest of the password.

Note: Cisco switches send VTP messages and Cisco Discovery Protocol (CDP) messages on trunks using VLAN 1.

Caveats When Moving Away from Default VTP Configuration

The default behavior of VTP introduces the possibility of problems when first configuring VTP. To see why, consider the following five points about VTP:

■   The default VTP configuration on Cisco switches is VTP server mode with a null domain name.

■   With all default settings, a switch does not send VTP updates, even over trunks, but the switch can be configured with VLANs because it is in server mode.

- After configuring a domain name, that switch immediately starts sending VTP updates over all its trunks.

- If a switch that still has a (default) null domain name receives a VTP update—which by definition lists a domain name—and no password was used by the sending switch, the receiving switch starts using that VTP domain name.

- When the previous step occurs, the switch with the higher VLAN database revision number causes the switch with the lower revision number to overwrite its VLAN database.

Example 26-5 progresses through these same five facts. Example 26-5 begins with trunking enabled between the two switches, but with default VTP settings (items 1 and 2 from the list preceding this paragraph). As soon as SW1 configures its VTP domain name, SW1 sends VTP messages over the trunk to SW2 (item 3). SW2 reacts by starting to use the VTP domain name listed in the received VTP update (Freds-domain, in this case). By the time the **vtp domain Freds-domain** command was issued on SW2 in Example 26-5, SW2 was already using the dynamically learned domain name Freds-domain, so Cisco IOS on SW2 issued the response "Domain name already set to Freds-domain" (item 4). Finally, SW2, with a lower VTP revision number, synchronized its VLAN database to match SW1 (item 5).

The process worked exactly as intended in Example 26-5. However, this same process allows an engineer to innocently configure a switch's VTP domain name and completely crash a switched LAN. For example, imagine that SW2 had configured VLAN 4 and assigned several interfaces to VLAN 4, but SW1 does not have a definition for VLAN 4. Following this same process, when SW2 synchronizes its VLAN database to match SW1, SW2 overwrites the old database, losing the definition of VLAN 4. At that point, SW2 can no longer forward frames in VLAN 4, and all the users of VLAN 4 might start calling the help desk.

This same process could be used to perform a denial of service (DoS) attack using VTP. With only default VTP settings, any attacker that can manage to bring up a trunk between an attacking switch and the existing legitimate switch can cause the existing switches to synchronize to the attacking switch's VLAN database, which might well have no VLANs configured. So, for real networks, if you do not intend to use VTP when installing a switch, it is worth the effort to simply configure it to be a VTP transparent mode switch, as is covered in the next section. By doing so, the configuration of a VTP domain name on that new switch will not impact the existing switches, and the configuration of a domain name on another switch will not impact this new switch.

Note: The later section "Troubleshooting VTP" explains how to recognize when VTP might have caused problems like those mentioned in this section.

Avoiding VTP: Configuring Transparent Mode

To avoid using VTP, you need to configure VTP transparent mode. In transparent mode, a switch never updates its VLAN database based on a received VTP message, and never causes other switches to update their databases based on the transparent mode switch's

VLAN database. The only VTP action performed by the switch is to forward VTP messages received on one trunk out all the other trunks, which allows other VTP clients and servers to work correctly.

Configuring VTP transparent mode is simple: Just issue the **vtp mode transparent** command in global configuration mode. You do not need a domain name or a password.

Troubleshooting VTP

VTP can have an enormous impact on a campus LAN built using Cisco switches, both a negative and positive impact. The following sections examine three aspects of VTP troubleshooting. First, the text suggests a process by which to troubleshoot VTP when VTP does not appear to be distributing VLAN configuration information (adds/deletions/changes). Following that, the text examines a common class of problems that occur when a trunk comes up, possibly triggering the neighboring switches to send VTP updates and overwrite one of the switch's VLAN database. This topic ends with suggested best practices for preventing VTP problems.

Determining Why VTP Is Not Currently Working

The first step in troubleshooting VTP should be to determine whether a problem exists in the first place. For switches that should be using VTP, in the same domain, a problem can first be identified when any two neighboring switches have different VLAN databases. In other words, they know about different VLAN IDs, with different names, and with a different configuration revision number. After identifying two neighboring switches whose VLAN databases do not match, the next step is to check the configuration and the operational trunking mode (not the administrative mode), and to correct any problems. The following list details the specific steps:

Step 1.   Confirm the switch names, topology (including which interfaces connect which switches), and switch VTP modes.

Step 2.   Identify sets of two neighboring switches that should be either VTP clients or servers whose VLAN databases differ with the **show vlan** command.

Step 3.   On each pair of two neighboring switches whose databases differ, verify the following:

    a.   At least one operational trunk should exist between the two switches (use the **show interfaces trunk**, **show interfaces switchport**, or **show cdp neighbors** command).

    b.   The switches must have the same (case-sensitive) VTP domain name (**show vtp status**).

    c.   If configured, the switches must have the same (case-sensitive) VTP password (**show vtp password**).

    d.   Although VTP pruning should be enabled or disabled on all servers in the same domain, having two servers configured with opposite pruning settings does not prevent the synchronization process.

Step 4.   For each pair of switches identified in Step 3, solve the problem by either troubleshooting the trunking problem or reconfiguring a switch to correctly match the domain name or password.

> **Note:** For real campus LANs, besides the items in this list, also consider the intended VTP design as well.

Although the process does spell out several steps, it mainly shows how to attack the problem with knowledge covered earlier in this chapter. The process basically states that if the VLAN databases differ, and the switches should be either VTP clients or servers, that a VTP problem exists—and the root cause is usually some VTP configuration problem. However, because you might not always be allowed to use enable mode where you can view the configuration, you need to be ready to troubleshoot problems using only **show** command output. For example, consider a problem in which three switches (SW1, SW2, and SW3) all connect to each other, and you need to find the root cause of the current problems, based only on the output of **show** commands like those in Example 26-6.

> **Note:** It would be a good exercise to read the example and apply the troubleshooting steps listed at the beginning of this section before reading any of the explanations that follow the example.

Example 26-6   *VTP Troubleshooting Example*

```
SW1# show cdp neighbors
Capability Codes: R - Router, T - Trans Bridge, B - Source Route Bridge
                  S - Switch, H - Host, I - IGMP, r - Repeater, P - Phone

Device ID          Local Intrfce      Holdtme  Capability   Platform   Port ID
SW2                Gig 0/1              163        S I       WS-C2960-2Gig 0/2
SW3                Gig 0/2              173        S I       WS-C3550-2Gig 0/1
SW1# show vlan brief

VLAN Name                             Status    Ports
---- -------------------------------- --------- -------------------------------
1    default                          active    Fa0/1, Fa0/2, Fa0/3, Fa0/4
                                                Fa0/5, Fa0/6, Fa0/7, Fa0/8
                                                Fa0/9, Fa0/10, Fa0/13, Fa0/14
                                                Fa0/15, Fa0/16, Fa0/17, Fa0/18
                                                Fa0/19, Fa0/20, Fa0/21, Fa0/22
                                                Fa0/23, Fa0/24, Gi0/2
3    VLAN0003                         active    Fa0/11
4    VLAN0004                         active
5    VLAN0005                         active
49   VLAN0049                         active
50   VLAN0050                         active
1002 fddi-default                     act/unsup
1003 trcrf-default                    act/unsup
1004 fddinet-default                  act/unsup
1005 trbrf-default                    act/unsup
```

```
SW1# show interfaces trunk

Port        Mode         Encapsulation  Status        Native vlan
Gi0/1       desirable    802.1q         trunking      1


Port        Vlans allowed on trunk
Gi0/1       1-4094


Port        Vlans allowed and active in management domain
Gi0/1       1,3-5,49-50


Port        Vlans in spanning tree forwarding state and not pruned
Gi0/1       3-5,49-50
SW1# show vtp status
VTP Version                     : 2
Configuration Revision          : 131
Maximum VLANs supported locally : 255
Number of existing VLANs        : 10
VTP Operating Mode              : Client
VTP Domain Name                 : Larry
VTP Pruning Mode                : Disabled
VTP V2 Mode                     : Enabled
VTP Traps Generation            : Disabled
MD5 digest                      : 0x1D 0x27 0xA9 0xF9 0x46 0xDF 0x66 0xCF
Configuration last modified by 1.1.1.3 at 3-1-93 00:33:38
! SW2 next
SW2# show cdp neighbors
Capability Codes: R - Router, T - Trans Bridge, B - Source Route Bridge
                  S - Switch, H - Host, I - IGMP, r - Repeater, P - Phone

Device ID           Local Intrfce     Holdtme  Capability  Platform     Port ID
SW1                 Gig 0/2           175          S I     WS-C2960-2Gig 0/1
SW3                 Gig 0/1           155          S I     WS-C3550-2Gig 0/2
SW2# show vlan brief

VLAN Name                            Status    Ports
---- -------------------------------- --------- -------------------------------
1    default                          active    Fa0/1, Fa0/2, Fa0/3, Fa0/4
                                                Fa0/5, Fa0/6, Fa0/7, Fa0/8
                                                Fa0/9, Fa0/10, Fa0/11, Fa0/12
                                                Fa0/13, Fa0/14, Fa0/15, Fa0/16
                                                Fa0/17, Fa0/18, Fa0/19, Fa0/20
                                                Fa0/21, Fa0/22, Fa0/23, Fa0/24

3    VLAN0003                         active
1002 fddi-default                     act/unsup
```

```
1003 trcrf-default                 act/unsup
1004 fddinet-default               act/unsup
1005 trbrf-default                 act/unsup
SW2# show vtp status
VTP Version                   : 2
Configuration Revision        : 0
Maximum VLANs supported locally : 255
Number of existing VLANs      : 6
VTP Operating Mode            : Server
VTP Domain Name               : larry
VTP Pruning Mode              : Disabled
VTP V2 Mode                   : Enabled
VTP Traps Generation          : Disabled
MD5 digest                    : 0x8C 0x75 0xC5 0xDE 0xE9 0x7C 0x2D 0x8B
Configuration last modified by 1.1.1.2 at 0-0-00 00:00:00
Local updater ID is 1.1.1.2 on interface Vl1 (lowest numbered VLAN interface found)
! SW3 next
SW3# show vlan brief


VLAN Name                            Status    Ports
---- -------------------------------- --------- ------------------------------
1    default                         active    Fa0/1, Fa0/2, Fa0/3, Fa0/4
                                                Fa0/5, Fa0/6, Fa0/7, Fa0/8
                                                Fa0/9, Fa0/10, Fa0/11, Fa0/12
                                                Fa0/14, Fa0/15, Fa0/16, Fa0/17
                                                Fa0/18, Fa0/19, Fa0/20, Fa0/21
                                                Fa0/22, Fa0/23, Fa0/24, Gi0/1
3    VLAN0003                        active    Fa0/13
4    VLAN0004                        active
5    VLAN0005                        active
20   VLAN20                          active
1002 fddi-default                    act/unsup
1003 trcrf-default                   act/unsup
1004 fddinet-default                 act/unsup
1005 trbrf-default                   act/unsup
SW3# show interfaces trunk


Port      Mode         Encapsulation  Status       Native vlan
Gi0/2     desirable    n-802.1q       trunking     1
```

```
Port          Vlans allowed on trunk
Gi0/2         1-4094


Port          Vlans allowed and active in management domain
Gi0/2         1,3-5,20


Port          Vlans in spanning tree forwarding state and not pruned
Gi0/2         1,3-5,20
SW3# show vtp status
VTP Version                     : 2
Configuration Revision          : 134
Maximum VLANs supported locally : 1005
Number of existing VLANs        : 9
VTP Operating Mode              : Server
VTP Domain Name                 : Larry
VTP Pruning Mode                : Disabled
VTP V2 Mode                     : Enabled
VTP Traps Generation            : Disabled
MD5 digest                      : 0x1D 0x27 0xA9 0xF9 0x46 0xDF 0x66 0xCF
Configuration last modified by 1.1.1.3 at 3-1-93 01:07:29
Local updater ID is 1.1.1.3 on interface Vl1 (lowest numbered VLAN interface found)
```

For Step 1, the **show cdp neighbors** and **show interfaces trunk** commands provide enough information to confirm the topology as well as show which links are operating as trunks. The **show interfaces trunk** command lists only interfaces in an operationally trunking state. Alternately, the **show interfaces switchport** command lists the operational mode (trunk or access) as well. Figure 26-12 shows the network diagram. Note also that the link between SW1 and SW3 does not currently use trunking.

For Step 2, a quick review of the **show vlan brief** command output from each switch shows that all three switches have different VLAN databases. For example, all three switches know about VLAN 3, whereas SW1 is the only switch that knows about VLAN 50, and SW3 is the only switch that knows about VLAN 20.

Because all three pairs of neighboring switches have different VLAN databases, Step 3 of the troubleshooting process suggests that each pair be examined. Starting with SW1 and SW2, a quick look at the **show vtp status** command on both switches identifies the problem: SW1 uses the domain name Larry, whereas SW2 uses larry, and the names differ because of the different case of the first letter. Similarly, SW3 and SW2 have difficulties because of the mismatched VTP domain name. Because SW2 is the only switch with lowercase larry, a solution would be to reconfigure SW2 to use Larry as the domain name.

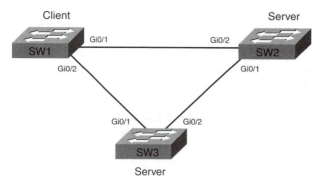

Figure 26-12 *Switched Network Topology in Example 26-6*

Continuing Step 3 for SW1 and SW3, the two switches have the same domain name (Step 3B), but a look at Step 3A shows that no trunk is connecting SW1 to SW3. CDP confirms that SW1's Gi0/2 interface connects to SW3, but the **show interfaces trunk** command on SW1 does not list the Gi0/2 interface. As a result, neither switch can send VTP messages to each other. The root cause of this problem is most likely an oversight in the configuration of the **switchport mode** interface subcommand.

Although the example did not have any problems because of VTP password mismatches, it is important to know how to check the passwords. First, the password can be displayed on each switch with the **show vtp password** command. Additionally, the **show vtp status** command lists an MD5 hash derived from both the VTP domain name and VTP password. So, if two switches have the same case-sensitive domain name and password, the MD5 hash value listed in the **show vtp status** command output will be the same. However, if two switches list different MD5 hash values, you then need to examine the domain names. If the domain names are the same, the passwords must have been different because the MD5 hashes are different.

Before moving on to the next topic, here is a quick comment about VTP version and how it should not prevent switches from working. If you examine the **show vtp status** command output again in Example 26-6, note the headings VTP Version and V2 Mode Enabled. The first line lists the highest VTP version supported by that switch's software. The other line shows what the switch is currently using. If a switch has the VTP version 2 command configured, overriding the default of version 1, the switch will use **vtp version 2**— but only if the other switches in the domain also support version 2. So, a mismatch of the configured VTP version means that the switches work, but they would use VTP version 1, and the line reading "VTP V2 Mode" would list the word *disabled*, meaning that VTP version 1 is used.

Problems When Connecting New Switches and Bringing Up Trunks

VTP can be running just fine for months, and then one day, a rash of calls to the help desk describe cases in which large groups of users can no longer use the network. After further examination, it appears that most every VLAN in the campus has been deleted. The switches still have many interfaces with **switchport access vlan** commands that refer to the now-deleted VLANs. None of the devices on those now-deleted VLANs work, because Cisco switches do not forward frames for nonexistent VLANs.

This scenario can and does happen occasionally, mainly when a new switch is connected to an existing network. Whether this problem happens by accident or as a denial of service (DoS) attack, the root cause is that when a new VLAN trunk (ISL or 802.1Q) comes up between two switches, and the two switches are either VTP servers or clients, the switches send VTP updates to each other. If a switch receives a VTP advertisement that has the same domain name and was generated with the same VTP password, one or the other switch overwrites its VLAN database as part of the synchronization process. Specifically, the switch that had the lower revision number synchronizes its VLAN database to match the neighboring switch (which has the higher revision number). Summarizing the process more formally:

Step 1.   Confirm that trunking will occur on the new link (refer to Table 26-4 for details).

Step 2.   Confirm that the two switches use the same case-sensitive VTP domain name and password.

Step 3.   If Steps 1 and 2 confirm that VTP will work, the switch with the lower revision number updates its VLAN database to match the other switch.

For example, Example 26-6 and Figure 26-12 show that the SW1-to-SW3 link is not trunking. If this link were to be configured to trunk, SW1 and SW3 would send VTP messages to each other, using the same VTP domain name and the same VTP password. So, one switch would update its VLAN database to match the other. Example 26-6 shows SW1 with revision number 131 and SW3 with revision number 134, so SW1 will overwrite its VLAN database to match SW3, thereby deleting VLANs 49 and 50. Example 26-7 picks up the story at the end of Example 26-6, showing the trunk between SW1 and SW3 coming up, allowing VTP synchronization, and resulting in changes to SW1's VLAN database.

Example 26-7   *VTP Troubleshooting Example*

```
SW1# configure terminal
Enter configuration commands, one per line.  End with CNTL/Z.
SW1(config)# interface gi0/2
SW1(config-if)# switchport mode dynamic desirable
SW1(config-if)# ^Z
SW1#
01:43:46: %SYS-5-CONFIG_I: Configured from console by console
01:43:46: %LINEPROTO-5-UPDOWN: Line protocol on Interface GigabitEthernet0/2,
changed state to down
SW1#01:43:49: %LINEPROTO-5-UPDOWN: Line protocol on Interface GigabitEthernet0/2,
changed state to up
SW1# show vlan brief
```

```
VLAN Name                             Status      Ports
---- -------------------------------- ----------  ----------------------------
1    default                          active      Fa0/1, Fa0/2, Fa0/3, Fa0/4
                                                  Fa0/5, Fa0/6, Fa0/7, Fa0/8
                                                  Fa0/9, Fa0/10, Fa0/13, Fa0/14
                                                  Fa0/15, Fa0/16, Fa0/17, Fa0/18
                                                  Fa0/19, Fa0/20, Fa0/21, Fa0/22
                                                  Fa0/23, Fa0/24, Gi0/1
3    VLAN0003                         active      Fa0/11
4    VLAN0004                         active
5    VLAN0005                         active
20   VLAN20                           active
1002 fddi-default                     act/unsup
1003 trcrf-default                    act/unsup
1004 fddinet-default                  act/unsup
1005 trbrf-default                    act/unsup
```

In real life, you have several ways to help reduce the chance of such problems when installing a new switch to an existing VTP domain. In particular, before connecting a new switch to an existing VTP domain, reset the new switch's VTP revision number to 0 by one of the following methods:

■ Configure the new switch for VTP transparent mode and then back to VTP client or server mode.

■ Erase the new switch's vlan.dat file in flash and reload the switch. This file contains the switch's VLAN database, including the revision number.

Avoiding VTP Problems Through Best Practices

Besides the suggestion of resetting the VLAN database revision number before installing a new switch, a couple of other good VTP conventions, called best practices, can help avoid some of the pitfalls of VTP. These are as follows:

■ If you do not intend to use VTP, configure each switch to use transparent mode.

■ If using VTP server or client mode, always use a VTP password.

■ Disable trunking with the **switchport mode access** and **switchport nonegotiate** commands on all interfaces except known trunks, preventing VTP attacks by preventing the dynamic establishment of trunks.

By preventing the negotiation of trunking to most ports, the attacker can never see a VTP update from one of your switches. With a VTP password set, even if the attacker manages to get trunking working to an existing switch, the attacker would then have to know the password to do any harm. And by using transparent mode, you can avoid the types of problems described earlier, in the section "Caveats When Moving Away from Default VTP Configuration."

Chapter Review

Review Key Topics

Review the most important topics from inside the chapter, noted with the Key Topic icons in the outer margin of the page. Table 26-7 lists these key topics and the page numbers on which each is found.

Table 26-7 *Key Topics for Chapter 26*

Key Topic Element	Description	Page Number
List	Reasons for using VLANs	644
Figure 26-2	Diagram of VLAN trunking	645
Figure 26-4	802.1Q header	647
Table 26-1	Comparisons of 802.1Q and ISL	648
Figure 26-6	VTP synchronization process concepts	650
List	Requirements for VTP to work between two switches	651
Table 26-2	VTP features summary	655
List	Configuration checklist for configuring VLANs and assigning to interfaces	656
List	Default VTP and VLAN configuration	656
Table 26-3	Options of the **switchport mode** command	661
Table 26-4	Expected trunking results based on the configuration of the **switchport mode** command	665
List	Four reasons why a trunk does not pass traffic for a VLAN	665
Table 26-5	Voice and data VLAN configuration and terms	668
List	Recommendations for how to protect unused switch ports	669
List	VTP configuration checklist	670
Table 26-6	VTP and VLAN configuration commands, and where they are stored	673
List	VTP troubleshooting process used when VTP is not performing as desired	675
List	Predicting what will happen with VTP when a new switch connects to a network	681
List	VTP best practices for preventing VTP problems	682

Key Topic

Define Key Terms

Define the following key terms from this chapter, and check your answers in the glossary:

802.1Q, ISL, trunk, trunking administrative mode, trunking operational mode, VLAN, VLAN configuration database, vlan.dat, VTP, VTP client mode, VTP pruning, VTP server mode, VTP transparent mode

Review Command Reference to Check Your Memory

Although you should not necessarily memorize the information in the tables in this section, this section does include a reference for the configuration and EXEC commands covered in this chapter. Practically speaking, you should memorize the commands as a side effect of reading the chapter and doing all the activities in this "Chapter Review" section. To check to see how well you have memorized the commands as a side effect of your other studies, cover the left side of the table with a piece of paper, read the descriptions in the right side, and see whether you remember the command.

Table 26-8   *Chapter 26 Configuration Command Reference*

Command	Description
vlan *vlan-id*	Global config command that both creates the VLAN and puts the CLI into VLAN configuration mode
name *vlan-name*	VLAN subcommand that names the VLAN
shutdown	VLAN subcommand that prevents that one switch from forwarding traffic in that VLAN
shutdown vlan *vlan-id*	Global config command that administratively disables a VLAN, preventing the switch from forwarding frames in that VLAN
vtp domain *domain-name*	Global config command that defines the VTP domain name
vtp password *password*	Global config command that defines the VTP password
vtp mode {server | client | transparent}	Global config command that defines the VTP mode
vtp pruning	Global config command that tells the VTP server to tell all switches to use VTP pruning
switchport mode {access | dynamic {auto | desirable} | trunk}	Interface subcommand that configures the trunking administrative mode on the interface
switchport trunk allowed vlan {add | all | except | remove} *vlan-list*	Interface subcommand that defines the list of allowed VLANs
switchport access vlan *vlan-id*	Interface subcommand that statically configures the interface into that one VLAN

Table 26-8   *Chapter 26 Configuration Command Reference*

Command	Description
switchport trunk encapsulation {dot1q | isl | negotiate}	Interface subcommand that defines which type of trunking to use, assuming that trunking is configured or negotiated
switchport voice vlan *vlan-id*	Interface subcommand that defines the VLAN used for frames sent to and from a Cisco IP phone
switchport nonegotiate	Interface subcommand that disables the negotiation of VLAN trunking

Table 26-9   *Chapter 26 EXEC Command Reference*

Command	Description
show interfaces *interface-id* switchport	Lists information about any interface regarding administrative settings and operational state
show interfaces *interface-id* trunk	Lists information about all operational trunks (but no other interfaces), including the list of VLANs that can be forwarded over the trunk
show vlan [brief | id *vlan-id* | name *vlan-name* | summary]	Lists information about the VLAN
show vlan [*vlan*]	Displays VLAN information
show vtp status	Lists VTP configuration and status information
show vtp password	Lists the VTP password

Answer Review Questions

Answer the following review questions:

1. In a LAN, which of the following terms best equates to the term *VLAN*?

   a. Collision domain

   b. Broadcast domain

   c. Subnet domain

   d. Single switch

   e. Trunk

2. Imagine a switch with three configured VLANs. How many IP subnets are required, assuming that all hosts in all VLANs want to use TCP/IP?

   a. 0

   b. 1

   c. 2

   d. 3

   e. You can't tell from the information provided.

3. Which of the following fully encapsulates the original Ethernet frame in a trunking header rather than inserting another header inside the original Ethernet header?

   a. VTP

   b. ISL

   c. 802.1Q

   d. Both ISL and 802.1Q

   e. None of the other answers are correct.

4. Which of the following adds the trunking header for all VLANs except one?

   a. VTP

   b. ISL

   c. 802.1Q

   d. Both ISL and 802.1Q

   e. None of the other answers are correct.

5. Which of the following VTP modes allow VLANs to be configured on a switch?

   a. Client

   b. Server

   c. Transparent

   d. Dynamic

   e. None of the other answers are correct.

6. Imagine that you are told that switch 1 is configured with the auto parameter for trunking on its Fa0/5 interface, which is connected to switch 2. You have to configure switch 2. Which of the following settings for trunking could allow trunking to work?

   a. Trunking turned **on**

   b. **Auto**

   c. **Desirable**

   d. **Access**

   e. None of the other answers are correct.

7. A switch has just arrived from Cisco. The switch has never been configured with any VLANs, VTP configuration, or any other configuration. An engineer gets into configuration mode and issues the **vlan 22** command, followed by the **name Hannahs-VLAN** command. Which of the following is true?

    a. VLAN 22 is listed in the output of the **show vlan brief** command.

    b. VLAN 22 is listed in the output of the **show running-config** command.

    c. VLAN 22 is not created by this process.

    d. VLAN 22 does not exist in that switch until at least one interface is assigned to that VLAN.

8. Which of the following commands list the operational state of interface Gigabit 0/1 in regard to VLAN trunking?

    a. show interfaces gi0/1

    b. show interfaces gi0/1 switchport

    c. show interfaces gi0/1 trunk

    d. show trunks

9. An engineer has just installed four new 2960 switches and connected the switches to each other using crossover cables. All the interfaces are in an "up and up" state. The engineer configures each switch with the VTP domain name Fred and leaves all four switches in VTP server mode. The engineer adds VLAN 33 at 9:00 a.m., and then within 30 seconds, issues a **show vlan brief** command on the other three switches, but does not find VLAN 33 on the other three switches. Which answer gives the most likely reason for the problem in this case?

    a. VTP requires that all switches have the same VTP password.

    b. The engineer should have been more patient and waited for SW1 to send its next periodic VTP update.

    c. None of the links between the switches trunk because of the default 2960 trunking administrative mode of auto.

    d. None of the other answers are correct.

10. Switches SW1 and SW2 connect through an operational trunk. The engineer wants to use VTP to communicate VLAN configuration changes. The engineer configures a new VLAN on SW1, VLAN 44, but SW2 does not learn about the new VLAN. Which of the following configuration settings on SW1 and SW2 would *not* be a potential root cause why SW2 does not learn about VLAN 44?

    a. VTP domain names of larry and LARRY, respectively

    b. VTP passwords of bob and BOB, respectively

    c. VTP pruning enabled and disabled, respectively

    d. VTP modes of server and client, respectively

This chapter covers the following subjects:

- **PPP Concepts:** This section examines PPP concepts, including control protocols and PAP/CHAP.

- **PPP Configuration:** This section looks at how to configure a simple PPP serial link, as well as how to configure CHAP.

- **Troubleshooting Serial Links:** This section examines the overall serial link troubleshooting process, including typical reasons why an interface has a particular status code.

CHAPTER 27

Point-to-Point WANs

The first few units of this book introduced the basics of WANs and LANs in enough detail to understanding routing. After spending the majority of the book on topics related to IP routing, Unit 9 then examined LANs in more depth. Similarly, Unit 10 takes a much deeper look at WANs, with particular emphasis on the data link layer protocols. Specifically, this unit examines High-Level Data Link Control (HDLC), PPP, and Frame Relay.

This particular chapter focuses on the aptly named Point-to-Point Protocol, a popular data link layer protocol used on point-to-point WAN links. This chapter starts by explaining the many PPP features available on routers, followed by PPP configuration, including the configuration of PPP authentication. The chapter ends with a section on troubleshooting serial links, covering a wide variety of topics, including PPP.

This chapter assumes that you recall the basic WAN information discussed in Chapter 3, "WAN Fundamentals," so you might want to review that chapter before beginning this chapter.

PPP Concepts

PPP provides several basic but important functions that are useful on a leased line that connects two devices, as reviewed in the following list:

Key
Topic

- Definition of a header and trailer that allows delivery of a data frame over the link

- Support for both synchronous and asynchronous links

- A protocol type field in the header, allowing multiple Layer 3 protocols to pass over the same link

- Built-in authentication tools: Password Authentication Protocol (PAP) and Challenge Handshake Authentication Protocol (CHAP)

- Control protocols for each higher-layer protocol that rides over PPP, allowing easier integration and support of those protocols

The next several pages take a closer look at the protocol field, authentication, and the control protocols.

The PPP Protocol Field

One of the more important features included in the PPP standard, but not in the HDLC standard, is the protocol field. The protocol field identifies the type of packet inside the frame. When PPP was created, this field allowed packets from the many different Layer 3 protocols to pass over a single link. Today, the protocol type field still provides the same function, even for the support of two different versions of IP (IPv4 and IPv6). Figure 27-1 compares the framing details of HDLC and PPP, showing the proprietary HDLC Protocol field and the standardized PPP Protocol field.

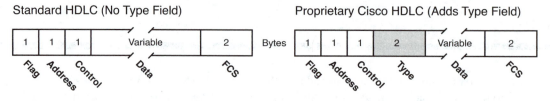

Figure 27-1 *PPP and HDLC Framing*

PPP defines a set of Layer 2 control messages that perform various link control functions. These control functions fall into two main categories:

■ Those needed regardless of the Layer 3 protocol sent across the link

■ Those specific to each Layer 3 protocol

The PPP *Link Control Protocol (LCP)* implements the control functions that work the same regardless of the Layer 3 protocol. For features related to any higher-layer protocols, typically Layer 3 protocols, PPP uses a series of PPP *control protocols (CP)*, such as IP Control Protocol (IPCP). PPP uses one instance of LCP per link, and one CP for each Layer 3 protocol defined on the link. For example, on a PPP link using IPv4, IPv6, and Cisco Discovery Protocol (CDP), the link uses one instance of LCP, plus IPCP (for IPv4), IPv6CP (for IPv6), and CDPCP (for CDP).

The next section first summarizes the functions of LCP and then explains one of those functions, authentication, in more detail.

PPP Link Control Protocol (LCP)

LCP provides four notable features, which are covered in this chapter. Table 27-1 summarizes the functions, gives the LCP feature names, and describes the features briefly. Following the table, the text explains each feature in more detail. Note that the features listed in the table are optional and are disabled by default.

Table 27-1 *PPP LCP Features*

Function	LCP Feature	Description
Looped link detection	Magic number	Detects if the link is looped, and disables the interface, allowing rerouting over a working route.
Error detection	Link Quality Monitoring (LQM)	Disables an interface that exceeds an error percentage threshold, allowing rerouting over better routes.

Table 27-1 *PPP LCP Features*

Function	LCP Feature	Description
Multilink support	Multilink PPP	Load-balances traffic over multiple parallel links.
Authentication	PAP and CHAP	Exchanges names and passwords so that each device can verify the identity of the device on the other end of the link.

Looped Link Detection

Error detection and looped link detection are two key features of PPP. Looped link detection allows for faster convergence when a link fails because it is looped. What does "looped" mean? Well, to test a circuit, the phone company might loop the circuit. The telco technician can sit at his desk and, using commands, cause the phone company's switch to loop the circuit. This means that the phone company takes the electrical signal sent by the CPE device and sends the same electrical current right back to the same device.

The routers cannot send bits to each other while the link is looped, of course. However, the router might not notice that the link is looped, because the router is still receiving something over the link! PPP helps the router recognize a looped link quickly so that it can bring down the interface and possibly use an alternative route.

In some cases, routing protocol convergence can be sped up by LCP's recognition of the loop. If the router can immediately notice that the link is looped, it can put the interface in a "down and down" status, and the routing protocols can change their routing updates based on the fact that the link is down. If a router does not notice that the link has been looped, the routing protocol must wait for timeouts—things such as not hearing from the router on the other end of the link for some period of time.

LCP notices looped links quickly using a feature called *magic numbers*. When using PPP, the router sends PPP LCP messages instead of Cisco-proprietary keepalives across the link; these messages include a magic number, which is different on each router. If a line is looped, the router receives an LCP message with its own magic number instead of getting a message with the other router's magic number. When a router receives its own magic number, that router knows that the frame it sent has been looped back, so the router can take down the interface, which speeds convergence.

Enhanced Error Detection

Similar to many other data-link protocols, PPP uses an FCS field in the PPP trailer to determine if an individual frame has an error. If a frame is received in error, it is discarded. However, PPP can monitor the frequency with which frames are received in error so that it can take down an interface if too many errors occur.

PPP LCP analyzes the error rates on a link using a PPP feature called Link Quality Monitoring (LQM). LCP at each end of the link sends messages describing the number of correctly received packets and bytes. The router that sent the packets compares this number of in-error frames to the number of frames and bytes it sent, and it calculates percentage loss. The router can take down the link after a configured error rate has been exceeded.

The only time LQM helps is when you have redundant routes in the network. By taking down a link that has many errors, you can cause packets to use an alternative path that might not have as many errors.

PPP Multilink

When multiple PPP links exist between the same two routers—referred to as parallel links—the routers must then determine how to use those links. With HDLC links, and with PPP links using the simplest configuration, the routers must use Layer 3 load balancing. This means that the routers have multiple routes for the same destination subnets. For example, the upper part of Figure 27-2 shows the load-balancing effect on R1 when forwarding packets to subnet 192.168.3.0/24.

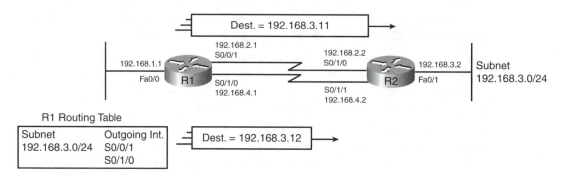

Figure 27-2   *Load Balancing Without Multilink PPP*

The figure shows two packets, one large and one small. Using Layer 3 logic, the router can choose to send one packet over one link, and the next packet over another. However, because the packets might be of different sizes, the router might not balance the traffic equally over each link. In some cases, particularly when most packets are sent to just a few destination hosts, the numbers of packets sent over each link might not even be balanced, which can overload one of the links and leave another link idle.

Multilink PPP load-balances the traffic equally over the links while allowing the Layer 3 logic in each router to treat the parallel links as a single link. When encapsulating a packet, PPP fragments the packet into smaller frames, sending one fragment over each link. For example, for the network shown in Figure 27-2, with two links, R1 would create two frames for each Layer 3 packet, with each frame holding roughly half the original packet. Then, PPP sends one fragment of each original packet over each of the two links. By sending about half of each packet over each link, multilink PPP can more evenly load-balance the traffic. As an added benefit, multilink PPP allows the Layer 3 routing tables to use a single route that refers to the combined links, keeping the routing table smaller. For example, in Figure 27-2, R1 would instead use one route for subnet 192.168.3.0/24, referring to the group of interfaces as a concept called a *multilink group*.

PPP Authentication

The term *authentication* refers to a set of security functions that help one device confirm that the other device should be allowed to communicate and is not some imposter. For instance, if R1 and R2 are supposed to be communicating over a serial link, R1 might want R2 to somehow prove that it really is R2. Authentication provides a way to prove one's identity.

WAN authentication is most often needed when dial lines are used. However, the configuration of the authentication features remains the same whether a leased line or dial line is used.

PAP and CHAP authenticate the endpoints on either end of a point-to-point serial link. CHAP is the preferred method today because the identification process uses values hidden with a Message Digest 5 (MD5) one-way hash, which is more secure than the clear-text passwords sent by PAP.

Both PAP and CHAP require the exchange of messages between devices. When a dialed line is used, the dialed-to router expects to receive a username and password from the dialing router with both PAP and CHAP. With a leased line, typically both routers mutually authenticate the other router. Whether leased line or dial, with PAP, the username and password are sent in the first message. With CHAP, the protocol begins with a message called a *challenge*, which asks the other router to send its username and password. Figure 27-3 outlines the different processes in the case where the links are dialed. The process works the same when the link uses a leased line.

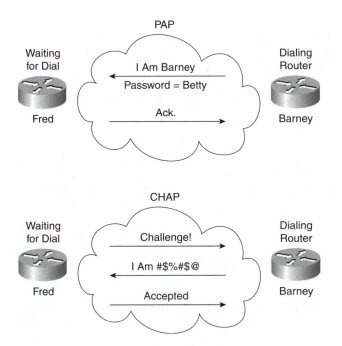

Figure 27-3 *PAP and CHAP Authentication Process*

PAP flows are much less secure than CHAP because PAP sends the hostname and password in clear text in the message. These can be read easily if someone places a tracing tool in the circuit. CHAP instead uses a one-way hash algorithm, with input to the algorithm being a password that never crosses the link, plus a shared random number. The CHAP challenge states the random number; both routers are preconfigured with the password. The challenged router runs the hash algorithm using the just-learned random number and the secret password and sends the results back to the router that sent the challenge. The router that sent the challenge runs the same algorithm using the random number (sent across the link) and the password (not sent across the link). If the results match, the passwords must match.

The most interesting part of the CHAP process is that at no time does the password itself ever cross the link. With the random number, the hash value is different every time. So even if someone sees the calculated hash value using a trace tool, the value is meaningless as a way to break in next time. CHAP authentication is difficult to break, even with a tracing tool on the WAN link.

PPP Configuration

This section examines how to configure PPP and then how to add CHAP configuration. At the same time, this section also examines a couple of commands that help verify if PPP is up and working.

Basic PPP Configuration

Configuring PPP requires only the **encapsulation ppp** command on both ends of the link. To change back to use the default of HDLC, the engineer just needs to use the **encapsulation hdlc** command on both ends of the link as well. However, besides this basic configuration, the physical serial link needs to be ordered and installed. This section assumes that the physical link has been installed and is working. If you want to read more details about the physical link, refer to Chapter 3.

Example 27-1 shows a simple configuration using the two routers shown in Figure 27-4. The example includes the IP address configuration, but the IP addresses do not have to be configured for PPP to work. Because most installations will use IP, the configuration is added for some perspectives in the **show** commands in the second part of the example.

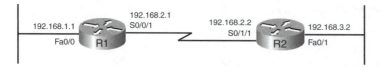

Figure 27-4   *Two-Router Internetwork Used in PPP Examples*

Example 27-1 *Basic PPP Configuration*

```
! The example starts with router R1
interface Serial0/0/1
 ip address 192.168.2.1 255.255.255.0
 encapsulation ppp
 clockrate 1536000
! Next, the configuration on router R2
interface Serial0/1/1
 ip address 192.168.2.2 255.255.255.0
 encapsulation ppp
! Back to router R1 again
R1# show interfaces serial 0/0/1
Serial0/0/1 is up, line protocol is up
  Hardware is GT96K Serial
  Internet address is 192.168.2.1/24
  MTU 1500 bytes, BW 1544 Kbit, DLY 20000 usec,
     reliability 255/255, txload 1/255, rxload 1/255
  Encapsulation PPP, LCP Open
  Open: CDPCP, IPCP, loopback not set
! lines omitted for brevity
```

This example shows the simple configuration, with both routers needing to use PPP encapsulation. If either router defaulted to use HDLC, and the other configured PPP as shown, the link would not come up, staying in an "up and down" interface state.

The **show interfaces** command at the bottom of the example shows the normal output when the link is up and working. The second interface status code typically refers to the data-link status, with the "up" value meaning that the data link is working. Additionally, a few lines into the output, the highlighted phrases show that PPP is indeed configured, and that LCP has completed its work successfully, as noted with the "LCP Open" phrase. Additionally, the output lists the fact that two CPs, CDPCP and IPCP, have also successfully been enabled—all good indications that PPP is working properly.

CHAP Configuration and Verification

The simplest version of CHAP configuration requires only a few commands. The configuration uses a password configured on each router. As an alternative, the password could be configured on an external Authentication, Authorization, and Accounting (AAA) server outside the router. The configuration steps are as follows:

Key Topic

Step 1.   Configure the routers' hostnames using the **hostname** *name* global configuration command.

Step 2.   Configure the name of the other router, and the shared secret password, using the **username** *name* **password** *password* global configuration command.

Step 3.   Enable CHAP on the interface on each router using the **ppp authentication chap** interface subcommand.

Example 27-2 shows a sample configuration, using the same two routers as the previous example (see Figure 27-4).

Example 27-2 *CHAP Configuration Example*

```
hostname R1                            hostname R2

username R2 password mypass            username R1 password mypass
!                                      !
interface serial 0/0/1                 interface serial 0/1/1
 encapsulation ppp                      encapsulation ppp
 ppp authentication chap                ppp authentication chap
```

The commands themselves are not complicated, but it is easy to misconfigure the hostnames and passwords. Notice that each router refers to the other router's hostname in the **username** command, but both routers must configure the same password value. Also, not only are the passwords (mypass in this case) case-sensitive, but the hostnames, as referenced in the **username** command, also are also case-sensitive.

Because CHAP is a function of LCP, if the authentication process fails, LCP does not complete, and the interface falls to an "up and down" interface state.

Configuring HDLC

Chapter 3 introduces the main concepts of HDLC. Briefly, HDLC acts like PPP in many ways. It works on point-to-point serial links. It adds both a header and trailer when encapsulating IP packets, and includes an FCS field in the trailer. And because HDLC and PPP differ, the two routers on both ends of the link must use the same WAN data link protocol (either HDLC or PPP).

Because Cisco IOS defaults to use HDLC on serial interfaces, most of the examples in this book have shown HDLC. However, before leaving the topic of WAN configuration, you should know a little more about HDLC configuration. This section discusses the HDLC WAN configuration details and reviews a couple of commands from earlier in this book.

IOS defaults to use HDLC as the data-link protocol, so there are no required commands that relate to Layer 2. However, many optional commands exist for serial links. The following list outlines some configuration steps, listing the conditions for which some commands are needed, plus commands that are purely optional:

Key Topic

Step 1. Configure the interface IP address using the **ip address** interface subcommand.

Step 2. The following tasks are required only when the specifically listed conditions are true:

  a. If an **encapsulation** *protocol* interface subcommand that lists a protocol besides HDLC already exists on the interface, use the **encapsulation hdlc** interface subcommand to enable HDLC.

  b. If the interface line status is administratively down, enable the interface using the **no shutdown** interface subcommand.

    c.   If the serial link is a back-to-back serial link in a lab (or a simulator), configure the clocking rate using the **clock rate** *speed* interface subcommand, but only on the one router with the DCE cable (per the **show controllers serial** *number* command).

Step 3.   The following steps are always optional, and have no impact on whether the link works and passes IP traffic:

    a.   Configure the link's speed using the **bandwidth** *speed-in-kbps* interface subcommand.

    b.   For documentation purposes, configure a description of the purpose of the interface using the **description** *text* interface subcommand.

In practice, when you configure a Cisco router with no pre-existing interface configuration, and install a normal production serial link with CSU/DSUs, the **ip address** command is likely the one configuration command you would need. Figure 27-5 shows a sample internetwork, and Example 27-3 shows the configuration. In this case, the serial link was created with a back-to-back serial link in a lab, requiring Steps 1 (**ip address**) and 2c (**clock rate**) from the preceding list, plus optional Step 3b (**description**).

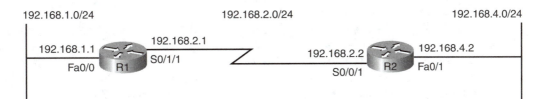

Figure 27-5 *Typical Serial Link Between Two Routers*

Example 27-3 *HDLC Configuration*

```
R1# show running-config
! Note - only the related lines are shown
interface FastEthernet0/0
 ip address 192.168.1.1 255.255.255.0
!
interface Serial0/1/1
 ip address 192.168.2.1 255.255.255.0
 description link to R2
 clockrate 1536000
!
router rip
 version 2
 network 192.168.1.0
 network 192.168.2.0
R1# show controllers serial 0/1/1
Interface Serial0/1/1
Hardware is GT96K
```

```
  DCE V.35, clock rate 1536000
! lines omitted for brevity
R1# show interfaces s0/1/1
Serial0/1/1 is up, line protocol is up
  Hardware is GT96K Serial
  Description: link to R2
  Internet address is 192.168.2.1/24
  MTU 1500 bytes, BW 1544 Kbit, DLY 20000 usec,
     reliability 255/255, txload 1/255, rxload 1/255
  Encapsulation HDLC, loopback not set
  Keepalive set (10 sec)
  Last input 00:00:06, output 00:00:03, output hang never
  Last clearing of "show interface" counters never
  Input queue: 0/75/0/0 (size/max/drops/flushes); Total output drops: 0
  Queueing strategy: weighted fair
  Output queue: 0/1000/64/0 (size/max total/threshold/drops)
     Conversations  0/1/256 (active/max active/max total)
     Reserved Conversations 0/0 (allocated/max allocated)
     Available Bandwidth 1158 kilobits/sec
  5 minute input rate 0 bits/sec, 0 packets/sec
  5 minute output rate 0 bits/sec, 0 packets/sec
     70 packets input, 4446 bytes, 0 no buffer
     Received 50 broadcasts, 0 runts, 0 giants, 0 throttles
     0 input errors, 0 CRC, 0 frame, 0 overrun, 0 ignored, 0 abort
     73 packets output, 5280 bytes, 0 underruns
     0 output errors, 0 collisions, 5 interface resets
     0 output buffer failures, 0 output buffers swapped out
     0 carrier transitions
     DCD=up  DSR=up  DTR=up  RTS=up  CTS=up
R1# show ip interface brief
Interface              IP-Address     OK? Method Status                Protocol
FastEthernet0/0        192.168.1.1    YES manual up                    up
FastEthernet0/1        unassigned     YES NVRAM  administratively down down
Serial0/0/0            unassigned     YES NVRAM  administratively down down
Serial0/0/1            unassigned     YES manual administratively down down
Serial0/1/0            unassigned     YES manual administratively down down
Serial0/1/1            192.168.2.1    YES manual up                    up
R1# show interfaces description
Interface              Status         Protocol Description
Fa0/0                  up             up
Fa0/1                  admin down     down
Se0/0/0                admin down     down
Se0/0/1                admin down     down
Se0/1/0                admin down     down
Se0/1/1                up             up       link to R2
```

The configuration on R1 is relatively simple. The matching configuration on R2's S0/0/1 interface simply needs an **ip address** command, plus the default settings of **encapsulation hdlc** and **no shutdown**. The **clock rate** command would not be needed on R2, as R1 has the DCE cable, so R2 must be connected to a DTE cable.

The rest of the example lists the output of a few **show** commands. First, the output from the **show controllers** command for S0/1/1 confirms that R1 indeed has a DCE cable installed. The **show interfaces S0/1/1** command lists the various configuration settings near the top, including the default encapsulation value (HDLC) and default bandwidth setting on a serial interface (1544, meaning 1544 kbps or 1.544 Mbps). At the end of the example, the **show ip interface brief** and **show interfaces description** commands display a short status of the interfaces, with both listing the line status and protocol status codes.

Troubleshooting Serial Links

This section discusses how to isolate and find the root cause of problems related to topics covered earlier in this chapter, as well as some point-to-point WAN topics covered in Chapter 3. Also, this section does not attempt to repeat the IP troubleshooting coverage in earlier units of this book, but it does point out some of the possible symptoms on a serial link when a Layer 3 subnet mismatch occurs on opposite ends of a serial link, which prevents the routers from routing packets over the serial link.

A simple **ping** command can determine whether a serial link can or cannot forward IP packets. A ping of the other router's serial IP address—for example, a working **ping 192.168.2.2** command on R1 in Figure 27-4—proves that the link either works or does not.

If the ping does not work, the problem could be related to functions at OSI Layer 1, 2, or 3. The best way to isolate which layer is the most likely cause is to examine the interface status codes described in Table 27-2. (As a reminder, router interfaces have two status codes—line status and protocol status.)

Table 27-2 *Interface Status Codes and Typical Meanings When a Ping Does Not Work*

Key Topic

Line Status	Protocol Status	Likely Reason/Layer
Administratively down	Down	Interface is shut down
Down	Down	Layer 1
Up	Down	Layer 2
Up	Up	Layer 3

The serial link verification and troubleshooting process should begin with a simple three-step process:

Step 1.   From one router, ping the other router's serial IP address.

Step 2. If the ping fails, examine the interface status on both routers, and investigate problems related to the likely problem areas listed in Table 27-3 (shown later in this chapter).

Step 3. If the ping works, also verify that any routing protocols are exchanging routes over the link.

> **Note:** The interface status codes can be found using the **show interfaces, show ip inter-face brief**, and **show interfaces description** commands.

The rest of this chapter explores the specific items to be examined when the ping fails, based on the combinations of interface status codes listed in Table 27-2.

Troubleshooting Layer 1 Problems

The interface status codes, or interface state, play a key role in isolating the root cause of problems on serial links. In fact, the status on both ends of the link can differ, so it is important to examine the status on both ends of the link to help determine the problem.

One simple and easy-to-find Layer 1 problem occurs when either one of the two routers has administratively disabled its serial interface with the **shutdown** interface subcom-mand. If a router's serial interface is in an administratively down line status, the solution is simple—just configure a **no shutdown** interface configuration command on the interface. Also, if one router's interface has a line status of down, the other router might be shut down, so check both sides of the link.

The combination of a *down* line status on both ends of the serial link typically points to a Layer 1 problem. The following list describes the most likely reasons:

Key Topic

- The leased line is down (a telco problem).

- The line from the telco is not plugged in to either or both CSU/DSUs.

- A CSU/DSU has failed or is misconfigured.

- A serial cable from a router to its CSU/DSU is disconnected or faulty.

The details of how to further isolate these four problems is beyond the scope of this book.

Interestingly, one other common physical layer problem can occur that results in both routers' interfaces being in an up/down state. On a back-to-back serial link, if the required **clock rate** command is missing on the router with a DCE cable installed, both routers' se-rial interfaces will fail and end up with a line status of up but a line protocol status of down. Example 27-4 shows just such an example, pointing out a couple of ways to check to see if a missing **clock rate** command is the problem. The two best ways to find this problem are to notice the absence of the **clock rate** command on the router with the DCE cable, and to note the "no clock" phrase in the output of the **show controllers serial** com-mand. (This example shows R1 from Figure 27-4, with the **clock rate** command removed.)

Example 27-4   *Problem: No* **clock rate** *Command on the DCE End*

```
R1# show controller s0/0/1
Interface Serial0/0/1
Hardware is PowerQUICC MPC860
  Internet address is 192.168.2.1/24
DCE V.35, no clock
! lines omitted for brevity
R1# show running-config interface S0/0/1
Building configuration...

Current configuration : 42 bytes
!
interface Serial0/0/1
 ip address 192.168.2.1 255.255.255.0
end
```

Note: Some recent IOS releases actually prevent the user from removing the **clock rate** command on the interface if a DCE cable or no cable is installed, in an effort to prevent the unintentional omission of the **clock rate** command. Also, IOS sometimes spells the **clock rate** command as the **clockrate** command; both are acceptable.

Troubleshooting Layer 2 Problems

When both routers' serial line status is up, but at least one of the routers' line protocol status (the second interface status code) either is down or continually switches between up and down, the interface probably has one of two types of data link layer problems. This section explains both problems, which are summarized in Table 27-3.

Table 27-3   *Likely Reasons for Data-Link Problems on Serial Links*

Key Topic

Line Status	Protocol Status	Likely Reason
Up	Down (stable) on both ends Or Down (stable) on one end, flapping between up and down on the other	Mismatched **encapsulation** commands
Up	Down on one end, up on the other	Keepalive is disabled on the end in an up state
Up	Down (stable) on both ends	PAP/CHAP authentication failure

Note: As with the other troubleshooting topics in this book, Table 27-3 lists some of the more common types of failures but not all.

The first of these two problems—a mismatch between the configured data-link protocols—is easy to identify and fix. The **show interfaces** command lists the encapsulation type in the seventh line of the output, so using this command on both routers can quickly identify the problem. Alternatively, a quick look at the configuration, plus remembering that HDLC is the default serial encapsulation, can confirm whether the encapsulations are mismatched. The solution is simple—reconfigure one of the two routers to match the other router's **encapsulation** command.

The other two root causes require a little more discussion to understand the issue and determine if they are the real root cause. The next two headings take a closer look at each.

Keepalive Failure

The second item relates to a feature called *keepalive*. The *keepalive* feature helps a router recognize when a link is no longer functioning so that the router can bring down the interface, hoping to then use an alternative IP route.

The keepalive function (by default) causes routers to send keepalive messages to each other every 10 seconds (the default setting). (Cisco defines a proprietary HDLC keepalive message, with PPP defining a keepalive message as part of LCP.) This 10-second timer is the keepalive interval. If a router does not receive any keepalive messages from the other router for a number of keepalive intervals (three or five intervals by default, depending on the IOS version), the router brings down the interface, thinking that the interface is no longer working.

For real networks, it is useful to just leave keepalives enabled. However, you can make a mistake and turn off keepalives on one end of a serial link, leave them enabled on the other, and cause the link to fail. For example, if R1 were configured with the **no keepalive** interface subcommand, disabling keepalives, R1 would no longer send the keepalive messages. If R2 continued to default to use keepalives, R2 would keep sending keepalive messages, plus R2 would expect to receive keepalive messages from R1. After several keepalive intervals pass, R2, having not received any keepalive messages from R1, would change the interface to an "up and down" state. Then, R2 would continually bring the link back up, still not get any keepalives from R1, and then fall back to an "up and down" state again, and flapping up and down repeatedly. R1, not caring about keepalives, would leave the interface in an "up and up" state the whole time. Example 27-5 shows this exact example, again with the routers in Figure 27-4.

Example 27-5   *Line Problems Because of Keepalive Only on R2*

```
! R1 disables keepalives, and remains in an up/up state.
R1# configure terminal
Enter configuration commands, one per line.  End with CNTL/Z.
R1(config)# interface s 0/0/1
R1(config-if)# no keepalive
R1(config-if)# ^Z
R1# show interfaces s0/0/1
Serial0/0/1 is up, line protocol is up
  Hardware is PowerQUICC Serial
```

```
    Internet address is 192.168.2.1/24  MTU 1500 bytes, BW 1544 Kbit, DLY 20000 usec,
        reliability 255/255, txload 1/255, rxload 1/255
    Encapsulation HDLC, loopback not set
    Keepalive not set
 ! lines omitted for brevity
 ! Below, R2 still has keepalives enabled (default)
 R2# show interfaces S0/1/1
 Serial0/1/1 is up, line protocol is down
    Hardware is PowerQUICC Serial
    Internet address is 192.168.2.2/24
    MTU 1500 bytes, BW 1544 Kbit, DLY 20000 usec,
        reliability 255/255, txload 1/255, rxload 1/255
    Encapsulation HDLC, loopback not set
    Keepalive set (10 sec)
 ! lines omitted for brevity
```

Note: It is a configuration mistake to enable keepalives on only one end of a point-to-point serial link. It appears that some very recent IOS versions notice when the keepalives are mistakenly disabled on one end of a link and prevent the problem described here from happening. Just be aware that keepalives should be enabled on both ends of the link, or disabled on both ends.

PAP and CHAP Authentication Failure

As mentioned earlier, a failure in the PAP/CHAP authentication process results in both routers falling to an "up and down" state. To discover whether a PAP/CHAP failure is really the root cause, you can use the **debug ppp authentication** command. For perspective, Example 27-6 shows the output of this command when CHAP has been configured as in earlier Example 27-2, with CHAP working correctly in this case.

Example 27-6 *Debug Messages Confirming the Correct Operation of CHAP*

Key Topic

```
R1# debug ppp authentication
PPP authentication debugging is on
R1#
*May 21 18:26:55.731: Se0/0/1 PPP: Using default call direction
*May 21 18:26:55.731: Se0/0/1 PPP: Treating connection as a dedicated line
*May 21 18:26:55.731: Se0/0/1 PPP: Authorization required
*May 21 18:26:55.731: Se0/0/1 CHAP: O CHALLENGE id 16 len 23 from "R1"
*May 21 18:26:55.731: Se0/0/1 CHAP: I CHALLENGE id 49 len 23 from "R2"
*May 21 18:26:55.735: Se0/0/1 CHAP: Using hostname from unknown source
*May 21 18:26:55.735: Se0/0/1 CHAP: Using password from AAA
*May 21 18:26:55.735: Se0/0/1 CHAP: O RESPONSE id 49 len 23 from "R1"
*May 21 18:26:55.735: Se0/0/1 CHAP: I RESPONSE id 16 len 23 from "R2"
*May 21 18:26:55.735: Se0/0/1 PPP: Sent CHAP LOGIN Request
*May 21 18:26:55.735: Se0/0/1 PPP: Received LOGIN Response PASS
```

```
*May 21 18:26:55.735: Se0/0/1 PPP: Sent LCP AUTHOR Request
*May 21 18:26:55.735: Se0/0/1 PPP: Sent IPCP AUTHOR Request
*May 21 18:26:55.735: Se0/0/1 LCP: Received AAA AUTHOR Response PASS
*May 21 18:26:55.739: Se0/0/1 IPCP: Received AAA AUTHOR Response PASS
*May 21 18:26:55.739: Se0/0/1 CHAP: O SUCCESS id 16 len 4
*May 21 18:26:55.739: Se0/0/1 CHAP: I SUCCESS id 49 len 4
```

CHAP uses a three-message exchange, as shown back in Figure 27-3, with a set of messages flowing for authentication in each direction by default. The three highlighted lines show the authentication process by which R1 authenticates R2; it begins with R1 sending a challenge message. The first highlighted message in Example 27-6 lists an "O," meaning "output." This indicates that the message is a challenge message and that it was sent from R1. The next highlighted message is the received response message (noted with an "I" for input), from R2. The last highlighted line is the third message, sent by R1, stating that the authentication was successful. You can see the same three messages for R2's authentication of R1 in the output as well, but those messages are not highlighted in the example.

When CHAP authentication fails, the **debug** output shows a couple of fairly obvious messages. Example 27-7 shows the results using the same two-router internetwork shown in Figure 27-4, this time with the passwords misconfigured, so CHAP fails.

Example 27-7   *Debug Messages Confirming the Failure of CHAP*

```
R1# debug ppp authentication
PPP authentication debugging is on
! Lines omitted for brevity
*May 21 18:24:03.171: Se0/0/1 PPP: Sent CHAP LOGIN Request
*May 21 18:24:03.171: Se0/0/1 PPP: Received LOGIN Response FAIL
*May 21 18:24:03.171: Se0/0/1 CHAP: O FAILURE id 15 len 25 msg is "Authentication
failed"
```

Troubleshooting Layer 3 Problems

This chapter suggests that the best starting place to troubleshoot serial links is to ping the IP address of the router on the other end of the link—specifically, the IP address on the serial link. Interestingly, the serial link can be in an "up and up" state but the ping can still fail because of Layer 3 misconfiguration. In some cases, the ping might work, but the routing protocols might not be able to exchange routes. This short section examines the symptoms, which are slightly different depending on whether HDLC or PPP is used, and the root cause.

First, consider an HDLC link on which the physical and data-link details are working fine. In this case, both routers' interfaces are in an "up and up" state. However, if the IP addresses configured on the serial interfaces on the two routers are in different subnets, a ping to the IP address on the other end of the link will fail, because the routers do not have a matching route. For example, in Figure 27-4, if R1's serial IP address remained 192.168.2.1, and R2's was changed to 192.168.3.2 (instead of 192.168.2.2), still with a mask of /24, the two routers would have connected routes to different subnets. They would not have a route matching the opposite router's serial IP address.

Finding and fixing a mismatched subnet problem with HDLC links is relatively simple. You can find the problem by doing the usual first step of pinging the IP address on the other end of the link, and failing. If both interface status codes on both routers' interfaces are up, the problem is likely this mismatched IP subnet.

For PPP links, with the same IP address/mask misconfiguration, both routers' interfaces also are in an "up and up" state, but the ping to the other router's IP address actually works. As it turns out, a router using PPP advertises its serial interface IP address to the other router, with a /32 prefix, which is a route to reach just that one host. So, both routers have a route with which to route packets to the other end of the link, even though two routers on opposite ends of a serial link have mismatched their IP addresses. For example, in Figure 27-4 again, if R2's IP address were 192.168.4.2/24, while R1's remained 192.168.2.1/24, the two addresses would be in different subnets, but the pings would work because of PPP's advertisement of the host routes. Example 27-8 shows this exact scenario.

Note: A route with a /32 prefix, representing a single host, is called a *host route*.

Example 27-8 *PPP Allowing a Ping Over a Serial Link, Even with Mismatched Subnets*

```
R1# show ip route
Codes: C - connected, S - static, R - RIP, M - mobile, B - BGP
       D - EIGRP, EX - EIGRP external, O - OSPF, IA - OSPF inter area
       N1 - OSPF NSSA external type 1, N2 - OSPF NSSA external type 2
       E1 - OSPF external type 1, E2 - OSPF external type 2
       i - IS-IS, su - IS-IS summary, L1 - IS-IS level-1, L2 - IS-IS level-2
       ia - IS-IS inter area, * - candidate default, U - per-user static route
       o - ODR, P - periodic downloaded static route

C    192.168.1.0/24 is directly connected, FastEthernet0/0
C    192.168.2.0/24 is directly connected, Serial0/0/1
     192.168.4.0/32 is subnetted, 1 subnets
C       192.168.4.2 is directly connected, Serial0/0/1
R1# ping 192.168.4.2

Type escape sequence to abort.
Sending 5, 100-byte ICMP Echos to 192.168.4.2, timeout is 2 seconds:
!!!!!
Success rate is 100 percent (5/5), round-trip min/avg/max = 1/2/4 ms
```

The first highlighted line in the example shows the normal connected route on the serial link, for network 192.168.2.0/24. R1 thinks this subnet is the subnet connected to S0/0/1 because of R1's configured IP address (192.168.2.1/24). The second highlighted line shows the host route created by PPP, specifically for R2's new serial IP address (192.168.4.2). (R2 will have a similar route for 192.168.2.1/32, R1's serial IP address.) So, both routers have a route to allow them to forward packets to the IP address on the other end of the link, which allows the ping to the other side of the serial link to work in spite of the addresses on each end being in different subnets.

Although the ping to the other end of the link works, the routing protocols still do not advertise routes because of the IP subnet mismatch on the opposite ends of the link. So, when troubleshooting a network problem, do not assume that a serial interface in an up/up state is fully working, or even that a serial interface over which a ping works is fully working. Also make sure the routing protocol is exchanging routes and that the IP addresses are in the same subnet. Table 27-4 summarizes the behavior on HDLC and PPP links when the IP addresses on each end do not reside in the same subnet but no other problems exist.

Table 27-4   *Summary of Symptoms for Mismatched Subnets on Serial Links*

Symptoms When IP Addresses on a Serial Link Are in Different Subnets	HDLC	PPP
Does a ping of the other router's serial IP address work?	No	Yes
Can routing protocols exchange routes over the link?	No	No

Chapter Review

Review Key Topics

Review the most important topics from this chapter, noted with the Key Topic icons. Table 27-5 lists these key topics and where each is discussed.

Table 27-5   *Key Topics for Chapter 27*

Key Topic Element	Description	Page Number
List	PPP features	689
Table 27-1	PPP LCP features	690
Figure 27-3	Comparison of messages sent by PAP and CHAP	693
List	Configuration checklist for CHAP	695
List	Configuration checklist for HDLC	696
Table 27-2	List of typical combinations of serial interface status codes, and the typical general reason for each combination	699
List	Common reasons for Layer 1 serial link problems	700
Table 27-3	Common symptoms and reasons for common Layer 2 problems on serial links	701
Example 27-6	Sample **debug** messages showing a successful CHAP authentication process	703

Define Key Terms

Define the following key terms from this chapter, and check your answers in the glossary:

CHAP, IP control protocol, keepalive, Link Control Protocol

Command Reference to Check Your Memory

Although you should not necessarily memorize the information in the tables in this section, this section does include a reference for the configuration and EXEC commands covered in this chapter. Practically speaking, you should memorize the commands as a side effect of reading the chapter and doing all the activities in this "Chapter Review" section. To see how well you have memorized the commands as a side effect of your other studies, cover the left side of the table, read the descriptions on the right side, and see if you remember the command.

Table 27-6 *Chapter 27 Configuration Command Reference*

Command	Description
encapsulation {hdlc | ppp}	Interface subcommand that defines the serial data-link protocol.
ppp authentication {pap | chap | pap chap | chap pap}	Interface subcommand that enables only PAP, only CHAP, or both (order-dependent).
username *name* password *secret*	Global command that sets the password that this router expects to use when authenticating the router with the listed hostname.

Table 27-7 *Chapter 27 EXEC Command Reference*

Command	Description
show interfaces [*type number*]	Lists statistics and details of interface configuration, including the encapsulation type.
debug ppp authentication	Generates messages for each step in the PAP or CHAP authentication process.
debug ppp negotiation	Generates **debug** messages for the LCP and NCP negotiation messages sent between the devices.

Answer Review Questions

Answer the following review questions:

1. Which of the following PPP authentication protocols authenticates a device on the other end of a link without sending any password information in clear text?

    a. MD5

    b. PAP

    c. CHAP

    d. DES

2. Which of the following PPP protocols controls the operation of CHAP?

    a. CDPCP

    b. IPCP

    c. LCP

    d. IPXCP

3. Two routers have no initial configuration whatsoever. They are connected in a lab using a DTE cable connected to R1 and a DCE cable connected to R2, with the DTE and DCE cables then connected to each other. The engineer wants to create a working PPP link. Which of the following commands are required on R1 for the link to reach a state in which R1 can ping R2's serial IP address, assuming that the physical back-to-back link physically works?

    a.   encapsulation ppp

    b.   no encapsulation hdlc

    c.   clock rate

    d.   ip address

4. Imagine that two routers, R1 and R2, have a leased line between them. Each router had its configuration erased and was then reloaded. R1 was then configured with the following commands:

```
hostname R1
interface s0/0
 encapsulation ppp
 ppp authentication chap
```

Which of the following configuration commands can complete the configuration on R1 so that CHAP can work correctly? Assume that R2 has been configured correctly and that the password is fred.

    a.   No other configuration is needed.

    b.   **ppp chap** (global command)

    c.   **username R1 password fred**

    d.   **username R2 password fred**

    e.   **ppp chap password fred**

5. Consider the following excerpt from the output of a **show** command:

```
Serial0/0/1 is up, line protocol is up
  Hardware is GT96K Serial
  Internet address is 192.168.2.1/24
  MTU 1500 bytes, BW 1544 Kbit, DLY 20000 usec,
    reliability 255/255, txload 1/255, rxload 1/255
  Encapsulation PPP, LCP Open
  Open: CDPCP, IPCP, loopback not set
```

Which of the following are true about this router's S0/0/1 interface?

    a.   The interface is using HDLC.

    b.   The interface is using PPP.

    c.   The interface currently cannot pass IPv4 traffic.

    d.   The link should be able to pass PPP frames at the present time.

6. Consider the following excerpt from the output of a **show interfaces** command on an interface configured to use PPP:

```
Serial0/0/1 is up, line protocol is down
  Hardware is GT96K Serial
  Internet address is 192.168.2.1/24
```

A ping of the IP address on the other end of the link fails. Which of the following are reasons for the failure, assuming that the problem listed in that answer is the only problem with the link?

a.   The CSU/DSU connected to the other router is not powered on.

b.   The IP address on the router at the other end of the link is not in subnet 192.168.2.0/24.

c.   CHAP authentication failed.

d.   The router on the other end of the link has been configured to use HDLC.

e.   None of the other answers is correct.

7. Two routers have a serial link between them, with the link configured to use PPP, and with EIGRP configured correctly for all interfaces. The engineer can ping the IP address on the other end of the link, but not the IP address of the other router's LAN interface. Which of the following answers is a likely cause of the problem?

a.   The CSU/DSU connected to the other router is not powered on.

b.   The serial IP address on the router at the other end of the link is not in the same subnet as the local router.

c.   CHAP authentication failed.

d.   The router on the other end of the link has been configured to use HDLC.

This chapter covers the following subjects:

- **Frame Relay Overview:** This section introduces the terminology, functions, and purpose of Frame Relay protocols.

- **Frame Relay Addressing:** This section examines the DLCI, the Frame Relay data-link address, and how it is used to transfer frames over the Frame Relay cloud.

- **Network Layer Concerns with Frame Relay:** This section mainly examines the various options for the use of Layer 3 subnets over a Frame Relay network.

CHAPTER 28

Frame Relay Concepts

Frame Relay defines a set of WAN standards that create a more efficient WAN service as compared to point-to-point links, while still allowing pairs of routers to send data directly to each other. With leased lines, a router can send packets to only one other router over that WAN link. With Frame Relay, the router can connect to the Frame Relay service over one physical serial interface and send IP packets to multiple other routers. For example, a company with one central site and ten remote sites would require ten leased lines to communicate with the main site and ten serial interfaces on the central site router. With Frame Relay, the main site could have a single leased line connecting it to the Frame Relay service and a single serial interface on the router at the central site, and still be able to communicate with each of the ten remote-site routers.

The first section of this chapter focuses on the basics of Frame Relay, including a lot of new terminology. The second section examines Frame Relay data-link addressing. This topic requires some attention because Frame Relay addresses are needed for both router configuration and troubleshooting. The last major section of this chapter examines some network layer concerns when using Frame Relay.

Frame Relay Overview

Frame Relay networks provide more features and benefits than simple point-to-point WAN links, but to do that, Frame Relay protocols are more detailed. For example, Frame Relay networks are multiaccess networks, which means that more than two devices can attach to the network, similar to LANs. Unlike with LANs, you cannot send a data link layer broadcast over Frame Relay. Therefore, Frame Relay networks are called *nonbroadcast multiaccess* (*NBMA*) networks. Also, because Frame Relay is multiaccess, it requires the use of an address that identifies to which remote router each frame is addressed.

Figure 28-1 outlines the basic physical topology and related terminology in a Frame Relay network.

Figure 28-1 shows the most basic components of a Frame Relay network. A leased line is installed between the router and a nearby Frame Relay switch; this link is called the *access link*. To ensure that the link is working, the device outside the Frame Relay network, called the *data terminal equipment* (*DTE*), exchanges regular messages with the Frame Relay switch. These keepalive messages, along with other messages, are defined by the Frame Relay *Local Management Interface* (*LMI*) protocol. The routers are considered DTE, and the Frame Relay switches are *data communications equipment* (*DCE*).

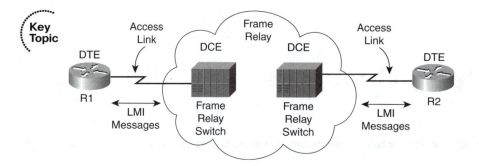

Figure 28-1 *Frame Relay Components*

Whereas Figure 28-1 shows the physical connectivity at each connection to the Frame Relay network, Figure 28-2 shows the logical, or virtual, end-to-end connectivity associated with a virtual circuit (VC).

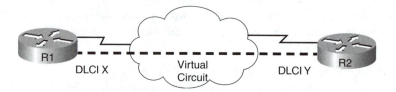

Figure 28-2 *Frame Relay PVC Concepts*

The logical communications path between each pair of DTEs is a VC. The trio of parallel lines in the figure represents a single VC; this book uses a thick dashed line style to make sure you notice the line easily. Typically, the service provider preconfigures all the required details of a VC; predefined VCs are called permanent virtual circuits (PVC).

Routers use the data-link connection identifier (DLCI) as the Frame Relay address; it identifies the VC over which the frame should travel. So, in Figure 28-2, when R1 needs to forward a packet to R2, R1 encapsulates the Layer 3 packet into a Frame Relay header and trailer and then sends the frame. The Frame Relay header includes the correct DLCI so that the provider's Frame Relay switches correctly forward the frame to R2.

Table 28-1 lists the components shown in Figures 28-1 and 28-2 and some associated terms. After the table, the most important features of Frame Relay are described in further detail.

Table 28-1 *Frame Relay Terms and Concepts*

Term	Description
Virtual circuit (VC)	A logical concept that represents the path that frames travel between DTEs. VCs are particularly useful when you compare Frame Relay to leased physical circuits.

Table 28-1 *Frame Relay Terms and Concepts*

Term	Description
Permanent virtual circuit (PVC)	A predefined VC. A PVC can be equated to a leased line in concept.
Switched virtual circuit (SVC)	A VC that is set up dynamically when needed. An SVC can be equated to a dial connection in concept.
Data terminal equipment (DTE)	DTEs are connected to a Frame Relay service from a telecommunications company. They typically reside at sites used by the company buying the Frame Relay service.
Data communications equipment (DCE)	Frame Relay switches are DCE devices. DCEs are also known as data circuit-terminating equipment. DCEs are typically in the service provider's network.
Access link	The leased line between the DTE and DCE.
Access rate (AR)	The speed at which the access link is clocked. This choice affects the connection's price.
Committed Information Rate (CIR)	The speed at which bits can be sent over a VC, according to the business contract between the customer and provider.
Data-link connection identifier (DLCI)	A Frame Relay address used in Frame Relay headers to identify the VC.
Nonbroadcast multiaccess (NBMA)	A network in which broadcasts are not supported, but more than two devices can be connected.
Local Management Interface (LMI)	The protocol used between a DCE and DTE to manage the connection. Signaling messages for SVCs, PVC status messages, and keepalives are all LMI messages.

Frame Relay Standards

The definitions for Frame Relay are contained in documents from the International Telecommunications Union (ITU) and the American National Standards Institute (ANSI). The Frame Relay Forum, a vendor consortium, originally defined several Frame Relay specifications, many of which predate the original ITU and ANSI specifications, with the ITU and ANSI picking up many of the forum's standards. (The Frame Relay Forum has disbanded, because its mission was complete.) Table 28-2 lists the most important of these specifications.

Table 28-2   *Frame Relay Protocol Specifications*

What the Specification Defines	ITU Document	ANSI Document
Data-link specifications, including LAPF header/trailer	Q.922 Annex A (Q.922-A)	T1.618
PVC management, LMI	Q.933 Annex A (Q.933-A)	T1.617 Annex D (T1.617-D)
SVC signaling	Q.933	T1.617
Multiprotocol encapsulation (originated in RFC 1490/2427)	Q.933 Annex E (Q.933-E)	T1.617 Annex F (T1.617-F)

Virtual Circuits

Frame Relay provides significant advantages over simply using point-to-point leased lines. The primary advantage has to do with virtual circuits. Consider Figure 28-3, which shows a typical Frame Relay network with three sites.

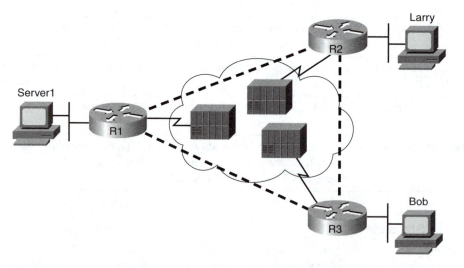

Figure 28-3   *Typical Frame Relay Network with Three Sites*

A virtual circuit defines a logical path between two Frame Relay DTEs. The term *virtual circuit* describes the concept well. It acts like a point-to-point circuit, providing the ability to send data between two endpoints over a WAN. There is no physical circuit directly between the two endpoints, so it's virtual. For example, R1 terminates two VCs—one whose other endpoint is R2, and one whose other endpoint is R3. R1 can send traffic directly to either of the other two routers by sending it over the appropriate VC.

VCs share the access link and the Frame Relay network. For example, both VCs terminating at R1 use the same access link. In fact, many customers share the same Frame Relay network. Originally, people with leased-line networks were reluctant to migrate to Frame Relay, because they would be competing with other customers for the provider's capacity inside the cloud. To address these fears, Frame Relay is designed with the concept of a committed information rate (CIR). Each VC has a CIR, which is a guarantee by the provider that a particular VC gets at least that much bandwidth. So you can migrate from a leased line to Frame Relay, getting a CIR of at least as much bandwidth as you previously had with your leased line.

Interestingly, even with a three-site network, it's probably less expensive to use Frame Relay than to use point-to-point links. Imagine an organization with 100 sites that needs any-to-any connectivity. How many leased lines are required? 4950! And besides that, the organization would need 99 serial interfaces per router if it used point-to-point leased lines. With Frame Relay, an organization could have 100 access links to local Frame Relay switches, one per router, and have 4950 VCs running over them. That requires a lot fewer actual physical links, and you would need only one serial interface on each router!

Service providers can build their Frame Relay networks more cost-effectively than for leased lines. As you would expect, that makes it less expensive for the Frame Relay customer as well. For connecting many WAN sites, Frame Relay is simply more cost-effective than leased lines.

Two types of VCs are allowed—permanent (PVC) and switched (SVC). PVCs are predefined by the provider; SVCs are created dynamically. PVCs are by far the more popular of the two. Frame Relay providers seldom offer SVCs as a service. (The rest of this chapter, as well as Chapter 29, "Frame Relay Configuration," ignore SVCs.)

When the Frame Relay network is engineered, the design might not include a VC between each pair of sites. Figure 28-3 includes PVCs between each pair of sites; this is called a full-mesh Frame Relay network. When not all pairs have a direct PVC, it is called a partial-mesh network. Figure 28-4 shows the same network as Figure 28-3, but this time with a partial mesh and only two PVCs. This is typical when R1 is at the main site and R2 and R3 are at remote offices that rarely need to communicate directly.

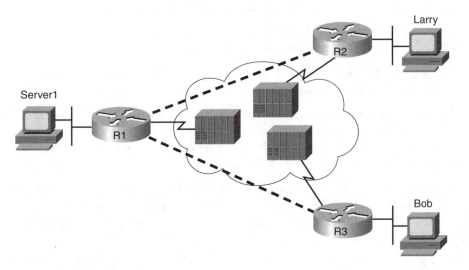

Figure 28-4   *Typical Partial-Mesh Frame Relay Network*

The partial mesh has some advantages and disadvantages compared to a full mesh. The primary advantage is that partial mesh is cheaper, because the provider charges per VC. The downside is that traffic from R2's site to R3's site must go to R1 first and then be forwarded. If that's a small amount of traffic, it's a small price to pay. If it's a lot of traffic, a full mesh is probably worth the extra money, because traffic going between two remote sites would have to cross R1's access link twice.

One conceptual hurdle with PVCs is that there is typically a single access link across which multiple PVCs flow. For example, consider Figure 28-4 from R1's perspective. Server1 sends a packet to Larry. It comes across the Ethernet. R1 gets it and matches Larry's routing table, which tells him to send the packet out Serial0, which is R1's access link. He encapsulates the packet in a Frame Relay header and trailer and then sends it. Which PVC does it use? The Frame Relay switch should forward it to R2, but why does it?

To solve this problem, Frame Relay uses an address to differentiate one PVC from another. This address is called a data-link connection identifier (DLCI). The name is descriptive: The address is for an OSI Layer 2 (data-link) protocol, and it identifies a VC, which is sometimes called a *virtual connection*. So, in this example, R1 uses the DLCI that identifies the PVC to R2, so the provider forwards the frame correctly over the PVC to R2. To send frames to R3, R1 uses the DLCI that identifies the VC for R3. DLCIs and how they work are covered in more detail later in this chapter.

LMI and Encapsulation Types

When you're first learning about Frame Relay, it's often easy to confuse the LMI and the encapsulation used with Frame Relay. The LMI is a definition of the messages used between the DTE (for example, a router) and the DCE (for example, the Frame Relay switch owned by the service provider). The encapsulation defines the headers used by a DTE to communicate some information to the DTE on the other end of a VC. The switch and its connected router care about using the same LMI; the switch does not care about the encapsulation. The endpoint routers (DTE) do care about the encapsulation.

Key Topic

The LMI status inquiry message plays an important role in the fundamental operation of Frame PVCs. Status messages perform two key functions:

- They perform a keepalive function between the DTE and DCE. If the access link has a problem, the absence of keepalive messages implies that the link is down.

- They signal whether a PVC is active or inactive. Even though each PVC is predefined, its status can change. An access link might be up, but one or more VCs could be down. The router needs to know which VCs are up and which are down. It learns that information from the switch using LMI status messages.

Three LMI protocol options are available in Cisco IOS software: Cisco, ITU, and ANSI. Each LMI option is slightly different and therefore is incompatible with the other two. As long as both the DTE and DCE on each end of an access link use the same LMI standard, LMI works fine.

The differences between LMI types are subtle. For example, the Cisco LMI calls for the use of DLCI 1023, whereas ANSI T1.617-D and ITU Q.933-A specify DLCI 0. Some of the messages have different fields in their headers. The DTE simply needs to know which of the three LMIs to use so that it can use the same one as the local switch.

Configuring the LMI type is easy. Today's most popular option is to use the default LMI setting. This setting uses the LMI autosense feature, in which the router simply figures out which LMI type the switch is using. So you can simply let the router autosense the LMI and never bother coding the LMI type. If you choose to configure the LMI type, the router disables the autosense feature.

Table 28-3 outlines the three LMI types, their origin, and the keyword used in the Cisco IOS software **frame-relay lmi-type** interface subcommand.

Table 28-3 *Frame Relay LMI Types*

Name	Document	IOS LMI-Type Parameter
Cisco	Proprietary	cisco
ANSI	T1.617 Annex D	**ansi**
ITU	Q.933 Annex A	**q933a**

Key Topic

A Frame Relay–connected router encapsulates each Layer 3 packet inside a Frame Relay header and trailer before it is sent out an access link. The header and trailer are defined by the Link Access Procedure Frame Bearer Services (LAPF) specification, ITU Q.922-A. The sparse LAPF framing provides error detection with an FCS in the trailer, as well as the DLCI, DE, FECN, and BECN fields in the header (which are discussed later). Figure 28-5 diagrams the frame.

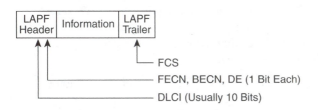

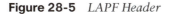

Figure 28-5   *LAPF Header*

However, the LAPF header and trailer do not provide all the fields typically needed by routers. In particular, Figure 28-5 does not show a Protocol Type field. Each data-link header needs a field to define the type of packet that follows the data-link header. If Frame Relay is using only the LAPF header, DTEs (including routers) cannot support multiprotocol traffic, because there is no way to identify the type of protocol in the Information field.

Two solutions were created to compensate for the lack of a Protocol Type field in the standard Frame Relay header:

■ Cisco and three other companies created an additional header, which comes between the LAPF header and the Layer 3 packet shown in Figure 28-5. It includes a 2-byte Protocol Type field, with values matching the same field Cisco uses for HDLC.

■ RFC 1490 (which was later superceded by RFC 2427; you should know both numbers), *Multiprotocol Interconnect over Frame Relay*, defined the second solution. RFC 1490 was written to ensure multivendor interoperability between Frame Relay DTEs. This RFC defines a similar header, also placed between the LAPF header and Layer 3 packet, and includes a Protocol Type field as well as many other options. ITU and ANSI later incorporated RFC 1490 headers into their Q.933 Annex E and T1.617 Annex F specifications, respectively.

Figure 28-6 outlines these two alternatives.

Key Topic

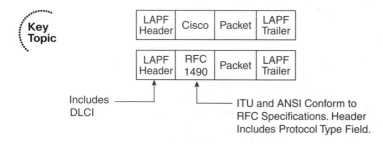

Figure 28-6   *Cisco and RFC 1490/2427 Encapsulation*

DTEs use and react to the fields specified by these two types of encapsulation, but Frame Relay switches ignore these fields. *Because the frames flow from DTE to DTE, both DTEs should agree on the encapsulation used. The switches don't care.* However, each VC can use a different encapsulation. In the configuration, the encapsulation created by Cisco is called **cisco**, and the other one is called ietf.

Now that you have a broad understanding of Frame Relay concepts and terminology, the next section takes a much closer look at Frame Relay DLCIs.

Frame Relay Addressing

Frame Relay defines the rules by which devices deliver Frame Relay frames across a Frame Relay network. Because a router uses a single access link that has many VCs connecting it to many routers, there must be something to identify each of the remote routers—in other words, an address. The DLCI is the Frame Relay address.

DLCIs work slightly differently from the other data-link addresses discussed in this book. This difference is mainly because of the use of the DLCI and the fact that *the header has a single DLCI field, not both Source and Destination DLCI fields.*

Frame Relay Local Addressing

You should understand a few characteristics of DLCIs before we get into their use. Frame Relay DLCIs are locally significant; this means that the addresses need to be unique only on the local access link. A popular analogy that explains local addressing is that there can be only a single street address of 2000 Pennsylvania Avenue in Washington, DC, but there can be a 2000 Pennsylvania Avenue in every town in the United States. Likewise, DLCIs must be unique on each access link, but the same DLCI numbers can be used on every access link in your network. For example, in Figure 28-7, notice that DLCI 40 is used on two access links to describe two different PVCs. No conflict exists, because DLCI 40 is used on two different access links.

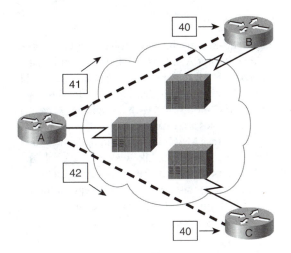

Figure 28-7   *Frame Relay Addressing with Router A Sending to Routers B and C*

Local addressing, which is the common term for the fact that DLCIs are locally significant, is a fact. It is how Frame Relay works. Simply put, a single access link cannot use the same DLCI to represent multiple VCs on the same access link. Otherwise, the Frame Relay switch would not know how to forward frames correctly. For instance, in Figure 28-7, Router A must use different DLCI values for the PVCs on its local access link (41 and 42 in this instance).

Frame Relay Global Addressing

Most people get confused about DLCIs the first time they think about the local significance of DLCIs and the existence of only a single DLCI field in the Frame Relay header. Global addressing solves this problem by making DLCI addressing look like LAN addressing in concept. Global addressing is simply a way of choosing DLCI numbers when planning a Frame Relay network so that working with DLCIs is much easier. Because local addressing is a fact, global addressing does not change these rules. Global addressing just makes DLCI assignment more obvious—as soon as you get used to it.

Here's how global addressing works: The service provider hands out a planning spreadsheet and a diagram. Figure 28-8 is an example of such a diagram, with the global DLCIs shown.

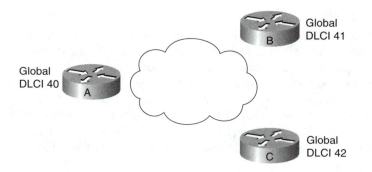

Figure 28-8   *Frame Relay Global DLCIs*

Global addressing is planned as shown in Figure 28-8, with the DLCIs placed in Frame Re-lay frames as shown in Figure 28-9. For example, Router A uses DLCI 41 when sending a frame to Router B, because Router B's global DLCI is 41. Likewise, Router A uses DLCI 42 when sending frames over the VC to Router C. The nice thing is that global addressing is much more logical to most people, because it works like a LAN, with a single MAC ad-dress for each device. On a LAN, if the MAC addresses are MAC-A, MAC-B, and MAC-C for the three routers, Router A uses destination address MAC-B when sending frames to Router B and uses MAC-C as the destination to reach Router C. Likewise, with global DL-CIs 40, 41, and 42 used for Routers A, B, and C, respectively, the same concept applies. Because DLCIs address VCs, the logic is something like this when Router A sends a frame to Router B: "Hey, local switch! When you get this frame, send it over the VC that we agreed to number with DLCI 41." Figure 28-9 outlines this example.

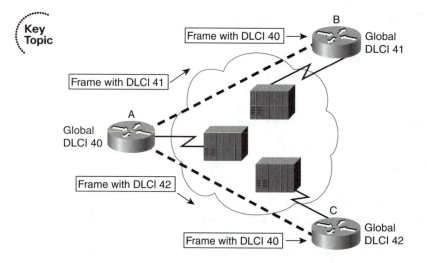

Figure 28-9   *Frame Relay Global Addressing from the Sender's Perspective*

Router A sends frames with DLCI 41, and they reach the local switch. The local switch sees the DLCI field and forwards the frame through the Frame Relay network until it reaches the switch connected to Router B. Then Router B's local switch forwards the frame out the access link to Router B. The same process happens between Router A and Router C when Router A uses DLCI 42. The beauty of global addressing is that you think of each router as having an address, like LAN addressing. If you want to send a frame to someone, you put his or her DLCI in the header, and the network delivers the frame to the correct DTE.

The final key to global addressing is that the Frame Relay switches actually change the DLCI value before delivering the frame. Did you notice that Figure 28-9 shows a different DLCI value as the frames are received by Routers B and C? For example, Router A sends a frame to Router B, and Router A puts DLCI 41 in the frame. The last switch changes the field to DLCI 40 before forwarding it to Router B. The result is that when Routers B and C receive their frames, the DLCI value is actually the sender's global DLCI. Why? Well, when Router B receives the frame, because the DLCI is 40, it knows that the frame came in on the PVC between itself and Router A. In general, the following are true when using the global addressing convention:

■ The sender treats the DLCI field as a destination address, using the destination's global DLCI in the header.

■ The receiver thinks of the DLCI field as the source address, because it contains the global DLCI of the frame's sender.

Figure 28-9 describes what happens in a typical Frame Relay network. Service providers supply a planning spreadsheet and diagrams with global DLCIs listed. Table 28-4 gives you an organized view of what DLCIs are used in Figure 28-9.

Table 28-4 *DLCI Swapping in the Frame Relay Cloud of Figure 28-9*

The Frame Sent by Router	With DLCI Field	Is Delivered to Router	With DLCI Field
A	41	B	40
A	42	C	40
B	40	A	41
C	40	A	42

Global addressing makes DLCI addressing more intuitive for most people. It also makes router configuration more straightforward and lets you add new sites more conveniently. For instance, examine Figure 28-10, which adds Routers D and E to the network shown in Figure 28-9. The service provider simply states that global DLCIs 43 and 44 are used for these two routers. If these two routers also have only one PVC to Router A, all the DLCI planning is complete. You know that Router D and Router E use DLCI 40 to reach Router A and that Router A uses DLCI 43 to reach Router D and DLCI 44 to reach Router E.

The remaining examples in this chapter use global addressing in any planning diagrams unless otherwise stated. One practical way to determine whether the diagram lists the local DLCIs or the global DLCI convention is this: If two VCs terminate at the same DTE, and a single DLCI is shown, it probably represents the global DLCI convention. If one DLCI is shown per VC, local DLCI addressing is depicted.

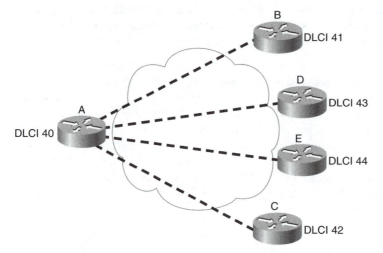

Figure 28-10   *Adding Frame Relay Sites: Global Addressing*

Now that you have a better understanding of how Frame Relay uses DLCIs to address each VC, causing the correct delivery of frames over a Frame Relay cloud, the next section moves up to Layer 3, examining the IP addressing conventions that can be used over Frame Relay.

Network Layer Concerns with Frame Relay

Frame Relay networks have both similarities and differences as compared to LAN and point-to-point WAN links. These differences introduce some additional considerations for passing Layer 3 packets across a Frame Relay network. You need to concern yourself with a couple of key issues relating to Layer 3 flows over Frame Relay:

■   Choices for Layer 3 addresses on Frame Relay interfaces

■   Broadcast handling

In particular, the Frame Relay implementation in Cisco defines three different options for assigning subnets and IP addresses on Frame Relay interfaces:

■   One subnet containing all Frame Relay DTEs

■   One subnet per VC

■   A hybrid of the first two options

This section examines the three main options for IP addressing over Frame Relay, as well as broadcast handling, which impacts how routing protocols work over Frame Relay.

Frame Relay Layer 3 Addressing: One Subnet Containing All Frame Relay DTEs

Figure 28-11 shows the first alternative, which is to use a single subnet for the Frame Relay network. This figure shows a fully meshed Frame Relay network because the single-subnet option is typically used when a full mesh of VCs exists. In a full mesh, each router has a VC to every other router, meaning that each router can send frames directly to every other router. This more closely resembles how a LAN works. So, a single subnet can be used for all the routers' Frame Relay interfaces, as configured on the routers' serial interfaces. Table 28-5 summarizes the addresses used in Figure 28-11.

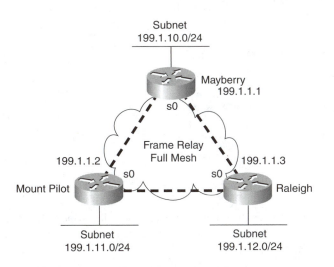

Figure 28-11   *Full Mesh with IP Addresses*

Table 28-5   *IP Addresses with No Subinterfaces*

Router	IP Address of Frame Relay Interface
Mayberry	199.1.1.1
Mount Pilot	199.1.1.2
Raleigh	199.1.1.3

The single-subnet alternative is straightforward, and it conserves your IP address space. It also looks like what you are used to with LANs, which makes it easier to conceptualize. Unfortunately, most companies build partial-mesh Frame Relay networks, and the single-subnet option has some deficiencies when the network is a partial mesh.

Frame Relay Layer 3 Addressing: One Subnet Per VC

The second IP addressing alternative, having a single subnet for each VC, works better with a partially meshed Frame Relay network, as shown in Figure 28-12. Boston cannot forward frames directly to Charlotte, because no VC is defined between the two. This is a more typical Frame Relay network, because most organizations with many sites tend to group applications on servers at a few centralized locations, and most of the traffic is between each remote site and those servers.

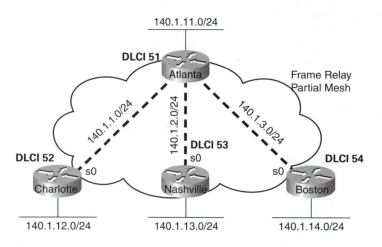

Figure 28-12   *Partial Mesh with IP Addresses*

The single-subnet-per-VC alternative matches the logic behind a set of point-to-point links. Using multiple subnets instead of one larger subnet wastes some IP addresses, but it overcomes some issues with distance vector routing protocols.

Table 28-6 shows the IP addresses for the partially meshed Frame Relay network shown in Figure 28-12.

Table 28-6   *IP Addresses with Point-to-Point Subinterfaces*

Router	Subnet	IP Address
Atlanta	140.1.1.0	140.1.1.1
Charlotte	140.1.1.0	140.1.1.2
Atlanta	140.1.2.0	140.1.2.1
Nashville	140.1.2.0	140.1.2.3
Atlanta	140.1.3.0	140.1.3.1
Boston	140.1.3.0	140.1.3.4

Cisco IOS Software has a configuration feature called *subinterfaces* that creates a logical subdivision of a physical interface. Subinterfaces allow the Atlanta router to have three IP addresses associated with its Serial0 physical interface by configuring three separate subinterfaces. A router can treat each subinterface, and the VC associated with it, as if it were a point-to-point serial link. Each of the three subinterfaces of Serial0 on Atlanta would be assigned a different IP address from Table 28-6 (Chapter 29 shows several sample configurations).

Note: The example uses IP address prefixes of /24 to keep the math simple. In production networks, point-to-point subinterfaces typically use a prefix of /30 (mask 255.255.255.252), because that allows for only two valid IP addresses—the exact number needed on a point-to-point subinterface. Of course, using different masks in the same network means your routing protocol must also support VLSM.

Frame Relay Layer 3 Addressing: Hybrid Approach

The third alternative for Layer 3 addressing is a hybrid of the first two alternatives. Consider Figure 28-13, which shows a trio of routers with VCs between each of them, as well as two other VCs to remote sites.

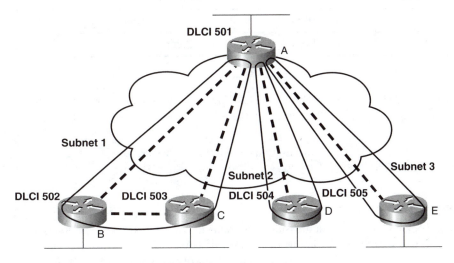

Figure 28-13 *Hybrid of Full and Partial Mesh*

Two options exist for Layer 3 addressing in this case. The first is to treat each VC as a separate Layer 3 group. In this case, five subnets are needed for the Frame Relay network. However, Routers A, B, and C create a smaller full mesh between each other. This allows Routers A, B, and C to use one subnet. The other two VCs—one between Routers A and D and one between Routers A and E—are treated as two separate Layer 3 groups. The result is a total of three subnets.

To accomplish either style of Layer 3 addressing in this third and final case, subinterfaces are used. Point-to-point subinterfaces are used when a single VC is considered to be all that is in the group—for instance, between Routers A and D and between Routers A and

E. Multipoint subinterfaces are used when more than two routers are considered to be in the same group—for instance, with Routers A, B, and C.

Multipoint subinterfaces logically terminate more than one VC. In fact, the name "multipoint" implies the function, because more than one remote site can be reached via a VC associated with a multipoint subinterface.

Table 28-7 summarizes the addresses and subinterfaces that are used in Figure 28-13.

Table 28-7   *IP Addresses with Point-to-Point and Multipoint Subinterfaces*

Router	Subnet	IP Address	Subinterface Type
A	140.1.1.0/24	140.1.1.1	Multipoint
B	140.1.1.0/24	140.1.1.2	Multipoint
C	140.1.1.0/24	140.1.1.3	Multipoint
A	140.1.2.0/24	140.1.2.1	Point-to-point
D	140.1.2.0/24	140.1.2.4	Point-to-point
A	140.1.3.0/24	140.1.3.1	Point-to-point
E	140.1.3.0/24	140.1.3.5	Point-to-point

What will you see in a real network? Most of the time, point-to-point subinterfaces are used, with a single subnet per PVC, although the other options are used occasionally.

Note: Chapter 29 provides full configurations for all three cases illustrated in Figures 28-11, 28-12, and 28-13.

Layer 3 Broadcast Handling

After contending with Layer 3 addressing over Frame Relay, the next consideration is how to deal with Layer 3 broadcasts. Frame Relay can send copies of a broadcast over all VCs, but there is no equivalent to LAN broadcasts. In other words, no capability exists for a Frame Relay DTE to send a single frame into the Frame Relay network and have that frame replicated and delivered across multiple VCs to multiple destinations. However, routers need to send broadcasts for several features to work. In particular, routing protocol updates are either broadcasts or multicasts.

The solution to the Frame Relay broadcast dilemma has two parts. First, Cisco IOS software sends copies of the broadcasts across each VC, assuming that you have configured the router to forward these necessary broadcasts. If there are only a few VCs, this is not a big problem. However, if hundreds of VCs terminate in one router, for each broadcast, hundreds of copies could be sent.

As the second part of the solution, the router tries to minimize the impact of the first part of the solution. The router places the copies of the broadcasts in a different output queue than the one for user traffic so that the user does not experience a large spike in delay each time a broadcast is replicated and sent over every VC. Cisco IOS software can also be configured to limit the amount of bandwidth that is used for these replicated broadcasts.

Although this book does not discuss scalability issues in detail, a short example shows the significance of broadcast overhead. If a router knows 1000 routes, uses RIP, and has 50 VCs, the router sends 1.072 MB (that's megabytes) of RIP updates every 30 seconds. That averages out to 285 kbps. (The math is as follows: 536-byte RIP packets, with 25 routes in each packet, for 40 packets per update, with copies sent over 50 VCs. 536 * 40 * 50 = 1.072 MB per update interval. 1.072 * 8 / 30 seconds = 285 kbps.) That's a lot of overhead!

Knowing how to tell the router to forward these broadcasts to each VC is covered in the section "Frame Relay Configuration and Verification" in Chapter 29.

Chapter Review

Review Key Topics

Review the most important topics from this chapter, noted with the Key Topic icons. Table 28-8 lists these key topics and where each is discussed.

Key Topic

Table 28-8 *Key Topics for Chapter 28*

Key Topic Element	Description	Page Number
Figure 28-1	Figure listing several terms related to a Frame Relay topology	714
Table 28-1	Table listing key Frame Relay terms and definitions	714
List	Two important functions of the Frame Relay LMI	718
Table 28-3	Frame Relay LMI types and LMI type configuration keywords	719
Figure 28-6	Figure showing headers and positions for the Cisco and IETF additional Frame Relay headers	720
Figure 28-9	Figure showing the concept of Frame Relay global addressing	722
List	Three options of subnets used on a Frame Relay network	724

Define Key Terms

Define the following key terms from this chapter, and check your answers in the glossary:

access link, access rate, Committed Information Rate (CIR), data-link connection identifier (DLCI), Frame Relay DCE, Frame Relay DTE, Local Management Interface (LMI), nonbroadcast multiaccess (NBMA), permanent virtual circuit (PVC), virtual circuit (VC)

Answer Review Questions

Answer the following review questions:

1. Which of the following is a protocol used between the Frame Relay DTE and the Frame Relay switch?

   a. VC

   b. CIR

   c. LMI

   d. Q.921

   e. DLCI

   f. FRF.5

   g. Encapsulation

2. Which of the following statements about Frame Relay are true?

   a. The DTE typically sits at the customer site.

   b. Routers send LMI messages to each other to signal the status of a VC.

   c. A frame's source DLCI must remain unchanged, but the frame's destination DLCI is allowed to change, as the frame traverses the Frame Relay cloud.

   d. The Frame Relay encapsulation type on the sending router should match the encapsulation type on the receiving router for the receiving router to be able to understand the frame's contents.

3. What does DLCI stand for?

   a. Data-link connection identifier

   b. Data-link connection indicator

   c. Data-link circuit identifier

   d. Data-link circuit indicator

4. Router R1 receives a frame from router R2 with DLCI value 222 in it. Which of the following statements about this network is the most accurate?

   a. 222 represents Router R1.

   b. 222 represents Router R2.

   c. 222 is the local DLCI on R1 that represents the VC between R1 and R2.

   d. 222 is the local DLCI on R2 that represents the VC between R1 and R2.

5. A Frame Relay planning diagram shows the number 101 beside R1, 102 by R2, 103 by R3, and 104 by R4. No other DLCIs are listed. The lead network engineer tells you that the planning diagram uses global DLCI addressing and that a full mesh of VCs exists. Which of the following are true?

a. Frames sent by R1 to R2, as they cross R2's access link, have DLCI 102.

b. Frames sent by R1 to R2, as they cross R2's access link, have DLCI 101.

c. Frames sent by R3 to R2, as they cross R3's access link, have DLCI 102.

d. Frames sent by R3 to R1, as they cross R3's access link, have DLCI 101.

6. FredsCo has five sites, with routers connected to the same Frame Relay network. Virtual circuits (VC) have been defined between each pair of routers. What is the fewest subnets that FredsCo could use on the Frame Relay network?

a. 1

b. 2

c. 3

d. 4

e. 5

f. 10

7. BarneyCo has five sites, with routers connected to the same Frame Relay network. VCs have been defined between each pair of routers. Barney, the company president, will fire anyone who configures Frame Relay without using point-to-point subinterfaces. What is the fewest subnets that BarneyCo could use on the Frame Relay network?

a. 1

b. 4

c. 8

d. 10

e. 12

f. 15

This chapter covers the following subjects:

■ **Frame Relay Configuration and Verification:** This section shows you how to configure the required and optional Frame Relay features, with basic verification of each feature.

■ **Frame Relay Troubleshooting:** This section examines a process by which an engineer can find the root cause of why one Frame Relay router cannot ping another Frame Relay router.

CHAPTER 29

Frame Relay Configuration

Chapter 28, "Frame Relay Concepts," introduced and explained the main concepts behind Frame Relay. This chapter shows you how to configure the features on Cisco routers, how to verify that each feature works, and how to troubleshoot problems with forwarding packets over a Frame Relay network.

Frame Relay Configuration and Verification

Frame Relay configuration can be very basic or somewhat detailed, depending on how many default settings can be used. By default, Cisco IOS automatically senses the LMI type and automatically discovers the mapping between DLCI and next-hop IP addresses (using Inverse ARP). If you use all Cisco routers, the default to use Cisco encapsulation works without any additional configuration. If you also design the Frame Relay network to use a single subnet, you can configure the routers to use their physical interfaces without any subinterfaces—making the configuration shorter still. In fact, using as many default settings as possible, the only new configuration command for Frame Relay, as compared to point-to-point WANs, is the **encapsulation frame-relay** command.

Building a comfortable skill set with Frame Relay configuration can be a bit challenging. First, Frame Relay configuration includes many optional settings, so figuring out when to use some settings, and not other settings, can be a challenge. Second, many experienced network engineers have experience with only one of the three main options for Frame Relay configuration (physical, multipoint, or point-to-point), but they might not know much about the other two options. This section examines the basics of each of these three options, including some of the optional configuration commands.

Planning a Frame Relay Configuration

Engineers must do a fair amount of planning before knowing where to start with the configuration. Although most modern Enterprises already have some Frame Relay connections, when planning for new sites, you must consider the following items and communicate them to the Frame Relay provider, which in turn has some impact on the routers' Frame Relay configurations:

- Define which physical sites need a Frame Relay access link installed, and define the clock rate (access rate) used on each link

- Define each VC by identifying the endpoints and setting the CIR

- Agree to an LMI type (usually dictated by the provider)

Additionally, the engineer must choose the particular style of configuration based on the following. For these items, the enterprise engineer does not need to consult the Frame Relay provider:

■ Choose the IP subnetting scheme: one subnet for all VCs, one subnet for each VC, or a subnet for each fully meshed subset.

■ Pick whether to assign the IP addresses to physical, multipoint, or point-to-point subinterfaces.

■ Choose which VCs need to use IETF encapsulation instead of the default value of "cisco." IETF encapsulation is typically used when one router is not a Cisco router.

After the planning has been completed, the configuration steps flow directly from the choices made when planning the network. The following list summarizes the configuration steps, mainly as a tool when studying for any tests. Feel free to refer to this list as the upcoming examples show you how to configure the various options. (There is no need to memorize the steps; the list is just a tool to help organize your thinking about the configuration.)

Key Topic

Step 1. Configure the physical interface to use Frame Relay encapsulation (**encapsulation frame-relay** interface subcommand).

Step 2. Configure an IP address on the interface or subinterface (**ip address** subcommand).

Step 3. (Optional) Manually set the LMI type on each physical serial interface (**frame-relay lmi-type** interface subcommand).

Step 4. (Optional) Change from the default encapsulation of **cisco** to **ietf** by doing the following:
   a. For all VCs on the interface, add the **ietf** keyword to the **encapsulation frame-relay** interface subcommand.
   b. For a single VC, add the **ietf** keyword to the **frame-relay interface-dlci** interface subcommand (point-to-point subinterfaces only) or to the **frame-relay map** command.

Step 5. (Optional) If you aren't using the (default) Inverse ARP to map the DLCI to the next-hop router's IP address, define static mapping using the **frame-relay map ip** *ip-address dlci* **broadcast** subinterface subcommand.

Step 6. On subinterfaces, associate one (point-to-point) or more (multipoint) DLCIs with the subinterface in one of two ways:
   a. Using the **frame-relay interface-dlci** *dlci* subinterface subcommand.
   b. As a side effect of static mapping using the **frame-relay map ip** *dlci ip-address* **broadcast** subinterface subcommand.

The rest of this section shows examples of all these configuration steps, along with some discussion about how to verify that the Frame Relay network is working correctly.

A Fully Meshed Network with One IP Subnet

The first example shows the briefest possible Frame Relay configuration, one that uses just the first two steps of the configuration checklist in this chapter. The design for the first example includes the following choices:

■ Install an access link into three routers.

■ Create a full mesh of PVCs.

■ Use a single subnet (Class C network 199.1.1.0) in the Frame Relay network.

■ Configure the routers using their physical interfaces.

Take the default settings for LMI, Inverse ARP, and encapsulation. Examples 29-1, 29-2, and 29-3 show the configuration for the network shown in Figure 29-1.

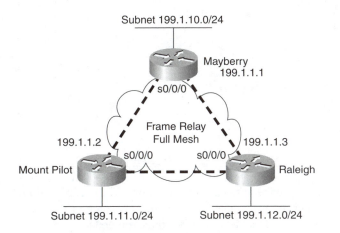

Figure 29-1   *Full Mesh with IP Addresses*

Example 29-1   *Mayberry Configuration*

```
interface serial0/0/0
 encapsulation frame-relay
 ip address  199.1.1.1  255.255.255.0
!
interface fastethernet 0/0
 ip address  199.1.10.1  255.255.255.0
!
router eigrp 1
 network 199.1.1.0
 network 199.1.10.0
```

Example 29-2 *Mount Pilot Configuration*

```
interface serial0/0/0
 encapsulation frame-relay
 ip address  199.1.1.2  255.255.255.0
 !
interface fastethernet 0/0
 ip address  199.1.11.2   255.255.255.0
 !
router eigrp 1
 network 199.1.1.0
 network 199.1.11.0
```

Example 29-3 *Raleigh Configuration*

```
interface serial0/0/0
 encapsulation frame-relay
 ip address  199.1.1.3  255.255.255.0
 !
interface fastethernet 0/0
 ip address  199.1.12.3   255.255.255.0
 !
router eigrp 1
 network 199.1.1.0
 network 199.1.12.0
```

The configuration is simple in comparison with the protocol concepts. The **encapsulation frame-relay** command tells the routers to use Frame Relay data-link protocols instead of the default, which is HDLC. Note that the IP addresses on the three routers' serial interfaces are all in the same Class C network. Also, this simple configuration takes advantage of the following IOS default settings:

Key Topic

■   The LMI type is automatically sensed.

■   The (default) encapsulation is Cisco instead of IETF.

■   PVC DLCIs are learned via LMI status messages.

■   Inverse ARP is enabled (by default) and is triggered when the status message declaring that the VCs are up is received.

Configuring the Encapsulation and LMI

In some cases, the default values are inappropriate. For example, you must use IETF encapsulation if one router is not a Cisco router. For the purpose of showing an alternative configuration, suppose that the following requirements were added:

■   The Raleigh router requires IETF encapsulation on both VCs.

■   Mayberry's LMI type should be ANSI, and LMI autosense should not be used.

To change these defaults, the steps outlined as optional configuration Steps 3 and 4 in the configuration checklist should be used. Examples 29-4 and 29-5 show the changes that would be made to Mayberry and Raleigh.

Example 29-4   *Mayberry Configuration with New Requirements*

```
interface serial0/0/0
 encapsulation frame-relay
 frame-relay lmi-type ansi
 frame-relay interface-dlci 53 ietf
 ip address 199.1.1.1  255.255.255.0
! rest of configuration unchanged from Example 29-1.
```

Example 29-5   *Raleigh Configuration with New Requirements*

```
interface serial0/0/0
 encapsulation frame-relay ietf
 ip address  199.1.1.3  255.255.255.0

! rest of configuration unchanged from Example 29-3.
```

These configurations differ from the previous ones (in Examples 29-1 and 29-2) in two ways. First, Raleigh changed its encapsulation for both its PVCs with the **ietf** keyword on the **encapsulation** command. This keyword applies to all VCs on the interface. However, Mayberry cannot change its encapsulation in the same way, because only one of the two VCs terminating in Mayberry needs to use IETF encapsulation, and the other needs to use Cisco encapsulation. So, Mayberry is forced to code the **frame-relay interface-dlci** command, referencing the DLCI for the VC to Raleigh, with the **ietf** keyword. With that command, you can change the encapsulation setting per VC, as opposed to the configuration on Raleigh, which changes the encapsulation for all VCs.

The second major change is the LMI configuration. The LMI configuration in Mayberry would be fine without any changes, because the default use of LMI autosense would recognize ANSI as the LMI type. However, by coding the **frame-relay lmi-type ansi** interface subcommand, Mayberry must use ANSI, because this command not only sets the LMI type, it also disables autonegotiation of the LMI type.

Note: The LMI setting is a per-physical-interface setting, even if subinterfaces are used, so the **frame-relay lmi-type** command is always a subcommand under the physical interface.

Mount Pilot needs to configure a **frame-relay interface-dlci** command with the **ietf** keyword for its VC to Raleigh, just like Mayberry. This change is not shown in the examples.

Frame Relay Address Mapping

Figure 29-1 does not even bother listing the DLCIs used for the VCs. The configurations work as stated, and frankly, if you never knew the DLCIs, this network would work! However, for real networking jobs, you need to understand an important concept related to Frame Relay—Frame Relay address mapping. Figure 29-2 shows the same network, this time with global DLCI values shown.

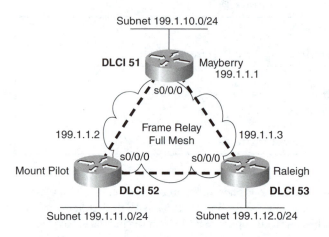

Figure 29-2 *Full Mesh with Global DLCIs Shown*

Frame Relay "mapping" creates a correlation between a Layer 3 address and its corresponding Layer 2 address. The concept is similar to the ARP cache for LAN interfaces. For example, the IP Address Resolution Protocol (ARP) cache used on LANs is an example of Layer 3-to-Layer 2 address mapping. With IP ARP, you know the IP address of another device on the same LAN, but not the MAC address; when the ARP completes, you know another device's LAN (Layer 2) address. Similarly, routers that use Frame Relay need a mapping between a router's Layer 3 address and the DLCI used to reach that other router.

This section discusses the basics of why mapping is needed for LAN connections and Frame Relay, with a focus on Frame Relay. Here's a more general definition of mapping:

Key Topic

> The information that correlates to the next-hop router's Layer 3 address, and the Layer 2 address used to reach it, is called mapping. Mapping is needed on multiaccess networks.

Thinking about routing helps make the need for mapping more apparent. Imagine that a host on the Mayberry Ethernet sends an IP packet to a host on the Mount Pilot Ethernet. The packet arrives at the Mayberry router over the LAN, and Mayberry discards the Ethernet header and trailer. Mayberry looks at the routing table, which lists a route to

199.1.11.0, outgoing interface Serial 0/0/0, and next-hop router 199.1.1.2, which is Mount Pilot's Frame Relay IP address.

The next decision that the router must make to complete the process points out the need for mapping: What DLCI should Mayberry put in the Frame Relay header? We configured no DLCIs. However, it would work as configured! To see the answer, consider Example 29-6, which shows some important commands that can be used to see how Mayberry makes the right choice for the DLCI.

Example 29-6   show *Commands on Mayberry, Showing the Need for Mapping*

```
Mayberry# show ip route
Codes: C - connected, S - static, I - IGRP, R - RIP, M - mobile, B - BGP
       D - EIGRP, EX - EIGRP external, O - OSPF, IA - OSPF inter area
       N1 - OSPF NSSA external type 1, N2 - OSPF NSSA external type 2
       E1 - OSPF external type 1, E2 - OSPF external type 2, E - EGP
       i - IS-IS, L1 - IS-IS level-1, L2 - IS-IS level-2, ia - IS-IS inter area
       * - candidate default, U - per-user static route, o - ODR
       P - periodic downloaded static route

Gateway of last resort is not set

D    199.1.11.0/24 [90/2195456] via 199.1.1.2, 00:00:26, Serial0/0/0
C    199.1.10.0/24 is directly connected, Fastethernet0/0
D    199.1.12.0/24 [90/2185984] via 199.1.1.3, 00:01:04, Serial0/0/0
C    199.1.1.0/24 is directly connected, Serial0/0/0
C    192.68.1.0/24 is directly connected, Fastethernet0/0
C    192.168.1.0/24 is directly connected, Fastethernet0/0

Mayberry# show frame-relay pvc
PVC Statistics for interface Serial0/0/0 (Frame Relay DTE)

                Active     Inactive     Deleted      Static
  Local         2          0            0            0
  Switched      0          0            0            0
  Unused        0          0            0            0

DLCI = 52, DLCI USAGE = LOCAL, PVC STATUS = ACTIVE, INTERFACE = Serial0/0/0

   input pkts 46            output pkts 22          in bytes 2946
   out bytes 1794           dropped pkts 0          in FECN pkts 0
   in BECN pkts 0           out FECN pkts 0         out BECN pkts 0
   in DE pkts 0             out DE pkts 0
   out bcast pkts 21        out bcast bytes 1730
   pvc create time 00:23:07, last time pvc status changed 00:21:38

DLCI = 53, DLCI USAGE = LOCAL, PVC STATUS = ACTIVE, INTERFACE = Serial0/0/0
```

```
   input pkts 39         output pkts 18        in bytes 2564
   out bytes 1584        dropped pkts 0        in FECN pkts 0
   in BECN pkts 0        out FECN pkts 0       out BECN pkts 0
   in DE pkts 0          out DE pkts 0
   out bcast pkts 18     out bcast bytes 1584
   pvc create time 00:23:08, last time pvc status changed 00:21:20


Mayberry# show frame-relay map
Serial0/0/0 (up): ip 199.1.1.2 dlci 52(0x34,0xC40), dynamic,
          broadcast,, status defined, active
Serial0/0/0 (up): ip 199.1.1.3 dlci 53(0x35,0xC50), dynamic,
          broadcast,, status defined, active
```

The example highlights all the related information on Mayberry for sending packets to network 199.1.11.0/24 off Mount Pilot. Mayberry's route to 199.1.11.0 refers to outgoing interface Serial 0/0/0 and to 199.1.1.2 as the next-hop address. The **show frame-relay pvc** command lists two DLCIs, 52 and 53, and both are active. How does Mayberry know the DLCIs? Well, the LMI status messages tell Mayberry about the VCs, the associated DLCIs, and the status (active).

Which DLCI should Mayberry use to forward the packet? The **show frame-relay map** command output holds the answer. Notice the highlighted phrase "ip 199.1.1.2 dlci 52" in the output. Somehow, Mayberry has mapped 199.1.1.2, which is the next-hop address in the route, to the correct DLCI, which is 52. So, Mayberry knows to use DLCI 52 to reach next-hop IP address 199.1.1.2.

Mayberry can use two methods to build the mapping shown in Example 29-6. One uses a statically configured mapping, and the other uses a dynamic process called *Inverse ARP*. The next two small sections explain the details of each of these options.

Inverse ARP

Inverse ARP dynamically creates a mapping between the Layer 3 address (for example, the IP address) and the Layer 2 address (the DLCI). The end result of Inverse ARP is the same as IP ARP on a LAN: The router builds a mapping between a neighboring Layer 3 address and the corresponding Layer 2 address. However, the process used by Inverse ARP differs for ARP on a LAN. After the VC is up, each router announces its network layer address by sending an Inverse ARP message over that VC. This works as shown in Figure 29-3.

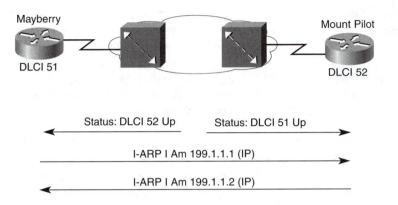

Figure 29-3 *Inverse ARP Process*

As shown in Figure 29-3, Inverse ARP announces its Layer 3 addresses as soon as the LMI signals that the PVCs are up. Inverse ARP starts by learning the DLCI data link layer address (via LMI messages), and then it announces its own Layer 3 addresses that use that VC. Inverse ARP is enabled by default.

In Example 29-6, Mayberry shows two different entries in the **show frame-relay map** command output. Mayberry uses Inverse ARP to learn that DLCI 52 is mapped to next-hop IP address 199.1.1.2 and that DLCI 53 is mapped to next-hop IP address 199.1.1.3. Interestingly, Mayberry learns this information by receiving an Inverse ARP from Mount Pilot and Raleigh, respectively.

Table 29-1 summarizes what occurs with Inverse ARP in the network shown in Figure 29-2.

Table 29-1 *Inverse ARP Messages for Figure 29-2*

Sending Router	DLCI When the Frame Is Sent	Receiving Router	DLCI When the Frame Is Received	Information in the Inverse ARP Message
Mayberry	52	Mount Pilot	51	I am 199.1.1.1.
Mayberry	53	Raleigh	51	I am 199.1.1.1.
Mount Pilot	51	Mayberry	52	I am 199.1.1.2.
Mount Pilot	53	Raleigh	52	I am 199.1.1.2.
Raleigh	51	Mayberry	53	I am 199.1.1.3.
Raleigh	52	Mount Pilot	53	I am 199.1.1.3.

To understand Inverse ARP, focus on the last two columns of Table 29-1. Each router receives some Inverse ARP "announcements." The Inverse ARP message contains the sender's Layer 3 address, and the Frame Relay header, of course, has a DLCI in it. These two values are placed in the Inverse ARP cache on the receiving router. For example, in the third row, Mayberry receives an Inverse ARP. The DLCI is 52 when the frame arrives at Mayberry, and the IP address is 199.1.1.2. This is added to the Frame Relay map table in Mayberry, which is shown in the highlighted part of the **show frame-relay map** command in Example 29-6.

Static Frame Relay Mapping

You can statically configure the same mapping information instead of using Inverse ARP. In a production network, you probably would just go ahead and use Inverse ARP. However, if you take the time to understand how to configure the same information using static mapping, you will better understand the information learned by Inverse ARP. Example 29-7 lists the static Frame Relay map for the three routers shown in Figure 29-2, along with the configuration used to disable Inverse ARP.

Example 29-7 *frame-relay map Commands*

```
Mayberry
interface serial 0/0/0
 no frame-relay inverse-arp
 frame-relay map ip 199.1.1.2 52 broadcast
 frame-relay map ip 199.1.1.3 53 broadcast
Mount Pilot
interface serial 0/0/0
 no frame-relay inverse-arp
 frame-relay map ip 199.1.1.1 51 broadcast
 frame-relay map ip 199.1.1.3 53 broadcast
Raleigh
interface serial 0/0/0
 no frame-relay inverse-arp
 frame-relay map ip 199.1.1.1 51 broadcast
 frame-relay map ip 199.1.1.2 52 broadcast
```

The **frame-relay map** command entry for Mayberry, referencing 199.1.1.2, is used for packets in Mayberry going to Mount Pilot. When Mayberry creates a Frame Relay header, expecting it to be delivered to Mount Pilot, Mayberry must use DLCI 52. Mayberry's **frame-relay map** statement correlates Mount Pilot's IP address, 199.1.1.2, to the DLCI used to reach Mount Pilot—namely, DLCI 52. Likewise, a packet sent back from Mount Pilot to Mayberry causes Mount Pilot to use its **map** statement to refer to

Mayberry's IP address of 199.1.1.1. Mapping is needed for each next-hop Layer 3 address for each Layer 3 protocol being routed. Even with a network this small, the configuration process can be laborious.

Note: The **broadcast** keyword is required when the router needs to send broadcasts or multicasts to the neighboring router—for example, to support routing protocol messages such as Hellos.

A Partially Meshed Network with One IP Subnet Per VC

The second sample network, based on the environment shown in Figure 29-4, uses point-to-point subinterfaces. Examples 29-8 through 29-11 show the configuration for this network. The command prompts are included in the first example because they change when you configure subinterfaces.

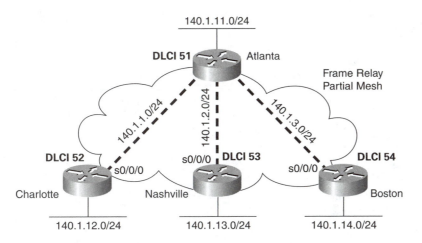

Figure 29-4 *Partial Mesh with IP Addresses*

Example 29-8 *Atlanta Configuration*

```
Atlanta(config)# interface serial0/0/0
Atlanta(config-if)# encapsulation frame-relay

Atlanta(config-if)# interface serial 0/0/0.1 point-to-point
Atlanta(config-subif)# ip address 140.1.1.1 255.255.255.0
Atlanta(config-subif)# frame-relay interface-dlci 52

Atlanta(config-fr-dlci)# interface serial 0/0/0.2 point-to-point
Atlanta(config-subif)# ip address 140.1.2.1 255.255.255.0
Atlanta(config-subif)# frame-relay interface-dlci 53
```

```
Atlanta(config-fr-dlci)# interface serial 0/0/0.3 point-to-point
Atlanta(config-subif)# ip address 140.1.3.1 255.255.255.0
Atlanta(config-subif)# frame-relay interface-dlci 54

Atlanta(config-fr-dlci)# interface fastethernet 0/0
Atlanta(config-if)# ip address 140.1.11.1 255.255.255.0
```

Example 29-9 *Charlotte Configuration*

```
interface serial0/0/0
 encapsulation frame-relay
!
interface serial 0/0/0.1 point-to-point
 ip address 140.1.1.2  255.255.255.0
 frame-relay interface-dlci 51
!
interface fastethernet 0/0
 ip address 140.1.12.2 255.255.255.0
```

Example 29-10 *Nashville Configuration*

```
interface serial0/0/0
 encapsulation frame-relay
!
interface serial 0/0/0.2 point-to-point
 ip address 140.1.2.3 255.255.255.0
 frame-relay interface-dlci 51
!
interface fastethernet 0/0
 ip address 140.1.13.3 255.255.255.0
```

Example 29-11 *Boston Configuration*

```
interface serial0/0/0
encapsulation frame-relay
!
interface serial 0/0/0.3 point-to-point
ip address 140.1.3.4 255.255.255.0
frame-relay interface-dlci 51
```

```
!
interface fastethernet 0/0
ip address 140.1.14.4  255.255.255.0
```

Again, defaults abound in this configuration, but some defaults are different than when you're configuring on the physical interface. The LMI type is autosensed, and Cisco encapsulation is used, which is just like the fully meshed examples. Inverse ARP is not really needed on point-to-point subinterfaces, but it is enabled by default in case the router on the other end of the VC needs to use Inverse ARP, as explained later in this section.

Two new commands create the configuration required with point-to-point subinterfaces. First, the **interface serial 0/0/0.1 point-to-point** command creates logical subinterface number 1 under physical interface Serial 0/0/0. The **frame-relay interface-dlci** subinterface subcommand then tells the router which single DLCI is associated with that subinterface.

An example of how the **frame-relay interface-dlci** command works can help. Consider router Atlanta in Figure 29-4. Atlanta receives LMI messages on Serial0/0/0 stating that three PVCs, with DLCIs 52, 53, and 54, are up. Which PVC goes with which subinterface? Cisco IOS software needs to associate the correct PVC with the correct subinterface. This is accomplished with the **frame-relay interface-dlci** command.

The subinterface numbers do not have to match on the router on the other end of the PVC, nor does the DLCI number. In this example, I just numbered the subinterfaces to be easier to remember. In real life, it is useful to encode some information about your network numbering scheme into the subinterface number. For example, a company might encode part of the carrier's circuit ID in the subinterface number so that the operations staff could find the correct information to tell the telco when troubleshooting the link. Many sites use the DLCI as the subinterface number. Of course, useful troubleshooting information, such as the DLCI, the name of the router on the other end of the VC, and so on, could be configured as text with the **description** command as well. In any case, there are no requirements for matching subinterface numbers. This example just matches the subinterface number to the third octet of the IP address.

Assigning a DLCI to a Particular Subinterface

As mentioned in the configuration checklist at the beginning of the "Frame Relay Configuration and Verification" section, earlier in this chapter, when configuring subinterfaces, the DLCIs must be associated with each subinterface in one of two ways. Examples 29-8 through 29-11 showed how to associate the DLCIs using the **frame-relay interface-dlci** subinterface subcommand. The alternative configuration would be to use the **frame-relay map** command as a subinterface subcommand on multipoint subinterfaces or as a physical interface subcommand. This command would both associate a DLCI with the subinterface and statically configure a mapping of Layer 3 next-hop IP address to that DLCI.

The router disables Inverse ARP on a subinterface when the **frame-relay map** command is configured. So, when using static maps on the router on one end of the VC, keep in mind that the router on the other end of the VC will not receive any Inverse ARP messages and might also then need to be configured with the **frame-relay map** command.

Comments About Global and Local Addressing

When a figure for a question shows three or more routers connected to Frame Relay, you should be able to easily decide whether the figure implies local or global DLCI values. For instance, Figure 29-4 shows a main site with three PVCs, one to each remote site. However, only one DLCI is shown beside the main site router, implying the use of global addressing. If local DLCIs were used, the figure would need to show a DLCI for each PVC beside the main site router.

In cases where a figure for a question shows only two routers, the figure might not imply whether local or global DLCI addressing is used. In those cases, look for clues in the question, answers, and any configuration. The best clues relate to the following fact:

On any given router, only local DLCI values are in the configuration or **show** commands.

Again, consider Figure 29-4 along with Examples 29-8 through 29-11. The figure shows global DLCIs, with DLCI 51 beside the Atlanta router. However, the **frame-relay interface-dlci** commands on the Atlanta router (refer to Example 29-8) and the Atlanta **show** commands in upcoming Example 29-12 list DLCIs 52, 53, and 54. Although Figure 29-4 makes it obvious that global addressing is used, even if only two routers had been shown, the **show** commands and configuration commands could have helped identify the correct DLCIs to use.

Frame Relay Verification

Example 29-12 shows the output from the most popular Cisco IOS software Frame Relay EXEC commands for monitoring Frame Relay, as issued on router Atlanta.

Example 29-12   *Output from EXEC Commands on Atlanta*

```
Atlanta# show frame-relay pvc

PVC Statistics for interface Serial0/0/0 (Frame Relay DTE)

               Active     Inactive     Deleted       Static
  Local          3           0            0             0
  Switched       0           0            0             0
  Unused         0           0            0             0
DLCI = 52, DLCI USAGE = LOCAL, PVC STATUS = ACTIVE, INTERFACE = Serial0/0/0.1

  input pkts 843          output pkts 876         in bytes 122723
  out bytes 134431        dropped pkts 0          in FECN pkts 0
  in BECN pkts 0          out FECN pkts 0         out BECN pkts 0
  in DE pkts 0            out DE pkts 0
  out bcast pkts 876       out bcast bytes 134431
```

```
  pvc create time 05:20:10, last time pvc status changed 05:19:31
 —More—
DLCI = 53, DLCI USAGE = LOCAL, PVC STATUS = ACTIVE, INTERFACE = Serial0/0/0.2

  input pkts 0            output pkts 875          in bytes 0
  out bytes 142417        dropped pkts 0           in FECN pkts 0
  in BECN pkts 0          out FECN pkts 0          out BECN pkts 0
  in DE pkts 0            out DE pkts 0
  out bcast pkts 875       out bcast bytes 142417
  pvc create time 05:19:51, last time pvc status changed 04:55:41
 —More—
DLCI = 54, DLCI USAGE = LOCAL, PVC STATUS = ACTIVE, INTERFACE = Serial0/0/0.3

  input pkts 10           output pkts 877          in bytes 1274
  out bytes 142069        dropped pkts 0           in FECN pkts 0
  in BECN pkts 0          out FECN pkts 0          out BECN pkts 0
  in DE pkts 0            out DE pkts 0
  out bcast pkts 877       out bcast bytes 142069
  pvc create time 05:19:52, last time pvc status changed 05:17:42


Atlanta# show frame-relay map
Serial0/0/0.3 (up): point-to-point dlci, dlci 54(0x36,0xC60), broadcast
          status defined, active
Serial0/0/0.2 (up): point-to-point dlci, dlci 53(0x35,0xC50), broadcast
          status defined, active
Serial0/0/0.1 (up): point-to-point dlci, dlci 52(0x34,0xC40), broadcast
          status defined, active


Atlanta# debug frame-relay lmi
Frame Relay LMI debugging is on
Displaying all Frame Relay LMI data

Serial0/0/0(out): StEnq, myseq 163, yourseen 161, DTE up
datagramstart = 0x45AED8, datagramsize = 13
FR encap = 0xFCF10309
00 75 01 01 01 03 02 A3 A1

Serial0/0/0(in): Status, myseq 163
RT IE 1, length 1, type 1
KA IE 3, length 2, yourseq 162, myseq 163
```

The **show frame-relay pvc** command lists useful management information. For instance, the packet counters for each VC, plus the counters for FECN and BECN, can be particularly useful. Likewise, comparing the packets/bytes sent on one router versus the counters of what is received on the router on the other end of the VC is also quite useful. This reflects the number of packets/bytes lost inside the Frame Relay cloud. Also, the PVC status is a great place to start when troubleshooting.

The **show frame-relay map** command lists mapping information. With the earlier example of a fully meshed network, in which the configuration did not use any subinterfaces, a Layer 3 address was listed with each DLCI. In this example, a DLCI is listed in each entry, but no mention of corresponding Layer 3 addresses is made. The whole point of mapping is to correlate a Layer 3 address to a Layer 2 address, but there is no Layer 3 address in the **show frame-relay map** command output! The reason is that the information is stored somewhere else. Subinterfaces require the use of the **frame-relay interface-dlci** configuration command. Because these subinterfaces are point-to-point, when a route points out a single subinterface, the DLCI to use to send frames is implied by the configuration. Mapping via Inverse ARP or static **frame-relay map** statements is needed only when more than two VCs terminate on the interface or subinterface, because those are the only instances in which confusion about which DLCI to use might occur.

The **debug frame-relay lmi** output lists information for the sending and receiving LMI inquiries. The switch sends the status message, and the DTE (router) sends the status inquiry. The default setting with Cisco IOS software is to send, and to expect to receive, these status messages. The Cisco IOS software **no keepalive** command is used to disable the use of LMI status messages. Unlike other interfaces, Cisco keepalive messages do not flow from router to router over Frame Relay. Instead, they are simply used to detect whether the router has connectivity to its local Frame Relay switch.

A Partially Meshed Network with Some Fully Meshed Parts

You can also choose to use multipoint subinterfaces for a Frame Relay configuration. This last sample network, based on the network shown in Figure 29-5, uses both multipoint and point-to-point subinterfaces. Examples 29-13 through 29-17 show the configuration for this network. Table 29-2 summarizes the addresses and subinterfaces used.

Table 29-2   *IP Addresses with Point-to-Point and Multipoint Subinterfaces*

Router	Subnet	IP Address	Subinterface Type
A	140.1.1.0/24	140.1.1.1	Multipoint
B	140.1.1.0/24	140.1.1.2	Multipoint
C	140.1.1.0/24	140.1.1.3	Multipoint

Table 29-2   *IP Addresses with Point-to-Point and Multipoint Subinterfaces*

Router	Subnet	IP Address	Subinterface Type
A	140.1.2.0/24	140.1.2.1	Point-to-point
D	140.1.2.0/24	140.1.2.4	Point-to-point
A	140.1.3.0/24	140.1.3.1	Point-to-point
E	140.1.3.0/24	140.1.3.5	Point-to-point

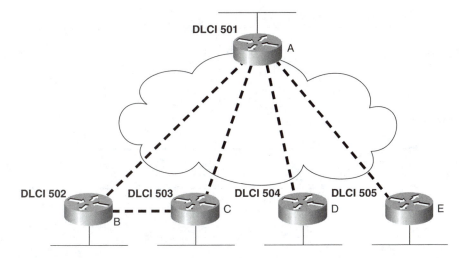

Figure 29-5   *Hybrid of Full and Partial Mesh*

Example 29-13   *Router A Configuration*

```
interface serial0/0/0
 encapsulation frame-relay
!
interface serial 0/0/0.1 multipoint
 ip address 140.1.1.1  255.255.255.0
 frame-relay interface-dlci 502
 frame-relay interface-dlci 503
!
interface serial 0/0/0.2 point-to-point
 ip address 140.1.2.1 255.255.255.0
 frame-relay interface-dlci 504
!
interface serial 0/0/0.3 point-to-point
 ip address 140.1.3.1 255.255.255.0
 frame-relay interface-dlci 505
```

Example 29-14 *Router B Configuration*

```
interface serial0/0/0
 encapsulation frame-relay
!
interface serial 0/0/0.1 multipoint
 ip address 140.1.1.2  255.255.255.0
 frame-relay interface-dlci 501
 frame-relay interface-dlci 503
```

Example 29-15 *Router C Configuration*

```
interface serial0/0/0
 encapsulation frame-relay
!
interface serial 0/0/0.1 multipoint
 ip address 140.1.1.3  255.255.255.0
 frame-relay interface-dlci 501
 frame-relay interface-dlci 502
```

Example 29-16 *Router D Configuration*

```
interface serial0/0/0
encapsulation frame-relay
!
interface serial 0/0/0.1 point-to-point
 ip address 140.1.2.4  255.255.255.0
 frame-relay interface-dlci 501
```

Example 29-17 *Router E Configuration*

```
interface serial0/0/0
 encapsulation frame-relay
!
interface serial 0/0/0.1 point-to-point
 ip address 140.1.3.5 255.255.255.0
 frame-relay interface-dlci 501
```

Multipoint subinterfaces work best when you have a full mesh between a set of routers. On Routers A, B, and C, a multipoint subinterface is used for the configuration referencing the other two routers, because you can think of these three routers as forming a fully meshed subset of the network.

The term *multipoint* simply means that there is more than one VC, so you can send and receive to and from more than one VC on the subinterface. Like point-to-point subinterfaces, multipoint subinterfaces use the **frame-relay interface-dlci** command. Notice that there are two commands for each multipoint subinterface in this case, because each of the two PVCs associated with this subinterface must be identified as being used with that subinterface.

Router A is the only router using both multipoint and point-to-point subinterfaces. On Router A's multipoint Serial0/0/0.1 interface, DLCIs for Router B and Router C are listed. On Router A's other two subinterfaces, which are point-to-point, only a single DLCI needs to be listed. In fact, only one **frame-relay interface-dlci** command is allowed on a point-to-point subinterface, because only one VC is allowed. Otherwise, the configurations between the two types are similar.

No mapping statements are required for the configurations shown in Examples 29-13 through 29-17, because Inverse ARP is enabled on the multipoint subinterfaces by default. No mapping is ever needed for the point-to-point subinterface, because the only DLCI associated with the interface is statically configured with the **frame-relay interface-dlci** command.

Example 29-18 lists another **show frame-relay map** command, showing the mapping information learned by Inverse ARP for the multipoint subinterface. Notice that the output now includes the Layer 3 addresses, whereas the same command when using point-to-point subinterfaces (in Example 29-12) did not. The reason is that the routes might refer to a next-hop IP address reachable out a multipoint interface, but because more than one DLCI is associated with the interface, the router needs mapping information to match the next-hop IP address to the correct DLCI.

Example 29-18   *Frame Relay Maps and Inverse ARP on Router C*

```
RouterC# show frame-relay map
Serial0/0/0.1 (up): ip 140.1.1.1 dlci 501(0x1F5,0x7C50), dynamic,
              broadcast,, status defined, active
Serial0/0/0.1 (up): ip 140.1.1.2 dlci 502(0x1F6,0x7C60), dynamic,
              broadcast,, status defined, active


RouterC# debug frame-relay events
Frame Relay events debugging is on

RouterC# configure terminal
Enter configuration commands, one per line.  End with Ctrl-Z.
RouterC(config)# interface serial 0/0/0.1
RouterC(config-subif)# shutdown
RouterC(config-subif)# no shutdown
RouterC(config-subif)# ^Z
RouterC#

Serial0/0/0.1: FR ARP input
Serial0/0/0.1: FR ARP input
Serial0/0/0.1: FR ARP input
datagramstart = 0xE42E58, datagramsize = 30
```

```
FR encap = 0x7C510300
80 00 00 00 08 06 00 0F 08 00 02 04 00 09 00 00
8C 01 01 01 7C 51 8C 01 01 03

datagramstart = 0xE420E8, datagramsize = 30
FR encap = 0x7C610300
80 00 00 00 08 06 00 0F 08 00 02 04 00 09 00 00
8C 01 01 02 7C 61 8C 01 01 03
```

The messages about Inverse ARP in the **debug frame-relay events** output are not so obvious. One easy exercise is to search for the hex version of the IP addresses in the output. These addresses are highlighted in Example 29-18. For example, the first 4 bytes of 140.1.1.1 are 8C 01 01 01 in hexadecimal. This field starts on the left side of the output, so it is easy to recognize.

Frame Relay Troubleshooting

As with most any router feature, to troubleshoot a Frame Relay problem, you need to understand the existing configuration and then compare that to what you think the correct configuration should look like. The LMI types must match or be autosensed, the Layer 3 mapping information has been learned or statically mapped, the right DLCI values have been associated with each subinterface, and so on. So, to be well prepared to find Frame Relay problems, you should review and memorize the many Frame Relay configuration options and understand what each option means.

However, you might need to find the root cause of a Frame Relay problem without looking at the configuration. To help you learn how to troubleshoot without the configuration, this second major section of this chapter examines Frame Relay troubleshooting, with emphasis on how to use **show** commands, along with the symptoms of a problem, to isolate the root cause of the problem.

A Suggested Frame Relay Troubleshooting Process

To isolate a Frame Relay problem, the process should start with some pings. Optimally, pings from an end-user host on a LAN, to another host on a remote LAN, can quickly determine if the network currently can meet the true end goal of delivering packets between computers. If that ping fails, a ping from one router to the other router's Frame Relay IP address is the next step. If that ping works, but the end user's ping failed, the problem probably has something to do with Layer 3 issues, and troubleshooting those issues was well covered Chapter 15, "Troubleshooting IP Routing," Chapter 20, "Troubleshooting IP Routing II," and Chapter 22, "Troubleshooting EIGRP and OSPF." However, if a ping from one router to another router's Frame Relay IP address fails, the problem is most likely related to the Frame Relay network.

This section focuses on troubleshooting problems when a Frame Relay router cannot ping another router's Frame Relay IP address. At that point, the engineer should ping the Frame Relay IP addresses of all the other routers on the other end of each VC to determine the following:

> Do the pings fail for all remote routers' Frame Relay IP addresses, or do some pings
> fail and some pings work?

For example, Figure 29-6 shows a sample Frame Relay network that will be used with the remaining examples in this chapter. If R1 tried to ping R2's Frame Relay IP address (10.1.2.2 in this case) and failed, the next question is whether R1's pings to R3 (10.1.34.3) and R4 (10.1.34.4) work.

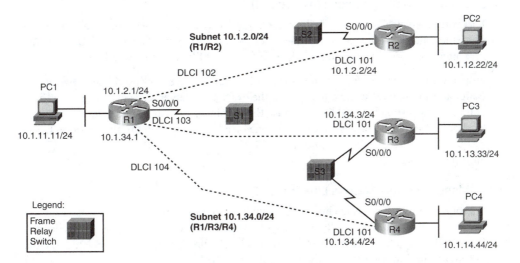

Figure 29-6   *Sample Frame Relay Network for the Troubleshooting Examples*

This chapter organizes its explanations of how to troubleshoot Frame Relay based on this first problem isolation step. The following list summarizes the major actions, with each step in the following list being examined in order following the list.

If a Frame Relay router's pings fail for all remote routers whose VCs share a single access link, do the following:

Step 1.   Check for Layer 1 problems on the access link between the router and the local Frame Relay switch (all routers).

Step 2.   Check for Layer 2 problems on the access link, particularly encapsulation and LMI.

After resolving any problems in the first two steps, or if the original ping tests showed that the Frame Relay router can ping some, but not all, of the other Frame Relay routers whose VCs share a single access link, follow these steps:

Step 3.   Check for PVC problems based on the PVC status and subinterface status.

Step 4.   Check for Layer 2/3 problems with both static and dynamic (Inverse ARP) mapping.

Step 5.   Check for Layer 2/3 problems related to a mismatch of end-to-end encapsulation (cisco or ietf).

Step 6.   Check for other Layer 3 issues, including mismatched subnets.

The rest of this chapter explains some of the details of each step of this suggested troubleshooting process.

Layer 1 Issues on the Access Link (Step 1)

If a router's physical interface used for the Frame Relay access link is not in an "up and up" state, the router cannot send any frames over the link. If the interface has a line status (the first interface status code) of down, the interface most likely has a Layer 1 issue.

From a Layer 1 perspective, a Frame Relay access link is merely a leased line between a router and a Frame Relay switch. As such, the exact same Layer 1 issues exist for this link as for a point-to-point leased line. Because the possible root causes and suggested troubleshooting steps mirror what should be done on a leased line, refer to the section "Troubleshooting Layer 1 Problems" in Chapter 27, "Point-to-Point WANs," for more information about this step.

Layer 2 Issues on the Access Link (Step 2)

If a router's physical interface line status is up, but the line protocol status (second status code) is down, the link typically has a Layer 2 problem between the router and the local Frame Relay switch. With Frame Relay interfaces, the problem is typically related to either the **encapsulation** command or the Frame Relay LMI.

The potential problem related to the **encapsulation** command is very simple to check. If a router's serial interface configuration omits the **encapsulation frame-relay** interface subcommand, but the physical access link is working, the physical interface settles into an up/down state. If the configuration is unavailable, the **show interfaces** command can be used to see the configured encapsulation type, which is listed in the first few lines of command output.

The other potential problem relates to the LMI. LMI status messages flow in both directions between a router (DTE) and Frame Relay switch (DCE) for two main purposes:

Key Topic

■   For the DCE to inform the DTE about each VC's DLCI and its status

■   To provide a keepalive function so that the DTE and DCE can easily tell when the access link can no longer pass traffic

A router places the physical link in an up/down state when the link physically works but the router ceases to hear LMI messages from the switch. With the interface not in an up/up state, the router does not attempt to send any IP packets out the interface, so all pings should fail at this point.

A router might cease to receive LMI messages from the switch because of both legitimate reasons and mistakes. The normal legitimate purpose for the LMI keepalive function is that if the link really is having problems, and cannot pass any data, the router can notice the loss of keepalive messages and bring the link down. This allows the router to use an alternative route, assuming that an alternative route exists. However, a router might cease to receive LMI messages and bring down the interface because of the following mistakes:

- Disabling LMI on the router (with the **no keepalive** physical interface subcommand), but leaving it enabled on the switch—or vice versa

- Configuring different LMI types on the router (with the **frame-relay lmi-type** *type* physical interface subcommand) and the switch

You can easily check for both encapsulation and LMI using the **show frame-relay lmi** command. This command lists only output for interfaces that have the **encapsulation frame-relay** command configured, so you can quickly confirm whether the **encapsulation frame-relay** command is configured on the correct serial interfaces. This command also lists the LMI type used by the router, and it shows counters for the number of LMI messages sent and received. Example 29-19 shows an example from router R1 in Figure 29-6.

Example 29-19   show frame-relay lmi *Command on R1*

```
R1# show frame-relay lmi

LMI Statistics for interface Serial0/0/0 (Frame Relay DTE) LMI TYPE = ANSI
   Invalid Unnumbered info 0          Invalid Prot Disc 0
   Invalid dummy Call Ref 0           Invalid Msg Type 0
   Invalid Status Message 0           Invalid Lock Shift 0
   Invalid Information ID 0           Invalid Report IE Len 0
   Invalid Report Request 0           Invalid Keep IE Len 0
   Num Status Enq. Sent 122           Num Status msgs Rcvd 34
   Num Update Status Rcvd 0           Num Status Timeouts 88
   Last Full Status Req 00:00:04      Last Full Status Rcvd 00:13:24
```

For this example, router R1 was statically configured with the **frame-relay lmi-type ansi** interface subcommand, with switch S1 still using LMI type cisco. When the LMI configuration was changed, the router and switch had exchanged 34 LMI messages (of type cisco). After that change, R1's counter of the number of status enquiry messages sent kept rising (122 when the **show frame-relay lmi** command output was captured), but the counter of the number of LMI status messages received from the switch remained at 34. Just below that counter is the number of timeouts, which counts the number of times the router expected to receive a periodic LMI message from the switch but did not. In this case, the router was actually still receiving LMI messages, but they were not ANSI LMI messages so the router did not understand or recognize them.

If repeated use of the **show frame-relay lmi** command shows that the number of status messages received remains the same, the likely cause, other than a truly nonworking link, is that the LMI types do not match. The best solution is to allow for LMI autosense by configuring the **no frame-relay lmi-type** *type* physical interface subcommand, or alternatively, configuring the same LMI type that is used by the switch.

If you troubleshoot and fix any problems found in Steps 1 and 2, on all Frame Relay connected routers, all the routers' access link physical interfaces should be in an up/up state. The last four steps examine issues that apply to individual PVCs and neighbors.

PVC Problems and Status (Step 3)

The goal at this step in the troubleshooting process is to discover the DLCI of the PVC used to reach a particular neighbor and then find out if the PVC is working. To determine the correct PVC, particularly if little or no configuration or documentation is available, you have to start with the failed **ping** command. The **ping** command identifies the IP address of the neighboring router. Based on the neighbor's IP address, a few **show** commands can link the neighbor's IP address with the associated connected subnet, the connected subnet with the local router's interface, and the local router's interface with the possible DLCIs. Also, the Frame Relay mapping information can identify the specific PVC. Although this book has covered all the commands used to find these pieces of information, the following list summarizes the steps that take you from the neighbor's IP address to the correct local DLCI used to send frames to that neighbor:

Step 3a.   Discover the IP address and mask of each Frame Relay interface/subinterface (**show interfaces, show ip interface brief**), and calculate the connected subnets.

Step 3b.   Compare the IP address in the failed **ping** command, and pick the interface/subinterface whose connected subnet is the same subnet.

Step 3c.   Discover the PVC(s) assigned to that interface or subinterface (**show frame-relay pvc**).

Step 3d.   If more than one PVC is assigned to the interface or subinterface, determine which PVC is used to reach a particular neighbor (**show frame-relay map**).

Note: As a reminder, lists like this one are meant for convenient reference when you read the chapter. It's easy to find the list when you study and want to remember a particular part of how to attack a given problem. You do not need to memorize the list, or practice it until you internalize the information.

Steps 3a, 3b, 3c, and 3d discover the correct PVC to examine. After it is discovered, Step 3 in the suggested troubleshooting process interprets the status of that PVC, and the associated interface or subinterface, to determine the cause of any problems.

This section takes a closer look at an example in which R1 cannot ping R2's 10.1.2.2 Frame Relay IP address. Before focusing on the process to determine which VC is used, it is helpful to see the final answer, so Figure 29-7 lists some of the details. For this example, R1's **ping 10.1.2.2** command fails in this case.

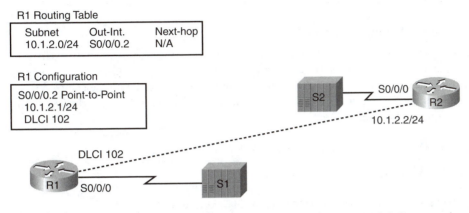

Figure 29-7   *Configuration Facts Related to R1's Failed* **ping 10.1.2.2** *Command*

Find the Connected Subnet and Outgoing Interface (Steps 3a and 3b)

The first two substeps to find R1's PVC (DLCI) connecting to R2 (Substeps 3a and 3b) should be relatively easy, assuming that you are reading this book sequentially. Any time you ping the Frame Relay IP address of a neighboring router, that IP address should be in one of the subnets also connected to the local router. To find the interface used on a local router when forwarding packets to the remote router, you just have to find that common connected subnet.

In this example, with R1 pinging 10.1.2.2, Example 29-20 shows a few commands that confirm that R1's S0/0/0.2 subinterface is connected to subnet 10.1.2.0/24, which includes R2's 10.1.2.2 IP address.

Example 29-20   *Finding Subnet 10.1.2.0/24 and Subinterface S0/0/0.2*

```
R1> show ip interface brief
Interface            IP-Address      OK? Method Status                   Protocol
FastEthernet0/0      10.1.11.1       YES NVRAM  up                       up
FastEthernet0/1      unassigned      YES NVRAM  administratively down    down
Serial0/0/0          unassigned      YES NVRAM  up                       up
Serial0/0/0.2        10.1.2.1        YES NVRAM  down                     down
Serial0/0/0.5        10.1.5.1        YES manual down                     down
Serial0/0/0.34       10.1.34.1       YES NVRAM  up                       up
R1# show interfaces s 0/0/0.2
Serial0/0/0.2 is down, line protocol is down
  Hardware is GT96K Serial
  Internet address is 10.1.2.1/24
  MTU 1500 bytes, BW 1544 Kbit, DLY 20000 usec,
```

```
    reliability 255/255, txload 1/255, rxload 1/255
 Encapsulation FRAME-RELAY
 Last clearing of "show interface" counters never
```

Find the PVCs Assigned to That Interface (Step 3c)

The **show frame-relay pvc** command directly answers the question of which PVCs have been assigned to which interfaces and subinterfaces. If the command is issued with no parameters, the command lists about ten lines of output for each VC, with the end of the first line listing the associated interface or subinterface. Example 29-21 lists the beginning of the command output.

Example 29-21   *Correlating Subinterface S0/0/0.2 to the PVC with DLCI 102*

```
R1> show frame-relay pvc

PVC Statistics for interface Serial0/0/0 (Frame Relay DTE)

              Active     Inactive     Deleted      Static
   Local        1           2            0            0
   Switched     0           0            0            0
   Unused       0           0            0            0

DLCI = 102, DLCI USAGE = LOCAL, PVC STATUS = INACTIVE, INTERFACE = Serial0/0/0.2

   input pkts 33           output pkts 338        in bytes 1952
   out bytes 29018         dropped pkts 0         in pkts dropped 0
   out pkts dropped 0          out bytes dropped 0
   in FECN pkts 0          in BECN pkts 0         out FECN pkts 0
   out BECN pkts 0         in DE pkts 0           out DE pkts 0
   out bcast pkts 332      out bcast bytes 28614
   5 minute input rate 0 bits/sec, 0 packets/sec
   5 minute output rate 0 bits/sec, 0 packets/sec
   pvc create time 00:30:05, last time pvc status changed 00:04:14

DLCI = 103, DLCI USAGE = LOCAL, PVC STATUS = INACTIVE, INTERFACE = Serial0/0/0.34

   input pkts 17           output pkts 24         in bytes 1106
   out bytes 2086          dropped pkts 0         in pkts dropped 0
   out pkts dropped 0          out bytes dropped 0
   in FECN pkts 0          in BECN pkts 0         out FECN pkts 0
   out BECN pkts 0         in DE pkts 0           out DE pkts 0
   out bcast pkts 11       out bcast bytes 674
   5 minute input rate 0 bits/sec, 0 packets/sec
```

```
 5 minute output rate 0 bits/sec, 0 packets/sec
 pvc create time 00:30:07, last time pvc status changed 00:02:57


DLCI = 104, DLCI USAGE = LOCAL, PVC STATUS = ACTIVE, INTERFACE = Serial0/0/0.34

 input pkts 41              output pkts 42            in bytes 2466
 out bytes 3017             dropped pkts 0            in pkts dropped 0
 out pkts dropped 0             out bytes dropped 0
 in FECN pkts 0             in BECN pkts 0            out FECN pkts 0
 out BECN pkts 0            in DE pkts 0              out DE pkts 0
 out bcast pkts 30          out bcast bytes 1929
 5 minute input rate 0 bits/sec, 0 packets/sec
 5 minute output rate 0 bits/sec, 0 packets/sec
 pvc create time 00:30:07, last time pvc status changed 00:26:17
```

To find all the PVCs associated with an interface or subinterface, just scan the highlighted parts of the output in Example 29-21. In this case, S0/0/0.2 is listed with only one PVC, the one with DLCI 102, so only one PVC is associated with S0/0/0.2 in this case.

Determine Which PVC Is Used to Reach a Particular Neighbor (Step 3d)

If the router's configuration associates more than one PVC with one interface or subinterface, the next step is to figure out which of the PVCs is used to send traffic to a particular neighbor. For instance, Example 29-21 shows R1 uses a multipoint subinterface S0/0/0.34 with DLCIs 103 and 104, with DLCI 103 used for the PVC to R3, and DLCI 104 for the PVC connecting to R4. So, if you were troubleshooting a problem in which the **ping 10.1.34.3** command failed on R1, the next step would be to determine which of the two DLCIs (103 or 104) identifies the VC connecting R1 to R3.

Unfortunately, you cannot always find the answer without looking at other documentation. The only **show** command that can help is **show frame-relay map**, which can correlate the next-hop IP address and DLCI. Unfortunately, if the local router relies on Inverse ARP, the local router cannot learn the mapping information right now either, so the mapping table might not have any useful information in it. However, if static mapping is used, the correct PVC/DLCI can be identified.

In the example of R1 failing when pinging 10.1.2.2 (R2), because only one PVC is associated with the correct interface (S0/0/0.2), the PVC has already been identified, so you can ignore this step for now.

PVC Status

At this point in major troubleshooting Step 3, the correct outgoing interface/subinterface and correct PVC/DLCI have been identified. Finally, the PVC status can be examined to see if it means that the PVC has a problem.

Routers use four different PVC status codes. A router learns about two of the possible status values, *active* and *inactive*, via LMI messages from the Frame Relay switch. The switch's LMI message lists all DLCIs for all configured PVCs on the access link, and whether the PVC is currently usable (active) or not (inactive).

The first of the two PVC states that is not learned using LMI is called the *static* state. If the LMI is disabled, the router does not learn any information from the switch about PVC status. So, the router lists all its configured DLCIs in the *static* state, meaning statically configured. The router does not know if the PVCs will work, but it can at least send frames using those DLCIs and hope that the Frame Relay network can deliver them.

The other PVC state, *deleted*, is used when LMI is working but the switch's LMI message does not mention anything about a particular DLCI value. If the router has configuration for a DLCI (for example, in a **frame-relay interface-dlci** command), but the switch's LMI message does not list that DLCI, the router lists that DLCI in a deleted state. This state means that the router has configured the DLCI, but the switch has not. In real life, the deleted state might mean that the router or switch has been misconfigured, or that the Frame Relay switch has not yet been configured with the correct DLCI. Table 29-3 summarizes the four Frame Relay PVC status codes.

Key Topic

Table 29-3 *PVC Status Values*

Status	Active	Inactive	Deleted	Static
The PVC is defined to the Frame Relay network	Yes	Yes	No	Unknown
The router will attempt to send frames on a VC in this state	Yes	No	No	Yes

As noted in the last row of the table, routers only send data over PVCs in an active or static state. Also, even if the PVC is in a static state, there is no guarantee that the Frame Relay network can actually send frames over that PVC, because the static state implies that LMI is turned off, and the router has not learned any status information.

The next step in the troubleshooting process is to find the status of the PVC used to reach a particular neighbor. Continuing with the problem of R1 failing when pinging R2 (10.1.2.2), Example 29-22 shows the status of the PVC with DLCI 102, as identified earlier.

Example 29-22 show frame-relay pvc *Command on R1*

```
R1> show frame-relay pvc 102

PVC Statistics for interface Serial0/0/0 (Frame Relay DTE)
```

```
DLCI = 102, DLCI USAGE = LOCAL, PVC STATUS = INACTIVE, INTERFACE = Serial0/0/0.2

    input pkts 22           output pkts 193         in bytes 1256
    out bytes 16436         dropped pkts 0          in pkts dropped 0
    out pkts dropped 0            out bytes dropped 0
    in FECN pkts 0          in BECN pkts 0          out FECN pkts 0
    out BECN pkts 0         in DE pkts 0            out DE pkts 0
    out bcast pkts 187      out bcast bytes 16032
    5 minute input rate 0 bits/sec, 0 packets/sec
    5 minute output rate 0 bits/sec, 0 packets/sec
    pvc create time 01:12:56, last time pvc status changed 00:22:45
```

In this case, R1 cannot ping R2 because the PVC with DLCI 102 is in an inactive state.

To further isolate the problem and find the root cause, you need to look deeper into the reasons why a PVC can be in an inactive state. First, as always, repeat the same troubleshooting steps on the other router—in this case, R2. If no problems are found on R2, other than an inactive PVC, the problem might be a genuine problem in the Frame Relay provider's network, so a call to the provider can be the next step. However, you might find some other problem on the remote router. For example, to create the failure and **show** commands in this section, R2's access link was shut down, so a quick examination of troubleshooting Step 1 on router R2 would have identified the problem. However, if further troubleshooting shows that both routers list their ends of the PVC in an inactive state, the root cause lies within the Frame Relay provider's network.

Finding the root cause of a problem related to a PVC in a deleted state is relatively easy. The deleted status means that the Frame Relay switch's configuration and the router's configuration do not match, with the router configuring a DLCI that is not also configured on the switch. Either the provider said it would configure a PVC with a particular DLCI, and did not, or the router engineer configured the wrong DLCI value.

Subinterface Status

Subinterfaces have a line status and protocol status code, just like physical interfaces. However, because subinterfaces are virtual, the status codes and their meanings differ a bit from physical interfaces. This section briefly examines how Frame Relay subinterfaces work and how IOS decides if a Frame Relay subinterface should be in an up/up state or a down/down state.

Frame Relay configuration associates one or more DLCIs with a subinterface using two commands: **frame-relay interface-dlci** and **frame-relay map**. Of all the DLCIs associated with a subinterface, IOS uses the following rules to determine the status of a subinterface:

- **down/down:** All the DLCIs associated with the subinterface are inactive or deleted, or the underlying physical interface is not in an up/up state.

- **up/up:** At least one of the DLCIs associated with the subinterface is active or static.

Key
Topic

For example, to cause the problems shown in Example 29-22, R2 and R3 simply shut down their Frame Relay access links. Figure 29-8 shows the next LMI status message that switch S1 sends to R1.

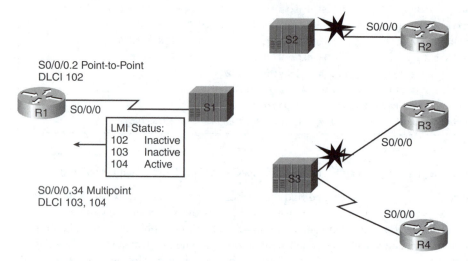

Figure 29-8   *Results of Shutting Down R2 and R3 Access Links*

As shown in the figure, R1 uses a point-to-point subinterface (S0/0/0.2) for the VC connecting to R2, and a multipoint subinterface (S0/0/0.34) associated with the VCs to R3 and R4 (103 and 104, respectively). The beginning of Example 29-20 shows that S0/0/0.2 is in a down/down state, which is because the only DLCI associated with the subinterface (102) is inactive. However, S0/0/0.34 has two DLCIs, one of which is active, so IOS leaves S0/0/0.34 in an up/up state.

It is useful to look at subinterface status when troubleshooting, but keep in mind that just because a subinterface is up, if it is a multipoint subinterface, the up/up state does not necessarily mean that all DLCIs associated with the subinterface are working.

Frame Relay Mapping Issues (Step 4)

If you follow the first three steps of the troubleshooting process suggested in this chapter and resolve the problems at each step, at this point each router's access link interfaces should be in an up/up state, and the PVC between the two routers should be in an active (or static) state. If the routers still cannot ping each other's Frame Relay IP addresses, the next thing to check is the Frame Relay address mapping information, which maps DLCIs to next-hop IP addresses.

This section does not repeat the detailed coverage of address mapping that appears in both Chapter 28 and this chapter. However, for perspective, the following list points out some tips and hints as reminders when you perform this troubleshooting step:

On point-to-point subinterfaces:

■ These subinterfaces do not need Inverse ARP or static mapping, because IOS simply thinks that the subnet defined on the subinterface is reachable via the only DLCI on the subinterface.

■ The **show frame-relay map** command output still lists these subinterfaces, but with no next-hop IP address.

On physical interfaces and multipoint subinterfaces:

■ They need to use either Inverse ARP or static mapping.

■ The **show frame-relay map** command should list the remote router's Frame Relay IP address and the local router's local DLCI for each PVC associated with the interface or subinterface.

■ If you're using static mapping, the **broadcast** keyword is needed to support a routing protocol.

For completeness, Example 29-23 shows the output of the **show frame-relay map** command on router R1 from Figure 29-6, with no problems with the mapping. (The earlier problems that were introduced have been fixed.) In this case, interface S0/0/0.2 is a point-to-point subinterface, and S0/0/0.34 is a multipoint, with one Inverse ARP-learned mapping and one statically configured mapping.

Example 29-23   show frame-relay map *Command on R1*

```
R1# show frame-relay map
Serial0/0/0.34 (up): ip 10.1.34.4 dlci 104(0x68,0x1880), static,
              broadcast,
              CISCO, status defined, active
Serial0/0/0.34 (up): ip 10.1.34.3 dlci 103(0x67,0x1870), dynamic,
              broadcast,, status defined, active
Serial0/0/0.2 (up): point-to-point dlci, dlci 102(0x66,0x1860), broadcast
          status defined, active
```

End-to-End Encapsulation (Step 5)

The end-to-end encapsulation on a PVC refers to the headers that follow the Frame Relay header, with two options: the Cisco-proprietary header and an IETF standard header. The configuration details were covered earlier in this chapter, in the section "Configuring the Encapsulation and LMI."

As it turns out, a mismatched encapsulation setting on the routers on opposite ends of the link might cause a problem in one particular case. If one router is a Cisco router, using Cisco encapsulation, and the other router is a non-Cisco router, using IETF encapsulation, pings can fail because of the encapsulation mismatch. However, two Cisco routers can understand both types of encapsulation, so it should not be an issue in networks with only Cisco routers.

Mismatched Subnet Numbers (Step 6)

At this point, if the problems found in the first five of the six troubleshooting steps have been resolved, all the Frame Relay problems should be resolved. However, if the two routers on either end of the PVC have mistakenly configured IP addresses in different subnets, the routers will not be able to ping one another, and the routing protocols will not become adjacent. So, as a last step, you should confirm the IP addresses on each router, and the masks, and ensure that they connect to the same subnet. To do so, just use the **show ip interface brief** and **show interfaces** commands on the two routers.

Chapter Review

Review Key Topics

Review the most important topics from this chapter, noted with the Key Topic icons. Table 29-4 lists these key topics and where each is discussed.

Table 29-4   *Key Topics for Chapter 29*

Key Topic Element	Description	Page Number
List	Frame Relay configuration checklist	736
List	Default Frame Relay settings in IOS	738
Definition	Frame Relay address mapping concept and definition	740
Figure 29-3	Frame Relay Inverse ARP process	743
List	Six-step Frame Relay troubleshooting checklist	755
List	Summary of the two main functions of LMI	756
Table 29-3	List of PVC status values and their meanings	762
List	Reasons for subinterfaces to be up/up or down/down	763
List	Summary of mapping information seen on point-to-point subinterfaces	765
List	Summary of mapping information seen on multipoint subinterfaces	765

Review Command Reference to Check Your Memory

Although you should not necessarily memorize the information in the tables in this section, this section does include a reference for the configuration and EXEC commands covered in this chapter. Practically speaking, you should memorize the commands as a side effect of reading the chapter and doing all the activities in this "Chapter Review" section. To see how well you have memorized the commands as a side effect of your other studies, cover the left side of the table, read the descriptions on the right side, and see if you remember the command.

Table 29-5   *Chapter 29 Configuration Command Reference*

Command	Description
encapsulation frame-relay [ietf]	Interface configuration mode command that defines the Frame Relay encapsulation that is used rather than HDLC, PPP, and so on.
frame-relay lmi-type {ansi | q933a | cisco}	Interface configuration mode command that defines the type of LMI messages sent to the switch.
bandwidth *num*	Interface subcommand that sets the router's perceived interface speed.
frame-relay map {*protocol protocol-address dlci*} [broadcast] [ietf | cisco]	Interface configuration mode command that statically defines a mapping between a network layer address and a DLCI.
keepalive *sec*	Interface configuration mode command that defines whether and how often LMI status inquiry messages are sent and expected.
interface serial *number.sub* [point-to-point | multipoint]	Global configuration mode command that creates a subinterface or references a previously created subinterface.
frame-relay interface-dlci *dlci* [ietf | cisco]	Subinterface configuration mode command that links or correlates a DLCI to the subinterface.

Table 29-6   *Chapter 29 EXEC Command Reference*

Command	Description
show interfaces [*type number*]	Shows the physical interface status.
show frame-relay pvc [interface *interface*][*dlci*]	Lists information about the PVC status.
show frame-relay lmi [*type number*]	Lists LMI status information.
debug frame-relay lmi	Displays the contents of LMI messages.
debug frame-relay events	Lists messages about certain Frame Relay events, including Inverse ARP messages.

Answer Review Questions

Answer the following review questions:

1. Imagine two Cisco routers, R1 and R2, using a Frame Relay service. R1 connects to a switch that uses LMI type ANSI T1.617, and R2 connects to a switch that uses ITU Q.933a. What keywords could be used in the R1 and R2 configuration so that the LMIs work correctly?

   a. ansi and itu

   b. T1617 and q933

   c. ansi and q933

   d. T1617 and itu

   e. This won't work with two different types.

2. BettyCo has five sites, with routers connected to the same Frame Relay network. VCs have been defined between each pair of routers. Betty, the company president, will fire anyone who configures anything that could just as easily be left as a default. Which of the following configuration commands, configured for the Frame Relay network, would get the engineer fired?

   a. ip address

   b. encapsulation

   c. lmi-type

   d. frame-relay map

   e. frame-relay inverse-arp

3. WilmaCo has some routers connected to a Frame Relay network. R1 is a router at a remote site, with a single VC back to WilmaCo's headquarters. The R1 configuration currently looks like this:

   ```
   interface serial 0/0
     ip address 10.1.1.1 255.255.255.0
     encapsulation frame-relay
   ```

   Wilma, the company president, has heard that point-to-point subinterfaces are cool, and she wants you to change the configuration to use a point-to-point subinterface. Which of the following commands do you need to use to migrate the configuration?

   a. no ip address

   b. interface-dlci

   c. no encapsulation

   d. encapsulation frame-relay

   e. frame-relay interface-dlci

4. WilmaCo has another network, with a main site router that has ten VCs connecting to the ten remote sites. Wilma now thinks that multipoint subinterfaces are even cooler than point-to-point. The current main site router's configuration looks like this:

```
interface serial 0/0
  ip address 172.16.1.1 255.255.255.0
  encapsulation frame-relay
```

Wilma wants you to change the configuration to use a multipoint subinterface. Which of the following do you need to use to migrate the configuration? (Note: DLCIs 101 through 110 are used for the ten VCs.)

   a.   interface-dlci 101 110

   b.   interface dlci 101-110

   c.   Ten different **interface-dlci** commands

   d.   frame-relay interface-dlci 101 110

   e.   frame-relay interface dlci 101-110

   f.   Ten different **frame-relay interface-dlci** commands

5. Which of the following commands lists the information learned by Inverse ARP?

   a.   show ip arp

   b.   show arp

   c.   show inverse arp

   d.   show frame-relay inverse-arp

   e.   show map

   f.   show frame-relay map

6. Which of the following are Frame Relay PVC status codes for which a router sends frames for the associated PVC?

   a.   Up

   b.   Down

   c.   Active

   d.   Inactive

   e.   Static

   f.   Deleted

7. Central site router RC has a VC connecting to ten remote routers (R1 through R10), with RC's local DLCIs being 101 through 110, respectively. RC has grouped DLCIs 107, 108, and 109 into a single multipoint subinterface S0/0.789, whose current status is "up and up." Which of the following must be true?

    a. Serial 0/0 could be in an up/down state.

    b. The PVC with DLCI 108 could be in an inactive state.

    c. The **show frame-relay map** command lists mapping information for all three VCs.

    d. At least one of the three PVCs is in an active or static state.

8. Frame Relay router R1 uses interface S0/0 to connect to a Frame Relay access link. The physical interface is in an up/down state. Which of the following could cause this problem?

    a. The access link has a physical problem and cannot pass bits between the router and switch.

    b. The switch and router are using different LMI types.

    c. The router configuration is missing the **encapsulation frame-relay** command on interface S0/0.

    d. The router received a valid LMI status message that listed some of the DLCIs as inactive.

Numeric Reference Tables

This appendix provides several useful reference tables that list numbers used throughout this book. Specifically:

Table A-1:   A decimal-binary cross reference, useful when converting from decimal to binary and vice versa

Table A-1   *Decimal-Binary Cross Reference, Decimal Values 0–255*

Decimal Value	Binary Value	Decimal Value	Binary Value	Decimal Value	Binary Value	Decimal Value	Binary Value
0	00000000	32	00100000	64	01000000	96	01100000
1	00000001	33	00100001	65	01000001	97	01100001
2	00000010	34	00100010	66	01000010	98	01100010
3	00000011	35	00100011	67	01000011	99	01100011
4	00000100	36	00100100	68	01000100	100	01100100
5	00000101	37	00100101	69	01000101	101	01100101
6	00000110	38	00100110	70	01000110	102	01100110
7	00000111	39	00100111	71	01000111	103	01100111
8	00001000	40	00101000	72	01001000	104	01101000
9	00001001	41	00101001	73	01001001	105	01101001
10	00001010	42	00101010	74	01001010	106	01101010
11	00001011	43	00101011	75	01001011	107	01101011
12	00001100	44	00101100	76	01001100	108	01101100
13	00001101	45	00101101	77	01001101	109	01101101
14	00001110	46	00101110	78	01001110	110	01101110
15	00001111	47	00101111	79	01001111	111	01101111
16	00010000	48	00110000	80	01010000	112	01110000
17	00010001	49	00110001	81	01010001	113	01110001
18	00010010	50	00110010	82	01010010	114	01110010
19	00010011	51	00110011	83	01010011	115	01110011
20	00010100	52	00110100	84	01010100	116	01110100
21	00010101	53	00110101	85	01010101	117	01110101
22	00010110	54	00110110	86	01010110	118	01110110
23	00010111	55	00110111	87	01010111	119	01110111
24	00011000	56	00111000	88	01011000	120	01111000
25	00011001	57	00111001	89	01011001	121	01111001
26	00011010	58	00111010	90	01011010	122	01111010
27	00011011	59	00111011	91	01011011	123	01111011
28	00011100	60	00111100	92	01011100	124	01111100
29	00011101	61	00111101	93	01011101	125	01111101
30	00011110	62	00111110	94	01011110	126	01111110
31	00011111	63	00111111	95	01011111	127	01111111

Decimal Value	Binary Value	Decimal Value	Binary Value	Decimal Value	Binary Value	Decimal Value	Binary Value
128	10000000	160	10100000	192	11000000	224	11100000
129	10000001	161	10100001	193	11000001	225	11100001
130	10000010	162	10100010	194	11000010	226	11100010
131	10000011	163	10100011	195	11000011	227	11100011
132	10000100	164	10100100	196	11000100	228	11100100
133	10000101	165	10100101	197	11000101	229	11100101
134	10000110	166	10100110	198	11000110	230	11100110
135	10000111	167	10100111	199	11000111	231	11100111
136	10001000	168	10101000	200	11001000	232	11101000
137	10001001	169	10101001	201	11001001	233	11101001
138	10001010	170	10101010	202	11001010	234	11101010
139	10001011	171	10101011	203	11001011	235	11101011
140	10001100	172	10101100	204	11001100	236	11101100
141	10001101	173	10101101	205	11001101	237	11101101
142	10001110	174	10101110	206	11001110	238	11101110
143	10001111	175	10101111	207	11001111	239	11101111
144	10010000	176	10110000	208	11010000	240	11110000
145	10010001	177	10110001	209	11010001	241	11110001
146	10010010	178	10110010	210	11010010	242	11110010
147	10010011	179	10110011	211	11010011	243	11110011
148	10010100	180	10110100	212	11010100	244	11110100
149	10010101	181	10110101	213	11010101	245	11110101
150	10010110	182	10110110	214	11010110	246	11110110
151	10010111	183	10110111	215	11010111	247	11110111
152	10011000	184	10111000	216	11011000	248	11111000
153	10011001	185	10111001	217	11011001	249	11111001
154	10011010	186	10111010	218	11011010	250	11111010
155	10011011	187	10111011	219	11011011	251	11111011
156	10011100	188	10111100	220	11011100	252	11111100
157	10011101	189	10111101	221	11011101	253	11111101
158	10011110	190	10111110	222	11011110	254	11111110
159	10011111	191	10111111	223	11011111	255	11111111

Table A-2:   A hexadecimal-binary cross reference, useful when converting from hex to binary, and vice versa

Table A-2   *Hex-Binary Cross Reference*

Hex	4-Bit Binary
0	0000
1	0001
2	0010
3	0011
4	0100
5	0101
6	0110
7	0111
8	1000
9	1001
A	1010
B	1011
C	1100
D	1101
E	1110
F	1111

Table A-3:   Powers of 2, from 2^0 through 2^{32}

Table A-3 *Powers of 2*

X	2^x	X	2^x
1	2	17	131,072
2	4	18	262,144
3	8	19	524,288
4	16	20	1,048,576
5	32	21	2,097,152
6	64	22	4,194,304
7	128	23	8,388,608
8	256	24	16,777,216
9	512	25	33,554,432
10	1024	26	67,108,864
11	2048	27	134,217,728
12	4096	28	268,435,456
13	8192	29	536,870,912
14	16,384	30	1,073,741,824
15	32,768	31	2,147,483,648
16	65,536	32	4,294,967,296

Table A-4:   Table of all 33 possible subnet masks, in all three formats

Table A-4   *All Subnet Masks*

Decimal	Prefix	Binary
0.0.0.0	/0	00000000 00000000 00000000 00000000
128.0.0.0	/1	10000000 00000000 00000000 00000000
192.0.0.0	/2	11000000 00000000 00000000 00000000
224.0.0.0	/3	11100000 00000000 00000000 00000000
240.0.0.0	/4	11110000 00000000 00000000 00000000
248.0.0.0	/5	11111000 00000000 00000000 00000000
252.0.0.0	/6	11111100 00000000 00000000 00000000
254.0.0.0	/7	11111110 00000000 00000000 00000000
255.0.0.0	/8	11111111 00000000 00000000 00000000
255.128.0.0	/9	11111111 10000000 00000000 00000000
255.192.0.0	/10	11111111 11000000 00000000 00000000
255.224.0.0	/11	11111111 11100000 00000000 00000000
255.240.0.0	/12	11111111 11110000 00000000 00000000
255.248.0.0	/13	11111111 11111000 00000000 00000000
255.252.0.0	/14	11111111 11111100 00000000 00000000
255.254.0.0	/15	11111111 11111110 00000000 00000000
255.255.0.0	/16	11111111 11111111 00000000 00000000
255.255.128.0	/17	11111111 11111111 10000000 00000000
255.255.192.0	/18	11111111 11111111 11000000 00000000
255.255.224.0	/19	11111111 11111111 11100000 00000000
255.255.240.0	/20	11111111 11111111 11110000 00000000
255.255.248.0	/21	11111111 11111111 11111000 00000000
255.255.252.0	/22	11111111 11111111 11111100 00000000
255.255.254.0	/23	11111111 11111111 11111110 00000000
255.255.255.0	/24	11111111 11111111 11111111 00000000
255.255.255.128	/25	11111111 11111111 11111111 10000000
255.255.255.192	/26	11111111 11111111 11111111 11000000
255.255.255.224	/27	11111111 11111111 11111111 11100000
255.255.255.240	/28	11111111 11111111 11111111 11110000
255.255.255.248	/29	11111111 11111111 11111111 11111000
255.255.255.252	/30	11111111 11111111 11111111 11111100
255.255.255.254	/31	11111111 11111111 11111111 11111110
255.255.255.255	/32	11111111 11111111 11111111 11111111

This appendix covers the following subjects:

- **Standard IP Access Control Lists:** This section explains how standard IP ACLs work and how to configure them.

- **Extended IP Access Control Lists:** This section examines the deeper complexity of extended IP ACLs, including how to configure them.

- **Advances in Managing ACL Configuration:** This section examines the nuances of two major enhancements to ACL configuration over the years: named ACLs and sequence numbers.

IP Access Control Lists

Network security is one of the hottest topics in networking today. Although security has always been important, the explosion of the size and scope of the Internet has created more security exposures. In years past, most companies were not permanently connected to a global network—a network through which others could attempt to illegally access their networks. Today, because most companies connect to the Internet, many companies receive significant income through their network-based facilities—facts that increase the exposure and increase the impact when security is breached.

Cisco routers can be used as part of a good overall security strategy. One of the most important tools in Cisco IOS Software used as part of that strategy is access control lists (ACL). ACLs define rules that can be used to prevent some packets from flowing through the network. Whether you simply want to restrict access to the payroll server to only people in the payroll department, or whether you are trying to stop Internet hackers from bringing your e-commerce web server to its knees, IOS ACLs can be a key security tool that is part of a larger security strategy.

Cisco IOS has supported IP ACLs almost since the original commercial Cisco routers were introduced in the late 1980s. Because of the historical progression of Cisco support for ACLs, this book still covers a lot of the same information and configuration commands that have been used with Cisco routers for almost 20 years. To support all that history, this appendix spends most of its time explaining IP ACLs—numbered IP ACLs—using the same commands and syntax available in IOS for a long time.

In particular, this appendix begins with a description of the simplest types of numbered IP ACLs—standard IP ACLs. The second major section then examines the more-complex extended IP ACLs, which can be used to examine many more fields inside an IP packet. Following that, the next section of the appendix describes the deepening support for ACLs in IOS—both the introduction of support for named ACLs with IOS version 11.2, and the later addition of support for ACL sequence numbers and enhanced ACL editing with IOS 12.3. The appendix concludes by covering miscellaneous ACL topics.

Standard IP Access Control Lists

IP ACLs cause a router to discard some packets based on criteria defined by the network engineer. The goal of these filters is to prevent unwanted traffic in the network—whether preventing hackers from penetrating the network or just preventing employees from using systems they shouldn't. Access lists should simply be part of an organization's security policy.

By the way, IP access lists can also be used to filter routing updates, to match packets for prioritization, to match packets for Virtual Private Network (VPN) tunneling, and to match packets for implementing quality of service features. However, this appendix focuses on the use of ACLs to filter IP packets.

This appendix covers two main categories of IOS IP ACLs—standard and extended. Standard ACLs use simpler logic, and extended ACLs use more-complex logic. The first section of this appendix covers standard IP ACLs, followed by a section on extended IP ACLs. Several sections related to both types of ACLs close the appendix.

IP Standard ACL Concepts

Engineers need to make two major choices for any ACL that will filter IP packets: which packets to filter, and where in the network to place the ACL. Figure B-1 serves as an example. In this case, imagine that Bob is not allowed to access Server1, but Larry is.

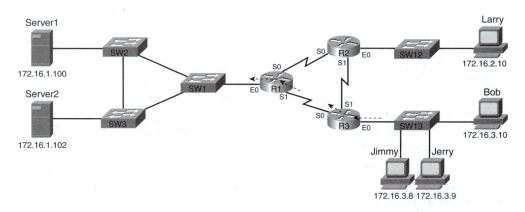

Figure B-1 *Locations Where Access List Logic Can Be Applied in the Network*

Filtering logic could be configured on any of the three routers and on any of their interfaces. The dotted arrowed lines in the figure show the most appropriate points at which to apply the filtering logic in an ACL. Because Bob's traffic is the only traffic that needs to be filtered, and the goal is to stop access to Server1, the access list could be applied at either R1 or R3. And because Bob's attempted traffic to Server1 would not need to go through R2, R2 would not be a good place to put the access list logic. For the sake of discussion, assume that R1 should have the access list applied.

Cisco IOS Software applies the filtering logic of an ACL either as a packet enters an interface or as it exits the interface. In other words, IOS associates an ACL with an interface, and specifically for traffic either entering or exiting the interface. After you have chosen the router on which you want to place the access list, you must choose the interface on which to apply the access logic, as well as whether to apply the logic for inbound or outbound packets.

For instance, imagine that you want to filter Bob's packets sent to Server1. Figure B-2 shows the options for filtering the packet.

Router R1

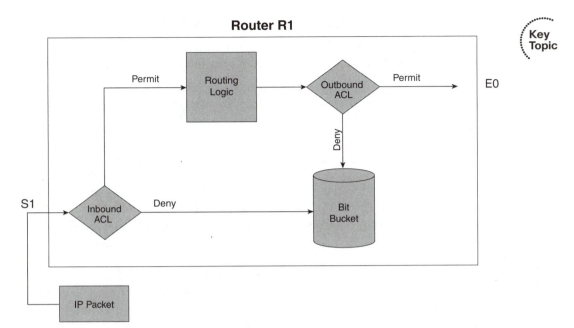

Figure B-2 *Internal Processing in R1 in Relation to Where R1 Can Filter Packets*

Filtering logic can be applied to packets entering S1 or to packets exiting E0 on R1 to match the packet sent by Bob to Server1. In general, you can filter packets by creating and enabling access lists for both incoming and outgoing packets on each interface. Here are some key features of Cisco access lists:

■ Packets can be filtered as they enter an interface, before the routing decision.

■ Packets can be filtered before they exit an interface, after the routing decision.

■ *Deny* is the term used in Cisco IOS software to imply that the packet will be filtered.

■ *Permit* is the term used in Cisco IOS software to imply that the packet will not be filtered.

■ The filtering logic is configured in the access list.

■ At the end of every access list is an implied "deny all traffic" statement. Therefore, if a packet does not match any of your access list statements, it is blocked.

For example, you might create an access list in R1 and enable it on R1's S1 interface. The access list would look for packets that came from Bob. Therefore, the access list would need to be enabled for inbound packets, because in this network, packets from Bob enter S1, and packets to Bob exit S1.

Access lists have two major steps in their logic: matching and action. Matching logic examines each packet and determines whether it matches the **access-list** statement. For instance, Bob's IP address would be used to match packets sent from Bob. IP ACLs tell the router to take one of two actions when a statement is matched: deny or permit. Deny means to discard the packet, and permit implies that the packet should continue on its way.

So the access list for preventing Bob's traffic to the server might go something like this:

Look for packets with Bob's source IP address and Server1's destination IP address. When you see them, discard them. If you see any other packets, do not discard them.

Not surprisingly, IP ACLs can get a lot more difficult than those in real life. Even a short list of matching criteria can create complicated access lists on a variety of interfaces in a variety of routers. I've even heard of a couple of large networks with a few full-time people who do nothing but plan and implement access lists!

Cisco calls its packet-filtering features "access control lists" in part because the logic is created with multiple configuration commands that are considered to be in the same list. When an access list has multiple entries, IOS searches the list sequentially until the first statement is matched. The matched statement determines the action to be taken. The two diamond shapes in Figure B-2 represent the application of access list logic.

The logic that IOS uses with a multiple-entry ACL can be summarized as follows:

Key Topic

1. The matching parameters of the **access-list** statement are compared to the packet.
2. If a match is made, the action defined in this **access-list** statement (permit or deny) is performed.
3. If a match is not made in Step 2, repeat Steps 1 and 2 using each successive statement in the ACL until a match is made.
4. If no match is made with an entry in the access list, the deny action is performed.

Wildcard Masks

IOS IP ACLs match packets by looking at the IP, TCP, and UDP headers in the packet. Extended access lists can check source and destination IP addresses, as well as source and destination port numbers, along with several other fields. However, standard IP access lists can examine only the source IP address.

Regardless of whether you use standard or extended IP ACLs, you can tell the router to match based on the entire IP address or just a part of the IP address. For instance, if you wanted to stop Bob from sending packets to Server1, you would look at the entire IP address of Bob and Server1 in the access list. But what if the criteria were to stop all hosts in Bob's subnet from getting to Server1? Because all hosts in Bob's subnet have the same numbers in their first 3 octets, the access list could just check the first 3 octets of the address to match all packets with a single **access-list** command.

Cisco *wildcard masks* define the portion of the IP address that should be examined. When defining the ACL statements, as you'll see in the next section of this appendix, you can define a wildcard mask along with the IP address. The wildcard mask tells the router which part of the IP address in the configuration statement must be compared with the packet header.

For example, suppose that one mask implies that the whole packet should be checked and another implies that only the first 3 octets of the address need to be examined. (You might choose to do that to match all IP hosts in the same subnet when using a subnet mask of 255.255.255.0.) To perform this matching, Cisco access lists use wildcard masks.

Wildcard masks look similar to subnet masks, but they are not the same. Wildcard masks represent a 32-bit number, as do subnet masks. However, the wildcard mask's 0 bits tell the router that those corresponding bits in the address must be compared when performing the matching logic. The binary 1s in the wildcard mask tell the router that those bits do not need to be compared. In fact, many people call these bits the "don't care" bits.

To get a sense of the idea behind a wildcard mask, Table B-1 lists some of the more popular wildcard masks, along with their meanings.

Table B-1   *Sample Access List Wildcard Masks*

Wildcard Mask	Binary Version of the Mask	Description
0.0.0.0	00000000.00000000.00000000.00000000	The entire IP address must match.
0.0.0.255	00000000.00000000.00000000.11111111	Just the first 24 bits must match.
0.0.255.255	00000000.00000000.11111111.11111111	Just the first 16 bits must match.
0.255.255.255	00000000.11111111.11111111.11111111	Just the first 8 bits must match.
255.255.255.255	11111111.11111111.11111111.11111111	Automatically considered to match any and all addresses.
0.0.15.255	00000000.00000000.00001111.11111111	Just the first 20 bits must match.
0.0.3.255	00000000.00000000.00000011.11111111	Just the first 22 bits must match.

The first several examples show typical uses of the wildcard mask. As you can see, it is not a subnet mask. A wildcard of 0.0.0.0 means that the entire IP address must be examined, and be equal, to be considered a match. 0.0.0.255 means that the last octet automatically matches, but the first three must be examined, and so on. More generally, the wildcard mask means the following:

> Bit positions of binary 0 mean that the access list compares the corresponding bit position in the IP address and makes sure it is equal to the same bit position in the address configured in the **access-list** statement. Bit positions of binary 1 are "don't care" bits. Those bit positions are immediately considered to be a match.

The last two rows of Table B-1 show two reasonable, but not obvious, wildcard masks. 0.0.15.255 in binary is 20 binary 0s followed by 12 binary 1s. This means that the first 20 bits must match. Similarly, 0.0.3.255 means that the first 22 bits must be examined to find out if they match. Why are these useful? If the subnet mask is 255.255.240.0, and you want to match all hosts in the same subnet, the 0.0.15.255 wildcard means that all network and subnet bits must be matched, and all host bits are automatically considered to match. Likewise, if you want to filter all hosts in a subnet that uses subnet mask 255.255.252.0, the wildcard mask 0.0.3.255 matches the network and subnet bits. In general, if you want a wildcard mask that helps you match all hosts in a subnet, invert the subnet mask, and you have the correct wildcard mask.

A Quicker Alternative for Interpreting Wildcard Masks

Both IP standard ACLs (source IP address only) and extended ACLs (both source and destination addresses) can be configured to examine all or part of an IP address based on the wildcard mask. However, working with the masks in binary can be slow and laborious unless you master binary-to-decimal and decimal-to-binary conversions. This section suggests an easier method of working with ACL wildcard masks that works well if you have already mastered subnetting math.

In many cases, an ACL needs to match all hosts in a particular subnet. To match a subnet with an ACL, you can use the following shortcut:

■   Use the subnet number as the address value in the **access-list** command.

■   Use a wildcard mask found by subtracting the subnet mask from 255.255.255.255.

For example, for subnet 172.16.8.0 255.255.252.0, use the subnet number (172.16.8.0) as the *address* parameter, and then do the following math to find the wildcard mask:

```
  255.255.255.255
- 255.255.252.0
    0.  0.  3.255
```

Often, you do not create the ACL, but you need to interpret existing **access-list** commands. Typically, these questions list preconfigured ACL statements, or you need to display the contents of an ACL from a router simulator, and you need to decide which statement a particular packet matches. To do that, you need to determine the range of IP addresses matched by a particular address/wildcard mask combination in each ACL statement.

If you have mastered subnetting math using any of the decimal shortcuts, avoiding binary math, another shortcut can be used to analyze each existing address/wildcard pair in each ACL command. To do so:

Step 1.   Use the address in the **access-list** command as if it were a subnet number.

Step 2.   Use the number found by subtracting the wildcard mask from 255.255.255.255 as a subnet mask.

Step 3.   Treat the values from the first two steps as a subnet number and subnet mask, and find the broadcast address for the subnet. The ACL matches the range of addresses between the subnet number and broadcast address, inclusively.

The range of addresses identified by this process is the same range of addresses matched by the ACL. So, if you can already find a subnet's range of addresses quickly and easily, using this process to change an ACL's math might help you find the answer more quickly. For example, with the command **access-list 1 permit 172.16.200.0 0.0.7.255**, you would first think of 172.16.200.0 as a subnet number. Then you could calculate the assumed subnet mask of 255.255.248.0, as follows:

```
255.255.255.255
- 0.  0.  7.255
255.255.248.0
```

From there, using any process you like, use subnetting math to determine that the broadcast address of this subnet would be 172.16.207.255. So, the range of addresses matched by this ACL statement would be 172.16.200.0 through 172.16.207.255.

Standard IP Access List Configuration

ACL configuration tends to be simpler than the task of interpreting the meaning and actions taken by an ACL. To that end, this section presents a plan of attack for configuring ACLs. Then it shows a couple of examples that review both the configuration and the concepts implemented by those ACLs.

The generic syntax of the standard ACL configuration command is

> **access-list** *access-list-number* {**deny** | **permit**} *source* [*source-wildcard*]

A standard access list uses a series of **access-list** commands that have the same number. The **access-list** commands with the same number are considered to be in the same list, with the commands being listed in the same order in which they were added to the configuration. Each **access-list** command can match a range of source IP addresses. If a match occurs, the ACL either allows the packet to keep going (**permit** action) or discards the packet (**deny** action). Each standard ACL can match all, or only part, of the packet's source IP address. Note that for standard IP ACLs, the number range for ACLs is 1 to 99 and 1300 to 1999.

The following list outlines a suggested configuration process. You do not need to memorize the process; it is simply listed here as a convenient study review aid.

Step 1. Plan the location (router and interface) and direction (in or out) on that interface:

a. Standard ACLs should be placed near to the destination of the packets so that it does not unintentionally discard packets that should not be discarded.

b. Because standard ACLs can only match a packet's source IP address, identify the source IP addresses of packets as they go in the direction that the ACL is examining.

Step 2. Configure one or more **access-list** global configuration commands to create the ACL, keeping the following in mind:

a. The list is searched sequentially, using first-match logic. In other words, when a packet matches one of the **access-list** statements, the search is over, even if the packet would match subsequent statements.

b. The default action, if a packet does not match any of the **access-list** commands, is to **deny** (discard) the packet.

Key Topic

Step 3.   Enable the ACL on the chosen router interface, in the correct direction, using
the **ip access-group** *number* {**in** | **out**} interface subcommand.

Next, two examples of standard ACLs are shown.

Standard IP ACL: Example 1

Example B-1 attempts to stop Bob's traffic to Server1. As shown in Figure B-1, Bob is not
allowed to access Server1. In Example B-1, the configuration enables an ACL for all packets going out R1's Ethernet0 interface. The ACL matches the source address in the
packet—Bob's IP address. Note that the **access-list** commands are at the bottom of the example because the **show running-config** command also lists them near the bottom, after
the interface configuration commands.

Example B-1   *Standard Access List on R1 Stopping Bob from Reaching Server1*

```
interface Ethernet0
 ip address 172.16.1.1 255.255.255.0
ip access-group 1 out
!
access-list 1 remark stop all traffic whose source IP is Bob
access-list 1 deny 172.16.3.10 0.0.0.0
access-list 1 permit 0.0.0.0 255.255.255.255
```

First, focus on the basic syntax of the commands. Standard IP access lists use a number in
the range of 1 to 99 or 1300 to 1999. This example uses ACL number 1 versus the other
available numbers for no particular reason. (There is absolutely no difference in using one
number or another, as long as it is in the correct range. In other words, list 1 is no better or
worse than list 99.) The **access-list** commands, under which the matching and action logic
are defined, are global configuration commands. To enable the ACL on an interface and
define the direction of packets to which the ACL is applied, the **ip access-group** command is used. In this case, it enables the logic for ACL 1 on Ethernet0 for packets going
out the interface.

ACL 1 keeps packets sent by Bob from exiting R1's Ethernet interface, based on the
matching logic of the **access-list 1 deny 172.16.3.10 0.0.0.0** command. The wildcard
mask of 0.0.0.0 means "match all 32 bits," so only packets whose IP address exactly
matches 172.16.3.10 match this statement and are discarded. The **access-list 1 permit
0.0.0.0 255.255.255.255** command, the last statement in the list, matches all packets, because the wildcard mask of 255.255.255.255 means "don't care" about all 32 bits. In other
words, the statement matches all IP source addresses. These packets are permitted.

Finally, note that the engineer also added an **access-list 1 remark** command to the ACL.
This command allows the addition of a text comment, or remark, so that you can track the
purpose of the ACL. The remark only shows up in the configuration; it is not listed in
show command output.

Although it's a seemingly simple example, in this case access list 1 also prevents Bob's
packets sent to Server2 from being delivered. With the topology shown in Figure B-1, an
outbound standard ACL on R1's E0 interface cannot somehow deny Bob access to Server1

while permitting access to Server2. To do that, an extended ACL is needed that can check both the source and destination IP addresses.

Interestingly, if the commands in Example B-1 are entered in configuration mode, IOS changes the configuration syntax of a couple of commands. The output of the **show running-config** command in Example B-2 shows what IOS actually places in the configuration file.

Example B-2 *Revised Standard Access List Stopping Bob from Reaching Server1*

```
interface Ethernet0
 ip address 172.16.1.1 255.255.255.0
 ip access-group 1 out

access-list 1 remark stop all traffic whose source IP is Bob
access-list 1 deny host 172.16.3.10
access-list 1 permit any
```

The commands in Example B-1 are changed based on three factors. Cisco IOS allows both an older style and newer style of configuration for some parameters. Example B-1 shows the older style, and the router changes to the equivalent newer-style configuration in Example B-2. First, the use of a wildcard mask of 0.0.0.0 does indeed mean that the router should match that specific host IP address. The newer-style configuration uses the **host** keyword in *front* of the specific IP address. The other change to the newer-style configuration involves the use of wildcard mask 255.255.255.255 to mean "match anything." The newer-style configuration uses the keyword **any** to replace both the IP address and 255.255.255.255 wildcard mask. **any** simply means that any IP address is matched.

Standard IP ACL: Example 2

The second standard IP ACL example exposes more ACL issues. Figure B-3 and Examples B-3 and B-4 show a basic use of standard IP access lists, with two typical oversights in the first attempt at a complete solution. The criteria for the access lists are as follows:

■ Sam is not allowed access to Bugs or Daffy.

■ Hosts on the Seville Ethernet are not allowed access to hosts on the Yosemite Ethernet.

■ All other combinations are allowed.

Example B-3 *Yosemite Configuration for Standard Access List Example*

```
interface serial 0
ip access-group 3 out
!
access-list 3 deny host 10.1.2.1
access-list 3 permit any
```

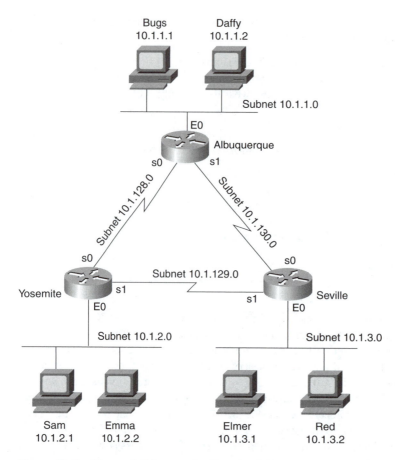

Figure B-3   *Network Diagram for Standard Access List Example*

Example B-4   *Seville Configuration for Standard Access List Example*

```
interface serial 1
ip access-group 4 out
!
access-list 4 deny 10.1.3.0    0.0.0.255
access-list 4 permit any
```

At first glance, these two access lists seem to perform the desired function. ACL 3, enabled for packets exiting Yosemite's S0 interface, takes care of criterion 1, because ACL 3 matches Sam's IP address exactly. ACL 4 in Seville, enabled for packets exiting its S1 interface, takes care of criterion 2, because ACL 4 matches all packets coming from subnet 10.1.3.0/24. Both routers meet criterion 3: A wildcard **permit any** is used at the end of each access list to override the default, which is to discard all other packets. So, all the criteria appear to be met.

However, when one of the WAN links fails, some holes can appear in the ACLs. For example, if the link from Albuquerque to Yosemite fails, Yosemite learns a route to 10.1.1.0/24 through Seville. Packets from Sam, forwarded by Yosemite and destined for hosts in Albuquerque, leave Yosemite's serial 1 interface without being filtered. So criterion 1 is no longer met. Similarly, if the link from Seville to Yosemite fails, Seville routes packets through Albuquerque, routing around the access list enabled on Seville, so criterion 2 is no longer met.

Example B-5 illustrates an alternative solution, with all the configuration on Yosemite— one that works even when some of the links fail.

Example B-5 *Yosemite Configuration for Standard Access List Example: Alternative Solution to Examples B-3 and B-4*

```
interface serial 0
 ip access-group 3 out
!
interface serial 1
 ip access-group 3 out
!
interface ethernet 0
 ip access-group 4 out
!
access-list 3 remark meets criteria 1
access-list 3 deny host 10.1.2.1
access-list 3 permit any
!
access-list 4 remark meets criteria 2
access-list 4 deny 10.1.3.0 0.0.0.255
access-list 4 permit any
```

The configuration shown in Example B-5 solves the problem from Examples B-3 and B-4. ACL 3 checks for Sam's source IP address, and it is enabled on both serial links for outbound traffic. So, of the traffic that is rerouted because of a WAN link failure, the packets from Sam are still filtered. To meet criterion 2, Yosemite filters packets as they exit its Ethernet interface. Therefore, regardless of which of the two WAN links the packets enter, packets from Seville's subnet are not forwarded to Yosemite's Ethernet.

Extended IP Access Control Lists

Extended IP access lists have both similarities and differences compared to standard IP ACLs. Just like standard lists, you enable extended access lists on interfaces for packets either entering or exiting the interface. IOS searches the list sequentially. The first statement matched stops the search through the list and defines the action to be taken. All these features are true of standard access lists as well.

The one key difference between the two is the variety of fields in the packet that can be compared for matching by extended access lists. A single extended ACL statement can examine multiple parts of the packet headers, requiring that all the parameters be matched correctly to match that one ACL statement. That matching logic is what makes extended access lists both much more useful and much more complex than standard IP ACLs.

This section starts with coverage of the extended IP ACL concepts that differ from standard ACLs—namely, the matching logic. Following that, the configuration details are covered.

Extended IP ACL Concepts

Extended access lists create powerful matching logic by examining many parts of a packet. Figure B-4 shows several of the fields in the packet headers that can be matched.

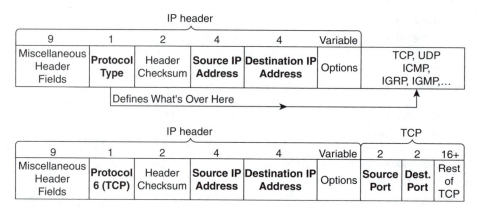

Figure B-4   *Extended Access List Matching Options*

The top set of headers shows the IP protocol type, which identifies what header follows the IP header. You can specify all IP packets, or those with TCP headers, UDP headers, ICMP, and so on, by checking the Protocol field. You can also check both the source and destination IP addresses, as shown. The lower part of the figure shows an example with a TCP header following the IP header, pointing out the location of the TCP source and destination port numbers. These port numbers identify the application. For instance, the web uses port 80 by default. If you specify a protocol of TCP or UDP, you can also check the port numbers.

Table B-2 summarizes the most commonly used fields that can be matched with an extended IP ACL, as compared with standard IP ACLs.

Table B-2   *Standard and Extended IP Access Lists: Matching*

Type of Access List	What Can Be Matched
Both standard and extended ACLs	Source IP address
	Portions of the source IP address using a wildcard mask
Only extended ACLs	Destination IP address

Key Topic

Table B-2   *Standard and Extended IP Access Lists: Matching*

Type of Access List	What Can Be Matched
	Portions of the destination IP address using a wildcard mask
	Protocol type (TCP, UDP, ICMP, IGRP, IGMP, and others)
	Source port
	Destination port
	All TCP flows except the first
	IP TOS
	IP precedence

Knowing what to look for is just half the battle. IOS checks all the matching information configured in a single **access-list** command. Everything must match for that single command to be considered a match and for the defined action to be taken. The options start with the protocol type (IP, TCP, UDP, ICMP, and others), followed by the source IP address, source port, destination IP address, and destination port number. Table B-3 lists several sample **access-list** commands, with several options configured and some explanations. Only the matching options are shaded.

Table B-3   *Extended access-list Commands and Logic Explanations*

access-list Statement	What It Matches
access-list 101 deny ip any host 10.1.1.1	Any IP packet, any source IP address, with a destination IP address of 10.1.1.1.
access-list 101 deny tcp any gt 1023 host 10.1.1.1 eq 23	Packets with a TCP header, any source IP address, with a source port greater than (**gt**) 1023, a destination IP address of exactly 10.1.1.1, and a destination port equal to (**eq**) 23.
access-list 101 deny tcp any host 10.1.1.1 eq 23	The same as the preceding example, but any source port matches, because that parameter is omitted in this case.
access-list 101 deny tcp any host 10.1.1.1 eq telnet	The same as the preceding example. The **telnet** keyword is used instead of port 23.
access-list 101 deny udp 1.0.0.0 0.255.255.255 lt 1023 any	A packet with a source in network 1.0.0.0, using UDP with a source port less than (**lt**) 1023, with any destination IP address.

Matching TCP and UDP Port Numbers

Extended IP ACLs allow for the matching of the IP header protocol field, as well as matching the source and destination TCP or UDP port numbers. However, many people have difficulty when first configuring ACLs that match port numbers, particularly when matching the source port number.

When considering matching using TCP or UDP ports, keep the following key points in mind:

Key Topic

- The **access-list** command must use protocol keyword **tcp** to be able to match TCP ports and the **udp** keyword to be able to match UDP ports. The **ip** keyword does not allow for matching the port numbers.

- The source port and destination port parameters on the **access-list** command are positional. In other words, their location in the command determines if the parameter examines the source or destination port.

- Remember that ACLs can match packets sent to a server by comparing the destination port to the well-known port number. However, ACLs need to match the source port for packets sent by the server.

- It is useful to memorize the most popular TCP and UDP applications, and their well-known ports, as listed in Table B-4, as shown later in this appendix.

For example, consider the simple network shown in Figure B-5. The FTP server sits on the right, with the client on the left. The figure shows the syntax of an ACL that matches

- Packets that include a TCP header

- Packets sent from the client subnet

- Packets sent to the server subnet

- Packets with TCP destination port 21

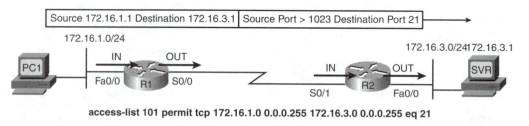

access-list 101 permit tcp 172.16.1.0 0.0.0.255 172.16.3.0 0.0.0.255 eq 21

Figure B-5   *Filtering Packets Based on Destination Port*

To fully appreciate the matching of the destination port with the **eq 21** parameter, consider packets moving left to right, from PC1 to the server. If the server is using well-known port 21 (FTP control port), the packet sent by PC1, in the TCP header, has a destination port value of 21. The ACL syntax includes the **eq 21** parameter *after* the destination IP address, with this position in the command implying that this parameter matches the destination port. As a result, the ACL statement shown in the figure would match this packet, and the destination port of 21, if used in any of the four locations implied by the four thick arrowed lines in the figure.

Conversely, Figure B-6 shows the reverse flow, with a packet sent by the server back toward PC1. In this case, the packet's TCP header has a source port of 21, so the ACL must check the source port value of 21, and the ACL must be located on different interfaces.

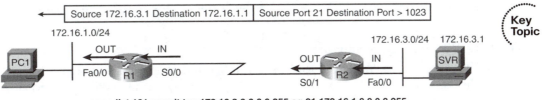

access-list 101 permit tcp 172.16.3.0 0.0.0.255 eq 21 172.16.1.0 0.0.0.255

Figure B-6   *Filtering Packets Based on Source Port*

When using ACLs that match port numbers, first consider whether the question requires that the ACL be placed in a certain location and direction. If so, you can then determine if that ACL would process packets either sent to the server or sent by the server. At that point, you can decide whether you need to check the source or destination port in the packet.

For reference, Table B-4 lists many of the popular port numbers and their transport layer protocols and applications. Note that the syntax of the **access-list** commands accepts both the port numbers and a shorthand version of the application name.

Table B-4   *Popular Applications and Their Well-Known Port Numbers*

Port Number(s)	Protocol	Application	Application Name Keyword in access-list Command Syntax
20	TCP	FTP data	ftp-data
21	TCP	FTP control	ftp
22	TCP	SSH	—
23	TCP	Telnet	telnet
25	TCP	SMTP	smtp
53	UDP, TCP	DNS	domain
67, 68	UDP	DHCP	bootps(67) bootpc(68)
69	UDP	TFTP	tftp
80	TCP	HTTP (WWW)	www
110	TCP	POP3	pop3

Table B-4 *Popular Applications and Their Well-Known Port Numbers*

Port Number(s)	Protocol	Application	Application Name Keyword in access-list Command Syntax
161		SNMP	snmp
443	TCP	SSL	—
16,384–32,767	UDP	RTP-based voice (VoIP) and video	—

Extended IP ACL Configuration

Because extended ACLs can match so many different fields in the various headers in an IP packet, the command syntax cannot be easily summarized in a single generic command. For reference, Table B-5 lists the syntax of the two most common generic commands.

Table B-5 *Extended IP Access List Configuration Commands*

Command	Configuration Mode and Description
access-list *access-list-number* {deny | permit} *protocol source source-wildcard destination destination-wildcard* [log | log-input]	Global command for extended numbered access lists. Use a number between 100 and 199 or 2000 and 2699, inclusive.
access-list *access-list-number* {deny | permit} {tcp | udp} *source source-wildcard* [*operator* [*port*]] *destination destination-wildcard* [*operator* [*port*]] [established] [log]	A version of the access-list command with TCP-specific parameters.

The configuration process for extended ACLs mostly matches the same process used for standard ACLs. The location and direction should be chosen first so that the ACL's parameters can be planned based on the information in the packets flowing in that direction. The ACL should be configured with **access-list** commands. Then the ACL should be enabled with the same **ip access-group** command used with standard ACLs. All these steps remain the same as with standard ACLs. However, the differences in configuration are summarized as follows:

Key Topic

- Extended ACLs should be placed as close as possible to the source of the packets to be filtered, because extended ACLs can be configured so that they do not discard packets that should not be discarded. So filtering close to the source of the packets saves some bandwidth.

- All fields in one **access-list** command must match a packet for the packet to be considered to match that **access-list** statement.

- The extended **access-list** command uses numbers between 100–199 and 2000–2699, with no number being inherently better than another.

The extended version of the **access-list** command allows for matching of port numbers using several basic operations, such as equal-to and less-than. However, the commands use abbreviations, so Table B-6 lists the abbreviations and a fuller explanation.

Table B-6   *Operators Used When Matching Port Numbers*

Operator in the access-list Command	Meaning
eq	Equal to
neq	Not equal to
lt	Less than
gt	Greater than
range	Range of port numbers

Extended IP Access Lists: Example 1

This example focuses on understanding the basic syntax. In this case, Bob is denied access to all FTP servers on R1's Ethernet, and Larry is denied access to Server1's web server. Figure B-7 is a reminder of the network topology. Example B-6 shows the configuration on R1.

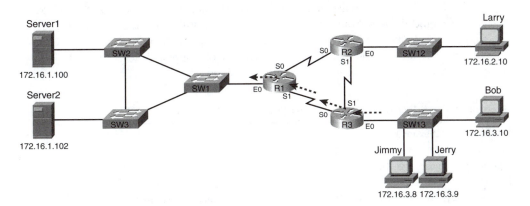

Figure B-7   *Network Diagram for Extended Access List Example 1*

Example B-6   *R1's Extended Access List: Example 1*

```
interface Serial0
 ip address 172.16.12.1 255.255.255.0
ip access-group 101 in
 !
interface Serial1
ip address 172.16.13.1 255.255.255.0
ip access-group 101 in
```

```
!
access-list 101 remark Stop Bob to FTP servers, and Larry to Server1 web
access-list 101 deny tcp host 172.16.3.10 172.16.1.0 0.0.0.255 eq ftp
access-list 101 deny tcp host 172.16.2.10 host 172.16.1.100 eq www
access-list 101 permit ip any any
```

In Example B-6, the first ACL statement prevents Bob's access to FTP servers in subnet 172.16.1.0. The second statement prevents Larry's access to web services on Server1. The final statement permits all other traffic.

Focusing on the syntax for a moment, there are several new items to review. First, the access list number for extended access lists falls in the range of 100 to 199 or 2000 to 2699. Following the **permit** or **deny** action, the *protocol* parameter defines whether you want to check for all IP packets or just those with TCP or UDP headers. When you check for TCP or UDP port numbers, you must specify the TCP or UDP protocol.

This example uses the **eq** parameter, meaning "equals," to check the destination port numbers for FTP control (keyword **ftp**) and HTTP traffic (keyword **www**). You can use the numeric values—or, for the more popular options, a more obvious text version is valid. (If you were to enter **eq 80**, the config would show **eq www**.)

In this first extended ACL example, the access lists could have been placed on R2 and R3 instead of on R1. As you will read near the end of this appendix, Cisco makes some specific recommendations about where to locate IP ACLs. With extended IP ACLs, Cisco suggests that you locate them as close as possible to the source of the packet. Therefore, Example B-7 achieves the same goal as Example B-6 of stopping Bob's access to FTP servers at the main site, and it does so with an ACL on R3.

Example B-7   *R3's Extended Access List Stopping Bob from Reaching FTP Servers Near R1*

```
interface Ethernet0
 ip address 172.16.3.1 255.255.255.0
 ip access-group 101 in

access-list 101 remark deny Bob to FTP servers in subnet 172.16.1.0/24
access-list 101 deny tcp host 172.16.3.10 172.16.1.0 0.0.0.255 eq ftp
access-list 101 permit ip any any
```

ACL 101 looks a lot like ACL 101 from Example B-6, but this time, the ACL does not bother to check for the criteria to match Larry's traffic, because Larry's traffic will never enter R3's Ethernet 0 interface. Because the ACL has been placed on R3, near Bob, it watches for packets Bob sends that enter its Ethernet0 interface. Because of the ACL, Bob's FTP traffic to 172.16.1.0/24 is denied, with all other traffic entering R3's E0 interface making it into the network. Example B-7 does not show any logic for stopping Larry's traffic.

Extended IP Access Lists: Example 2

Example B-8, based on the network shown in Figure B-8, shows another example of how to use extended IP access lists. This example uses the same criteria and network topology as the second standard IP ACL example, as repeated here:

■ Sam is not allowed access to Bugs or Daffy.

■ Hosts on the Seville Ethernet are not allowed access to hosts on the Yosemite Ethernet.

■ All other combinations are allowed.

Example B-8 *Yosemite Configuration for Extended Access List Example 2*

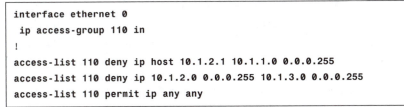

```
interface ethernet 0
 ip access-group 110 in
!
access-list 110 deny ip host 10.1.2.1 10.1.1.0 0.0.0.255
access-list 110 deny ip 10.1.2.0 0.0.0.255 10.1.3.0 0.0.0.255
access-list 110 permit ip any any
```

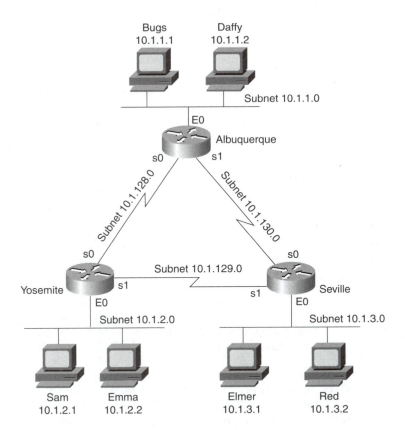

Figure B-8 *Network Diagram for Extended Access List Example*

This configuration solves the problem with few statements while keeping to Cisco's design guideline of placing extended ACLs as close as possible to the source of the traffic. The ACL filters packets that enter Yosemite's E0 interface, which is the first router interface that packets sent by Sam enter. The issue of having packets "routed around" access lists on serial interfaces is taken care of with the placement on Yosemite's only Ethernet interface. Also, the filtering mandated by the second requirement (to disallow Seville's LAN hosts from accessing Yosemite's) is met by the second **access-list** statement. Stopping packet flow from Yosemite's LAN subnet to Seville's LAN subnet stops effective communication between the two subnets. Alternatively, the opposite logic could have been configured at Seville.

Advances in Managing ACL Configuration

Now that you have a good understanding of the core concepts in IOS IP ACLs, this next section examines a couple of enhancements to IOS support for ACLs: named ACLs and ACL sequence numbers. Although both features are useful and important, neither adds any function as to what a router can and cannot filter, as compared to the numbered ACLs already covered in this appendix. Instead, named ACLs and ACL sequence numbers provide the engineer with configuration options that make it easier to remember ACL names and easier to edit existing ACLs when an ACL needs to change.

Named IP Access Lists

Named ACLs, introduced with IOS version 11.2, can be used to match the same packets, with the same parameters, that can be matched with standard and extended IP ACLs. Named IP ACLs do have some differences, however, some of which make them easier to work with. The most obvious difference is that IOS identifies named ACLs using names you make up, as opposed to numbers—and you have a better chance of remembering names.

In addition to using more memorable names, the other major advantage of named ACLs over numbered ACLs, at the time they were introduced into IOS, was that you could delete individual lines in a named IP access list. Throughout the history of numbered IP ACLs and the **access-list** global command, until the introduction of IOS 12.3, a single line in a numbered ACL could not be deleted. For example, if you had earlier configured the **access-list 101 permit tcp any any eq 80** command, and then you entered the **no ip access-list 101 permit tcp any any eq 80** command, the whole ACL 101 would be deleted! The advantage of the introduction of named ACLs is that you can enter a command that removes individual lines in an ACL.

> **Note:**   With IOS 12.3, Cisco expanded IOS to be able to delete individual lines in numbered ACLs, making IOS support for editing both named and numbered ACLs equivalent. These details are explained in the next section.

The configuration syntax is very similar between named and numbered IP access lists. The items that can be matched with a numbered standard IP access list are identical to the items that can be matched with a named standard IP access list. Likewise, the items are identical with both numbered and named extended IP access lists.

Two important configuration differences exist between old-style numbered ACLs and the newer named access lists. One key difference is that named access lists use a global command that places the user in a named IP access list submode, under which the matching and permit/deny logic is configured. The other key difference is that when a named matching statement is deleted, only that one statement is deleted.

Example B-9 shows an example that uses named IP ACLs. It shows the changing command prompt in configuration mode, showing that the user has been placed in ACL configuration mode. It also lists the pertinent parts of the output of a **show running-config** command. It ends with an example of how you can delete individual lines in a named ACL.

Example B-9   *Named Access List Configuration*

```
conf t
Enter configuration commands, one per line.  End with Ctrl-Z.
Router(config)# ip access-list extended barney
Router(config-ext-nacl)# permit tcp host 10.1.1.2 eq www any
Router(config-ext-nacl)# deny udp host 10.1.1.1 10.1.2.0 0.0.0.255
Router(config-ext-nacl)# deny ip 10.1.3.0 0.0.0.255 10.1.2.0 0.0.0.255
! The next statement is purposefully wrong so that the process of changing
! the list can be seen.
Router(config-ext-nacl)# deny ip 10.1.2.0 0.0.0.255 10.2.3.0 0.0.0.255

Router(config-ext-nacl)# deny ip host 10.1.1.130 host 10.1.3.2
Router(config-ext-nacl)# deny ip host 10.1.1.28 host 10.1.3.2
Router(config-ext-nacl)# permit ip any any
Router(config-ext-nacl)# interface serial1
Router(config-if)# ip access-group barney out
Router(config-if)# ^Z
Router# show running-config
Building configuration...

Current configuration:

.
. (unimportant statements omitted)
.
interface serial 1
 ip access-group barney out
!
ip access-list extended barney
permit tcp host 10.1.1.2 eq www any
 deny    udp host 10.1.1.1 10.1.2.0 0.0.0.255
 deny    ip 10.1.3.0 0.0.0.255 10.1.2.0 0.0.0.255
 deny    ip 10.1.2.0 0.0.0.255 10.2.3.0 0.0.0.255
 deny    ip host 10.1.1.130 host 10.1.3.2
 deny    ip host 10.1.1.28 host 10.1.3.2
```

```
  permit ip any any
Router# conf t
Enter configuration commands, one per line.  End with Ctrl-Z.
Router(config)# ip access-list extended barney
Router(config-ext-nacl)#no deny ip 10.1.2.0 0.0.0.255 10.2.3.0 0.0.0.255
Router(config-ext-nacl)# ^Z
Router# show access-list

Extended IP access list barney
    10 permit tcp host 10.1.1.2 eq www any
    20 deny   udp host 10.1.1.1 10.1.2.0 0.0.0.255
    30 deny   ip 10.1.3.0 0.0.0.255 10.1.2.0 0.0.0.255
    50 deny   ip host 10.1.1.130 host 10.1.3.2
    60 deny   ip host 10.1.1.28 host 10.1.3.2
    70 permit ip any any
```

Example B-9 begins with the creation of an ACL named barney. The **ip access-list extended barney** command creates the ACL, naming it barney and placing the user in ACL configuration mode. This command also tells the IOS that barney is an extended ACL. Next, seven different **permit** and **deny** statements define the matching logic and action to be taken upon a match. The **permit** and **deny** commands use the exact same syntax that the numbered **access-list** commands use, starting with the **deny** and **permit** keywords. In this example, a comment is added just before the command that is deleted later in the example.

The **show running-config** command output lists the named ACL configuration before the single entry is deleted. Next, the **no deny ip...** command deletes a single entry from the ACL. Notice that the output of the **show running-config** command still lists the ACL, with six **permit** and **deny** commands instead of seven.

Editing ACLs Using Sequence Numbers

Numbered ACLs have existed in IOS since the early days of Cisco routers. From their creation, up through IOS version 12.2, the only way to edit an existing numbered ACL—for example, to simply delete a line from the ACL—was to delete the whole ACL and then reconfigure the entire ACL. Besides being an inconvenience to the engineer, this process also caused some unfortunate side effects. When deleting the ACL, it is important to disable the ACL from all interfaces, and then delete it, reconfigure it, and enable it on the interface. Otherwise, during the reconfiguration process, before all the statements have been reconfigured, the ACL will not perform all the checks it should, sometimes causing problems, or exposing the network to various attacks.

As mentioned in the preceding section, the original IOS support for named ACLs, introduced in IOS 11.2, solved some of the editing problem. The original commands for named ACLs allowed the engineer to delete a line from an ACL, as shown in the preceding section in Example B-9. However, the configuration commands did not allow the user to insert a new **permit** or **deny** command into the list. All new commands were added to the end of the ACL.

With IOS 12.3, Cisco introduced several more configuration options for ACLs—options that apply to both named and numbered IP ACLs. These options take advantage of an ACL sequence number that is added to each ACL **permit** or **deny** statement, with the numbers representing the sequence of statements in the ACL. ACL sequence numbers provide the following features for both numbered and named ACLs:

Key
Topic

■   An individual ACL **permit** or **deny** statement can be deleted just by referencing the sequence number, without deleting the rest of the ACL.

■   Newly added **permit** and **deny** commands can be configured with a sequence number, dictating the location of the statement within the ACL.

■   Newly added **permit** and **deny** commands can be configured *without* a sequence number, with IOS creating a sequence number and placing the command at the end of the ACL.

To take advantage of the ability to delete and insert lines in an ACL, both numbered and named ACLs must use the same overall configuration style and commands used for named ACLs. The only difference in syntax is whether a name or number is used. Example B-10 shows the configuration of a standard numbered IP ACL, using this alternative configuration style. The example shows the power of the ACL sequence number for editing. In this example, the following occurs:

Step 1.   Numbered ACL 24 is configured, using this new-style configuration, with three **permit** commands.

Step 2.   The **show ip access-list** command shows the three permit commands, with sequence numbers 10, 20, and 30.

Step 3.   The engineer deletes only the second **permit** command, using the **no 20** ACL subcommand, which simply refers to sequence number 20.

Step 4.   The **show ip access-list** command confirms that the ACL now has only two lines (sequence numbers 10 and 30).

Step 5.   The engineer adds a new **permit** command to the beginning of the ACL, using the **5 deny 10.1.1.1** ACL subcommand.

Step 6.   The **show ip access-list** command again confirms the changes, this time listing three **permit** commands, sequence numbers 5, 10, and 30.

Note: For this example, note that the user does not leave configuration mode, instead using the **do** command to tell IOS to issue the **show ip access-list** EXEC command from configuration mode.

Example B-10   *Editing ACLs Using Sequence Numbers*

```
! Step 1: The 3-line Standard Numbered IP ACL is configured.
R1# configure terminal
Enter configuration commands, one per line.  End with Ctrl-Z.
R1(config)# ip access-list standard 24
```

```
R1(config-std-nacl)#permit 10.1.1.0 0.0.0.255
R1(config-std-nacl)#permit 10.1.2.0 0.0.0.255
R1(config-std-nacl)#permit 10.1.3.0 0.0.0.255
! Step 2: Displaying the ACL's contents, without leaving configuration mode.
R1(config-std-nacl)# do show ip access-list 24
Standard IP access list 24
    10 permit 10.1.1.0, wildcard bits 0.0.0.255
    20 permit 10.1.2.0, wildcard bits 0.0.0.255
    30 permit 10.1.3.0, wildcard bits 0.0.0.255
! Step 3: Still in ACL 24 configuration mode, the line with sequence number 20 is
! deleted.
R1(config-std-nacl)# no 20
! Step 4: Displaying the ACL's contents again, without leaving configuration mode.
! Note that line number 20 is no longer listed.
R1(config-std-nacl)# do show ip access-list 24
Standard IP access list 24
    10 permit 10.1.1.0, wildcard bits 0.0.0.255
    30 permit 10.1.3.0, wildcard bits 0.0.0.255
! Step 5: Inserting a new first line in the ACL.
R1(config-std-nacl)# 5 deny 10.1.1.1
! Step 6: Displaying the ACL's contents one last time, with the new statement
! (sequence number 5) listed first.
R1(config-std-nacl)# do show ip access-list 24
Standard IP access list 24
    5 deny   10.1.1.1
    10 permit 10.1.1.0, wildcard bits 0.0.0.255
    30 permit 10.1.3.0, wildcard bits 0.0.0.255
```

Interestingly, numbered ACLs can be configured with the new-style configuration, as shown in Example B-10, or with the old-style configuration, using **access-list** global configuration commands, as shown in the first several examples in this appendix. In fact, you can use both styles of configuration on a single ACL. However, no matter which style of configuration is used, the **show running-config** command output still shows the old-style configuration commands. Example B-11 demonstrates these facts, picking up where Example B-10 ended, with the following additional steps:

Step 7. The engineer lists the configuration (**show running-config**), which lists the old-style configuration commands—even though the ACL was created with the new-style commands.

Step 8. The engineer adds a new statement to the end of the ACL, using the old-style **access-list 24 permit 10.1.4.0 0.0.0.255** global configuration command.

Step 9. The **show ip access-list** command confirms that the old-style **access-list** command from the previous step followed the rule of being added only to the end of the ACL.

Step 10. The engineer displays the configuration to confirm that the parts of ACL 24 configured with both new-style commands and old-style commands are all listed in the same old-style ACL (**show running-config**).

Example B-11 *Adding to and Displaying a Numbered ACL Configuration*

```
! Step 7: A configuration snippet for ACL 24.
R1# show running-config
! The only lines shown are the lines from ACL 24
access-list 24 deny    10.1.1.1
access-list 24 permit 10.1.1.0 0.0.0.255
access-list 24 permit 10.1.3.0 0.0.0.255


! Step 8: Adding a new access-list 24 command
R1# configure terminal
Enter configuration commands, one per line.  End with CNTL/Z.
R1(config)#access-list 24 permit 10.1.4.0 0.0.0.255
R1(config)# ^Z
! Step 9: Displaying the ACL's contents again, with sequence numbers. Note that even
! the new statement has been automatically assigned a sequence number.
R1# show ip access-list 24
Standard IP access list 24
    5 deny    10.1.1.1
    10 permit 10.1.1.0, wildcard bits 0.0.0.255
    30 permit 10.1.3.0, wildcard bits 0.0.0.255
    40 permit 10.1.4.0, wildcard bits 0.0.0.255
!
! Step 10: The numbered ACL configuration remains in old-style configuration commands.
R1# show running-config
! The only lines shown are the lines from ACL 24
access-list 24 deny    10.1.1.1
access-list 24 permit 10.1.1.0 0.0.0.255
access-list 24 permit 10.1.3.0 0.0.0.255
access-list 24 permit 10.1.4.0 0.0.0.255
```

Appendix Review

Review Key Topics

Review the most important topics from this appendix, noted with the Key Topic icons. Table B-7 lists these key topics and where each is discussed.

Table B-7   *Key Topics for Appendix B*

Key Topic Element	Description	Page Number
Figure B-2	Logic diagram showing when a router examines packets with inbound and outbound ACLs	783
List	Four steps that describe how a router processes a multiline ACL	784
Table B-1	Explains sample wildcard masks and their meanings	785
List	Shortcut to find values in the access-list command to match a subnet number, given the subnet number and subnet mask	786
List	Shortcut to interpret the address and wildcard mask in an **access-list** command as a subnet number and mask	786
List	ACL planning and configuration checklist	787
Table B-2	List of IP packet fields matchable with standard and extended ACLs	792
List	Hints and tips on matching TCP and UDP ports using IP ACLs	794
Figure B-6	Shows a packet with source and destination port, with the corresponding location of the source port parameter in the **access-list** command	795
List	Three items that differ between standard and extended IP ACLs	796
Table B-6	List of operators that can be used when comparing port numbers in extended **access-list** commands	797
List	Features for both numbered and named ACLs provided by ACL sequence numbers	803

Define Key Terms

Define the following key terms from this appendix, and check your answers in the glossary:

extended access list, named access list, standard access list, wildcard mask

Review Command Reference to Check Your Memory

Although you should not necessarily memorize the information in the tables in this section, this section does include a reference for the configuration and EXEC commands covered in this appendix. Practically speaking, you should memorize the commands as a side effect of reading the appendix and doing all the activities in this "Appendix Review" section. To see how well you have memorized the commands as a side effect of your other studies, cover the left side of the table, read the descriptions on the right side, and see whether you remember the command.

Table B-8   *Appendix B Configuration Command Reference*

Command	Description
access-list *access-list-number* {**deny** | **permit**} *source* [*source-wildcard*] [**log**]	Global command for standard numbered access lists. Use a number between 1 and 99 or 1300 and 1999, inclusive.
access-list *access-list-number* {**deny** | **permit**} *protocol source source-wildcard destination destination-wildcard* [**log**]	Global command for extended numbered access lists. Use a number between 100 and 199 or 2000 and 2699, inclusive.
access-list *access-list-number* {**deny** | **permit**} **tcp** *source source-wildcard* [*operator* [*port*]] *destination destination-wildcard* [*operator* [*port*]] [**log**]	A version of the **access-list** command with TCP-specific parameters.
access-list *access-list-number* **remark** *text*	Defines a remark that helps you remember what the ACL is supposed to do.
ip access-group {*number* | *name* [**in** | **out**]}	Interface subcommand to enable access lists.
access-class *number* | *name* [**in** | **out**]	Line subcommand to enable either standard or extended access lists.
ip access-list {**standard** | **extended**} *name*	Global command to configure a named standard or extended ACL and enter ACL configuration mode.
{**deny** | **permit**} *source* [*source-wildcard*] [**log**]	ACL mode subcommand to configure the matching details and action for a standard named ACL.
{**deny** | **permit**} *protocol source source-wildcard destination destination-wildcard* [**log**]	ACL mode subcommand to configure the matching details and action for an extended named ACL.
{**deny** | **permit**} **tcp** *source source-wildcard* [*operator* [*port*]] *destination destination-wildcard* [*operator* [*port*]] [**log**]	ACL mode subcommand to configure the matching details and action for a named ACL that matches TCP segments.
remark *text*	ACL mode subcommand to configure a description of a named ACL.

Table B-9   *Appendix B EXEC Command Reference*

Command	Description
show ip interface [*type number*]	Includes a reference to the access lists enabled on the interface.
show access-lists [*access-list-number* | *access-list-name*]	Shows details of configured access lists for all protocols.
show ip access-list [*access-list-number* | *access-list-name*]	Shows IP access lists.

Answer Review Questions

Answer the following review questions:

1. Barney is a host with IP address 10.1.1.1 in subnet 10.1.1.0/24. Which of the following are things that a standard IP ACL could be configured to do?

   a.   Match the exact source IP address

   b.   Match IP addresses 10.1.1.1 through 10.1.1.4 with one **access-list** command without matching other IP addresses

   c.   Match all IP addresses in Barney's subnet with one **access-list** command without matching other IP addresses

   d.   Match only the packet's destination IP address

2. Which of the following wildcard masks is most useful for matching all IP packets in subnet 10.1.128.0, mask 255.255.255.0?

   a.   0.0.0.0

   b.   0.0.0.31

   c.   0.0.0.240

   d.   0.0.0.255

   e.   0.0.15.0

   f.   0.0.248.255

3. Which of the following wildcard masks is most useful for matching all IP packets in subnet 10.1.128.0, mask 255.255.240.0?

   a.   0.0.0.0

   b.   0.0.0.31

   c.   0.0.0.240

   d.   0.0.0.255

   e.   0.0.15.255

   f.   0.0.248.255

4. Which of the following fields cannot be compared based on an extended IP ACL?

   a. Protocol

   b. Source IP address

   c. Destination IP address

   d. TOS byte

   e. URL

   f. Filename for FTP transfers

5. Which of the following **access-list** commands permits traffic that matches packets going from host 10.1.1.1 to all web servers whose IP addresses begin with 172.16.5?

   a. access-list 101 permit tcp host 10.1.1.1 172.16.5.0 0.0.0.255 eq www

   b. access-list 1951 permit ip host 10.1.1.1 172.16.5.0 0.0.0.255 eq www

   c. access-list 2523 permit ip host 10.1.1.1 eq www 172.16.5.0 0.0.0.255

   d. access-list 2523 permit tcp host 10.1.1.1 eq www 172.16.5.0 0.0.0.255

   e. access-list 2523 permit tcp host 10.1.1.1 172.16.5.0 0.0.0.255 eq www

6. Which of the following **access-list** commands permits traffic that matches packets going to any web client from all web servers whose IP addresses begin with 172.16.5?

   a. access-list 101 permit tcp host 10.1.1.1 172.16.5.0 0.0.0.255 eq www

   b. access-list 1951 permit ip host 10.1.1.1 172.16.5.0 0.0.0.255 eq www

   c. access-list 2523 permit tcp any eq www 172.16.5.0 0.0.0.255

   d. access-list 2523 permit tcp 172.16.5.0 0.0.0.255 eq www 172.16.5.0 0.0.0.255

   e. access-list 2523 permit tcp 172.16.5.0 0.0.0.255 eq www any

7. Which of the following fields can be compared using a named extended IP ACL but not a numbered extended IP ACL?

   a. Protocol

   b. Source IP address

   c. Destination IP address

   d. TOS byte

   e. None of the other answers are correct.

8. In a router running IOS 12.3, an engineer needs to delete the second line in ACL 101, which currently has four commands configured. Which of the following options could be used?

   a. Delete the entire ACL and reconfigure the three ACL statements that should remain in the ACL.

   b. Delete one line from the ACL using the **no access-list...** command.

   c. Delete one line from the ACL by entering ACL configuration mode for the ACL and then deleting only the second line based on its sequence number.

   d. Delete the last three lines from the ACL from global configuration mode, and then add the last two statements back into the ACL.

Glossary

10BASE-T The 10-Mbps baseband Ethernet specification using two pairs of twisted-pair cabling (Categories 3, 4, or 5): One pair transmits data and the other receives data. 10BASE-T, which is part of the IEEE 802.3 specification, has a distance limit of approximately 100 m (328 feet) per segment.

100BASE-TX A name for the IEEE Fast Ethernet standard that uses two-pair copper cabling, a speed of 100 Mbps, and a maximum cable length of 100 meters.

1000BASE-T A name for the IEEE Gigabit Ethernet standard that uses four-pair copper cabling, a speed of 1000 Mbps (1 Gbps), and a maximum cable length of 100 meters.

802.11a The IEEE standard for wireless LANs using the U-NII spectrum, OFDM encoding, at speeds of up to 54 Mbps.

802.11b The IEEE standard for wireless LANs using the ISM spectrum, DSSS encoding, and speeds of up to 11 Mbps.

802.11g The IEEE standard for wireless LANs using the ISM spectrum, OFDM or DSSS encoding, and speeds of up to 54 Mbps.

802.11i The IEEE standard for wireless LAN security, including authentication and encryption.

802.1Q The IEEE standardized protocol for VLAN trunking.

A

AAA Authentication, Authorization, and Accounting. Authentication confirms the identity of the user or device. Authorization determines what the user or device is allowed to do. Accounting records information about access attempts, including inappropriate requests.

ABR Area Border Router. A router using OSPF in which the router has interfaces in multiple OSPF areas.

access interface A LAN network design term that refers to a switch interface connected to end-user devices.

access link In Frame Relay, the physical serial link that connects a Frame Relay DTE device, usually a router, to a Frame Relay switch. The access link uses the same physical layer standards as do point-to-point leased lines.

access point   A wireless LAN device that provides a means for wireless clients to send data to each other and to the rest of a wired network, with the AP connecting to both the wireless LAN and the wired Ethernet LAN.

access rate   *See* AR.

accounting   In security, the recording of access attempts. *See* AAA.

ACL   Access control list. A list configured on a router to control packet flow through the router, such as to prevent packets with a certain IP address from leaving a particular interface on the router.

ad hoc mode   In wireless LANs, a method or mode of operation in which clients send data directly to each other without the use of a wireless access point (AP).

adjacent-layer interaction   The general topic of how on one computer, two adjacent layers in a networking architectural model work together, with the lower layer providing services to the higher layer.

administrative distance   In Cisco routers, a means for one router to choose between multiple routes to reach the same subnet when those routes were learned by different routing protocols. The lower the administrative distance, the better the source of the routing information.

administrative mode   *See* trunking administrative mode.

ADSL   Asymmetric digital subscriber line. One of many DSL technologies, ADSL is designed to deliver more bandwidth downstream (from the central office to the customer site) than upstream.

alternate port   In RSTP 802.1w, a port role used to denote an interface that is currently receiving an inferior Hello BPDU, making it a possible replacement for the root port. Also used in the Cisco 802.1d STP implementation.

Anti-X   The term used by Cisco to refer to a variety of security tools that help prevent various attacks, including antivirus, anti-phishing, and anti-spam.

AR   Access Rate. In Frame Relay, the speed at which bits are sent over an access link.

Area Border Router   *See* ABR.

ARP   Address Resolution Protocol. An Internet protocol used to map an IP address to a MAC address. Defined in RFC 826.

ASBR   Autonomous System Border Router. A router using OSPF in which the router learns routes via another source, typically another routing protocol, exchanging routes that are external to OSPF with the OSPF domain.

asymmetric   A feature of many Internet access technologies, including DSL, cable, and modems, in which the downstream transmission rate is higher than the upstream transmission rate.

asynchronous   Describes a convention for sending data with digital signals. The sender and receiver operate at the same speeds, but no attempt is made to dynamically cause the sender and receiver to adjust their speeds based on the other device's speed.

ATM   Asynchronous Transfer Mode. The international standard for cell relay in which multiple service types (such as voice, video, and data) are conveyed in fixed-length (53-byte) cells. Fixed-length cells allow cell processing to occur in hardware, thereby reducing transit delays.

authentication   In security, the verification of the identity of a person or a process. *See* AAA.

authorization   In security, the determination of the rights allowed for a particular user or device. *See* AAA.

autonomous system   An internetwork in the administrative control of one organization, company, or governmental agency, inside which that organization typically runs an Interior Gateway Protocol (IGP).

Autonomous System Border Router   *See* ASBR.

autosummarization   A routing protocol feature in which a router that connects to more than one classful network advertises summarized routes for each entire classful network when sending updates out interfaces connected to other classful networks.

auxiliary port   A physical connector on a router that is designed to be used to allow a remote terminal, or PC with a terminal emulator, to access a router using an analog modem.

B

back-to-back link   A serial link between two routers, created without CSU/DSUs, by connecting a DTE cable to one router and a DCE cable to the other. Typically used in labs to build serial links without the expense of an actual leased line from the telco.

backup designated router   An OSPF router connected to a multiaccess network that monitors the work of the designated router (DR) and takes over the work of the DR if the DR fails.

backup port   In RSTP 802.1w, a port role used when multiple interfaces on one switch connect to a single collision domain. This makes one interface the designated port (DP), and one or more others become available to replace the DP (backup role).

balanced hybrid   A term that refers to a general type of routing protocol algorithm, the other two being distance vector and link state. The Enhanced Interior Gateway Routing Protocol (EIGRP) is the only routing protocol that Cisco classifies as using a balanced hybrid algorithm.

bandwidth   A reference to the speed of a networking link. Its origins come from earlier communications technology in which the range, or width, of the frequency band dictated how fast communications could occur.

basic service set (BSS)   In wireless LANs, a WLAN with a single access point.

Bc   Committed burst. A Frame Relay term referring to the number of bits that can be sent during a defined time interval. This helps measure if/when the DTE has, on average, sent more data over a VC than the speed defined in the traffic contract.

BECN   Backward explicit congestion notification. The bit in the Frame Relay header that implies that congestion is occurring in the opposite (backward) direction from the frame. Switches and DTEs can react by slowing the rate at which data is sent in that direction.

bitwise Boolean AND   A Boolean AND between two numbers of the same length in which the first bit in each number is ANDed, and then the second bit in each number, and then the third, and so on.

Blocking state   In 802.1d STP, a port state in which no received frames are processed, and the switch forwards no frames out the interface, with the exception of STP messages.

Boolean AND   A math operation performed on a pair of one-digit binary numbers. The result is another one-digit binary number. 1 AND 1 yields 1; all other combinations yield a 0.

boot field   The low-order 4 bits of the configuration register in a Cisco router. The value in the boot field in part tells the router where to look for a Cisco IOS image to load.

BPDU   Bridge protocol data unit. The generic name for Spanning Tree Protocol messages.

BPDU Guard   A Cisco switch feature that listens for incoming STP BPDU messages, disabling the interface if any are received. The goal is to prevent loops when a switch connects to a port expected to only have a host connected to it.

BRI   Basic Rate Interface. An ISDN interface composed of two 64-kbps bearer (B) channels and one 16-kbps data (D) channel for circuit-switched communication of voice, video, and data.

bridge ID (BID)   An 8-byte identifier for bridges and switches used by STP and RSTP. It is composed of a 2-byte priority field followed by a 6-byte System ID field that is usually filled with a MAC address.

bridge protocol data unit   *See* BPDU.

broadcast address   *See* subnet broadcast address.

broadcast domain   A set of all devices that receive broadcast frames originating from any device within the set. Devices in the same VLAN are in the same broadcast domain.

broadcast frame   An Ethernet frame sent to destination address FFFF.FFFF.FFFF, meaning that the frame should be delivered to all hosts on that LAN.

broadcast subnet   When subnetting a Class A, B, or C network, the one subnet in each classful network for which all subnet bits have a value of binary 1. The subnet broadcast address in this subnet has the same numeric value as the classful network's network-wide broadcast address.

bus   A common physical signal path composed of wires or other media across which signals can be sent from one part of a computer to another.

C

CDP   Cisco Discovery Protocol. A media- and protocol-independent device discovery protocol that runs on most Cisco-manufactured equipment, including routers, access servers, and switches. Using CDP, a device can advertise its existence to other devices and receive information about other devices on the same LAN or on the remote side of a WAN.

CDP neighbor   A device on the other end of some communications cable that is advertising CDP updates.

CHAP   Challenge Handshake Authentication Protocol. A security feature defined by PPP that allows either or both endpoints on a link to authenticate the other device as a particular authorized device.

CIDR   An RFC-standard tool for global IP address range assignment. CIDR reduces the size of Internet routers' IP routing tables, helping deal with the rapid growth of the Internet. The term classless refers to the fact that the summarized groups of networks represent a group of addresses that do not confirm to IPv4 classful (Class A, B, and C) grouping rules.

CIDR notation   *See* prefix notation.

CIR   Committed Information Rate. In Frame Relay and ATM, the average speed at which bits can be transferred over a virtual circuit according to the business contract between the customer and the service provider.

circuit switching   The switching system in which a dedicated physical circuit path must exist between the sender and the receiver for the duration of the "call." Used heavily in the telephone company network.

classful addressing   A concept in IPv4 addressing that defines a subnetted IP address as having three parts: network, subnet, and host.

classful network   An IPv4 Class A, B, or C network; called a classful network because these networks are defined by the class rules for IPv4 addressing.

classful routing   A variation of the IPv4 forwarding (routing) process that defines the particulars of how the default route is used. The default route is used only if the classful network in which the packet's destination address resides is missing from the router's routing table.

classful routing protocol   An inherent characteristic of a routing protocol. Specifically, the routing protocol does not send subnet masks in its routing updates. This requires the protocol to make assumptions about classful networks and makes it unable to support VLSM and manual route summarization.

classless addressing   A concept in IPv4 addressing that defines a subnetted IP address as having two parts: a prefix (or subnet) and a host.

classless interdomain routing (CIDR)   *See* CIDR.

classless routing   A variation of the IPv4 forwarding (routing) process that defines the particulars of how the default route is used. The default route is always used for packets whose destination IP address does not match any other routes.

classless routing protocol   An inherent characteristic of a routing protocol, specifically that the routing protocol does send subnet masks in its routing updates, thereby removing any need to make assumptions about the addresses in a particular subnet or network, making it able to support VLSM and manual route summarization.

CLI   Command-line interface. An interface that enables the user to interact with the operating system by entering commands and optional arguments.

clock rate   The speed at which a serial link encodes bits on the transmission medium.

clock source   The device to which the other devices on the link adjust their speed when using synchronous links.

clocking   The process of supplying a signal over a cable, either on a separate pin on a serial cable or as part of the signal transitions in the transmitted signal, so that the receiving device can keep synchronization with the sending device.

codec   Coder-decoder. An integrated circuit device that transforms analog voice signals into a digital bit stream and then transforms digital signals back into analog voice signals.

collision domain   A set of network interface cards (NICs) for which a frame sent by one NIC could result in a collision with a frame sent by any other NIC in the same collision domain.

command-line interface   *See* CLI.

Committed Information Rate (CIR)   *See* CIR.

configuration mode   A part of the Cisco IOS Software CLI in which the user can type configuration commands that are then added to the device's currently used configuration file (running-config).

configuration register   In Cisco routers, a 16-bit, user-configurable value that determines how the router functions during initialization. In software, the bit position is set by specifying a hexadecimal value using configuration commands.

connection establishment   The process by which a connection-oriented protocol creates a connection. With TCP, a connection is established by a three-way transmission of TCP segments.

console port   A physical socket on a router or switch to which a cable can be connected between a computer and the router/switch, for the purpose of allowing the computer to use a terminal emulator and use the CLI to configure, verify, and troubleshoot the router/switch.

contiguous network   In IPv4, a internetwork design in which packets being forwarded between any two subnets of a single classful network only pass through the subnets of that classful network.

convergence   The time required for routing protocols to react to changes in the network, removing bad routes and adding new, better routes so that the current best routes are in all the routers' routing tables.

counting to infinity   An unfortunate side effect of distance vector routing protocols in which the routers slowly increase the metric for a failed route until the metric reaches that routing protocol's finite definition of a maximum metric (called infinity).

CPE   Customer premises equipment. Any equipment related to communications that is located at the customer site, as opposed to inside the telephone company's network.

crossover cable   An Ethernet cable that swaps the pair used for transmission on one device to a pair used for receiving on the device on the opposite end of the cable. In 10BASE-T and 100BASE-TX networks, this cable swaps the pair at pins 1,2 to pins 3,6 on the other end of the cable, and the pair at pins 3,6 to pins 1,2 as well.

CSMA/CA   Carrier sense multiple access with collision avoidance. A media-access mechanism that defines how devices decide when they can send, with a goal of avoiding collisions as much as possible. IEEE WLANs use CSMA/CA.

CSMA/CD   Carrier sense multiple access collision detect. A media-access mechanism in which devices ready to transmit data first check the channel for a carrier. If no carrier is sensed for a specific period of time, a device can transmit. If two devices transmit at once, a collision occurs and is detected by all colliding devices. This collision subsequently delays retransmissions from those devices for some random length of time.

CSU/DSU   Channel service unit/data service unit. A device that connects a physical circuit installed by the telco to some CPE device, adapting between the voltages, current, framing, and connectors used on the circuit to the physical interface supported by the DTE.

cut-through switching   One of three options for internal processing on some models of Cisco LAN switches in which the frame is forwarded as soon as possible, including forwarding the first bits of the frame before the whole frame is received.

D

Database Description   An OSPF packet type that lists brief descriptions of the LSAs in the OSPF LSDB.

data-link connection identifier (DLCI)   *See* DLCI.

DCE   Data communications equipment. From a physical layer perspective, the device providing the clocking on a WAN link, typically a CSU/DSU, is the DCE. From a packet-switching perspective, the service provider's switch, to which a router might connect, is considered the DCE.

DE   Discard eligible. The bit in the Frame Relay header that, if frames must be discarded, signals a switch to choose this frame to discard instead of another frame without the DE bit set.

Dead Timer   In OSPF, a timer used for each neighbor. A router considers the neighbor to have failed if no Hellos are received from that neighbor in the time defined by the timer.

decapsulation   On a computer that receives data over a network, the process in which the device interprets the lower-layer headers and, when finished with each header, removes the header, revealing the next-higher-layer PDU.

default gateway/default router   On an IP host, the IP address of some router to which the host sends packets when the packet's destination address is on a subnet other than the local subnet.

default mask   The mask used in a Class A, B, or C network that does not create any subnets; specifically, mask 255.0.0.0 for Class A networks, 255.255.0.0 for Class B networks, and 255.255.255.0 for Class C networks.

default route   On a router, the route that is considered to match all packets that are not otherwise matched by some more specific route.

demarc   The legal term for the demarcation or separation point between the telco's equipment and the customer's equipment.

denial of service (DoS)   A type of attack whose goal is to cause problems by preventing legitimate users from being able to access services, thereby preventing the normal operation of computers and networks.

deny   An action taken with an ACL that implies that the packet is discarded.

designated port   In both STP and RSTP, a port role used to determine which of multiple interfaces, each connected to the same segment or collision domain, should forward frames to the segment. The switch advertising the lowest-cost Hello BPDU onto the segment becomes the DP.

designated router   In OSPF, on a multiaccess network, the router that wins an election and is therefore responsible for managing a streamlined process for exchanging OSPF topology information between all routers attached to that network.

DHCP   Dynamic Host Configuration Protocol. A protocol used by hosts to dynamically discover and lease an IP address, and learn the correct subnet mask, default gateway, and DNS server IP addresses.

Diffie-Hellman Key Exchange   A key exchange protocol in which two devices can exchange information over a public network. Combined with some preexisting secrets, this allows them to calculate a symmetric key known only to them.

Diffusing Update Algorithm (DUAL)   *See* DUAL.

Dijkstra Shortest Path First (SPF) algorithm   The name of the algorithm used by link-state routing protocols to analyze the LSDB and find the least-cost routes from that router to each subnet.

Direct Sequence Spread Spectrum (DSSS)   A method of encoding data for transmission over a wireless LAN in which the device uses 1 of 11 (in the USA) nearby frequencies in the 2.4-GHz range.

directed broadcast address   *See* subnet broadcast address.

disabled port   In STP, a port role for nonworking interfaces—in other words, interfaces that are not in a connect or up/up interface state.

Discarding state   An RSTP interface state in which no received frames are processed, and the switch forwards no frames out the interface, with the exception of RSTP messages.

discontiguous network   In IPv4, a internetwork design in which packets being forwarded between two subnets of a single classful network must pass through the subnets of another classful network.

distance vector   The logic behind the behavior of some interior routing protocols, such as RIP. Distance vector routing algorithms call for each router to send its entire routing table in each update, but only to its neighbors. Distance vector routing algorithms can be prone to routing loops but are computationally simpler than link-state routing algorithms.

DLCI   Data-Link Connection Identifier. The Frame Relay address that identifies a VC on a particular access link.

DNS   Domain Name System. An application layer protocol used throughout the Internet for translating hostnames into their associated IP addresses.

DS0   Digital signal level 0. A 64-kbps line or channel of a faster line inside a telco whose origins are to support a single voice call using the original voice (PCM) codecs.

DS1   Digital signal level 1. A 1.544-Mbps line from the telco, with 24 DS0 channels of 64 kbps each, plus an 8-kbps management and framing channel. Also called a T1.

DSL   Digital subscriber line. Public network technology that delivers high bandwidth over conventional telco local-loop copper wiring at limited distances. Typically used as an Internet access technology, connecting a user to an ISP.

DTE   Data terminal equipment. From a Layer 1 perspective, the DTE synchronizes its clock based on the clock sent by the DCE. From a packet-switching perspective, the DTE is the device outside the service provider's network, typically a router.

DUAL   Diffusing Update Algorithm. A convergence algorithm used in EIGRP when a route fails and a router does not have a feasible successor route. DUAL causes the routers to send EIGRP Query and Reply messages to discover alternate loop-free routes.

dual stacks   In IPv6, a mode of operation in which a host or router runs both IPv4 and IPv6.

dynamic ACL   A type of ACL that goes beyond traditional IP ACLs to dynamically permit traffic from a host if the host's user first connects to the router via Telnet and passes an authentication process.

E

E1   Similar to a T1, but used in Europe. It uses a rate of 2.048 Mbps and 32 64-kbps channels, with one channel reserved for framing and other overhead.

EIGRP   Enhanced Interior Gateway Routing Protocol. An advanced version of IGRP developed by Cisco. Provides superior convergence properties and operating efficiency and combines the advantages of link-state protocols with those of distance vector protocols.

enable mode   A part of the Cisco IOS CLI in which the user can use the most powerful and potentially disruptive commands on a router or switch, including the ability to then reach configuration mode and reconfigure the router.

encapsulation   The placement of data from a higher-layer protocol behind the header (and in some cases, between a header and trailer) of the next-lower-layer protocol. For example, an IP packet could be encapsulated in an Ethernet header and trailer before being sent over an Ethernet.

encoding   The conventions for how a device varies the electrical or optical signals sent over a cable to imply a particular binary code. For instance, a modem might encode a binary 1 or 0 by using one frequency to mean 1 and another to mean 0.

encryption   Applying a specific algorithm to data to alter the appearance of the data, making it incomprehensible to those who are not authorized to see the information.

error detection   The process of discovering whether or not a data-link level frame was changed during transmission. This process typically uses a Frame Check Sequence (FCS) field in the data-link trailer.

error disabled   An interface state on LAN switches that is the result of one of many security violations.

error recovery   The process of noticing when some transmitted data was not successfully received and resending the data until it is successfully received.

EtherChannel   A Cisco-proprietary feature in which up to eight parallel Ethernet segments between the same two devices, each using the same speed, can be combined to act as a single link for forwarding and Spanning Tree Protocol logic.

Ethernet   A series of LAN standards defined by the IEEE, originally invented by Xerox Corporation and developed jointly by Xerox, Intel, and Digital Equipment Corporation.

extended access list   A list of IOS **access-list** global configuration commands that can match multiple parts of an IP packet, including the source and destination IP address and TCP/UDP ports, for the purpose of deciding which packets to discard and which to allow through the router.

extended ping   An IOS command in which the **ping** command accepts many other options besides just the destination IP address.

Extended Service Set (ESS)   In wireless LANs, a WLAN with multiple access points to create one WLAN, allowing roaming between the APs.

exterior gateway protocol (EGP)   A routing protocol that was designed to exchange routing information between different autonomous systems.

F

feasibility condition   In EIGRP, when a router has learned of multiple routes to reach one subnet, if the best route's metric is X, the feasibility condition is another route whose reported distance is <= X.

feasible distance   In EIGRP, the metric of the best route to reach a subnet.

feasible successor In EIGRP, a route that is not the best route (successor route) but that can be used immediately if the best route fails, without causing a loop. Such a route meets the feasibility condition.

FECN Forward explicit congestion notification. The bit in the Frame Relay header that signals to anything receiving the frame (switches and DTEs) that congestion is occurring in the same direction as the frame.

filter Generally, a process or a device that screens network traffic for certain characteristics, such as source address, destination address, or protocol, and determines whether to forward or discard that traffic based on the established criteria.

firewall A device that forwards packets between the less secure and more secure parts of the network, applying rules that determine which packets are allowed to pass, and which are not.

Flash A type of read/write permanent memory that retains its contents even with no power applied to the memory, and uses no moving parts, making the memory less likely to fail over time.

flooding The result of the LAN switch forwarding process for broadcasts and unknown unicast frames. Switches forward these frames out all interfaces, except the interface in which the frame arrived. Switches also forward multicasts by default, although this behavior can be changed.

flow control The process of regulating the amount of data sent by a sending computer toward a receiving computer. Several flow control mechanisms exist, including TCP flow control, which uses windowing.

forward To send a frame received in one interface out another interface toward its ultimate destination by way of an internetworking device.

forward acknowledgment A process used by protocols that do error recovery in which the number that acknowledges data lists the next data that should be sent, not the last data that was successfully received.

forward delay An STP timer, defaulting to 15 seconds, used to dictate how long an interface stays in both the Listening state and Learning state. Also called the forward delay timer.

forward route From one host's perspective, the route over which a packet travels from that host to some other host.

Forwarding state An STP and RSTP port state in which an interface operates unrestricted by STP.

four-wire circuit A line from the telco with four wires, composed of two twisted-pair wires. Each pair is used to send in one direction, so a four-wire circuit allows full duplex communication.

fragment-free switching One of three internal processing options on some Cisco LAN switches in which the first bits of the frame may be forwarded before the entire frame is received, but not until the first 64 bytes of the frame are received, in which case, in a well-designed LAN, collision fragments should not occur as a result of this forwarding logic.

frame   A term referring to a data-link header and trailer, plus the data encapsulated between the header and trailer.

Frame Relay   An international standard data-link protocol that defines the capabilities to create a frame-switched (packet-switched) service, allowing DTE devices (typically routers) to send data to many other devices using a single physical connection to the Frame Relay service.

Frame Relay DCE   The Frame Relay switch.

Frame Relay DTE   The customer device connected to a Frame Relay access link, typically a router.

Frame Relay mapping   The information that correlates, or maps, a Frame Relay DLCI to the Layer 3 address of the DTE on the other end of the VC identified by the local DLCI.

framing   The conventions for how Layer 2 interprets the bits sent according to OSI Layer 1. For example, after an electrical signal has been received and converted to binary, framing identifies the information fields inside the data.

Frequency Hopping Spread Spectrum   A method of encoding data on a wireless LAN in which consecutive transmissions occur on different nearby frequency bands as compared with the prior transmission. Not used in modern WLAN standards.

FTP   File Transfer Protocol. An application protocol, part of the TCP/IP protocol stack, used to transfer files between network nodes. FTP is defined in RFC 959.

full duplex   Generically, any communication in which two communicating devices can concurrently send and receive data. Specifically for Ethernet LANs, the ability of both devices to send and receive at the same time. This is allowed when there are only two stations in a collision domain. Full duplex is enabled by turning off the CSMA/CD collision detection logic.

full mesh   A network topology in which more than two devices can physically communicate and, by choice, all pairs of devices are allowed to communicate directly.

Full state   In OSPF, a neighbor state that implies that the two routers have exchanged the complete (full) contents of their respective LSDBs.

full update   With IP routing protocols, the general concept that a routing protocol update lists all known routes. *See also* partial update.

fully adjacent   In OSPF, a characterization of the state of a neighbor in which the two neighbors have reached the Full state.

G

global unicast address   A type of unicast IPv6 address that has been allocated from a range of public globally unique IP addresses as registered through ICANN, its member agencies, and other registries or ISPs.

H

half duplex   Generically, any communication in which only one device at a time can send data. In Ethernet LANs, the normal result of the CSMA/CD algorithm that enforces the rule that only one device should send at any point in time.

HDLC   High-Level Data-Link Control. A bit-oriented synchronous data link layer protocol developed by the International Organization for Standardization (ISO). Derived from synchronous data-link control (SDLC), HDLC specifies a data encapsulation method on synchronous serial links using frame characters and checksums.

head end   The upstream, transmit end of a cable TV (CATV) installation.

Hello   (Multiple definitions) 1) A protocol used by OSPF routers to discover, establish, and maintain neighbor relationships. 2) A protocol used by EIGRP routers to discover, establish, and maintain neighbor relationships. 3) In STP, refers to the name of the periodic message sourced by the root bridge in a spanning tree.

Hello BPDU   The STP and RSTP message used for the majority of STP communications, listing the root's Bridge ID, the sending device's Bridge ID, and the sending device's cost with which to reach the root.

Hello interval   With OSPF and EIGRP, an interface timer that dictates how often the router should send Hello messages.

Hello timer   In STP, the time interval at which the root switch should send Hello BPDUs.

holddown   A Distance Vector protocol state assigned to a route placed so that routers neither advertise the route nor accept advertisements about it for a specific length of time (the holddown timer). Holddown is used to flush bad information about a route from all routers in the network. A route typically is placed in holddown when a link in that route fails.

host   Any device that uses an IP address.

host address   The IP address assigned to a network card on a computer.

host part   A term used to describe a part of an IPv4 address that is used to uniquely identify a host inside a subnet. The host part is identified by the bits of value 0 in the subnet mask.

host route   A route with a /32 mask, which by virtue of this mask represents a route to a single host IP address.

HTML   Hypertext Markup Language. A simple document-formatting language that uses tags to indicate how a given part of a document should be interpreted by a viewing application, such as a web browser.

HTTP   Hypertext Transfer Protocol. The protocol used by web browsers and web servers to transfer files, such as text and graphic files.

hub   A LAN device that provides a centralized connection point for LAN cabling, repeating any received electrical signal out all other ports, thereby creating a logical bus. Hubs do not interpret the electrical signals as a frame of bits, so hubs are considered to be Layer 1 devices.

I

ICMP   Internet Control Message Protocol. A TCP/IP network layer protocol that reports errors and provides other information relevant to IP packet processing.

IEEE   Institute of Electrical and Electronics Engineers. A professional organization that develops communications and network standards, among other activities.

IEEE 802.11   The IEEE base standard for wireless LANs.

IEEE 802.2   An IEEE LAN protocol that specifies an implementation of the LLC sublayer of the data link layer.

IEEE 802.3   A set of IEEE LAN protocols that specifies the many variations of what is known today as an Ethernet LAN.

IEEE 802.1ad   The IEEE standard for the functional equivalent of the Cisco-proprietary EtherChannel.

IEEE 802.1d   The IEEE standard for the original Spanning Tree Protocol.

IEEE 802.1Q   The IEEE-standard VLAN trunking protocol. 802.1Q includes the concept of a native VLAN, for which no VLAN header is added, and a 4-byte VLAN header is inserted after the original frame's type/length field.

IEEE 802.1s   The IEEE standard for Multiple Instances of Spanning Tree (MIST), which allows for load balancing of traffic among different VLANs.

IEEE 802.1w   The IEEE standard for an enhanced version of STP, called Rapid STP, which speeds convergence.

IGRP   Interior Gateway Routing Protocol. An old, no-longer-supported Interior Gateway Protocol (IGP) developed by Cisco.

inactivity timer   For switch MAC address tables, a timer associated with each entry, which counts time upwards from 0 and is reset to 0 each time a switch receives a frame with the same MAC address. The entries with the largest timers can be removed to make space for additional MAC address table entries.

inferior Hello   When comparing two or more received Hello BPDUs, a Hello that lists a numerically larger root Bridge ID than another Hello, or a Hello that lists the same root Bridge ID but with a larger cost.

infinity   In the context of IP routing protocols, a finite metric value defined by the routing protocol that is used to represent an unusable route in a routing protocol update.

infrastructure mode   A mode of wireless LAN (WLAN) operation in which WLAN clients send and receive data with an access point (AP), which allows the clients to communicate with the wired infrastructure through the AP. Clients do not send data to each other directly; the AP must receive the data from one client, and then send the data to the other WLAN client.

inside global   A NAT term referring to the IP address used for a host inside the trusted part of the network, but in packets as they traverse the global (untrusted) part of the network.

inside local   A NAT term referring to the IP address used for a host inside the trusted part of the network, but in packets as they traverse the local (trusted) part of the network.

interior gateway protocol (IGP)   A routing protocol designed to be used to exchange routing information inside a single autonomous system. *See* interior routing protocol.

interior routing protocol   A routing protocol designed for use within a single organization.

Inter-Switch Link (ISL)   The Cisco-proprietary VLAN trunking protocol that predated 802.1Q by many years. ISL defines a 26-byte header that encapsulates the original Ethernet frame.

intrusion detection system (IDS)   A security function that examines more complex traffic patterns against a list of both known attack signatures and general characteristics of how attacks may be carried out, rating each perceived threat and reporting the threats.

intrusion prevention system (IPS)   A security function that examines more complex traffic patterns against a list of both known attack signatures and general characteristics of how attacks may be carried out, rating each perceived threat and reacting to prevent the more significant threats.

Inverse ARP   A Frame Relay protocol with which a router announces its Layer 3 address over a VC, thereby informing the neighbor of useful Layer-3-to-Layer-2 mapping information.

IOS   Cisco operating system software that provides the majority of a router's or switch's features, with the hardware providing the remaining features.

IOS Image   A file that contains the IOS.

IP   Internet Protocol. The network layer protocol in the TCP/IP stack, providing routing and logical addressing standards and services.

IP address   In IP Version 4 (IPv4), a 32-bit address assigned to hosts using TCP/IP. Each address consists of a network number, an optional subnetwork number, and a host number. The network and subnetwork numbers together are used for routing, and the host number is used to address an individual host within the network or subnetwork.

IP Control Protocol (IPCP)   A control protocol defined as part of PPP for the purpose of initializing and controlling the sending of IPv4 packets over a PPP link.

IPsec   The term referring to the IP Security Protocols, which is an architecture for providing encryption and authentication services, typically when creating VPN services through an IP network.

ISDN   Integrated Services Digital Network. A service offered by telephone companies that permits telephone networks to carry data, voice, and other traffic. Often used as an Internet access technology, as well as dial backup when routers lose their normal WAN communications links.

ISL   Inter-Switch Link. A Cisco-proprietary protocol that maintains VLAN information as traffic flows between switches and routers.

ISO   International Organization for Standardization. An international organization that is responsible for a wide range of standards, including many standards relevant to networking. The ISO developed the OSI reference model, a popular networking reference model.

ISP prefix   In IPv6, the prefix that describes an address block that has been assigned to an ISP by some Internet registry.

K

keepalive   A feature of many data-link protocols in which the router sends messages periodically to let the neighboring router know that the first router is still alive and well.

L

L4PDU   The data compiled by a Layer 4 protocol, including Layer 4 headers and encapsulated high-layer data, but not including lower-layer headers and trailers.

LAPF   Link Access Procedure Frame Bearer Services. Defines the basic Frame Relay header and trailer. The header includes DLCI, FECN, BECN, and DE bits.

Layer 3 protocol   A protocol that has characteristics like OSI Layer 3, which defines logical addressing and routing. IP, IPX, and AppleTalk DDP are all Layer 3 protocols.

learning   The process used by switches for discovering MAC addresses, and their relative location, by looking at the source MAC address of all frames received by a bridge or switch.

Learning state   In STP, a temporary port state in which the interface does not forward frames, but it can begin to learn MAC addresses from frames received on the interface.

leased line   A serial communications circuit between two points, provided by some service provider, typically a telephone company (telco). Because the telco does not sell a physical cable between the two endpoints, instead charging a monthly fee for the ability to send bits between the two sites, the service is considered to be a leased service.

Link Control Protocol   A control protocol defined as part of PPP for the purpose of initializing and maintaining a PPP link.

link local address   A type of unicast IPv6 address that represents an interface on a single data link. Packets sent to a link local address cross only that particular link and are never forwarded to other subnets by a router. Used for communications that do not need to leave the local link, such as neighbor discovery.

link state   A classification of the underlying algorithm used in some routing protocols. Link-state protocols build a detailed database that lists links (subnets) and their state (up, down), from which the best routes can then be calculated.

link-state advertisement (LSA)   In OSPF, the name of the data structure that resides inside the LSDB and describes in detail the various components in a network, including routers and links (subnets).

link-state database (LSDB)   In OSPF, the data structure in RAM of a router that holds the various LSAs, with the collective LSAs representing the entire topology of the network.

link-state request   An OSPF packet used to ask a neighboring router to send a particular LSA.

link-state update   An OSPF packet used to send an LSA to a neighboring router.

Listening state   A temporary STP port state that occurs immediately when a blocking interface must be moved to a Forwarding state. The switch times out MAC table entries during this state. It also ignores frames received on the interface and doesn't forward any frames out the interface.

LLC   Logical Link Control. The higher of the two data link layer sublayers defined by the IEEE. Synonymous with IEEE 802.2.

local loop   A line from the premises of a telephone subscriber to the telephone company CO.

Local Management Interface (LMI)   A Frame Relay protocol used between a DTE (router) and DCE (Frame Relay switch). LMI acts as a keepalive mechanism. The absence of LMI messages means that the other device has failed. It also tells the DTE about the existence of each VC and DLCI, along with its status.

logical address   A generic reference to addresses as defined by Layer 3 protocols, which do not have to be concerned with the physical details of the underlying physical media. Used mainly to contrast these addresses with data-link addresses, which are generically considered to be physical addresses because they differ based on the type of physical medium.

LSA   *See* link-state advertisement.

M

MAC   Media Access Control. The lower of the two sublayers of the data link layer defined by the IEEE. Synonymous with IEEE 802.3 for Ethernet LANs.

MAC address   A standardized data link layer address that is required for every device that connects to a LAN. Ethernet MAC addresses are 6 bytes long and are controlled by the IEEE. Also known as a *hardware address*, a *MAC layer address*, and a *physical address*.

mask   *See* subnet mask.

MaxAge   In STP, a timer that states how long a switch should wait when it no longer receives Hellos from the root switch before acting to reconverge the STP topology. Also called the MaxAge Timer.

metric   A unit of measure used by routing protocol algorithms to determine the best route for traffic to use to reach a particular destination.

microsegmentation   The process in LAN design by which every switch port connects to a single device, with no hubs connected to the switch ports, creating a separate collision domain per interface. The term's origin relates to the fact that one definition for the word "segment" is "collision domain," with a switch separating each switch port into a separate collision domain or segment.

MLP   Multilink Point-to-Point Protocol. A method of splitting, recombining, and sequencing frames across multiple point-to-point WAN links.

modem   Modulator-demodulator. A device that converts between digital and analog signals so that a computer may send data to another computer using analog telephone lines. At the source, a modem converts digital signals to a form suitable for transmission over analog communication facilities. At the destination, the analog signals are returned to their digital form.

MTU   Maximum transmission unit. The maximum packet size, in bytes, that a particular interface can handle.

multimode   A type of fiber-optic cabling with a larger core than single-mode cabling, allowing light to enter at multiple angles. Such cabling has lower bandwidth than single-mode fiber but requires a typically cheaper light source, such as an LED rather than a laser.

N

name server   A server connected to a network that resolves network names into network addresses.

named access list   An ACL that identifies the various statements in the ACL based on a name, rather than a number.

NAT   Network Address Translation. A mechanism for reducing the need for globally unique IP addresses. NAT allows an organization with addresses that are not globally unique to connect to the Internet by translating those addresses into public addresses in the globally routable address space.

NAT overload   *See* Port Address Translation (PAT).

NAT-PT   An IPv6 feature in which packets are translated between IPv4 and IPv6.

NBMA   *See* nonbroadcast multiaccess.

neighbor   In routing protocols, another router with which a router decides to exchange routing information.

Neighbor Discovery Protocol (NDP)   A protocol that is part of the IPv6 protocol suite, used to discover and exchange information about devices on the same subnet (neighbors). In particular, it replaces the IPv4 ARP protocol.

neighbor table   For OSPF and EIGRP, a list of routers that have reached neighbor status.

network   A collection of computers, printers, routers, switches, and other devices that can communicate with each other over some transmission medium.

network address   *See* network number.

network broadcast address   In IPv4, a special address in each classful network that can be used to broadcast a packet to all hosts in that same classful network. Numerically, the address has the same value as the network number in the network part of the address, and all 255s in the host octets—for example, 10.255.255.255 is the network broadcast address for classful network 10.0.0.0.

network number   A number that uses dotted decimal notation like IP addresses, but the number itself represents all hosts in a single Class A, B, or C IP network.

network part   The portion of an IPv4 address that is either 1, 2, or 3 octets/bytes long, based on whether the address is in a Class A, B, or C network.

networking model   A generic term referring to any set of protocols and standards collected into a comprehensive grouping that, when followed by the devices in a network, allows all the devices to communicate. Examples include TCP/IP and OSI.

nonbroadcast multiaccess (NBMA)   A characterization of a type of Layer 2 network in which more than two devices connect to the network, but the network does not allow broadcast frames to be sent to all devices on the network.

NVRAM   Nonvolatile RAM. A type of random-access memory (RAM) that retains its contents when a unit is powered off.

O

ordered data transfer   A networking function, included in TCP, in which the protocol defines how the sending host should number the data transmitted, defines how the receiving device should attempt to reorder the data if it arrives out of order, and specifies to discard the data if it cannot be delivered in order.

Orthogonal Frequency Division Multiplexing   A method of encoding data in wireless LANs that allows for generally higher data rates than the earlier FHSS and DSSS encoding methods.

OSI   Open System Interconnection reference model. A network architectural model developed by the ISO. The model consists of seven layers, each of which specifies particular network functions, such as addressing, flow control, error control, encapsulation, and reliable message transfer.

OSPF   Open Shortest Path First. A popular link-state IGP that uses a link-state database and the Shortest Path First (SPF) algorithm to calculate the best routes to reach each known subnet.

outside global   A NAT term referring to an IP address used for a host in the outside (untrusted) part of the network, for packets as they traverse the outside part of the network, which is usually the global Internet.

outside local   A NAT term referring to an IP address used for a host in the outside (untrusted) part of the network, for packets as they traverse the inside (trusted), or local, part of the network.

overlapping subnets An (incorrect) IP subnet design condition in which one subnet's range of addresses includes addresses in the range of another subnet.

P

packet A logical grouping of information that includes the network layer header and encapsulated data, but specifically does not include any headers and trailers below the network layer.

packet switching A WAN service in which each DTE device connects to a telco using a single physical line, with the possibility of being able to forward traffic to all other sites connected to the same service. The telco switch makes the forwarding decision based on an address in the packet header.

PAP Password Authentication Protocol. A PPP authentication protocol that allows PPP peers to authenticate one another.

partial mesh A network topology in which more than two devices could physically communicate but, by choice, only a subset of the pairs of devices connected to the network is allowed to communicate directly.

partial update With IP routing protocols, the general concept that a routing protocol update lists a subset of all known routes. *See also* full update.

PAT *See* Port Address Translation.

PCM Pulse code modulation. A technique of encoding analog voice into a 64-kbps data stream by sampling with 8-bit resolution at a rate of 8000 times per second.

PDU Protocol data unit. An OSI term to refer generically to a grouping of information by a particular layer of the OSI model. More specifically, an L*x*PDU would imply the data and headers as defined by Layer *x*.

periodic update With routing protocols, the concept that the routing protocol advertises routes in a routing update on a regular periodic basis. This is typical of distance vector routing protocols.

permanent virtual circuit (PVC) A preconfigured communications path between two Frame Relay DTEs, identified by a local DLCI on each Frame Relay access link, that provides the functional equivalent of a leased circuit, but without a physical leased line for each VC.

permit An action taken with an ACL that implies that the packet is allowed to proceed through the router and be forwarded.

ping Packet Internet groper. An Internet Control Message Protocol (ICMP) echo message and its reply; ping often is used in IP networks to test the reachability of a network device.

pinout The documentation and implementation of which wires inside a cable connect to each pin position in any connector.

poison reverse A distance vector poisoned route advertisement for a subnet that would not have been advertised because of split-horizon rules but is now advertised as a poison route.

poisoned route   A route in a routing protocol's advertisement that lists a subnet with a special metric value, called an infinite metric, that designates the route as a failed route.

port   (Multiple definitions) 1) In TCP and UDP, a number that is used to uniquely identify the application process that either sent (source port) or should receive (destination port) data. 2) In LAN switching, another term for switch interface.

Port Address Translation (PAT)   A NAT feature in which one inside global IP address supports over 65,000 concurrent TCP and UDP connections.

port number   A field in a TCP or UDP header that identifies the application that either sent (source port) or should receive (destination port) the data inside the data segment.

PortFast   A switch STP feature in which a port is placed in an STP Forwarding state as soon as the interface comes up, bypassing the Listening and Learning states. This feature is meant for ports connected to end-user devices.

positive acknowledgment and retransmission (PAR)   A generic reference to how the error recovery feature works in many protocols, including TCP, in which the receiver must send an acknowledgment that either implies that the data was (positively) received, or send an acknowledgment that implies that some data was lost, so the sender can then resend the lost data.

Power-on Self Test (POST)   The process on any computer, including routers and switches, in which the computer hardware first runs diagnostics on the required hardware before even trying to load a bootstrap program.

PPP   Point-to-Point Protocol. A data-link protocol that provides router-to-router and host-to-network connections over synchronous and asynchronous circuits.

prefix notation   A shorter way to write a subnet mask in which the number of binary 1s in the mask is simply written in decimal. For instance, /24 denotes the subnet mask with 24 binary 1 bits in the subnet mask. The number of bits of value binary 1 in the mask is considered to be the prefix length.

PRI   Primary Rate Interface. An Integrated Services Digital Network (ISDN) interface to primary rate access. Primary rate access consists of a single 64-kbps D channel plus 23 (T1) or 30 (E1) B channels for voice or data.

private addresses   IP addresses in several Class A, B, and C networks that are set aside for use inside private organizations. These addresses, as defined in RFC 1918, are not routable through the Internet.

private IP network   One of several classful IPv4 network numbers that will never be assigned for use in the Internet, meant for use inside a single enterprise.

private key   A secret value used in public/private key encryption systems. Either encrypts a value that can then be decrypted using the matching public key, or decrypts a value that was previously encrypted with the matching public key.

problem isolation   The part of the troubleshooting process in which the engineer attempts to rule out possible causes of the problem, narrowing the possible causes until the root cause of the problem can be identified.

protocol data unit (PDU)   A generic term referring to the header defined by some layer of a networking model, and the data encapsulated by the header (and possibly trailer) of that layer, but specifically not including any lower-layer headers and trailers.

protocol type   A field in the IP header that identifies the type of header that follows the IP header, typically a Layer 4 header, such as TCP or UDP. ACLs can examine the protocol type to match packets with a particular value in this header field.

Protocol Type field   A field in a LAN header that identifies the type of header that follows the LAN header. Includes the DIX Ethernet Type field, the IEEE 802.2 DSAP field, and the SNAP protocol Type field.

PSTN   Public Switched Telephone Network. A general term referring to the variety of telephone networks and services in place worldwide. Sometimes called *POTS*, or Plain Old Telephone Service.

PTT   Post, telephone, and telegraph. A government agency that provides telephone services. PTTs exist in most areas outside of North America and provide both local and long-distance telephone services.

public IP address   An IP address that is part of a registered network number, as assigned by an Internet Assigned Numbers Authority (IANA) member agency, so that only the organization to which the address is registered is allowed to use the address. Routers in the Internet should have routes allowing them to forward packets to all the publicly registered IP addresses.

public key   A secret value used in public/private key encryption systems. Either encrypts a value that can then be decrypted using the matching private key, or decrypts a value that was previously encrypted with the matching private key.

PVC   *See* permanent virtual circuit.

R

RAM   Random-access memory. A type of volatile memory that can be read and written by a microprocessor.

Rapid Spanning Tree Protocol (RSTP)   Defined in IEEE 802.1w. Defines an improved version of STP that converges much more quickly and consistently than STP (802.1d).

reflexive ACL   A type of ACL that goes beyond traditional IP ACLs to monitor the addition of new user sessions. The router reacts to add an ACL entry that matches that session's IP addresses and TCP or UDP port numbers.

Regional Internet Registry (RIR)   The generic term for one of five current organizations that are responsible for assigning the public, globally unique IPv4 and IPv6 address space.

registry prefix   In IPv6, the prefix that describes a block of public, globally unique IPv6 addresses assigned to a Regional Internet Registry by ICANN.

reported distance   From one EIGRP router's perspective, the metric for a subnet as calculated on a neighboring router and reported in a routing update to the first router.

reverse route   From one host's perspective, for packets sent back to the host from another host, the route over which the packet travels.

RFC   Request For Comments. A document used as the primary means for communicating information about the TCP/IP protocols. Some RFCs are designated by the Internet Architecture Board (IAB) as Internet standards, and others are informational. RFCs are available online from numerous sources, including http://www.rfc-editor.org/.

RIP   Routing Information Protocol. An Interior Gateway Protocol (IGP) that uses distance vector logic and router hop count as the metric. RIP Version 1 (RIP-1) has become unpopular, with RIP Version 2 (RIP-2) providing more features, including support for VLSM.

RJ-45   A popular type of cabling connector used for Ethernet cabling. It is similar to the RJ-11 connector used for telephone wiring in homes in the United States. RJ-45 allows the connection of eight wires.

ROM   Read-only memory. A type of nonvolatile memory that can be read but not written by the microprocessor.

ROMMON   A shorter name for ROM Monitor, which is a low-level operating system that can be loaded into Cisco routers for several seldom needed maintenance tasks, including password recovery and loading a new IOS when Flash memory has been corrupted.

root bridge   *See* root switch.

root cause   A troubleshooting term that refers to the reason why a problem exists, specifically a reason for which, if changed, the problem would either be solved or changed to a different problem.

root port   In STP, the one port on a nonroot switch in which the least-cost Hello is received. Switches put root ports in a Forwarding state.

root switch   In STP, the switch that wins the election by virtue of having the lowest Bridge ID, and, as a result, sends periodic Hello BPDUs (the default is 2 seconds).

routable protocol   *See* routed protocol.

route summarization   The process of combining multiple routes into a single advertised route, for the purpose of reducing the number of entries in routers' IP routing tables.

routed protocol   A Layer 3 protocol that defines a packet that can be routed, such as IPv4 and IPv6. Examples of routed protocols include AppleTalk, DECnet, and IP.

router ID (RID)   In OSPF, a 32-bit number, written in dotted decimal, that uniquely identifies each router.

Router Security Device Manager   The administrative web-based interface on a router that allows for configuration and monitoring of the router, including the configuration of DHCP and NAT/PAT.

routing protocol   A set of messages and processes with which routers can exchange information about routes to reach subnets in a particular network. Examples of routing protocols include the Enhanced Interior Gateway Routing Protocol (EIGRP), the Open Shortest Path First (OSPF) protocol, and the Routing Information Protocol (RIP).

routing table   A list of routes in a router, with each route listing the destination subnet and mask, the router interface out which to forward packets destined to that subnet, and, as needed, the next-hop router's IP address.

routing update   A generic reference to any routing protocol's messages in which it sends routing information to a neighbor.

RSTP   *See* Rapid Spanning Tree Protocol.

running-config file   In Cisco IOS switches and routers, the name of the file that resides in RAM memory, holding the device's currently used configuration.

RxBoot   A limited-function version of IOS stored in ROM in some older models of Cisco routers, for the purpose of performing some seldom needed low-level functions, including loading a new IOS into Flash memory when Flash has been deleted or corrupted.

S

same-layer interaction   The communication between two networking devices for the purposes of the functions defined at a particular layer of a networking model, with that communication happening by using a header defined by that layer of the model. The two devices set values in the header, send the header and encapsulated data, with the receiving device(s) interpreting the header to decide what action to take.

secondary IP address   The second (or more) IP address configured on a router interface, using the **secondary** keyword on the **ip address** command.

Secure Shell (SSH)   A TCP/IP application layer protocol that supports terminal emulation between a client and server, using dynamic key exchange and encryption to keep the communications private.

Secure Sockets Layer (SSL)   A security protocol that is integrated into commonly used web browsers that provides encryption and authentication services between the browser and a website.

segment   In TCP, a term used to describe a TCP header and its encapsulated data (also called an *L4PDU*). Also in TCP, the process of accepting a large chunk of data from the application layer and breaking it into smaller pieces that fit into TCP segments. In Ethernet, a segment is either a single Ethernet cable or a single collision domain (no matter how many cables are used).

segmentation   The process of breaking a large piece of data from an application into pieces appropriate in size to be sent through the network.

serial cable   A type of cable with many different styles of connectors used to connect a router to an external CSU/DSU on a leased-line installation.

Service Set Identifier (SSID)   A text value used in wireless LANs to uniquely identify a single WLAN.

setup mode   An option on Cisco IOS switches and routers that prompts the user for basic configuration information, resulting in new running-config and startup-config files.

shared Ethernet   An Ethernet that uses a hub, or even the original coaxial cabling, which results in the devices having to take turns sending data, sharing the available bandwidth.

shared key   A reference to a security key whose value is known by both the sender and receiver.

single-mode   A type of fiber-optic cabling with a narrow core that allows light to enter only at a single angle. Such cabling has a higher bandwidth than multimode fiber but requires a light source with a narrow spectral width (such as a laser).

site prefix   In IPv6, the prefix that describes a public globally unique IPv6 address block that has been assigned to an end-user organization (for example, an Enterprise or government agency). The assignment typically is made by an ISP or Internet registry.

sliding windows   For protocols such as TCP that allow the receiving device to dictate the amount of data the sender can send before receiving an acknowledgment—a concept called a window—a reference to the fact that the mechanism to grant future windows is typically just a number that grows upwards slowly after each acknowledgment, sliding upward.

SLSM   Static-length subnet mask. The usage of the same subnet mask for all subnets of a single Class A, B, or C network.

SONET   Synchronous Optical Network. A standard format for transporting a wide range of digital telecommunications services over optical fiber.

Spanning Tree Protocol (STP)   A protocol defined by IEEE standard 802.1d. Allows switches and bridges to create a redundant LAN, with the protocol dynamically causing some ports to block traffic, so that the bridge/switch forwarding logic will not cause frames to loop indefinitely around the LAN.

split horizon   A distant vector routing technique in which information about routes is prevented from exiting the router interface through which that information was received. Split horizon updates are useful in preventing routing loops.

SSL   *See* Secure Sockets Layer.

standard access list   A list of IOS global configuration commands that can match only a packet's source IP address for the purpose of deciding which packets to discard and which to allow through the router.

star   A network topology in which endpoints on a network are connected to a common central device by point-to-point links.

startup-config file   In Cisco IOS switches and routers, the name of the file that resides in NVRAM memory, holding the device's configuration that will be loaded into RAM as the running-config file when the device is next reloaded or powered on.

stateful DHCP   A term used in IPv6 to contrast with stateless DHCP. Stateful DHCP keeps track of which clients have been assigned which IPv6 addresses (state information).

stateless autoconfiguration   A feature of IPv6 in which a host or router can be assigned an IPv6 unicast address without the need for a stateful DHCP server.

stateless DHCP   A term used in IPv6 to contrast with stateful DHCP. Stateless DHCP servers don't lease IPv6 addresses to clients. Instead, they supply other useful information, such as DNS server IP addresses, but with no need to track information about the clients (state information).

store-and-forward switching   One of three internal processing options on some Cisco LAN switches in which the Ethernet frame must be completely received before the switch can begin forwarding the first bit of the frame.

STP   Shielded twisted pair. Shielded twisted-pair cabling has a layer of shielded insulation to reduce electromagnetic interference (EMI).

straight-through cable   In Ethernet, a cable that connects the wire on pin 1 on one end of the cable to pin 1 on the other end of the cable, pin 2 on one end to pin 2 on the other end, and so on.

subinterface   One of the virtual interfaces on a single physical interface.

subnet   Subdivisions of a Class A, B, or C network, as configured by a network administrator. Subnets allow a single Class A, B, or C network to be used instead of multiple networks, and still allow for a large number of groups of IP addresses, as is required for efficient IP routing.

subnet address   *See* subnet number.

subnet broadcast address   A special address in each subnet, specifically the largest numeric address in the subnet, designed so that packets sent to this address should be delivered to all hosts in that subnet.

subnet mask   A 32-bit number that numerically describes the format of an IP address by representing the combined network and subnet bits in the address with mask bit values of 1, and representing the host bits in the address with mask bit values of 0.

subnet number   In IP v4, a dotted decimal number that represents all addresses in a single subnet. Numerically, the smallest value in the range of numbers in a subnet, reserved so that it cannot be used as a unicast IP address by a host.

subnet part   In a subnetted IPv4 address, interpreted with classful addressing rules, one of three parts of the structure of an IP address, with the subnet part uniquely identifying different subnets of a classful IP network.

subnet prefix   In IPv6, a term for the prefix that is assigned to each data link, acting like a subnet in IPv4.

subnetting   The process of subdividing a Class A, B, or C network into smaller groups called subnets.

successor   In EIGRP, the route to reach a subnet that has the best metric and should be placed in the IP routing table.

summary route   A route created via configuration commands to represent routes to one or more subnets with a single route, thereby reducing the size of the routing table.

SVC Switched virtual circuit. A VC that is set up dynamically when needed.

switch A network device that filters, forwards, and floods frames based on each frame's destination address. The switch operates at the data link layer of the Open System Interconnection (OSI) reference model.

switched Ethernet An Ethernet that uses a switch, and particularly not a hub, so that the devices connected to one switch port do not have to contend to use the bandwidth available on another port. This term contrasts with *shared Ethernet*, in which the devices must share bandwidth, whereas switched Ethernet provides much more capacity, as the devices do not have to share the available bandwidth.

symmetric A feature of many Internet access technologies in which the downstream transmission rate is the same as the upstream transmission rate.

synchronous The imposition of time ordering on a bit stream. Practically, a device will try to use the same speed as another device on the other end of a serial link. However, by examining transitions between voltage states on the link, the device can notice slight variations in the speed on each end and can adjust its speed accordingly.

T

T1 A line from the telco that allows transmission of data at 1.544 Mbps, with the ability to treat the line as 24 different 64-kbps DS0 channels (plus 8 kbps of overhead).

TCP Transmission Control Protocol. A connection-oriented transport layer TCP/IP protocol that provides reliable data transmission.

TCP/IP Transmission Control Protocol/Internet Protocol. A common name for the suite of protocols developed by the U.S. Department of Defense in the 1970s to support the construction of worldwide internetworks. TCP and IP are the two best-known protocols in the suite.

telco A common abbreviation for telephone company.

Telnet The standard terminal-emulation application layer protocol in the TCP/IP protocol stack. Telnet is used for remote terminal connection, enabling users to log in to remote systems and use resources as if they were connected to a local system. Telnet is defined in RFC 854.

TFTP Trivial File Transfer Protocol. An application protocol that allows files to be transferred from one computer to another over a network, but with only a few features, making the software require little storage space.

topology database The structured data that describes the network topology to a routing protocol. Link-state and balanced hybrid routing protocols use topology tables, from which they build the entries in the routing table.

trace Short for traceroute. A program available on many systems that traces the path that a packet takes to a destination. It is used mostly to debug routing problems between hosts.

transparent bridge   The name of a networking device that was a precursor to modern LAN switches. Bridges forward frames between LAN segments based on the destination MAC address. Transparent bridging is so named because the presence of bridges is transparent to network end nodes.

triggered update   A routing protocol feature in which the routing protocol does not wait for the next periodic update when something changes in the network, instead immediately sending a routing update.

trunk   In campus LANs, an Ethernet segment over which the devices add a VLAN header that identifies the VLAN in which the frame exists.

trunk interface   On a LAN switch, an interface that is currently using either 802.1Q or ISL trunking.

trunking   Also called *VLAN trunking*. A method (using either the Cisco ISL protocol or the IEEE 802.1q protocol) to support multiple VLANs that have members on more than one switch.

trunking administrative mode   The configured trunking setting on a Cisco switch interface, as configured with the **switchport mode** command.

trunking operational mode   The current behavior of a Cisco switch interface for VLAN trunking.

twisted pair   Transmission medium consisting of two insulated wires, with the wires twisted around each other in a spiral. An electrical circuit flows over the wire pair, with the current in opposite directions on each wire, which significantly reduces the interference between the two wires.

two-way state   In OSPF, a neighbor state that implies that the router has exchanged Hellos with the neighbor, and all required parameters match.

U

UDP   User Datagram Protocol. Connectionless transport layer protocol in the TCP/IP protocol stack. UDP is a simple protocol that exchanges datagrams without acknowledgments or guaranteed delivery.

unique local address   A type of IPv6 unicast address meant as a replacement for IPv4 private addresses.

unknown unicast frame   An Ethernet frame whose destination MAC address is not listed in a switch's MAC address table, so the switch must flood the frame.

up and up   Jargon referring to the two interface states on a Cisco IOS router or switch (line status and protocol status), with the first "up" referring to the line status, and the second "up" referring to the protocol status. An interface in this state should be able to pass data-link frames.

update timer   The time interval that regulates how often a routing protocol sends its next periodic routing updates. Distance vector routing protocols send full routing updates every update interval.

URL Universal Resource Locator. A standard for how to refer to any piece of information retrievable via a TCP/IP network, most notably used to identify web pages. For example, http://www.cisco.com/univercd is a URL that identifies the protocol (HTTP), hostname (www. cisco.com), and web page (/univercd).

user mode A mode of the user interface to a router or switch in which the user can type only nondisruptive EXEC commands, generally just to look at the current status, but not to change any operational settings.

UTP Unshielded twisted pair. A type of cabling, standardized by the Electronics Industry Alliance (EIA) and Telecommunications Industry Association (TIA), that holds twisted pairs of copper wires (typically four pair), and does not contain any shielding from outside interference.

V

variable-length subnet masking (VLSM) Also represents variable-length subnet masks. *See* VLSM.

variable-length subnet masks (VLSM) The capability to specify a different subnet mask for the same Class A, B, or C network number on different subnets. VLSM can help optimize available address space.

variance IGRP and EIGRP compute their metrics, so the metrics for different routes to the same subnet seldom have the exact same value. The variance value is multiplied with the lower metric when multiple routes to the same subnet exist. If the product is larger than the metrics for other routes, the routes are considered to have "equal" metric, allowing multiple routes to be added to the routing table.

VC Virtual circuit. A logical concept that represents the path that frames travel between DTEs. VCs are particularly useful when comparing Frame Relay to leased physical circuits.

virtual circuit In packet-switched services like Frame Relay, VC refers to the ability of two DTE devices (typically routers) to send and receive data directly to each other, which supplies the same function as a physical leased line (leased circuit), but doing so without a physical circuit. This term is meant as a contrast with a leased line or leased circuit.

virtual LAN (VLAN) A group of devices, connected to one or more switches, with the devices grouped into a single broadcast domain through switch configuration. VLANs allow switch administrators to separate the devices connected to the switches into separate VLANs without requiring separate physical switches, gaining design advantages of separating the traffic without the expense of buying additional hardware.

virtual private network (VPN) A set of security protocols that, when implemented by two devices on either side of an unsecure network such as the Internet, can allow the devices to send data securely. VPNs provide privacy, device authentication, anti-replay services, and data integrity services.

VLAN *See* virtual LAN.

VLAN configuration database   The name of the collective configuration of VLAN IDs and names on a Cisco switch.

vlan.dat   The default file used to store a Cisco switch's VLAN configuration database.

VLAN Trunking Protocol (VTP)   A Cisco-proprietary messaging protocol used between Cisco switches to communicate configuration information about the existence of VLANs, including the VLAN ID and VLAN name.

VLSM   *See* variable-length subnet masks.

VoIP   Voice over IP. The transport of voice traffic inside IP packets over an IP network.

VPN   *See* virtual private network.

VPN client   Software that resides on a PC, often a laptop, so that the host can implement the protocols required to be an endpoint of a VPN.

VTP   *See* VLAN Trunking Protocol.

VTP client mode   One of three VTP operational modes for a switch with which switches learn about VLAN numbers and names from other switches, but which does not allow the switch to be directly configured with VLAN information.

VTP pruning   The VTP feature by which switches dynamically choose interfaces on which to prevent the flooding of frames in certain VLANs when the frames do not need to go to every switch in the network.

VTP server mode   One of three sets of operating characteristics (modes) in VTP. Switches in server mode can configure VLANs, tell other switches about the changes, and learn about VLAN changes from other switches.

VTP transparent mode   One of three sets of operating characteristics (modes) in VTP. Switches in transparent mode can configure VLANs, but they do not tell other switches about the changes, and they do not learn about VLAN changes from other switches.

W

web server   Software, running on some computer, that stores web pages and sends those web pages to web clients (web browsers) that request the web pages.

web VPN   A tool offered by Cisco in which a user can use any common web browser to securely connect using SSL to a web VPN server, which then connects to the user's Enterprise web-based applications—applications that may or may not support SSL.

well-known port   A TCP or UDP port number reserved for use by a particular application. The use of well-known ports allows a client to send a TCP or UDP segment to a server, to the correct destination port for that application.

Wi-Fi Alliance An organization formed by many companies in the wireless industry (an industry association) for the purpose of getting multivendor certified-compatible wireless products to market in a more timely fashion than would be possible by simply relying on standardization processes.

Wi-Fi Protected Access (WPA) A trademarked name of the Wi-Fi Alliance that represents a set of security specifications that predated the standardization of the IEEE 802.11i security standard.

wildcard mask The mask used in Cisco IOS ACL commands and OSPF and EIGRP **network** commands.

window The term window represents the number of bytes that can be sent without receiving an acknowledgment.

wired equivalent privacy (WEP) An early WLAN security specification that used relatively weak security mechanisms, using only preshared keys and either no encryption or weak encryption.

WLAN client A wireless device that wants to gain access to a wireless access point for the purpose of communicating with other wireless devices or other devices connected to the wired internetwork.

WPA2 The Wi-Fi Alliance trademarked name for the same set of security specifications defined in the IEEE 802.11i security standard.

Z

zero subnet For every classful IPv4 network that is subnetted, the one subnet whose subnet number has all binary 0s in the subnet part of the number. In decimal, the zero subnet can be easily identified because it is the same number as the classful network number.

Index

B

I

O

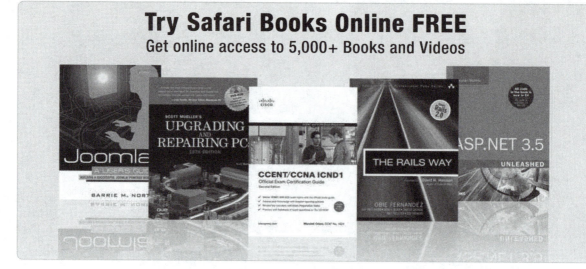

·ı|ıı·ı|ıı·
CISCO™

ciscopress.com: Your Cisco Certification and Networking Learning Resource

Subscribe to the monthly Cisco Press newsletter to be the first to learn about new releases and special promotions.

Visit **ciscopress.com/newsletters.**

While you are visiting, check out the offerings available at your finger tips.

– Free Podcasts from experts:
  - OnNetworking
  - OnCertification
  - OnSecurity

View them at **ciscopress.com/podcasts.**

– Read the latest author **articles** and **sample chapters** at ciscopress.com/articles.

– Bookmark the Certification Reference Guide available through our partner site at **informit.com/certguide.**

Connect with Cisco Press authors and editors via Facebook and Twitter, visit **informit.com/socialconnect.**

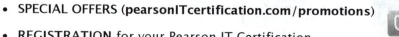